THE NEW NATURALIST
A SURVEY OF BRITISH NATURAL HISTORY

BRITISH BIRDS OF PREY

The aim of this series is to interest the general reader
in the wild life of Britain by recapturing the inquiring
spirit of the old naturalists. The Editors believe that
the natural pride of the British public in the native fauna
and flora, to which must be added concern for their
conservation, is best fostered by maintaining a high
standard of accuracy combined with clarity of exposition
in presenting the results of modern scientific research.

THE NEW NATURALIST

BRITISH BIRDS
OF PREY

A study of Britain's 24 diurnal raptors

LESLIE BROWN

COLLINS
ST JAMES'S PLACE, LONDON

William Collins Sons & Co Ltd
London · Glasgow · Sydney · Auckland
Toronto · Johannesburg

To

SPOFF and SALLY

First published April 1976
Reprinted October 1976
© Leslie Brown, 1976

ISBN 0 00 219405 8

Made and Printed in Great Britain by
William Collins Sons & Co Ltd Glasgow

CONTENTS

CONTENTS

PLATES

vii

PLATES

EDITORS' PREFACE

To many, hawks and eagles have become symbols of freedom. In these days, when the world is coming more and more under man's domination, and when the total destruction of our natural environment is increasingly feared, these magnificent birds achieve an even greater importance in our imagination. As long as they retain a significant place among our wildlife, everything does not appear to be lost. But they have an even greater, and more practical, importance. These birds are also increasingly recognised as 'indicator species', particularly susceptible to damage from man-made pollution. As long as they remain we know that the struggle for the conservation of both our wildlife and of our environment is worth pursuing.

Yet this love of our birds, particularly our birds of prey, has not always been so prevalent. In the nineteenth century, when environmental pressures were far less intense than they are today, birds like the Osprey and the Sea Eagle were exterminated in Britain, largely by persecution by man. In this ornithologists, by stealing innumerable eggs and by wholesale shooting to obtain skins for their collections, played a significant part. They undoubtedly prevented many new species which might have colonised this country from obtaining a toe hold. But it was the growth of game preservation which did most harm to our hawks. Landowners and gamekeepers believed that any bird with a hooked bill endangered their pheasants, so hawks were shot, trapped inhumanely and their nests were destroyed over most of the country. Sheep farmers in the Highlands of Scotland persecuted the Golden Eagle, in the belief that it carried off their lambs. Pigeon fanciers had a particular enmity for the Peregrine, which undoubtedly prevented some homing birds from reaching their destination.

All these birds are now protected by law. Many landowners, and even some gamekeepers, realise that they are often less harmful to game birds than are the rats and other small rodents on which the hawks largely feed. Although the inhuman pole trap is still used, and many birds are illegally poisoned, the law, and a greater knowledge of predator ecology, is having some effect. Most people are now in favour of supporting the law. But in the last twenty years a new danger has arisen from pesticides and other pollutants. In many countries species of hawks and eagles have been wiped out over large areas. In Britain, although the Sparrowhawk has ceased to breed in most counties where arable farming predominates, and the Peregrine only breeds successfully in the remoter parts of Scotland, the situation would seem to be less catastrophic. The most recent records show some improvement in the numbers, distribution and breeding success of most of our endangered species. This is largely due to the vigilance of our naturalists, who established the danger, and the co-operation of our Government, our farmers and our industrialists, who took action to control the most dangerous uses of the most toxic pesticides before it was too late.

Many of us, even naturalists familiar with other forms of wildlife, are sadly ignorant about most of the birds described in this book, so it should be of real value to its readers. The only species we can expect to see at all often is the Kestrel, so well named the 'Windhover' or 'Windcheater', for this has taken to soaring over our motorways when hunting the voles which have found a perfect new habitat in the grass verges. In Wales and the West Country we may see a Buzzard, and, with luck, a Golden Eagle on a visit to the Highlands. The eleven other species which breed in Britain, and the ten others which have been recorded as regularly visiting our shores, are almost unknown except to the few. This is not entirely surprising when we realise how small are the numbers of most species. Only three have over 500 breeding pairs, and some could be counted, if not on our fingers, then on our fingers and toes.

Leslie Brown's book will do much to enlighten us. Though it contains a wealth of scientific information, this is presented in a manner which will make it readily assimilated. The author is perhaps unduly modest about the part he has played in amassing the original information. He tells us that he has lived for much of his life in East Africa and other countries, and that he has only devoted a fraction of his time to first-hand field studies in Britain. However, all those who know him recognise him as an authority on the predatory birds of the world, and value his ability to compare and extend his British studies with those in other countries. Also no one person, no matter how talented and diligent, could become the infallible authority on such a large subject as that covered by this book. Leslie Brown has been able to make full and critical use of the observation of others, and the confidence other ornithologists have in him is clear from their willingness to provide him with this information.

It is a truism to say that all our wildlife in Britain is in danger from our growing and more affluent (and more mobile) population. We believe that the books in the *New Naturalist* series make their contribution, by helping to educate the public, to the safeguarding and conservation of that wildlife. Our hawks and eagles are clearly one of the groups most endangered, so this book is particularly important at this time, for it will make a substantial contribution to the knowledge of those engaged in protection and conservation. It should also add to their enjoyment, first as it is a pleasure to read, and secondly as it will do much to sharpen their appreciation of the countryside.

AUTHOR'S PREFACE

WHEN first I mentioned, to Chris Perrins at the Edward Grey Institute, that I had been asked to write this book he observed 'Poaching, aren't you?'; and, in a sense, I am. However, I have gathered that several British ornithologists who might have liked to sink their teeth into this particular cock pheasant have not felt able to spare the time and effort from other more essential tasks to bag it legitimately. So it has fallen to me to climb over the fence with my concealed weapon and snatch the bird from under the noses of British experts. Those who know me well will merely observe that I am a creature of habit, and would not be able to resist it. However, when they have seen me making off with the bird they have all encouraged me in my nefarious task and, if I faltered, have plied me with meat and drink, bed and board, that I might poach the better.

In short, I could not have written this book alone. I know a lot about birds of prey in Africa but am not really expert on many British species and (dare I admit it) there are even species that I haven't succeeded in seeing in Britain though I know them elsewhere. This being so I have descended shamelessly on my friends and colleagues in various parts of Britain, ruthlessly picked their brains for unpublished information, and taken up their time. One and all have drawn deep on their knowledge and imparted it freely, with the result that in many a good day in the field my own knowledge of birds of prey has been both broadened and sharpened by this critical contact with other enthusiasts and specialists. I like to hope that these advantages have been to some extent mutual.

Much work is in progress and as yet unpublished on British birds of prey, and I have tried, by these personal contacts, to include as much as possible of this work in this book. I think most agree that it would be absurd to write a book based only on published material, which is sometimes very scanty and out of date. I have not been able to see everybody and read everything, because I could only allocate limited periods to the task; but what I have been able to gather by personal contact has immensely enhanced the value of the text. I have to some extent anticipated publication of several major current field studies, for instance on the kite and the hen harrier, but I hope it will be obvious that this is not due to any desire to pirate other people's research, but solely because I, and most others, see little point in writing a reference work without including available knowledge because of the dictates of scientific punctilio. In the case of the common buzzard in Speyside I have had to work on interim reports, augmented by personal contacts, and have had no access to the final detailed results, which are in preparation. In the case of the Speyside ospreys, I have not had access to the detailed analysis of the R.S.P.B. record books which is in preparation; these two chapters are necessarily the poorer for lack of this important material.

The manuscript of this book was finished in December 1972 and thereafter no major changes have been made, though the bibliography has been brought up to date as papers then in draft were published, and a few other minor inconsistencies ironed out. Montagu's harrier has now ceased to breed in Britain, so that statements on the status of that species are at present inaccurate, one hopes not permanently.

I must first express my gratitude to the late Dr David Lack and to Dr Christopher Perrins of the Edward Grey Institute, where it is always such a pleasure to work. Dr J. M. Flegg and his staff at the British Trust for Ornithology (hereafter abbreviated as the B.T.O.) have been abundantly helpful, especially Chris Mead (who actually volunteered to draw maps for me), Robert Spencer, and Robert Morgan. They have given me free access to nest record cards and to migration records, which have made a vital contribution to the chapters on several species. Finally, I have spent time at the offices of the Royal Society for Protection of Birds (R.S.P.B.) and benefited greatly from the advice and help of Dr James Cadbury, Mike Everett, and Richard Porter, while Dorothy Rooke was especially helpful in locating literature for me. Hermann Heinzel kindly drew the heads on page 2 and the feet on pages 14 and 15.

The experts who have helped with the chapters on particular species or subjects, and whom I have relentlessly pursued to their lairs from Orkney and wettest Wales to the New Forest include my colleague Dr Dean Amadon of the American Museum of Natural History, on classification; Douglas Weir on the osprey, common buzzard, golden eagle, and peregrine falcon; Dr Colin Tubbs on the honey buzzard, common buzzard, and hobby; Peter Davis and Peter Walters Davies on the red kite; Bert Axell and John Buxton on the marsh harrier; the late Eddie

Balfour and Dr James Cadbury on the hen harrier; Dr Ian Newton, especially on the sparrowhawk and goshawk, but also on other species; Dr Peter Dare on the buzzard; Dr Adam Watson, especially on the golden eagle, but also on moorland and grouse research generally; David Merrie on the golden eagle; Dr Derek Ratcliffe on the peregrine falcon; Dr Staffan Ulfstrand on boreal migrants and Dr Norman Moore on pesticides. All these experts have been good enough not only to spend time with me, but also to read the chapters concerning their particular subjects and comment on them. The revised versions which appear here may therefore be taken as having been vetted by them. I have also had stimulating discussions with Dr David Jenkins, Dr Morton Boyd, Nick Picozzi, and many others. All have contributed generously to making this book a more valuable and informative compilation than I could have written without their aid.

Then – there are those long-suffering wives, on whom I descend, monopolising their husbands' time, glowering at the children, and expecting regular satisfaction of the appetite of a biggish boa-constrictor. Though they may get little out of it, they too have done much for this book. Special thanks are due to Angela Davis, Bridget Buxton, Helena Newton, and Penny Weir. Last, but far from least, Vee Mead, who looked after me for weeks while I was wrestling to complete the text. The text itself has been impeccably typed by Chris Salmon and Carol Bonham of the B.T.O.

If I have disagreed with any of my advisers on particular species that is my affair alone; the book has been a joint effort but any shortcomings are my responsibility. As I have said at several points in the text I have been surprised to find quite large gaps in our knowledge of British birds of prey. In trying to fill these gaps myself I have been obliged by the time factor to limit my reading to the main British journals and reference works, with important papers and books in the Continental literature. Inevitably, this means that some suggestive titbits of interesting information will have been missed.

I have tried to identify all important sources and personal communications, but in order to avoid cluttering the text with full quotes of references (which to my mind makes any reader lose the thread of what is written) the information has been identified in a bibliography attached to each chapter, either by number (main references), or a letter (shorter references and personal communications). The first time a main reference appears it is quoted in full; but several appear many times, and are thereafter quoted 'op. cit.', with the chapter and number where they originally appeared. Shorter references are given in abbreviated form to save space; but all are readily identifiable. In this way I hope it will be relatively painless to read the book while the published information should be easily identifiable. I have drawn freely on my personal contacts, and here and there have made an original observation myself.

Nowadays, it is customary in all scientific work to use the metric system, expressing weights in grams or kilograms and distance and area in metres, kilometres, hectares, and square kilometres, rather than in feet, yards, miles, acres and square miles. I am told that the British are at present unable to grasp the intricacies of this infinitely simpler system. Small weights, in particular, cannot be as easily expressed in British units as they can in grams; 250 grams=0.25 kg= about 8.7 oz, if you find that any easier. To get over such difficulties, I have here and there quoted important weights or measurements of area or distance in both units. Those who wish to look more closely at tabulated figures may use a conversion table, available in many pocket diaries today. *Box 24916, Karen, Kenya.*

AUTHOR'S NOTE TO THE REPRINT

Since the manuscript was completed in late 1972 no substantial changes have been made. However, the status of certain species has altered since I completed the text, and I give details below. Also, some ongoing studies have been published, while others are awaiting publication. The following are additional details relevant to certain species so far as I know them from correspondence with friends in Britain.

Chapter 4. The Osprey. Ospreys have continued to increase; and I believe there were fourteen pairs in 1975. An analysis of the results from the R.S.P.B. daily logbooks has been done, and awaits publication. (J. Cadbury, in litt.)

Chapter 6. The Red Kite. Kites have, as forecast, continued to increase slowly. In 1975 there were 28 pairs with about 30 non-breeding birds so that the total population now approaches 90. In 1974 more than 20 young were reared. Welsh kites continue to be illegally shot outside their home areas; one was shot in Kircudbright in 1975. The study on which Chapter 6 was based has been published (Bibliography, Chapter 2, 4.), and other studies continue. Changes in land use as they affect the kite are being studied, and a study of the kite in relation to other predators is in progress. (P. E. Davis and P. Walters Davies, in litt.)

Chapter 7. The Sea Eagle. A new attempt is being made to reintroduce the sea eagle, by hacking young birds back to the wild, on Rhum. The attempt has run into some management difficulties, and one of the young was electrocuted some distance from the release point, but others have apparently survived after release. If long enough continued and in sufficient numbers, this may result in establishing a small population. The alternative of placing eggs in golden eagles' eyries, which I thought preferable, was apparently rejected on grounds of costs, and the uncertainty that it would result in fledged young not imprinted on their golden eagle foster parents. (J. Morton Boyd, pers. comm.)

Chapter 8. The Marsh Harrier. Has increased to seven pairs, unexpectedly, of which four were at Minsmere, and two at Horsey, where a warden has now been appointed to care for them and keep people away from their haunts. They have still not re-established themselves in Dorset; but the position is slightly more hopeful than it was in 1972. (B. Buxton, H. E. Axell, in litt.)

Chapter 9. The Hen Harrier. The total number of pairs is still conjectural, and studies of food have not yet been published. Further large-scale afforestation projects should temporarily benefit this species, while the trees are young. In 1975 I saw more hen harriers on mainland Scotland than in the rest of my life together. The main study of hen harriers, by Cadbury and Balfour, in Mss in 1970, has never been published, and should be; it has been delayed by Eddie Balfour's untimely death.

Chapter 10. Montagu's Harrier. This species has, unexpectedly, become extinct as a regular breeding species in Britain since 1972. The decline is evidently widespread over much of northern Europe; and at the second International Conference on

Birds of Prey at Vienna in October 1975 several European countries expressed concern on this issue. It is feared that Montagu's harriers might be collecting pesticides in their winter quarters, in which case their situation is analogous to the migrant races of sub-Arctic peregrines. (I. Prestt and others; I.C.B.P. Conference on Birds of Prey; proceedings in prep.)

Chapter 11. The Goshawk. Has been successfully established in Britain and is increasing. The number of pairs known could now be more than twenty, though their whereabouts is still secret. Studies on goshawks hacked back to the wild by falconers, and their effect on prey and mortality are being written up for publication. (I. Prestt; I. Newton; R. E. Kenward; in litt. and pers. comm.)

Chapter 13. The Buzzard. The first part of the Speyside studies has now been published in *British Birds*; others are awaited. A new study on buzzards in Wales, related to their relations with kites and changes in land use has been started. (P. E. Davis, in litt.)

Chapters 15-18. The Kestrel, Hobby, Merlin, and Peregrine Falcon. Some further studies have been done on all of these, not yet published. The peregrine falcon has been bred in captivity very successfully by Professor T. J. Cade of Cornell and others; and attempts at reintroducing it in areas of the United States where it had become extinct show some promise. The status of peregrines in Britain has somewhat improved; but eyries are still robbed by falconers illegally, including some only recently re-occupied. (P. Dare, in litt.)

Chapter 27. Conservation. Some people have expressed the view that I am too hard on gamekeepers. I do not believe I am. Here in Kenya, where I make no attempt to obtain details of such matters, I have been told within the last two months, by people who would wish to remain nameless, of a gamekeeper who urged a young naturalist to shoot any hen harriers he could in Orkney, of all places; my informant was outraged and refused. I have also been told of an estate in Scotland (which I am unable to pinpoint, but which should receive attention as a persistent offender against the law) which openly bragged about killing golden eagles in 1975. If I can hear these echoes 5000 miles away, the details at close quarters must be quite clearly audible. Gamekeepers are not alone to blame; falconers and egg collectors (the Loch Garten osprey eyrie was again robbed, as I understand) have also offended; and the fines inflicted upon such people are still inadequate to check such abuses.

This is in the nature of stop-press news. When some more water has run under the bridge, and some more unpublished studies have appeared in print, there will be cause to rewrite the text more substantially.

PUBLISHER'S NOTE TO THE REPRINT

Mr Desmond Nethersole-Thompson has drawn our attention to certain passages on page 22, page 229 and page 243, which he claims impute that he is an egg-collector. The author wishes to make it quite clear that all these passages refer specifically to the year 1931, and it was not intended that they should imply that Mr Nethersole-Thompson is an egg-collector now. The author recognises that Mr Nethersole-Thompson is accepted as one of the foremost field ornithologists in the British Isles.

CHAPTER I

BIRDS OF PREY AND THEIR WAY OF LIFE

IN theory any species of bird that preys or feeds upon other living creatures is a bird of prey. Such a broad definition, however, would include all those species that eat insects, crustacea, fish, frogs and reptiles as well as the more powerful, swift and rapacious species that kill large mammals and birds. Song thrushes and buzzards alike feed a good deal on earthworms but, although the song thrush is probably a more important predator on earthworms than is the buzzard, the latter is a bird of prey while the song thrush is not. The mainly insectivorous shrikes also eat small reptiles and mammals, or young birds, and the name 'butcher bird' applied to the red-backed shrike (now a rare bird in Britain and slowly decreasing) testifies to its predatory function. The dividing line between some of the large gulls, feeding on auks on sea-cliffs, and eagles in the same areas is a tenuous one. Both prey upon sea-birds, but the gulls are not birds of prey proper.

When it comes to fish, sea eagles and ospreys feed mainly or entirely on them; but so do auks, grebes, divers, cormorants, shags and gannets, ducks such as mergansers, terns, and most gulls. One may well wonder why the term 'bird of prey' is applied to the sea eagle and not to the much more voracious cormorant. All of these are more important predators on fish than are the rare ospreys or sea eagles, certainly in Britain where they are numbered in aggregate by the million against about a dozen resident ospreys and even rarer visiting sea eagles. The osprey and the sea eagle were once widespread and presumably effective predators on fish but both were exterminated in Britain in the nineteenth century. Only the osprey has come back, in small numbers, so that, although these are birds of prey proper, their predatory effect is at present negligible.

When we think of the sea eagle, however, or the golden eagle which is nearly as large and probably a more vigorous predator, the meaning of the term becomes clearer. These very powerful species are the only birds in Britain regularly capable of killing large active wild animals such as hares, or the young of deer or seals. The great falcons, the gyrfalcon which is a scarce winter visitor, and the unmatched and unmatchable peregrine, the prince of all flying birds, are the only predators that can snatch or strike dead in flight a swift flying gamebird or a wild duck – or even a wild goose. The goshawk, also a winter visitor and a very scarce breeder in Britain, catches and kills large birds such as woodpigeons and crows in the woods and rabbits and even hares in the open and conveys, while doing so, an impression of savage speed and force equalled by only a few small swift tropical eagles. Other birds of prey may be smaller, and much less agile or fierce, feeding on insects, but are obviously related anatomically to these large powerful species; so they too are birds of prey proper.

The birds of prey proper include two orders of birds which have certain features in common. With a few exceptions, they have powerful grasping feet with the toes ending in long sharp curving talons, used both to kill the prey by piercing and gripping it, and to hold it down when feeding. A great black-backed gull feeding on a puffin can neither kill the puffin as cleanly, nor hold it firmly to the ground with its webbed foot. In Britain vultures are only rare vagrants, but in these mainly tropical

PLATE 2. FLIGHT. *Above left,* a white-tailed sea eagle's broad wings show eight emarginated primaries at the tip, here bending under heavy load as the eagle flaps its wings; *right,* hovering kestrels fan the tail and poise the body at an angle to increase lift; the alula shows on the left wing. *Below,* a buzzard has a 'generalised' wing, moderately long and broad, with primaries not extremely emarginated.

scavengers, which do not need to kill, the strong talons are reduced and the foot more resembles that of a hen than that of an eagle; but vultures retain the other main feature of true birds of prey – a powerful hooked beak useful for tearing the flesh of the animal which has been found dead or has been killed. True birds of prey are those which kill their prey with the grasping talons and tear it up with the hooked beak. Gulls and cormorants, and some shrikes too, have something of a hooked bill, and shrikes can even carry quite large prey in their claws; but in none of these is the armoury developed to perfection, and in action these others may appear relatively clumsy and inept. Cormorants, indeed, swallow their prey whole and the hook on the bill is only for holding the prey, not for tearing it up.

The two groups included in this narrower definition are the eagles, falcons, hawks and vultures, comprising the order Falconiformes or diurnal birds of prey; and the owls, order Strigiformes, the nocturnal birds of prey. Despite the possession of common attributes such as talons and hooked beaks they are not closely allied to one another and are usually sharply differentiated by their habits. The nearest relatives of the hawks are on the one hand ducks and on the other gamebirds, on both of which groups they feed extensively. The nearest relatives of the owls are the nightjars on one side, and on the other cuckoos. Nightjars and owls share nocturnal habits, but a cuckoo resembles an owl almost as little as a duck does a hawk.

In practice such niceties of classification mean only that the hawks and owls are both old groups which diverged from their near relatives a very long time ago and have become highly specialised for their predatory function. The fact that both owls and hawks, not closely related to one another, share some of the same characters is due to what is called convergent evolution, through which the same structures can evolve for a particular purpose in unrelated groups of animals. The crocodile, the pike, the cormorant, otter, seal and killer whale all prey on fish and all except the cormorant have sharp teeth for catching, holding and chewing flesh; the cormorant does not need them because it swallows its prey whole.

In general these two groups of birds of prey divide the hunting time of the 24-hour day between them, the hawks feeding by day and the owls by night. Among British species this division is generally very clear, though the small insectivorous hobby falcons often catch prey in the dusk when tawny and even more certainly little owls are already astir. In other countries the division may be less exact, and there are hawks that feed exclusively on bats almost in the dark, while the hawk owl of northern woods is largely diurnal and has lost some of the typical night-adapted characters of other owls, just as vultures have lost their talons.

In this book I am discussing only the diurnal British species so that from now on we can forget about owls, except for a brief comparative mention here and there. I am not an expert on British owls while other people are, so that it would be an impertinence on my part to attempt a discussion of their particular field. Moreover, it is in any case hard enough to compress the available material on British diurnal species into the compass of a moderate sized book. So I largely part company with the owls here, though they are none the less true birds of prey.

The diurnal birds of prey have developed certain characters to aid them in locating and killing their prey. Foremost among these is the sense of sight, which in all the species is marvellously developed. So acute is the sense of sight that there is little need for any other sense, such as smell, though the diurnal birds of prey also possess acute hearing and sometimes use it, particularly in heavily wooded localities, to help them locate their prey. They locate their prey by sight, occasionally assisted by hearing, but never by smell (even vultures do not locate their prey by smell) and they kill it by the use of their other special attributes – sheer speed and agility in flight. Owls, in contrast, do not have particularly acute sight, though their eyes are adapted for night vision and detecting movement. Their hearing is so extraordinarily acute and well adapted that they can kill a mouse by ear alone in pitch darkness; like diurnal birds of prey they have no sense of smell. Neither group needs a sense of smell, for they can efficiently detect and catch their prey by the use of other senses.

Both hawks or falcons and owls often make use of an element of surprise in catching their prey. In the diurnal species this is best achieved by sheer speed or superior agility. In strong daylight a pigeon attacked by a falcon must be able to hear the rushing sound made by its attacker in full stoop for, although falcons can travel very fast, they cannot penetrate the sound barrier, and the noise of their stoop reaches the pigeon before they do; but it may be killed before it has properly comprehended its danger. A goshawk, flitting quietly between the branches with speed and dexterity that has to be seen to be believed, is even more dangerous than a falcon to a pigeon. Owls cannot achieve the element of surprise in such ways but manage, by silent flight, to come upon their prey before it has even thought to escape.

In the detailed exercise of their functions there is a degree of overlap between these two groups of birds. However a combination of special attributes for day and night hunting and a degree of overlap at dusk and dawn means that these two groups can hunt a variety of animals throughout the 24 hours. It does not profit the prey to be exclusively nocturnal or diurnal. A nocturnal wood mouse may escape the diurnal buzzard but will be in even greater danger from the even more numerous and widespread tawny owl.

For the diurnal birds of prey acute sight and/or speed or agility are the most important attributes enabling them to kill their prey. All need acute sight, but the speed or agility they must display depends very largely on the type of prey taken. Some prey on relatively slow moving animals that require neither speed nor agility to catch; neither is required to catch a mole (when it appears above ground or very close to the surface), but an insectivorous small falcon such as the hobby depends entirely on speed to catch dragonflies and can easily catch even swifts in full flight. For a less specialised bird of prey such as the buzzard or the kite, with a wide variety of diet, a turn of speed may not often be necessary but is a useful attribute when, for instance, trying to catch a starling in flight crossing an estuary.

The term 'eagle-eyed' is used to denote unusually keen vision, for it has long been recognised that the diurnal birds of prey, including eagles, have very remarkable eyesight. Neither eagles nor other birds of prey see any further than we do, and probably they see the same colours as we do, but they are able to see detail very much more clearly than do human beings. A buzzard, only about a fiftieth of a man's weight, has an eye very nearly the same size as that of a man, so that it is fifty times as large in relation to the bird's body as is our own eye to ourselves. It is as if we had eyes the size of large oranges. The buzzard's very large eye is also nearly immovable in its socket, capable of only minor adjustments to improve binocular vision. We can move our eyes from side to side, but to achieve the same effect a buzzard must keep moving its head around to see in all directions. It may even turn its head upside down to look at objects otherwise out of its line of vision. However, by the use of its flexible neck (much more flexible than ours, which we

4

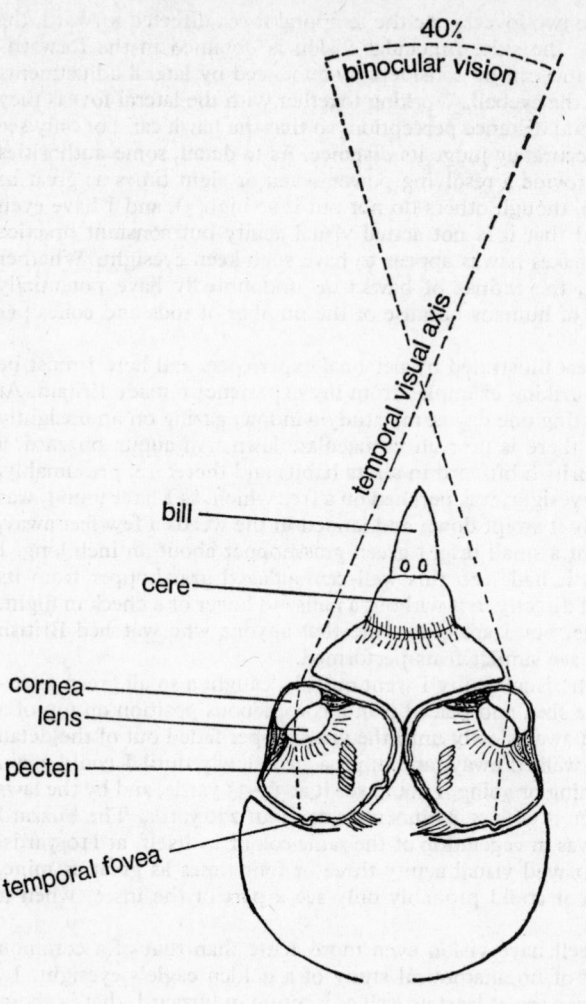

40%

binocular vision

temporal visual axis

bill

cere

cornea

lens

pecten

temporal fovea

FIG. I. A bird of prey's head (*Buteo* sp.) to show binocular vision.

cannot turn to look directly behind us) it can achieve 360 degree vision with greater economy of movement than can a human.

The proverbial keenness of vision is due to the structure of the retina, the sensitive surface at the back of the eyeball on which the image of the seen object is cast. The amount of detail perceived by the retina depends on the number of specialised visual cells, known as rods and cones, per unit area – the more rods and cones the better the perception of detail. The common buzzard has the grand champion in visual acuity of all vertebrate eyes, with rods and cones enabling it to see detail at least twice as well as even a keen-sighted human being[4].

Moreover, in the retinas of buzzards and other diurnal raptors there are structures known as foveas, in which the number of rods and cones is still greater. In the retinas of hawks there are two foveas, one the temporal fovea directed forward, the other the lateral fovea to the side. Binocular vision is obtained in the forward-directed temporal fovea and can be considerably enhanced by lateral adjustments through a few degrees of the eyeball. Working together with the lateral foveas they also provide unusually good distance perception, so that the hawk can not only see its prey clearly but can accurately judge its distance. As to detail, some authorities believe that the foveas provide a resolving power seven or eight times as great as that of the human eye(4), though others do not put it so high(3), and I have even heard the view expressed that it is not actual visual acuity but constant practice and use of the eye that makes hawks appear to have such keen eyesight. Whether the latter is true or not, the retinas of hawks do undoubtedly have potentially keener vision than those of humans because of the number of rods and cones per unit area.

This visual acuity is best illustrated by personal experience, and here I must be forgiven if I draw upon striking examples from my experience outside Britain. At Karen in Kenya I was sitting one day at my study window, gazing on an unsightly expanse of weeds where there is now an immaculate lawn. An augur buzzard, a bird very similar to the British buzzard in all its habits and therefore, presumably, similarly equipped as to eyesight, was perched on a tree which, as I later found, was 110 yards away. Suddenly it swept down and landed in the weeds a few feet away, where I saw it had caught a small bright green grasshopper about an inch long. I had no doubt at all that it had seen this well-camouflaged grasshopper from its perch, for it had swooped directly to it without a pause to hover or a check in flight. It seemed barely credible, but I am quite sure that anyone who watched British buzzards for long would see similar feats performed.

In order to test my own visual acuity I went outside, caught a small green grasshopper of about the same size, and placed it in a conspicuous position on top of a fence post. I then backed away slowly until the grasshopper faded out of the detail I could perceive. I then walked away, and approached slowly until I could again see the grasshopper. Coming or going, I could see it at 33–35 yards, and by the laws of optics I could have seen it with × 8 binoculars at about 270 yards. The buzzard had seen it, hidden as it was in vegetation of the same colour as itself, at 110 yards, and accordingly had displayed visual acuity three or four times as great as mine, and doubtless better, for it could probably only see a part of the insect when it launched its attack.

A golden eagle may well have vision even more acute than that of a common buzzard, though I know of no anatomical study of a golden eagle's eyesight. I , however, a golden eagle can see at least as well as a common buzzard, that is about four times as well as a human being, and maybe eight times as well, then it is easy to calculate the distance at which a golden eagle could see a mountain hare, an animal about fifteen inches long when crouched, and a good deal bigger when walking or running. On the analogy of the grasshopper I would be able to see the hare at a range of 500 yards – and I am quite sure I *have* seen hares at near that range once they move. A golden eagle should therefore be able to see a hare at a range of 2000 yards or 6000 feet, and maybe at twice these distances. From 1500 feet above Ben Nevis it could see a cat in a garden at Inverlochy. It needs no great exercise of the imagination, therefore, to believe that an eagle, soaring along a ridge 1500 feet above a wide glen, is able to see any hare or grouse that moves in the bottom of that glen with ease, for such large mammals and birds would be well within the theoretical limits of its visual acuity.

Vultures are commonly believed to have marvellous eyesight and, though they are unimportant in Britain as carrion feeders, their place is to some extent taken by golden eagles, which feed on carrion in winter and spring. A dead sheep is about three or four feet long and white, in strong contrast to the general dark colour of the environment. It stands out very clearly, even though it does not move. Using the same principles, a golden eagle should be able to see a dead sheep at a range of about 5000 yards, or three miles. It requires no marvellous eyesight to be able to locate such a source of food in an eagle's home range, and nor do vultures need marvellous eyesight; eyes such as mine would serve. Both eagles and vultures may often be attracted to such nourishment in the first place by the movements of crows or ravens near the carcase.

Speed and/or agility are the other main special requirements of the diurnal birds of prey. The large falcons such as the peregrine and the gyrfalcon display a combination of speed and precision that is little short of miraculous. This speed and agility may not only be used in the act of killing, but will be shown in the spectacular courtship flights of large falcons. A pair of peregrines, above a sea-cliff with a good wind blowing, perform magnificent stoops at one another in spring courtship, and no one who watches their mastery can doubt that, if brought into play with lethal intent, it must be highly effective. Yet other birds, particularly waders in estuaries, often do escape the peregrine by the use of even more rapid twists and turns than the falcon can manage. Lapwings are very common in many peregrine haunts, but are seldom killed because they can so easily dodge the falcon. The gyrfalcon is not so marvellous a flier as the peregrine; it too is capable of magnificent feats and, being heavier, is probably actually faster. However, it tends to take more of its prey on the ground than does the peregrine, which normally kills in full flight.

I have seen a British peregrine kill a rock dove that was flying low along the base of a sea-cliff; and my brother George saw a wigeon duck killed in a northern estuary in winter. Neither of these kills was a breath-taking piece of speed or agility, but both were good workman-like examples of what a peregrine can do. The rock dove was flying along the base of the cliff, hugging the rock face, perhaps knowing its danger from the falcon perched on the sunlit cliff top among the flowering thrift. The peregrine just dropped off and with its added momentum, quickly overhauled the rock dove from behind, seized it, and carried it to a ledge a little further away. I was too far above the action to be certain, but I fancy the peregrine swung rather below the dove, and that it swooped upwards at the last moment to seize its prey. The duck, on a dull misty November day, when George was crouching half frozen behind a fucus-encrusted boulder in Castle Stewart Bay, waiting for something edible to come his way, was flying along the tide edge several hundred feet above the mud. Out of the sky came the peregrine, straightening out of a curving dive behind the duck, overhauling it and grasping it before the quarry seemed to be aware of its presence. The wigeon was as heavy as the peregrine, which laboured shorewards after binding to its prey, disappearing in the grey murk before he saw it land.

If neither of these kills were first class examples of the peregrine's powers of flight, I have twice seen peregrines in Africa perform evolutions that left me breathless with excitement and admiration, both times in play or aggression. Once, when I was at an eyrie the falcon, perched 100 feet or so above me, took exception to a bull terrier bitch who had reluctantly accompanied me down to the ledge and was standing, her tongue lolling at her mad *bwana*, just above me and a few feet from my face. The falcon dived from her perch and, when just above the dog's back, turned at right angles, lowered her foot, and drew the hind claw through the hair from tail to shoulders, just drawing blood all along, and putting the fear of God into a brave bull terrier who enjoyed nothing better than to attack a rhinoceros. Travelling with the aid of gravity the falcon would have achieved nearly a hundred miles an hour by the time she reached us, and at that speed showed a combination of agility in the right angle turn and hairbreadth accuracy that I have not seen bettered. After such a performance, given in aggression just in front of my face, I could not doubt that a peregrine can kill whenever a fair chance presents itself.

Almost better still, I was one day on the summit rocks of Eagle Hill in Embu district with friends. We were watching a pair of Ayres's eagles, themselves magnificent fliers, in nuptial display. The male, from several hundred feet above us, stooped in play at his mate, who was soaring round the lower slopes of the hill. He had perhaps a thousand feet to fall and as he accelerated in the dive he pressed his wingtips close to his tail and whizzed like a heart-shaped bullet through the air. We held him in the field of our binoculars, entranced by his speed. Then, just as he was reaching his mate, into the circular field of view shot a peregrine – an immature at that – which flashed past the eagle with the ease of an Aston Martin overhauling a family saloon. I yield to none in my admiration for Ayres's eagle; but that peregrine seemed to be saying, 'Fly can you! I'll show you!' This too was not done with intent to kill, but only in play.

At such extreme speeds, of course, real agility in turning is hardly to be expected; a slow biplane can very easily outmanoeuvre a supersonic jet and the lapwing and peregrine demonstrate this principle in the wild. The real masters of agility are the sparrowhawk and goshawk, which catch their prey in thick cover or by using the lie of the land, haystacks, buildings, or bushes, to come up to prey unseen and snatch one before it can get away. One would be lucky to see a goshawk do it, but anyone who lives in the country has the chance of seeing a sparrowhawk kill. The favoured method is to fly low along the ground, silently, and showing a fair turn of speed. The hawk flips up over a hedgerow, and on the far side surprises a flock of sparrows or chaffinches feeding. Before they can escape a lightning turn is made, a long leg is thrust out, and the wide-open needle-like talons of the sparrowhawk seize and grasp the luckless prey.

Sparrowhawks usually kill prey very much smaller than themselves, but goshawks will often attack rabbits or even young hares, and kill them with a powerful grip. If one compares the legs of the goshawk and the sparrowhawk one can see that they are of the same basic design, very long, so that they can be thrust far out to grab a prey desperately trying to escape. However, the legs and feet of the goshawk are relatively very much thicker and stronger than those of the sparrowhawk, and the talons more solid and stiff, less needle-like. One need only examine these feet to judge that the goshawk, relative to its own weight, can normally kill and carry prey relatively much heavier than can the sparrowhawk. Even so, the goshawk too normally kills prey well within its strength, and it can display agility in the quick turn and snatch very little inferior to that of the lighter bird.

Eagles, of which our golden eagle is a good example, require not only speed and some agility but also great strength to subdue the large prey they sometimes tackle. Normally a golden eagle, like other raptors, kills prey of half its own weight or less, and with such an advantage of power the prey has very little chance when seized. A falconer, carrying an eagle on his fist, must wear a heavy horsehide gauntlet for protection from the bird's grip. Even then, if it is suddenly alarmed or angered, the eagle may contract its foot in the killing grasp. The falconer is then helpless, unable to withdraw his hand or unlock the crushing talons, and must wait, slowly growing numb, till the great bird relents. By the time an eagle relents, a wild hare is already dead.

Another special attribute of the eagle is a wing designed for efficient soaring, rather long and narrow, with the primary feathers much emarginated on both webs, so that when fully extended they are well separated, like the fingers of a spread hand. An eagle's wing is not as efficient for soaring as is that of an albatross or even a gull, both of which have very long and narrow wings like those of a gliding sail-plane. However, it would be inconvenient for the eagle to have an 11-foot wingspan like a wandering albatross, for it would hinder the eagle when catching prey on the ground or in manoeuvring to land on cliff ledges or the branches of trees. The eagle's wing is a compromise, enabling both masterful soaring flight and a fair degree of manoeuvrability close to the ground.

The emarginated wingtip primaries help in this, in the following way. Primary feathers may be emarginated not at all, on only one web, or on both webs. When they are not emarginated at all short V-shaped notches are formed between their tips when the wing is spread. When, as in the common buzzard, four or five primaries are somewhat emarginated, these notches are deeper but are still V-shaped. When all six or seven primaries forming the wingtip are deeply emarginated on both webs the notches are not only deeper but are squarer in form, more U-shaped. The notches function in the same way as wing slots, reducing turbulence and increasing wingtip lift. It appears that square wing slots are the most efficient for this purpose, and in effect that is what a large eagle has. Vultures display these structures to even greater degree.

In addition, one theory is that the very deep notches enable the spread primaries to bend to a varying degree under the varying aerodynamic load they experience, so that they lie one above another in level flight and help to give the wingtip some of the extra lift characterised by biplanes or triplanes(2). In this case each separate feather acts as an individual aerofoil or flying surface, so that the spread wing has, in effect, several little wings attached to its tip(5). These structures are displayed semi-diagramatically in Fig. 2.

The use that a golden eagle makes of its wingtips was demonstrated to me clearly one day on the summit of Ben a Chlachair, an obscure Munro of the Ben Alder group. It was one of those rare hot hazy days of summer when one can light a pipe on the summit of the hill without shielding the match against the wind. As I was sitting there a golden eagle hunted slowly along the face of the hill a couple of hundred feet below me. He – it was a male – was riding with ease upcurrents imperceptible to me or my match and as he did so he continually flexed his wingtips, the spread primaries opening and closing a little as he delicately adjusted them in the light airs of that summer day. His body, and most of his wing surface, were as stable as the fuselage of a VC10, but his wingtips moved constantly, fingering, as it were, the faint currents I could not perceive.

The golden eagle may not be able to perform quite the spectacular stooping feats of the peregrine, but is a master of easy gliding and precise timing. Once, with my father, I was having tea on the slope of a Scottish mountain on a warm spring afternoon. We had our backs to a big rock, and were watching, across a deep glen where a snow-fed burn rushed in white water below us, a female eagle brooding on her eyrie, sitting tight in the afternoon sun, and blinking occasionally in the strong light. Five hundred feet or so above us her mate poised, riding a breeze with wings partly closed, swinging a little this way and that. After a while the female rose,

9

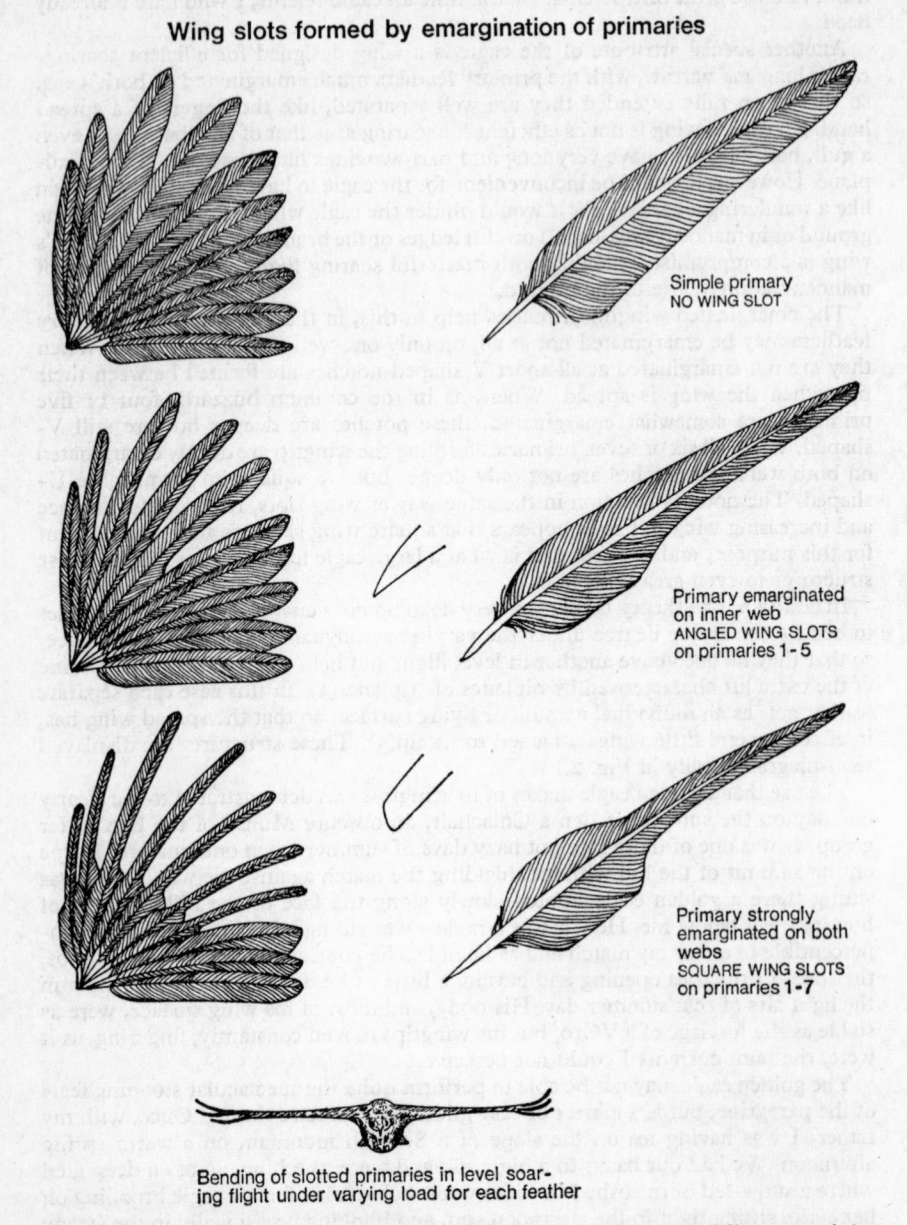

Wing slots formed by emargination of primaries

Simple primary
NO WING SLOT

Primary emarginated
on inner web
ANGLED WING SLOTS
on primaries 1 - 5

Primary strongly
emarginated on both
webs
SQUARE WING SLOTS
on primaries 1 - 7

Bending of slotted primaries in level soaring flight under varying load for each feather

FIG. 2. Adaptations for soaring flight: emargination of primaries (semi-diagrammatic).

stepped unhurried to the edge of the eyrie, and glided away down the glen. As she left the male plunged almost vertically from his high poise, shot with wings closed right into the bottom of the glen, several hundred feet below the eyrie, turned up again just above the foaming burn, and swept up to the nest to land with the last of his momentum, wings still closed, on the ledge his mate had just left. Doubtless he had often done it, and knew his ground; but it was a 1500-foot curving swoop of unforgettably perfect timing and grace.

Golden eagles can also be agile, and their agility is shown perfectly when in display. Not long ago I was perched on the summit of Ben More of Mull, on another of those marvellous sunny days that are experienced so seldom, and are all the more welcome for that. Four eagles, the resident pair, a neighbouring male, and a stranger immature female, performed a spectacular aerial battle in the sky to the west. They would soar in circles for a while to gain height, and then one would suddenly stoop with electrifying speed at another, perhaps two or three hundred feet below. The bird under attack must always have been aware of the antagonist rushing at it from behind for, at the last moment, it would flip over in a lightning roll and present claws to the attacker's feet. This is a normal movement in the mutual nuptial display of eagles and many other species of raptors, but here was done by two males to one another, and by all three adults to the immature which, for some reason, attacked all the others in turn. At length, after twenty minutes of magnificent flying, they separated, the home pair soaring back towards me, the other male leaving in the direction of his nest, and the immature flying south until it faded from view in the field of my binoculars, seven or eight miles away over the Ross of Mull. Watching these twirling feats of agility performed in play, without a feather lost or a single violent contact (potentially dangerous in such powerfully armed birds), I could never imagine the eagle as clumsy or not manoeuvrable, despite its size and weight.

Many diurnal raptors require neither speed nor agility to kill their small and easily caught prey. Examples are the kestrel and the buzzard, which live very largely on voles. When hunting these both the kestrel and the buzzard often make use of the technique of hovering. In kestrels this is the most usual way of catching prey and in buzzards it is a method much used in spring and summer, one of several ways in which this versatile and successful hawk hunts.

When hovering the kestrel or buzzard hangs, head to wind, over a slope or a field, usually 50–100 feet up, but on occasion as much as 300 feet and often much lower than 50 feet. A slow motion film of a hovering bird (and the technique is used also by, for instance, terns and kingfishers) shows that the head is maintained dead level and steady while the body and wings absorb all the buffets of the air currents. In effect, the hover is an aerial perch in open country lacking tall trees. The buzzard, being heavier, is more stable in a hover than a kestrel, having the same sort of advantage that a heavy aircraft possesses in bumpy air over a light plane. If the wind is strong the wings may not be flapped to maintain height and position, but the buzzard or kestrel partly closes them and hangs there without a wing flap. This mode of flight can be called 'poising' rather than 'hovering'. Actually the bird is then gliding slightly downwards against the wind, its airspeed being equivalent to the windspeed and the lift it obtains compensating exactly for its attitude in a gentle downward glide. Just so a salmon hangs in a current of water, neither moving forwards nor back, and hardly flipping its tail.

From such a hover, or from a perch on a tree, a buzzard or kestrel adopts much the same method of killing. It glides down gently till it is nearly above the quarry, and may check once or more in flight, finally raising its wings above its back and dropping feet first on the prey. Its action then actually resembles an osprey catching a fish in a loch, and ospreys also hover briefly when sighting a fish. In the case of the osprey the prey is relatively very much more agile and able to escape to the depths than is the vole that the buzzard or kestrel is after, which perhaps explains why the osprey usually makes a swift precipitate dive once it has really started, while the buzzard and the kestrel can check briefly to make certain that they have judged aright before making the final plunge.

The kestrel and the buzzard search their hunting ground systematically, inch by inch, from a series of hovers, or high perches on trees. They know their ground from experience, and know and defend against others of their kind (at least in the case of the buzzard) certain advantageous perches. Another method of systematic search for small creatures is slow flight, and this is normally the method used by the three species of British harriers. Harriers are a very distinct, well-adapted, and cosmopolitan group of ground-nesting raptors which have specialised in hunting long grass, reedbeds, or other rather long rank vegetation. To do so effectively they have not only developed a rather characteristic slow, buoyant, flapping mode of flight but are among the few diurnal raptors which have unusually keen hearing. They have to some extent evolved the specialised hearing aids brought to perfection in some owls. Their external ear openings are large, sometimes with a pronounced conch, and they have partial facial discs which give them an owlish look when facing the observer. These structures must enhance the normally keen hearing of birds of prey, and it is only among harriers and some aberrant forest falcons of South America that these special structural adaptations are found. Extra keen hearing would evidently be an advantage to a harrier slowly flying over dense vegetation, helping it to locate an unseen vole, check in flight, hover briefly, and drop upon the prey when its position is finally fixed.

The advantage of slow flight can be illustrated by the analogy of a man looking for a lost golf ball. He does not pace about rapidly from place to place, but walks slowly, head bent, searching the ground inch by inch. The hunting harrier zigzags slowly over the moor, usually flying into wind or at an angle to it, only a few feet above the ground. Against a strong breeze its ground speed may be little above a human walking pace, for its normal flight speed in still air is not more than twenty miles an hour. Thus it can search minutely a transect of ground a few yards wide, and can in this way locate small mammals or large insects, the latter especially in tropical winter quarters.

Slow flight and manoeuvrability are both enhanced by low wing loading, that is, the weight supported by any unit area of wing surface, usually expressed in grams per square centimetre. Harriers are, for their apparent size and wing area, remarkably light birds, weighing only a pound or a pound and a half, and having wing loading less than half that of the exceedingly swift but relatively much less manoeuvrable peregrine – which benefits from its high wing loading in a steep dive. The wing loading of harriers varies from 0·21–0·30 gr./sq.cm., that of a large heavy female marsh harrier being greater than that of a light male Montagu's. In sparrowhawks of comparable weight it is nearly double this, 0·4–0·45 gr./sq.cm., and in the peregrine it is 0·63 gr./sq.cm. Admittedly the peregrine is a heavier bird and wing loading increases automatically with increase in bodyweight; but a study of graphs shows that harriers have wing loading relatively lower than would be found in other raptors of comparable weight.

Harriers, then, are adapted for slow buoyant flapping flight low over the ground,

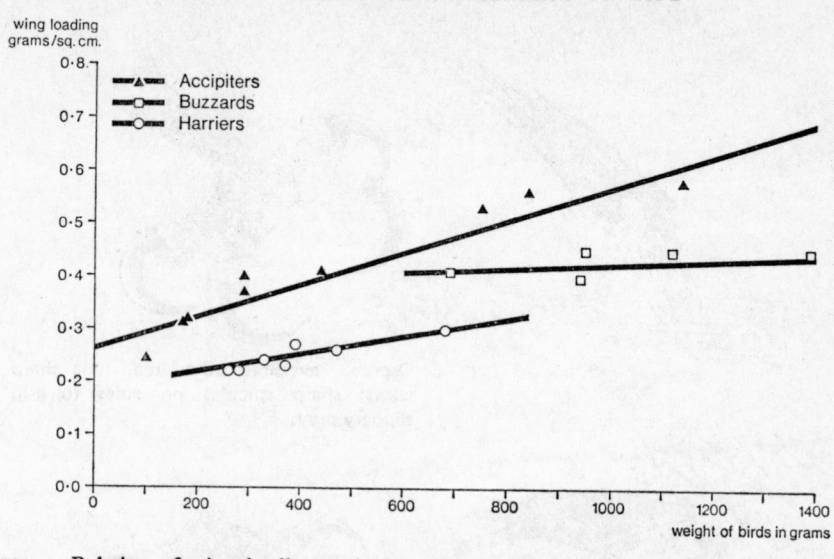

FIG. 3. Relation of wing loading to body weight in harriers, accipiters and buzzards. Harriers show lower wing loading per unit weight than either buzzards or accipiters. (Data from Brown and Amadon, 1969.)

and they hardly need to make use of air currents in normal hunting, though it probably helps them to travel against a moderate wind because of the slow ground-speed they then attain. Their low wing loading and flapping mode of flight also enables them to cross large stretches of water such as the Mediterranean Sea on migration more easily than can soaring birds, which avoid such crossings because of the lack of thermal upcurrents over the sea. Rising thermal bubbles enable soaring birds easily to gain height, several hundred or thousand feet in a few minutes, and then to glide on effortlessly for miles, to pick up another thermal later. Harriers do not normally use thermals at all when hunting or on migration, though they may make use of aircurrents to soar in nuptial display. They can flap over the waves just as easily as they can over a moor on a still day but cannot, of course, perch to rest. All the same, migrant Montagu's harriers normally leave and enter Europe by the same constricted migration routes at Gibraltar and Suez as do soaring species.

The honey buzzard and red kite also have relatively low wing loading for their size, and both possess special remarkable adaptations fitting them to their regular mode of life. The honey buzzard regularly migrates across the Mediterranean via Malta, where it is all too often greeted with senseless wanton charges of shot. It has been seen to use the rising air of thunder clouds to enable it to gain height at Malta and is apparently the largest raptor that regularly makes this crossing in numbers. Perhaps its relatively low wing loading (and I am rather guessing here because not many honey buzzards among the thousands shot have been examined from this viewpoint) may help it to make this crossing when the common buzzard, with rather higher wing loading, does not usually cross by this route.

Osprey: reversible outer toe; long sharp claws; sharp spicules on soles to grip slippery prey.

Honey buzzard: claws short, blunted by digging; foot with little grasping power.

Sparrowhawk: leg long, thin; foot wide-spreading; long sharp talons aid grasping agile prey.

Buzzard: moderately strong, long-clawed, rather powerful foot for killing mammals.

FIG. 4. Feet and mode of killing in British raptors.

Harrier: long legs for reaching; toes shorter; relatively stronger than in sparrowhawk; less spread.

Golden eagle: powerful foot; heavy sharp talons for killing large, even dangerous, mammals.

Peregrine falcon: powerful foot on short leg adapted to strike large birds dead in flight.

Hobby: foot proportioned like peregrine's, but relatively slender, for catching small birds and insects.

The main specialisation of the honey buzzard is connected with its chief prey – wasp larvae, taken from nests dug out of the ground. Through digging, the honey buzzard has lost the long sharp talons of most birds of prey; its feet are more like a hen's than an eagle's. The wasps are not large, but possess a vicious sting, and become infuriated when their nest is attacked by the honey buzzard, frequently venting their fury on other animals, including humans, that may pass. Most birds of prey have bare or nearly bare patches of skin on the lores, between the eye and the beak, and this may be associated with a rather messy, bloody diet, necessitating frequent cleaning of this area, which would be difficult if it was feathered. The honey buzzard does not have a bloody, messy diet, and has the lores covered with small, hard, scale-like feathers, which may serve as protection against wasp stings. Whether this is so, or whether all birds of prey at one time had feathered lores and have lost them, as the honey buzzard has lost its claws, because of their messy diet is a matter for conjecture, and it must be admitted that the honey buzzard pays little attention to the wasps buzzing about its face.

The red kite is possibly the most graceful and manoeuvrable of all our larger birds of prey. It glides effortlessly on the wind above a slope, or moves along a few feet above the ground against a breeze, searching methodically in the manner of a harrier, but without the wing flaps. As it travels along the long forked tail is constantly twisted or canted this way and that, and the bird appears almost as responsive to aircurrents as a blown leaf. The kite is an opportunist feeder, catching any small mammal that comes its way, eating carrion, taking a good many birds in spring, for which a turn of speed plus manoeuvrability in the manner of a sparrowhawk would be an asset.

The forked tail is used constantly for steering purposes, but, when partly or fully spread, also probably acts as an additional aerofoil, giving the kite some of the manoeuvrability at slow speeds possessed by a biplane as compared to a monoplane. Many other raptors increase the area of their flying surfaces by spreading the tail. The buzzard and kestrel spread it when hovering, and it is spread and used by a soaring eagle, or used as a brake when landing on prey. A descending long-tailed sparrowhawk or goshawk can be seen to 'slip' air from the undersurface by raising or lowering the tail a little, the effect being to increase or decrease the angle of dive. However, no British raptor uses the tail quite as flexibly and constantly as does the red kite.

Although British birds of prey are not as many and various as are found in some other countries or on the continent of Europe they do include representative members of several groups which demonstrate the main hunting techniques of raptors the world over. Masterful soaring flight, by buzzard or eagle; agile manoeuvring at speed by sparrowhawk and goshawk, members of the largest genus of raptorial birds and one of the most successful, world-wide; slow buoyant flight by the harriers and a combination of uniquely beautiful gliding and buoyancy by the kite; hovering by kestrel, buzzard and osprey; and finally spectacular killing in the grand manner, striking the prey dead in the air by the peregrine, modified in the equally swift and even more graceful hobby to catch smaller but sometimes swifter aerial prey, such as insects and swallows or swifts.

When actually killing prey, it is the feet that are important, and here too the similarities of evolved structure in diurnal species and owls become most apparent. Whatever the method of hunting the killing is normally done with the feet, and these are adapted for the job. The strength of grasp exerted by even quite a small raptor has to be felt to be believed, and a large eagle can exert a crushing force far more than sufficient to drive the breath from the body of a hare and to thrust the huge rear talon like a dagger into the body, which is held against the hind claw by the grip of the three forward directed toes on each foot.

Only in falcons is the beak used to assist in killing. Falcons have notches, or 'teeth' on the upper mandibles and it has been considered that these are used in killing prey that has been seized and carried still alive to a perch. Where the prey is struck dead in full flight, as often happens with the peregrine, mandibular, or properly 'toral', teeth are unnecessary. But often a peregrine seizes and carries its prey, 'binds to it' as falconers say, and then it will use the beak to break the neck of its quarry which may be strong, and nearly or quite as heavy as itself. The precise function of these toral teeth, however, is still a matter for debate, because it has been shown in some shrikes (which also possess them and are also strongly predatory) that the shrike can manage nearly or quite as well if the teeth are filed off(1).

The feet of diurnal raptors are modified in various ways to assist in grasping and killing their prey. The legs of sparrowhawks and goshawks are very long, able to stretch out at an angle to reach elusive quick-moving prey. Their talons are long and needle-like, and the shanks of sparrowhawks, especially males, are thin and apparently frail, though those of females, and of goshawks are heavier, enabling them to cope with larger prey. Sparrowhawks can be sexed as fledglings by examining their shanks. The legs of harriers are also long and thin, ending in needle-sharp talons, equipping them for a lightning snatch at some small mammal moving in thick vegetation where a shorter, stouter leg might not be able to reach. Since they live mainly on small prey they do not require very powerful feet though those of the marsh harrier are relatively stronger.

The golden eagle and the sea eagle have powerful, thick legs and feet giving them a killing grasp of tremendous force. The inside of the toes of the sea eagle are equipped with sharp spicules, which enable them to grasp and hold slippery prey. This device is still further specialised in the osprey, which eats nothing but fish, whereas the sea eagle also eats birds, mammals and carrion, and could probably manage on these alone even if it could not get fish. Raptors that kill a wide variety of prey, from earthworms and small frogs to medium-sized rabbits, crows, or even young owls and other birds of prey, such as the common buzzard or red kite, have a more generalised style of foot, moderately strong, on the end of a moderately long leg. Those of the kite are, again, more harrier like, long and thin, with needle-sharp talons, more specialised to that mode of hunting than are the feet of the buzzard.

In Britain one cannot observe in wild birds the highly specialised modifications possessed by, for instance, the ambulatory African secretary bird or the double-jointed harrier hawks and crane hawks, equipped respectively for walking on plains and thrusting a foot into all manner of awkward cavities, but among our rather small raptorial fauna there is nevertheless plenty of variety in the feet with which the killing is done. No two even closely related species, such as the sparrowhawk and goshawk or the hobby and peregrine, are quite alike. The foot of the peregrine, which can strike a grouse dead in the air and must withstand this heavy impact at high speed, is relatively much thicker and stronger than that of the mainly insectivorous hobby.

Although we can, in such ways, deduce a lot about the methods of hunting and killing adopted by our birds of prey we still have remarkably few field observations on which to found these partly conjectural views. Few people ever see a bird of prey kill, and most of us who have spent a lifetime in the study of raptors have seen it happen only a few times, and that by chance. One may search the literature, largely in vain, for even a few examples, and some of these are clearly apocryphal, or an imaginative interpretation of observed facts. There is a great field for pure – and admittedly very difficult – field research into the precise ways in which the evolved and specialised adaptations of birds of prey are actually put to use in catching and killing the animals on which they feed.

PLATE 3. OSPREYS. *Above,* the male osprey spends many hours perched close to his sitting mate, suggesting little difficulty in catching fish. *Below,* an osprey feeding; the legs and feet are very powerful for a raptor of this size.

PLATE 4. HONEY BUZZARD; the claws of this individual are less blunted by digging for wasps nests than in some.

CHAPTER 2

THE BRITISH SPECIES

BRITAIN is not a country rich in birds of prey, and at least within historical times probably never was, compared to the adjacent continent of Europe. 24 species of diurnal raptors occur, or have been known to occur in Britain, as compared with 37 on the continent of Europe and 33–34 in the European countries bordering the English Channel and North Sea – France, Belgium, Holland, Germany, Denmark, Norway and Sweden. Admittedly the comparison is unfair since the combined area of these countries is very much greater than that of Britain, while their span of latitude is from arctic Norway to the sub-tropics of the South of France.

However, Britain is unquestionably a poor country in which to study the biology of birds of prey, for not only are there few species, but some of these are very much rarer than in Europe and many of the remainder have been and still are severely persecuted or are subject to human population pressures much more intense than in many parts of continental Europe. Britain is, and has been for centuries, one of the most densely populated countries in Europe and the world. This means that all British birds of prey live in an environment radically altered from its original state by man, to whose company they have had to adapt, with varying success. Of course, this does not mean that there is no interesting work on birds of prey being done or still to do in Britain; there is plenty, as I hope to show. Indeed I have been very surprised to find how great are the gaping lacunae in our knowledge of the few British birds of prey.

Of the 24 species of British diurnal birds of prey, eight, the black kite, white-tailed eagle, Egyptian and griffon vultures, pallid harrier, spotted eagle, lesser kestrel and red-footed falcon, are scarce or very scarce vagrants or visitors, and cannot be regarded as significant members of the British bird of prey fauna. With one exception, the white-tailed eagle, which once was common but was lost to the British Isles by persecution in the late nineteenth and early twentieth centuries, I cannot believe that any of them were ever important predators or scavengers in Britain. Of the other seven, the most likely one to have been a resident in Britain within the last three thousand years or so may have been the spotted eagle. It is an inhabitant of rather boggy forested country with glades such as may have existed in England in pre-Roman times, and it may then have occurred and died out, un-recorded, through changes in habitat brought about by the increasing human population and agriculture. I see no reason to suppose that any of the other six ever were common in Britain. The black kite, the Egyptian vulture, the griffon, the pallid harrier, the lesser kestrel and red-footed falcon are all species of mainly tropical or sub-tropical distribution, dependent on warm climates at least in summer. The pallid harrier and red-footed falcon breed further north than the others but the harrier usually requires open steppe to nest.

Of the six, if I were asked to forecast, the only one that seems to me at all likely to breed in Britain in the future is the black kite. This extraordinarily adaptable and successful raptor, almost certainly the most numerous of Old World birds of prey, is spreading and becoming more abundant in Europe. Of the twelve British records seven have been since 1960 (four in 1966, one in 1968, and two in 1971) and two others since 1942; these include records from Orkney and Shetland to the Scilly Isles. Red-footed falcons, too, have been seen with increasing frequency in recent years, and there are certainly abundant corvid nests, mainly rooks', in which they could breed. However, they might not be able to get enough insect food in our cool summer climate.

Part of the reason for the more frequent records of black kites and red-footed falcons in the British Isles may be the great interest in recording rare birds which has developed in recent years. A black kite is likely to be quickly spotted by today's army of skilled bird-watchers. However, several of the other recorded rarities are due to the gamekeeper and his gun, or the ardent skin collector, and date from times when birds of prey, if not bird-watchers, were more numerous in Europe than they are now. If kites ever breed again in Grays Inn they might well be black kites and not the red kites that formerly nested there. The black kite is quite capable of spreading in the manner of the collared dove, if not quite so fast.

Discounting these rare vagrants or visitors there are 16 species which are either breeding birds or regular migrants, sometimes both, as in the case of the goshawk and the harriers. Of these, 14 actually breed in Britain, and two – the rough-legged buzzard and the gyrfalcon – are more or less regular winter visitors in small numbers from arctic tundras. When they visit Britain nowadays they may be fractionally less likely to be greeted with a charge of shot than they were 30 or 40 years ago, but only fractionally. In 1972 a magnificent gyrfalcon was injured by gunshot in Anglesey and died despite efforts to save it; and I imagine that any misguided rough-legged buzzard that tried to hunt voles on a Breckland heath would get short shrift.

It cannot be said that the survival of the few individuals of these two species that visit Britain is crucially important to their survival in the main parts of their range. Neither is at present endangered, and they are much more likely to be endangered by pesticide residues in their prey than by being shot on their rare visits to Britain. Nevertheless it is a pity wantonly to destroy harmless and spectacular raptors such as these; even if they are out of their ecological range when they come here, probably driven south by food shortage, and quite likely would anyhow not survive to return to the arctic and breed. At present, neither rough-legged buzzards nor gyrfalcons are important members of the British winter raptor fauna. They are just scarce and spectacular winter visitors that ought to be given a chance and left alone.

Of the 14 present breeders, four, the osprey, honey buzzard, marsh harrier and goshawk, are represented by less than ten pairs, and cannot be considered important, countrywide, as predators on any particular sort of prey. Three of them, the marsh harrier, the goshawk, and the osprey, have each become extinct as breeders in Britain within the last 70 years, the osprey about 1910(3) and the marsh harrier about 1917 in Ireland and before 1900 in England: it probably never bred regularly in Scotland(2).

The marsh harrier re-established itself between the two World Wars and under protection rose to a maximum of about twenty pairs, but is now on the way down again, and may actually be the rarest regular breeder among our birds of prey, with less than five pairs. The osprey re-established itself in a blaze of well-judged publicity in 1954 or 1955 and has since increased to seven pairs in 1971(3,b). Both it and the marsh harrier must formerly have been much more common in Britain than they are now, and were reduced to their present case by, in the osprey, persecution pure and simple, and in the marsh harrier by a combination of persecution and destruction of habitat through fen drainage. The osprey, left to itself, should certainly now make a come-back perhaps to 100 pairs. The marsh harrier, however, may well be on the fringe of its range like its relative, Montagu's harrier, and might not be able to increase very much whatever protection it was offered. Nor can its habitat be restored, though the way in which it has adapted to Minsmere, its present sole regular breeding place, which was artificially flooded in the Second World War and is consequently a habitat only 35 years old, indicates how it could recolonise, given a chance.

I cannot find convincing evidence that the goshawk has been a common breeder in Britain at any time in the last two centuries, and I can find no definite published proof that the pairs that have undoubtedly bred in British woodlands in the last two decades are other than falconers' escapes or at best first generation descendants of these. This I do find odd, for I should have thought that there are plenty of tracts of private and state woodland large enough to support a pair or two of goshawks. When the extensive Forestry Commission plantations of the last 20 years become more mature there will be far more potential goshawk habitat than there was in 1799. This powerful aggressive hawk is not a specialised feeder, and can live in deciduous and coniferous woodland alike, though perhaps it thrives best in extensive coniferous forests such as those of Finland or Russia. It has been highly susceptible, like other bird eaters, to the effects of pesticide residues, and the Southern and Central European populations are in decline. It needs 5000–8000 acres (2000–3500 ha.) of mixed woodland and open country per pair, and there are few undisturbed tracts of this size in Britain. However, I still find it odd that goshawks do not regularly breed in some of the extensive conifer forests that now exist. Perhaps they do, but the whole affair is so shrouded in secrecy that no ordinary person or scientific investigator comes to hear of it. I have heard estimates of 2–20 pairs, but it seems best to conclude that there are less than ten, perhaps far fewer.

The honey buzzard, on the other hand, definitely is a specialist feeder on wasp grubs during the breeding season, and could not thrive unless there is an adequate supply of wasp grubs. Where it does breed in Britain I am told that it is highly successful, rearing a high proportion of young from eggs laid and, because of its very secretive ways in the incubation period, suffering small losses from egg collectors. On its breeding performance it ought to be able to spread in our more enlightened age (when every new-generation gamekeeper should be able to tell a honey buzzard from a common buzzard at a glance); but it does not, and this must be because it is a specialised feeder confined to certain localities where it can find enough wasps. All the same, it may well be the most numerous of the four breeding species represented by less than ten pairs in Britain, for it is very easily overlooked.

Two species, the red kite and Montagu's harrier, are represented by 10–50 pairs in Britain. The exact number of either is hard to discover from published literature, but the kite is now very well documented by the Nature Conservancy and Royal Society for Protection of Birds (R.S.P.B.), and totals about seventy birds of which at least fifty-two – 26 pairs – are mature breeding adults(4). The kite and Montagu's harrier make a nice parallel with the osprey and marsh harrier. The kite was formerly much more widespread and was the species spoken of by late-sixteenth-century travellers as being almost as common in the streets of London as the black kite was in Cairo – and that would be common indeed. It was eliminated, mainly by gamekeepers, from most of Britain before the end of the nineteenth century, but a small remnant survived in Wales. This remnant has increased significantly in the last 20 years, despite breeding success apparently lower than that of continental European red kites, even without the ravages of egg collectors. Since 1950 the population of kites has about doubled, and there can be no doubt that, if left to itself and not persecuted, the kite would slowly spread to other parts of Britain. There is plenty of suitable habitat in the rest of Wales, Devon, Western Scotland, or even East Anglia and Sussex.

Montagu's harrier, on the other hand, seems also to be another of those species that are on the northern fringe of their range and fluctuate in numbers from ecological causes. It probably was not ever very common in Britain, represented in the thirties by about twenty-five pairs(7). It increased to about forty–fifty pairs by 1957, this increase being mainly due to the spread of suitable breeding habitat in young forestry plantations. At the right stage of growth, these abound in voles and provide the right sort of dense cover for nesting harriers. Montagu's harrier took advantage of this situation, and bred successfully for a time, but with increased age the plantations became less suitable and the Montagu's harriers ceased breeding in them. When it has bred this harrier seems to have been generally rather successful, rearing good broods and being little persecuted; so its scarcity must be attributed largely to natural causes, though no doubt sporadic persecution has played some part.

Only one British species, the hobby, falls into the bracket 50–100 pairs. It may just exceed 100 pairs, but no accurate census is available, so that it seems safer to place it here. This beautiful little falcon is a largely insectivorous summer visitor and in relation to its numbers is one of the least known of British birds of prey. There is no good published account of the breeding behaviour of the hobby in Britain in the last thirty years or so, the best available being that of the egg collector Nethersole Thompson in 1931(6). The hobby does not even get a mention in the index of many volumes of British Birds. Many bird photographers have taken pictures of hobbies in this period, and I have been infuriated by a laconic reference, by one author, to having 'studied the hobby for fourteen years', without writing more than a paragraph or two about it(a).

Ignorant as we are about British hobbies it seems clear that the factors controlling this falcon are natural, not due to persecution or egg collecting. It is a summer visitor, arriving late, breeding late in wooded country, and leaving in autumn. It is therefore naturally confined to the drier and warmer parts of S.E. England, especially Hampshire, where about a quarter of the total population breed. There may be more hobbies than we suppose, for they are not easy to locate and quite easy to overlook. Whatever the causes of their low numbers they are nowhere sufficiently dense to be regarded as effective predators in the natural environment. 100 pairs scattered over even the six southern counties most commonly inhabited by hobbies means a density of 50–100 square miles or more per pair (130–260 sq.km.), far more than a pair actually needs for hunting. Hobbies in Britain are quite scarce, and are unlikely ever to have been anything else, or to increase very markedly in the future.

The next group of species, of 100–500 pairs, includes the hen harrier, golden eagle, peregrine falcon and merlin. Prior to 1950 the peregrine was represented by more than 500 pairs, but it has declined to just below that figure since the introduction of persistent organo-chlorine pesticides in agriculture. Each of these four species except perhaps the merlin is probably at capacity numbers (by which I mean the largest population any given area could support) in some parts of its range even today, and they are accordingly worth studying as effective predators in the environment, as well as worth watching just as magnificent raptors. The least known of the four is the merlin, which is a little better known than the hobby. The best known is the hen harrier, due almost entirely to the long-term researches of one man, Eddie Balfour, in Orkney. The golden eagle and peregrine are less well known, and there are surprising gaps in the published information on these species, even in subjects such as breeding biology which one would have thought might have been effectively studied. In the golden eagle, much more information is probably available than has been published in the scientific literature, and the continuous watch being kept on the only English breeding pair should soon provide information to fill many gaps in our knowledge of the breeding behaviour.

Of these four species the peregrine and the merlin are or were decreasing, though the peregrine has made something of a come-back in 1971–72. The main reasons for the decrease of the peregrine are agricultural pesticides and increasing human interference, often casual, in that order of importance(9). It is not clear why the merlin is decreasing – or even whether it really is. If it were not for this recent decrease the peregrine and the merlin would be found to be as common as they could be, in their rather limited areas of habitat – mountain country and sea-cliffs for the peregrine and open rolling moorland for the merlin. The merlin is so little studied that its population ecology is virtually unknown. A full study might well show that there are more than 500 pairs in Britain as a whole, though I doubt it. I have walked a great many miles over suitable Scottish moors and seen very few merlins. I see far more golden eagles, and it would not surprise me to learn that there are far fewer than 500 pairs of merlins.

The golden eagle is still at capacity numbers in much of its Highland range, and would undoubtedly spread to new areas if allowed to. It has demonstrated its potential for increase in recent years by recolonising Ireland briefly, re-establishing itself in Orkney, and breeding, perhaps for the first time, in the Lake District. It is not in acute danger, though its fortunes could be adversely affected very easily and quickly, as discussed in greater detail later. The hen harrier may actually be the second most numerous of this particular group, being represented by perhaps 450 pairs. Moreover, it is the only one of the four which is actually increasing, despite pesticides, severe persecution in its winter haunts, and other factors. Like Montagu's harrier its increase has in places been helped and hastened by the availability of young conifer plantations, unkeepered and rich in voles, as breeding habitat in several parts of Britain. In the focus of its range, in Orkney, it has long been about as numerous as it could be.

There remain three species, the buzzard, sparrowhawk, and kestrel which are resident over very large tracts of Britain in numbers exceeding 500 pairs. Of the three the kestrel and the sparrowhawk occur almost wherever there is suitable habitat though the sparrowhawk has disappeared from some suitable areas. The kestrel at least may be at capacity numbers in many parts of the country. This vole-eating falcon is less affected by agricultural pesticides than is the bird-eating sparrowhawk, which has undoubtedly decreased sharply in England in the last two decades though it may now be recovering again. These two small and widespread hawks are really the only British diurnal birds of prey that would have to be considered as regular predators in all suitable environments in Britain.

The kestrel is probably the commonest bird of prey in Britain, but locally the buzzard can be more numerous, occurring at higher breeding densities of up to three pairs per square mile. It is even possible that the buzzard may be the most effective raptor in Britain in terms of weight, and it is certainly at capacity numbers in a good many areas. However, as we shall see later, the range of the buzzard is

Table 1 Summarised Research Data British Birds of Prey

Recorded Information. A Good or very good. B Fair. C Poor.

	Population Status	General Ecology	Food Preferences	Breeding Behaviour	Breeding Statistics (Clutch & Brood size etc)	Ringing results and movements	General state of knowledge	General knowledge with additional European data	Notes on research needs etc.
Osprey	A	C	A	A	A	B	AB	A	Observations on feeding behaviour needed.
Honey Buzzard	C	C	C	C	C	C	C	AB	Available unpublished information needs publishing.
Red Kite	A	A	A	B	A	B	AB	AB	Additional breeding studies needed.
Marsh Harrier	A	A	C	C	B	B	B	A	Research impracticable because of small population.
Montagu's Harrier	B	C	C	B	C	B	BC	AB	Breeding biology and statistics needed.
Hen Harrier	A	A	A	A	A	A	A	A	Apparently rather little left to learn.
Sparrowhawk	A	A	A	B	B	B	AB	A	Much information unpublished.
Goshawk	C	C	C	C	C	C	C	AB	If this species breeds in Britain the fact should be recorded.
Buzzard	A	A	A	B	A	A	AB	A	Good breeding behaviour studies needed. Food data needed.
Golden Eagle	A	B	B	B	A	C	B	B	Breeding biology: quantitative food studies.
Kestrel	B	B	B	C	C	A	B	A	Breeding behaviour relatively poorly studied.
Merlin	C	C	C	C	C	B	C	C	Population data and breeding biology lacking.
Hobby	B	B	C	C	C	C	BC	A	Population data and breeding biology lacking.
Peregrine	A	A	A	B	A	B	AB	AB	Good breeding studies needed.

Data from British sources (columns 1–8)

restricted, not by pesticides or by land use methods, but by the persistent destructive activities of gamekeepers, in defiance of the law of the land.

Some of the details given above are summarised in Table 1. In sum, of 24 species that occur eight can be discounted as rare or very rare vagrants, and another two (rough-legged buzzard and gyrfalcon) are scarce but regular winter visitors never numerous enough to have much effect as predators. Of the 14 breeding species four (osprey, honey buzzard, marsh harrier and goshawk) are so rare that their total predatory effect on the British environment is negligible. Two others (kite and Montagu's harrier), if not quite so rare, are also so uncommon that their predatory effect is only noticeable in small local areas; one of these is limited by ecological factors rather than persecution. The hobby, fairly widespread, and little persecuted, is still so scarce, with less than 100 pairs, that it cannot have very much real effect on its prey animals. Only seven species, four (peregrine, merlin, golden eagle and hen harrier) restricted in range, and three (buzzard, sparrowhawk and kestrel) potentially or actually widespread over most of Britain can be regarded as effective natural predators on other animals inhabiting the same environment.

I think these figures underline the relative poverty of the British bird of prey fauna, even compared to Europe, where several species rare with us are still quite abundant, if decreasing. It is, no doubt, still more unfair to compare Britain with a tropical African country, and I do so merely as an example. In Kenya, where I live, 70 species of diurnal raptors occur, either as residents or as winter migrants. Of this large number none is seriously affected by persecution, and only the winter migrants are likely to be affected by pesticides, not acquired, at least to any substantial extent, in Kenya. Some of the Kenyan species undoubtedly have adapted to man-made environment, and some, such as the black kite, are without doubt commoner therein. However, in every case one can observe the raptor concerned and be pretty certain that only natural factors affect its abundance or predatory behaviour. If it is rare, it is not because it has been savagely persecuted out of existence at some time in the past; and a common large eagle such as the fish eagle or crowned eagle may even behave as it naturally should, showing very little fear of man. This too direct comparison is certainly unfair to Britain; but I think it makes the point that in Britain we are studying a beleaguered population of a few species inhabiting only man-made or man-affected environments, and which is probably, therefore, not ideal as a subject for the study of the bionomics of birds of prey as such. Nevertheless the British work does demonstrate some remarkable findings.

Given this limited range of species and the controversy that has surrounded their activities in the environment one would think that the last word would have been said long ago on the behaviour of most British birds of prey. This is very far from being the case. Up to about 1950, research on British birds of prey was minimal, largely confined to observation and photography at the nest by a few individuals, several of them egg collectors, who recorded the details of the laying intervals only because they waited for the clutch to be completed before taking it while it was still fresh and easily blown. They may also have recorded details of courtship behaviour; but that is not what they went there for.

The bird photographers usually waited until the young had hatched before putting up their hides and taking photographs. They recorded oddments of interest about the fledging periods of birds of prey, items of food and so on, but although many of them claim to have kept detailed notes they seldom published much detail on what they had seen in scientific journals. If one were to study the back numbers of the *Field*, or *Country Life*, one could perhaps find quite a lot of data which would supplement, if rather unsystematically, that available in scientific journals, and in the field notebooks of bird photographers there must be many an interesting detail tucked away that will never see the searching light of scientific print. When I record that little is known about the breeding behaviour of, say, the merlin, there will be some who snort with fury and say 'rubbish'. However I know that if I ask these same people for quantitative data on the share of the sexes in incubation, bringing food, or the amount and type of prey brought, only minimal factual data will be forthcoming. I've tried it, and given up, not in disgust, for I have been a bird photographer myself and know what they are after – the finest trophy photograph they can get – but in despair that much of real value will be produced.

On a world wide or African basis I classify our knowledge of the breeding cycle of birds of prey under five heads: (i) Unknown; the nest never having been found. (ii) Little known; a few nests having been found and the eggs described, but no sustained observations made. (iii) Well known; a good general idea of the nest and nest site, clutch size, etc., derived from many nests, and a few sustained observations covering part of a breeding cycle in at least one case. (iv) Very well known; the general nesting behaviour is understood and detailed accurate observations are available throughout most of the breeding cycle at at least one nest, leaving only a few details to add. (v) Intimately known; observations in detail over many years or at many nest sites, including such advanced detail as changes of mates among adults and survival rates of the young.

If this classification is applied to the breeding cycle of the 14 British breeding species none are unknown or little known; all have been better studied than that. However, if we stick entirely to British published literature, most of the species are no better than well known; to obtain a good picture of the breeding cycle British information must be supplemented from continental sources. While it is likely that buzzards at the nest in Britain behave like buzzards in Germany or Belgium, there is no good published account of a British buzzard's breeding cycle in a scientific journal on which to base this conclusion.

In the case of the extremely rare British species – the honey buzzard, osprey, marsh harrier and goshawk – reluctance to study the species at the nest is understandable. Harm could be done to a scarce and struggling breeding population by such interference. Yet one of the only two intimately known species in Britain is the osprey, the Loch Garten pair having been watched intensively day and night since they began to breed. They have been watched more intensively than any other pair of raptors anywhere in the world. Yet the results of this very detailed study have never yet been published, and in 1972 I was distressed to find that the observations recorded daily at the Loch Garten eyrie had not been summarised day by day or year by year as the study progressed. This analysis is now being done, but the results have not been available for this book, and this account of the osprey is accordingly the poorer. It is virtually certain that, in the course of analysis of this mass of important material, it will become evident that the watchers could easily have recorded additional information of several sorts, but did not, because they were not guided by results of day to day analysis. Good research has been done; but the opportunity to do a really first class piece of research on this pair of ospreys has unquestionably been lost.

All the other three of these four rare species can be upgraded to at least the very well-known category by consulting the continental literature; and I believe that there is, in the case of the honey buzzard, a mass of unpublished British material which is not published for security reasons alone. In my opinion this is misguided, for the main facts of breeding biology can be brought out without giving away sites of nests in any detail, or even in such a way that the field of search for an egg collector would be narrowed. It is to be hoped that the possessors of this information will change their minds and publish it, for we need it; and it need give away no more secrets about localities than have already been detailed in the published literature.

The two species with 10–50 pairs, Montagu's harrier and the red kite, are both very well known, but in the case of the harrier we have to depend mainly on the continental literature though there are some useful observations in Britain too. The breeding behaviour of the kite has until recently been shrouded in secrecy, but the main details have now been published by the Nature Conservancy, and I was earlier privileged to be allowed to include a summary of this information in this book(4). Otherwise, from published British information I could only have written a few words about the red kite.

The hobby is little known in Britain, but again the continental literature enables us to call it very well, but not intimately known. Hobbies probably behave in Britain as they do in Holland, but equally they are certainly on the fringe of their range in Britain and may, accordingly, be expected to show some differences in, for instance, breeding success or brood size. If they do not, it will be the harder to understand why hobbies are not more common than they are.

It is among the commoner species that one finds the most surprising gaps. I cannot find a really good account of the breeding behaviour of the merlin or, much more surprising, of the magnificent and much publicised peregrine falcon anywhere in the world. The peregrine is, in some ways, the most admired and studied of all birds of prey; but I have not read a good modern account of the breeding biology at a single nest throughout the season, with the type of quantitative data available for many African raptors, in any journal in any language. One must go back to Francis Heatherly, in 1910, to find a fairly good British account.

The golden eagle, likewise, is poorly recorded in Britain, though I hope some of the gaps can be filled by the detailed observations on the Lake District birds. Undoubtedly wide knowledge about its breeding biology is already available, in the notebooks of the grand old man of eagle studies, Seton Gordon. However, from what he has published it is still not possible to give other than rather a general account of the breeding behaviour of golden eagles(5). Possibly he might say that he is not greatly interested in the scientific aspects but simply loves eagles, and that is understandable but regrettable. I love eagles too, but I think I love and understand them better by reason of recording in detail the scientific facts, and I think I could claim to have stimulated others to do likewise, perhaps to the overall benefit of the species concerned. The detailed quantitative data on the food of the golden eagle provided by recent American studies are a far more telling conservation argument than any amount of general statements or views.

It is odder still to find that none of the three commonest species – the buzzard, kestrel and sparrowhawk – have been studied in detail at the nest in Britain in the last 30 years. Again, we can push them all into the very-well-known category, if not the intimately known, by recourse to the continental literature. The best accounts of breeding biology of any of these three species were published by J. H. Owen on the sparrowhawk in British Birds in 1927 and earlier, and these observations are good. There is much recent information on the sparrowhawk awaiting publication, but a good breeding behaviour study of both the kestrel and the buzzard in Britain is needed. In these two species there is no reason to defer such studies because they are rare, for they are not. Anyway, as has been shown in the case of the osprey, such studies can with care be done on rare species without causing disaster.

The limitations of research on birds of prey in Britain as regards the breeding cycle do not apply so strongly with regard to population status and general ecology, at least for some species. The plight of birds of prey resulting from the use of organo-chlorine pesticides in agriculture triggered off a spate of status and population surveys, several of them continuing and as yet unpublished (1, 8). In the case of several species the population is fairly accurately known, or could be computed from available records. There is also much more information on the ecology of some of these species, and their food preferences, than on breeding biology. Even in these respects, however, the population ecology and feeding behaviour of some species, such as the hobby and merlin is little known or studied. One cannot find good published data on the food of either, almost nothing has recently been published on their local population density, and we do not really know what controls their numbers in Britain.

It would certainly not be true, therefore, to say that the last word has been said on British birds of prey, even on the common species where restrictions on study for security reasons can be minimal. It would however be true to say, unfortunately, that current research is too often hampered by illegal interference, mainly from gamekeepers; scarcely any research project is free of such interference. In this chapter and in the species accounts which follow I have attempted to set out the state of knowledge as I know it. In doing so I may well have overlooked odd items of data in some of the lesser journals, but I have consulted the major British journals and the standard published works on British birds without locating any more than I record herein and I have been able to make use of much unpublished material. There is still scope for a wide field of research on British raptors, just as there is for many other British species.

An army of keen ornithologists setting out all together to study raptors in the field could well, in a densely populated country like Britain, do at least as much harm as good. One pair of ospreys is said to have been destroyed, not because the proprietor of the estate was against them as such, but because he did not want his land invaded by swarms of bird-watchers 'twitching' ospreys for their lists. Such people are the worst threat to breeding success in the few remaining pairs of marsh harriers. It would therefore be desirable for any research which is done to be controlled, organised, and directed to obtain the maximum benefit in new knowledge for the least disturbance. There is no reason for this to be onerous or restrictive, and it can lead to more rewarding results.

There is a very good case for extending the methods used in the case of the osprey to certain other species. Kites, golden eagles, peregrine falcons are all spectacular raptors, and all could be observed at certain breeding sites without causing desertion through disturbance. Indeed, in both the kite and the golden eagle, one can think of breeding sites that would actually be more likely to succeed if organised watches were kept at nests from hides that could be used by interested members of the public to see these magnificent species at close quarters. They might be less of a draw than the osprey, but it would be worth trying and, in the case of the only English pair of golden eagles a continuous watch is being kept which can be guided to provide much more data on breeding behaviour than is available from other sources,

It is unnecessary to be a professional ornithologist or doctorate scientist to make good accurate observations during the breeding cycle, and most of the best work in this respect, world wide, has been done by enthusiastic individuals or teams of amateurs. Balfour's detailed work on hen harriers in Orkney is a classic case of this. Britain is probably richer in enthusiastic amateur ornithologists than any other country in the world; and I do not believe that *none* of these, or even that few of them are sufficiently dedicated or interested to brave the rigours of the Scottish spring to obtain detailed factual data on the breeding cycle of the golden eagle or peregrine falcon. With hides built in the winter of semi-permanent waterproof materials observations spells need not be too rigorous. Essentially, however, good studies of birds of prey at the nest are best tackled by teams of three or four people rather than one man alone; the necessity to eat and sleep means that a single observer finds it most difficult to keep the nest under observation all the hours of daylight, let alone through the night in a northern summer. It is easier for a single man to undertake local status surveys, food analyses, and similar research that can be done in odd spare hours at any time of the year.

Ideally, of course, studies at the nest itself should be accompanied by parallel studies at the same time of where and when the male or female hunts for food, and by habitat analysis and population counts of available prey animals. There is scope to bring together the undoubtedly available talent of geologists, botanists, mammalogists and herpetologists in the study of the whole home range of a pair of raptors over several years. Such work could probably be undertaken by county bird clubs, perhaps in conjunction with Universities, and co-ordinated by the National Environmental Research Council. I would not like to believe that no one in Britain, other than professional salaried ornithologists, would be prepared to do such work; and I am sure that to extend our knowledge of British birds of prey by taking part in effectively co-ordinated research would be more rewarding for many people than driving all over the country merely to tick off a rarity or two on a list.

CHAPTER 3

CLASSIFICATION AND FIELD IDENTIFICATION

I HAVE grouped these two rather knotty subjects in one chapter since there may be people who feel uninterested in the relations of birds of prey to one another, or who are certain they can identify any species on the British list without hesitation – which I myself should never claim. For those who are uninterested, skip from here to the next chapter and return later if you feel inclined.

When it comes to identification I must say at the outset that I have not the space to make this into an identification manual for British and European birds of prey as well as a general account of the biology of British species. Identification is the province of the field guide book, and there are many available, while a particularly good series of identification papers has recently appeared in British Birds(5). As regards identification, therefore, I confine myself to a few remarks on each species in Britain. As I myself seldom have much difficulty if I have a good view of a bird of prey I am probably not the best person to advise those who find identification of birds of prey difficult.

The classification of the diurnal birds of prey, the Falconiformes, is not wholly satisfactory. Few arrangements agree, and in many reference works to which one turns for enlightenment the species are listed in an order almost as dependent on the author's personal whims as on the most generally agreed classification based on established relationships. This is highly confusing to the average reader, and would make Linnaeus turn in his grave. Presumably, the idea of a standard classification of genera and species is to simplify and codify relationships within families and larger groups. If attempts at classification make confusion worse confounded they had better be abandoned, and we should go for that counsel of despair, the list in alphabetical order that obscures any possible relationships between species. I find it hard to understand how a reference work, such as Bannerman's *Birds of the British Isles*(1), can insist on listing the falcons first when, in all accepted modern systematic lists, the latest of which is the British Ornithologists Union's Records Committee's standard list 'The Status of Birds in Britain and Ireland'(12), they are listed last. I can pick any three or four reference works off my own shelves and find the falcons in a different place and order each time. Such methods, derived from the inability of systematists to agree among themselves, or sheer indifference, can only confuse rather than clarify.

Changes of scientific name brought about, for instance, by the lumping or splitting of species, or the discovery of a long lost work of reference which happens to pre-date existing nomenclature should only be forced on the long-suffering ornithological public with very good reasons indeed, and these reasons should be clearly and cogently stated. Frequent changes of this sort make classification into an abstruse, difficult and irritating exercise in pedantry to the average ornithologist, whereas the idea really is to clarify relationships within groups and so, for instance, to provide a helpful springboard for comparative biological studies of related species and genera and their behaviour patterns. There is much to be said for the *nomina conservanda* (names which cannot be changed); and the day when a systematist could give a bird a new name just because he thought fit is surely past. Personally,

I should treat any such arbitrary change with the contempt I think it deserves, and fortunately it seldom happens nowadays among European or British birds of prey.

The most familiar arrangement of the Falconiformes, and the one used for instance by the British Museum, is that of the 1931 Peters List(10). This is based on the Wetmore classification, which puts the recently evolved passerines last, and is now generally adopted in preference to the old British Handbook classification which puts passerines first and leaps abruptly from sandmartins to the not closely related swifts. The Peters List begins with the primitive New World vultures, passes on to honey buzzards and kites, and ends with falcons. Anyone going through this list who is familiar with the behaviour or anatomy of the birds listed will at once locate points in it at which the logical linear sequence of relationships breaks down and becomes inexplicable. A particular family or genus follows another to which it is not obviously very similar or closely related.

This cannot be avoided in the classification of any large group. One is faced with a mass of birds, in this case all obviously diurnal birds of prey, and one tries to put them into the most logical order possible. There are bound to be gaps, caused for instance by the extinction during geological time (which in diurnal raptors extends back more than 70 million years) of intermediate linking forms. Such gaps not only affect particular species, such as the osprey, which must be put in a family of its own, but entire large families such as the falcons, which are not at all obviously related to the secretary bird except that they too have hooked beaks. Such difficulties will strike anyone who strives to understand this knotty subject, and all one can say is that systematists do their best, but don't always agree with one another – indeed very seldom do.

The two main modern classifications of the Falconiformes suffer also from this drawback. There may even be doubt that the Falconiformes should all be grouped in one Order at all. If and when the modern technique of egg-white or other protein electrophoresis has attained sufficient refinement and accuracy to give a clearer insight into really basic relationships it may, for instance, show that the falcons and caracaras, the family Falconidae, are so different from other diurnal raptors that they deserve to be in a separate Order. To quote my favourite author 'The logical mind bends almost double under the weight of so dire a catastrophe'. Fortunately, the likelihood of this happening before I am dead seems at present remote.

The two most modern arrangements are those of the late Professor Erwin Stresemann of Berlin and of my friend and colleague Dr Dean Amadon of the American Museum. The latter made fewer radical departures from, but seemed to us to clear up some, but not all, of the existing anomalies in the Peters List(4). Naturally, nothing is perfect; but we felt that this was the best we could do. The rationale of our arrangement is illustrated in Fig. 5.

Dr Stresemann's list, published in 1960(13), depended very largely on the single character of the order of wing moult. He arranged the Falconiformes according to whether they moult their primaries in one of three ways; (i) ascendant, beginning with the fourth primary and moulting outwards to primary 1 and inwards to the innermost; (ii) descendant, beginning with the innermost primary and moulting in regular sequence to the outermost at the tip of the wing; and (iii) irregular, moulting the primaries from several centres. In this last case immatures sometimes moult in regular descendant sequence and adults irregularly(13).

When one examines the matter, one finds that, except in the Falconidae, which all moult in the same way, large or very large birds with high wing loading tend

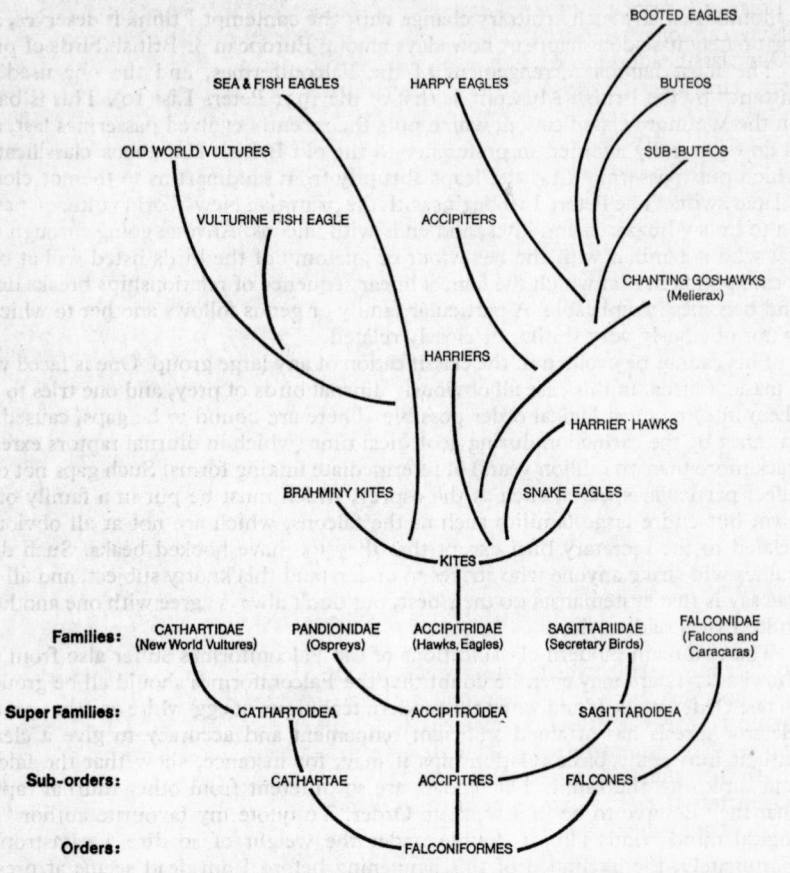

FIG. 5. Basis of the Amadon classification of Falconiformes, with detail of Accipitridae. (From Brown and Amadon, 1969.) In this classification of the Accipitridae the Old World vultures, sea eagles, harpy eagles and booted eagles are each regarded as the culmination of a particular line of evolution.

to moult irregularly while smaller species moult in regular descendant series. In arranging his families mainly according to wing moult Stresemann began with the New and Old World vultures, went on to harriers, snake eagles, sparrowhawks, buzzards, and large eagles, and placed the sea eagles and kites near the end of the order close to the osprey and falcons. We felt we could not fully accept this proposed classification so far as the arrangement of genera is concerned and suggested our own. This is essentially that of Dr Amadon, but with any points at issue thoroughly thrashed out between us.

Moreover, the standard practice nowadays in classifying any group is to start with the most primitive member and end with the most highly evolved and specialised.

This is the principle of the Wetmore classification of birds, used for instance in the New Dictionary of Birds(7), and is what Dr Amadon and I have also tried to do. Our classification has recently been used in the recent B.O.U. Records Committee standard work on the status of birds in Britain and Ireland, and is likely to be accepted for the revised version of the Peters List. If it can be shown, at a later date, that our arrangement is radically in error, with clear and cogent reasons stated, I shall be happy at least to argue my views to which, otherwise, I intend to stick like glue.

Of course, someone has to decide what is primitive and what is not, a difficult decision which I am glad is not normally mine. Which, for instance, is the more primitive falcon, the sexually dimorphic kestrel or the powerful peregrine, normally regarded as the more advanced. I cannot avoid a sneaking feeling that the peregrine is regarded as more advanced partly because it is bigger, fiercer, and more spectacular in its way of killing than the vole-eating kestrel. In the opinion of mediaeval falconers the kestrel was a relatively despicable bird. 'Cowardly as a koystril' said one of W. Shakespeare's characters; and has this undeserved stigma stuck, as Aristotle's crude estimate of the incubation period of the golden eagle was repeated for 2200 years(9) ? Why should the osprey or the honey buzzard, both very highly specialised raptors filling a particular ecological niche, be placed very early in the whole order, immediately after the apparently primitive New World vultures, and accordingly be regarded as more primitive than the relatively unspecialised and versatile buzzard. There may be good reasons, but they are often not clearly stated by any modern systematist. Does it even matter, or should we just give up trying to sort out this sort of tangle and list everything in alphabetical order anyhow ?

One must face the fact that to the ordinary ornithologist these niceties do not matter much. He wants to know what a bird of prey is, what and how much it eats, and how it lives. The first essential to the average person is recognition; and only when a deeper study of comparative anatomy or behaviour is made does it seem necessary to ascertain more accurately what is a particular bird's nearest relation. Even then there are systematists who say that behaviour, or voice, are such plastic characters that they cannot be used to demarcate fundamental relationships anyhow. It sometimes seems to me that the Dockers' Union does not have a monopoly of curious ideas about what is proper!

When it comes to recognition and identification in the field, I am always surprised to find how many people think the birds of prey are a difficult group in this respect. I suppose long practice has made me unable to appreciate other people's difficulties. I am not able to understand how anyone can identify small warblers or, even worse, pipits and larks, and have difficulty with great big, often clearly marked diurnal birds of prey soaring about in the sky or perching on a conspicuous crag or bough. In Britain, even allowing for immature and subadult plumages there really should be no difficulty at all. In any one area the maximum number of species likely to be observed together is not more than five in summer and a couple more in winter, all of them clearly differentiated from one another by size, colouring, habitat preference, mode of flight, and other easily observable characters.

I suppose part of the feeling that it is imperative accurately to recognise a rarity at a glance, even in a thick fog on a freezing saltmarsh, derives from the modern preoccupation with listing which, to my mind, has been admirably epitomised by the slang word 'twitching'. Rarities are of interest, certainly, for they may be the probing forerunners of resident species of the future. However, they are not the most important members of the British bird of prey fauna today, and I have not treated them as such, but have concentrated in the text on the commoner species likely to be seen more often and for longer, and about which more information is available. I seek to stimulate interest in what we have here now rather than in rare exotics; and I think and hope I have shown that there is still much that is obscure here, even among common species such as the kestrel.

British ornithologists these days go far more to the continent. For this reason I have tried to include in the tabulated information many continental figures to amplify the often scanty British data, and have drawn extensively on comparative behaviour studies from Europe. I have also included in the 'English' or vernacular names some alternatives likely to be proposed or used for very wideranging species which also occur in North America. On the Continent it is true that a large falcon might be a lanner or saker as well as a gyr or peregrine, while a dark-brown buzzard-sized bird might be a dark booted eagle instead of a honey, common, rough-legged, or long-legged buzzard. Obviously, if I were to go into the niceties of identification of all the continental species as well it would take up half this book, and I am quite sure I could not do it any better or even as well as several other authors already in print. Accordingly, I have mainly attempted to give a few brief ideas as to how to identify the *British species in Britain.* Even here, those who really know these birds are likely to criticise my own methods harshly; and those who don't will do better to take up a standard field guide first.

Many people have great difficulty in identifying certain species, and, if it is any comfort to them, so do I. I would never attempt to state with certainty whether a particular female harrier two hundred yards away was a pallid or a Montagu's, though I like to think I could distinguish both with certainty from a female hen harrier – though perhaps not in a freezing saltmarsh on a foggy day. When asked what a certain raptor may be, one should not be ashamed to say 'I do not know'. Equally, one should not claim to have seen a rough-legged buzzard kill an adult shelduck in full flight unless absolutely certain that that unlikely event had actually been witnessed.

ORDER **FALCONIFORMES**
Sub-order ACCIPITRES
Family **Pandionidae**
Genus *Pandion* Savigny

Osprey. *Pandion haliaetus* (Linnaeus)

The osprey is the sole member of the family Pandionidae, which in the Amadon classification comes before the primitive kites in the whole list of Falconiformes. Some other authorities have thought it might be related to the very primitive New World vultures; but in the past it has usually been placed between the larger and more advanced eagles and the falcons, which are generally considered to be the most highly evolved diurnal raptors. I think everyone agrees that the osprey deserves a family to itself, for it has no obvious close relatives at all; but whether it is more closely related to kites or falcons is a moot point.

Similarities with kites include, for instance, the shape of the wings, with a pronounced angle at the carpal joint in flight; the whistling sort of voice; the building of a large stick nest; the greenish inside eggshell; and certain primitive anatomical features, such as the lack of a bony ridge above the eye. Differences from the falcons include the making of a large stick nest, laying eggs with a green, not buff, inner shell and again, the voice; the voices of all falcons are harsh or rasping, and of the family Falconidae only the South American caracaras and near relatives build their own nests.

All British ospreys, whether vagrants in winter, or residents in summer belong to the nominate race *P.h. haliaetus*, which inhabits the whole of Europe and Asia and migrates to Africa in winter. Two other races, *P.h. carolinensis* of the Americas, and *P.h. cristatus* of Australasia are separated by minor characters of plumage and size. Neither is likely to be seen in Britain. In Britain ospreys are distinguished by their mainly aquatic habitat, large size, and conspicuous white heads with dark line through the pale yellow, rather bulbous looking eye. The beak is very sharply hooked, and in flight the angle at the carpal joint of the wings distinguishes the osprey from all but kites. Kites are brown below and have forked tails, while ospreys have square tails and are mainly white with dark markings under the wing, which in flight shows a blackish patch at the carpal joint. Immatures resemble adults, but are browner. I think it is easier to confuse ospreys with large subadult gulls than with any other diurnal raptor.

The osprey has a distinctive yelping voice, 'cheuk-cheuk' or 'kyip-kyip', quite unlike that of eagles or buzzards; a male in display utters a high pitched frenzied 'cherreeek-chereeeek'; but he is then so conspicuous as to be unmistakable.

Family **Accipitridae**

Genus *Pernis* Cuvier

Honey Buzzard. *Pernis apivorus* (Linnaeus)

Honey buzzards are primitive members of the family Accipitridae which include also kites, Old World vultures, hawks, harriers, buzzards and eagles. They and their near relatives were formerly separated in a subfamily Perninae, which was a convenient and good idea and has been abandoned, rather to my sorrow, mainly because present knowledge does not permit division into clear-cut subfamilies. Among the nearest relatives of honey buzzards are other primitive 'kites' such as the cuckoo falcons and bazas (*Aviceda*), the Cayenne and American swallow-tailed kites (*Leptodon, Elanoides*) and the falcon-like crepuscular bat hawk (*Machaerhamphus*). Many of these birds are, although apparently all relatively primitive, very highly specialised, feeding on particular species of types of prey, quite unlike the omnivorous true kites (*Milvus*), which are regarded as less primitive.

Honey buzzards are Old World forms inhabiting the whole of Europe and Asia, visiting but not breeding in Africa, and represented in some East Indian islands by other species, the barred and long-tailed honey buzzards (*Pernis celebensis* and *Henicopernis* spp.). The continental, Asian and European forms can be regarded as three species *P. apivorus*, *P. orientalis* and *P. ruficollis* respectively; or all three can be regarded as races of one species, *P. apivorus*. I prefer the latter since the similarities of behaviour and plumage are great; however, the tropical Indian and Malaysian races of *P.a. ruficollis* (or *P. ruficollis*), some of which are island forms, may merit specific rank. Certainly *P.a. ruficollis* and especially the Malaysian *P.a. torquatus* are more distinct than either of the other two races from each other.

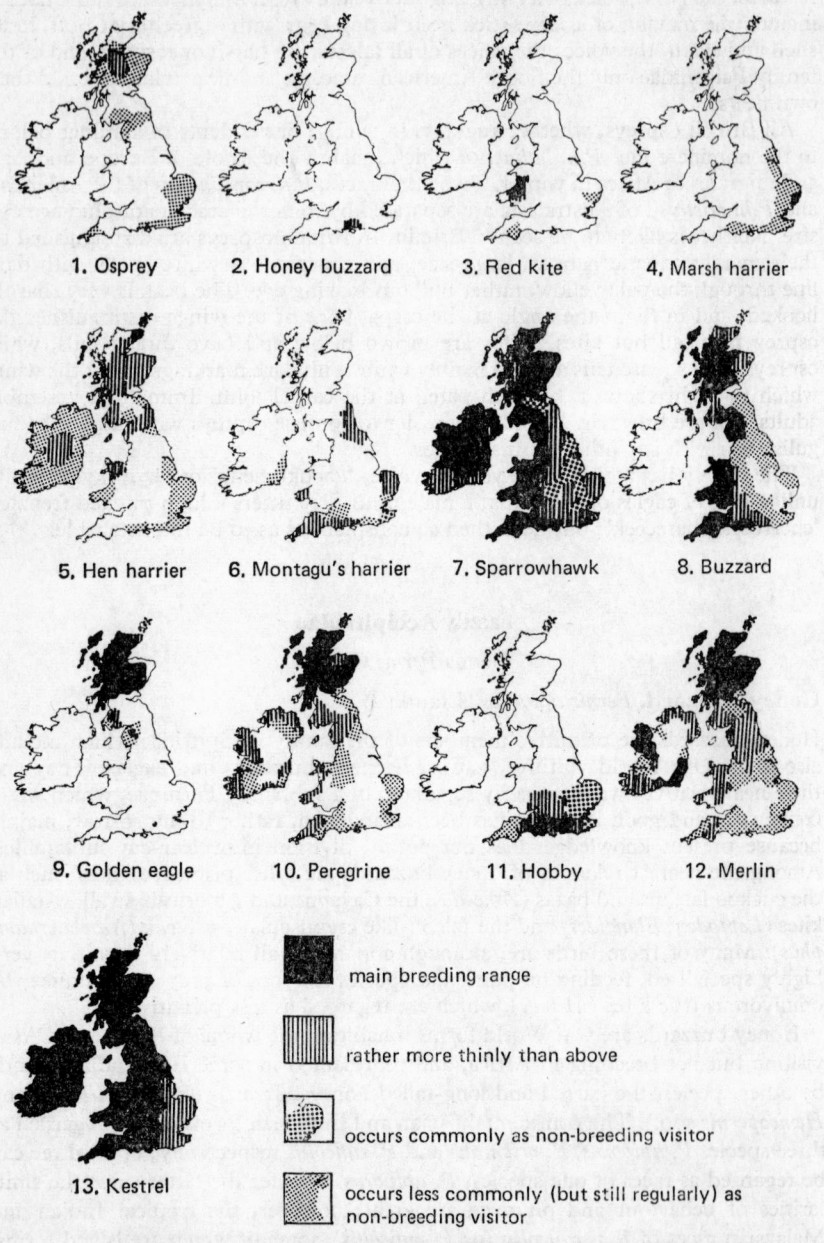

1. Osprey   2. Honey buzzard   3. Red kite   4. Marsh harrier

5. Hen harrier   6. Montagu's harrier   7. Sparrowhawk   8. Buzzard

9. Golden eagle   10. Peregrine   11. Hobby   12. Merlin

13. Kestrel

- main breeding range
- rather more thinly than above
- occurs commonly as non-breeding visitor
- occurs less commonly (but still regularly) as non-breeding visitor

MAPS I – 13. Distribution Maps. By kind permission of John Parslow, from *The Birds of Britain and Europe* by Heinzel, Fitter and Parslow (Collins).

The other species occurring alongside *P. apivorus* is *P. celebensis* of Celebes; both it and a form of *P. apivorus* occur in the Philippines.

All British and European honey buzzards belong to the typical race *P.a. apivorus*; no other is likely to be seen, and it only occurs from May to September as a high summer migrant. In Britain it can hardly be confused with any other species but the common buzzard which is about the same size and lives also in woodlands. Honey buzzards are intensely variable, but are often paler below and darker above than the common buzzard, but much more strongly barred on the breast and under wing coverts. The tail has a characteristic pattern with two dark bars near the base separated from a broad terminal bar by a mottled greyish area. In flight the honey buzzard tends to hold its wings flatter, with less of a dihedral, and appears to have a slimmer narrower head and relatively longer tail. It also twists the tail about like a kite, and flaps its wings slowly below the horizontal. The bright yellow eye and feathered cheeks would be diagnostic at close quarters but difficult to see at any distance.

The voice of the honey buzzard is not well described; some utterances are mewing whistles 'kuwiee-ee-ee-eiu' like those of the buzzard but shriller, while the male at the nest utters a clicking or popping noise like a stick being held against the spokes of a rotating bicycle wheel, if that sound can be imagined in this age of motor transport. At the nest too sounds like a spitting cat are uttered, 'Pyow' or 'Pya'.

Genus *Milvus* Lacepede

Black Kite. *Milvus migrans* (Boddaert)

Red Kite. *Milvus milvus* (Linnaeus)

These two species are omnivorous, scavenging kites inhabiting vast tracts of the Old World. The black kite is possibly the most numerous bird of prey, certainly the most numerous large raptor, occurring in almost incredible numbers in India and the East. It is divided into geographical races inhabiting Europe and Western Asia, Asia north of the Himalayas, India, Egypt and N.E. Africa, tropical Africa, and Australasia. The largest race is *M.m. lineatus* inhabiting North Asia and migrating to India, and the smallest *M.m. affinis* of Australasia. All the races are both gregarious and migratory or nomadic to some extent. Any black kites seen in Britain or Europe belong to the nominate race *M.m. migrans*, which breeds from southern Europe to Western Asia and migrates into Africa in winter.

The red kite is larger, more elegant, but less successful than the black. It inhabits woodlands in Southern Europe along with *M. migrans* and has only one continental race, which extends rarely as far as Western India. A smaller race *M.m. fasciicauda* inhabits the Cape Verde Islands.

Both these kites have slender bodies, long wings angled sharply at the carpal joint in flight, and forked tails constantly flexed and twisted when in soaring flight. They are buzzard-sized, but very distinct. The forked tail and angled wings at once distinguish adults from anything else, and the immature red kite also has a strongly forked tail. The immature black kite shows a forked tail when at rest but when spread in soaring flight it is straight across or only slightly dished; however, the angled wings are distinctive. Both species have a notably graceful leisurely flight, but are capable of swift manoeuvring close to the ground or among trees. The black kite is not black but dark brown, almost uniform in the adult with barring visible on wings and tail, streaked paler below on the body in the immature. The red kite is definitely brightish red, with conspicuous large pale patches on the underwing in flight, and a much longer more strongly forked tail. Both utter long drawn quavering whistling calls, sometimes preceded by sharp high-pitched short notes, repeated. They cannot really be mistaken for anything else, and are easily distinguished from each other.

Genus *Haliaeetus* Savigny

White-tailed Sea Eagle. *Haliaeetus albicilla* (Linnaeus)

Sea eagles are related to kites rather than to the true or booted eagles of the genus *Aquila* and related genera. The connecting link is the eastern brahminy kite *Haliastur indus* which strongly resembles in appearance some of the smaller *Haliaeetus* species, especially the African fish eagle. One American authority has even called the African fish eagle 'only a great big brahminy kite'. The brahminy kite looks very different to the huge European sea eagle; but apart from anatomical or plumage features in common sea eagles and kites share scavenging and piratical habits, robbing other raptors; and they are the most likely of all species to perform certain nuptial displays, notably the spectacular downward whirling displays with feet locked.

The sea eagle has two races, the nominate *H.a. albicilla* of Europe and *H.a. groenlandicus* of Greenland. The former is the only member of the genus likely to be seen as a rare vagrant in Britain. It can scarcely be confused with anything but a golden eagle, from which it is distinguished in adult plumage by its short, white, wedge-shaped tail, broader wings, and generally paler upperparts, though this varies. At close quarters the heavy yellow bill and bare yellow tarsus are distinctive. In immature plumage the sea eagle is all dark brown, whereas the immature golden eagle has a very marked pale base to the tail and large pale patches at the carpal joint of the wing. An immature sea eagle is much larger and darker than an adult golden eagle, the wings broader, the tail shorter and wedge-shaped and the head and bill coarser. The sea eagle is also more likely to be found near water, especially along coastlines.

The golden eagle and the sea eagle do not seem to be vocal so calls are not much help; the golden eagle especially seldom utters. When it does, its call is a loud clear yelp, or more often what the cognoscenti describe as a 'typical *Aquila* cluck'. The sea eagle emits more of a repeated bark; and if it flings its head backwards and upwards as it calls the unknown bird is certainly a sea eagle.

Genus *Neophron* Savigny and *Gyps* Savigny

Egyptian Vulture. *Neophron percnopterus* (Linnaeus)

European Griffon Vulture. *Gyps fulvus* (Hablizl)

Vultures are of two families, the Old World vultures including these two species, and the New World vultures, Cathartidae, the most primitive of all birds of prey and not closely related to the Old World vultures. The two groups share a similar scavenging function and many anatomical characters through convergent evolution. The Old World vultures used to be separated in a family of their own Aegypiidae, or a sub-family Aegypiinae; again, I regret that this convenient arrangement has been abandoned, for they are so distinct that they do not easily link on to either sea eagles on one side of their nearest relations or the snake eagles on the other.

The Egyptian vulture is thought to be fairly closely related to an aberrant African sea eagle, the vulturine fish eagle or palm-nut vulture *Gypohierax angolensis*, a real oddity that lives on oil palm fruit. I keep a pretty open mind on this myself, but accept that on present knowledge it is the most likely link. The palm nut vulture has certainly not been studied sufficiently thoroughly from all angles to encourage any dogmatism, but shares certain features with other Old World vultures such as a bare face (which may be merely a coincidence due to eating oily or messy food) and a very long fledging period for its size. It resembles fish eagles or sea eagles in colour sequence of immature and adult plumages, and aquatic habits; so at present it will do as a link.

The Egyptian and griffon vultures are widespread in the subtropical and tropical Old World from Southern Europe and North Africa to India. The griffon is one of a group of seven species of large gregarious and colonial flesh-eaters but the Egyptian vulture is solitary and unlike any other vulture. Both have other races in India and Pakistan; but in Britain and Europe only the nominate races *N.p. percnopterus* and *G.f. fulvus* of each have ever been recorded, and so rarely that we need hardly consider them as probable British species at any time.

The Egyptian and griffon vultures are both obviously vultures, with bare or partly bare heads and necks, scavenging habits, and weak feet which have largely lost the grip and talons of the large powerful raptors from which they perhaps sprang, having found that carrion feeding paid better than hunting for oneself. The Egyptian is a small, weak species that snatches most of its living from among the feet of other larger vultures, but also has the very rare ability to use a tool – a stone hurled with the bill – to break open ostrich eggs. The griffon is a typical large broad-winged vulture adapted for soaring and for eating the soft flesh of a large rotting carcase, with a long bare neck which can be thrust far into any aperture to reach the meat inside. Vultures are generally neither beautiful nor admired, but are useful; in the words of a Scottish minister who used to preach to my father; 'Were it not for the vultures the air would be filled with abominable stenches'. Declaim in the Doric for best effect!

The adult Egyptian vulture is slim, graceful in flight, strikingly black and white, with a long diamond or wedge-shaped tail, completely unmistakable. The immature is the same shape, but dark brown. The slim bare head, thin beak, and long wedge-shaped tail would distinguish it from, for instance a dark common buzzard or a golden eagle; if it visited Britain it would almost certainly associate with man, and be shot for its confidence.

The griffon is huge, as big as or bigger than a sea eagle, with very broad wings, very short tail, and, in flight, the head drawn back into the forward edge of the wing and not projecting as far as would that of an eagle. No one who saw a griffon perched could possibly mistake it for anything else, and it is superfluous to say more.

Genus *Circus* Lacepede

Marsh Harrier. *Circus aeruginosus* Linnaeus

Hen Harrier. *Circus cyaneus* Linnaeus

Montagu's Harrier. *Circus pygargus* Linnaeus

Pallid Harrier. *Circus macrourus* (Gmelin)

The harriers are a very distinctive group whose specialised hunting habits of slow flapping flight over open grassland or moorland have opened the door to them world-wide. They are not obviously closely related to vultures at all, but in the overall classification of birds of prey are related to African harrier hawks *Polyboroides* and the American crane hawk *Geranospiza*; both these appear related to the snake eagles of the oriental genus *Spilornis* in the old subfamily Circaetinae, another of those convenient groupings which have to my sorrow been abandoned. Although listed next to vultures the snake eagles themselves do not bear much resemblance to vultures, either anatomically or in habits. In placing them here we find one of those gaps in the logical sequence, derived no doubt from specialised evolution away from a common ancestor in the dim and distant past, which we cannot now adequately bridge.

The marsh harrier is the most widespread of the four, occurring over a vast range in Europe and Asia, on some Indian Ocean islands, in North Africa, and in Australasia. It can be divided into eight races or at least four or five species, according to whether one is a lumper or a splitter. To those races accepted by, for instance, Vaurie in the Birds of the Palearctic Fauna some would add the African marsh harrier, which I regard somewhat dubiously as a distinct species, *Circus ranivorus*. We need not enumerate all these races and forms here except to say that if *C.a. spilonotus* of eastern Asia is regarded as a race, and not as a species *C. spilonotus*, then it is logical to think of all as races. Some of the forms are so little studied that one cannot really say what is the correct position. So far as British ornithologists are concerned the only race they are likely to see in Britain or Europe is the nominate *C.a. aeruginosus*; but in north Africa the large and beautiful race *C.a. harterti* occurs. It, however, is obviously a race of *C. aeruginosus*.

All marsh harriers are rather bigger and heavier than their relatives, and less strongly dimorphic, though the male European marsh harrier is much greyer than the female, and some of the eastern males are black and white. They frequent marshes and reedbeds in Europe, and in Britain may occur in marshes alongside both Montagu's and hen harriers.

The hen harrier is the next most widespread, having a wide distribution all over northern Europe, and being represented also by a race in America, *C.c. hudsonius*, known there confusingly as the marsh hawk. It is so known because, being the only harrier in N. America, it has monopolised the marshland hunting niche, though it also hunts over moorland like a true European hen harrier. There is one recent and to my mind very doubtful sight record of an immature American hen harrier in East Anglia(a). One would expect this race, if at all, to appear in Ireland or West Scotland and I cannot help thinking that this individual was just an unusual plumage phase, so probable in the variable harriers. Otherwise, all the hen harriers recorded in Britain are of the nominate race *C.c. cyaneus*. All hen harriers are inhabitants of marshes and moorlands rather than grasslands.

The pallid and Montagu's harriers are more closely related to one another than they are to the marsh or hen harriers. Both are smaller and slimmer, breed mainly in southern or Central European and West Asian latitudes, are monotypic with no races, and strongly migratory, wintering in tropical Africa and India. The males are very distinct, but the females are so alike that I think it unwise to advise anyone that they can certainly be distinguished in the field, even in good light. I myself am not really able to see, for instance, the fine differences shown in the recent identification papers in British Birds. Apparently, the male harriers themselves have this difficulty, for there are at least two records of female Montagu's harriers successfully soliciting male pallids(8). These females at least should have known better, for it is not easy to mistake the males.

The four British harriers are, in adult plumage, and excepting females of the pallid and Montagu's, not too difficult to distinguish from one another. Marsh harriers are all larger, heavier, broader winged in flight, and darker plumaged in both sexes than the others. A big female marsh harrier is almost as big as a buzzard and somewhat resembles a black kite, both perched and in flight, until one sees the square tail and notes the strong dihedral at which the wings are held when floating over swampland. Immatures are almost uniformly dark, but the adult female has a distinctive creamy head and a creamy patch on the upper wing coverts. The male, according to age, shows patches of silvery grey on the upper wing; and a full-plumaged old male has a quiet distinction about his dress that other harriers lack.

In all the other three the males are grey, the females brown, streaked and barred below. The hen harrier is a good deal larger than the others in fact, but this difference would easily elude one in the field. The male hen harrier has a pronounced white rump contrasting with his basic grey plumage. The male Montagu's has a slender black wing bar at the base of the flight quills, both above and below; but a much better distinction is the chestnut streaks on the underwing and underside; this is even useful in sub-adult plumage. The adult male pallid is a gloriously beautiful bird, *much* paler than either of the others, almost as white as a gull, with a narrow sliver of black at the wingtip, and no other noticeable markings at all.

The female hen harrier is distinguishable from the other two by her generally paler brown or greyer colour, a dark trailing edge to the wing, heavier barring, and larger pale patches in the wing. All three have white rumps, that of the hen harrier being the most obvious. As I have said, I would not undertake certainly to distinguish female pallid and Montagu's; the pallid is said to have a dark line separating the facial ruff from a white crescent behind it, but I have never been able to see this distinction myself, even in strong light in Africa. Perhaps I'm just bad at it. No female pallid harrier I have seen has this feature as strongly marked as that depicted for instance by G. E. Lodge in Volume V of Bannerman's *Birds of the British Isles*(1).

Immatures are also very hard to recognise; but the first immature Montagu's harrier is a beautiful unstreaked rich rufous below, and should be quite easy to distinguish. Finally, neither pallid nor Montagu's harriers will normally be seen in Britain in the winter, when the only problem is to distinguish the hen from the marsh harrier; this is not too difficult. Any grey male from October to April is almost certainly a hen harrier; and the female hen harrier is smaller, paler, more streaky and barred than the female marsh harrier, and has a white rump. I do not think any of the harriers could be distinguished by any published description of their voice; they all say 'chek-ek-ek-ek' or variations thereof in anger or annoyance, and utter whistling cries in display or when soliciting food. Only someone familiar with the calls in the field would be able to use them.

Genus *Accipiter* Brisson

Goshawk. *Accipiter gentilis* (Linnaeus)

Sparrowhawk. *Accipiter nisus* (Linnaeus)

Goshawks and sparrowhawks are much more obviously related to harriers than the latter are to vultures. There are evident similarities in the long legs and sharp claws. However, whereas the long-winged slim harriers are specialised for hunting in the open the genus *Accipiter* specialises in hunting in woodland, scrub, or forest. *Accipiter* is the largest genus of Falconiform birds, with about forty-five species distributed world wide. It was formerly divided into two genera, *Astur*, including the heavy-legged goshawk, and *Accipiter*, including the thin-shanked longer-toed sparrowhawk. However, as more species became known it grew plain that there were so many intermediates that they should all be merged into one genus, *Accipiter*. English names ending in 'goshawk' for the genus *Astur* have been applied to a variety of small species which have strong legs but otherwise bear little resemblance in power or size to the true goshawk, which is the largest of all. In my opinion it is best to describe all members of this genus as 'Accipiters' instead of trying to decide whether their thin or thick shanks should entitle them sparrowhawks or goshawks.

The goshawk occurs all over Europe, Asia, and North America from the limit of the treeline to subtropical climates; hence the alternative name 'northern goshawk' may be more descriptive. It has been divided into nine races, some doubtfully valid, and in Eurasia there is a general cline of increasing size and paler colour from West to East and South to North. Most of the British goshawks are of the nominate European race *A.g. gentilis* (Linnaeus), and these are also the only goshawks most people would see in Europe, except for Corsica and Sardinia where *A.g. arrigonii* occurs. Five individuals of the American goshawk *A.g. atricapillus* have been obtained in Britain, four in Ireland and one in the Scilly Isles. Some would say that the American goshawk deserves full specific rank as *A. atricapillus*; but this view is not generally accepted.

The sparrowhawk occurs over most of Europe and Asia wherever there is woodland, but is replaced by closely allied forms in India (*A. virgatus*), Africa south of the Sahara (*A. rufiventris*), North America (*A. striatus*), and elsewhere. It has been divided into six geographical races, the only one of which occurring in Britain or continental Europe is the nominate *A.n. nisus*. Other races occur abroad, *A.n. wolterstorfii* in Corsica and Sardinia, and *A.n. punicus* in North Africa, but are very unlikely to visit Britain.

All members of the genus *Accipiter*, have short broad wings, long tails, long legs, usually with long toes and sharp talons, and live in woodland or forest, emerging into the open circumspectly, to hunt, and to display in the breeding season. They are distinguished from other raptors by these features and by their usually silent, secretive ways which persist even in tropical forests where they are never persecuted. The goshawk is large, a female being almost the size of a buzzard, while the male sparrowhawk is the lightest of all British birds of prey, though it does not appear the smallest in flight because of its broad wings. In all members of this genus the size difference between male and female is great; a male sparrowhawk is little more than half the female's weight.

In adult plumage sparrowhawks and goshawks are blue-grey or dark grey above, narrowly barred blackish and white below; and in immature plumage are brown, heavily barred on wings and tail with dark streaks on the underside of the body. Adult females are always browner than males and have a more or less visible white eyebrow while males are more narrowly barred below; the male sparrowhawk also has a rufous rather than white barred underside.

Goshawks and sparrowhawks call 'kew-kew-kew' or variants thereof, shriller or deeper toned according to size and sex; the voices of females, as in most birds of prey, are deeper than those of the smaller males. Some other members of the genus, notably the Levant sparrowhawk *Accipiter brevipes*, the only other *Accipiter* species likely to be seen in Europe, have a completely different voice, a shrill 'kewick-kewick'. The Levant sparrowhawk is also more heavily barred in the body, but in flight the underwing is almost unbarred white, with a black wingtip, and the tail has fewer bars.

Genus *Buteo* Lacepede

Common Buzzard. *Buteo buteo* (Linnaeus)

Rough-legged Buzzard. *Buteo lagopus* (Pontoppidan)

The buzzards are another large and extremely successful group of large soaring hawks, occurring world wide except for Australasia, but found in greatest variety in South America, where certain of them have grown to the size of eagles, and are usually called eagles, while others are as small as sparrowhawks and are sometimes described as 'sub-buteonines'. There is actually an almost continuous series of linking forms between a typical buzzard and typical sparrowhawk, and here at least the present overall order of classification makes sense.

The largest buzzards of this genus are as big as a small eagle and almost as predatory; the smallest are smaller than a goshawk. Buzzards like a mixture of woodland and open country, hunting most in the latter but breeding in the woodland, or on cliffs. They are a very good example of a 'generalised' design, neither very big nor very small, able to feed on almost anything from an earthworm or beetle to the carcase of a bull, with moderately broad wings, moderately powerful feet and bills, and so on. Since they are so versatile they are naturally successful, and one species of *Buteo* or another is likely to be among the commonest large birds of prey seen in almost any part of the Old or New World, always excepting the ubiquitous black kite in the Old World, and excepting Australasia where large aberrant kites and small eagles fill the 'buzzard niche'.

Of three species of buzzards in Europe two, the common buzzard *B. buteo* and the rough-legged buzzard *B. lagopus* occur in Britain; the second is only a scarce winter migrant. The honey buzzard is only so called because it is about the same size and shape as a common buzzard; it is not closely related. The long-legged buzzard *B. rufinus* of eastern Europe and North Africa does not occur in Britain.

I am far from happy about the classification of the genus *Buteo*, which seems to me to have suffered more than some others from lumping and splitting of forms. Some species that may actually be good species are regarded as races, and vice versa. This situation, however, applies to the classification of British buzzards only insofar as it affects the validity of the steppe buzzard *Buteo vulpinus* or, as most authorities now agree, *B. buteo vulpinus*. For long it was regarded as a separate species and still is by, for instance, Bannerman, on the grounds that the two species overlap in their breeding range. However Vaurie, in the *Birds of the Palearctic Fauna*, regards the steppe buzzard as a race of the common buzzard, and most agree with this view(15). According to Russian literature quoted by Bannerman the two races or species in fact intergrade and interbreed on the boundaries of their range, and accordingly they cannot be good species(1). The steppe buzzard, race or species, has only occurred once in Britain, more than a century ago in 1864, in Wiltshire. It occurs fairly commonly in continental Europe on migration, in the range of the typical common buzzard, but this is of no significance as to its relationships.

Apart from this one straggler all British buzzards belong to the nominate race of the common buzzard *B.b. buteo*, which also extends over Western Europe. Other races, *B.b. japonicus* and *B.b. toyoshimae*, of this bird occur further east, and perhaps in Africa, where there is similar argument over the validity as a species of the African mountain buzzard *B. oreophilus* or *B.b. oreophilus*. These questions are, however, only of rather academic interest to British ornithologists.

The rough-legged buzzard is an Arctic species, circumpolar, with other races in N.E. Asia and N. America. Those that visit Britain belong to the nominate race *B.l. lagopus* which, extending East to the Yenisei is also the only one likely to be seen by any British ornithologist in Europe.

Buzzards as such are large or medium-sized birds of prey, much given to soaring, but able to hover gracefully at need, or hunting from perches. In flight they usually soar with a marked dihedral, and the tail is normally fully spread when soaring so that it makes a nearly continuous flying surface with the wings. Perched, buzzards have large heads, short, rather heavy looking bodies, and rather short tails. These characters are shared by most members of the genus. The rough-legged buzzard is so called because it has a feathered tarsus (lagopus = hare-footed) resembling that of a typical booted eagle. However, this is an adaptation to the Arctic climate, and is not easy to see in the field.

In Britain buzzards can only be confused with each other, and with golden eagles and honey buzzards. From eagles they are distinguished by the more unsteady erratic flight, much smaller size, broader more rounded-looking wings, and loud mewing calls. One may say that it is possible to confuse a buzzard with an eagle for a few moments, but not vice versa. The square tail and straight leading edge of the wing instantly distinguishes them from the kite, and the short tail and relatively longer wings from a soaring goshawk, which is almost as large.

Rough-legged buzzards are about the same size as common buzzards but are paler, and generally slimmer and lighter looking in flight. The tail is basally almost plain white with a broad terminal bar whereas that of the common buzzard is barred all along with a dark tip. The rough-legged buzzard is generally paler below with a broad dark band across the breast, while the common buzzard is barred brown and white over the whole underside. However, one may see very pale or very dark individuals of each species, and confusion is always possible in poor light. Rough-legged buzzards are, of course, only likely to be seen in winter, and rarely then. 'When in doubt say common buzzard' is a good motto to adopt.

If a buzzard utters a call it immediately proclaims its identity. The normal calls of the common buzzard are loud clear whistles or mews 'Peee-oo'. Those of the rough-legged buzzard are described as squalling, mewing, or screeching, terminating on a lower note, 'kee-wee-uk', louder and lower pitched in general than the common buzzard. The rough-legged buzzard is unlikely to call in Britain.

Genus *Aquila* Brisson

Greater Spotted Eagle. *Aquila clanga* Pallas

Golden Eagle. *Aquila chrysaetos* (Linnaeus)

The genus *Aquila* is the largest and most widespread genus of the true or booted eagles, which have the tarsus feathered to the toes. This is, in this case, not an adaptation to an arctic climate for it also occurs in the tropical eagles of the genus *Spizaetus* which inhabit warm moist forests. These small eagles, together with some others for instance of the genus *Hieraaetus* are often called hawk eagles because they have similar proportions to Accipiters, with long tails and short wings. Recently, some authors have tended to lump *Hieraaetus* and others with *Aquila*(2); but this is going altogether too far in my opinion, it does not simplify but rather complicates the situation, and ignores many behavioural characteristics and such useful identification aids as voice.

The genus *Aquila* is related to buzzards through a group of large or very large eagles with bare tarsi inhabiting tropical forests in South America and parts of tropical Asia and Australasia. These are just big and rapacious buzzards and include the huge harpy eagle *Harpia harpya* and the Philippine monkey-eating eagle *Pithecophaga jefferyi*. A possible connecting link is the rather odd Indian black eagle *Ictinaetus malayensis*, which is in some respects kite-like, but has been too little studied in the field to be certain of its true affinities. *Aquila* eagles are generally large, long-winged species inhabiting open country, and include the tawny eagle *A. rapax* which is probably the most abundant medium-sized eagle in the world, and the golden eagle which is the most widespread and probably the most numerous large eagle.

The golden eagle breeds all over Europe, Asia, North Africa, and North America from the Arctic south to the subtropics. It has close relatives in Africa south of the Sahara (the magnificent black *A. verreauxi*), in New Guinea (*A. gurneyi*), and in Australia (the wedge-tailed eagle *A. audax*). All these are about the same size and form a nice superspecies, a convenient arrangement applied to a group of several closely similar species, insufficiently differentiated from their near relatives to be a full genus. All British and north European golden eagles belong to the typical race *A.c. chrysaetos* but in Spain and North Africa the smaller and darker *A.c. homeryi* occurs.

The other British *Aquila* species, the greater spotted eagle, is a rare vagrant, which has occurred only twice in the twentieth century (never since 1915), and only a dozen times altogether. It may once, before historical times, have bred in British deciduous forests. This species is relatively common still in eastern and Central Europe, but has decreased in the last half century to a point where there is alarm in some countries for its future. It prefers swampy valleys in woodland or forest to other habitat, is monotypic, and migrates to Africa north of the equator and India in winter.

These two species could hardly be confused, for the golden eagle is much larger than the spotted and occurs in mountainous open habitat. The adult spotted eagle is very dark plain brown, sometimes almost purplish, but the immature has large whitish drop-shaped spots on the upper wing coverts, which should instantly distinguish it. In Britain the golden eagle can really only be confused with the sea

45

eagle; I have mentioned field distinctions under that species. In the field it is much larger, more stately and longer winged in flight than the common buzzard which often shares its habitat; when one actually sees an eagle there is little doubt about it. Immature golden eagles are darker generally than adults but have conspicuous white tail bases and large white patches at the carpal joint of the wing. By the amount of white in these areas it is possible to age golden eagles in the field into first-year immatures, subadults, and full adults, in which the white is greatly reduced.

In Europe the golden eagle can most easily be confused with the large imperial eagle, which is rather smaller and darker, generally inhabits lowlands, and in the adult has conspicuous white epaulettes on the wings, while the immature is very clearly streaked below. The spotted eagle is extremely hard to distinguish in adult plumage from the adult steppe or tawny eagle *A. rapax* and from the lesser spotted eagle *A. pomarina*; this is almost impossible, even in some museum specimens. The adult spotted eagle is generally much darker than the lesser spotted, but many adult steppe eagles are also very dark. The immature steppe eagle has white tips to the greater and lesser upper wing coverts which produce two marked pale bars along the wing, whereas in the immatures of spotted eagles the wing coverts are spotted, not barred. In the lesser spotted eagle the spots are small, in the spotted eagle, large. The fine distinctions between the steppe and the two spotted eagles will baffle anyone lacking experience of all the species in the field, and it would be a rash man who could say he infallibly could distinguish all individuals of any species.

Sub-order FALCONES

Family **Falconidae**

Genus *Falco*

Lesser Kestrel. *Falco naumanni* Fleischer

Common Kestrel. *Falco tinnunculus* Linnaeus

Red-footed Falcon. *Falco vespertinus* Linnaeus

Merlin. *Falco columbarius* Linnaeus

Hobby. *Falco subbuteo* Linnaeus

Gyrfalcon. *Falco rusticolus* Linnaeus

Peregrine Falcon. *Falco peregrinus* Tunstall

The seven British falcons, four of which breed in Britain, form the largest genus of birds of prey in Britain, and include between a fifth and a quarter of all the genus *Falco*, a world-wide genus of 38 species, the second largest genus of Falconiformes. The true falcons of the genus *Falco*, and the pigmy falcons and falconets, *Polihierax* and *Microhierax*, are all that occur in the Old World. In the New World, especially in South America, *Falco* is related to the apparently primitive nest-building, carrion-eating caracaras by a variety of extremely curious intermediate forms such as the laughing falcon *Herpetotheres cachinnans* (which eats snakes) and members of the genus *Micrastur* which live in the gloomy undergrowth of tropical forests, behave more like Accipiters than peregrines, and have even developed some of the enhanced hearing powers of harriers.

The family Falconidae in general is so different from other birds of prey that Dr Amadon considered it should be separated in a suborder; and further research may yet indicate that it should be a full Order(11). Differences from other birds of prey include a buffish, not greenish or yellowish inner eggshell, a different sequence of moulting the wing quills (which is invariable in all the genera, however unlike one another they may otherwise be) and certain differences in behaviour. For instance, no true falcon builds a nest; all except caracaras breed in holes, cliff ledges, or old nests of other birds. Falcons allow their droppings to fall below the perch instead of raising the tail and squirting the excrement away horizontally; and the predatory bird-eating members of the genus *Falco* have two 'teeth' on the mandible which are used for breaking the necks of their prey before starting to feed. The true falcons also have blunt heads, slim bodies, and long narrow pointed wings, adapting them for speedy flight, and in all British and European species producing a flight silhouette unlike that of other diurnal raptors, except the aberrant bat hawk *Machaerhamphus*.

This large and otherwise rather unwieldy genus splits itself conveniently into a number of groups or superspecies, so distinct that by some authors they have been named as genera, e.g. *Cerchneis* for the dimorphic kestrels; this rather convenient arrangement has now been abandoned. The British falcons are represented in all the main superspecies; the lesser kestrel, common kestrel, and red-footed falcon are in the kestrel group, with which some include a number of very aberrant African members wrongly placed with the dimorphic typical kestrels. The merlin is, for reasons completely obscure to me, sometimes placed in a species group with the red-necked falcon *F. chicquera*, which is not at all similar in most of its habits and like the merlin really does not fit with any other. The hobby fits well with other similar small, long-winged insect and bird-eating swift falcons occurring world wide. The gyrfalcon is the largest and most spectacular member of a group of 'great falcons' which includes also sakers, *F. cherrug*, lanners *F. biarmicus*, laggars *F. jugger*, and prairie falcons *F. mexicanus*. The peregrine is the dominant member of a smaller group including the richly coloured orange-breasted falcon *F. deiroleucus* and the diminutive and extremely rare Teita falcon of Africa *F. fasciinucha*. Those who have read my comments on the systematic arrangement of the falcons in my book *African Birds of Prey*(3) will see that it is far from ideal; but again, some of the species are so little known that it is at present difficult to suggest any marked improvement.

The kestrel group includes the lesser and common kestrel and the red-footed falcon. These are generally very distinct in their breeding quarters, the lesser kestrel normally breeding colonially in buildings or cliffs; the common kestrel normally breeding singly in holes or the old nests of other birds; and the red-footed falcon breeding colonially in rooks' nests. All are migratory or nomadic, and sexually dimorphic, with the males more brightly coloured than the females. All three are gregarious on migration, and although the lesser kestrel looks more like a common kestrel than a red-footed falcon it behaves on migration rather more like the latter, and often accompanies it. Thus, although the male red-footed falcon has an entirely different colour scheme to the males of the two kestrels, being entirely slate grey with rich red thighs as opposed to chestnut, barred and spotted with black, in other respects it fits well with kestrels; the immature plumages of red-footed falcons are more similar to kestrels.

Lesser kestrels were formerly divided into two races, but the eastern race *F.n. pekinensis* has now been abandoned. Common kestrels have 11 races, four of which are island forms, four African, and two oriental, breeding in the Himalayas and India. All European and British kestrels belong to the nominate race *F.t. tinnunculus*, which in Britain is quite sedentary but in some other parts of its range is strongly nomadic or migratory. The red-footed falcons occurring in Britain or Europe are all of the nominate western race *F.v. vespertinus*. The eastern race *F.v. amurensis* is by many thought to be a separate species; it is certainly very distinct, and performs the most remarkable migrations of any bird of prey, apparently hopping, no one knows how, across the Indian Ocean from N.E. India to S. Tanzania. The western race is also migratory, and its northward migration brings it further west than its southward journey; it is then that most of the British individuals are seen.

The merlin is a very successful and widespread species breeding throughout much of North Europe, Asia, and North America (where it is called the pigeon hawk), with seven geographical races, three of them American and the others Eurasian. Two of the latter occur in Britain, the European merlin *F.c. aesalon* and the Iceland merlin *F.c. subaesalon* which is only rather doubtfully distinct. Only the former breeds in Britain, but our population is augmented by migrants of both races. As *F.c. aesalon* extends east to the Yenisei no other race is likely to be seen in Europe either. As mentioned, in the general classification the merlin is rather uneasily paired with the red-necked falcon *F. chicquera*, which is usually associated with fan palms, *Borassus* spp., a fact which severely and inexplicably limits its actual distribution. I dislike this arrangement, and prefer to regard the merlin as unique.

The hobby is a typical member of a well-defined group of falcons occurring world wide; other members include the African and Asian hobbies *F. cuvieri* and *F. severus*; the Australian little falcon *F. longipennis*; and the Aplomado falcon *F. femoralis*. These are evidently closely allied to Eleanora's and the sooty falcon *F. eleanorae* and *F. concolor*, which have specialised in feeding on migrant passerines in summer; and less closely allied to the Australian brown falcon *F. berigora* and the New Zealand falcon *F. novaezeelandiae*, and possibly others such as the Australian black falcon *F. subniger*, which is as big as a peregrine but flies like a hobby. Typical hobbies are all long-winged, small or medium-sized, and extremely swift, feeding mainly on insects outside the breeding season, when they eat birds. The European hobby extends east to China, is migratory throughout its range, and has been divided into a number of races, most of which are doubtfully valid. In Europe or Britain any hobby is of the typical race *F.s. subbuteo*.

Gyrfalcons are superficially rather like huge peregrines but are normally included in a different species group with other large falcons, which are even more like peregrines in their general appearance and behaviour but differ in certain other characters, such as voice. Of these, all but the prairie falcon are bigger than peregrines and tend to dominate peregrines where they occur together, though gyrfalcons breed in the Arctic alongside races of peregrines. Gyrfalcons used to be divided into seven or more races of which three, the gyrfalcon itself *F.r. rusticolus*, the Iceland falcon *F.r. islandus*, and the Greenland falcon *F.r. candicans* have occurred as vagrants in Britain; these races have recently all been lumped by Vaurie in one form *F. rusticolus*, since their measurements overlap and paler or darker forms may be found in all areas, though the nearly white birds are commonest in high arctic latitudes. As the races are not clearly distinct this seems a better and simpler arrangement. If this is accepted no lister need worry about what race of gyrfalcon he sees in Britain. However, the more northern forms of extreme Arctic climates are the more inclined to migrate, and hence white birds of the Greenland form *candicans* are most often observed here.

The peregrine falcon is the dominant member of its superspecies which includes three other rather rare or little known species. The peregrine is cosmopolitan, and has been divided into eighteen or nineteen races of which five are island forms, two Australasian, three American, one African, and the rest Eurasian. Vaurie considers that two races, the barbary falcon and the shaheen, *F.p. pelegrinoides* and *F.p. babylonicus*, should be separated in a different species *F. pelegrinoides*(14); however the evidence against this is at least as good as that for it, and accordingly it seems to me preferable to continue to regard these as small desert-adapted races of the peregrine.

In Britain two races, the nominate *F.p. peregrinus* of Europe and the American peregrine or duck hawk *F.p. anatum* have occurred, the latter only twice, in 1891 and 1910. It is unlikely that the duck hawk will occur again since it is now practically extinct in eastern north America south of Greenland and Baffin Land through pesticide poisoning(6). British ornithologists visiting the Mediterranean will see *F.p. brookei*, and in North Africa *F.p. pelegrinoides*; and a summer's observation in Morocco could solve the problem of whether *F. pelegrinoides* is a good species or not. If it breeds separately alongside *brookei* it is; if not, not. It's as simple as that.

Falcons are generally easy to distinguish from other birds of prey by their wing silhouettes and habitat, normally in open country. It is just possible to confuse a merlin momentarily with a sparrowhawk, but a quick view of a few wingflaps will inevitably show the broad wings of the hawk. From each other, British falcons are not hard to distinguish. The kestrels, male and female, are rufous coloured birds that live in mixed woodland and open country and hunt hovering over open ground. Common kestrels are very difficult to distinguish from lesser kestrels, which are rare summer vagrants. Male lesser kestrels have unspotted chestnut backs, bluer heads and tails than common kestrels, but by far the most useful distinction is the almost unspotted or barred plain white underwing in flight. Females and juveniles are very difficult to distinguish from common kestrels, but appear smaller, slimmer, and generally paler in flight, with unstreaked breasts in some females. From above, one may see a slate blue or grey patch on the lesser kestrel's secondaries and, if one can see the feet on a perch, the white or pale claws are distinctive. Kestrels are less easily confused with red-footed falcons. Male red-footed falcons are unmistakable slate grey with red thighs, the latter not always easy to see, and females have a grey, not brown, barred back and a conspicuous grey, barred tail. Red-footed falcons are also only summer migrants, and in flight have something of the grace of the hobby.

The hobby is a little like the red-footed falcon, but slimmer and longer winged, and appears like a huge swift in flight. Both sexes are dark slate grey or dark brown above, with streaked undersides and prominent moustachial streaks, visible even in immatures. The reddish thighs are hard to see in the field, especially in flight. Merlins are a little like hobbies in a museum skin, but lack the moustachial streaks and the reddish thighs. In the field they fly in a totally different manner, very swift and dashing but usually near the ground, with rapid wingbeats contrasting strongly with the hobby's leisurely strokes. The habitat of the merlin is open country, that of the hobby woodland, and the hobby is only a summer migrant. Merlins and kestrels tend to share the same habitat year-round, but are easily distinguishable by the reddish colour of the kestrel and the mode of flight, very distinct, swift and dashing in the merlin, slower and repeatedly stopping to hover in the kestrel. It is easy to magnify the difficulty of distinguishing these small falcons from one another, but if a reasonable view is obtained there should be no doubt.

Peregrines inhabit wild open country with merlins and kestrels, and might of course be seen elsewhere, for instance in farmlands, especially in winter. They are large, dark-headed, with a heavy black moustachial streak, grey-blue above and buffy white barred black below in the adults, browner, and streaked below in immatures. The raucous, angry, hacking voice is distinctive and freely used, especially near nesting cliffs. If the view obtained is so bad that one cannot distinguish the peregrine from the merlin or kestrel then one ought to say 'don't know' anyhow. Gyrs are much larger than peregrines, lack the blackish moustachial streaks, and are always much paler, almost white with sparse black markings in the Greenland form which visits Britain most commonly. A female gyr is more nearly the size of a male buzzard or a goshawk than a peregrine, heavy bodied and blunt headed, with a noticeably slow deliberate wingbeat in flight. Gyrs are only rare winter visitors; peregrines permanent residents.

There is really no substitute for experience in the identification of falcons or any other British or European birds of prey. An inexperienced observer will do well to conclude that any species he has seen is most likely, on the laws of probability, to be one of the three commonest, the buzzard if it is a soaring bird, kestrel if a falcon, and sparrowhawk if an Accipiter. If one feels certain it is not one of these then the next most likely are the golden eagle if a soaring bird, peregrine or merlin if a falcon, and hen harrier. Difficulties can be further minimised by knowledge of range and occurrence at different times of the year. It would doubtless be possible to see a hobby in, for instance, Leicestershire, in winter; but if I did I should appeal for a miracle, in which case the suspect hobby would probably resolve itself into a small male peregrine which had tried catching a wader in a pool of sewage and so got its thighs stained brown.

CHAPTER 4

THE OSPREY

ALTHOUGH still one of the rarest, with a maximum of seven pairs breeding in 1971, the osprey is probably the most famous, if not the best known of all British diurnal birds of prey. Certainly none has been more closely observed at the nest, though these data are not published. It had been extinct in Britain as a breeding bird, occurring only in small numbers as a fairly regular visitor, from about 1910–1954. It then re-established itself with one breeding pair in Speyside, near Loch Garten, and probably bred first in 1954. This nest was carefully watched, and despite one failure through the maniac efforts of an egg collector which might have halted the entire process of re-establishment, the pair persisted and the site is occupied to this day, observed day and night, and by many thousands of people annually, hundreds of thousands in total since this pair appeared. Never can any individual pair of birds anywhere in the world have given so much pleasure to so many people, and never can any pair of birds done more for the cause of bird conservation. The re-establishment of the osprey is a remarkable triumph of organisation, supported by enthusiastic public interest, and should perhaps be taken as an object lesson as to what can be done with a rare bird without harming it(4).

The osprey well deserves the interest and enthusiasm it has aroused, for it is a magnificent creature. It is larger, with a five-foot wingspan, than any other resident British species except the golden eagle and, while I am not going to admit that it is as magnificent as an eagle, it comes a good second in Britain. With its nearly white head and underside and mottled white underwing in flight it is far more conspicuous than is the eagle, and it is also very much bolder. It will sit, relatively unperturbed, in full view with observers not very far away, and the Loch Garten birds must be aware of the cars and people near their nest. Many ospreys visiting Britain in winter have caught fish while watched by people at close range on waters such as reservoirs easily accessible from large population centres. In many of its natural north European haunts the osprey has no occasion to fear man; and in some other countries, notably North America, has been so welcomed that artificial nest sites, such as cartwheels on top of poles, have been erected for its use. It loses popularity when, for instance, it nests on top of electricity installations, perhaps plunging large areas into darkness; but effective action can be taken against this sort of over-familiarity without harming the ospreys.

Until very recently the osprey never aroused this kind of enthusiasm in Britain, but was relentlessly persecuted. Even now I have heard that certain proprietors are already claiming that there are too many ospreys in Speyside, and that 'we must get our priorities right', an example of mental arrogance that would be hard to beat. For most people the priority is that the osprey should be left alone to flourish; there cannot be too many ospreys, at least for a very long time to come. All credit to those proprietors who have protected and are proud of their ospreys; they have set a fine example and helped the ospreys to succeed.

The story of the extinction of the osprey in Britain is the usual one of ruthless, senseless reduction of a formerly fairly numerous and widespread population to a small remnant by gamekeepers, followed by intensive egg and skin collecting, which gave this remnant the *coup de grâce*. The last few pairs lingered in certain rather remote lochs in Sutherland, at Loch an Eilein in Speyside, and at Loch Arkaig. The Sutherland birds were virtually eliminated by two collectors, Charles St John and William Dunbar, who visited the lochs concerned with the avowed object of collecting the last surviving ospreys if they could – not for themselves but for others(8). They were successful, and the osprey became extinct on the lonely lochs of this part of the Highlands, Loch Mor Ceann na Saile and Loch na Claise Carnaich. Other highland lochs which supported a pair of ospreys were sometimes named Loch an Iasgair, and can still be located on the ordnance map. Charles St John, who seems otherwise to have been a sporting gentleman, wrote of these exploits with sickening hypocrisy, shedding crocodile tears on paper over his vile deeds. To do him justice, he probably realised how vile they were, heralding the osprey's extinction. But his mentality was typical of his day, and is at least equalled in modern times by the egg collectors who robbed the Loch Garten nest in 1971.

The ospreys nesting on the old castle at Loch an Eilein in Speyside persisted to a later date, but were repeatedly robbed by the same William Dunbar, who swam over to the island at night, climbing the walls of the castle ruins to take the eggs. This nest site was robbed by other collectors too, and can hardly ever have succeeded in rearing young. Yet a succession of different birds continued to try for many years until finally only one bird visited the eyrie in spring. Then it too vanished and the Loch an Eilein eyrie was finally deserted. It is said that the Loch an Eilein eyrie is now too public a place for ospreys to succeed there; but I doubt this and live in hope that they may yet reoccupy the old castle, a romantic but quite typical osprey nesting site.

Other pairs persisted, in less well-known localities, until 1908 at Loch Arkaig and 1916 at Loch Loyne(4). The area round Loch Loyne must then have been better wooded than it is now, for at present there are no trees in the area suitable for an osprey, nor were there before the present dam raised the water level by many feet. These nesting sites were apparently less savagely persecuted than the others and were even offered some protection, in the shape of wire round the tree at Loch Arkaig. But the protection was inadequate, and this last population group failed to rear enough young year by year to maintain itself.

Thereafter, from 1910 onwards, the osprey was a scarce passage visitor to Britain in winter. The migrants came, and still come mainly from Sweden, as the ringing recoveries prove (Map 14). Up to the 1930s at least the osprey was still persecuted in European countries too, but it was then given protection in Sweden and began to increase again. It was probably helped by the Second World War, when movement was restricted and people had other things to do. Usually, among these birds of passage two or three ospreys might be seen in Britain each year, but there were some records of unusual interest such as a party of six seen by P. A. Clancey at Carmunnock, Lanarkshire(b), and one which remained most of one summer at Loch Fad in Bute(a), where it was watched by many people. These visiting ospreys were not shy, frequently stayed for some days or even weeks at their temporary homes, and fished in the normal manner. Usually they were not actively persecuted in Britain but probably some were shot and they all disappeared in due course. One immature which visited Ireland in 1944 was unlucky. It had the misfortune to alarm some turkeys, which of course it could not and did not intend to eat; but a Mrs Collier urged her husband to shoot it, which he did(c). In 1944 at least six separate birds visited Britain, two in spring, one summering, and three in autumn;

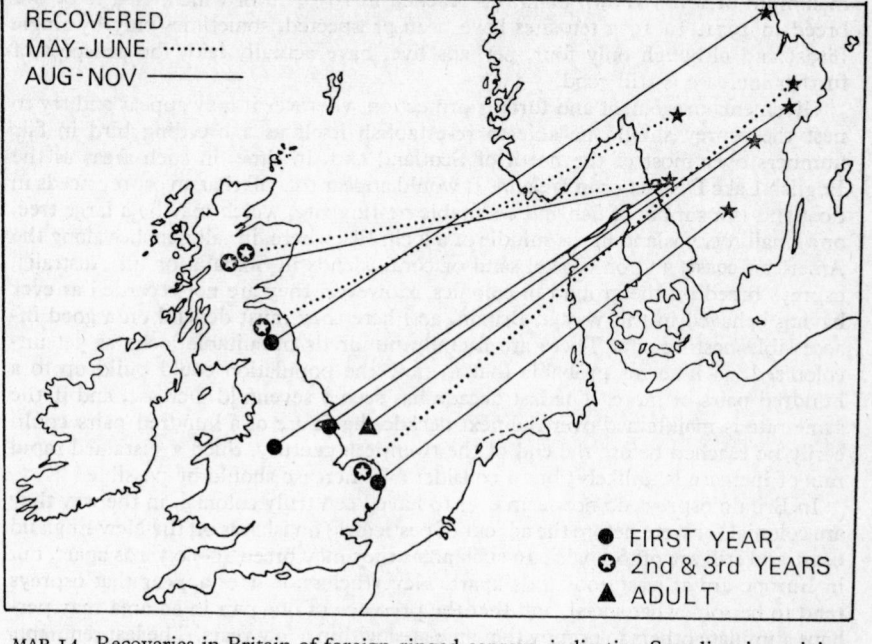

RECOVERED
MAY-JUNE ········
AUG-NOV ————

● FIRST YEAR
◉ 2nd & 3rd YEARS
▲ ADULT

MAP 14. Recoveries in Britain of foreign-ringed ospreys, indicating Scandinavian origins.

one was shot, but the others were apparently objects of interest and were un-molested.

In 1955 I first heard rumours of ospreys nesting in Speyside. That year there was a typical osprey-like nest near Loch Morlich in a dead pine. There were said to be castings below it, but when I visited it I found beneath it only the droppings of a fox, composed by a strange coincidence entirely of fish bones (which an osprey would completely digest). Consequently I was inclined to doubt the rumours at the time, but I was wrong. The osprey was about to – indeed already had re-established itself as a breeding bird. In the following year, 1956, it was first certainly proven to breed, though it almost certainly bred in 1954. In 1956 the eggs were robbed by a collector in a daring night raid. His aberrant mentality can only be compared with that of the collectors who robbed the nest in 1971, despite a 24-hour watch by volunteer wardens organised by the R.S.P.B. His maniac effort might have halted the entire process of re-colonisation of Britain by the osprey, and there were some who would have thought it quite proper if he had succeeded. Fortunately he did not deter the ospreys, which first reared young in 1957, a triumphant moment for the many volunteers who had given their time to protect the birds(4).

In 1963 a second pair undoubtedly laid eggs, but in all the nine years this eyrie has been occupied the eggs have been infertile. This would suggest that the same female was always involved, but this is certainly not so, for one female here was ringed and another not(i). In 1965 a third pair appeared, in a different area some forty miles from the two existing sites, and in the following year they laid and bred successfully there. From then on there were new pairs almost every year until a maximum of seven known pairs was reached in 1970, all of which tried to or did breed in 1971. In 1972 ten sites have been prospected, sometimes only by single birds, and although only four, perhaps five, have actually laid, the prospect of further increase is still good.

Given encouragement and further protection wherever it may appear and try to nest the osprey should be able to re-establish itself as a breeding bird in fair numbers over most of the north of Scotland and, in time, in such areas as the English Lake District or in Ireland. It would appear that all that an osprey needs in Scotland is a supply of fish and a suitable nesting site, which may be a large tree, or a small rocky island in the middle of a loch. Elsewhere, in salt marshes along the American coast, and on coastal sand or coral islands in Somalia or off Australia, ospreys breed on the ground in colonies. However, they are not recorded as ever having behaved in this way in Britain, and here they must depend on a good in-accessible nesting site. There are literally hundreds of suitable lochs as yet un-colonised, so it seems probable that in time the population could build up to a hundred pairs or more. The last decade has seen a sevenfold increase, and if the same rate is maintained over the next decade the figure of a hundred pairs could easily be reached before the end of the twentieth century. Such a sustained rapid rate of increase is unlikely; but a considerable increase should be possible.

In Britain ospreys do not seem ever to have been truly colonial, in the way they are colonial (or were before the advent of pesticides) on islands off the New England coast and still are off Somalia. In such areas they may breed 40–60 yards apart, but in Europe are at least 400 yards apart. Nevertheless, it does appear that ospreys tend to be somewhat social, and that the presence of one pair in an area may per-haps stimulate others to occupy the same area within a few years. The last remnants of the osprey population lingered on in three main localities or groups so it seems possible that the anticipated spread, if and when it occurs, may follow a similar pattern, with small groups developing from an original colonising pair.

It is not strictly correct to say that all an osprey needs is a food supply of fish and a nesting site, because the species does not breed at all in the southern hemi-sphere except in Australasia. It winters as far south as Chile in S. America and in Africa south to the Cape Province but, although there are a few apparently authentic instances of breeding in South Africa, there are no recent records and a persistent rumour of breeding at Lake Naivasha in Kenya must, in my opinion, be dis-counted. Ospreys summer regularly at Lake Naivasha but none have bred or even displayed, although there is an abundant supply of fish and plenty of good nesting trees. It is even more strange that the osprey does not breed in some of the coastal lagoons, creeks, and brackish South African marshes, which are not at all unlike places in temperate Europe or North America where it does breed. This is a curious and apparently inexplicable quirk of the osprey's breeding distribution.

In its winter quarters, where I know it best, I can often observe ospreys fishing at leisure. Its mode of hunting is entirely aerial. It perches much on trees, but it hunts exclusively in flight, unlike its piratical neighbour the African fish eagle, which catches most of its prey from a perch. The osprey flies about in circles or figures of eight, or if the breeze is strong enough, glides and soars against it, about a hundred to two hundred feet above the water of a lake, lagoon, river or creek. On sighting a fish it checks briefly in flight, sometimes hovers for a moment or two, then plunges nearly vertically towards the prey. It appears to dive head first, and early accounts indicated that it plunged like a gannet, but actually at the last moment the feet are thrown forward in front of the head and the osprey crashes in feet first, usually with a heavy splash. The osprey appears to be sighting the prey through or between its own outstretched feet. It may sometimes snatch a fish near the surface with relatively little commotion, but on occasion plunges in so deep that only the wingtips remain above the water. In such instances it must be seizing fish well below the surface, perhaps two or three feet down.

The feet of the osprey are very strong and the tarsi short and thick, while the toes are lined with sharp spicules and the talons long, stiff and sharply curved. The cere is enlarged and can apparently close at will over the nostrils. All these are specialised adaptations for withstanding a heavy impact, grasping and holding slippery prey, and not getting water up the nose! The shock of impact which, as everyone knows who has jumped off a high diving board is considerable, must be cushioned by the depth of water between the surface and the fish itself. Otherwise the osprey would probably break its legs, for its impact-energy at the water surface must be about 3000–4000 foot pounds, equivalent to the muzzle energy of a heavy rifle bullet.

Emerging from the water, after a few initial wingflaps to rise from the surface, the osprey shivers to rid its plumage of surplus droplets. It normally carries its prey head first, one foot gripping the fish behind the other, so that it offers minimal resistance to the air, like a torpedo slung below an aircraft. Very rarely it may carry the fish transversely or in its bill. It makes for a perch on a tree or rock where it can feed at leisure but while doing so is very often robbed of its catch by the much larger sea eagles and fish eagles which regularly share its habitat. At least five species victimise the osprey, the largest the European sea eagle; it is usually unable to resist their piratical attacks, though it can throw off similar attacks by smaller kites and gulls. Robbed of its fish, the osprey must return for more, and may be obliged to capture several before it manages to retain one for itself.

Opinions differ on the degree of success enjoyed by fishing ospreys. One American observer thought that the birds were successful on almost every occasion when they tried, but Scottish experience suggests that an osprey makes two–four unsuccessful plunges for every successful catch, averaging about one fish in four attacked. Much depends on how one interprets the osprey's actions. If it checks briefly in flight but does not plunge this is hardly a serious attempt, but if it dives to near the surface and then swoops up again without actual immersion this is presumably a determined attack abandoned only when it clearly would not succeed. Immersion in water does not seem to discommode an osprey for long, but repeated immersion would no doubt necessitate a rest to dry the feathers before hunting in flight could be resumed.

My own experience indicates that an osprey makes three or four unsuccessful plunges for every occasion when it succeeds in catching a fish, and that on most of the successful occasions the fish is taken close to the surface so that the osprey only wets its legs, not the whole body and wings. If a fish close to the surface can be caught it is preferred but an osprey is certainly capable of taking fish swimming two to three feet below the surface, deeper than can any other fish-eating raptor. When it takes a fish deep in this way it submerges all but the upstretched wingtips, sometimes perhaps entirely.

The fish taken are mainly those that tend to bask near the surface, or rise to the surface in search of their own prey. In Britain pike, carp, grey mullet, bream, trout (brown, sea and rainbow), small salmon (grilse), roach, and perch are recorded(4). The Loch Garten pair feed mainly on pike and trout. The Loch Arkaig ospreys flew to the sea to obtain grey mullet and in suitable estuarine waters mullet, which often shoal near the surface, were and are favoured prey. One in Devon took a bass *Morone labrax*, carrying this large fish transversely afterwards(f); and in an ornamental pond in a Scottish glen goldfish were exterminated by a visiting osprey(i).

In Europe ospreys take many other species and in their tropical wintering and breeding quarters the list of fish taken must include hundreds of species. The huge majority of the food is living fish caught in open water; ospreys do not normally scavenge dead fish as do fish eagles and sea eagles. They catch a small number of aquatic birds and there are at least two British records of young lapwings, while one on a Kentish reservoir fed on a young rabbit, which it perhaps did not itself catch(d,h).

Ospreys were persecuted out of existence in Britain largely because of the supposed damage they do to trout and salmon fishery interests. This has undoubtedly been exaggerated, but equally it is pointless to deny that ospreys catch trout when they can. In many Scottish lochs the only available food would be trout; but in many such lochs trout are too numerous and undersized, so that they could do with thinning out. However, ospreys catch pike more easily than trout because pike are more inclined to bask motionless near the surface. In killing pike they probably do more good to the trout fishing interests than they do harm by catching some trout and in any case they are still so rare that there is no warrant whatever for objecting to their presence on these grounds.

The size of fish taken by ospreys is also sometimes exaggerated. They are credited with being able to take fish up to four pounds' weight (1·8 kg.), but this must be exceedingly rare. In Speyside the fish taken normally weigh 10–12 oz. and often less than half a pound, while the largest fish recorded in 16 years would not have been more than four pounds. It is extremely doubtful that an osprey could normally lift such a fish, about its own weight. With several hundred records to work from this is a good index of the preference and abilities of the osprey. In African winter quarters the vast majority of the fish I have seen taken by ospreys weigh less than a pound.

Ospreys, like fish eagles, are sometimes also reputed to perish through locking their claws in a fish much too large for them to handle, being dragged under, and drowned. Why the osprey does not simply let go (as would be natural) is never explained. A remarkable photograph exists of a large carp caught in a net, with the skeleton of an osprey still attached(e). In this photograph the skin of the osprey's legs is only partly decomposed, and although the flesh of the body has rotted off the skeleton is entire. It appears to me barely credible that a carp could swim about in a pool for the period necessary to achieve this stage of decomposition without detaching the osprey, whose muscles must at some stage have relaxed. The skeleton would probably also soften and disintegrate in water. Accordingly, my opinion is that this photograph, published in *British Birds* in 1945, is a hoax. It looks to me as if the skeleton of the osprey could have been later attached by the feet to the dead body of the carp.

The food requirement of an osprey is theoretically about 10% of its body weight, that is, about 140–160 grams (5–6 oz.). A pair normally feed on each other's kills, and digestion of fish is practically complete, bones and all. Waste is minimal, the only matter cast up in pellets being the scales, though sometimes the head and backbone of large fish are not eaten. In the ordinary way an osprey can satisfy this food requirement in a short period of daily hunting, by catching one half-pound fish. Outside the nesting season ospreys spend the majority of the day perched, not hunting. Even when there are young in the nest, and the female is tied to the vicinity of the eyrie, the male, who then has to feed himself and the equivalent of at least three other ospreys, can still manage to spend many hours perched and idle.

Ospreys do not seem to defend a home range or well defined territory, either in winter or in breeding quarters. In areas where they are colonial ospreys passing over other ospreys' nests are tolerated, and the birds from the whole colony fish in the same waters(1). In Britain an osprey can scarcely have any clearly defined range, for its only fishing grounds are widely separated tracts of water, sometimes with miles of dry land between. Doubtless the Loch Garten pair fish mainly in Loch Garten and in adjacent stretches of the river Spey, which is often broad and sluggish in that part of Speyside. Odd other ospreys visit the nest sites during the breeding season, usually without exciting violent reaction. If and when the osprey population builds up to larger numbers some regular pattern of espacement between breeding sites may become apparent, but at present there is none, at least in part because the birds are too few, while males fishing some distance from their own nest sites may tolerate the presence of other ospreys on these fishing grounds. More data are needed on the fishing ranges and behaviour of the Speyside ospreys.

British ospreys, derived from Scandinavian stock, are migrants, and are absent from the breeding area from September to April. New pairs tend to arrive about 10–15 April, but old established pairs take up residence earlier and earlier each year, though not normally before 1 April(4). This also was the traditional arrival date of the unfortunate Loch an Eilein pair. The male normally arrives first, but is joined in a few days by the female. The same birds return year after year to the same eyrie, unless one of them is killed or dies during the winter, when the survivor will presumably obtain another mate if it can. Females tend to be replaced about every four years but one ringed bird is still present after five years. Strange ospreys visit the nesting sites during the early stages of courtship and nest building; they are apparently tolerated by the resident birds of the opposite sex, but are often repelled by birds of the same sex, from which one might deduce that they are surplus unmated adults seeking a partner(i).

The period of nuptial display in Speyside ospreys is rather short, since the birds only arrive in the first few days of April and eggs are sometimes laid by 20 April. The male performs spectacular displays over the site, sometimes alone, sometimes to the female who may be perched below or also on the wing. He soars high, then dives and swoops up again in rather deep, steep undulations, calling loudly and shrilly. Such undulating displays are typical of many large raptors and are thrilling to watch. Sometimes the male carries a fish in his feet in the undulating display. Occasionally he performs a display exclusive to the osprey, in which he flaps his wings vigorously, several hundred feet above the ground, dangles his feet, often holding a fish, and calls in a frenzied manner 'chereeek-chereeek-chereeek'. He may actually fly backwards during this display which very quickly attracts attention. Although given to the female during courtship, this display is also performed by a nesting male apparently to distract intruders, whether human beings or, for instance, large passing gulls. It is accordingly one of the very few true distraction displays performed by any diurnal raptor.

During courtship the male feeds the female who generally remains near the nest and does no fishing for herself. Two to three fish are brought most days, occasionally one only, and the feeding rate at this stage is similar to that during the incubation period. The pair mate on the nest or on trees close to it. The male is decidedly uxorious and she, apparently, nothing loath. Mating begins on the day the female arrives, increases to as many as seven times daily before egg laying, but is reduced after the second egg is laid. In 1970, for instance, the pair mated or attempted to mate 106 times between 5 and 25 April, with about half the attempts successful(7). Sometimes the male presents the female with a fish and copulation follows, and it may also be associated with bringing nest material, but it often occurs without these preliminaries. This very frequent mating has not been recorded elsewhere but is doubtless typical, and ensures that the eggs have every chance of being fertile.

All Scottish nests and most European are at present in trees, but in former times Scottish ospreys also bred on small rocky islands in the middle of lochs where they were safe from all but human predators. The nests, wherever they are, are used repeatedly and, especially on the ground, become huge, in some cases larger than those of the largest eagles. The famous Loch Garten nest is relatively very small for an osprey. Both sexes build, the male starting as soon as he arrives, the female as soon as she joins him. At first they collect sticks, which are usually collected from the ground near by, or may be broken off another tree, sometimes in flight. Ospreys do not normally line the nest with green branches as egg laying approaches, but may add chips of bark, sphagnum moss, reeds, heather or dead grass. Sticks and other nesting material continue to be brought through the whole nesting cycle, fewer towards the end of the fledging period. In the later stages, after the hatch, the female brings more material than the male(4,7).

Two to four eggs are laid, usually two or three; 11 British clutches average 2·64. As in most large raptors the eggs are laid at intervals of about two days, but the details are not exactly recorded in British nests because of the need not to disturb the birds. The onset of incubation can be deduced by the behaviour of the female, who begins to sit as soon as or shortly after the first egg is laid. Speyside ospreys normally begin incubating 20–30 April(i). The female does most of the incubation by day, the male relieving her for spells of up to two hours, for a total of 30–35% of the daylight hours. Since the female invariably sits all night she actually does about four-fifths of all the incubation. As incubation progresses both birds tend to sit for longer periods and nest reliefs, which at first occur rather often, become less frequent.

Although the female is certainly off the nest for long enough spells to be able to hunt for herself she is apparently fed by the male throughout the incubation period(4,7). The food brought to the nest in this period varies from one to five fish per day and averages 1·7–1·8. In 1970 86 fish were brought in the incubation period, an average of 2·3/day(7). The male perhaps obtains some vocal or behavioural clue from the female as to whether she needs food or not, for he spends long idle periods perched near the nest interspersed with bouts of hunting. When he brings food the female often leaves the nest to eat it, and he may then relieve her on the eggs for periods of varying length; or she may feed on the nest. It should be possible to make a detailed quantitative analysis of the available data on the incubation period, and this is now being done.

Incubation in Europe lasts 35–38 days and in Speyside the period has been estimated as 35–37 days for each egg, again by observing the behaviour of the female. An early record of 33 days is incorrect(4). When the young hatch she tends to sit higher in the nest and repeatedly looks beneath her. The young hatch at intervals corresponding to the laying interval and can be heard cheeping before they emerge from the egg. Although they hatch at intervals of several days, and there is some variation in size they are not normally aggressive to one another. Consequently, any losses that reduce the brood are not due to fratricidal strife, but to such factors as shortage of food or disease.

At first the young are relatively inactive and remain invisible beneath the female. By 14 days old, however, they are active and move about the nest. When danger threatens they lie down and remain very still; their colour at this stage, brownish, with brown mottled feathers showing through the down, tones rather well with the interior of the nest and may thus have some survival value. By 28 days old they have started to grow feathers, which cover the body by 40 days. Thereafter they are mostly alone in the nest, standing or squatting and, as they grow older, performing wing-flapping exercises. They make their first flights at 50–59 days, usually 52–55, without any parental coaxing in most cases. The late Col. Richard Meinertzhagen recorded coaxing behaviour with fish by the parents to induce the young to leave a Swedish nest, but his observations are unique and need confirmation(5).

During the fledging period the role of the sexes in the adults is clearly defined. For the first thirty days, until the young have begun to grow feathers, the female remains on the nest with them or perches very close to it. She broods them continually at first, but by day ceases to brood them much after ten days and, as they grow bigger, stands over them rather than broods them and later stands beside them or on a tree branch, though she will return to brood them during heavy rain or cold. She broods at night till the young are about 30 days old. Throughout this time the male brings all the fish, and only the female feeds the young, herself eating some of the fish brought by the male.

As soon as the young hatch the rate of catching fish is about doubled. In 1970, for instance, it rose from 2·3/day during incubation to 3·9/day in the first ten days of the fledging period, reached a peak of 6·3/day between days 21 and 30, and then fell off gradually to 4·8/day just before the young flew. During the whole fledging period a total of 273 fish were brought on 55 days, averaging 4·9/day overall. The fish were eaten by the parents as well as by the brood. It is possible that the male, when absent from the nest area fishing, may have caught and eaten some prey himself without bringing it to the nest, but this seems rather unlikely.

The food requirement of a normal brood of two or three, with their parents, may be estimated at 750–950 grams daily, according to the number of chicks and assuming that each chick on average eats as much as an adult. This is equivalent to four or five half-pound trout. Allowing for some waste, this approximates the number of fish actually brought. However, if a more careful estimate is made, as in Text Table 2 for 1970, it appears that the daily food consumption is actually higher, approaching twice the theoretical requirement. Unfortunately, no figures are available for captive ospreys; but it seems unlikely that ospreys would in fact eat twice their theoretical requirement. Accordingly, it seems likely that the observers are overestimating the size of the fish brought in; an error of only one inch too large would mean that the real requirement is only 102 kg. (252 lb) instead of 138 kg. (302 lb). The daily food intake would then be about 260 grams, nearer the theoretical need. Although, therefore, careful analysis of the R.S.P.B. record books should give a good idea of the number of fish of each species taken, it is doubtful if they can give more than a very approximate quantitative picture of the food requirements of an osprey pair and their brood.

Fish may be brought at almost any time of the day from early morning soon after 4 a.m. to very late evening at 11.30 p.m. when almost dark(7). However, for an hour or two just after the dawn light begins to increase few are brought, perhaps because the fishing male needs some fishing time to catch them. More fish are caught after midday than during the morning, and the osprey, like everyone else, fishes the evening rise of trout. If the available data were more critically

Table 2 Estimated Size and Weight of Fish Brought by
Loch Garten Ospreys, 1973

(Data extracted from R.S.P.B. record book for that year)

Incubation. 37 days. 2 adults only	10"	10"–11"	12"–13"	14"–15"	16"–17"	18"+	Total
			Size of fish in inches				
Pike	4	10	9	9	1	4	37
Trout	2	8	16	5	0	1	32
Other	9	4	4	0	0	0	17
Total	15	22	29	14	1	5	86
Est. av. weight, grs.	150	200	320	450	800	1,200	
Total weight	2,250	4,400	9,280	6,300	800	6,000	29,030
Fledging. 56 days. 2 adults + 3 young							
Pike	3	9	29	19	2	7	69
Trout	24	18	40	24	10	15	131
Other	30	10	20	10	0	3	73
Total	57	37	89	53	12	25	273
Est. av. weight, grs.	150	200	320	450	800	1,200	
Total weight	8,550	7,400	28,480	24,850	9,600	30,000	104,880
Grand total weight	10,800	11,800	37,760	31,150	10,400	36,000	137,910

NOTE Many small fish unidentifiable; included in 'other'.
Total weight in incubation period 29·03 kg (64 lb).
Estimated daily catch/adult 392 gr. Waste, 10%. Eaten, 353 gr.
Total weight taken in fledging period, 104·9 kg (221 lb).
Estimated daily catch/osprey, 374 gr. Waste, 10%. Eaten, 337 gr.
Total weight taken in whole cycle, 137·9 kg (302 lb).
Estimated daily catch/osprey, 389 gr. Waste, 10%. Eaten, 350 gr.

analysed they would probably show a fishing peak about two or three hours before
dark, and another peak an hour or two after dawn. On available knowledge it is not
really possible to correlate times of bringing fish to the nest with fish activity, and
in any case if the male has been fishing at some distance he may not arrive at the
nest with his catch until an hour or so later, perhaps more.

The female continues to feed the young until they are about 42 days old, after
which they can feed themselves, though they will still beg her for food if she is in
the neighbourhood and she may still occasionally respond by feeding them; she
may even feed young after they have left the nest, and throughout this time takes
little part herself in hunting for the brood. In the middle of the fledging period the
male must kill up to five times his own food requirements to satisfy his family, and
can apparently do so without special difficulty.

Young ospreys roost in the nest for about a week after they make their first
flight, normally in late July. They remain in the general area thereafter for about
a month, and are at first still dependent on their parents for food, though as they
become stronger on the wing they accompany the adults to the fishing grounds and

do not wait for the food to be brought to the nest area. These aspects of breeding biology have been less well observed in the Speyside ospreys than some others, and are naturally more difficult to watch, since the young are no longer easily located at a fixed point.

It appears normal for young ospreys to learn to fish for themselves over a rather long period, gradually becoming independent of parental care. Again, Col. R. Meinertzhagen records a unique case of a brood of young being taught to fish by their parents within a week of leaving the nest; no one else has seen any such thing, and it probably is not normal(5). However, careful observations on such points are needed.

Up to the end of 1971 47 young ospreys had been reared to flying stage in the seven known Scottish eyries, from 21 successful nests out of 35 in which eggs were known to have been laid(i). If the mean clutch size of 2·64 is applicable to all nests in which eggs were laid, the mean resulting brood size of 1·34 per pair which laid is a little more than half the total number of eggs laid (47/92). The average size of brood is 2·24 per successful nest and, taking all pairs into consideration, including non-breeding pairs, almost exactly one young per pair per annum. Most of the failures were due to females which habitually laid infertile eggs, one nest having failed to produce any young for nine years. If these infertile females are discounted the average brood size would have been 1·64 per pair which laid and about 1·4/pair/year overall. These figures are not inferior to European broods of ospreys, and are very much superior to breeding success observed on the eastern coasts of America, where the osprey is becoming more or less rapidly extinct, apparently through the effects of organochlorine pesticides(2). These substances may be the cause of the infertility of two of the Speyside females, though the amounts found in the eggs have been low.

In mid September and October young and adults leave the area and migrate to Africa. Not all the Speyside young have been ringed, but of 32 ringed a rather high proportion, five altogether, have been recovered. One was recovered in Portugal, two (from the same nest in successive years) in Spain, and two nest mates ringed in 1971 were both recovered in Mauretania, one dead, the other caught alive. These records and others show that Speyside ospreys not only originally came from Scandinavia but follow the same sort of route south as do Swedish ospreys on their winter migrations (Map 15). There is a definite tendency for the recoveries to be on the western fringe of the main Swedish migration path(i).

It is possible to compute the overall life spans of ospreys in the wild state from European and American ringing recoveries. Ospreys mature in their third year, and losses among the young in their first winter are heavy, about 55% of all those reared. Less than one young bird in three becomes sexually mature(6). Although the adult life span can be up to 23 years, making the total life in this case 26 years, this is very rare. The average adult life span is estimated at only about 1·8 years, or barely two breeding seasons(6). In that time, with an average brood size of about 1·5 per pair which laid, two adults can produce only three young, only one of which will survive to become sexually mature. At this rate, it would be impossible for the osprey to increase – as it undoubtedly has, both in Europe and in Britain, in the last 20 years.

This would apply even more strongly if the average overall productivity of Scottish eyries, about one young per pair per annum is taken into account. At the same mortality rate this would necessitate an average life span of eight years as adults to keep the population stable, let alone increase. Accordingly, it appears

Table 3 Breeding success: Speyside Ospreys 1954-71

Nest series	Years occupied	Years pairs present	Years pairs known laid	No. succ. nests	Total young fledged	Notes
A1	1954-71 (17)	17	16	11	25	twice robbed by egg collectors
A2	1963-71 (9)	8	7	0	0	infertile eggs
A3	1968-71 (4)	4	1	0	0	
B1	1966-71 (6)	6	5	5	10	
B2	1968-71 (4)	3	3	2	8	
C1	1968-71 (4)	3	1	1	2	
C2	1969-71 (3)	3	2	2	2	
	1954-71 (48)	45	35	21	47	

= 0·98 young/occupied territory/year.
  1·04 ,, /active pair/year.
  1·34 ,, /pair which bred.
  2·24 ,, /successful nest.

NOTE In 1973 13 pairs of ospreys attempted to nest in Scotland, rearing 21 young; 29 young have now been reared from nest A.1.

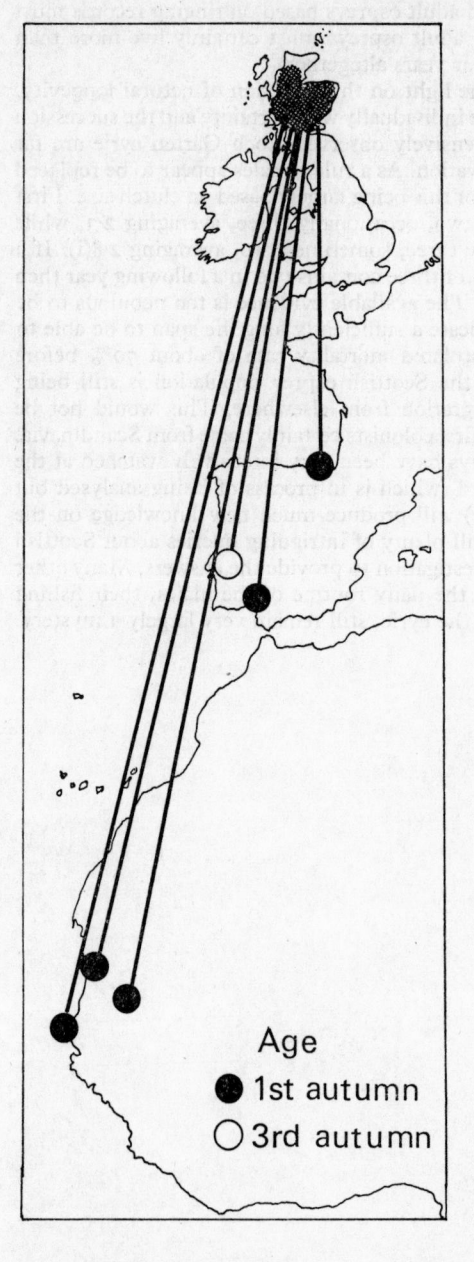

Age

● 1st autumn

○ 3rd autumn

MAP 15. Foreign recoveries of British-ringed ospreys.

that estimates of the life span of wild adult ospreys based on ringing records must be too pessimistic, and that healthy adult ospreys must certainly live more than 1·8 years as adults and more than four years altogether.

The data from Speyside shed little light on this question of natural longevity. Ospreys are not very easy to recognise individually with certainty and the succession of changes of mate, even at the intensively observed Loch Garten eyrie are far from clear over the 17 years of observation. As a rule females appear to be replaced every four years or so, the evidence for this being largely based on clutch size. First clutches by any female are usually two, occasionally three, averaging 2·3, while second and later clutches are usually three, sometimes two, averaging 2·8(i). If a nest which has generally had a clutch of three contains two in a following year then a new female is likely to be present. The available evidence is too nebulous to be worth much, yet does not so far indicate a sufficiently long life span to be able to maintain the population at the postulated mortality rate of about 70% before sexual maturity. If this is so, then the Scottish osprey population is still being maintained and expanded by immigration from elsewhere. This would not be surprising in view of the fact that the first colonists certainly came from Scandinavia.

Thus, although the Scottish ospreys have been very intensively watched at the nest, and although the 17-year record (which is in process of being analysed but which has not been available to me) will produce much new knowledge on the osprey's breeding habits there are still plenty of intriguing queries about Scottish ospreys that will stimulate future investigation to provide the answers. Many other aspects of the osprey's life, such as the daily routine of the males, their fishing ranges and success when away from the eyrie, still remain very largely a mystery.

CHAPTER 5

THE HONEY BUZZARD

ACCORDING to the published literature, the honey buzzard is one of the two rarest British breeding birds of prey, rarer than the osprey or probably the goshawk (if that really breeds here regularly) and until recently even rarer than the marsh harrier. It is also extremely local, most of the population breeding in one small area of southern England. There are those who say that it must be commoner than is generally admitted in its main haunt, and that because of its secretive habits it probably breeds unobserved in other parts of England, and they may be right. However, a judgement based on what is actually published indicates that there are probably less than ten pairs in Britain, a few regular in Hampshire and odd other pairs less regular in Central England and towards the Welsh borders. Apparently it almost certainly bred in Fife in 1949, and has bred in Aberdeenshire and Easter Ross in the nineteenth century. It has never bred in Ireland(8).

The honey buzzard probably was not very numerous in Britain in the recent past for lack of large stretches of suitable habitat. However, in far off times when most of southern England was covered with natural forest it must have been a much more common bird than it is today. In the last two hundred years it probably never has exceeded a score of more or less severely harried pairs. It undoubtedly would have been persecuted without reason, like other raptors in the great game preserving era, and even today the population in Hampshire is largely confined to unkeepered areas. However the main limiting factors on the honey buzzard in Britain are its migratory habit and specialised diet of wasp and bee grubs, while its need for peace and quiet in the breeding season may also be a factor in overcrowded southern England.

Like Montagu's harrier and the hobby the honey buzzard is a summer migrant, arriving in May and leaving again in September. However, it differs from Montagu's harrier in that in Europe it breeds much further north, as far as 68°N, apparently in large numbers. Enormous numbers pass Falsterbo and Heligoland on the southern migration in autumn; 4000 may be seen in a day and 20,000 may be seen in a season, and it is safe to assume that many more pass unseen(11). Allowing for the fact that these migrants include both adults and young, it seems fairly safe to assume that there must be at least ten thousand pairs breeding somewhere north of Falsterbo, perhaps not only in Norway and Sweden but also further east.

It may seem odd that if the honey buzzard is ecologically limited, in the British Isles, to the warmer wooded parts, that it can breed much further north in Europe. However, continental countries often enjoy weeks of fine hot weather in summer at times when depression after depression comes in to the British Isles from the Atlantic, bringing in rain and cool weather. There are also very much larger continuous tracts of natural woodland than in Britain, so that both from the viewpoint of available habitat and summer warmth Europe is more likely to attract honey buzzards.

In Britain the honey buzzard is probably limited both by habitat and its food habits. It requires large tracts of mixed woodland with natural glades in which it can hunt its prey, wasp nests. Apparently it does not thrive so well in country which is alternately cultivated fields and woodland in Europe, so presumably this is also the case in Britain. Perhaps this is because cultivation destroys underground wasps' nests. There are many areas in England where quite large tracts of secluded woodland alternate with intensively farmed land, but comparatively few where woodland alternates with large natural openings. It is also quite possible that soil type would affect a species that must dig for its food; it may only be possible to dig out enough wasps' nests in light sandy or loamy soil, not in heavy clay.

The honey buzzard is badly named, for it is neither a buzzard nor does it eat honey. It feeds almost entirely on the grubs of wasps and bumble bees, with an occasional frog or lizard to vary the diet. When eating the wasps' nests and grubs some of the comb is consumed, perhaps for roughage, and the honey buzzard does also eat a few birds. However, unless it can find enough wasps' nests it cannot live and breed. One estimate is that a honey buzzard pair with the brood require 90,000 wasp grubs per year, and this seems quite realistic(2). Such a quantity of wasps' nests will evidently most easily be found in areas with a warm or hot summer and sufficient moisture, which perhaps explains why the honey buzzard does not breed commonly if at all in Mediterranean France, Spain, or Portugal, where the summers are hot but dry.

The dependence of the honey buzzard on wasps is well illustrated by an analysis of stomach contents in Norway by Hagen(4). Among a total of 15,978 listed items, 14,345 were the contents of wasp cells and 1283 wasps and bees, while other insects totalled 338, mostly larvae; there were only 12 vertebrates, 10 frogs and 2 birds. These would be more important by weight, each amounting to several hundred wasp grubs; but nevertheless the dependence on wasps and their grubs is obvious. Holstein in Denmark records, in 104 identifiable items brought to the nest, 61 wasp combs, 15 bumble-bee nests, 19 frogs, 2 birds, 2 worms, and a lizard(5). This contains a higher proportion of vertebrate material, perhaps associated with the fledging period. Also, perhaps more vertebrate food must be eaten in a year when wasps are scarce.

In Europe honey buzzards in France can find enough food to breed in quite small areas of woodland. In Lorraine the breeding range of pairs is given as 64–150 hectares, and two pairs attempted to breed in a wood of 80 hectares, with four pairs of common buzzards; one of the pairs of honey buzzards did not persevere(9). In Denmark, over nine years, there were 23 nests in a wood of 1890 hectares, averaging overall about 650 hectares (1620 acres) per nest, but in some years less, 360 hectares (890 acres)(5). The honey buzzards in all these cases probably also fed at some distance from the nest. In other parts of Europe honey buzzards are reported to forage over larger areas, up to 5 km. (3 miles) from the nests. Probably the number of honey buzzards able to breed depends on the density of wasps' nests available; but as this is extremely hard to estimate accurately the two factors have never been connected. In Britain, with a wet Atlantic climate and relatively scarce wasps, it seems likely that the birds would have to forage over much larger areas in order to obtain their requirements. They could also have been adversely affected recently by the use of agricultural pesticides in the more intensively cultivated parts of south-east England, which are the main areas where the climate is likely to be sufficiently warm for abundant wasps permitting honey buzzards to nest.

The honey buzzard is anatomically adapted to its peculiar diet. Killing no large animals or birds, it requires no sharp talons, and its claws are blunt and nearly straight, like those of a hen. Such a foot is, however, much more efficient for walking on the ground and digging than would be a foot with long curved talons; all eagles, for instance, are noticeably awkward when walking. The honey buzzard's face, bare in most birds of prey, is covered with stiff short scale-like feathers, and it has usually been assumed that this is to protect these areas from wasp stings. However, it appears that wasps, angry though they may be, seldom actually attempt to sting the honey buzzard's face, but hover round its head without stinging, and are even caught and eaten with impunity by the bird. The advantage of the scale-like feathers is thus not fully proven.

A honey buzzard digging out a wasps' nest apparently locates it first by perching at the edge of a wood and watching acutely for passing wasps. If workers are seen returning to their nest along a certain route the bird follows, and, having located the nest, begins to dig. It digs with its feet, scratching away the ground cover first, and gradually digging a deeper and deeper trench like a terrier until it can finally excavate the nest. It may disappear underground completely while digging, and is so preoccupied with its task that it may be closely approached(10). It may return to the same place day after day for several days until no remnant remains of a large nest or cluster of nests, and eventually entirely removes all the comb. The papery wasps' nests do not contain honey and it is the grubs in the individual brood cells that the bird is after. When these have been extracted the comb also is discarded and its base is not eaten, though the papery cells apparently are. The wasps and bees are unable to do anything to prevent the removal of their nest and are themselves sometimes eaten. The bird catches them by the middle and nips off the sting before swallowing them. The wasps and bees become very angry and aggressive, however, and may attack other animals or human beings passing in the neighbourhood of a colony that is being robbed. Any ornithologist suddenly and unreasonably attacked by wasps may, if he perseveres, find a honey buzzard working near by.

In Europe, honey buzzards also eat a few frogs, lizards, and birds, and other insects, principally larvae and grubs. They presumably catch the lizards and frogs on the ground, and it seems not impossible that they may pick up the birds as carrion, for they would not seem to be well equipped to catch them alive. However, there are no direct observations on the point. In winter quarters in Africa honey buzzards eat insects caught on the ground and the grubs in the nests of wasps and hornets, which frequently hang below tree branches, under cliffs, or from the eaves of houses in dozens. The diet in Africa is not really well known because the winter quarters are still not fully established and the honey buzzards are seldom observed.

All European and British honey buzzards winter in tropical Africa, but the main wintering ground is not adequately known. The autumn migration in September and October enters Africa through Gibraltar, Suez, and down the length of Italy, while some birds also occur in Malta, where they are relentlessly shot. Although, from the records of migration stations it seems certain that at least scores of thousands of honey buzzards must enter Africa they are very unobtrusive there in winter. They are said to be more common in the west than in the east, but Bannerman quotes very few definite records for the west coast countries between Gambia and Cameroon, all of which contain large tracts of tropical forest or savanna, suitable habitat for the honey buzzard(1). In Kenya I have myself seen two in twenty-six years both in my own property; and there is no doubt that the honey buzzard is a scarce migrant east of the main Congo forests. It is said to be quite common in Gabon and in the Brachystegia woodland of Rhodesia and Zambia between November and March and, as is confirmed by the paucity of records, it is also said to be very quiet and unobtrusive even there in its habits. Even so, it is extraordinary how so many of these large birds seem to disappear in the vast area of forest and savanna available to them.

The southward autumn migration into Africa is perhaps less concentrated at Mediterranean entry points than the northward spring movement. Although greater numbers must pass south in autumn they are less obvious in the Mediterranean basin, though apparently they are even more obvious than in spring at certain northern migration stations such as Falsterbo and Heligoland. The southward move begins as soon as breeding is complete, or earlier in the case of old birds which have not bred or have failed; these are on the move south by mid August, while the young of the year and their parents do not move south till early September. The birds travel south in small parties or sometimes in larger flocks, and on favourable days a continuous stream passes over, with peaks of five or six hundred in an hour, and flocks of eighty to a hundred or more birds. Once they reach Africa or even before they apparently split up into small parties and finally become single. Although it has been suggested that in the breeding season the same birds return to the same place to nest each year the pair bond is apparently not maintained in the African winter quarters. However, so little is known about honey buzzards in Africa that one would not want to be dogmatic about such matters.

The return migration in spring is evidently performed by a smaller number of birds, owing to winter mortality, but is more concentrated and easier to observe in the Mediterranean. Again, the birds enter Europe at certain spots, Gibraltar, across the Mediterranean via Malta, and to Sicily and Italy. The spring migration may follow a more westerly course than the southward autumn movement. At Malta the migration occurs in two main waves, the first and largest in early (5–15) May, with a smaller flight in late May or early June(3). It seems likely that the birds which are going to breed might be those which come in the first wave, those which follow later being doubtful breeders, for they would possibly arrive in breeding grounds too late to succeed in completing the cycle. Alternatively, those breeding further north may migrate north earlier than those breeding in, for instance, Southern France. Data are inadequate to answer such queries.

In the Mediterranean the spring migration occurs in certain weather conditions, usually calm, though I have also seen what I took to be honey buzzards crossing the Straits of Gibraltar against a strong wind, with Montagu's harriers. At Malta they apparently use the lift obtained from thunderclouds to gain height to make the crossing, and they are the largest birds of prey at all common on migration at Malta(3). This suggests certain flight adaptations, such as low wing loading; on scanty evidence honey buzzards have lower wing loading than other raptors of the same size. In Sicily the spring migration is apparently greeted by gunfire, and honey buzzards are even reputed to be good to eat; since they are not flesh-eaters this may well be so.

The main spring migration crosses the Mediterranean in early May, and the birds arrive on their breeding grounds in Britain and in other parts of Europe at the same latitude in late May and early June. The speed of the migration probably means that the birds migrate fasting, and there is little evidence that they stop to feed, though migrants arriving in Britain have been found to have insects in their stomachs. They are perhaps unable to subsist easily at first in breeding quarters and may have to eat more frogs and other insects until mid June when wasp and bumble bee nests are likely to be plentiful. The nests, comb and grubs are of course available before the wasps themselves are very abundant. At any rate, the whole breeding cycle is rather compressed, especially in courtship and nest building, which normally takes a month or so in smaller raptors, but in the honey buzzard is very brief.

Nuptial display in the honey buzzard is absolutely characteristic. The male is said to arrive two to seven days before the female in Denmark, though in some cases the birds arrive paired(5). Holstein suggests that the male selects the nesting place and at once begins nest building. The most common form of display is for the male to rise in circles and, having gained height, to fly forward in a straight line and at intervals rise steeply upward, so that he gains further height in a series of steps. At the top of each upward swoop he raises his wings nearly vertically above the back and flicks them through a short arc two or three times, apparently defying gravity in this posture. Sometimes he trails his feet and some observers say that he claps his wings together over his back several times; however this has not been seen in Britain. Females perform a similar display, less often than males; in their case the straight flight is gently undulating and there is no or less gain in height. The pair also soar together high up, the male above the female; he may dive at her and swoop up again, raising his wings above his back. The raising of the wings vertically above the back is absolutely diagnostic in this species. Rarely males also perform a headlong vertical stoop with closed wings. Display is usually silent, but occasionally a loud high-pitched mew, 'peee-uw' is uttered, resembling calls of the common buzzard but shriller and more resonant.

Hardly anything has been published about the breeding behaviour of honey buzzards in Britain, so we must assume that it resembles that of the species in Denmark or Germany, where whole books have been written about this very intriguing bird(5,6). The nests are apparently built high up in trees, usually deciduous, but sometimes coniferous, with beech a favourite. When built by the honey buzzards alone they are small structures, but are often built on top of the old nest of a crow or common buzzard, when they are larger and more obvious. The same general area is used, but not usually the same nest, though this has been known. Nests are usually built near the edge of a wood, often near a path, road, or human habitation, and the birds are secretive and quiet rather than shy.

The male brings most of the material, while the female remains in the nest and works it into the structure. Although some dead branches are brought most of the material is green leafy twigs, so that the nest develops a characteristic appearance. Days of building are interspersed with periods in which no building is done, perhaps to allow the green material to wither and dry; similar intermittent building is seen, for instance, among African weaver birds that make nests of green grass. Most of the building is done in the early morning and evening, leaving the middle of the day free for hunting prey. The birds do not roost near the nest, but fly in silently one or two hours after sunrise, build for a time, and then cease after six o'clock, when the male at least goes hunting, while the female may remain near the nest site. Building is resumed in the evening. The finished nest is small, 2–2½ ft across and 8 in. to 1 ft deep with a leafy central cup 10 in. to 1 ft across. Besides the nest eventually used, other nests may be built up, and these may be added to after eggs are laid. Non-breeding pairs may build up a nest one year and use it the next year.

The female sometimes begins to brood in the nest before egg laying. When wanting to mate she flies to a branch near by and solicits the male, uttering a loud wailing shriek during the act. Mating occurs up to five times daily for 10–12 days usually in the morning. The whole courtship, nest building and mating period occupies only two weeks or a little more, unusually short, but evidently biologically desirable in so large a bird with such a specialised diet, only able to live in temperate latitudes in high summer when wasps and their larvae are abundant.

There are no accurate data on egg laying dates in Britain, but presumably they are laid in early June, as in Denmark, where the earliest clutches are normally laid by about 4 June and few after 15 June. In 63 cases Holstein recorded only two clutches in May(5). One to three eggs, usually two, are laid at three-day intervals, and since they are very handsomely marked they are in heavy demand by egg collectors, who were one of the main causes of reduction of the honey buzzard in Britain in the late nineteenth century, and are now the main reason why available British knowledge is never published.

Both sexes incubate, beginning with the first egg, and the male takes a large share, 20–50% of the daylight hours. Individual spells vary from 50 minutes to 20 hours, for a female. The female is said to sit at night, and the male does not normally relieve her for his first spell before 05.00 when the sun is well up, or after 17.30 in the evening when she settles for the night. Since the female is off long enough to hunt her own prey the male does not feed her. The birds are extremely silent and unobtrusive all through the incubation period, even at nest relief, which is brief, one bird flying in and the other away.

At this stage, and at other times the male and female are said by Holstein to be distinguishable by their voices. The male makes a sound like a piece of cardboard being held against the spokes of a slowly rotating bicycle wheel, and the female a melodious whistling howl. Other attempts to describe these peculiar utterances suggest a rapid clicking or popping by the male and a high-pitched whistling mew by the female, also, a sound like a spitting cat. The amount of calling varies between pairs, some being quite noisy. According to Holstein, who is apt to cite longer incubation periods than other observers of the same species, incubation takes 34–38 days, but elsewhere in the literature is estimated at 28–35 days; estimates for each egg are from 31–37 days. The young hatch 24 hours after chipping the shell and the empty eggshells are removed by the parents.

Few eggs fail to hatch as the parents are very close sitters and the nest is scarcely ever left unattended, except through human disturbance, to permit carrion crows or other predators to get at the eggs. However, when two young hatch one is usually lost early in the fledging period and there is at least one record of the elder relentlessly attacking the younger, possibly killing it later. There is a considerable difference in size due to the laying interval of three days, and the younger is much weaker and smaller than the elder. It seems a little curious that this feature, regularly associated with large and aggressive eagles, should also occur in a comparatively inoffensive insectivorous species.

For the first 10 days of the fledging period one or other of the parents is always on the nest. Both sexes brood and feed the young, and the male is even said to feed them with the female present, most unusual in birds of prey. Daytime brooding is reduced after 3–4 days, but continues at night for up to 10 days longer. During the first 10 days the female brings about 10% of the food, the male 90%. The female then remains mainly on the nest, while the male alone hunts and brings in wasps' nests and other prey. Wasp grubs are fed to the young one by one, and the empty comb is trodden into the nest in fragments. Frogs are skinned, then torn up for the young, as in other large raptors.

The male continues hunting alone until about day 24–25, when the young are quite strong and can remove grubs from wasp nests for themselves. The female is then released to take part in hunting for the brood or single young bird. She then brings in about a third of the prey, the male the remaining two-thirds. The parents continue to bring food to the young in the nest after they have made their first flight at about 40–45 days, for about another 10 days.

The young are very feeble at first, but by 13 days old are vigorous and active, moving about the nest and flapping their stumps of wings. Feathers are evident at about 19 days and about the same time the young learn to extract grubs from wasps' nests and thereafter require less parental assistance. By 28 days they are covered with feathers and are practising wing flapping and from 35 days onwards climb out on to branches of the nest tree and make short flights from branch to branch. They make their first flights at 40–45 days, but remain near it for another 10 days, returning to it to be fed by either adult. By the time they are large and well feathered they are not quarrelsome, and if two survive to that stage both will probably be reared. There are no adequate data from Holstein or other sources, but it seems likely that 1·2–1·4 young per pair which breed are reared, or 1–1·2 per pair overall, including some non-breeders.

The whole nesting cycle, from egg laying in early June, to the stage at which the young move away from the nest takes 90–95 days, about the same as for the common buzzard from laying to first flight of the young from the nest, but compressed in the nest building and the post-fledging period, each only two weeks or so, while in the common buzzard both occupy a month or more. The young move away from the nest area and can fly strongly about 5–10 September in Europe, by which time wasps and their larvae are becoming scarcer. There is some suggestion that in the later stages of the fledging period more frogs and reptiles may be fed to the young than earlier, during the peak of abundance of wasp larvae.

The young must accordingly leave the nesting area to migrate almost as soon as they can fly well. Since, in some other species, it has been shown that the young can catch insects before they can catch birds or more powerful prey, these young can presumably find enough food to maintain themselves almost as soon as they start on the southward journey. There is at any rate no evidence that migrating young are still heavily dependent on their parents for food when they pass south over Falsterbo and Heligoland in great streams in early to mid September.

A few of these migrating European honey buzzards reach Britain. The records for Ireland are for passage migrants in summer and autumn. Most of the Irish birds were moving north in June, but a few also occur moving south in autumn, as late as November. The last two recorded in Ireland were shot in 1967(8). Honey buzzards have appeared as autumn stragglers at Fair Isle, and in small numbers on the east coast of England, but the number that stray from the main migratory routes is small. The southward migration of honey buzzards is unusually concentrated at least until it reaches France and Spain, where large numbers are shot on their southward journey before they reach Africa.

No doubt these may include a few of the small British population, but there is at present no way of telling what happens to these. It would be nice to think that the climate of opinion in Britain may change sufficiently to make publication of available knowledge possible, but at present there seems little likelihood of that either.

CHAPTER 6

THE RED KITE

THE red kite is the best British example of a species brought to the verge of extinction here by eighteenth and nineteenth-century persecution, but which survived as a beleaguered remnant in a remote part of Wales and is now, from this last stronghold, apparently making a slow and difficult come-back. Although it is far too early to say that the kite is out of danger we can take comfort from the fact that in 1972 the known numbers are about double those of twenty years previously, while the average number of young reared in each of the last three years is four times as many as were reared in 1945. A record number of pairs (26 known) nested in 1972, but four of these were robbed by egg collectors, including one pair which has reared large broods in each of the previous three years. The kite is not now the rarest British breeding raptor, and may even be commoner than Montagu's harrier, the other member of its group of 10–50 pairs; but its position is still precarious and it must be nurtured with care if it is once again to become common and widespread in Britain.

The story of the near extinction of the kite is a melancholy one and has been told by many authors(1). Up to the end of the eighteenth century it was common or abundant, and it was this species, not the black kite (which occupies the town scavenger niche in most of the Old World), which was abundant in the streets of London in the sixteenth century. One sixteenth-century traveller, Le Cluse, likened its numbers to those of black kites in Cairo(b). Assuming that Egyptians were at least as insanitary in 1570 as they are today that must have been common indeed. In the seventeenth century protection afforded to it because of its useful scavenging habits ceased to be effective, but according to Pennant it still bred in Gray's Inn in 1777, and was then common throughout Britain.

In the late eighteenth century the era of intensive game preservation began and the kite was quickly exterminated in most of its range. It had probably already declined due to some improvements in sanitation, refuse disposal, and loss of suitable breeding habitat through enclosures, but still must have been quite abundant. Living as it often did close to the haunts of and in association with men (as 90–95% of tropical black kites do today) it was both easily shot and trapped, while its carrion feeding habits made it easy to poison. Thus it was wiped out in England by 1870, greatly reduced in Scotland by 1850 and extirpated there by 1900(1). Even in Wales, where it survived better, it was wiped out in S. Wales after the 1830s and a merciless campaign was still directed against the remnant in the '90s. A few pairs survived in the wilder unkeepered parts of Central Wales, and in 1903 an endeavour was made to give these last remnants special protection. The onslaughts of egg collectors and skin collectors may have reduced the remnant to as few as four to five surviving pairs, though some doubt that it was ever quite as rare as that and consider that there were at least eight or nine pairs in 1905(3).

Efforts to conserve the remnant after that appear to have been bedevilled by personality conflicts and by extreme forms of secrecy, which may have been necessary but which on occasion appear to have acted against the kite. Partly as a result of this good population data are hard to come by and little of any value was recorded about the ecology or behaviour of Welsh kites at that time. Rewards were paid to farmers on whose land young kites were reared, thus foreshadowing the more widespread R.S.P.B. reward scheme of today. Breeding success was very low in those days, one or two young being all that were known to be reared in some years. The fact that the kite could recover at all from this low ebb gives cause for some cautious optimism today.

The full story of these efforts at conservation has been told by Colonel H. Morrey Salmon and need not be repeated here(3). The kites, like other raptors in Britain, certainly benefited from the Second World War, which reduced the number and mobility of persons able or willing to reach the breeding areas to persecute the birds. However, even in 1945, only the same number of young, four, from two out of five known nests, were known to have been reared as in 1905. In fact, there were probably more for immediately after the war other pairs were found in outlying areas besides the restricted area watched in wartime. By 1951 breeding records were more complete, and in that year there were thought to be 13 pairs with nests plus at least 4 non-breeding adults, 8 successful nests, and 11 young reared. An ecological and population study of the kite was then undertaken in 1957 by the Welsh Nature Conservancy team, and it is on the results of this study, prepared in draft and since published by Peter Davis and Peter Walters Davies, that this account is based(2).

Since then the kite has made a shaky gradual climb to its present numbers of about 70 known adults, young, and immatures. The period has been marked by several major setbacks. Myxomatosis in the rabbit population in 1954–55 drastically reduced the numbers of pairs which bred from 10 to 6, and only one young was reared. However the situation improved the following year and thereafter until 1963, when the severe winter probably caused poor breeding success in the 14 pairs which bred, for they reared only 4 young. The adverse effects of the use of dieldrin as sheep dip in 1961–67 clearly reduced breeding success and slowed the recovery but did not affect the kite as badly as was first feared at the time, though breeding success fell. In 1967 the magic figure of 20 breeding pairs was for the first time exceeded and 22 pairs bred rearing 11 young.

Since then only in one year has the breeding population been below this figure (Text Table 4). In every year some nests have been lost to egg collectors and others to natural causes, and the breeding success of kites in Wales continues to be below average for the species in its main European haunts. In 1972 the egg collector menace sharply worsened but despite this there was a record breeding season, as one pair re-laid, for the first time on record, and reared two young(2).

At present the kite habitat consists of four main vegetation or land use types: (i) oakwoods, of mainly sessile oak; a type which formerly covered most of Wales up to 1200 ft, and is now reduced to small remnant hanging woods, vital to the kite both for roosting and nesting: (ii) marginal hill land; partly enclosed rough pasture, sometimes indistinguishable from (iii) mountain sheepwalk; unenclosed, unimproved rough pasture which was probably formerly birch scrub but has been converted to grassland by overgrazing and too frequent burning: and (iv) lowland valley farmland, a mosaic of small grass fields and riverside marshlands with homesteads, hedges, walls, etc., but very little arable land. There are also small oakwoods along steep stream banks in the valleys.

All four zones are used by kites for feeding, hunting, roosting or nesting. They hunt very little in the oakwoods, and still less in plantations of conifers. Oak woodlands provide very little food other than some sheep carrion and some young

Table 4 Breeding Success: Red Kite, 1951-72

(Highest and lowest figs. **bold**)

Year	Pairs with nests	Non-breeding adults	Success-ful nests	Young reared	Young/pair overall Note (1)	Young/pair which bred	Young/success-ful nest	Notes
1951	13	4	8	11	0·73	0·84	1·4	
1952	10	8	6	7	0·50	0·70	1·2	
1953	11	5	7	11	**0·84**	1·0	1·6	
1954	10	14	8	12	0·72	1·2	1·5	(2)
1955	7	13	1	1	**0·074**	**0·14**	**1·0**	(3)
1956	9	6	5	6	0·50	0·66	1·2	
1957	7	10	6	7	0·58	1·0	1·2	
1958	11	8	5	5	0·33	0·45	1·0	
1959	12	3	7	9	0·69	0·74	1·3	
1960	10	6	8	10	0·76	**1·0**	1·25	
1961	13	4	5	6	0·4	0·46	1·2	
1962	11	9	5	6	0·43	0·54	1·2	
1963	14	5	3	4	0·25	0·29	1·3	(4)
1964	14	10	6	7	0·32	0·5	1·2	(5)
1965	17	8	10	11	0·52	0·65	1·1	,,
1966	15	6	8	11	0·61	0·73	1·4	,,
1967	22	4	7	11	0·42	0·50	**1·6**	
1968	19	16	9	12	0·44	0·63	1·3	
1969	24	13	10	16	0·53	0·66	**1·6**	
1970	24	11	11	17	0·58	0·71	1·5	
1971	22	13	12	16	0·57	0·72	1·3	
1972	26	13	14	19	0·58	0·73	1·4	(6)
Total 22 yrs.	321	189	161	215				
Means					0·52	0·67	1·32	

NOTES (1) is an indicative figure calculated from the total number of adults that could form pairs (known pairs + non-breeding adults divided by 2); fluctuates from 0·07–0·84, i.e. by 900%, cf. 1·0–1·6 for young per successful nest (60%).

(2)(3) Years of myxomatosis, depressed severely the pairs which bred but did not affect number of adults so much.

(4) Severe winter of 1963 depressed the number of adults breeding but did not affect young per successful nest.

(5) Dieldrin in sheep dip depressed breeding to some extent 1964–66 but not severely.

(6) 1972, a record year in all ways, including number of pairs, number of young reared, and number of nests robbed; but for this last the expected number of young reared would have been 22–23.

corvids in spring. From their oakwood roosts and nesting haunts kites forage mainly uphill into the open country, travelling 6–8 miles (10–13 km.) from the nest and up to 15 miles (24 km.) from winter roosts. Typically, a pair of kites' home range is long and narrow, with its focus at the nest site in the oakwood. Its total extent is hard to determine, for adjacent pairs tolerate one another and their ranges overlap. However, an average pair of kites probably requires about 6–10 square miles (2580 ha.) of ground in the breeding season, and forage far outside this area in winter. In winter individuals have been seen at points 6 miles (10 km.) apart on the same day and 11 miles (18 km.) apart on different days.

In the spring and summer kites forage mainly in the marginal hill land and sheep-walks, largely because of the availability of sheep carrion in these areas. The average stocking rate is about one ewe to 3 acres, so that in any home range there may be about 1000–1200 ewes. As in other mountain range habitats about 10–15 lambs per 100 ewes will be lost each year through starvation or bad weather, while adult sheep also die, so that in a typical kite home range 100–120 dead lambs may be found each spring, with a steady supply of mutton carrion at other times. These upland areas are also the breeding haunts of, for instance, black-headed gulls, and some kites exploit this source of food. The rough pasture also provides a good supply of voles. For all these items kites must compete with other resident predators and scavengers, notably the common buzzard and the raven, both very much more numerous than the kite.

The lowland farmland is potentially rich in prey, but carrion is less available because most sheep carcases are buried. Young corvids are however relatively abundant in lowlands. Kites mainly forage in this habitat in late autumn and winter, preferring water meadows and open stream banks to enclosures. Rivers provide frogs, fish, and carrion after spates, and roads provide carrion, while kites also frequent rubbish tips, farm middens, collect slaughterhouse refuse and, in winter, may even take scraps put out for other birds. They attend the hay harvest, catching small invertebrates and mammals after the grass is cut. Although the main feeding habitat is still the uplands kites have made more use of the lowlands in recent times and may yet adapt to such areas again if left alone. They already display a marked tendency to associate with man.

The most usual method of hunting is to soar and circle over open country, often at a considerable height, but frequently also gliding low over the ground against or across the wind, thus travelling rather slowly and searching the area thoroughly somewhat like a harrier. If carrion is sighted the kite descends in circles, and alights some distance off before finally walking or flying up to the carcase. The sighting of live prey results in a steep dive with closed wings, landing with feet outstretched. If the prey runs away the kite may pursue, but not for long. Prey is usually caught by surprise rather than speed, but some items such as woodpigeons and small birds must require a turn of speed and considerable agility. Quantitative data are lacking, but kites are unsuccessful far more often than they are successful when trying to catch live prey.

Kites may also hunt from perches, or walk about on the ground seeking in-vertebrates; they are ungainly on the ground because of the long tail and small feet. They hawk some insects on the wing, or catch such small prey after slow flapping close to the ground, landing frequently for long periods. They perch and walk about less than do buzzards, but can hover briefly close to the ground when taking small prey. They are pirates, as are black kites, taking morsels of carrion or other prey particularly from corvids. When scavenging they must compete with foxes, farm dogs, ravens, buzzards, and other smaller predatory mammals and birds; of these foxes, buzzards and ravens can all open a carcase before a kite can. When kites, buzzards and corvids all meet at carrion the hierarchy is not specifically determined. In some cases the kite is dominant, in others the raven or buzzard; probably this depends on which was at the carcase first, or the degree of hunger. The bird first in possession has an advantage over others, but a very hungry bird may drive away one less hungry, as happens among gregarious vultures. Kites tolerate other kites at a carcase without quarrelling, but will not feed quietly with buzzard and raven. They tend to take repeated small feeds rather than gorge heavily at once, and may fly some distance straight to a known source of food.

There is no real evidence that competition with any other avian predator at present limits the kite's ability to survive and breed. When compared to its most likely competitor, the buzzard, it is more wide ranging and more inclined to take dead fish, scraps, and carrion. The two compete for the available supply of rabbits and small mammals, but the kite breeds 7–10 days earlier than the buzzard, which enables it to feed its young largely on young corvids and gulls when these are abundant, while the buzzard is more dependent on young rabbits and voles.

Breeding kites may hunt at any hour from 5 in the morning to 8 at night, with a peak from 9 a.m. to midday and another, less marked, from 3–5 in the afternoon. After the breeding season kites leave their roosts well after sunrise, and often return quite early in the evening. Their hunting day may vary from as much as 15 hours when feeding young in summer to 4–5 hours in the short winter days. Within their range they are often quite predictable, their punctual appearance in certain areas suggesting a regular hunting routine. In winter pairs of kites may still roost close together but hunt alone.

The kite is a versatile predator taking a large variety of prey. The food has been studied by pellet analysis, direct observation at nests, and watching kites to see what they kill – the latter relatively unrewarding. Pellet analysis shows that kites feed heavily on sheep carrion all the year round, the proportion taken in summer and winter being about the same, 50·4 and 49·1% of pellets respectively containing sheep carrion. Probably, in terms of weight consumed, carrion is even more important than this. Other mammals, mainly voles, become more important in autumn and winter, when they are most numerous, occurring in 68·6% of autumn and winter pellets compared to 51·4% in spring and summer. Birds occur in 56·3% of spring and summer pellets but in only 18·9% in winter, while invertebrates are taken in much the same proportions all the year round.

The complete list of prey includes 22 mammal species (including such unlikely scraps as a pig tail only taken as carrion), 36 birds, 3 reptiles or amphibians, 3 fish, and at least 19 different invertebrates.

The largest live prey ever killed by a Welsh kite is probably a medium-sized half-grown rabbit or hare leveret. They take many moles and the importance of rabbit in the diet was reflected by a drastic reduction in breeding success after the myxomatosis epidemic of 1955. The kites now seem to have adjusted to this, and rabbits are also commoner once again.

In Europe sheep carrion is only a minor item of diet but in Wales it is of major importance. There is no evidence that kites ever take any but dead sheep; indeed, it would probably be impossible for the weak-footed kite to kill a lamb. They eat the placentas at lambing time, pick up docked tails and scrotal sacs, and even collect the red rubber rings used for docking.

The remains of prey at nests show that corvids are important in the nesting season. Thirty-nine nests all contained corvids, magpies, jackdaws, and crows being the commonest species, in that order. Other common bird prey includes wood pigeons, black-headed gulls, and blackbirds. At winter roosts remains of other birds have been found (including a turkey head taken as Christmas carrion) and a pied wagtail. Young kites eat their dead nest-mates, perhaps after killing them, but perhaps more likely after natural death. In Wales hardly any gamebirds are aken but they are anyway uncommon in kite habitat. Continental data, however, including 1966 items (Appendix Table 1) shows that even where gamebirds are better distributed and common the kite takes very few(4). It never deserved, and should never have received, the persecution which so nearly rendered it extinct, while its habit of eating young corvids, rats, and gulls should actually make it a welcome ally of the gamekeeper. It will take young poultry if these are not properly penned or housed, and are wandering in the fields.

Certain kites appear to specialise in certain types of prey, not necessarily the most abundant available. In the breeding season some feed largely on black-headed gulls or young corvids, but of two adjacent pairs with almost equally easy access to a gull colony only one hunted the gulls. Specialisation in prey appears to continue outside the breeding season, when some individuals are more likely to eat in vertebrates than are others with equal opportunity.

In winter kites move to lower ground, foraging more in the lowland habitat, and they disperse over a greater total area than the total breeding area of about 650 square miles (1690 sq. km.). They establish winter roosts well away from the nesting sites, including roosts in areas where few if any kites breed. At this time they forage more at rubbish tips, slaughterhouses, etc., and conceivably (provided crows did not get all the food), some programme of deliberate winter feeding might benefit the population and help it to increase more rapidly.

At times, notably at winter roosts and in aerial gatherings kites are quite strongly gregarious, in this respect resembling black kites, which also roost communally outside the breeding season. Winter roosts may include six to twelve or more kites, old and young, with pairs that have been hunting alone by day rejoining one another at roosting time. In late winter on fine days aerial gatherings of ten or more are frequently seen; up to 22 have been counted in one such gathering. The kites then soar and circle together in a small area and are not really aggressive though they may dive at one another. The purpose of these gatherings is not clear, but they could perhaps be a form of communal display, and it might be worth while correlating breeding success in the following year with the number and frequency of such gatherings observed; they are also typical of black kites in the tropics. There is also a suspicion that kites which nest in close proximity to one another, almost in a colony, may breed more successfully than do isolated pairs. However, the evidence for this is as yet very slender.

The breeding season begins early. Some breeding pairs remain in their home ranges the year round, others apparently disperse over a wide area. Most pairs are located near their nest site in January but in any case they return to the breeding area by early March and will not thereafter leave it till they have failed or reared young. Mated pairs probably stay together for many years, and though the pair bond is probably loosened during winter dispersion it is probably never severed except by death. If one of a pair has died in the winter the other returns to the home range in spring and in due course attracts another mate, perhaps a young bird which may be unable to breed for a year or two.

Kites are extremely conservative in their choice of breeding site, the same area, even the same tree being used for long periods. This fact is well known to egg collectors, and although it would make study more difficult it is a pity that the kite does not shift its nesting site more often, as do certain other raptors when repeatedly persecuted in this way. In the breeding area 37 territories or home ranges have been occupied in the period 1951–71; of these 15 have been used for more than 10 years, four for over 19 years, and three for over 21 years, while two date back to 1900.

In much of the breeding area kites, even if so inclined, are still too scarce to have developed the regular spatial distribution pattern characteristic of many other British raptors. There are many apparently suitable breeding sites as yet untenanted. However, locally they attain high densities, with breeding pairs only half a mile to a mile apart, and in one small area (now discovered by egg collectors) three pairs nest, two within 400 yards (360 metres) of one another. It seems likely that, with their tolerant attitude towards neighbouring pairs, overlapping ranges, and tendency to be gregarious, the pattern of nesting distribution in a 'capacity' population of kites would be quite different from that of the buzzard or golden eagle, where regular spatial distribution over a wide area is the rule.

Display, in March and early April consists of soaring and circling over the breeding site, especially early on fine mornings. No more vigorous aerobatics, such as the whirling display with feet locked, are described. The pair normally weave about in the sky, or pursue one another, often calling; but kites are less vocal than are buzzards at such times.

The nest site is usually in an oakwood, and only a small area round it is defended against other kites or corvids. The large number of tree-nesting ravens in the kite breeding area are a constant cause of strife. Most of the nests are in oak trees, but other broad-leaved trees such as beech, birch, or alder are sometimes used and conifers, mainly larch, are also used occasionally. Breeding success in larch is poorer than in broad-leaved species. The replacement of oakwood nesting sites with conifer plantation could well be serious for the kites.

Nests are invariably in trees; this species is not known to breed on rocks anywhere except in the Cape Verde Is. They are usually built on the foundation of an old crow's, raven's or buzzard's nest, added to by the kite. The same nest may be used year after year, or a new one made. Human disturbance or late snowfall can cause kites to move suddenly from a nest which has been started to another site. Nest repair or building begins in mid March, and is brief, being completed by 7 April when most eggs are laid. No green branches are brought but a lining of wool is added before laying. The nest is distinguished from those of other raptors by being decorated with bits of cloth, paper, plastic bags, and other oddments; this is typical of kites generally. Pairs have one to six alternate nest sites, usually one to three; successful and less often unsuccessful nests are often used again the following year. A nesting site may be reoccupied after a gap of as much as 20 years. Some pairs occupy ranges but do not build a nest, at least in the first year of occupation, or nests may be built but not used. Generally such a nest is used successfully in the following or a later year. Both sexes build, the share of the sexes in Wales not being accurately determined, for fear of disturbance.

One to three eggs are laid at three-day intervals in early April while the trees are still completely bare. Of 76 clutches 62 (82%) were of 2 eggs, 10 of 3, and 4 of 1; the average is 2·04 eggs per pair, well below the average of European clutches where 3 or 4 is normal and 5 recorded. The female does most of the incubation by day and sits all night; she probably does 90–95% of the total incubation. The male brings prey to the nest area, and may relieve the female for short spells while she is feeding, or when he pays a visit without bringing prey. Each egg hatches in 31–32 days. Nearly all eggs hatch in a 17-day period 4–21 May, with a peak 7–14 May when 82% hatch. This peak probably reflects experienced breeders which lay earlier than do young birds.

The young hatch at intervals, as in many other raptors. Hatching may be spread over nine days. The young are not apparently aggressive to each other, though this aspect of breeding behaviour has not been fully observed. They grow rapidly, and are partly feathered by 21 days, and feathered, with the head still downy, at 28 days. For the first two to three weeks the female remains much on the nest and the male brings all prey at this time. After this the female assists the male in foraging for the young.

Precise fledging data are lacking because nests have not been watched much, to avoid disturbance. Probably the period varies according to the food supply available, and broods of one certainly fly earlier than broods of two or three. Broods of two may fledge almost together, or at an interval of seven days and, in extreme cases, the third of a brood of three leaves the nest three weeks after the first. The latest fledging record is on 2 August, indicating a fledging period of over 65 days in this case as compared to the normal 49–56 days. Surviving young sometimes eat their nest mates, though it seems unlikely that they kill them first, but merely eat them after natural death.

Breeding success in Welsh kites is apparently rather poorer than on the Continent of Europe (Appendix Table 2). There are frequent failures, totalling 147 out of 294 nestings in 21 years(4). Of 111 nests studied the cause was unknown in 77. When the cause was known, 12 were due to deliberate and four to casual human disturbance, 11 to infertile eggs, and the remainder to the death of an adult, the weather, or interference from other species. Most of the failures occur in May, suggesting that young broods are very vulnerable. Possibly casual human disturbance causes more losses than are known to be due to this cause, but this is not consonant with losses especially of small young.

Between 1951 and 1972 161 nests with eggs succeeded, producing 215 young. Allowing for non-breeding pairs this is equivalent to about 0·52 per pair overall, 0·67 per pair which bred, and 1·32 per successful nest. Success varies from year to year and from one part of the breeding area to another. In one river catchment breeding success fell off seriously after 1960, though prior to that it had been as good as elsewhere. At the same time two pairs in another catchment increased to ten between 1955 and 1971 and bred successfully. Accordingly, reasons for variations in success are hard to ascribe.

There is apparently no such long series of continental records with which to compare this, but it seems certain that the success of Welsh kites is lower than in lowland European deciduous forests. In Germany, in 15 cases productivity was 1·2/pair overall, 1·4 per pair which bred and 3·0 per successful nest; and in 27 French pairs 0·92, 1·1, and 2·5/successful nest (Appendix Table 2). Productivity in Welsh kites is apparently about half that of European continental kites. However a fully comparable series of European records is needed before we can condemn the Welsh kites as poor breeders.

Pre-myxomatosis productivity was about 0·88 young per pair which bred, but this fell to 0·54 after 1955. In more recent years it has again risen to 0·71–0·73, but this is still apparently lower than in Europe. Productivity is not, apparently, affected by the location of nests, or type of tree, except that in larch nests appear to fail often, perhaps because they are insecure. In recent years some pairs have done much better than the average, though the reasons are not known.

It seems likely that the habitat of the Welsh kites is marginal for the species as a whole, as in Europe it appears to do best in lowland deciduous woods with access to swampy ground and large river beds; it might do better in Kent or Sussex, if allowed to survive and not shot as soon as it appears. However, it seems clear that the present overall productivity could to some extent be increased by reduction in avoidable unnecessary nest losses, caused by careless or malevolent humans, and that if even this small increase could be achieved the kite's recovery could be accelerated.

After leaving the nest the young continue to be dependent on their parents, remaining near the nest for one to three weeks, sometimes longer. They do not disperse until late August or September. Some then remain in or near the home range through the winter, and are tolerated by the adults while others leave the breeding area altogether. Analysis of 180 records of occurrence elsewhere in Britain from 1920 to 1970 (Map 16) shows that kites occur in all but two English and a few Scottish counties. The records show that there is an autumn movement east and south of the breeding area, mainly E.S.E. to England east and south of Wales, and to Devon across the Bristol Channel. A sparse scatter of winter records indicates a concentration along the east coast from Norfolk to Kent; some of these may be European kites, but they are more likely to be Welsh. Irish, Isle of Man, and Scottish records are also in winter. A kite spent a month in upper Speyside in the winter of 1971–72(c). Spring records indicate a wide dispersal, and a return movement towards Wales; Hartland Point and Lundy records then indicate a return northward crossing of the Bristol Channel. It is now clear, however, that Welsh kites do regularly move east and south into England, where they may be destroyed by gamekeepers.

Three ringing records have positively confirmed this movement. Of 26 young ringed up to 1970 one was recovered near Woodstock, Oxfordshire, 110 miles E.N.E.; one near Marlborough, Wiltshire, 115 miles E.S.E.; and one at Wrotham, Kent, 195 miles E.S.E. Two of them were on railway lines, and one had apparently been attracted by a dead parrot; none had certainly been shot (Maps 17–18). The numbers seen in wintering areas outside Central Wales has increased along with the known total increase in productivity of Welsh kites, rising from about one record per year in the 1920s to two in the '40s and about nine in the '60s.

Although from these data anyone seeing a kite in winter in Britain might reasonably conclude that it is one of the small Welsh stock, some passage of continental kites is also suspected. For instance, between 19 March and 27 April 1969 kites were seen in Essex, Suffolk, Norfolk, Bucks, Leicester, Lincoln, Derby, Lancashire, Kinross, Angus, and even in Sutherland. Moreover, in 1972 a kite ringed as a nestling in Schleswig-Holstein, at the northern extremity of the European range, was recovered in Wales(a)! This astonishing record indicates that perhaps the Welsh kites are not so genetically isolated as had been thought; on the other hand it may have been a genuine straggler, perhaps more likely as otherwise there would surely have been some earlier indications that continental kites were colonising Wales.

Kites are known to be long-lived in the wild state. Analysis of available ringing records shows that mortality in winter is heavy, but that once adult a kite can live quite a long time. A 26-year-old German red kite now holds the record for the longest-lived ringed wild predator. Indeed, if kites were not long-lived the Welsh population could not have increased, even as slowly as it has. Assuming maturity in the third year of life, and the level of breeding success maintained over the last four years, about 0.7 young/pair/annum, each Welsh breeding kite must live between five and six years to be able to replace itself. Since they do actually increase, their average life span must be longer, perhaps six or seven years as adults, and nine or ten altogether.

Factors affecting the future productivity of the kite include human interference

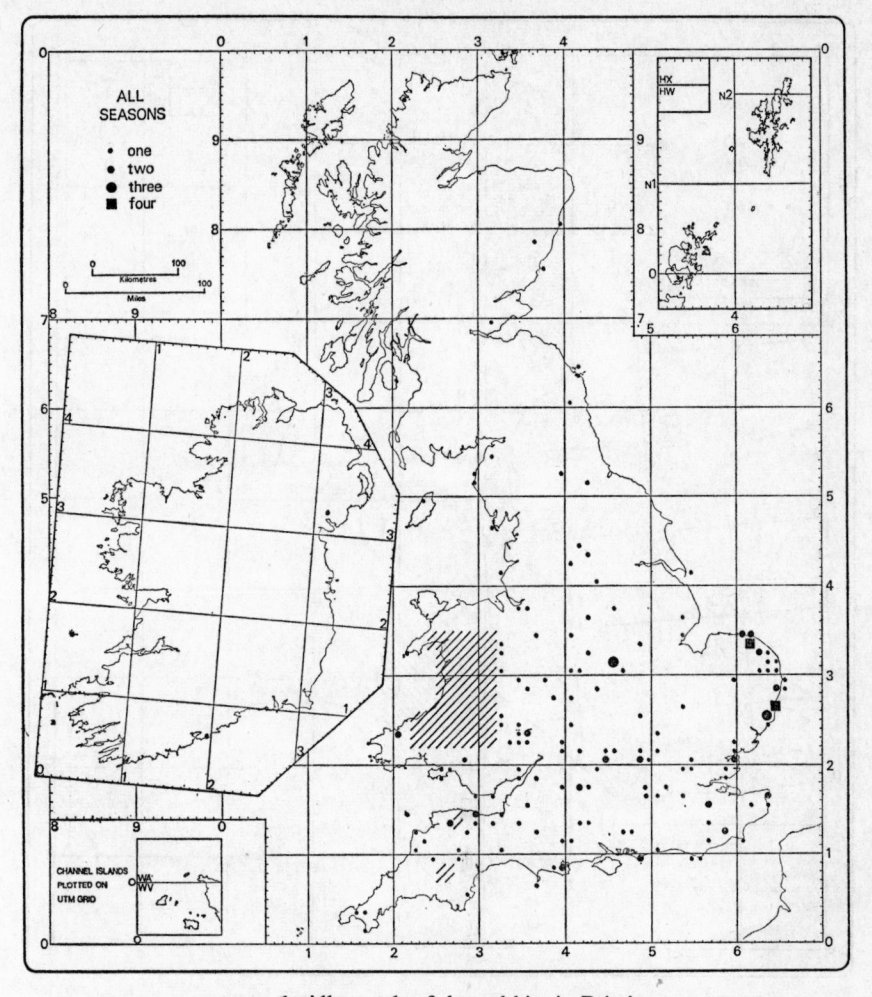

MAP 16. All records of the red kite in Britain.

and land use methods. Human interference is undoubtedly increasing due to the growth of the tourist industry in Central Wales. All deliberate human disturbance is due to egg collectors or bird watchers, especially at Easter, when kites are very vulnerable to disturbance. Probably many unexplained desertions are due to deliberate or unintentional human disturbance, but failures could also be due to corvids or other predators, though when eggs are sucked the offender can usually be identified. At least, an attempt should be made to reduce the level of human disturbance by more effective penalties for deliberate disturbance and, perhaps, enabling the interested ornithological public to watch a kite's nest from a hide, as has been so successful with ospreys. Keeping a continuous watch on certain nests which commonly fail might actually improve their chances of success.

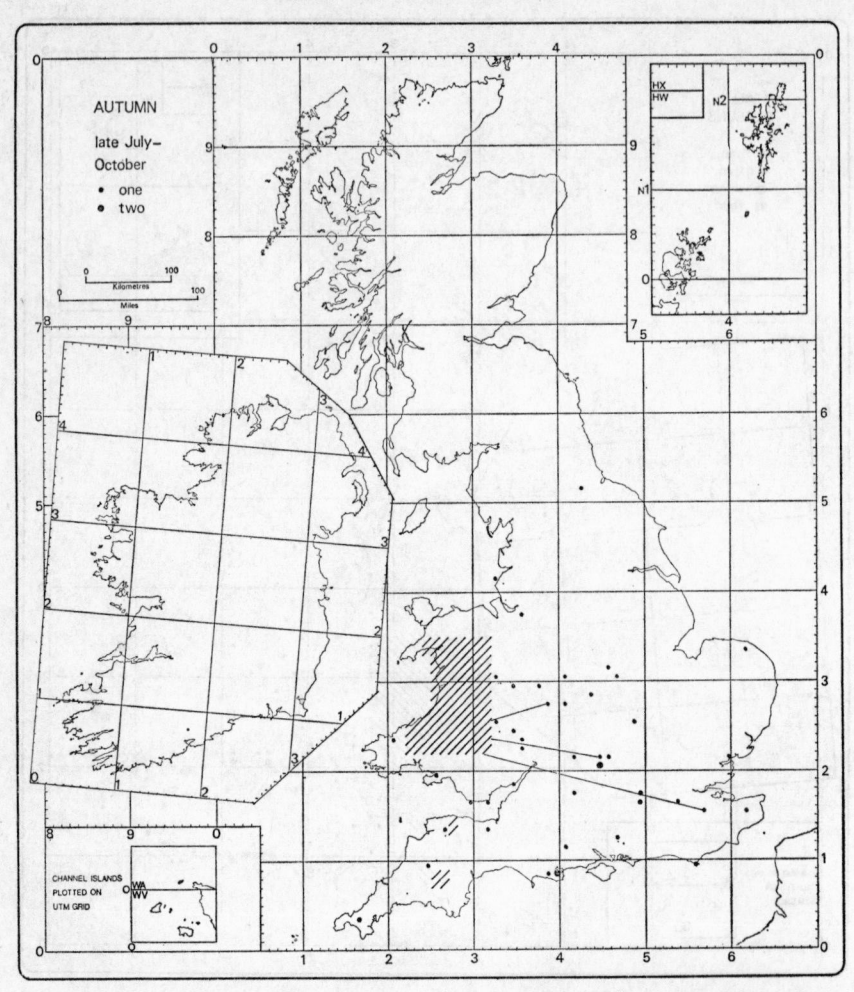

MAP 17. Autumn records of the red kite, with three British ringing recoveries.

Possibly changes in land use patterns are more important. Given freedom from disturbance kites will tolerate quite extensive change in land use patterns, but evidently would have difficulty in adjusting to changes which deprive them of necessary food supply. Among these are submergence of valleys under reservoirs, which has affected at least one pair; improved agricultural practices resulting in lowered sheep mortality and reduced availability of carrion; the use of toxic chemicals in the environment; and increased occupation of hill land with closely planted conifers. Of these forestry may improve the food supply for a few years, through a large increase in the vole population, but later reduces it because the kites are unable to hunt at all in dense conifer woods; they cannot at any time find carrion in forestry plantations since sheep are excluded. Accordingly extensive

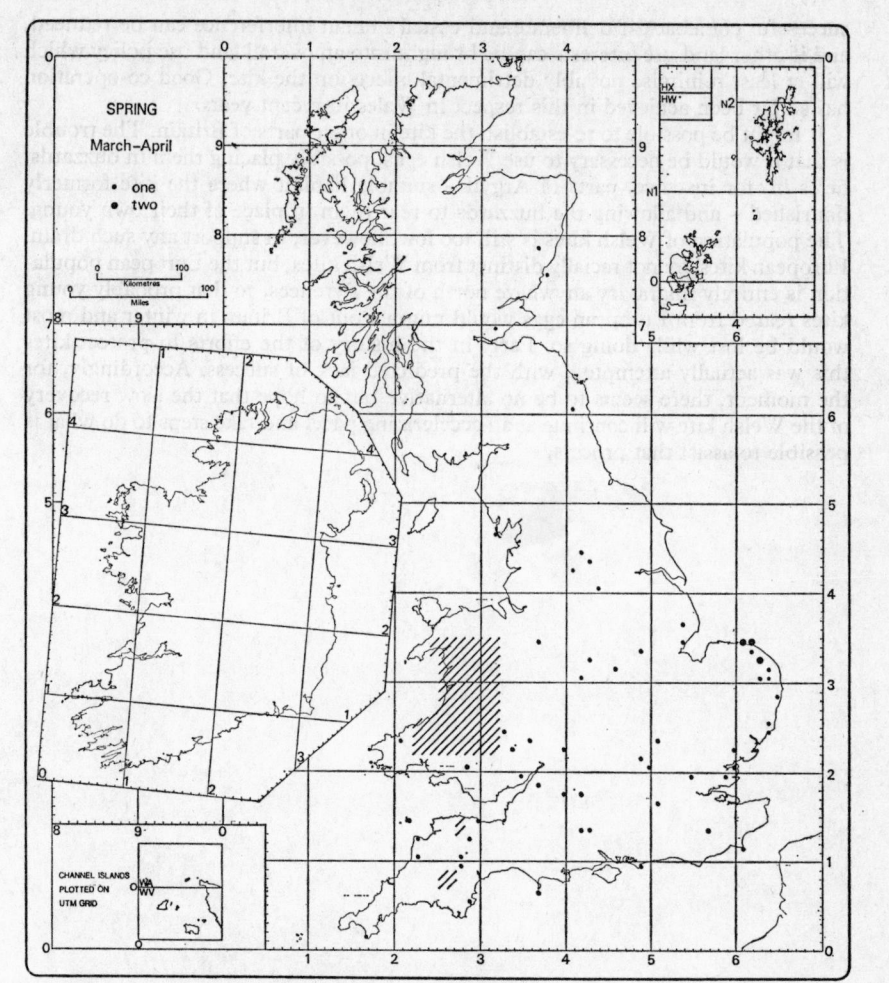

MAP 18. Spring records of the red kite, indicating more northerly distribution.

afforestation of uplands or replacement of nesting oakwoods with conifers is bound to harm the kite.

Toxic chemicals have had a serious but hopefully short term effect on productivity. There was an obvious reduction in breeding success from *c.* 0·8 to *c.* 0·5/pair in the period when dieldrin was in general use 1958–66 and an obvious connection between the ban on dieldrin post 1966 and the recovery to higher levels of breeding success, about 0·7/pair 1968–71. One dead kite examined had 15 parts per million in its liver, certainly a contributory cause of death; other specimens have not contained such high levels. The numbers examined are naturally small, but the evidence is suggestive.

It is clear, at any rate, that the Welsh kite will have a better chance of making a successful comeback if deliberate and casual human interference can be reduced, and if other land use interests can be brought into an overall land use policy which will at least minimise possibly detrimental effects on the kite. Good co-operation has so far been achieved in this respect in Wales in recent years.

It might be possible to re-establish the kite in other parts of Britain. The trouble is that it would be necessary to use Welsh eggs, possibly placing them in buzzards' nests in, for instance, parts of Argyll – suitable habitat where the kite formerly flourished – and allowing the buzzards to rear them in place of their own young. The population of Welsh kites is still too low, however, to support any such drain. European kites are not racially distinct from Welsh kites, but the European population is entirely migratory anywhere north of the Pyrenees, so that probably young kites reared from European eggs would migrate out of Britain in winter and most would be lost while doing so. Early in the history of the efforts to protect kites this was actually attempted, with the predicted lack of success. Accordingly, for the moment, there seems to be no alternative but to hope that the slow recovery of the Welsh kite will continue at an accelerating pace, and take steps to do what is possible to assist that process.

CHAPTER 7

THE SEA EAGLE

ALTHOUGH the sea eagle is now only a rare vagrant to Britain I shall discuss it as if it was a resident species because it once bred quite commonly here and because, if efforts to re-establish the species are successful, it may well breed here again. One unsuccessful attempt to re-establish sea eagles has already been made, but others are likely in future and may have a better chance of success. If so, then before this century is out there may again be sea eagles nesting along the Scottish highland coast, if not elsewhere.

In the past the sea eagle was said to be commoner than the golden eagle in the Highlands of Scotland, and it may well have been this species and not the golden eagle which formerly bred at Windermere(a). During the latter part of the nineteenth century after the Highland clearances it was ruthlessly exterminated in the interests of sheep farming. A pair lingered on in the Shetlands till 1908, and single birds thereafter till 1910, but the last pair said to have bred in Scotland was one which survived in Skye till 1916(2). Skye was always one of the main strongholds of the sea eagle, with eyries on almost every headland. However, it was probably quite a common species all along the West Coast and in the Hebrides, Orkneys and Shetlands.

Whether the sea eagle was actually more common than the golden eagle may now be only of academic importance, but since the fortunes of the two are likely to be closely interwoven in the event of any further attempts to re-introduce sea eagles it is perhaps worth thinking about this question. I doubt if the sea eagle really was commoner than the golden eagle. It seems to me much more likely that the sea eagle inhabited the coast and the golden eagle the much larger area of inland mountains. Near the coast sea eagles may have been locally more common than golden eagles but, taking the Highlands as a whole, I doubt if they were. This point cannot be settled at present, and it will be a great many years before any possible conflicts for living space, or interactions between sea and golden eagles can be worked out in the future, even if attempts at re-introduction succeed.

In Norway, where sea eagles are still relatively numerous, and where about three-quarters of the nest-sites known to be occupied in 1850 were still in use in 1950–60, the golden and sea eagles are ecologically separated(10). The sea eagle is common along the coast, breeding on the numerous small islands and skerries, with locally dense populations and pairs nesting 1–$1\frac{1}{2}$ miles ($1 \cdot 6$–$2 \cdot 4$ km.) apart, while the golden eagle lives inland. The feeding ground of sea eagles is mainly marine, and an archipelago of small islands in sheltered inland waters, with an abundance of both seafowl and fish seems to be the ideal habitat. The ranges of golden and sea eagles overlap at the edges, and here they could compete; if so, it appears that the smaller and lighter but probably swifter and fiercer golden eagle dominates any competition for nesting sites. However, as a rule the two do not overlap, and each dominates in its own preferred habitat.

Few golden eagle pairs are really dependent on marine habitat in Scotland today; they may breed on sea cliffs but most hunt inland. However, there are a few pairs that feed mainly on seabirds and which might be displaced if sea eagles again became established. Personally I can see no reason why the comparative ecology of sea and golden eagles should be any different in Scotland to that in Norway; and therefore I should always expect that if the sea eagle ever again becomes common here it will remain mostly coastal.

Sea eagles did breed in certain inland localities in Britain, for instance on Loch Ba in the Rannoch Moor(6) (which is not very far from the sea), and perhaps at Windermere. Some groups also breed inland in Sweden, Germany, Finland and elsewhere. However, the main habitat of sea eagles in Britain was more akin to coastal Norway than to the flat, forested and lake-studded inland regions of Germany or Finland which resemble the inland habitat of American bald eagles. If a population of sea eagles ever again became established in Scotland I would expect history to repeat itself. A few pairs of golden eagles might be displaced, but probably only a few, and as a species the golden eagle can survive in areas that would probably never be colonised by sea eagles at all.

We cannot now guess how many sea eagles may have existed in Britain in the past. However, eagles of the genus *Haliaeetus* generally seem to be able to live in comparatively small nesting ranges and are, in some species, almost sociable or semi-colonial. Where the habitat was suitable, therefore, I would expect the sea eagle to have been more abundant than the golden eagle, which demands a home range of 11–13,000 acres (4500–5300 ha.) per pair whether the food supply is abundant or not. If Scottish sea eagles behaved like the Norwegian birds they may only need 1500–2000 acres (600–800 ha.) per pair. I do not think that it is now possible to work out what the distribution of sea eagles in Skye might have been in 1800; but a coastal cliff named Stac na'h Iolaire is more likely to have been the rock of a sea eagle than of a golden eagle then, even if the golden eagle inhabits it now. Even so, the number of really suitable breeding cliffs in the Highlands and Islands is not very great; and I would be surprised if the maximum population of sea eagles was more than 200 pairs.

The sea eagle is considerably larger and probably more powerful than a golden eagle, and especially heavier(5). Individuals of either sex exceed the golden eagle in wingspan by only about 10–15%, but in weight by 35–40%. The golden eagle, however, is a swifter and more potent predator, while the sea eagle is more inclined, like other members of its genus, to be a pirate and a scavenger. It does not normally kill animals any larger than does the golden eagle, and is much more inclined to feed on dead fish, or carrion. However, it does kill many sea and water birds and can kill animals as large as a baby seal or a roe deer calf, while it also catches fish, usually near the surface, and its feet have sharp spicules on their inner surface to assist in grasping slippery prey. It also takes prey from ospreys by pursuing them and forcing them to drop their catch, a habit shared with most other members of the genus *Haliaeetus*.

It appears that if a sea eagle hunts a species of diving seabird such as an eider duck or a cormorant it probably can kill almost at will. The duck or cormorant dives when attacked, and is repeatedly harried whenever it surfaces, for the eagle can of course watch it under water and pursue it. In the end the luckless diver is too exhausted and out of breath to stay below, or even perhaps to fly when finally forced to surface, and it is caught. Sea eagles probably could not often catch such species if they flew at once when attacked instead of diving; but their instinct is to dive when threatened.

The sea eagles of Britain were exterminated because they were alleged to kill many lambs. To my mind the evidence that they ever were important pests of sheep farming is extremely slender, resembling the nebulous justification for killing golden eagles advanced by some Scottish shepherds today. No doubt the sea eagle did kill a few live lambs; but like the golden eagle, it could find abundant dead lambs in its home range in spring and accordingly would have no need to kill live ones. It therefore seems most unlikely that its extermination was justified, as in most other such cases. However, the sea eagle was reduced, like the osprey, to a few pairs by extermination campaigns. When these few pairs were all that survived they were inadequate to maintain the species, with only indifferent protection, and strong pressure on the surviving remnant from egg and skin collectors. For practical purposes the sea eagle disappeared from the Scottish scene at about the same time as the osprey, and for similar reasons.

The feeding ecology of the sea eagle in Norway has been thoroughly examined by Willgohs(10) and in Iceland by Ingolffson(9). Prey items listed by Willgohs included 576 fish of 29 species, the commonest being dogfish and lump suckers, with small numbers of economically important species such as cod or pollack, and only a few salmon and trout. In Alaska and Kamschatka the related American bald and Steller's sea eagles feed commonly on Pacific salmon kelts dying or dead after spawning and, although they technically eat salmon, these are of no interest at all to fishermen(3). 675 birds are listed, the commonest being eider ducks and auks, while the sea eagle is almost unique among European raptors in killing a considerable number of gulls (101 listed, mainly kittiwakes). This species thus might help to control the now over-abundant gull population of Britain. 167 mammals, varying from red deer calves to water voles include 80 remains of sheep and goats; but it is certain that most, and likely that all of these were taken as carrion, and in any case the number noted is a minute fraction of the total number of sheep and goats present in a vast tract of terrain. Apparently Norwegian farmers consider that the sea eagle is less injurious than the golden eagle to sheep, but advance very slender evidence against either, while whatever evidence is advanced is not borne out by careful factual investigation. In Scotland the sea eagle was said to do more harm to sheep rearing interests than did the golden eagle, no doubt because it was more inclined to scavenge dead lambs than the latter, which seldom picks up dead lambs even when they are abundant. Both Norwegian and Scottish farmers might learn from the people of Iceland, who apparently recognise that although the sea eagle does pick up dead lambs it so seldom kills a live one that it is not persecuted but protected and encouraged in Iceland(1). In Norwegian nests Willgohs himself found only ten pieces of only four separate sheep, all probably picked up dead and not killed by the eagle(10). Where other food such as seabirds abound sheep, dead or alive, are seldom taken by the eagle.

It would thus appear that, as usual, the extermination of the sea eagle in Britain was not justified by factual evidence, and that the expected outcry against its re-introduction could reasonably be resisted as baseless. Whether these considerations would influence vote-seeking politicians is another matter; the Norwegian Government, having protected eagles for some years, then again acceded without good evidence to renewed demands for their destruction but has now protected them again. We can observe in Europe the extraordinary, ridiculous, or pathetic paradox of frantic efforts, including artificial feeding, to maintain the dwindling population of Swedish and German sea eagles(7,8), while the Norwegian sea eagles are to some extent persecuted, and the Icelandic sea eagles are virtually – and rightly – left alone.

In all its continental haunts the sea eagle is a sedentary species; no young bird ringed in Norway was recovered more than about 60 miles from its place of ringing. The northern populations of the Lofoten Islands and other such places may move further than do those of southern Norway and the few vagrants that reach Britain must have travelled several hundred miles at least; but there is little hope that such vagrants will ever be numerous enough to establish themselves naturally in Britain. The osprey, which is very strongly migratory, was able to re-establish itself in Britain from a vigorous and increasing Scandinavian stock; but the same cannot be expected of the sea eagle which is dwindling steadily in Europe. If it is to be re-established in Britain, it will have to be by deliberate re-introduction, and soon, before it becomes so rare in Norway that it is rigorously protected.

When such a step is contemplated one must consider whether the effect upon other animals in the environment may be adverse, and whether it is in other respects a proper step to take. In the case of the sea eagle, and a few other species such as the goshawk, which were common here but were exterminated by man, there seems no good reason for not re-introducing the species, if the habitat is still ecologically suitable, and if the effects on other animals in it are not likely to be adverse. The habitat is still obviously viable for sea eagles; if they could exist in Skye in some numbers in the nineteenth century there is no reason why they should not today. Indeed, some of their possible seabird prey, such as gulls or fulmars, has increased very greatly since those days, and there should be plenty of sheep or deer carrion available in most areas. Sea eagles will undoubtedly feed upon certain seabirds such as puffins which may be subject to other severe pressures; but the effect of all the sea eagles in the world on populations of British seabirds is likely to be much less severe in aggregate, even over a year or two, than one large oil-tanker disaster such as that of the Torrey Canyon.

Sea eagles will be accused of killing lambs before they have seen one but, as suggested earlier, the justification of this view is at best slender. They might displace, by competition for nesting space and food supply, other relatively rare species such as the golden eagle, but the latter is well able to look after itself in competition with the sea eagle elsewhere, evolved alongside it, and will be able to survive with it in the foreseeable future. The re-introduction of the sea eagle is not therefore a question of whether to do it, but of how. It should and no doubt will be done; the only question is the best method.

The method attempted to date, of re-establishing mature young birds taken from Norwegian nests, has failed(4). It was only attempted on too small a scale, and on Fair Isle, an island perhaps not large enough to maintain a permanent population of sea eagles, though a pair was said to have nested there in the past. Fair Isle was chosen for several good reasons, amongst them its remoteness, and the fact that there was abundant food supply, while the resident warden could keep close control of the whole operation. It would have been desirable to choose a larger area, more similar to the coastal archipelagoes of Norway from whence the young birds came; but there is no such area in Britain where the attempt could be properly controlled from start to finish. Anywhere along the western Scottish coast the young sea eagles would be likely to wander out of the area of release and at once risk being shot or trapped.

Four young sea eagles were released on Fair Isle in early July 1968, two males and two females. They were first housed and fed in large cages on Erne's Hill, where the sea eagle last bred about 1840. No attempt was made to tame them, and they were flying well by the end of July. All were ringed before release, and were then up to average weight for wild males and females. The first, a female, was released on 16 September, the others on 2, 4 and 20 October. They at first fed on food placed near the cages, and later obtained some of their own prey elsewhere. One male, known as Johan, was not seen after 21 October and had either left the island or, more likely, died somewhere out of sight. The other three carried away prey put out for them but apparently could not kill their own. In this way all three survived into December, when they were flying strongly(4).

In January and February 1969 all three eagles were seen on 33/59 days. They were fed on rabbits or gulls and found some of their own food by eating carrion and feeding on dead animals on the beaches. They could fly well enough to perform the movements of nuptial display, including the spectacular whirling display with feet locked. They did not attempt to take live rabbits, but ate seabird carcases, some of them of oiled birds. One of the females became independent, finding her own food, about 6 March. The other two stayed together, perhaps forming a pair as has happened with wild golden eagles in immature plumage, and as happens in the closely related African fish eagle. The single female disappeared about 12 April; she had probably flown either to Orkney or Shetland. The other two remained; they began moulting in early April but, despite some possible handicap in flight from this they did not attack lambs during the lambing season, nor were they seen to carry away any dead lambs.

These two young birds were in the habit of soaring up to 2000 ft, whence they could evidently see Orkney or Shetland in good weather. The female disappeared in fine weather about 7 June, and had probably strayed to one of the adjacent island groups. An eagle seen briefly on 20 May may have been the other female, that had disappeared in March, returned; but this could not be confirmed. That left only one male on the island, and he was seen at intervals up to 18 August. On 19 August he was found in a cave, soaked with oil, probably the crop contents of nesting fulmars, regurgitated over the eagle when he tried to catch the fulmars for food. He was last seen on 28 August and probably died(4).

Thus none of the young eagles remained alive on Fair Isle 14 months after they arrived, and none was ever reported from anywhere in Orkney or Shetland. Probably, two at least, and possibly three of these young flew to these other island groups and should have been seen; probably they died but they may have been quietly destroyed. The fourth and last almost certainly died on Fair Isle, incapacitated by the effects of oil regurgitated by fulmars he was trying to kill for food.

Fair Isle was probably not the best place for such an attempt. The nature reserve on Rhum, much larger, equally controllable, and in an area where the sea eagle formerly thrived would undoubtedly have been a better place to try the experiment. Also, the release of mature young birds may not have been the best way of re-establishing the sea eagle, nor were only four enough to be able to establish the species without an incredibly high level of survival to maturity unlikely to be achieved in natural conditions. Normally, only one in four could expect to survive to sexual maturity. Evidently any further attempts should be made on a larger scale, and should be sustained over a period of perhaps ten years before being finally abandoned as failures.

My own view is that the sea eagle may best be re-established by placing sea eagles' eggs in golden eagles' nests and allowing these to hatch and rear the young. It would then only be necessary to transport the eggs from Norway to their foster parents' nests in Scotland. The displaced golden eagles' eggs could possibly be given to falconers to hatch in incubators and rear the young if they could (and eagles can be hand-reared). The young sea eagles would probably be readily accepted by the adult golden eagles, and would be fed by them on a diet only a little different to that which they would receive from adult Norwegian sea eagles; in the fledging period this consists more of seabirds than of fish. The process would probably make little or no difference to the sea eagle population of Norway, for the eggs could be taken from eyries likely to be persecuted anyhow, or in which one young would probably be killed by its nest mate or mates. It would presumably cost very much less in man-hours or work to do the experiment this way than to bring over young birds and hand-rear them for later release, and the saving in cost and time that could thus result might mean that the experiment could be continued for many years, if successful, until about a hundred young sea eagles had eventually taken wing in Scotland. That should result in a fair population of young sea eagles able to breed several years after they left the nest.

Many obstacles and difficulties can, of course, be foreseen. Much the worst would be the hostility shown to eagles in low-lying coastal crofting areas, which would probably result in illegal destruction of the young sea eagles after they left the nest, or even earlier, unless it can be brought under control. This hostility, based very largely on ignorance, at present has quite a serious effect on the population of golden eagles in these low-lying easily accessible coastal sites. This is the main reason why it is best to carry out such trials in areas which can be properly protected, even if they are not otherwise ideal. Then, again, the golden eagles might not take kindly to the young sea eagles or might feed them the wrong sort of food. Experiments now being made with young goshawks being reared in sparrowhawks' nests, and the successful rearing of young spotted eagles in Germany by black kites suggest that the first of these difficulties may not be serious. In the second case, golden eagles living along the sea coast do actually kill quite a few seabirds, and their diet is not too dissimilar to that of sea eagles in Norway or Iceland; so I would expect this difficulty not to be serious either.

It has also been suggested that young sea eagles reared by golden eagles would later try to mate with these, and not with their own kind so forming sterile pairs. I think that this too is improbable, because the innate forms of display, voice, and other behaviour patterns of sea eagles are sufficiently different to those of golden eagles to separate the species, even if the very distinct adult plumage did not. Only time can tell; but to my mind no other difficulty is as daunting as that of ensuring that the young sea eagles are not shot or trapped once they leave areas where they can be watched and protected.

For such an experiment to be successful, with a very large species such as the sea eagle which has a low reproductive rate, it would be necessary to obtain considerable numbers of eggs or young and introduce them over a long period, perhaps continuing for ten years. The sea eagle apparently rears larger average broods than the golden eagle, and the young are less inclined to kill each other in the nest. The number of young in Norwegian nests averaged 1·6(10), and in Iceland brood size is about 1·4 young per successful nest(9). Re-introduction by putting eggs into golden eagles' nests would inevitably result in some failures through eggs failing to hatch or being lost through some mishap, while mortality among the nestlings after hatching could also be expected. It seems likely that for every 100 eggs introduced 70–80 young might fly, and of these perhaps 20 at best might survive to maturity. If 20 eggs were brought over every year for ten years this could result in about 20 pairs of mature sea eagles 15 or 16 years after the experiment commenced. I am convinced that only by making the attempt on this sort of scale, and for this sort of time is it likely to succeed.

It might, of course, be possible to bring 50 eggs for four years and obtain a quicker result with a more concentrated population of more even age. This would, however, involve the sterilisation of about 50 pairs of golden eagles annually for the period of the experiment; and this is rather a large fraction of the total golden eagle population. I would therefore prefer to see a smaller number of golden eagles' nests used over a longer period to obtain the same total. It may also be possible, by supplementary feeding or other means, to induce golden eagles to rear two or even three young sea eagles per nest. Experiments with captive eagles and even with wild golden eagles suggest that they will readily adopt a young eagle and feed it with food given to them if they cannot catch enough. Certainly it would be desirable to speed up the experiment in this sort of way if possible; but it would inevitably mean more supervision and effort, either by permanent wardens or by volunteers. In the end, several methods may be used as experience dictates. However, this does not alter the need for a target figure of at least 200 eggs or young introduced over five to ten years to establish a viable mature population; and I would prefer to see the figure still larger.

If this project matures and the sea eagle is again established in Scotland it will no doubt breed mainly along the coast, only spreading to inland sites when all the suitable coastal eyrie sites are occupied. The last surviving sea eagle sites in Scotland were all on high cliffs, but a few known sites were on trees on islands in lochs. If undisturbed, the sea eagle will breed in Norway on very small cliffs or even on a gently sloping rock face or grassy bank(10). All the inland European nests in Germany and Sweden are in trees; normally pines(5). In Iceland some nest sites are on rocky columns projecting from steep volcanic valley slopes and the eagles cannot make a large nest for lack of suitable material(1). In Scotland, no doubt the nests would become huge, as they are in Norway and elsewhere in Europe where tree branches or heather is available.

In early spring Norwegian or Icelandic sea eagles soar over their nest site in display, often not very high up. The male dives at the female who turns over and presents her claws to his, sometimes grasping them firmly so that the two partners come whirling earthwards in a spectacular series of cartwheels(5). Members of this genus perform this whirling display more often than do any other eagles. They separate when only a few feet above the ground or water and soar up again, perhaps to repeat the performance. From all accounts the nuptial display of the sea eagle is less spectacular than that of the golden eagle, no doubt because the eagles themselves are more ponderous and stately fliers less inclined to aerobatics.

Both sexes may spend much time soaring or perched near the nest site without doing any building, but building or nest repair can be expected from very early spring onwards, reaching a peak in March. Both sexes build, collecting branches from near the nest and adding softer material such as rushes or dead grass as egg-laying approaches. Like other eagles most pairs have several nests, 1–11, averaging 2·4 in Norway and may build up more than one before egg laying. Coition usually occurs on the ground near the nest; when one or other of the pair lies down on its breast coition is likely to follow. It may rarely occur up to two miles from the nest site, usually nearer(10).

One to four eggs are laid at intervals of three days; the average of 65 Norwegian clutches is 2·18 and of 14 Icelandic 2·1(10,9). The sea eagle thus lays a somewhat larger clutch than a golden eagle, and in clutches of three the first and last egg would be separated by seven days. Both sexes incubate, the male taking a large share, 25–30% of the total time by day. Nest reliefs are frequent up to ten times daily, and when the male relieves the female he sometimes brings prey; however the female has not been seen to bring prey to the nest, though she is sometimes off long enough to hunt. The female sits all night so that in fact she does more than four-fifths of all incubation(10).

The eggs hatch in 38 days according to Willgohs; some other estimates are longer, up to 45 days(5), and 38 is certainly remarkably short for so large a bird. As incubation begins with the first egg there is a marked size difference between the young when the second or third eaglets hatch. Young sea eagles are perhaps less aggressive to one another than are young golden eagles, so that the weaker second young one has a better chance of being reared than in the golden eagle. The average of young per successful nest in Norway is 1·6 and in Iceland rather lower, 1·4, but still better than the golden eagles' 1·2–1·4. Three young are sometimes reared. Most observers of this species have not given details of non-breeding pairs or failures in any area. Including failures and non-breeding pairs the average productivity per pair is apparently about 0·65 young in Iceland, roughly the same as in the golden eagle in most of Scotland; but this may be too low a figure for more favourable Norwegian habitats(10).

The behaviour of the adults resembles that of other large raptors, but the male takes a larger share throughout than in many species. He both broods and feeds the young, but still brings most of the prey in the early part of the fledging period. A male has been seen to feed young almost as often in a day as the female (five times to her six)(10). Males have been known to catch prey at very short intervals, of ten minutes or less, indicating that at times they can kill almost at will, perhaps by concentrating on diving birds which can hardly escape.

In the early fledging period the female remains near the nest most of the time. Females observed by Willgohs spent more than five times as long on the nest by day as the males, although these did play a considerable part in brooding and feeding. The female normally feeds on pieces of prey brought by the male at this stage. After 35 days the female spends little time actually on the nest, and a little later both sexes leave the young alone and hunt for the entire brood. A female can probably kill and carry weightier items than can the male, but is perhaps less agile.

The fledging period lasts 70–90 days, and the one to three young make their first flight independent of parental coaxing. Since egg laying occurs normally in late March to early April in Norway, later further north, the young normally hatch in May and leave the nest in July or early August. In Britain the breeding dates could be expected to be rather earlier, laying in the first half of March and leaving the nest early in July, much like the golden eagle. The young remain near the nest, still dependent on the parents, for up to two months after making their first flight, and would normally become independent in October, perhaps even later.

The adults in most of Europe remain in or close to their breeding areas but the young disperse and wander in autumn(5). In Iceland adults also disperse. Sea eagles tend to be more sociable than most other large birds of prey, and may roost or feed in groups of five or six if food is abundant in a certain locality. Mortality in the first autumn is probably high and probably at least three-quarters of the young sea eagles hatched die before they are sexually mature at four or possibly five years old. If overall productivity is about 0·65 young per pair per annum and mortality 75 % before sexual maturity then an adult Icelandic sea eagle must live on average at least six years as an adult and probably ten or eleven years altogether if the population is to be maintained. Potentially, sea eagles can live for at least 40 years, and have lived for 45 years in captivity.

Such a high rate of mortality among young carefully re-introduced into Scotland would undoubtedly be depressing but would probably be inevitable, and a necessary hazard to be faced and planned for in any re-introduction programme. In the absence of a population of adults it is likely that the young would not have to disperse so far from the places where they were reared or released, and the mortality rate might be lower. However, it would be unwise to plan on any more than 40 or at best 50 young surviving to breed from 200 young reared to fledging; and that would necessitate placing 250–280 sea eagle eggs in suitable golden eagles' nests. Plainly, even if a determined effort to re-introduce the species is made, and destruction of the young reared can be contained or prevented, it will be many years before the sea eagle could be as common as it was said to be in Britain only about 150 years ago.

CHAPTER 8

THE MARSH HARRIER

THE marsh harrier may now be Britain's rarest regularly breeding diurnal raptor. It now breeds certainly only at Minsmere reserve in East Anglia, having abandoned several other formerly regular British haunts within the last decade(2). There has been an overall decrease since 1958, and still more recently there has been a further local decrease in Dorset; one formerly regular haunt has apparently been abandoned by the pairs that bred there. The explanation of this decrease is not perhaps as simple as it would appear at first glance, when disturbance of breeding haunts by excessive numbers of noisy, pleasure-seeking human beings leaps to mind as the most obvious reason. Marsh harriers are undoubtedly sensitive to disturbance in Britain, but have also ceased breeding in some apparently little disturbed localities.

Before 1700 the marsh harrier was very common in much of East Anglia, especially in the fens. It was also common, later than that, in Irish bogs and reedbeds, but it never appears to have been very common in Scotland where really suitable reedbed habitat is generally lacking. The reedbeds in which marsh harriers prefer to breed are essentially a feature of the warmer parts of Britain and of flat swampy terrain, lacking in Scotland. Undoubtedly, therefore, the main cause of the marsh harrier's decline has been the destruction of suitable habitat by fen drainage. This began on a big scale in the seventeenth century and continues up to the present day, when odd pieces of suitable reedbed are being reclaimed here and there for agriculture, or filled in for building. *Per contra*, the only present regular breeding haunt is an artificial one, and there are considerable new areas of wetland in Britain. It is probably at least as likely that those breeding haunts of the harrier lost within the last decade have been lost through other causes as through direct drainage or destruction.

Fen drainage largely preceded the great era of predator destruction, and a reduced stock of marsh harriers resulting from habitat destruction was then subject to intense persecution by gamekeepers. Once it had become relatively rare, egg collectors and skin collectors also played their part, as with other British raptors. The result was that the marsh harrier, abundant in East Anglia in 1800 had by 1850 been reduced to a beleaguered remnant and was extinct altogether in England by 1900. A few pairs lingered on in Ireland until 1917, but the marsh harrier was lost as a breeding species to England for a period at the end of the nineteenth and early twentieth centuries(13).

Marsh harriers attempted to recolonise Norfolk about 1908, but these early attempts failed. In 1915 a pair succeeded in rearing young at Hickling, but did not return (apparently rather common behaviour in British marsh harriers). The next recorded successful breeding was in 1921, and after 1927 there were up to four pairs, usually two or three. In 1939 they began to settle in Suffolk coastal marshes and probably bred there successfully before this was actually proved; there was a further increase during the Second World War, as in many other raptors. Minsmere Reserve, at present the only regular breeding haunt, was deliberately flooded as defence against enemy action; but the marsh harriers did not breed there till 1955.

By 1951 a few pairs bred regularly in Dorset, and by 1958 a maximum of 15 pairs were breeding, 4–6 in Norfolk, 8 in Suffolk, and about 5 pairs in other counties(13). Marsh harriers were then probably more numerous than at any time for a century or more, but even then bred regularly only in Norfolk, Suffolk, and Dorset, with sporadic breeding elsewhere. Once extinct in Ireland it did not become re-established there though there is probably at least as much suitable habitat in Ireland as in Great Britain, while the relatively thin human population should favour recolonisation. Perhaps any that try are still shot in Ireland.

Since its peak in 1958 the species has again declined to a maximum of five or six pairs, some of which do not breed, with only one certain breeding haunt. Such former regular haunts as Hickling and Horsey Mere, where the birds were carefully protected, have been abandoned. Horsey was last used in 1965, again by a pair which did not return. It is tempting to ascribe this decline, which coincides in time with that of many other British raptors, wholly or mainly to the increased use of agricultural pesticides; the few harriers that have been analysed have had high residue levels(12). However the continued occupation of one locality by a fairly successful and regular colony argues against pesticides as the sole reason.

Extensive destruction of formerly luxuriant reedbeds by coypus is also suggested as a cause(2,a). Coypus are large South American rodents which have escaped from fur farms (they are the source of the fur 'Nutria' which probably no one would buy if it was simply called 'coypu' just as people will buy 'lapin' but not 'rabbit') to become feral. In the absence of any of their natural predators they quickly increased in any suitable marshland habitat, and are only kept within bounds by control measures and by frosts, which, being of tropical origin, they cannot endure. The hard winter of 1963 greatly reduced them but the coypu is an adaptable animal and will probably remain a permanent part of the British fauna. Marsh harriers will have to learn to live with it if they are to survive as a breeding species, and in some European areas they can and do. Accordingly, perhaps, the coypu is less of a menace to marsh harriers than has been supposed.

Antagonism between bitterns and harriers is also suggested as a cause of decline(2). Bitterns have increased a lot in recent years, and they certainly are aggressive towards harriers, and vice versa. However, although losses in certain years can be attributed to bitterns, it is difficult to believe that the natural increase of a species which always has shared the same marshes could have had a decisive long term effect on the harriers.

The most likely cause of recent decline seems to be the increased mobility of the British public, the demand for aquatic recreation areas, and the consequent invasion of formerly quiet localities by speedboats, water skiers, fishermen, yachtsmen, and so on. Birdwatchers and photographers can be a serious menace, since they seek to reach nests. Personally, and although it seems the more likely reason at present, I do not find this explanation wholly satisfactory. Elsewhere in its extremely wide range the marsh harrier is able to live quite happily alongside dense populations of human beings. African marsh harriers (which are regarded as a different species but have very similar habits) do not seem to breed less successfully at Lake Naivasha in Kenya because of the recent invasion of pleasure boats and fishermen. Moreover, in at least one of the former breeding haunts, the marsh is more extensive and the disturbance probably no more than if not less than at Minsmere. However, in this area the nests were regularly examined while at Minsmere no one is allowed to approach them.

The marsh harrier is decreasing in some of its European haunts as well, and in some of these areas the decrease is almost certainly not due to increased use of water and marshlands for recreation. It is said that the marsh harrier requires large areas of undisturbed reedbeds to be able to breed in Britain, but elsewhere this is not the case and it will breed quite happily in small reedbeds, for instance in the Camargue or Morocco. However, in such areas one must admit that it has probably never been subjected to the intense persecution that characterised Britain up to the outbreak of the Second World War. British marsh harriers may be the nervous survivors of the era of persecution, more readily disturbed than in, for instance, southern France.

It would be tempting too to say that, like the Montagu's harrier, the marsh harrier is on the northern boundary of its ecological range and can hardly increase for that reason. Against that one must argue that it was formerly much more widespread and abundant, and is therefore more analogous to the osprey, kite and sea eagle than to Montagu's harrier or the honey buzzard. A bird which was formerly abundant in Norfolk and Suffolk ought to be able to re-establish itself again, given the protection it could nowadays expect in most suitable habitats. But it does not; indeed it continues to decrease.

Some records indicate that British marsh harriers breed less successfully than do those on the Continent of Europe, but this whole issue is obscured by the fact that it is often only the successful nests which are followed to completion while the fate of pairs which tried to breed and failed may be ignored. The average number of young fledged from all known nests at Minsmere in 15 years was 2·3, with 2·7 from 39 successful nests. The average brood from 18 successful nests at Horsey was 3·7; and from all recent British successful nests it has been 3·0. These figures may be compared with 2·2 for all nests in Sweden in 1956–59(3) and 3·2 per successful nest. More recent figures from Sweden give an average of 2·3 young in 67 successful nests(1). Broods per successful nest in Holland have averaged 3·3(8), in Germany 3·5(7), and in Lorraine, France 3·7(14); but in Finland only 2·35(9) and in the Camargue, France, only 1·9(d). Taking every pair into account Thiollay found in Lorraine that while successful nests reared on average 3·7 young the number per pair overall was only 1·57(14). In the Camargue, which anyone would regard as ideal marsh harrier habitat with a capacity population including a very large proportion (70%) of non-breeding subadults and immatures, breeding success is apparently lower still(14,d). Here the mean clutch size is no different, 4·6 eggs; but the number of young reared per successful nest is about 1·54 and the number per pair overall is only 0·7–0·8(d).

Thus, although breeding success at Minsmere is apparently lower than in some European localities at about the same latitude in others, including some which would be regarded as better habitat for marsh harriers, breeding success is actually a good deal lower than at Minsmere. Moreover, the breeding success of marsh harriers at Minsmere, 2·7 young per successful nest, is higher than the 2·4 young per successful nest recorded for Orkney hen harriers, which are increasing. Poor breeding success cannot therefore, in my opinion, be advanced as the reason for the decline of British marsh harriers. The fate of the young after they leave the nest must be more important.

One is left with the conclusion that there is no single very satisfactory reason for the recent decline, though it is probably not due to fundamental ecological reasons. No less than 111 young marsh harriers have been reared at Minsmere since 1955 and perhaps 150 in all Britain. One might suppose this adequate to result in some spread to other areas. However, it is fair to say that less disturbance in breeding haunts, the decreased use of agricultural pesticides, and effective penalties for any sporadic persecution by gamekeepers and egg collectors (which probably still occurs), would all help the marsh harrier to recover its pre-1958 position as a regular breeding bird in small numbers in extensive reedbeds. Sadly, it can never again become a really numerous breeding species in Britain because of the extensive destruction for agriculture of its main habitat, reedbeds.

Marsh harriers live in reedbeds, breeding and roosting therein, but forage widely outside this habitat and catch much of their prey in shorter vegetation, even in open country. The manner in which a marsh harrier hunts is similar to that of other harriers, that is, it systematically quarters, flapping and gliding over the habitat, travelling generally at slow speed against or across the wind, and drops into the reeds when it locates suitable prey. Before dropping it will often flap or hover for up to a minute or more, and make several false attempts before finally succeeding. If a good source of food, such as a brood of young birds, is discovered, the hunting marsh harrier will return again and again to the same spot. Although the marsh harrier is a much larger and more powerful bird than either of the other two British species, a female being almost as large and powerful as a buzzard, it actually does not take very much larger prey than the smaller harriers. It feeds principally on species that live near water, but also on, for instance young rabbits from warrens on dry ground near reedbeds(4). In Europe it apparently does not take even small coypus because the time of activity of these rodents is different to that of the harrier(c); but at Minsmere small coypus are active by day and are sometimes taken. However, marsh harriers could never effectively control coypus, whose natural South American predators are very much larger.

In their breeding haunts marsh harriers may hunt for long hours or shorter periods, depending largely on the stage of the breeding cycle. A male with two mates and broods to feed may have to hunt from early morning to evening, but when feeding incubating females alone the same bird spends long hours perched on bushes or on masses of floating vegetation, interspersing these with bouts of hunting in which he may catch several prey in a matter of minutes. One Hickling male visited the nest with prey three times in seven minutes. They may perch on trees or fence posts, and, when something is caught, either eat it where it is if the place is suitable or, more often carry it to a feeding place and eat it there.

The daily food requirement of a pair of marsh harriers is not exactly known, but based upon the known facts in hen harriers is probably about 12–15% of body-weight(6). A male would need about 60 grams and a female about 90 grams. Since marsh harriers lay large clutches and as a rule rear large broods (for a bird of prey) the food requirement of the brood in the nest is correspondingly large, and any food shortage is likely to reduce brood survival. This is, however, unlikely to be the cause of poor brood survival in Britain, since in the areas where marsh harriers breed there are plenty of young waterfowl on which to feed. In Holland the marsh harrier has been deliberately reduced in some areas because of the number of young wildfowl and waterfowl which it takes, in some cases in sanctuaries for other rare species.

Actual details of the food taken by British marsh harriers are scanty, because for reasons of protection the birds are usually left strictly alone at the nest. From a distance the usually small prey held in the foot cannot often be certainly identified. In one nest studied in Anglesey, where the birds bred for one year only, young moorhens were common in the early fledging period, brought by the male(5). In the later part of the fledging period, when the female was also hunting, larger items were brought, such as young rabbits and, it must be admitted, young pheasants. At a nest at Hickling in 1942 Hosking recorded 71 birds and 35 mammals, which included 29 young pheasants, 29 young partridges, and 22 young rabbits and hares(10). At Minsmere the harriers have been seen carrying small rodents, rabbits, and very small coypus; adult water rails and young duck, moorhens, coots, lapwings, and snipe are all taken(2). At nesting sites starlings, yellowhammers, and young partridges have been found.

Probably, in Britain, the main prey is small mammals and young water birds, with some young game-birds included amongst a variety of other birds taken. All harriers tend to live more on birds than has often been supposed, and the marsh harrier is no exception. It must be admitted that marsh harriers do take a number of young pheasants and partridges besides many young wild duck, but are not known to kill adult game-birds and, in view of their very small numbers, can do very little real harm to game preserving interests. The late Major Anthony Buxton, who zealously protected the marsh harriers at Horsey, was as keen a shooting man as any, but bore the harriers no grudge. Many of the young pheasants taken would not be hand reared but wild-reared in marshes and reedbeds, which are actually the natural haunt of the pheasant in its country of origin.

Better data are available for the marsh harrier in Europe. Here too it feeds mainly on small mammals and birds, but also takes many frogs and occasional snakes and lizards. Water snakes are taken less often than one might suppose from their numbers in some continental marshes. All European published records (Appendix Table I) indicate that very few game-birds are taken.

At Minsmere the 400-acre marshland section of the reserve includes some 20 meres totalling about 100 acres, the rest being reedbeds. The breeding habitat is extended by 50 acres of reedbeds outside the reserve, while much of the surrounding country is grass meadow subject to flooding, heathland, or cereal fields, all potentially good hunting terrain. The total range hunted by the two to three pairs that breed, and which are considered the maximum this marsh can support, is about 4000 acres (1620 ha.). The adults of adjacent pairs hunt over the breeding areas of other pairs without exciting animosity, except immediately round the nest. At Horsey and Hickling, where formerly at least two pairs bred regularly, there are 4000 acres of reedbeds and 2–300 of open water, with extensive marshlands and rough pastures in the neighbourhood.

These figures may be compared with the Camargue, where breeding marsh harriers hunt over total ranges of 270–420 ha. (670–1040 acres), of which only a part is actual reedbeds. The same range in the Camargue supports at least two non-breeding birds for every breeding marsh harrier, and the effective used area per harrier is only about 15 ha. (37 acres)(15). It would appear, therefore, that there must be other reedbeds and marshy areas in Britain of adequate size, and sufficiently quiet, to support one or two pairs of marsh harriers and it is all the more difficult to understand why the species does not colonise or re-colonise such areas.

A possible reason may be that all harriers, the marsh not excepted, tend to be somewhat gregarious, preferring to breed in small loose colonies rather than singly, and perhaps not persisting, even if they are successful, as single breeders. The pair mentioned in Anglesey bred only for one year, 1945, the first known breeding since the mid-nineteenth century(5). Four young hatched, and three flew, but only one was reared, and the adults did not breed again in this otherwise suitable locality where they were welcomed and protected. A recent suspected breeding attempt in Scotland was not repeated(b). Such instances may help to explain why

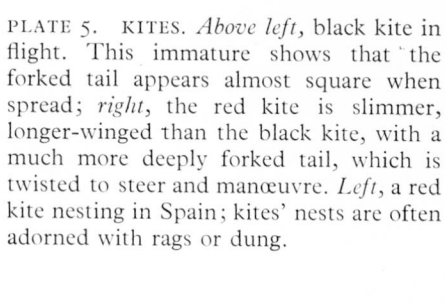

PLATE 5. KITES. *Above left,* black kite in flight. This immature shows that the forked tail appears almost square when spread; *right,* the red kite is slimmer, longer-winged than the black kite, with a much more deeply forked tail, which is twisted to steer and manœuvre. *Left,* a red kite nesting in Spain; kites' nests are often adorned with rags or dung.

PLATE 6. HARRIERS. *Above left*, the male Montagu's harrier in flight is at once distinguished by the narrow black bar on the upper wing and chestnut flecks below the wing; *right*, the creamy-headed female marsh harrier is the largest British harrier. *Right*, a female hen harrier perched on a post; the long legs and facial ruff are characteristic of harriers.

breeding away from East Anglia is still only sporadic, but do not explain why the marsh harrier does not extend its breeding haunts in E. Anglia where there are certainly other suitable breeding localities besides Minsmere.

Marsh harriers can probably breed in their second year, and certainly in their third year(4,16). Breeding by birds still showing traces of the immature plumage has been recorded, and seems to be quite typical of this and other harriers generally. In some European localities the males arrive at the breeding grounds well before the females, but at Minsmere and other British breeding areas the adults remain all winter and do not migrate, though the young do often leave in winter.

In nuptial display, which is very spectacular, males mount to several hundred feet above the marsh, a greater height than they attain at any other time except when on migration. From several hundred feet they tumble earthwards in spectacular dives, during which they twist violently from side to side, or spin through 360 degrees. These erratic movements display the contrasting grey and brown of their wings to advantage and the whole process is not only visible but the rushing sound made is audible for some distance. At the completion of the dive the male throws up, and mounts again steeply, to repeat the performance, sometimes after further aerobatics which may include looping the loop at the top of the swift steep upward swoop. This exceedingly spectacular display is performed repeatedly, especially in fine weather, and continues at intervals through much of the breeding season.

When the females arrive at or are present in the breeding haunt mutual displays are performed, in which the male, soaring above the female, dives at his mate. She then turns over and presents her claws in a symbolic movement she will later use for a real purpose in the food pass. As courtship progresses the male brings food to the female, who then tends to remain in one area on or near the nest while the male forages further afield. The food may be received by the female either on the ground, or she may rise to meet the male and receive it from him in the aerial food pass. As egg laying approaches the female ceases to hunt for herself and the male kills more prey for her(15).

The food pass, as it is called, is especially characteristic of harriers, being performed by all species; it is also less often performed by falcons and it is perhaps significant that both these groups of birds nest largely on the ground, or on cliff ledges, less often in trees. The male arriving with food calls the female off the nest with a characteristic mewing whistle 'keee-oo'. The female may answer with a higher-pitched whistle, rather more sibilant, 'pseeee-oo, psee-ooo' also slurred downward. She rises from her perch or, later in the season, from the nest and flies to meet the male. He often drops the food, which the female flying below him then catches with a dexterous twist in mid air. Sometimes however, she flies up to him, turns over, and receives the prey by a foot-to-foot pass, a spectacularly agile and beautifully timed movement. Often the male takes food to a feeding place in the marsh where the female joins him and eats it on the ground.

Possibly calling off the female to receive food may have biological value in reducing the danger of the nest being located and disturbed by possible predators. In the marsh and all the harriers the female is cryptically coloured, the male relatively conspicuous, and repeated visits with food to the nest by the male could reveal its position more easily. Also, once the female is off the nest, she need not and will not return at once if danger threatens; if she were to remain on it and be fed there it would be somewhat more easy to locate. However, it is doubtful if this is of any real significance in survival, as the only enemies of harriers likely to make use of such aids to locate the nest are human beings, and this behaviour pattern could scarcely have evolved with them in view.

The actual site of the nest is probably selected by the female, but both sexes bring nesting material to it. The same general area in the reedbed may be used year after year, but not normally the same actual site. The nest is a large platform of dead reeds and other suitable material, its size depending largely on whether it is built on dry ground, on floating vegetation, or in vegetation growing in water. In wet places it may be two feet across the top and built up to eighteen inches above water level; wet situations are preferred and are usually used.

All harriers lay unusually large clutches for birds of prey. The marsh harrier in Europe lays 3–8 eggs at 2–3-day intervals, with average clutches in Holland of 4·7, 5·57 in Lorraine, and 4·6 in the Camargue. It is not known whether British clutches are now on average smaller, because the nests are left strictly alone, but probably they are, since brood size is smaller and depends, primarily, on clutch size. However, seven Horsey clutches averaged 4·0 before 1965. A normal large clutch of 5–6 eggs takes 10 days or even more to deposit, and very large clutches still longer(16). This means that the young hatch over a long period, 5 young at Hickling in 1942 taking 10 days, 7–17 June(10). In one race of this species (in New Zealand) the female will cease to incubate the later laid eggs of a large clutch because the earlier hatched young become too active(e). However, this does not seem to happen in Europe or, presumably, Britain. In Europe the female continues to incubate the later eggs for at least 7 days after the first two hatch, which would be adequate for a clutch of 5–6 to hatch.

The role of the sexes in harriers in the breeding season is clearly defined. The female marsh harrier alone incubates, and may moult during incubation. She is fed by the male before and during incubation, and during the first third of the fledging period, for a total of perhaps 60 days; it is doubtful if she is prevented from hunting by her moult(2), and females can rear broods alone if the male disappears. The handsome male harriers are the despair of bird photographers, as they seldom actually visit the nest, though they sometimes bring food to the young, especially in the absence of the female, and never stay for more than a few seconds.

Incubation may not begin till the second or third egg has been laid, and consequently the first two young of a brood are usually the same size, hatched on the same day. The laying interval is reflected in the differing sizes of the later young. The incubation period is estimated at 36 days for each egg, but may be 32–38 days and, for a clutch of 5–6, would occupy about 48 days from laying the first egg to hatching the last.

The young are at first clad in buffy down, shorter and white on the crown. By 18 days feathers have begun to show through, and cover the body by 28 days. The eldest young of a large brood may be feathered when the smallest is still entirely downy. As soon as they can walk, at about 25 days, they are likely to scramble out of the nest into the surrounding vegetation, perhaps seeking shade. They return when a parent arrives with food, and require help in feeding for up to about 28 days, by which time they are feathered and active. At first they are aggressive to human visitors at the nest, lying on their backs and striking upwards with their talons but later, when they can walk, they hide in the surrounding vegetation. Apparently they are not aggressive to each other, at least in the early stages and as long as food is plentiful. Possibly, in the later stages, large feathered young may kill and eat weaker smaller downy young, though this has not been positively recorded. If abandoned by their parents by night they may die of cold and one youngster, reared in its own nest by Eric Hosking on food brought by its own parents, used to answer his call when he approached the nest and came rushing to meet him from its reedy hiding place(10).

During the early fledging period the female remains on the nest, incubating the later laid eggs after the first have hatched, and thereafter feeding the brood on prey brought by the male. Occasionally she leaves the nest earlier, and may kill only five days after the first egg has hatched; this, however, is rare. Once the larger young are feathered and active she leaves the nest and herself hunts, as well as the male. The appetite of a partly feathered brood of four young would probably be twice that of the adult pair, so that if the female did not then hunt the male would be hunting, in effect, for himself and five others. If, as sometimes happens, a male has two or more females, he may be responsible for feeding himself and 10–12 other harriers.

Clearly this could result in difficulty in obtaining enough prey, so that in harriers it seems especially desirable that the female should be able to hunt in the later fledging period. She may start to do so while still partially in moult, but perhaps then is not very successful or she may not feed the young at all. In the Anglesey brood observed, which fell from four hatched to one finally reared, the female failed to bring food to the nest after she left it, still partially in moult, and the male brought most of the prey to the young even in the late stages. This female did not visit the nest after 28 July, and from then until 15 August the young were apparently dependent on the male. Three survived to fly, but only one to the age at which it could catch prey for itself. At Hickling the single surviving young of a brood of five was fed mainly by the male in the later stages. In both these cases, however, the birds were disturbed by human observers near the nest(5,10).

Male marsh harriers are frequently bigamous, one male having been mated to two females in eight out of eighteen years at Minsmere(2). In theory, this should result in poorer breeding success in a species where the female both incubates alone and moults during incubation and early fledging so that she cannot hunt so effectively for herself, but must be fed by the male. However, the Minsmere records do not show any decrease in success in 'bigamous' years as opposed to years in which there were as many males as females, in fact the reverse. In eight 'bigamous' years 21 of 23 nests succeeded, rearing 56 young, equivalent to 2·44 per nest and 2·66 per successful nest. In ten 'non bigamous' years 21/26 nests reared 55 young, 2·1 per nest and 2·61 per successful nest. In one year with two males and three females three nests were all successful, rearing ten young. Any difference was largely due to a greater number of failures through desertion and to battles with bitterns in the non-bigamous nests. These small differences are undoubtedly fortuitous, but underline the fact that food shortage at Minsmere could hardly be responsible for small brood size, if males feeding two females and broods can do so as well or better than males with only one mate and brood to feed.

Continental records indicate that young marsh harriers make their first flight at 35 to 40 days, perhaps longer; one of the Anglesey young made its first flight when about 47 days old and one at Hickling at 45 days. After flying they are wholly or partly dependent on their parents for several weeks. The young Anglesey bird mentioned made its first flight on 11 August and was flying strongly around the lake by 21 and 25 August; it could then catch food brought to it by its parent in the air, but returned to the nest area to rest and roost. Minsmere marsh harriers normally can fly by 7–10 July

Even in Britain, where broods are sometimes smaller than on the Continent, the population of marsh harriers at the end of August is normally double or more that present in April, and can vary from one and a half times to three times as many. In southern France if all pairs over a larger area are considered however, including a proportion of pairs that probably or certainly do not breed, the increase is not as great. The rearing of large broods, perhaps biologically necessary in a raptor nesting on the ground, could also result in acute competition for winter food if all attempted to remain in the area. It is therefore no surprise to find that harriers are, almost without exception, migratory or partially migratory.

Young British marsh harriers are mainly migratory, though a few overwinter, as was demonstrated by one yearling recovered near where it was ringed in late December. Minsmere young do not winter there though adults do. Out of 15 ringing recoveries of birds ringed at Hickling, in Dorset, in Norfolk and at Minsmere 12 were recovered in Britain and three abroad. The latter included a bird ringed at Hickling and shot near Amiens, France in its first winter; one ringed at

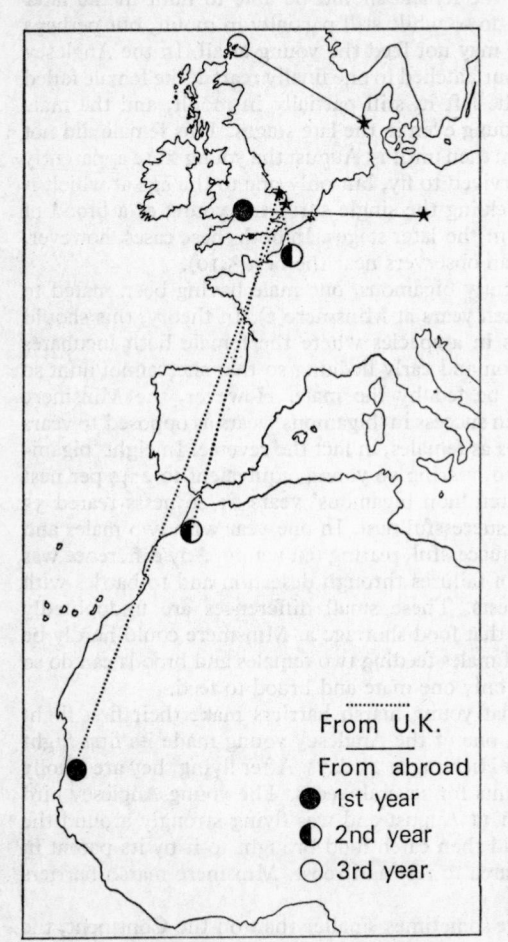

From U.K.
From abroad
● 1st year
◐ 2nd year
○ 3rd year

MAP 19. Recoveries abroad of British-ringed marsh harriers, and in Britain of foreign-ringed marsh harriers.

Horsey and recovered 50 miles east of Casablanca in its second spring; and the Minsmere bird, which was a young one reared at Walberswick, found later in a coypu trap, fed for two to three weeks and released, only to be killed the following spring on the Rosso River in Senegal. Continental marsh harriers are more strongly migratory; but only two European birds have been recovered in Britain(11).

Large numbers of marsh harriers have been killed in southern Europe each winter, and no doubt some of the British reared birds are among these, though the total British population is only a very small fraction of the continental, which probably numbers between 500 and 1000 pairs. Until this practice is stopped one feels that one need look no further for at least one main cause of the general decrease of European marsh harriers.

The age to which marsh harriers live may be calculated from brood size and from ringing records. The latter indicate that they live longer than other harriers, as one would expect from their larger size. The oldest record is of one which was nearly 15 years old. Winter mortality in the first year is severe, around 50–60% of young reared and amounts to about 75% before full maturity at two to three years. With a mean brood size of 2·3 from all nests, and 75% mortality before maturity, adult marsh harriers in Britain must breed for three to four years to replace themselves with sexually mature young. With a mean brood size of three or more, and the same level of mortality among the young continental marsh harriers could replace themselves in less than three years. This may be part of the reason why British marsh harriers are apparently unable to increase as we would all hope they might. However since 111 young have been reared at Minsmere in 18 years, and a few others elsewhere, one could have expected a total addition to the adult population of more than 35 birds, or at least two per year(2). With such a record of productivity, and bearing in mind that the 1972 Minsmere male was probably eight years old as an adult and 10 or 11 altogether, it still appears strange that there is no perceptible increase in the meagre total of less than five British breeding pairs.

CHAPTER 9

THE HEN HARRIER

THE hen harrier is unique among British birds of prey in several ways. In the first place, it is the only British species which has been actively and aggressively increasing in the last decade, when organochlorine pesticides have been prevalent in agriculture. Secondly, it has been continuously studied in detail in Orkney over more than twenty years, so that there is an unrivalled mass of data available on its behaviour and especially its population dynamics, perhaps more than for any bird of prey anywhere in the world. All this impressive field work has been done by one man, the late Eddie Balfour, the representative of the Royal Society for the Protection of Birds in Orkney. He published several classic papers and I have been privileged to see the recent unpublished results, collected by Dr James Cadbury (1,2,5,b). Thirdly, the hen harrier shows some extraordinarily interesting features in its breeding biology, notably the fact that it is strongly polygamous, perhaps because of an excess of females over males from the nestling stage onwards. Some males have as many as seven females attached to them. So far as I know this is unique among birds of prey anywhere, though other harriers, some falcons, and Accipiters often are also at least bigamous at the breeding sites.

The numbers of hen harriers have not been accurately estimated except in Orkney, where there may be about 65–70 breeding females with about 35–40 breeding males. At that, Orkney probably supports as many hen harriers as could survive there; accordingly if the species is to increase it must do so by recolonising the Scottish mainland. Here hen harriers certainly have been increasing since 1936, when they bred in Inverness-shire(e). They are certainly more numerous and widespread than is generally known, and they may actually be the most numerous of their particular group of British species, numbering 100–500 pairs. A rough recent estimate by Douglas Weir indicates that there may be 250 pairs on the mainland of Scotland north of the Tay(g) while, since there were at least 35 pairs in 1966, there could now be 50 pairs in Ireland(10). At that rate there should be at least 400 pairs in Britain and Ireland outside Orkney, and the hen harrier might even exceed five hundred pairs altogether. Personally, I doubt this; but the point can only be settled by a detailed inquiry. Any accurate census is difficult to achieve because the hen harrier breeds all over great areas of moorland and cannot be readily localised by any simple means.

It seems certain that without the continuing illegal persecution it receives from gamekeepers on grouse moors in eastern Scotland and no doubt elsewhere the hen harrier would quickly increase to well over a thousand pairs. The species has a more northerly distribution than other British harriers, occurring outside Britain over a vast tract of moorland, prairie and taiga in North America and northern Europe. Consequently, it was probably always the most numerous of British harriers, to be found wherever there was open moorland in Great Britain and Ireland. It may not have bred commonly in the fen country alongside the marsh harrier, and it may not have been common on southern moors such as Dartmoor, where Montagu's harrier may have replaced it; but there must have been many thousands of pairs before the era of game preservation began. Probably, until then, no one paid much attention to the hen harrier, for it is not a species that could possibly have any effect on other human interests and no doubt it mainly frequented uplands away from cultivated areas. As its name suggests it may have been a poultry thief; but probably only a few would have access to poultry.

Since 1800, however, there has been a huge decrease in the hen harrier population. The birds are easily shot off the nest, and can also be pole-trapped quite easily as they tend to settle on posts for a rest between periods of hunting flight. The destruction followed its usual totally indiscriminate course, harriers being exterminated everywhere whether or not they did any real damage, until in the twentienth century the species was reduced to a remnant breeding in Orkney, another very small population in the outer Hebrides and one to two pairs in Ireland(10). Possibly the more northerly populations may actually have been the most healthy and vigorous of the British stock, and were able to hang on for this reason, as well as because they were not so severely persecuted in Orkney, where attempts to maintain grouse moors were a failure and gamekeeping is almost unknown. In 1940 there may have been only forty or fifty pairs in Britain, but even at that the hen harrier was still at least twice as common as the other two British species, the marsh and Montagu's harriers, combined.

The recovery clearly dates from the establishment of effective protection for the species in Orkney. Here the population has been stable, and therefore probably at capacity numbers, since the fifties and there may even have been a slight decrease(b). However, if it had not increased through protection in Orkney it would probably not have been able to re-colonise the Scottish mainland, with or without the relaxation of persecution that followed the Second World War. The Orkney population was, however, healthy, and able to increase, and individuals from it colonised the Central Highlands in 1939. Immigration from continental sources is also a possibility. By the end of the war up to the early fifties several other small groups had developed, while at the same time there was a further marked increase in Orkney. By 1960 the hen harrier had spread to south-west Scotland, and by 1967 it bred in most Scottish counties and had re-established itself in small numbers in two Welsh and one English, counties(9). It is perhaps less successful in these southern areas than in its northern strongholds, suggesting that the Welsh mountains might actually be the southern fringe of its normal breeding range in Britain. However, the numbers involved are so small that no sound conclusions can be drawn on this point.

In Ireland too the species spread and increased. The very small remnant of one to two pairs retaining a precarious foothold in Ireland increased by 1950 to an unspecified but greater number, and by 1964 at least 34 pairs bred in six Irish counties(10). The fact that it also managed to spread in Ireland during the period 1939–50, when persecution by gamekeepers was reduced in Britain, suggests that other factors were also at work; persecution, if severe, was unlikely to have been relaxed in Ireland to the same extent as in Great Britain. Moreover, the species is still increasing in Britain despite a farily heavy level of persecution, which the existing legal provisions scarcely check.

The main other factor encouraging spread and colonisation was probably afforestation. In Ireland it seems that the hen harriers usually bred in recently afforested areas, where the young trees were of a certain height, and where there was a dense undergrowth of whins *Ulex gallii*(10). Plantations on rolling moorland, often on old red sandstone soils, were preferred. In Scotland also young plantations were and are used by the harriers, and small colonies of three or four pairs were formed in favoured places. However, in Scotland the species also bred in areas which had not recently been afforested, in open heather moorlands or even in sand dunes covered with long bent grasses. Afforestation was certainly important but not apparently crucial. In Britain Montagu's harrier also used the thick growth of the young plantations as nesting sites. Whether the hen harrier could have spread as rapidly without forestry must remain a matter of conjecture; but afforestation, with its attendant high populations of voles and other small mammals, certainly seems to have been the chief catalyst of the recent spread on the British mainland and in Ireland.

During the breeding season a male hen harrier takes up a territory or home range, wherein are also found a varying number of females, often two, three, or four, and occasionally up to five or even more. Seven have been known attached to one male(b). Adults normally remain in their home areas all the year round, but wander a good deal in winter and even in summer are not necessarily confined to a territory, which they do not actively defend against other harriers. The male does not necessarily arrive first in the breeding range in spring. The size of a male's breeding range may be as little as one square mile, with smaller individual ranges hunted over by the several females within the male's range.

Evidently the effect of the hen harrier on prey animals in its breeding range must depend on the number of females and their broods within it. A range with four females attached to the resident male may in theory have to support as many as 15–20 (in practice usually not more than ten) hen harriers late in the breeding season, a greater increase than occurs or is possible in any other known bird of prey, most of which are monogamous or at most doubtfully and rarely bigamous, and which rear smaller broods.

Hen harriers seldom fly very high above the ground, and if they are seen flying high they are not hunting. They very often inhabit windy uplands, where they can glide against the wind maintaining a low ground speed, which helps them to locate small prey in dense low cover. On still days they are obliged to hunt by steady flapping flight, but on windy days they usually glide with an occasional wingflap, the wings being held well above the horizontal. In a strong wind a harrier looks as if it is being blown about, but in fact it retains close control of its movements and can check and remain poised in a gale above possible prey for moments while it finally locates the quarry. It then drops quietly into the vegetation and either catches the prey or fails. Harriers can catch some birds in flight, but normally take nearly all their prey on the ground in this manner. The hunting methods of the hen harrier thus do not differ from those of other British harriers in open country, or of other species of harriers elsewhere in the world. However the hen harrier is a rather larger and more powerful species than is Montagu's and it may take rather larger prey.

Very little is recorded outside Orkney on what a hen harrier actually eats(4). If any massive lists of food taken in mainland Britain exist they have not been published. Small mammals and birds are probably the most important item throughout (Appendix Table I). Part of the reason for the success of the Orkney population may have been the Orkney vole, which, unlike most voles, does not appear to suffer violent fluctuations of population, so that it provides a steady reliable source of food for the breeding harriers. Hedgehogs, rats, and fair-sized young rabbits are taken, and if such mammalian prey is too large to carry entire it is dismembered and parts carried away. Large numbers of moorland birds are also taken, including for instance young waders such as curlews and lapwings; meadow pipits and other small passerines, notably starlings, and some young gamebirds. Young gulls, which are often common on northern moorlands, especially the young of common gulls which nest on open short heather or moorland, do not often seem to be taken, an indication that gulls are generally distasteful to the birds of prey sharing their habitat.

The justification, if any, for persecuting hen harriers on grouse moors rests on the numbers of young grouse taken in the breeding season and the disturbance caused at grouse drives later. A hen harrier cannot apparently kill an adult territorial red grouse, but can catch surplus adults in winter and takes some grouse chicks in summer when they are abundant and the harriers have young in the nest(d). A study of the effects of hen harrier predation on red grouse is in progress on a Kincardineshire moor by Nick Picozzi; preliminary indications are that quite a number of grouse chicks are taken. Whether the number taken makes any real difference to bags in the shooting season is doubtful, since these depend primarily on the ability of guns to hit what they aim at. In Fenno-Scandia rodents form the majority of the prey. Bergmann lists 333 mammals and 228 birds, but most of the birds were small passerines and young grouse composed only 7% of the total of birds. By weight, both in Britain and elsewhere, small mammals may be about equally important as birds (Appendix Table I).

Very occasionally a hen harrier may attack something larger. Recorded prey includes occasional adult water rails in winter quarters(a), and a female or immature has been seen to attack a wigeon duck, weighing 600–700 grams (1½ lb), and therefore much heavier than the harrier itself. The harrier did not succeed in picking up the duck, which escaped in the end, though doubtless injured, partly because gulls mobbed the harrier(c). Having failed twice to pick up the duck the harrier returned but did not make a third attempt.

In winter range, which may be upland moors or coastal marshes in Britain, hen harriers are not confined to any territory but can move freely over the whole country visible or available to them. They may nevertheless remain in a comparatively small area for some weeks at a time, regularly hunting the same tract of moorland or coastal marsh. The population of harriers in the winter range outside Orkney never approaches the full capacity of the environment to support, whereas in the breeding range in Orkney the population present may be as many as could be carried.

In Orkney and elsewhere the hen harrier roosts communally in winter, a habit shared by other migrant harriers. Roosts are regularly used in certain preferred localities, situated in long rank vegetation, and often swampy or waterlogged, but free of human disturbance. They are usually 15–20 ha. (40–60 acres) in extent, but sometimes the birds may spread over much larger areas. The harriers collect in these roost areas from some distance around, and the numbers using the roost vary from time to time, seasonally, and according to weather conditions. In America over 40 have been recorded using the same roost(6), but in S.W. Scotland, where this behaviour has been thoroughly studied, the maximum numbers at any roost rarely exceed thirty, and in Orkney usually less than fifteen hen harriers roost together.

In south-west Scotland, where several roosts have been studied(10), the harriers create trampled platforms of vegetation which remain more or less dry in wet surroundings. They may be used for many nights in succession possibly, but not certainly, by the same birds; this has also been suspected of migrant harriers in Africa. Preferred roosting platforms are defended against other harriers, and the whole roost area is defended with alarm calls from human intruders or possible predators such as foxes. Harriers begin to appear at the roosts in September, but reach peak numbers in October and November, suggesting that the birds using the roosts are mainly passage migrants rather than locally resident birds. One individual at least came from Kincardineshire, and others probably from Orkney.

The harriers flew in purposefully to their roost from up to $7\frac{1}{2}$ miles (11 km.) away; and some certainly hunted an area $5\frac{1}{2}$ miles (8 km.) away. They began to arrive at the roost up to $\frac{3}{4}$ hour before sunset and continued to arrive on some nights up to half an hour after sunset, with a spread of 12–74 minutes covering their arrival. Their departure in the early morning was usually more abrupt, taking 9–45 minutes, beginning up to half an hour before sunrise and continuing sometimes to half an hour after sunrise. Roosting behaviour varied with the weather, numbers present, and other factors, but the greatest numbers were recorded in mild conditions and the smallest on calm, cold nights. Possibly fine cold nights may stimulate the harriers to roost in or near future breeding areas, especially in late winter(10).

The time spent hunting by a hen harrier depends on the availability and vulnerability of the prey, and on the numbers of young that may have to be fed. The food requirement of an adult is estimated at about 90 grams by Picozzi, which may be too high. This is provided by two large voles or four small ones. Orkney voles weighing 34–63 grams are larger than mainland voles. It is thus evident that a single adult harrier does not have to hunt for very long in many areas before killing its requirement. The specialised, slow, steady hunting flight of the harrier enables it to locate such prey as voles in long grass or other rank vegetation, poise above it, and grasp it when the moment is favourable. Of course harriers do often fail to catch what they try to seize, but their apparently acute hearing probably helps them to locate invisible prey in long cover and they can then poise for a few moments if necessary before making the kill. The fact that they prefer to nest in afforested areas where the cover is unusually rank indicates that they can catch prey almost irrespective of the cover conditions. Indeed, if this were not so, it is difficult to see how a male could provide for several females and their broods, when he may have to kill ten to fifteen times his own requirements. Such a male would be obliged to spend most of a long summer day hunting; but a single bird in winter might easily obtain its food requirements in an hour or so.

Breeding pairs or groups of several females with one male are found in the breeding grounds from March onwards. The male does not necessarily arrive first, as appears to be so in more strongly migratory harriers. At that time the male displays with or to one or more females. The display is largely aerial, and in the later stages, extremely spectacular. At first the pair soar together, the male diving often at the female, who sometimes turns over and presents her claws to his. These displays are accompanied by calling a similar, staccato 'chek-ek-ek-ek' as will later be used to signify to the sitting female that the male has food. As courtship progresses the male performs undulating flights of increasing vigour, alone. Finally, in April, the most spectacular display is performed, in which the male hurls himself earthwards from a hundred feet or more above the ground, twisting or spinning in flight with threshing wings. The display is not only visible but audible at some distance, and is accompanied by 'chek-ek-ek-ek' calls not unlike alarm notes. Although the male appears out of control he checks within a few feet of the ground and then rises again to his former pitch, repeating the performance many times, often up to twenty, and rarely even over a hundred times. Normally this spectacular diving display, which is similar to that of other harriers, is performed immediately above a nesting station; but the displaying male may range over half a mile or so.

Females normally take no part in this spectacular display but remain perched on the ground. When the male eventually alights a female may fly to join him, and this is perhaps part of the process of nest selection. Some females, however, also perform this swift diving display, especially in sites where females outnumber males. This may be how individual females ensure separation of their own nest site from those of other females attached to the same male. The actual nest sites of the several females mated to one male are usually rather regularly spaced. Diving displays by the female continue into the late fledging period, which would tend to support the view that each female holds her own territory within the male's wider home range.

Diving displays by the male coincide with the period of nest selection and egg laying, and may be resumed later if a repeat clutch is laid or after failure. A typical nest site is a depression on a hillside, with rank bracken, rushes, or ferns, but relatively little heather, and always with some wet ground. Suitable nesting habitat is very characteristic. In such an area the vegetation is quite sparse at egg laying, but is luxuriant and rank by the end of the fledging period. Ideal nesting situations are used for many years in succession, and one female has been known to nest in the same area for six successive years.

Nest selection and laying is accompanied by food presentation by the male. The female remains in the nesting area and when the male flies over the food she rises and flies after him, calling in solicitation with a long drawn, gull-like call. The male either drops the food which is then dexterously caught by the female or passes it to her foot to foot. This may be done by both birds turning on their sides, or by the female turning upside down below the male. The female then returns to the nest to feed on the prey. If a bigamous or polygamous male is carrying prey not destined for a certain female he may fly over her high, so indicating that it is not for her; but such a male may sometimes be unable to decide which of two females should receive the prey and go from one to the other(b). Rarely, the male may leave food for the female on the ground near the nest site, and still more rarely a pass may occur away from the nest site. Females are often quite reluctant to leave the nest to receive food and may only jump a few feet in the air. A female may take prey from the male while herself carrying other food which she herself has caught.

Mating takes place on the ground in the nesting area, and occurs after nearly every food pass and until egg-laying is complete. As the male passes over in flight the female crouches with part opened wings. The male alights, she raises her tail. and the act is completed in a few seconds. The male then often alights and preens close by. Mating continues after egg laying, and presumably helps to maintain the pair bond(1).

The nest is on the ground in thick vegetation; about half the nests are in rushes and another half in heather, with only a few in shorter vegetation. The nest itself is a largish platform with a foundation of heather lined with finer material, formed into a shallow cup. In wet situations and long growth the nest is likely to be larger than on dry ground, and on a steep slope it is built up on the outer side so that the platform is level. Most of the nest building is done by the female, who collects the material within 50–150 yards of the nest itself. She picks up dead stems or may jump into the air trying to wrench off living heather gripped in her feet. Most of the material is carried in the feet, sometimes in the bill. Males also bring some material but do not spend much time building. The nest-building bird often flies back to the nest by a circuitous route, not direct, but must eventually land on the structure. Nest building may take only a few days or up to two weeks, and in extreme cases where a replacement clutch has been laid the nest was built in a matter of hours. Later on, the nest becomes a flattened pad of vegetation but it is kept surprisingly clean as egg shells and food remains are carried away by the parent female(4). It is not normally used for another year, though the same general area is used year after year, and nests in successive years may be within a few yards of each other.

All these manoeuvres make the nest of the hen harrier quite easy to locate, for its exact position is clearly marked by the behaviour of the female. Nevertheless, the actual site is sometimes not easy to find after eggs have been laid, as the female sits very tight and will allow close approach before flushing, almost at the intruder's feet.

In Orkney the first eggs are laid in the second half of April, and the majority of clutches between 1 and 20 May. Clutches laid later than this indicate repeat layings, and can be found into June. The laying date is affected by the weather, earlier in some years than others, but in all years the peak laying period is the first half of May. The largest clutches are also laid at this time, possibly by the most experienced females, breeding at an optimum period. Other British records do not indicate much variation from Orkney laying dates, though the information is meagre.

Normally 3–6 eggs, and occasionally 7, 8, even 10 or 12 are laid, each egg being laid at an interval of 48–72 hours, occasionally longer. No full Orkney clutches of less than 3 are known and any recorded may have been reduced from an earlier larger clutch. In Wales clutches of 2, apparently complete, have been recorded and the few records indicate that the average clutch size here is much smaller than the Orkney average, 10 clutches varying from 2 to 6, and averaging 3·5 eggs; however all clutches of less than 4 are doubtfully complete. The average of 29 clutches outside Orkney is about 4·6, while that of no less than 390 Orkney clutches is 4·57. Clutch size in Orkney varies from year to year, for instance from 3·8 in 1952 to 7·3 in 1953; but these differences, over a series, are not significant or related to any easily observable phenomenon(1). It suffices to say that a normal clutch is of 4–5 eggs, and that it takes 8–10 days to deposit. The very large clutches of 10 or more are repeat clutches laid on top of the first, not as apparently occurs in the sparrowhawk due to two females laying in the same nest.

Eggs are normally laid in the morning, between eight and midday. Incubation begins normally with the second, third, or fourth egg. There is much overlap between egg laying and the start of incubation, and perhaps the first periods spent by the female sitting on the nest are not full incubation. Only females incubate, being normally fed on the nest by the male. In cases of polygamy, however, females may be forced to leave the nest to hunt during the incubation period. A single Hebridean record of a male perhaps incubating was made in unusual circumstances, when the female had been sitting on addled eggs long after they should have hatched(f). Some males visit the nests during incubation but many do not even do that. If any mishap occurs, however, a male is more liable to visit the nest than if all proceeds normally.

The female is an extremely close sitter. She does not normally leave the nest except when the male brings prey and, if humans are visible in the vicinity, she will not then return to her eggs. Occasionally she calls from the nest, and occasionally one female visits or passes over another, which may result in a short aerial skirmish before they return to their respective nests. The female undergoes a partial moult during incubation, but no more than two flight quills are missing at a time from each wing, and some tail feathers. This amount of moult does not seriously affect her hunting ability. This sort of behaviour is typical of all the harriers that have been studied, but the detail available for the hen harrier in Britain is fuller than that for any other species. In some other species it is suggested that the moult might impair hunting efficiency; but the observations on which these suggestions are based are less critical than Balfour's in Orkney.

The incubation period varies from 29–37 days for each egg and for the entire clutch. Normally the hatching period is somewhat shorter than the laying period, since incubation does not normally begin till several eggs have been laid, but this varies a good deal. One clutch of 6 laid at 2-day intervals over 11 days between 24 April and 4 May hatched over 8 days from 27 May to 3 June; another clutch of 4 eggs, however, all hatched within 24 hours, though laid over at least a week; that particular female did not begin to sit till all 4 eggs had been laid. The longest recorded laying period is for a clutch of 7 laid over 12 days which hatched over 10 days; but only 5 of the 7 eggs hatched.

There are heavy losses among the eggs, unusually heavy for any bird of prey. Hatching success over 27 years 1944–71 has varied from 33 to 69% and averages overall 53·5%. The period concerned can be divided into four parts; before the general use of DDT up to 1946; with DDT in use from 1949–52; with dieldrin also in general use 1957–61, and with restrictions on the use of these compounds after 1961. Hatching success from 1949–52, when DDT was in general use, was lower than for the periods before or after that, but has been as high (62·6%) when dieldrin and other pesticides were in general use as it is in more recent times when these pesticides have been controlled if not banned (62·4%)(5). Variations in hatching success are apparently not, therefore, due to pesticides; and although some egg-eating was noticed in the fifties it has not recently been seen. A possible explanation is that in 1946–52, when hatching success was lowest, the increase of population then taking place may have resulted in a high proportion of young, inexperienced females, which laid smaller clutches and failed to hatch their eggs more often than the present capacity population of older females(5).

The young hatch over a period in most nests, so that the oldest is usually markedly larger than the youngest. Cases are recorded where the oldest was partly feathered while the smallest was still entirely downy. However, young harriers do not seem to be aggressive to one another and nestling losses are not normally due to inter-sibling strife. Dead nestlings are, however, eaten by their nest mates, especially in periods of bad weather which may reduce normal hunting success by the adults, leaving the nestlings hungry(1). Females continue to incubate the remaining eggs in a nest although they also have an increasing brood of young to cope with. One female continued to incubate addled eggs until her first hatched young was almost fully feathered. Even in large clutches hatching success is not much affected by clutch size. It is, however, adversely affected by polygamy, being lowest when a female shares a male with *two* others(5). Such differences are not easy to explain even if statistically significant, since hatching success when males have four females is once again higher. Possibly a young, merely bigamous male may have difficulty; but once he has reached the Bluebeard stage he has learned to surmount the difficulties of polygamy.

If the eggs fail to hatch the female may continue incubating for up to 70 days, twice the normal incubation period. However, when the eggs fail early in the incubation period a repeat clutch is often laid. Many late clutches are of this nature; they average smaller than normal clutches, those laid 10–20 June averaging only 3·33(1).

Males take a greater interest in the nest site at the hatch. Presumably they must then determine that there are young in it, and accordingly increase their rate of killing to provide food. Probably there is some as yet not understood method of communicating the presence of young to the male. In many birds of prey this is simply achieved because the male visits the nest, but in the case of harriers the male does not take prey to the nest and often may not even see what is in it, since the female comes off in response to his call and receives the prey some distance away. In this case the greater interest shown by the male at the hatch could therefore reveal to him the presence of visible chicks; but how he could know when to take a greater interest is obscure.

The females continue to brood the young closely for up to seven days, thereafter brooding them less closely and leaving the nest to take part in hunting. In theory it is at this point that the adverse effects of polygamy should appear. A male hen harrier with four females, which he must feed on the nest (for they do not regularly hunt for themselves while incubating) still only has to catch four or five times his own needs, if that, since the appetite of an incubating female may be rather less than that of an active male flying about. However, when all these females hatch their broods the male may then have to provide ten to fifteen times his own requirements.

In theory, this should be such a strain on his ability that his several females are forced to hunt for themselves and their broods earlier than would a female in a monogamous mating, so exposing the young to greater danger from predators, cold, rain, and other factors, resulting in increased brood mortality. Bigamy, much less polygamy, should not pay! Some of the earlier work indicated that, in bigamous or polygamous matings, the females were forced to leave the nests and hunt earlier than they would if the male was supporting only one female and brood, with consequently heavier losses among nestlings through bad weather(1). However, more recent work has not confirmed this view, though females in polygamous matings certainly do leave the nest to hunt for themselves if the male does not feed them enough(5).

It appears that in Orkney at least males can support at least four mates and their broods satisfactorily, breeding success in territories with four females being actually higher (66·0% fledging success) than in cases where there were two or three females(5). The losses of nests and eggs generally reduce the burden a male must face to manageable proportions. Only the older, more experienced males appear to be able to achieve this, however, and a very old male may not be able to continue in this way. Young males breeding before they have assumed fully adult dress are normally mated to only one female; no case where such a young male had three females is known, and only one with two, whereas older males sometimes acquire additional females formerly mated to younger males(b). Presumably, therefore, experienced males which may have occupied the same range for several years are able to hunt in it with sufficient success, helped by their mates, to supply even many times their own requirements.

Alternatively, it may be that this is an abnormal situation peculiar to Orkney, which may be optimum habitat for the hen harrier, with the Orkney vole a particularly suitable, reliable and easily caught prey species. Bigamous matings in hen harriers are known elsewhere(7), and are frequent in all harrier species that have been studied, while the importance of the Orkney vole is indicated by the small harrier population on Hoy, which has no voles. However, the multiple matings of Orkney hen harriers appear unique. The answer to the riddle of whether this polygamy is normal or not can only be found when comparable detailed work has been done in another area; and it will certainly be many years if ever before a comparable body of data is available from anywhere else.

Polygamy in itself suggests that there must be more adult females than males; in fact in Orkney there are an average of 1·96 females per male, varying from one mate only in about half of all cases to a maximum of seven, and also varying from 1·7–2·6 females per male in different years(5). Such a situation could only come about if (i) males live nearly twice as long as females on average, at least as adult breeding birds or (ii) there are more females than males in the population from fledging onwards.

In fact the answer appears to be a combination of both. Young hen harriers can be sexed in the nest by eye colour alone, that of a male chick being greyish while that of a female is brown(3). The difference persists into adult life, the young male always having a paler yellow eye than the female, while that of the female becomes paler as she grows older. Sexing nestlings by this means reveals that over a long period of years 1·2 females are reared for every male(5). Since this difference is not as great as that between the adult birds it seems clear that mortality soon after fledging must be higher in males. Both sexes may breed while still in immature plumage at less than two years old, females perhaps more readily than males. However, any difference in this respect is not sufficient to account for the difference between 1·2 young females reared per male and the observed adult ratio, which is almost two females per male.

Bigamous or not, there is heavy nesting mortality among all hen harrier nests. In 562 observed nests 231 have failed; of these 36 failed during laying, 58 during incubation, and in 45 all the young died. In other nests a proportion of the young die or eggs are addled(5). In 455 Orkney nests containing 2037 eggs 1091 young hatched (53·5%). Of 1068 young hatched 716 young were reared; and from 331 successful nests 794 young, an average of 2·4 young per nest, were reared. This is equivalent to an overall breeding success of about 1·58 per pair which bred: there are no records of non-breeding pairs in hen harriers, but it seems likely that some females attached to males do not lay and some females, including one albino, have not been attached to any male(b). Discarding this possibility, on average there are still nearly two breeding females for every adult male. In fact this number of young, 1·58 per nest, or 3·16 per male with two females is produced by three, not four adults, so that in the polygamous hen harrier 1·06 young per breeding adult per year results. This appears to be enough not only to maintain the Orkney population but also to allow vigorous spread to elsewhere, kept in check only by continued persecution.

Surviving young in the nest are covered by the female for up to seven days, after which time she ceases to brood them much, and can take part in hunting. She may hunt earlier if necessary. She will return to brood them during heavy rain, or at night, when she cannot hunt, and presumably the elder young, huddling together with the smaller later hatched chicks help to keep these warm by day. From 14 days onwards the young leave the nest and crawl away into the surrounding growth, but return when a parent brings food. They have by this time started to sprout feathers, which completely cover them by 25 days. They make their first flights, independent of parental coaxing, at about 35 days old, but will fly earlier if closely approached by human beings or other possible enemies. Males, smaller and lighter than females, fly earlier, at about 32 days on average, whereas females may remain in the nest for 42 days(1).

Despite the immense amount of other data available on Orkney hen harriers I cannot find any good accounts of the behaviour of either adults or young during the fledging period. It would be of interest to know just how soon a female sharing a mate with several others must start hunting to help provide the food, and how many hours a male with several broods to rear must hunt to provide for them. In the nearly related Montagu's harrier (for which there are also no good British data) the male provides 5–6 kills per day for the first 10 days, during which period the female and brood are entirely dependent on him. An Orkney polygamous male might have to kill as many as 20–25 voles to provide for his dependants, or at least one per hour during the whole of a long summer day. In theory, this does not sound impossible; but whether it occurs is still not clear and there is still plenty of scope for research into the precise regulation of such aspects of the hen harrier's breeding cycle.

Certainly it seems that in other parts of the British Isles hen harriers breed in very different conditions to those in Orkney. Virtually every nest in Orkney is at less than 500 feet (150 m.) above sea level, and this was true also of the small population in the Outer Hebrides. The most recent colonists of the Scottish mainland have in some cases bred on higher mountains, while in Wales only one nest among the B.T.O. nest record cards is at less than 1500 feet (450 m.) above sea level. Whether this is because the favoured type of habitat, recently planted forest with rank heather or other thick growth, is only or mainly found in Wales at such altitudes, or whether these new colonists can only survive persecution in more remote mountain areas is obscure. As already mentioned, both clutch and brood size in the small available sample of Welsh pairs seem well below the Orkney average, or that for the rest of mainland Britain. Again, this might be because Wales is towards the southern fringe of the hen harrier's normal breeding range, or because the species is forced by persecution to breed in unfavourable habitat. The possible answers to such conundrums will be subjects of intriguing speculation for many years to come.

About two-thirds of all young reared in Orkney each year are ringed(b). Available ringing results give a good idea of what happens to young hen harriers after they leave the nest (Maps). Some of them attempt to spend the autumn and winter in Orkney while others migrate to the Scottish mainland and elsewhere. Of 94 recoveries of birds ringed as young in the nest in Orkney 41 were recovered in their first winter or autumn in Orkney, and another 13 in Scotland. One first-winter young reached Ireland, a second England, and a third Denmark. 66/94 were recovered before they could reasonably have bred, indicating a mortality of 70% before sexual maturity. At that rate, with an average long-term productivity of 1·06 young per breeding adult, each adult must live on average over three and a half years as an adult to provide a replacement. Individual wild life spans have not been published, but one female is known to be alive at nine years, and several six-year-old birds are known(5,b). However, life tables based on ringing records tend to be unreliable because most of the recoveries are of birds which died unnatural deaths; this is actually less likely to have occurred among Orkney hen harriers than in some other species. However, who knows how many young hen harriers are shot or trapped and quietly buried, ringed or not ? Hen harriers are a species that should lend itself to quantitative evaluation of the population composition by age classes, either by observation or trapping. At present, 3–4 young males appear annually in

PLATE 7. HARRIERS at the nest. *Above*, a male marsh harrier alighting; it is exceptional for any male harrier to visit a nest. *Centre*, female hen harrier at a typical nest among heather, with four unmarked pale blue eggs. *Below*, Montagu's harrier nesting among rushes; one egg has failed to hatch, a a common feature in harriers.

PLATE 8.   GOSHAWK. The goshawk may nest in Britain in small numbers; the nest is large for the size of the bird, and the female remains with the downy chicks, fed by the male.

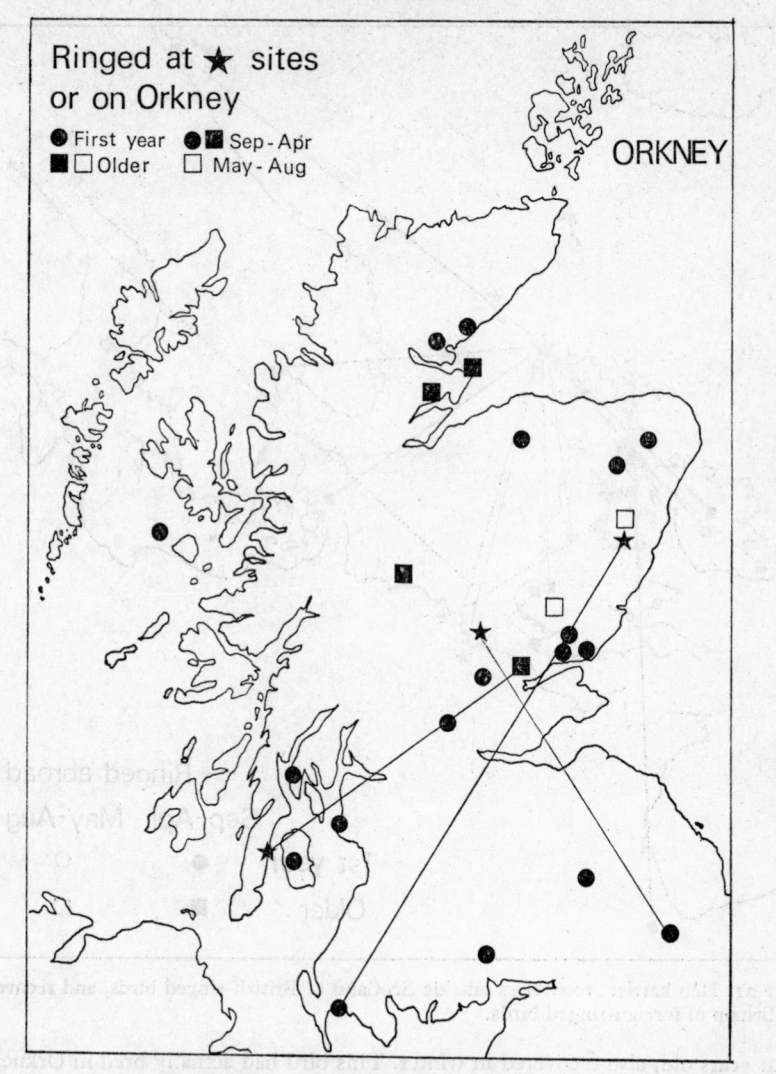

Ringed at ★ sites
or on Orkney

● First year ●◧ Sep-Apr
■ □ Older   □ May-Aug

ORKNEY

MAP 20. Recoveries of hen harriers ringed in Orkney and Scotland, which have been recovered, in Scotland, more than 100 km from ringing site.

the total of 15–20 adult males in the Orkney study area, suggesting a mean life span among adult males of about five years(b). This line of investigation should be worth pursuing.

The six Orkney-ringed young recovered as adults on the Scottish mainland were all in known breeding areas; one of them was in fact shot at a nest. Two other adults were recovered in Ireland in winter and two in the Netherlands. Of two Norwegian recoveries one was in its second winter and the other was more than

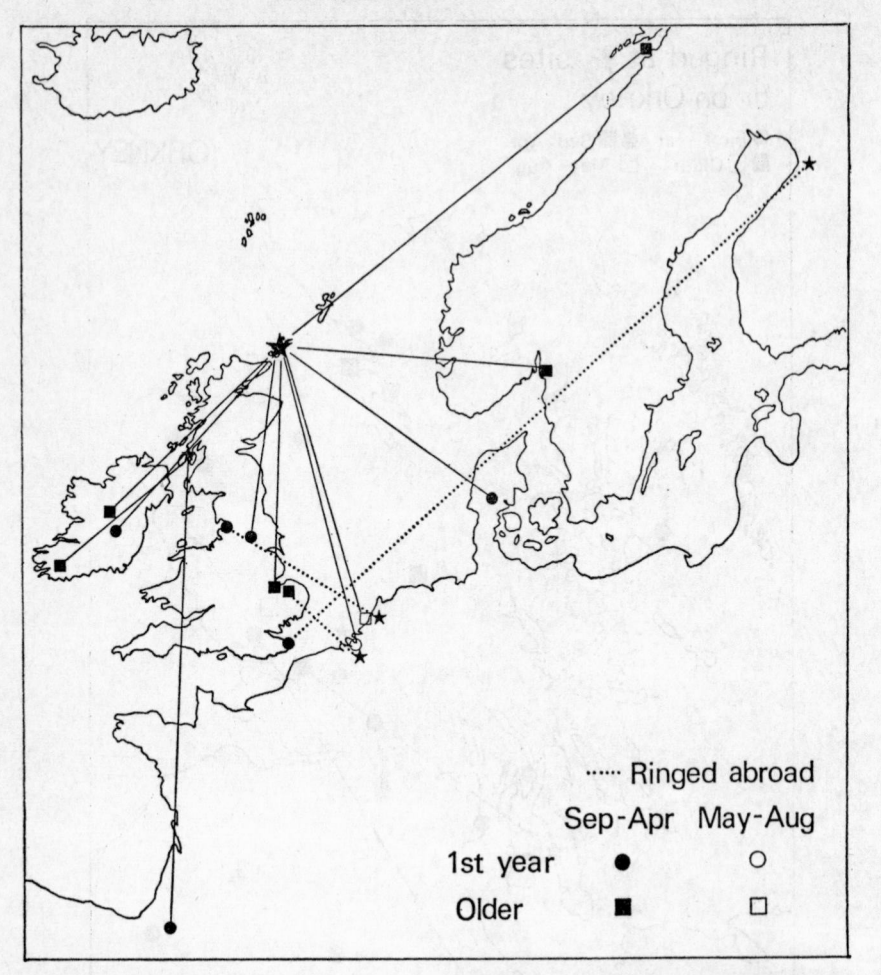

MAP 21. Hen harrier: recoveries outside Scotland of British-ringed birds, and recoveries in Britain of foreign-ringed birds.

four years old, also recovered in winter. This bird had actually bred in Orkney in 1968, but was apparently absent from its usual nesting area in 1969 and 1970, so that it may have mated with a Norwegian bird and stayed there during these two summers.

The main trend of movement from Orkney is thus to the Scottish mainland, with a few individuals travelling further afield, to England, Ireland, across the North Sea or to France(8). There is evidently some interchange between European and British populations for there are also three records of foreign-ringed birds recovered in Britain. One was ringed as a nestling in Finland and recovered the following spring in Kent, and two Dutch birds were recovered in Norfolk and Lancashire. Moreover, it is likely that the Orkney population is maintained by some foreign migration, since the proportion of ringed adults is always less than the two-thirds of young ringed annually, and this cannot wholly be explained by ring loss(b). Thus the hen harrier is somewhat like the osprey, with some interchange of migrant birds from the Continent, but with a stronger tendency to remain in the breeding areas through the winter and no indication of migration to Mediterranean or African countries.

All the indications are that the hen harrier will continue to increase if it is left alone and is not persecuted when it appears in a new breeding area. Since this is unlikely to happen unless the species can be shown to be relatively harmless to game preserving interests, and even then only with the greatest reluctance, and under heavy legal and other pressures, it is important that clear and objective analysis of the hen harrier's food needs and preferences in all parts of its range is soon obtained and published.

Even if it is found to take larger numbers of grouse chicks in eastern Scotland than is generally thought, there are still vast tracts of country in the north and west of Scotland, and in Ireland too, where grouse are too scarce to be worth preserving and the hen harrier feeds mainly on voles and moorland birds. Here it is at least neutral and unimportant to man's interests. If it were to become as numerous over the gently undulating bog flow country of Sutherland and Caithness as it is in Orkney the population could rise to several hundred pairs in these two counties alone. At least it is possible to look forward with some confidence to a time when the hen harrier is much more abundant than it is today. In this respect too the hen harrier is unique among British birds of prey.

CHAPTER 10

MONTAGU'S HARRIER

MONTAGU'S is the smallest, the most beautiful and graceful, and least known of all British harriers. It has not been studied in the same detail as has the hen harrier in Britain but more has been written about it in Britain than about the marsh harrier, and rather more people here have watched it and photographed it at the nest(6,12). Abroad, it is less well observed and described than the marsh harrier. It is a species that I know quite well in its winter quarters in Africa but which I have been unable to see in Britain. What follows, therefore, is derived entirely from the rather scanty British written accounts amplified from abroad. Probably much more is known about this harrier in Britain than has been published, no doubt for the usual reason that to publish would lead to undesirable publicity followed by interference with breeding localities by egg collectors and eager birdwatchers alike.

Montagu's harrier is quite definitely a summer migrant to Britain, breeding here and leaving again in the autumn. Unlike the other British harriers none winter here at all. Few of the individuals that migrate northwards each year through Gibraltar, Spain, and France ever reach Britain; and those that do are mainly confined, as might be supposed, to southern and eastern counties of England. In the past this species may have been much more common than it is at present or has been within the past twenty years; it may have been the common regular breeding harrier on southern heathlands, just as the hen harrier probably was on northern moors. However, there is scant evidence that Montagu's harrier ever was a very common breeding bird in England and Wales. In Scotland it has always been rather a rare migrant, occasionally breeding and in Ireland is only a very rare resident, represented annually by about two breeding pairs at most(11). Although undoubtedly the species has been and still is persecuted whenever it appears in game rearing areas it appears likely that its numbers were always rather small and that the main reasons for its relative scarcity are natural and ecological rather than human persecution.

In this century the numbers of Montagu's harriers have fluctuated from about 20 to perhaps as many as 50 pairs at its peak in the fifties. Several incomplete status surveys have been done at intervals and these give a fair idea of these fluctuations. In 1935 a survey by Witherby indicated 17–18 breeding pairs in England and Wales, with a few elsewhere; perhaps 20–25 in Britain as a whole. In 1945 it was not considered to have increased appreciably by Lack and Nicholson, and in 1967 Parslow's status survey of all British raptors indicated that its numbers then were still about 15–25 pairs, about the same as in the thirties. Between 1944 and 1967 the population had risen to a peak of about 40–50 pairs in the fifties, and this harrier bred as far north as Perth and Kirkcudbright between 1952 and 1955. In 1950 there were about 20 pairs, equivalent to the total British population of the thirties, in Devon and Cornwall alone. Between 1956 and 1965 it bred in 20 counties at least once, but since 1960 has bred annually in only six counties in England and Wales. One or two pairs are still said to breed fairly regularly in Ireland, but it has not bred in

Scotland since the fifties, and probably only breeds so far north in years when the population reaches a peak(11).

What causes these fluctuations is not at all clear. Since the exact number of breeding pairs is not known in most years it is not possible to plot them against weather conditions or such natural factors to see whether these have any effect. It seems probable that the increase to a peak of about forty to fifty pairs in the fifties was the result of a combination of factors. A decrease in persecution leading to an overall increase in the number of young reared in the war years combined with a reduction of shooting of migrants would have resulted in a greater population of mature breeding adults in the late forties and early fifties. Secondly, the sharp increase, after World War II, in the areas of young forestry plantations in southern England provided suitable areas of undisturbed breeding habitat, which was undoubtedly preferred and used by these harriers just as it is used by hen harriers today. The two combined could quite easily have doubled the population of this harrier which, like others, rears large broods, in a few years.

Since 1960 there has undoubtedly been a decline, perhaps to even lower levels than occurred in the thirties. It seems reasonable to suppose that at least part of the decline is due to the increased use of agricultural pesticides, which would affect the bird-eating harriers, and have been suspected as the cause of the decline of marsh harriers. However, it must be admitted that Montagu's harrier is as much a bird of undisturbed heathlands as is the hen harrier, and that the latter does not appear to be declining, is in fact increasing, despite pesticides. Montagu's harrier, however, probably faces worse hazards on migration than the hen harrier. If not shot in Britain first, it passes through regions of France and Spain where birds of prey are deliberately and systematically shot by gunners waiting for them; almost all the more distant ringing recoveries are obtained in this way. Such systematic persecution may be more severe than that meted out by gamekeepers to the hen harriers that move to the Scottish mainland in winter.

It is unlikely that any changes in the habitat or the land use patterns in winter quarters in Africa have had any appreciable effect on the status of Montagu's harrier. It is apparently still quite common as a migrant from October to March in West African savannas, though up to 1950 few had been recorded in West Africa and perhaps its habits are changing(7). In East Africa it is nearly as common as the pallid harrier, but both appear to have declined considerably since 1950(3). It is not likely that such a decline has been caused by any change in the habitat in the winter quarters; it is more probably due to greater persecution, pesticides, and other factors affecting the breeding population of both species in Europe. In Africa Montagu's harrier frequents open short grass savanna areas, and is not persecuted by Africans anywhere. It is unlikely that in any part of Africa, except perhaps in the intensively managed irrigated tracts of the Nile Valley in Sudan and Egypt, it would feed upon animals or birds seriously contaminated by pesticides; and Montagu's harrier seems rare in the Nile Valley anyhow(9). I believe therefore that any reasons for the decline of Montagu's harrier in Europe and Britain have to be sought there and not in Africa.

It now seems likely that the breeding population of Montagu's harrier in Britain is less rather than more than twenty pairs. In writing this book I have heard of only three localities in which they have regularly bred in the last few years, and have seen none in the only one of these areas I have been able to visit. Whether this low level of population will be permanent remains to be seen. There is probably less suitable nesting terrain available now than formerly, because the young plantations favoured in the fifties have now grown too tall and so reduced the total hunting area in favoured localities, while new planting is not proceeding at the same pace as a few years ago. Also, disturbance of probable nesting localities is undoubtedly worse in S. England. If all the southern heathlands were eventually covered with conifer forest Montagu's harrier would disappear as a breeding bird from Britain, apart from an odd pair that may nest in marshlands in Norfolk or Suffolk, as they used to but apparently no longer regularly do. What one may say is that a reduction in any persecution it may receive in Britain, together with a total stoppage of the senseless shooting of migrant raptors that still goes on in other countries along the main migration route would help the Montagu's harrier to make a comeback, if it is ecologically capable of doing so.

In its winter quarters, where I have good opportunities to observe it, Montagu's harrier behaves almost exactly like its close relative the pallid harrier. It is about the same size and just as slim and graceful in flight, while the rather darker grey male with the characteristic black wing bar and chestnut flecks on the underside is the only plumage in which I would wish to be dogmatic about distinguishing the two. In its winter quarters Montagu's harrier roosts communally in long grass or swampy places and counts at these roosts would give a good idea of the relative numbers of harriers from year to year. The birds come into the roost an hour to half an hour before dark, and settle in a particular place, making a sort of form like that of a hare in the long grass. Probably, the same bird uses the same place nightly, though it is hard to prove this(3). Before going to roost they often settle on a patch of bare ground some distance away, several resting and preening there for a time before making the final short flight into the roost. Communal roosting of this sort seems to be typical of all harriers; but little detailed study has been made of this interesting habit. The birds coming in to any particular roost may well travel ten or more miles to it, and the same roost areas are favoured year after year.

The Montagu's and other harriers leave the roost soon after dawn and fly out to hunting areas, which are short or tall grasslands and boggy places, or even cultivated fields. They do not seem to object to the presence of men and small farms and they can often be seen hunting in mixed cultivation and weedy places. Their method is exactly the same as that of other harriers. They fly low and slowly over the ground gliding against a wind if they can, but flying slowly with alternate wing flapping and gliding if there is no wind, repeatedly checking in flight, hovering briefly above suspected prey, and dropping into the grass to catch it if it is finally located, or passing on if it is not. No data are available on the number of unsuccessful attempts made for each successful strike, but in a species such as Montagu's harrier, which can often be watched and followed in completely open country for some time, it would be relatively easy to gather good quantitative data of this sort.

How far a hunting harrier travels by day is a matter of conjecture at present; but in tropical winter quarters the harriers may be on the wing for 9–10 hours each day, and travel at an airspeed of around 20 miles an hour. Theoretically, therefore, they could cover almost 200 air miles (320 km.) in a full day. It is unlikely that they are on the wing for more than half the day, however, as they spend long periods perched and resting on termite mounds, open bare spaces on the ground, or fence posts. In the absence of any detailed quantitative observations on diurnal behaviour it is not possible to say how long or how far a harrier flies, but I would suspect that a Montagu's harrier in Kenya flies between 50 and a 100 miles daily (80–160 km.). This could easily take it up to 10 miles (16 km.) from the roost.

When not hunting Montagu's and other harriers are inclined to fly higher, in a more direct and purposeful manner. When returning to the roost in the evening they often travel straight and quarter the ground much less than they would when hunting, but nevertheless give the impression that they are watching the ground all the time, and will undoubtedly drop on anything eatable seen in passing. In fact, except when they are crossing the sea or woodland, I doubt if harriers in Africa ever travel very far without at least being aware of possible prey in the grass or bushes beneath them. They migrate hunting all the time, so to speak.

In Africa I suspect that most of the prey caught by Montagu's harrier is large insects or small rodents living in the grass, but birds are also included. In its breeding haunts in Europe small mammals, notably voles, are the most important items of prey. In some areas Montagu's harrier lives almost entirely on voles. For instance, in the Vendée district of France, according to Thiollay, Montagu's harriers ate mainly voles, the individuals of a number of pairs coming up to 8 km. (5 miles) from their nesting places to areas where voles were abundant. At peak hunting periods, more than 50 Montagu's harriers might be seen hunting together(13). In forestry plantations in Britain the harriers must also feed very largely on voles.

However, elsewhere small birds are an important food item. Taking Europe as a whole, Uttendorfer lists at least 317 small mammals, 32 hares and rabbits (young), 257 small birds, 32 gamebirds, 88 reptiles, 20 frogs, and several hundred other items mainly large insects(14). Evidently, of all these items, small mammals would be the most important by weight, followed by small birds. A good many eggs are eaten, the shells appearing later in castings(f).

Montagu's harrier is, in fact, a very catholic feeder on any small animal it can get, probably concentrating on certain prey items such as voles or grasshoppers if these happen to be the most numerous and easily caught in a particular area. It cannot kill anything very large, the largest being a young rabbit or leveret, probably not as heavy as the harrier itself; and most bird prey is caught on the ground, not in flight. As in other harriers, although it does undoubtedly take some gamebird chicks, mainly wild bred marshland pheasants or partridges in open country, the proportion of these in the food supply as a whole is small. In Britain one pair at Hickling fed eight partridge chicks to their young one day; but this is not necessarily typical even of that pair. In Cornwall and Devon the main food appears to be reptiles, frogs, small mammals, and small moorland birds such as skylarks and meadow pipits(12). Pellet analysis in another locality in Cornwall in 1950 indicated that the main prey was small birds and reptiles. Although it must be admitted that some gamebirds are taken, it is altogether too sweeping to observe on the evidence of one day at one nest that 'there can be no two opinions as to the menace which this harrier is to game chicks in areas where partridges are really plentiful' as Dr David Bannerman does in his work on British Birds(1). The fact is that where partridges are really plentiful the few pairs of Montagu's harriers could take only a very small proportion of the available stock, while in other areas gamebirds form an insignificant fraction (2%) of the diet (Appendix Table I).

Montagu's and other harriers also use their ears when hunting, and it is recorded that Montagu's can be attracted by imitating the call of a quail; it is shot in Malta and perhaps elsewhere by this means(1). The use of hearing to locate small mammals moving in long dry grass where they might otherwise be quite invisible would obviously be of great value to the harriers, and would narrow the field of search in flight.

Montagu's harrier is present in its Equatorial East African and Southern African winter quarters from October to March; few are seen during April and stragglers that remain into May are probably non-breeding immatures. It is mainly a passage migrant in East Africa, most birds travelling on to winter further south, as far as Cape Province. The wintering quarters in Africa thus extend far further south than in Asia, where the species does not normally leave the mainland to the Indies or cross the Equator(4).

The adult males apparently both leave winter quarters earlier and tend to arrive later. I usually see a few females and immatures of both Montagu's and pallid harriers in October before any males arrive. The southward migration from Europe into winter quarters has been less well observed than the northward passage in spring. I myself have seen harriers, probably Montagu's but perhaps pallid, crossing the Mediterranean north of Cape Bon and west of Port Said, flying low over the waves in steady flapping flight. Since more birds must necessarily travel south in autumn than north in spring, when they are reduced by winter mortality, it seems curious that the movement has not been better observed. Presumably they are then less gregarious and travel on a broad front. It also seems likely that, as in some other raptors such as the red-footed falcon, the northward spring migration follows a more westerly course than the southward autumn migration.

It is especially odd that more Montagu's harriers have not often been recorded in West African savannas, where there were few records up to the fifties(7). The large number of Montagu's harriers crossing from Cape Spartel to Gibraltar each spring indicate that there must at that time be a great many in north West Africa. Either these birds must have been in West Africa all the winter, or they must have crossed Africa from East to West in February and March, at the height of the dry season in the northern West African savannas. Such a movement would increase the length of the migratory journey north by two to three thousand miles, involving at least a month in time as a harrier flies. It seems more likely, therefore, that Montagu's harriers have always wintered in some numbers in West Africa, and that their presence there among much greater numbers of pallid harriers, which are certainly the more numerous of the two species, has gone largely unrecorded until relatively recent times.

The spring move northwards across the straits is dramatic, and has been well described by Dr David Bannerman(2); I have also watched it myself. It normally takes place against a strong wind, the very conditions in which one would think the crossing most difficult. As they approach the straits, planing low over ridges thick with rock rose, broom and other shrubs, the harriers give the impression of being blown about and scarcely able to make progress, sometimes even moving backwards as they rise over a ridge and meet the suddenly increased force of the gale. A moment or so later, however, the same bird is moving purposefully forward again and, on reaching the sea, it sets out firmly across the turbulent straits. Dozens or scores of Montagu's harriers cross the straits in spring in this way between late March and mid April. Although it seems more difficult to cross against the wind in fact the harriers are merely gliding fast into the wind without effort whereas, if they crossed on a calm day, they would have to expend very much more energy in flapping flight. Their flight is strongly reminiscent of gulls moving easily against a strong wind.

There seems no doubt that in this strongly migratory species males arrive on the breeding grounds before the females. In Hungary, where this harrier has been well observed in the breeding season by Laszlo, males arrive four or five days before the females(8). In one area of Cornwall the males arrived about 27–28

April to be followed by females on 3, 9 and 13 May(12). It is normally after mid April or early in May before any Montagu's harriers arrive in Britain, and a record from Horsey on 9 April and two from Surrey on 8 April are unusually early(1). We must assume that all those coming to Britain have crossed the Straits of Gibraltar earlier, and that the flight from there to southern England has normally taken three to four weeks. This makes an East-West crossing of Africa before moving north all the more unlikely.

The breeding haunts of Montagu's harrier in Britain are quite varied and include heathery heathlands, reedbeds and sedge beds in Norfolk and Suffolk; upland grassy or heather moors in north England and Wales; and young forestry plantations with tall dense heather and, in the West of England, sometimes in a dense shrub cover of whins *Ulex gallii*, evidently the same sort of habitat as is used by Irish hen harriers. Montagu's, in fact, breeds in the same sort of terrain as both marsh and hen harriers, and this also seems to be true of parts of Europe. It is necessary, therefore, to identify the species concerned with care, and while this is not difficult in the case of the marsh harrier, Montagu's is much more difficult to distinguish from the hen harrier. However, these two species do not much overlap in their breeding range either in Britain or in Europe, and they might tend to be mutually exclusive. Altitudes of nests recorded on B.T.O. nest record cards are mainly below 250 ft A.S.L. whereas in the southern parts of its British breeding range the hen harrier commonly breeds at more than 1000 ft above the sea. Thus even where both occur Montagu's might be found in similar habitat but in lower and warmer localities. In Europe, Montagu's harrier seems to be able to breed in the same sort of terrain as does the pallid harrier, and cases are on record where female Montagu's have solicited and been fed by male pallid harriers(8).

Soon after arrival on the breeding ground the pair select a feeding and resting area close to the eventual nesting place; this is normally an open rock outcrop or patch of short vegetation. The female feeds here on prey brought by the male. Montagu's harrier is decidedly social wherever it occurs, breeding in Britain in small colonies or groups, with nests very close together, and outside Britain in much larger loose colonies of up to thirty pairs(8). Males are often at least bigamous, mated to two females, while a case is on record where two males occurred in the same area with only one female. In this case the second male was tolerated by the resident pair and lived close to them through the breeding season, but brought no prey to their nest(6). From all published accounts it seems clear that Montagu's harrier shows no very strong territorial behaviour and is considerably more inclined to social breeding in small or large colonies than is the hen harrier, or even the marsh harrier.

The full course of the breeding season has not been completely described anywhere, but a good account can be pieced together from British and European sources. Soon after the arrival of the females the pairs spend much time soaring over the nest site and performing mutual displays. As in other harriers these consist of the male diving towards the female who turns over and presents claws in a symbolic food-pass, a gesture similar to that used later in accepting prey from the male. Such displays may continue for many hours, with striking aerobatics, somersaulting or looping the loop. Alternatively, the male may soar alone above the nesting site, diving down with rapid wingbeats towards the female perched on the ground, and swinging up again to repeat the performance many times. The most spectacular display, performed usually by the male but sometimes also by the female, is a vertical plunge from 100 feet or more with half open wings, rapidly vibrated through a short arc, evidently very much like the vertical plunging display of the hen harrier, which is the culmination of nuptial display just before egg laying. Males usually perform this spectacular manoeuvre to a perched female or to another male; and females may do it to a perched male or by themselves. All these nuptial displays are accompanied by loud calling. The precise sequence, timing and function of these displays of varying intensity is not as yet clear in Montagu's harrier, but is probably similar to the hen harrier.

The nest site is usually 30–100 yards or metres from the feeding and resting area. Much slow soaring over the site precedes its final selection. Several pairs may nest very close together. The three females in one Cornish colony all nested within 1½ acres, two within 20 yards of each other(12). In the Vendée, France, 14 nests were found within 220 hectares (540 acres), and the same seems to be true elsewhere(13). Coition takes place near the nest while on the ground and, as in the hen harrier, the female solicits the male by crouching and uttering a high thin whistle(8,12). Mating takes about ten seconds, and occurs frequently before eggs are laid. The male normally glides straight on to the female's back and does not perch near first.

The nest, as befits a summer migrant arriving late to begin a rather long breeding cycle and with no time to waste is quickly completed. Both sexes bring material to the site, but the female does most of the building. Material if large is carried in the feet, or if small and light in the bill. The nest may be completed within 4–5 days, and is a flattish mound of heather, reeds etc. only about a foot or a foot and a half across and three inches deep, with a central cup lined with finer material about six inches across. It is very hard to find when placed in deep cover, but is obvious enough when placed in low reeds or long grass, as sometimes occurs. Judging from the data available on B.T.O. nest record cards marshy land is sometimes preferred to dry ground, but heather or thick growth inside forestry plantations is commoner, and nests have been recorded in wheatfields and hayfields. Young forestry plantations up to eight feet tall, with the trees covering much of the ground area and the nest hidden in deep cover may be used, or an entirely open site on sand-dunes(b).

Three to six eggs are normally laid, usually at 2-day intervals so that as in other harriers a large clutch may take 10 days to deposit. Occasionally very large clutches of 8 or 10 are recorded, and one of 10 at Hickling was laid over at least 20 days from 10–30 May, with even laying intervals of 2–3 days, so that it was unlikely to be either the product of two females or, as in hen harriers, a premature repeat clutch by the same female in the same nest(h). The mean of 18 British clutches is 4·16, which is up to the average recorded in Europe(b). Twelve Hungarian clutches of 3–6 average 4·7, but small clutches may have been omitted; Laszlo considered that clutches of 3 were laid only by young females. Eggs are not normally laid in Britain before late May: in Devon and Cornwall 13–28 May, Hants and Dorset 19 May to 6 June, Anglesey 15–31 May, and in one Yorkshire nest about 20 June. During egg laying the female remains near the nest, does not hunt, and is fed by the male. She begins to sit before the clutch is complete, but precise details are lacking on this aspect of behaviour.

Incubation, according to Laszlo, takes 29–30 days, and other estimates are from 27–30 days, about a week less than in other British harriers. The eggs hatch at intervals over up to 7 days, but as in the hen harrier the hatching period is normally shorter than the laying period, indicating that the female does not incubate properly before several eggs have been laid. One Hungarian clutch of 5 hatched 4 young on 18 June and the 5th on 22 June, indicating a laying interval of at least 4 days for the last egg(8). Hatching success, as in other harriers, is likely to be poor. In 19 nests in which 78 eggs were laid 52 (66·7%) hatched and 26 failed from various natural causes. More data are obviously needed on such aspects of breeding, but this record is not inferior to that of the hen harrier in a peak population in Orkney.

The young, at first clad in scanty buffish down, are helpless at first, but after five days acquire a thicker down coat and are then more active. The youngest of the brood usually dies early in the fledging period, not because of aggression by its nest-mates but because it is weak and small, or cannot get enough food. The chicks are not aggressive to one another and until about 12 days old remain in the nest; after that they can stagger about and begin to sprout feathers, which cover the body but not the head at 28 days. As soon as they can walk they move into the shade or shelter of surrounding vegetation, and can be killed by exposure to hot sun even when 20 days old and partly feathered(8). They make their first flights at 32–42 days after hatching, usually between 35 and 40 days.

The young in the nest can probably be sexed by eye colour in the same way as can hen harriers; that is, the males have grey eyes and the females brown. This is suggested by Laszlo but not positively proven, and is a point that should be checked by future observers. Since the adult females are markedly heavier than the males it should be possible to confirm this by weighing individuals of comparable age, on the basis of feather development or other such characters.

As in all other harriers known the roles of the adults are clear cut. Throughout building, egg laying, incubation, and the early fledging period the male feeds the female and the brood, and in some cases continues to do so throughout the fledging period as well. Bigamy occurs, but is perhaps rather uncommon as it has not often been noted(c). When it does occur it does not apparently result in poorer breeding success. One British case involved two females, each of which laid five eggs, and which reared four and three young(c). Neither of these females hunted much until the young were well-grown and most of the prey was brought by the male throughout. Clearly, in this case, the male must at one stage have been providing for himself and nine other harriers altogether, indicating that he had no great difficulty in feeding such a large family and that a normal male with one mate and brood should have no difficulty at all. Some males feed their mates and broods right up to the time of first flight; however a female has also been known to rear a brood in the absence of a male(g).

The amount of time spent hunting by harriers varies according to the stage of the nesting cycle, the number of the brood or broods, and the size of the prey obtainable. In the incubation period the male may feed the female 5 or 6 times per day, but this is increased as soon as the brood hatch and by the time they are 14 days old, when the female is still with them and not hunting, the male must bring at least 10–12 kills per day, averaging one every 1½ hours of a summer's day. At Horsey it was noted that little hunting took place very early or very late, and that one male brought on average 16 kills between 10·30 and 17·20, occasionally achieving up to 25 kills in that time, or better than three per hour(5).

On the other hand, in the Vendée of France Thiollay observed that harriers hunted most in the early hours of the morning and in the evening, with peaks soon after six o'clock and again between eight and nine in the evening(13). In this case the harriers rested in the heat of the day, when only 40% of maximum activity was noted. These observations were made in the first two weeks in July when the young in the nest were large and the females were beginning to take part in hunting. Thiollay estimated that the males brought 85% of the prey eaten by the young and

25% of that eaten by females, the latter providing 15% of the food of the young and three-quarters of their own. Feeding at the nest could occur at any time from sunrise at 05·22 to just after nine o'clock, an hour after sunset. An average family of male, female and three young required 23–26 small animals per day, and the hunting parents ate some prey away from the nest, especially in the evening. In this case 30 pairs of Montagu's harriers, or 60 birds, were feeding largely on the voles in about 2000 hectares (5000 acres) of land, and they took 18–22 items of prey to the nests per day in 23–25 visits by the males, or better than one per hour. Even so, this amounted to only 5·6 small mammals per hectare (2·3 per acre) per 15 days, about one-sixth to one-fifteenth of the available vole population. Thus even a dense population of harriers, hunting in a confined locality, and coming up to 5 miles (8 km.) to reach it, could have little real depressing effect on the population of voles.

Breeding success of the British Montagu's harriers appears to be up to the average elsewhere. The average brood size in 13 cases on B.T.O. cards where all the young were old enough to ring was 3·25, varying from 1–5; in 12 of these cases 38 young flew, averaging 3·16. This seems as good as in most continental areas, though Laszlo considered that average broods of four would be reared from clutches of five in Hungary, without giving precise details(8). These figures refer to successful nests only; the proportion of non-breeding birds is not established, though it seems to be small. The average clutch size in British nests is 5·15, and if 67% of these hatch (as indicated earlier) the average brood hatched, including all failures, will be 2·8. Fledging success, on the evidence of B.T.O. nest record cards for 13 broods is 28 young from 53 hatched (52·8%) so that from average broods of 2·8 it is 1·47 per pair which bred. This is probably nearer the true productivity of Montagu's harrier than records derived only from successful broods. Though the figures are too small to be able to draw very sound conclusions this is not inferior to the productivity of the hen harrier overall, (1·41 young per pair which bred), indicating that it is not poor breeding success which prevents Montagu's harrier from increasing in Britain, but probably other natural or artificial causes which may not be controllable.

Observations in Norfolk suggest that the young Montagu's harriers may actually be coaxed out of the nest by the parents. The oldest and most active young is said to be induced to fly towards the female, which it imagines has food, while the male feeds the remainder in the nest(5). The older young bird then returns to the nest, but is too late to get any prey. It then makes a flight for some distance and is at once rewarded with food. These observations, which are of their type unique except for Col. Meinertzhagen's observations at one osprey nest, and certainly very unusual for any bird of prey, require confirmation. Normally as soon as young Montagu's harriers can they fly to meet the parent bringing food to the nest; and quite evidently some will be unable to obtain food at first in this way for as long as young remain there the parent will go to the nest first. However, in the normal course of events all the young that fly soon become expert in receiving food from the adults by the aerial food pass technique. Leaving the nest in late July or early August, they remain in the area for three or four weeks, but start to leave in late August or early September on migration. By mid September no adults or young remain in Britain, and by early October some have reached Africa.

Immediately after leaving the nest area the young seem to perform a random dispersal, often moving west or east, not south, though eventually they move south-east towards Europe. Of those recovered in Britain three were dead in the nests, five had gone less than 20 miles, four 20–50 miles, four 50–100, three 100–200, and only one more than 200 miles (320 km.). The most interesting of these records was a six-year-old male shot in 1949 at Hickling, where it was reared in 1943 or 1944. Several young were recovered a year or more later, evidently as young adults or subadults about to breed. Thus one ringed in Anglesey in 1950 was shot in Yorkshire in the following August; another Anglesey youngster was found dead near a nest with four eggs at Dalry, Kirkcudbright in its second summer; one ringed on Dartmoor in 1948 was recovered alive in Anglesey the following August; one ringed in 1952 in the New Forest was recovered at Tresco, Scilly Isles in its second spring; and one ringed in Dorset in 1956 was shot as the female of a breeding pair at Fordingbridge, Hants, in 1958.

These records all indicate that the young, if they survive their first winter, may return to breed in Britain but not often to the area in which they themselves were bred. Unfortunately, they also show conclusively that many of those recovered are shot, even after 1954 when this harrier was completely protected. Two young ringed at Horsey in 1934 were both shot, one at Bawdsey, Suffolk the same summer and the other near King's Lynn the following summer, said to be carrying a pheasant chick. One young ringed at Stokeferry in Norfolk in 1958 was shot two summers later near Sandy, Bedfordshire, not, I assume, by any member of the R.S.P.B. The birds that were not admittedly shot were often 'found dead' which may mean that they had been shot earlier and left to decompose, or trapped. These are only the admitted cases; no doubt many are shot and quietly flung into bushes to rot. Only a few of the short distance recoveries probably mean natural death.

Only one foreign-ringed Montagu's harrier has been recovered in Britain. One ringed in Texel in 1928 was recovered in Suffolk the following June, indicating that it behaved like some of the British ringed young recovered in Britain and moved to another breeding area not close to where it was ringed(10). This record indicates that there is some interchange between the Dutch and British populations in our favour, for none of our Montagu's harriers have been recovered in Holland.

The foreign recoveries of British ringed birds are set out on Map 22. So far no British ringed Montagu's harrier has been recovered in Africa, which must presumably be their ultimate destination, though it is quite possible that the British population may not migrate so far as more northerly breeding birds. Most of the recoveries are from France, with a few from Portugal. Whenever the cause of death is openly stated the birds have been shot or have been killed; similar causes may be assumed where no statement of the cause is made. Numbers of migrating hawks are killed by gunners in south-west France each year, and when they cross the Pyrenees; one need look no further for the cause of death in many of the young British Montagu's harriers which do not return.

Looking at this record the cause of the recent decline of the Montagu's harrier in Britain seems clearer. Here we have a species which admittedly is probably ecologically restricted to the warmer parts of England as a regular breeder, but which can also breed successfully further north if left alone. It lays average clutches and rears average broods as large as the much more successful hen harrier or as continental Montagu's harriers, so that one cause of decline suspected in the marsh harrier does not appear to apply. But it is a migrant, and is shot too often in Britain soon after leaving the nesting area or, if not then, as soon as it reaches France. One may well wonder whether increased persecution is not the sole cause of the decline, and whether the peak population of the fifties was not solely due to

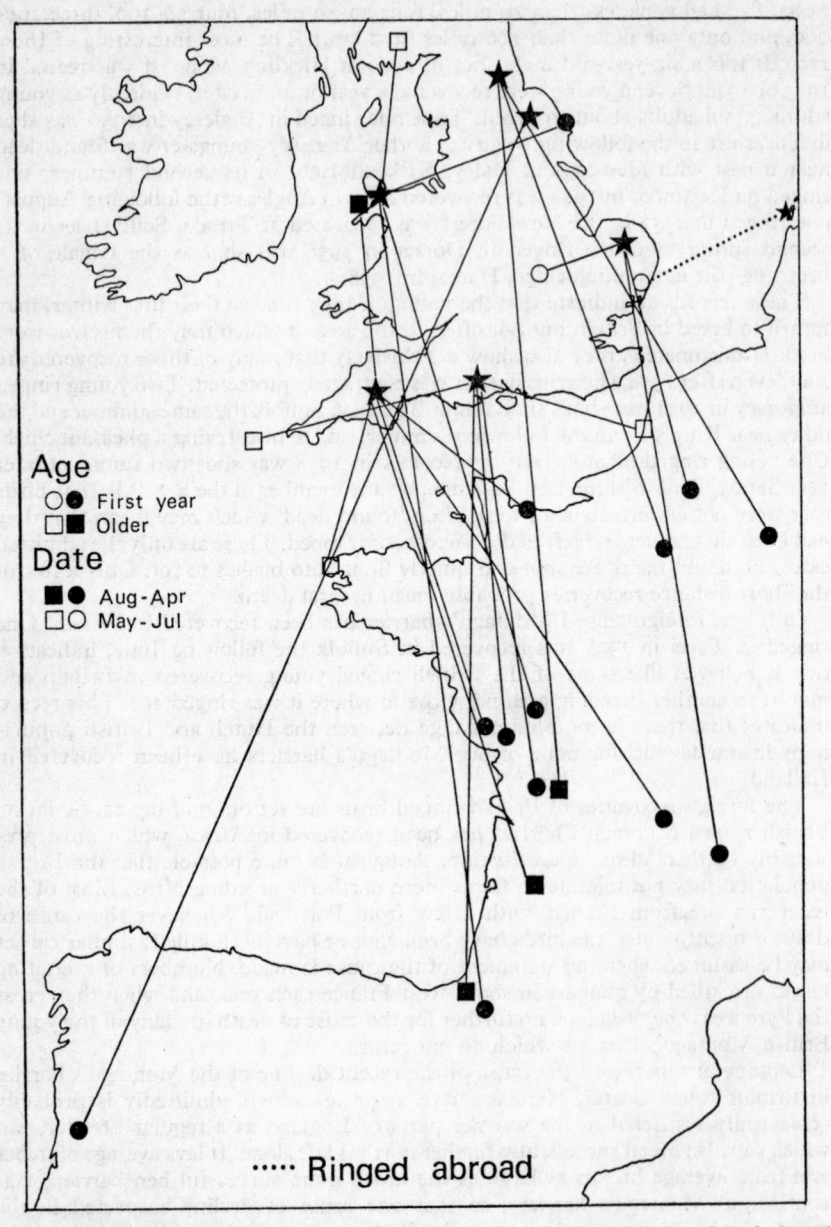

Age

○ ● First year
□ ■ Older

Date

■ ● Aug - Apr
□ ○ May - Jul

..... Ringed abroad

MAP 22. Montagu's harrier: recoveries of British-ringed birds, with one ringed abroad recovered in Britain.

a reduction of persecution during and just after World War II. At least reduced persecution is the first remedy to try if we want to have the Montagu's harrier back in the numbers existing in Britain twenty years ago.

Records do not indicate that Montagu's harrier is naturally a long-lived species. Since its breeding biology and replacement rate is very similar to that of the hen harrier it probably lives about as long as that species or slightly less. At an average brood size of 1·47 per pair which bred and 66% mortality in the first winter (which seems likely) an adult pair need only live two to three years to replace themselves. Montagu's harriers of either sex may be able to breed in their second summer, when just under a year old, and certainly can when they are just under two years old(8). Such young birds may lay smaller clutches and be less successful breeders than older birds. Males can be aged quite successfully, at least in the hand, by plumage characters; younger males are mottled or ringed with brown in the grey plumage. Thus it should be possible to estimate the age structure of breeding British Montagu's harriers and see whether this indicates a large predominance of young males. If so, this is a further indication that the species is in trouble, and that no surplus of subadults can build up to stimulate the type of spread and colonisation of new areas observed in the fifties, and which may simply have been due to less persecution than Montagu's harrier suffers at present.

THE GOSHAWK

THERE appears to be little point in writing at length about the goshawk in Britain since, although there have been persistent rumours of increased if sporadic breeding in this country for about the last three decades, factual evidence for this in the published literature is negligible. It would be completely impossible for anyone with access only to literary sources to make a good estimate of the number of breeding pairs that exist in Britain, if any. The sole recent contribution to the literature is a note by Col. Richard Meinertzhagen in 1950, in which he recorded probable breeding in a certain locality in southern England back to 1928(11), and Philip Brown in his book *Birds of Prey* records that he actually saw one occupied nest in England(2). But for the most part rumour prevails; and until it becomes fact or not no competent assessment of the goshawk's real status in Britain is possible.

The official British Ornithologists' Union List Committee's opinion on this subject is that the goshawk is a scarce winter visitor and a casual occasional breeder in Britain, or perhaps an extremely rare regular breeder(14). Pending publication of further factual data this view must be accepted. The number of breeding pairs may be anything from two to twenty, according to verbal estimates I have received, but I have thought it best to say here that there are probably less than ten. Whether any or all of these are genuine wild birds that have re-established themselves here from outside, or whether they are all falconers' escapes or the offspring of falconers' escapes is unknown; some of them certainly are falconers' escapes, for they have jesses and bells. However I personally can see no reason why the first generation offspring of falconers' escapes should not be regarded as wild British goshawks from now on, if they in fact exist.

Rumours of breeding pairs have recently come from Sussex, where several pairs were said to have bred up to 1951; these probably refer to Col. Meinertzhagen's pairs but I have heard no recent rumours from here. In preparing this book I have been told of breeding goshawks on the Welsh borders; in Northumberland; in Perthshire; and in the Spey basin in recent years, while in the summer of 1972 I also had reports of adults from the New Forest, Bute, and Kintail. If these breeding birds all exist in fact the goshawk is scarce but widespread as a breeding species in Britain. You may take your choice – two or twenty breeding pairs, according to taste; or be conservative like me and the B.O.U. list committee and say 'less than ten pairs, if any regular breeders exist'.

It seems to me tragic, and symptomatic of the utterly unrealistic attitude of the British towards their birds of prey that such a situation can exist at all. Here we have a magnificent raptor, undoubtedly formerly a resident of these islands, when they were better wooded than they are now, and when gamekeeping did not dominate the scene to the same extent, to whose existence no one will now openly admit for fear that a horde of egg collectors, game preservers and, not least, casual birdwatchers 'twitching' goshawks in which they have no real interest may descend on the spot and blight carefully nurtured hopes of re-establishment.

The situation of the goshawk is strictly comparable to that of the osprey. Both had become extinct in Britain in the nineteenth or early twentieth century, mainly through persecution(1). Both may have or have re-established themselves as scarce breeding birds since 1950. But the one is received with a blaze of publicity, reported on the B.B.C. and in the national press, and rigorously protected, while the other is the subject of unreliable rumour and might at once be blotted out of existence by game preserving interests or egg collectors if its whereabouts were revealed. Certainly one cannot compare the osprey and the goshawk directly, for one is an extremely accommodating aquatic species while the other is a relatively shy and secretive inhabitant of woodland and forest. However the parallel needs drawing and to me it underlines the nearly absolute lack of objective judgement directed by a race supposed to be both civilised and intelligent towards the wild creatures in their midst.

Certainly there are plenty of places in Britain where the goshawk could re-establish itself if given a chance. Goshawks are birds of woodland or forest, resembling sparrowhawks in most of their habits, but needing larger undisturbed tracts of forest in which to breed. In areas of Europe in our latitudes, where deciduous forest is the natural climax vegetation a pair needs 8000–12,000 acres (3500–5000 ha.) of mixed woodland and open country (of which one-fifth to one-quarter should be woodland) in which to hunt, and a large secluded tract of woodland in which to nest(3). Some of the larger planted forests of the Forestry Commission certainly provide the latter, as do some private woodlands. Ecologically, I can see nothing to stop goshawks breeding in, for instance, the Tay Valley between Rohallion and Pitlochry, where there is room for several pairs; or, further south, in Thetford Chase or Kielder Forest. Goshawks seem to prefer coniferous woodlands and to be most numerous in northern spruce and fir forests; so the dark uniform stands of Forestry Commission woodlands are not necessarily repellent or unsuitable, and the more open stands resulting (in rather rare instances) from a policy of amenity planting and thinning to produce large mature trees should be ideal.

There is also plenty of suitable prey. Britain swarms with unwanted woodpigeons, with corvids, starlings, and other birds that are common goshawk prey in ecologically comparable parts of Europe; and rabbits in Britain have now recovered sufficiently well from myxomatosis to be at least as abundant as they are in much of continental Europe, where goshawks feed on them. Goshawks could both breed and feed in Britain. Why don't they, in greater and greater numbers each year? Is it because some of the best habitat is on private estates where they are instantly killed when they appear; or is the explanation more complicated than that?

One possible reason is that it seems certain that the goshawk became extinct as a regular breeder long before the osprey. In Roman and Mediaeval times, when much of Britain was covered with continuous or large broken areas of deciduous or coniferous forest, goshawks must have been relatively numerous, as were sparrowhawks. However, most of this forest was cut down for industry or shipbuilding, or opened up for agriculture, especially after the enclosure acts brought about better husbandry practices(15). By 1700 forest and woodland had been reduced to 16% of the total area but this would still have been adequate for many goshawks. It was still further reduced till, in 1800 and shortly after, it fell to a low of only 5%(5). More than nine-tenths of the once abundant forests and woodlands of Britain had by then been cleared, and probably much of what remained was in scattered areas individually too small to support pairs of goshawks. The sparrowhawk can survive well in such country of small woodlands and open farmland but it is apparent that goshawks do require bigger tracts of deciduous or coniferous woodland. Thus it is likely that the goshawk was already extremely scarce and localised in Britain by 1800.

Then came the game preserving era, and the few remaining regular pairs would have been relentlessly pursued and blotted out. It seems improbable that the goshawk can have been anything but a very rare bird for around two hundred years. Ian Newton considers that the goshawk was as numerous as it could be in restricted areas of suitable habitat in Scotland between 1800-40, but had become extinct by 1900(12). However there appears to be no good ecological reason to suggest that it could have been numerous anywhere in Britain in the first half of the nineteenth century though it survived in patches of suitable habitat. In Ireland it is obvious that the goshawk has for a very long time been extremely scarce. There are only about fourteen records listed by Ruttledge since the beginning of the nineteenth century, and most or all of these are for winter migrants(13).

Natural recolonisation of Britain by goshawks from adjacent countries in Europe is also becoming more difficult, because in all these countries the goshawk has decreased sharply in the last twenty years principally through the effects of agricultural pesticides. At the I.C.B.P. conference at Caen in 1964, at which the status of European birds of prey was assessed, severe decreases in goshawks were recorded in Holland and Germany, less drastic but considerable decreases elsewhere(7). In northern taiga woodlands in Finland, and the Soviet Union the goshawk is still very abundant; 3000 are still shot annually on licence in Finland(a). However, these are more migratory northern forms, which are less likely to colonise Britain than would a surplus of breeding population from Holland, Germany or Denmark. Such a surplus does not now exist, if it ever did in recent times, so that genuine natural colonisation by surplus wild birds resulting from an increase of a continental population, which is apparently what happened in the case of the osprey, seems now very unlikely in the goshawk.

If natural colonisation is unlikely it remains to be seen what can be done by artificial re-introduction. British falconers often keep goshawks, obtaining their birds from Europe; and some of these escape. Owing to the increasing difficulty of obtaining wild European goshawks (though if 3000 a year are shot in Finland this is surely absurd) British falconers are anxious to re-establish the goshawk here. Probably any birds that bred in Britain in the fifties were actually falconer's escapes, though it is also possible that at that time, just after the Second World War, there may have been a small real surplus of wild birds from Europe.

I believe that falconers are, at present, attempting to re-establish the goshawk in several parts of Britain. Young have been obtained and are being hand reared for release in suitable areas. A steady programme of release over five years or more might establish a small population in suitable forested areas. It will then remain to be seen whether this population can stay alive and breed in these areas or whether it will move out, to be immediately exterminated by gamekeepers. No one else is likely to wipe it out, but it is possible that goshawks may not be able to survive permanently in dense young conifer plantations, which support abundant woodpigeons in summer but are short of suitable prey in winter. Goshawks might then be obliged to move into more open country, to meet with increased hazards from both guns and pesticides. However, we must hope that the efforts to re-establish the goshawk will succeed, and that we shall once again be able to count this magnificent raptor among our permanent residents.

There will evidently be strong opposition in some quarters as to the propriety of re-introducing goshawks at all. It seems to me reasonable to re-introduce species that once occurred in Britain but which have become extinct through persecution, if this can be done successfully; and the goshawk certainly deserves the effort, as does the sea eagle. However to allay possible fears it would be as well to assess carefully the likely ecological effects of goshawks in Britain, and to do this one must depend on other sources of information, for nothing worthwhile is recorded of the goshawk in Britain itself.

The goshawk has been extensively studied in Europe and in America, both from the viewpoint of its food requirements and feeding habits and its breeding ecology(4,8,9,10,16). The food requirement of a goshawk is about 150-200 grams per day, according to sex, females requiring more than males; one woodpigeon provides two days' rations. A recent ten-year ecological study of a pair of German goshawks showed that they could survive and breed in a summer range of 3600 hectares (11·6 square miles) which expanded to 5000 hactares (19·3 square miles)in winter(3). In this area 3875 recorded prey included 54 predatory birds and mammals (varying from shrikes to buzzards and domestic cats) and 404 game birds, mainly partridges (a very small fraction of those that existed). It was shown that goshawks had a selective effect on the partridge population by killing surplus males (as also happens, for instance with other predators in red grouse of either sex in Scotland). In America, goshawks also exert a selective effect in populations of woodland grouse by taking the displaying males(6).

However, the proportion of game birds in the diet in Germany is relatively very small. The majority (1435/3875 of all bird kills) were pigeons and doves, mainly woodpigeons; and other small birds (1059/3875) including many starlings and turdines. Goshawks also are effective killers of corvids up to the size of a carrion crow, and their extinction results in an increase of corvids in the general population. They also take many rabbits and an occasional hare.

This study concluded that there was little or no evidence that the goshawk was harmful to human interests, and that they fed mainly on the commonest prey available, which was usually pigeons or the larger passerines. Undoubtedly, in Britain, the goshawk would depend heavily on our over-abundant woodpigeon population; but it could not conceivably be an effective controlling agent in view of the relative abundance of hawks and pigeons, though this would need study. It would also kill numbers of corvids, some of which, at least, are regarded as harmful to game preserving interests or to sheep farmers. Although it must be freely admitted that the goshawk does kill gamebirds the total number killed is relatively small in relation to the total population. In the German study area concerned it amounted to about 40 per year in 8000 acres (5000 ha.), which had no significant effect. In any well stocked British game preserving area such a total would be negligible and would probably be counterbalanced by the other ecological effects of the goshawk, for instance in reducing the population of crows, jays, and even sparrowhawks.

Most other available studies of the ecological effects of the goshawk produce similar results. For instance, in Lorraine, of 510 food items, 495 were birds, but these included only two gamebirds(17). Other data are given in Appendix Table I. In Finland, in the northern coniferous forest zone, the goshawk does feed mainly on gamebirds(16). However, these conditions are not ecologically comparable to Britain, while German or French results should quite accurately indicate what might happen here.

There are therefore no really good grounds for opposition to the introduction of the species in suitable areas. Farmers, who are plagued by woodpigeons, should actually welcome the return of the goshawk, and for all others but game preservers the possible effects are essentially neutral. However, there is no evidence that anyone in Britain, other than a few knowledgeable scientists, is capable of judging such a situation objectively and many will certainly base their conclusions, as usual, on ingrained prejudice and bigoted ignorance.

In its breeding habits the goshawk is just like a big sparrowhawk. Favourite nesting sites are stable and used year after year by a succession of different birds(8). Such a site has several nests in a small area of woodland; these may be built afresh each year, or be used again and again for several years. The nests are usually 30–60 feet (10–20 m.) up, either in conifers or broad-leaved deciduous trees. As in the sparrowhawk they are broad flattish structures and, just before egg-laying, they are lined with chips of bark or sometimes with fresh green sprigs.

The neighbourhood of the nest is advertised, especially in early morning and evening, by display flights, which are very similar to those of the sparrowhawk, with soaring, slow wing-flapping, and some shallow undulating flights. The female is said to attract the male into the nesting area by perching there and calling. By one authority the male is said to do most of the nest building, but this would be very unusual in any raptor and needs confirmation(8). Mating begins with nest building, occurs up to ten times daily, and continues through most of the incubation period, for about 40–50 days altogether; this again would seem to need confirmation as it is unusual for mating to continue long after eggs are laid. Mating is often associated with the presentation of food and, as in the sparrowhawk, the female is dependent on the male for food during incubation, in which period she undergoes part of her annual moult.

One to five eggs are laid; clutches of 1 or 2 are probably abnormal and 3–5 is usual. Clutch size, and subsequent brood size is affected by the relative abundance of prey, at least in Finland(16). According to Holstein, in Denmark incubation proper does not begin till all the eggs are laid and the total period may be 45 days, of which only 25 days is true incubation(8). More usually, incubation is estimated at 36–38 days, and Holstein's findings need confirmation. The female only incubates, and the male brings prey. She usually leaves the nest to feed in answer to his call. The male spends much time perched near the nest and can apparently catch whatever prey is necessary at this stage in short hunting periods.

The young are said by Holstein to hatch almost simultaneously, but there is some difference in sizes in the nest partly because females grow more rapidly than males; like young sparrowhawks the young are not very aggressive to one another. They sprout feathers at 18 days, can feed themselves at 28 days, and are fully feathered by 38 days. They fly at about 45 days old, but have already moved out on to branches from the age of 35 days onwards. Males are smaller, lighter, more active, and fly earlier, as in the sparrowhawk.

The female broods the new hatched young closely for 8–10 days, and thereafter remains near the nest. At this stage she can be exceedingly aggressive to a human intruder, attacking vigorously and repeatedly with loud harsh calling and on occasion actually striking home. An angry female goshawk is decidedly alarming in thick forest. After 16 days the female stays further from the nest, but she still feeds the young up to 28 days old; if she were not present they would probably starve without her aid though captive young can feed themselves earlier. Up to this stage the male does not usually bring prey to the nest, but passes it to the female some distance away; after 28 days, when the young can feed themselves, either of the adults takes prey direct to the nest, where the young tear it up.

However, in some cases at least the female is said not to hunt regularly till the young can fly.

There are certain rather aberrant features in Holstein's account of the breeding cycle, notably the lengthy incubation period, the protraction of mating after laying, and the statement that the female does not hunt till the young can actually fly, which should be confirmed or refuted by fresh studies; but the general similarity to the breeding behaviour of the sparrowhawk will be evident.

After the young fly they remain partially or wholly dependent on the parents for another 50 days; after that they can kill for themselves, but are said not to be completely independent till 70 days after first flight(8). The goshawk thus has, as would be expected, a much longer nesting cycle than the sparrowhawk. In Britain, if eggs are laid in late April, they would hatch about the beginning of June, the young would fly in mid July, and would become independent in mid September. Captive young released have shown their ability to kill before the normal independence date, in the absence of parents.

The amount of food required naturally depends on the size of the brood. The male brings in an average of five or six kills a day during the fledging period, and for a brood of two young the food requirement in the nest is estimated at altogether 13 kg. (28½ lb)(8). However, broods are often more than two young; in 198 Finnish cases they varied from 3·1 in years of abundant food to 2·7 in years when food was not abundant(16). A brood of three would require about 20 kg. (44 lb) of food altogether while in the nest, and another 25 kg (55 lb) in the post-fledging period, when they are still mainly dependent on the adults. The requirement of the adults and their brood over the entire year up to independence of the young would be about 143 kg. (269½ lb). This is actually equivalent, allowing for waste, to about 300 full-grown woodpigeons; but in practice the requirement would be provided by much larger numbers of young woodpigeons and smaller birds. However, it seems clear that even quite a large population of goshawks with an average home range per pair of 8–10,000 acres (3–4000 ha.) would have little effect on the total woodpigeon populations, though they might selectively attack nesting pigeons in spring and summer.

Presumably it will be several years before any studies of breeding goshawks can be made in Britain. The majority of goshawks seen here are probably migrants. They occur mainly in the south, east, and north of Britain, and at two periods of peak migration, August to November and again March to May, presumably moving south or north respectively(14). Goshawks are usually seen annually, and nowadays when one is seen numbers of people try to go and identify it. However, since European goshawks are not racially distinct, it is never certain whether these birds are visitors from abroad, wanderers from unknown British breeding areas, or even falconers' escapes – though the last at least should be relatively easily identified, as they are likely to be tamer than true wild birds and may have jesses or bells still attached to their feet.

The goshawk is the commonest hawk now used in falconry in Britain; if it were not so difficult to train it would undoubtedly be still more popular, for it is an extremely effective killer of gamebirds and large mammals. It is flown at prey by throwing it from the hand direct, and is not released to wait on above the falconer like a peregrine. The smaller sparrowhawk is flown in just the same way, as are several other species of *Accipiter*. Goshawks are difficult to train because of their nervous temperament, which makes them inclined to tantrums, bating, and other faults. But once they are well trained they are very useful game-getters and can be flown at anything from partridges to hares; only a strong female can take a hare. Wild goshawks only kill hares occasionally; but they take many more ground mammals, especially rabbits, than do sparrowhawks.

In its manner of hunting the goshawk is similar to the sparrowhawk, but far more impressive. A female goshawk is almost as big as a buzzard, but infinitely swifter and more savage in general appearance. The flashing orange-yellow eye of an adult goshawk is especially beautiful. Goshawks are capable of astonishing bursts of speed over short distances, and combine this with an agility in the quick turn very little inferior to the much smaller sparrowhawk. Relatively, their feet and legs are very much more powerful than those of sparrowhawks, no doubt because they do occasionally need to subdue mammalian prey larger and heavier than they are themselves.

I fear that the time is still far distant when we can hope to see a goshawk hunting regularly in British woodland. If it ever comes about, it can only be through a determined and prolonged effort to reintroduce the species, in the sort of numbers that will permit the establishment of a viable breeding population in one or more centres, from which the species can then spread. This will need to be correlated with a far more realistic attitude towards birds of prey in general than at present exists in Britain, and a willingness on the part of gamekeepers and their employers to listen to reason and fact, obey the law, and not merely act from prejudice or ignorance. Personally, in view of the obstacles, I do not feel hopeful that the goshawk will be as successful in re-establishing itself as the osprey; but I would like to think that it might be so, and no one will be better pleased than I if the vague estimates of existing numbers I have given here prove grossly erroneous. I would very much like to be proved wrong in all these rather pessimistic forecasts, and to know that there are more than ten breeding pairs of goshawks in the British Isles.

CHAPTER 12

THE SPARROWHAWK

ALTHOUGH the sparrowhawk has decreased greatly in the last two decades, to the extent that not so long ago fears were expressed for its ultimate survival, it is still one of the commonest British diurnal raptors. Despite unremitting illegal persecution by gamekeepers and the adverse effects of toxic chemicals used in agriculture this adaptable and dashing little hawk still is found in some areas at very high breeding densities. Owing to its secretive habits it is often overlooked even when it is relatively common, and a deliberate search in any area not subject to the effects of pesticides will almost invariably reveal more sparrowhawks than were thought to exist.

Although it has been seriously affected by organo-chlorine pesticides it is not now thought to be in danger of extinction, and has lately shown remarkable powers of recovery from a low population point in the late fifties and early sixties; this recovery has coincided with reduced use of organo-chlorine pesticides in agriculture(6).

At one time, when most of Britain was wooded, the sparrowhawk must have been by a very large margin the most abundant British raptor. It would then have been much more abundant than its only possible rivals, the kestrel and the buzzard, since both of these prefer open country while sparrowhawks could thrive in dense woodland. Even in terrain of mixed woodlands and open fields the sparrowhawk still is almost as, or more numerous than, the kestrel, and where woodland predominates is the commoner species. It has the advantage of normally building its own nest, whereas the kestrel is completely dependent on natural cavities, cliff ledges, or the old nests of corvids or other birds of prey. In pesticide-free areas, therefore, the sparrowhawk is only limited by the availability of suitable nesting woods (which generally are available even in agricultural areas) whereas there are many areas of open moorland otherwise suited to kestrels in which these falcons are scarcer than they might be because of lack of nesting sites.

If sparrowhawks occurred in mediaeval Britain in the same breeding densities as they are found today in good habitat they could have been numbered by the hundred thousand. Breeding densities at present can reach a maximum of 5–6 pairs per square mile (2 per sq.km.), which, with their large broods late in the summer, mean 30–35 sparrowhawks per square mile (11–13 per sq.km.) altogether(6). In Great Britain and Ireland there might have been about 75,000 square miles of suitable habitat, so that at this peak density a figure of half a million breeding adults in the British Isles is by no means fanciful. However, present day or recent densities of breeding sparrowhawks in Europe do not normally approach 5 per square mile, partly because a healthy population of goshawks keeps the sparrowhawks in check(17). Density overall in Britain is therefore unlikely to have exceeded a pair per square mile. Perhaps there never were more than a quarter of a million British sparrowhawks. However, today's much reduced population must be thought of in relation to this now almost incredible former abundance.

Up to about 1800 the main factor adversely affecting the sparrowhawk was the reduction in extent of suitable nesting woodlands, as existing forests were felled without replanting, and more and more land was opened up for agriculture. Even then, a very large population must have remained. However, after 1800 it was, like every other raptor in Britain, subject to severe persecution in any area where game preserving took place. Owing to its native cunning and secretive ways the sparrow-hawk was able to survive the ravages of gamekeepers better than most raptors and it remained a relatively common predator. Persecution undoubtedly reduced the sparrowhawk population to a level far below the maximum that could have existed in any area, but there were always some pairs breeding in isolated undisturbed woodlands while the large broods reared by successful pairs meant a substantial increase in the population each summer(9). Where the adults were not as numerous as they could be these young probably had a better chance of survival and could breed in their first year, when eight to nine months old.

The persecution did greatly reduce the population, as was shown by the very marked and rapid increase that took place during and just after the Second World War, when gamekeepers were away and preserving reduced. At the end of the war in 1945 the number of young sparrowhawks ringed annually in relation to those of other birds was about seven times what it was in 1940(7). The sparrowhawk population in many areas must at least have quadrupled, and by 1945 this hawk may well have been more numerous than at any time since 1800.

After 1945 the return of gamekeepers and game preserving led to widespread decrease through renewed persecution. The sparrowhawk was the only British diurnal raptor not completely protected by the 1954 Bird Preservation Act. Since this Act has been and is singularly ineffective in preventing persecution of sparrow-hawks, or any other raptor, by gamekeepers it is doubtful if this exception had much long-term effect on the sparrowhawk's status. In any case, it was shortly to be varied in the sparrowhawk's favour because of an unprecedented decrease that became apparent soon after the Act was passed.

By 1955 a marked decline in the numbers of sparrowhawks, in areas where they had recently been common was already apparent, and by 1960 it had become catastrophic. So sudden and complete was the decline in many areas of Britain that it must have been due to wholesale deaths among the adults, and not only to the poor breeding success noted in sparrowhawks and other birds of prey at that time. The effects were worst in cereal growing districts, and in such counties as Lincoln the sparrowhawk became extinct by 1960(14). The decline was similar to that observed in other *Accipiter* species in other countries, and in other bird-eating raptors such as the peregrine falcon, and was clearly due to some new and hitherto unknown factor.

This decline in the sparrowhawk population is discussed more fully in the chapter on pesticides. Here it suffices to say that adults practically disappeared from cereal-growing districts in eastern England and lowland eastern Scotland, while breeding success also fell off drastically in any areas adjacent to cereal-growing fields. Before 1950, in the absence of persecution 100 pairs of sparrow-hawks could be expected to rear 400 fledglings per year, but by 1961–70 only 197; even this figure is probably rather higher than that for the late fifties, for which period there are few statistics(8). The reduction was due to increased failure to hatch complete or partial clutches, egg-eating and other related factors, and was not due to a reduction in mean clutch size.

After 1962 a voluntary ban was partially effective on the use of the more toxic seed dressings in spring, while the use of DDT was also reduced. Breeding success, in terms of the number of young reared per egg laid, is still much lower than in the period before 1950, but nevertheless there has certainly been some recovery in the numbers of sparrowhawks. They are still largely absent from eastern cereal-growing districts, but work in Dumfriesshire suggests that in borderline areas where cereal-growing gives way to grassland the population may actually have doubled within five years (though still much below full strength) while in the few areas remote from cereal-growing areas normal broods are still reared(8). Undoubtedly too the sparrowhawk has been favoured by the rapidly increasing acreage of planted coniferous forest which has grown up in recent years. Some of these planted forests are now very large, and at a certain stage of growth support dense populations of sparrowhawks. These not only increase the actual numbers in the areas concerned but can provide recruits to populate or re-populate areas where woods are small and scattered and game preserving is still carried on, with its attendant persecution of sparrowhawks.

The present-day distribution of the sparrowhawk in Britain is similar to that of the buzzard, common and perhaps increasing in western non-arable districts, and virtually absent from eastern cereal-growing areas. In the case of the sparrowhawk, however, its absence from the east is not wholly or even mainly due to persecution by gamekeepers (as is probably the case with the buzzard) for moderate populations of sparrowhawks were always able to survive in these eastern districts even when gamekeepers were both more numerous and more aggressive in their persecution of raptors than they are today. It is perhaps impossible at present to arrive at a good quick estimate of the total British population; but it would probably be fair to say that there may still be 20–30,000 square miles of suitable habitat supporting an average density of about one pair per 4 square miles (10 sq.km.), locally more, so that there may still be 10–15,000 sparrowhawks in spring increasing to about double that number in autumn. This may seem a very large figure; but is only a small fraction of what there might be in the absence of persecution or pesticides, and only a remnant of the number that must have flourished in the Middle Ages.

Despite its numbers the sparrowhawk is an unfamiliar bird to most people, even to those who live in the country. It is shy and secretive, a character not necessarily associated with constant persecution, for some tropical *Accipiter* species which are never persecuted are just as shy. The most that is normally seen of a sparrowhawk is a grey or grey-brown shape flitting low over an open field, or slipping along a hedgerow, crossing from side to side as it seeks prey. Those who rise early are more likely to see the soaring flights performed in spring display, and occasionally a sparrowhawk is observed, from some vantage point, circling to 100 feet (30 m.) or more above the ground, unaware of the observer(15). But for the most part, and especially during the early breeding season, the birds remain very unobtrusive, neither visible nor audible. When large young are in the nest they are noisy and easily located, and when these young are on the wing in late summer and early autumn they are generally more obvious than the adults.

Those who have the fortune to see a sparrowhawk at close quarters will find it a very rewarding bird. To me it gives an impression of nervous tension and capacity for sudden swift movement unequalled in any other raptor, except similar small *Accipiters*. Its plumage is a satisfying blend of uniform coloured upperparts, bluer in the male than in the female, and neatly barred underparts, while the fierce yellow or orange eye is arresting when seen at close quarters. It is not so very small and a female is both powerful for her size and ferocious, weighing only about 270–310 grams (10–11 oz) but capable of killing a woodpigeon twice her own weight. The male, as is also the case in several other small *Accipiter* species, is very much smaller than the female, about one-third smaller in all linear dimensions and only about half her weight(2). This means that he is unable to kill the larger prey that is regularly killed by females, and also that if he is confined in a cage with a female she is more likely than not to kill and eat him.

The sparrowhawk is not given to magnificent feats of flight in the manner of the large falcons or eagles, but catches most of its prey by a combination of agility and stealth, taking the victim by surprise at close range. Its hunting methods have been observed by J. H. Owen and others in Britain(12) and in Europe, especially by L. Tinbergen, whose classic study of the sparrowhawk in Holland is a model for all who wish to study any raptor species(17). Owen considered that sparrowhawks could fly at anything between 15 and 90 m.p.h. but the latter estimate is probably excessive even in a dive and others have thought that a sparrowhawk cannot exceed 60–65 m.p.h. The normal speed in full chase was estimated by Owen at 45–50 m.p.h. but others have thought 18–25 m.p.h. in hunting flight a more realistic figure, with which I would agree(15). A sparrowhawk often appears to be moving very fast but this is often because it is seen suddenly close to the observer, skimming only a few feet above the ground.

In Tinbergen's account the hunting sparrowhawk is shown as flying low over open ground, making use of any cover such as a bush, a hedge, or building to approach the prey, which is very often a flock of sparrows or finches feeding out in the open. Perhaps such flights are planned from some distance off, for Owen and others have described a 'prospecting' flight in which the bird rises in circles to as much as 120 feet above the ground, circling and flapping for perhaps 15 seconds before gliding off on a hunting flight close to the ground(15,12). Alternatively, the prey is often observed from a perch in dense cover, say at the edge of a wood, and then hunted in low, gliding flight. Speed is maintained in the low gliding flight partly by wing flapping three or four times at rather long intervals, but the sparrowhawk must also be a very efficient glider, losing little energy or speed even though it may travel over undulating country and dodge between or over obstacles. A hunting sparrowhawk often follows a similar route each day, and in hot pursuit of quarry may be very impetuous, dashing into brushwood at full speed and slipping through small openings between, for instance, vertical saplings or the bars of a gate. When attacking a flock of finches it often appears to select one from the flock, which may be fractionally less able to escape than the others, and pursues this one bird alone(17). However, it must also be able to catch and kill perfectly healthy birds, and often takes fledglings just out of the nest. It prefers to catch its prey in flight rather than on the ground but in some areas many young waders are taken on the ground. Its hunting efficiency is apparently unaffected by, for instance fog, which may allow it to approach its prey more easily unseen.

The actual kill is made with the feet, thrust out wide-open at the end of very long legs, often by turning over on the side or even on the back in flight. The sparrowhawk has long thin shanks and long toes with curving, needle-sharp talons, ideally adapted to snatching quick-moving prey at an angle. The degree of success in killing is not very clearly established, and again much depends on the observer's opinion as to whether the hawk is in earnest or not. Owen believed that if in earnest a hunting sparrowhawk was nearly always successful, but others consider that many unsuccessful attacks are made for every successful attempt(17). More systematic observations on this sort of point are needed; but while it seems plain that although a sparrowhawk can often manage to catch its food requirements relatively easily, some do undoubtedly die of starvation, indicating that they cannot catch their needs.

Extensive research in Europe has established the fact that an adult sparrowhawk requires on average about 53 grams of food, but that to obtain this amount it must kill about 82 grams(17,18). The actual amount needed varies according to sex, a female needing more than a male, and is equivalent to an average of two to three sparrow-sized birds per day per adult. If larger prey is killed it will evidently suffice for more than one day; female sparrowhawks are sometimes trapped returning to woodpigeons they have killed, but are unable to carry away. The huge majority of the prey taken weighs less than 50 grams per bird. In Tinbergen's study the average weight of all prey was 39 grams, and 82% of the victims weighed less than 50 grams(17). However, by weight the smaller prey made up only 47% of the total, and the 18% of larger prey accounted for the remaining 53% by weight and included birds up to 350 grams (13 oz) weight. Sparrowhawks actually can kill birds of up to 600 grams (1½ lb), but very rarely do(17).

From the data available it is possible to work out quite exactly the amount of prey needed or taken by a pair of sparrowhawks and their brood in the course of a year. In round figures each adult needs to kill about 30 kg. (66 lb) of food per year to survive, of which it will actually eat about 20 kg. (44 lb). This is made up of 750–800 average-sized (40 gram) birds, so that the pair requires 1500–1600 small birds per year. The amount eaten by the brood, in the dependent period of three months in summer, varies naturally according to brood size; but at present in Britain average brood size is about two per pair per year, so that the requirement of the growing brood is only a little more than that of a pair of adults over the same period, about 5 kg. (11 lb) eaten out of 7·5 kg. (16 lb) killed, or about 400 birds per year(17). If a particular pair eats a large proportion of large birds the numbers taken would correspondingly be reduced. Although this total requirement of about 2000–2200 birds per pair of sparrowhawks per year may seem very large there is no evidence that it causes more than a temporary or local decrease in the population of smaller birds in any area.

The hunting methods of sparrowhawks result in a strongly selective effect on the prey taken. Tinbergen's study showed that this was unrelated to the total numbers available of many common bird species, but was directly related to the ease with which they could be caught – their vulnerability to attack. Prey which is conspicuous either from size, numbers, or certain habits is preferred. Sparrows and finches which feed in flocks in the open are favourite items of prey, but skulking species such as the coal-tit, common in dense cover, were seldom eaten in Holland, though they were commonly taken in Dumfriesshire. Tinbergen calculated that sparrowhawks were responsible for half the total mortality of house sparrows in summer, a quarter of the chaffinches and great tits, but a negligible proportion of coal tits, which inhabit thicker cover. Swallows, which are abundant and conspicuous in summer, are seldom caught by sparrowhawks because of their superior powers of flight(17); but tree pipits, also given to aerial display, are highly vulnerable and heavily preyed upon.

Such effects must vary from place to place according to the type of prey available. There is also variation in the size of prey taken by the sexes, and the seasonal composition of the prey. In the nesting season. Tinbergen found that more woodland species were taken, and this has been confirmed in recent studies in Scotland by Ian Newton(e). He found that pairs living in forests ate more forest-living birds than did those that live in small woods, while after the breeding season most pairs fed more in open country on, for instance, young lapwings and meadow pipits than they ate early in the year. Tinbergen found that the smallest birds, such as goldcrests or long-tailed tits, were most often taken by males; that sparrow and lark-sized birds were taken about equally by both sexes; that both sexes took thrush and jay-sized birds but that the female tended to kill more of these; and that the heaviest prey such as full grown woodpigeons was only killed by females[17]. Likewise Ian Newton has found that males kill prey up to their own weight, including birds the size of a mistle thrush, while females regularly killed woodpigeons, as well as some well-grown pheasants and black grouse, and occasional adult red grouse and crows. In Dumfriesshire the most important prey in summer is songthrushes, blackbirds, chaffinches and starlings in terms of numbers, with lapwings and woodpigeons also important in terms of total weight(e).

A very large number of different species are recorded as taken by sparrowhawks, varying from the very small goldcrests to well-grown pheasants or full-grown woodpigeons, normally in the weight range 10–400 grams, but occasionally even more, up to 600 grams ($1\frac{1}{2}$ lb). Tinbergen recorded 75 species in his area, and in Europe and Britain the total known prey range exceeds 120 species[18]. A small number of mammals and other ground animals are taken; in Dumfriesshire bank voles and young rabbits are items of prey. In Tinbergen's study 3647 items included 3502 birds, 135 mammals, eight lizards, and two insects. Of the birds, 3384 were passerines, and 118 others included three young sparrowhawks, many turtle doves, but only 18 young gamebirds. A similar range of prey is recorded in all other studies of this species, and all such studies conclude that in areas well stocked with wild-bred gamebirds only a very small proportion of the prey consists of these. In Tinbergen's study it was less than 0·5% by numbers (18/3657) and much less than that by weight; and in Dumfriesshire young pheasants made up only 1·3% of 1282 prey items, and 1·5% by weight (Text Table 5). Other data on this point are given in Appendix Table I.

The burning question of whether the sparrowhawk is really a severe danger to game preserving is relatively simply answered. The fact is that a sparrowhawk cannot normally kill a pheasant poult of more than four weeks of age, when it weighs about 100 grams ($3\frac{1}{2}$ oz). This is about the normal upper limit for a male, and a female will not normally kill one of more than 300 grams (11 oz) weight. A half-grown young pheasant leaving a release pen weighs about 600 grams, and is beyond the powers of any normal sparrowhawk. Moreover, the female, who might kill an occasional larger pheasant poult, is normally fed by the male until the young are 18–21 days of age, in early–mid July. At that time wild-hatched pheasant poults, hatching about the end of May, are five to six weeks old and weigh about 200 grams (7 oz)(b).

Therefore, if poults in rearing pens are properly protected until they are a certain age they will not normally be eaten by sparrowhawks, because they are too heavy for the hawk to kill. Young pheasant poults are normally transferred from rearing to release pens when they are about six weeks old and weigh 200 grams; they fly from the release pens two or three weeks later. Recent experiments in Dumfries indicate that such released poults are more likely to be killed by perching young sparrowhawks just independent, about mid August; by that time young wild pheasants should be flying and too heavy for a sparrowhawk to kill(20).

Gamekeepers should therefore have little to fear from sparrowhawks if they site the rearing and release pens carefully, provide cover in the woods, and take other intelligent steps to minimise the likelihood of attack by sparrowhawks.

Table 5 Food of the Sparrowhawk, Numbers and Weight

Based on data from Dr I. Newton, Nature Conservancy, Edinburgh

Prey species	Number	% by number	Mean weight grams	Total weight grams	% by weight
Corvids (ii)	12	0·83	200	2,400	2·1
Finches/sparrows (iii)	316	24·6	40	12,640	11·4
Larks/pipits/wrens	109	8·5	30	3,270	2·9
Thrushes (iii)/wheatears	356	27·6	90	32,040	28·6
Starlings (iii)	135	10·4	80	10,800	9·7
Warblers/tits	138	10·6	15	2,070	1·8
Woodpigeons (ii)/pigeons (iii)	79	6·2	500	39,500	35·5
Waders/gulls	49	3·8	100	4,900	4·4
Gamebirds (mainly small)	17	1·3	100	1,700	1·5
Other non-passerines (i)	5	0·3	30	150	0·1
Unidentified	39	3·04	40	1,560	1·4
Total birds	1255	97·9		111,030	99·4
Mammals, etc.	27	2·1	25	675	0·6
Total, all prey	1282			111,705	

NOTES (i) Includes two adult male sparrowhawks.

(ii) Woodpigeons plus corvids = about 7% of kills by number but nearly 38% by weight.

(iii) Four commonest items (finches, thrushes, starlings, pigeons) = 85% by weight.

Sparrowhawks kill a fair number of corvids, especially jays, and are to this extent beneficial to game preserving, while they are also to a degree cannibals on their own young. Of course, if young pheasant poults are released into woods lacking cover close to a sparrowhawk's nest some trouble is inevitable.

Sparrowhawks live and breed mainly in woodlands, but often hunt far from their nest sites and there is no evidence that they defend a definite territory from other sparrowhawks. They hunt over a wide area, and several individuals may be found hunting in certain favoured places such as starling roosts, to reach which they must pass over the breeding areas of other pairs or individuals(e). Nevertheless the actual nest sites are regularly spaced with almost mathematical exactitude over any area of uniformly suitable habitat, which suggests that some form of territorial or spacing behaviour must operate to ensure these regular intervals. This is achieved with little overt territorial fighting so far as is known; such fighting is certainly not normal. The nest sites are very stable from year to year, and each site is normally used over a succession of years by different breeding individuals or pairs. Tinbergen found in Holland that most of the nest sites in his area were occupied continuously from 1941–43 and some for four to five years, and in Britain similar results have been noted in Dumfriesshire(6). A site may not be occupied in some years but may be reoccupied in other years by completely different birds.

To this extent a sparrowhawk does not have a regular 'home range' occupied by the pair all the year round and from which other pairs may be excluded. It has a nesting range, with a group of nest sites in it, but forages partly in common ground some distance outside this range, sometimes two or more miles from it. Outside the breeding season they hunt more in open country and in Scotland and Wales may then be observed several miles from trees; this, however, would be less usual in well wooded areas(e).

The spacing between nest sites varies greatly, and depends primarily on the availability of suitable woodland or plantations in which to nest. If the entire country is uniformly covered with suitable woodland of similar type the nest sites are regularly spaced all over it; but the distance between them varies at least four-fold. In forestry plantations in Dumfries each site is on average 0·4 miles (0·6 km.) from its neighbour; in southern Kincardine 0·7 miles (1·1 km.); in Central Wales 1·0 miles (1·6 km.), and in the Spey basin of Inverness 1·5 miles (2·4 km.)(9). The density of breeding pairs is not limited in plantations by the availability of suitable nesting cover but by the spacing behaviour of the birds themselves.

It may be that this variation is directly due to variation in the amount of food available; but a nesting territory distant 1½ miles from the next includes a potential hunting area more than fourteen times as great as that included in one 0·4 miles from its neighbour. In the absence of good quantitative evidence it is difficult to believe that the total abundance of prey in forestry plantations in Dumfries is fourteen times as great as that in the Spey basin. It is also difficult to believe that the prey is proportionately that much more vulnerable in forestry plantations in Dumfries than in Speyside. Evidently much more evidence is needed before the true reasons for this variation in spacing of nesting sites in British sparrowhawks can be understood.

Regular spacing breaks down in areas of mixed farmland and woodlands because there is then a shortage of suitable nesting sites(e). Sparrowhawks prefer rather dense woods with closed canopy for nesting and, where coniferous woods are available, they prefer these; however the availability of such suitable habitat varies from one part of the country to another. Where no suitable woods are available nests will be built in overgrown orchards, thorn thickets and overgrown hedges, scrub-filled gullies or riverside trees, but not in isolated trees or in single lines of trees. In undisturbed areas a less suitable or safe site than normal may be used, and sparrowhawks also nest in clumps of tall trees in towns.

The lack of suitable breeding habitat reduces the number of sparrowhawks able to breed in any area; in Dumfriesshire, for instance, the local density within a study area of about 200 square miles (500 sq.km.) varied from a maximum of five to six pairs per square mile in the most suitable habitat to one pair per more than 3 square miles in the least suitable woodland and farmland, with nil on open moors, and averaged about one per square mile overall(6). This was a fairly typical area of mixed woodland and farmland, with many small plantations, originally planted as pheasant covers (but also quite suitable for breeding sparrowhawks) with large tracts too of unsuitable open sheepwalk and dense young conifers. There are many other areas of Britain where similar conditions might apply. On this basis an average population in those parts of Britain still occupied by sparrowhawks of about one pair per square mile would seem reasonable if it were not known that densities elsewhere are, for some reason, much lower. An overall average of a pair to 4 square miles may be cautious, but is more realistic on present knowledge.

Although the sparrowhawk is a secretive and shy species more difficult to study than are most British raptors it is one of the few that has been studied here in fair detail at the nesting site, the results having been published in a series of pioneer papers by J. H. Owen between 1916 and 1922(10,11). No really comparable early work exists on any other British raptor, and it was unfortunate that so many of

Owen's nests were prevented from going any further than the egg stage by game-keepers. The breeding behaviour of the sparrowhawk has also been extensively studied in Europe by Tinbergen and others so that we know at least as much about this small and secretive raptor as about many much larger and more conspicuous species.

Sparrowhawks may normally be monogamous, but are sometimes at least bigamous; polygamy can be suspected. Sparrowhawks do not apparently live very long in the wild state and changes of mates are frequent; however this would not occur unless one or other of the partners had disappeared for some reason. Dutch ringing records indicate that the average age of birds finishing their final year is 2·5 years, but nesting territories are normally occupied by new birds each year; one partner often returns and attracts a new mate(17). Perhaps persistence of any formed pairs is as much due to attachment to the nesting site as through attachment of individual birds to each other.

The nesting sites, stable from year to year, are marked by groups of nests, easily recognisable with a little practice(9). In early spring some display is seen, but soaring display may occur at any time of the year, and is probably the means by which the regular espacement of nest sites is maintained. The three main elements of display are soaring with spread tail, slow flapping flight, and diving on half-closed or closed wings, sometimes towards the actual nest tree. In the slow flapping flight, which is analogous to the steeply undulating displays performed by many other raptors, a single bird or a pair may beat to and fro over the nesting area with slow deliberate wing beats, rising sharply at each turn. This may be followed by spiralling upwards, again with slow wingbeats, to about 200 feet, then increasing the speed of flight by a few wingbeats, rising abruptly for 20–30 feet, and finally plunging steeply down in a long dive with closed wings. Just above the nest-tree the displaying bird may swing up again, to repeat the performance several times before settling, and when a female is displaying in this way the male may be perched in the trees below, calling.

Such aerial displays are seen mainly in the early morning in sunny weather, and it is chiefly during such displays that the sparrowhawk becomes at all obvious(a,d). Such advertisement is probably necessary to locate a nesting area for other sparrow-hawks, and more than two birds may be seen displaying over such a nest site, perhaps establishing mutual boundaries. However, these displays probably have a dual function in stimulating mating behaviour. When a female sparrowhawk is ready to mate she flies downwards and alights with partly open wings, exposing, by ruffling her feathers, a white nape and eye stripe, and white areas on the back and rump. These visual signals no doubt convey to the male a state of submission in an otherwise formidable partner twice his weight, who could and sometimes does actually kill and eat him(5)! Mating takes place on branches near the nest site, usually well below the tree canopy, and is accompanied by calling and sometimes preceded by the presentation of food by the male(6).

Nests are built afresh each year, but in the same areas used in previous years. The nests are solid structures of twigs and sticks up to two feet across, and last for years, so that nesting sites can easily be located even when the birds are not breeding. A new nest is distinguished from old ones by the fact that one can see through it; the old nests collect masses of conifer needles or dead leaves in autumn and are opaque(6). Most nests are, if possible, built close to the trunk of an upright conifer where several small branches emerge at the same level; or, in pines, some-times out on a lateral limb. In deciduous trees the nest must be placed in a fork and is then often deeper than in a conifer. Nests may be at any height from 5–80 feet (1·5–25 m.) above the ground depending on the size of tree available, but are not usually more than 40 feet (12 m.) up. Nest building may commence two months before eggs are laid, and is done by the female, though the male also brings material at times. During laying the rather deep nest cup is lined with fresh twigs or chips of bark. The finished structure is up to two feet across with a deep cup in the centre in which the sitting female will later be nearly invisible though her tail usually projects. More material will be added during the breeding cycle until, by the time the young leave, the nest is a broad flattened platform with practically no suggestion of a nest cup, on which the young can exercise freely.

Three to seven, usually four to six eggs are laid, on alternate days or at three-day intervals, and at any time of day; Owen observed that eggs were laid at any time from 4 a.m. to midday(10). A full clutch of six thus takes eleven days to deposit, but incubation does not usually begin till at least the second egg has been laid, and sometimes not until the clutch is complete. This in turn means that when the young hatch they are more equal in size than would be the case if the female started to incubate as soon as the first egg is laid. Occasionally larger clutches of up to ten eggs have been recorded, but such are due to two females laying in the same nest with a bigamous male. If the eggs are removed one by one the female can be induced to lay a much larger number than normal; up to 23 have been recorded(e). If a clutch is lost or removed soon after egg laying is complete the female will usually lay another on a near-by old nest, and occasionally even a third. Such readiness to lay a repeat clutch, whatever egg collectors may say, is unusual in diurnal raptors, and applies mainly if the eggs are fresh; if incubation is well advanced repeat clutches are not laid. Second clutches are usually smaller than first clutches and contain more addled eggs.

Although the sparrowhawk is shy and elusive as a rule it is not a very difficult species to study at the nest, and like the hen harrier will tolerate a good deal of interference, enabling an observer to make repeated visits at different stages to ascertain clutch and brood sizes. Once the female has begun to sit she is dependent on the male for food, and she sits very tightly, often not leaving the nest until the tree is struck or the observer has climbed part way up it. This behaviour undoubtedly has survival value, for a nest will often pass as unoccupied when all the time the female is sitting tight. She undergoes part of her annual moult while incubating, but, as in hen harriers, not to the extent that she cannot hunt for herself if necessary(e).

Normally the male keeps the incubating female supplied with food, bringing, according to Tinbergen, an average of just over two kills per day in the first two weeks, nearly four per day in the third week, and just under three in the fourth week. If consistent, these variations may be connected with the stage of the female's moult. The male will normally have decapitated and partly eaten these kills himself before bringing them to the nest, so partly satisfying his own appetite. When he arrives he calls from a neighbouring perch and, in the early stages of incubation, the female leaves the nest to receive the prey from him. Later in incubation she may not leave the nest, and is also reluctant to do so if it is raining; the male then takes the prey to the nest if he fails to obtain the usual response to his food call(10). As incubation progresses the female, preening herself, deposits flecks of down on the nest edge and adhering to the surrounding branches, so that the stage of incubation can easily be gauged from below(e). Incubation takes 32–36 days, averaging 35 days for each egg.

Most sparrowhawks in Britain start to lay between late April and mid May, with the earliest southern clutches laid before the end of April and the latest northern clutches about the third week of May. As in several other raptors such as the buzzard there is less variation in laying date according to temperature and state of leafage on the trees than would seem likely; perhaps the frequent preference for nesting in the dense cover of conifers minimises temperature effects. The laying date means that the young emerge normally in early to mid June, and are in the nest at a time when fledgling songbirds just out of the nest are available in numbers and provide an abundant food supply. However, the timing of the nesting cycle may not necessarily be geared to food supply alone, but could be influenced by other factors.

The young hatch in 24 or more hours from first chipping the egg, sometimes over as long a period as four days. Depending on the stage at which the female began incubating there may be little or a marked size difference between them, as is also observed in the large clutches of harriers. The chicks are not aggressive to one another and there is little or no inter-sibling strife such as is seen in the larger eagles and buzzards. They are at first feeble, clad in down, but can open their eyes and stretch up for food. They are brooded continuously by the female, whose role at this stage is to remain on or near the nest tending young while the male brings prey. The female normally remains near the nest until the young are able to feed themselves which occurs after 18–21 days of age; they can pull at carcases earlier but are normally unable to feed without assistance till 18–21 days, rather later, proportionately, in the fledging period than in most birds of prey(2).

As soon as the young hatch the male immediately doubles his rate of killing prey, and with a normal brood brings in six kills a day in the first week of the fledging period, varying with the number of young hatched. He presumably satisfies his own hunger with parts of these, and the female feeds on portions not eaten by the young, so that this rate represents the actual amount taken by the entire family. The rate of killing is increased to nearly eight average (40 gram) kills per day in the third week of the fledging period. It rises still further thereafter to ten per day; but by then the female is also able to take part in killing, and kills larger prey than does the male. These figures apply only to normal broods and average-sized prey: a brood of even six could be satisfied with one woodpigeon killed by a female.

After the third week of the fledging period the pressure on the male, who has been feeding himself, his partner, and his young for at least eight weeks is reduced. The male in monogamous matings can apparently manage this duty without particular difficulty, but it will be evident that if he is bigamous he must then kill 12–18 birds per day during the fledging period and, if polygamous, still more. In such cases it is likely that the females would take to hunting at an earlier stage than normal, and observations in Dumfriesshire suggest that this is probably so(e). The effects of bigamy or polygamy are, however much more difficult to observe in the cover-loving sparrowhawk than in harriers which live in open country and among which it does not seem to be disadvantageous(3).

The female remains on the nest and covers the young almost continuously for the first two weeks; after that she perches near and remains ready to feed them when the male comes with prey, which she normally receives on a tree a little distance away. She may occasionally attempt to kill near the nest, but is still mainly dependent on the male for food. Owen, who had plenty of opportunity to observe this particular facet of behaviour in the Essex countryside, noted that if not on the nest she returned to brood the young in rain or would remain on the nest and refuse to leave to collect prey from the male(10). She eats anything that the young cannot eat or reject, and swallows pellets, droppings, and remaining pieces before returning to brood the chicks. According to Owen, she also removes the flecks of down which adhered to the nest rim and surrounding branches during incubation, but we must assume that this is not a belated conscious effort to aid concealment of the nest and its contents. The male may visit the nest during the fledging period, especially if the female does not leave it in response to his call, but he never feeds the young. A case is on record where the young, nine hours after a female had been shot, were found starving but nearly smothered by 16 freshly killed songbirds, all untouched(1). In this case the male had continued to bring prey, but had not fed the young, which at this age would starve in the presence of abundant food unless he obtained another female partner.

By the time the young are 20 days old feathers have covered their bodies, and after 18–21 days, when they can tear at food, they will survive if the female is shot or otherwise lost. Once they have learned to feed themselves the young remain in the nest for another week, but by 28 days old have learned to climb out on to branches and fly soon after that. After the young have learned to climb out on to branches they scramble back to the nest hurriedly when a parent comes with food. They are at this stage noisy, calling continuously for long periods; this is the only stage at which sparrowhawks' nests are really conspicuous and easily located by gamekeepers, who then frequently destroy broods which they have hitherto overlooked. The nest becomes covered with flecks of down and the surrounding branches spattered with droppings, while the nest platform is flattened and broken down as the young walk about on it.

Young sparrowhawks can be sexed in the nest by the size of their feet and legs (those of the female being much stronger and thicker) by one week old and later by weight; a female puts on weight almost twice as fast as a male(e). The sex ratio appears to be equal in the sparrowhawk, at least when little mortality occurs among the young in contrast to the hen harrier where it is slightly in favour of females in the nest. Young males leave the nest earlier than females, being slimmer and more active throughout.

The young become independent of their parents about three to four weeks after their first flight. During this post-fledging period they remain near the nest, frequently screaming for food, which they soon learn to take from their parents in flight, sometimes turning upside down and snatching it foot-to-foot. Most prey at this stage is brought by the female, who occasionally will not relinquish it to the young at once but forces them to chase her among the trees for a while before she drops it. Perhaps the young learn in this way to catch their own prey, and it is certainly a rather unusually clear example of coaxing behaviour by an adult raptor. Throughout Britain the young become independent of their parents during August.

Sparrowhawks in Britain are very sedentary. All the available ringing records indicate that most young do not move more than ten miles from the nesting site, few travel more than thirty miles, while until recently no young had been recovered from more than 100 miles (160 km.) away; there is now a record of more than 120 miles (190 km.)(e). The main mortality occurs in the first autumn when it is very easy for gamekeepers to trap young sparrowhawks in cage traps baited with small birds. First year birds are also frequently caught in such traps in March, indicating that at this time they are also moving about the countryside. Total mortality in the first year, derived from ringing records, is about 66%; but this

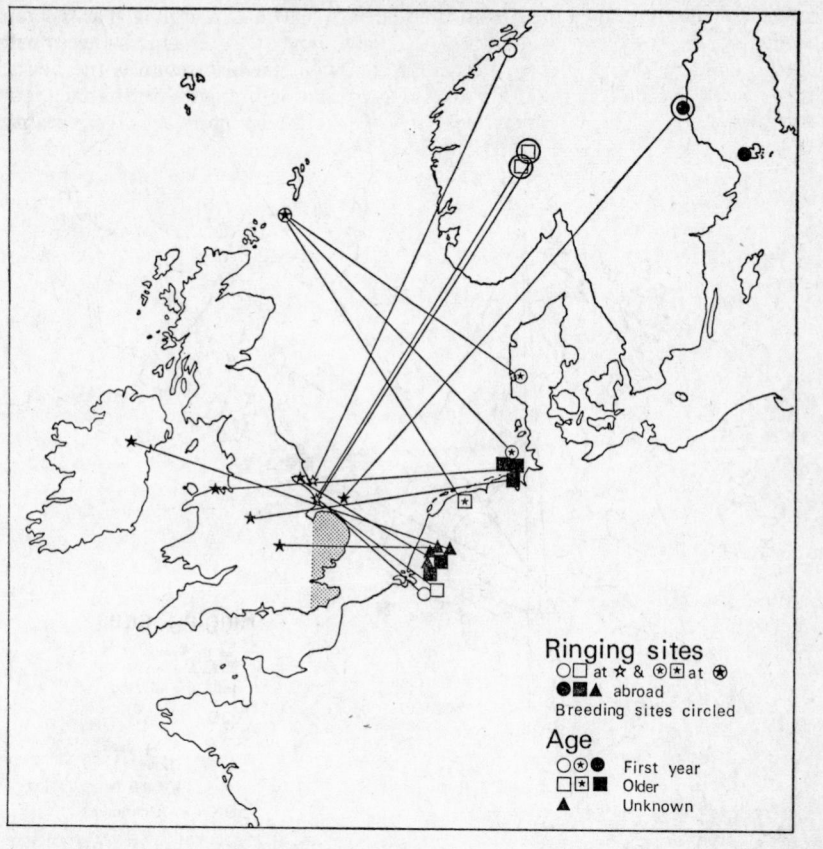

Ringing sites
○□ at ✶ & ⊙✦ at ✳
●▣▲ abroad
Breeding sites circled
Age
○⊙● First year
□✦▣ Older
▲ Unknown

MAP 23. Recoveries of 19 female sparrowhawks ringed in Britain and recovered abroad, or ringed abroad and recovered in Britain.

may not be entirely natural because many such records are of trapped or shot birds(4).

Sparrowhawks migrate in winter from more northern latitudes, sometimes reaching the Equator in Africa; I have seen a sparrowhawk in semi arid thornbush in Kenya. On migration they may fly in company with other birds, for instance crows or Levant sparrowhawks, and the sexes may be separated(2). Some of these migrants reach Britain each year, mainly along the east coast, but recorded from Fair Isle to Somerset and Kent, and even from Ireland. A few of these may spend the winter here. Fourteen foreign-ringed individuals include five from Holland, six from Germany, and others from Finland and Norway(16). Some of the migrants are ringed here and released, and a few have been recaptured or killed elsewhere. Three ringed at Gibraltar point, Lincolnshire, were recovered at Valdres, Norway, (2) and Jutland; and four ringed at Fair Isle were recovered in Vendée, France, Mayenne, France, Holland and Heligoland. Apparently, females may predominate among these migrant individuals, and in some years large numbers arrive in East

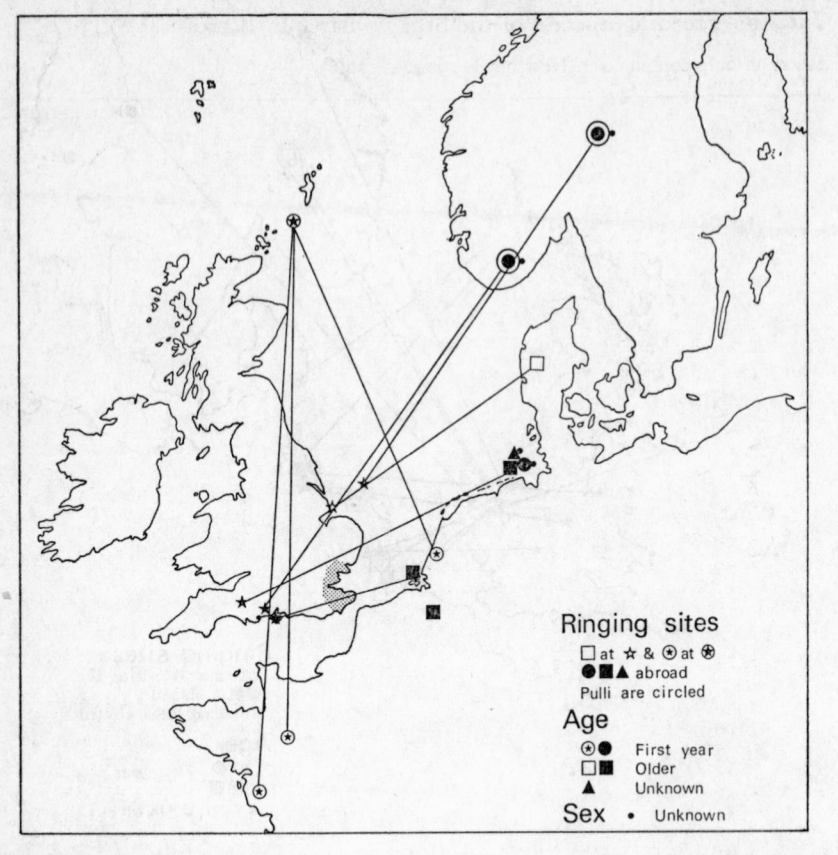

MAP 24. Recoveries of seven male and four unsexed sparrowhawks ringed in Britain and recovered abroad, or ringed abroad and recovered in Britain.

Anglia(4). However, as a whole, Britain is only touched by the fringe of the migratory movement of sparrowhawks from Europe. (Maps 23, 24.)

The breeding success of sparrowhawks, as brought out by recent studies in Dumfries by Newton(8), is now much lower than it was in the years before the First World War or up to 1950. Sparrowhawks at present lay about the same number of eggs as ever they did, with a mean overall clutch of 4·9–5·0, whether before 1950 or in 1960–71. However this mean size of the broods reared has fallen sharply. Pre-1950 the mean brood size per successful nest (others were usually not observed) was 4·0, but in arable farming areas had fallen to 3·4 in 1951–60 and to 2·9 in 1961–70. Prior to 1950 losses among eggs are known to have been slight, with few eggs addled and very few eaten or broken by the parents. After 1950 more entire clutches have been lost during incubation, and a greater proportion of eggs in clutches that partially hatched have been addled or broken. All these factors combined have reduced the productivity per 100 breeding pairs of sparrowhawks from about 400 young per year to 197; in other words, whereas every adult reared 2

Table 6   Breeding Success of the Sparrowhawk in Britain: 1900 to 1970

Based on data contained in Newton, I. 1974 (c): 12(8).

	Clutch size	Incidence of addled eggs	Brood size	% nests producing young	Young reared per 100 clutches
Farmland					
Pre-1951	5·0	0·64	4·0	100	400
1951–1960	4·9	0·75	3·4	50	190
1961–1970	4·9	1·66	2·9	68	180
Non-farmland					
1951–1960	5·0	?	(4·0)	100	(400)
1961–1970	5·0	0·73	3·8	100	380

NOTES   (1) Overall breeding success in farming areas has dropped from 4·0 young per pair per annum to 1·8 per pair per annum since 1950.
(2) No significant reduction in clutch size in any area.
(3) Much higher incidence of addled eggs in farmland as cf. non-farmland (1·66:0·73) in 1961–70.
(4) Figures do not include non-breeding birds or nests destroyed by humans.
(5) Figures in parentheses are estimated.

young per year in 1950 and earlier a successful adult now only rears one. Further, these figures take no account of non-breeding pairs, which are also more common now than in the past. No change in breeding success is noted in areas far from arable land.

With an annual mortality of 66% before the first breeding season at one year of age, when still in immature plumage, every adult before 1950 required to live for less than two years as an adult in order to be able to replace itself; in other words one year of breeding as a subadult and part of a second year as a full adult. At the present time it would appear that adults must live for up to four or five years as adults to be able to replace themselves if the first-year mortality estimated by ringing records of 66% is in fact correct.

There are as yet no age data available of breeding adults to show whether this is so or not, but on the available evidence it seems unlikely. Sparrowhawks are known that are at least three years old as adults, but to maintain an average breeding life span of four or five years some adults would have to live much longer than that, to ten or twelve years at least. There are no records of sparrowhawks of more than ten years old derived from wild ringed birds, a female of eight being the oldest known(c). Accordingly, it seems possible that first year mortality is not actually as great as the two-thirds indicated by ringing records, and must in fact be very considerably lower. However, definite conclusions on this sort of subject cannot be drawn without better evidence on survival in wild ringed birds.

Young sparrowhawks of either sex can breed in their first year, at about eight to nine months since they became independent. They are then in a distinctive plumage and the sexes can only be separated by size, not, as in the full adult plumage acquired in the following year, by plumage characters(6). In both sexes at this time the upper parts are brown, with rufous tinges to the feathers, producing an overall orange-brown appearance(6,20). The underparts are white to pale orange streaked, barred, or blotched with chocolate or orange brown. If a high proportion of breeding sparrowhawks in any area are in this stage of plumage it would presumably indicate a high level of adult mortality resulting in the necessity for frequent early replacements, in the breeding population, of adults by subadults. If, on the other hand, there are more full adults than subadults in the breeding population this would be a healthy sign.

It seems likely that before the days of pesticides there must always have been a large surplus of adults, or subadults capable of breeding, and that not all the sparrowhawks capable of breeding could find a nesting area in which to breed. There may not now be such a large surplus of non-breeding adults and subadults, and subadults may be able or obliged to breed earlier than would be the case in a completely normal population. However, such questions remain to be answered by future research.

The sparrowhawk, much hated by the gamekeeping fraternity in the past, continually persecuted then and to some extent illegally persecuted now, must nevertheless be admired as a thoroughly successful and adaptable species which has shown great vigour and ability to recover from many setbacks. It even appears to be able to maintain its numbers in many areas of Britain at the present time despite not only persecution but the effects of pesticides in reducing breeding success. Presumably we shall never again be able to number British sparrowhawks by the hundred thousand, for the necessary habitat is unlikely to be available for them, even if the effects of pesticides in the long term are reduced and they reoccupy areas at present lost to them. That they can and will there is no doubt, if left alone; and we must hope that an increasing awareness of their true predatory function and ability, which is mainly directed against small passerines and not against gamebirds, will reduce the senseless persecution which is still illegally meted out to this engaging little hawk.

CHAPTER 13

THE BUZZARD

IT will seem odd to those who, like myself, can remember the time when a buzzard was considered to be rather a rare bird when I say that it now is, in terms of live weight, perhaps the most important diurnal bird predator in Britain, and that it may even be the second commonest diurnal British bird of prey. It is probably exceeded in numbers by both the sparrowhawk and kestrel but it would not surprise me if a careful and thorough population survey proved that it was more numerous than the sparrowhawk. Moreover, a buzzard weighs 800–1200 grams (2–3 lb), occasionally up to 1400, so that every buzzard is equivalent to 4–5 sparrowhawks or kestrels. A possible population of 15,000 buzzards equals at least 60,000 sparrowhawks in weight. Now that the sparrowhawk has been seriously reduced by pesticides, and the kestrel occurs in rather small numbers over much of the country the buzzard possibly represents a greater weight of predators than either. All three species, buzzard, sparrowhawk and kestrel are very much more numerous than their next possible competitors, hen harrier, golden eagle, peregrine and merlin, all of which have less than 500 breeding pairs or 1000 adult birds in Britain.

The buzzard is also probably the best known and most studied British bird of prey. Detailed ecological studies have been done in several areas here and these may be compared with several fine European studies and with studies of the *Buteo* species in America(3,10,22). The buzzard is both large and majestic enough to command admiration and common enough to provide statistical data without too much effort; this explains the interest shown in its biology.

When I was young the buzzard was a relatively rare bird, confined mainly to the better wooded parts of western England, Wales, and West Scotland, and a good deal persecuted even in these areas. Its real recovery from persecution began in 1914, and there is no doubt that the Second World War gave it a further fillip. Its main enemy has been and still is gamekeepers and up to the early fifties of this century its main food supply in Britain, the rabbit, was still very abundant. The recent changes in its status reflect very largely local changes in the attitudes of gamekeepers and in the abundance of rabbits(11).

The overall past and present status of buzzards in Britain has been very thoroughly surveyed by Dr Norman Moore, who describes its past status in three phases(11). From the Pleistocene and recent geological times up to about AD 1100 Britain was mainly forested, and the rabbit had either not been introduced or was relatively rare. Buzzards were then probably less common than they are now. Between 1100 and 1799 most of Britain was cleared of forest and was later enclosed. Rabbits became numerous and, in the absence of other controls, rats and voles were probably also numerous. It seems clear that the buzzard was then common all over Britain, as would be natural for a *Buteo* species living in association with peasant agricultural people. A good many early records may have confused the buzzard with other species such as kites or hen harriers but it is certain that it was then widely present and quite abundant in areas from which it is now entirely absent.

Mild persecution began at quite an early stage. Henry VIII forbade egg stealing

153

but did not include buzzards in this order and in 1457 James I of Scotland ordered destruction of buzzards. Warreners interested in the abundance of rabbits probably persecuted the buzzard to some extent. From 1800–1915 waste lands were reclaimed, industrialisation spread, and game preservation became a major occupation, probably accelerating the increase of the rabbit by reduction of its natural enemies. The highlands of Scotland were opened up for sheep farming and sporting estates. At the beginning of the nineteenth century the buzzard probably bred all over the British Isles but by 1865 was almost exterminated in the midland and eastern counties. Its decline continued in England and Wales, in eastern Scotland where grouse moors are important, in Ireland, where it became extinct in Ulster about 1890 and earlier in the rest of Ireland, and to a lesser extent elsewhere.

From 1914–54 the buzzard largely recovered from the nadir reached about the beginning of the twentieth century. Keepering was reduced and collecting of specimens by naturalists began to be superseded by observation and photography. Probably, skin and egg collectors never had a very serious effect on the buzzard population for it would always have been easy to obtain skins from the many that were shot, and the bird never became so rare as, for instance the osprey or sea eagle. By 1918 the buzzard had returned to many of its old haunts in Devon, the Welsh borders and elsewhere. There must actually have been a healthy remnant population, especially in Wales, where it was never seriously endangered, for the buzzard to be able to return so fast. An isolated population free of excessive persecution survived in the New Forest(18). Scotland seems to have been worse documented throughout, but the buzzard was fairly common in the West Highlands where grouse moors were unimportant and where rabbits then abounded.

In 1929 the total Devon population was estimated at 900–1200 birds and 46 pairs were recorded in 306 square miles – a density of 1 per 6·7 square miles, which may be compared with many other less ideal areas in Britain at the present time, but is less than a third of the present-day Devon population, estimated in 1966 at 3707(12). By 1940 the buzzard had spread back into Hampshire, Dorset, Somerset, Shropshire, and Hereford and was numerous further west. It probably reached a peak about 1949, but there was little real decline before 1954.

The Second World War started a spectacularly rapid spread eastwards, at least in parts of Scotland. I recall, when on leave in 1946, locating a pair of buzzards in Glen Lossie near my home in Elgin, in a locality where predatory birds were never tolerated before the war. As a boy I lived in Devon, and often saw buzzards, but I never saw a buzzard in Speyside till the fifties, and by then it was common. It may still be spreading in Speyside where it has probably been prevented from reaching a natural balance at a peak population only by continued illegal persecution by gamekeepers. In the West Highlands it has for long been a characteristic bird, wherever woods and open country mix.

In 1952–55 myxomatosis was introduced into the rabbit population of Britain. A catastrophic epidemic resulted which almost eliminated rabbits. Agriculturally, it was no doubt justifiable; but it was bad luck for buzzards, which depend largely on rabbits in the breeding season. This epidemic started some further spread or scatter of buzzard populations, and the colonisation of certain Scottish areas dates from that time. Many pairs were said not to have bred at all, and those that did were said not to have reared such large broods. However, analysis of the B.T.O. nest record cards does not support this last contention and, at least in the more favourable areas such as Dartmoor, adult buzzards did not decrease by more than about 20%, though they did breed less successfully(3). Moore thought that myx-

THE BUZZARD

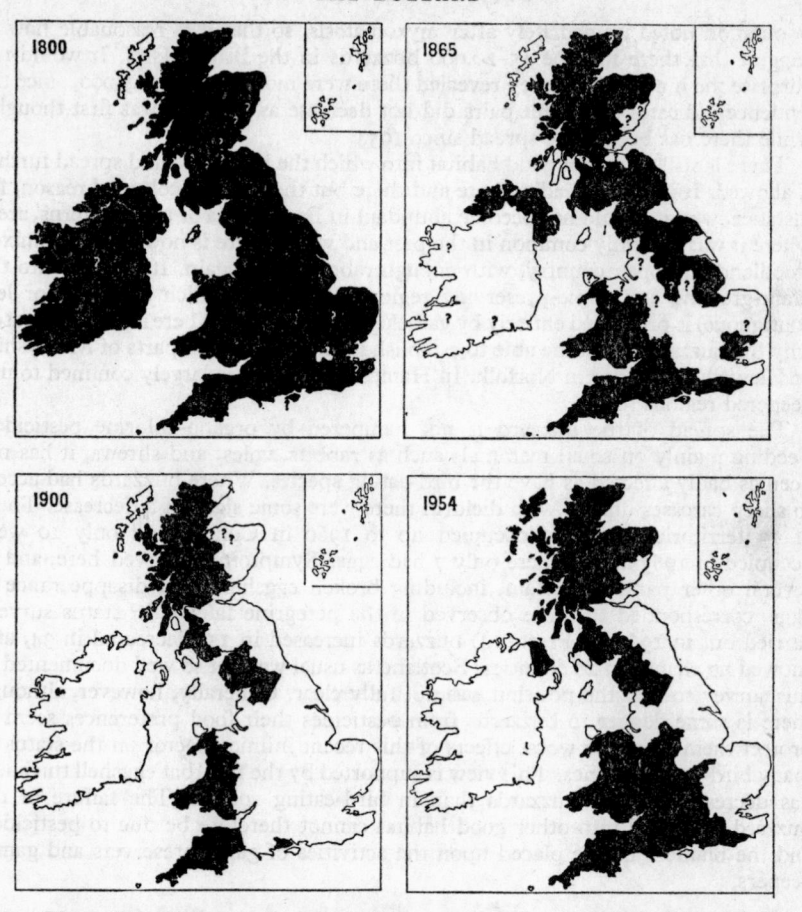

KEY: Black—Breeding proved, or good circumstantial evidence of breeding.
? on Black—Circumstantial evidence suggests that breeding probably took place.
? on White—Inadequate evidence of breeding.
White—No evidence of breeding.

MAPS 25, 26, 27 and 28. Breeding distribution of the buzzard in Britain: 1800 (maximum), 1865, 1900 (minimum) and 1954. (From N. W. Moore, 1957.)

omatosis might have reduced the buzzard population by about half overall; but other authorities think that the decline was not as drastic as that and I agree with this view(19).

The average density of population in Dr Moore's buzzard survey was one pair per 7·23 square miles (18·9 sq.km.), and on this basis he calculated that there were probably 12,000 pairs plus 2000 non-breeding birds in early 1954, about 20–30,000 altogether in the British Isles. He thought this might have fallen to 12,000 after myxomatosis. There has certainly been some recovery since the reduction of population noted immediately after myxomatosis, so that it is reasonable now to suggest that there may be 15–20,000 buzzards in the British Isles. It would not surprise me if a careful survey revealed there were more, perhaps 25,000, since the evidence indicates that adult pairs did not decrease as much as was first thought, while there has been some spread since 1954.

There is still abundant good habitat into which the buzzard could spread further if allowed. It is still spreading here and there but there is no ecological reason, for instance, why it should not become abundant in East Anglia or the Chilterns, areas where it was certainly common in the past and where there is now plenty of mixed woodland and open country, with enough rabbits once again. Its spread into the grain-growing and game-preserving regions of Britain (which are more or less contiguous) is prevented entirely by gamekeepers (Map 29). There is no other reason why the buzzard should be able to establish itself quite well in parts of Morayshire or Hampshire but not in Norfolk. In Hampshire itself it is largely confined to un-keepered regions (o).

The spread of the buzzard is not hampered by organo-chlorine pesticides. Feeding mainly on small mammals such as rabbits, voles, and shrews, it has not been as badly affected as have the bird-eating species. Where buzzards had access to sheep carcases dipped with dieldrin there were some signs of a decrease. Thus, of 13 territories regularly occupied up to 1960 in Cumberland only 10 were occupied in 1963 and of these only 7 had eggs. Symptoms observed here, and in several other parts of Britain, including broken eggshells and disappearance of eggs, corresponded to those observed in the peregrine falcon. In status surveys carried out in 1965 by Prestt(14) buzzards increased in 15, decreased in 34, and showed no change in 20 counties; Scotland as usual was not so well documented in this survey so that the position was not fully clear. Generally, however, although there is some danger to buzzards from pesticides their food preferences seem to protect them from the worst effects of this recent inimical factor on the status of many bird-eating species. This view is supported by the fact that eggshell thickness has decreased less in buzzards than in bird-eating species. The failure of the buzzard to spread into other good habitat cannot therefore be due to pesticides, and the blame must be placed upon the activities of game preservers and game-keepers.

KEY: Double cross-   — 3-6 gamekeepers per 100 square miles (see note).
       hatch

       Cross-hatch   — 1-2 gamekeepers per 100 square miles.

       Diagonal hatch   — 1 gamekeeper or more per 200 square miles but
                               less than 1 gamekeeper per 100 square miles.

       White   — Less than 1 gamekeeper per 200 square miles.

Note: These figures were kindly supplied by Major A. W. Neve, Secretary of the Gamekeepers' Association. They are relative, not absolute: they are based on membership of the Gamekeepers' Association, not on total numbers. Major Neve states that they give a fairly reliable picture of the situation south of the Border. They cease to be reliable where estates are very large. These are mainly in Red Grouse (*Lagopus scoticus*) shooting-areas. Therefore the principal grouse-preserving areas "G" have been superimposed on the map. These should be noted in conjunction with the pattern of game-keeper-density. The positions of the principal grouse-preserving areas are partly based on Leslie & Shipley (1911) and partly on information supplied by County Pest Officers and others.

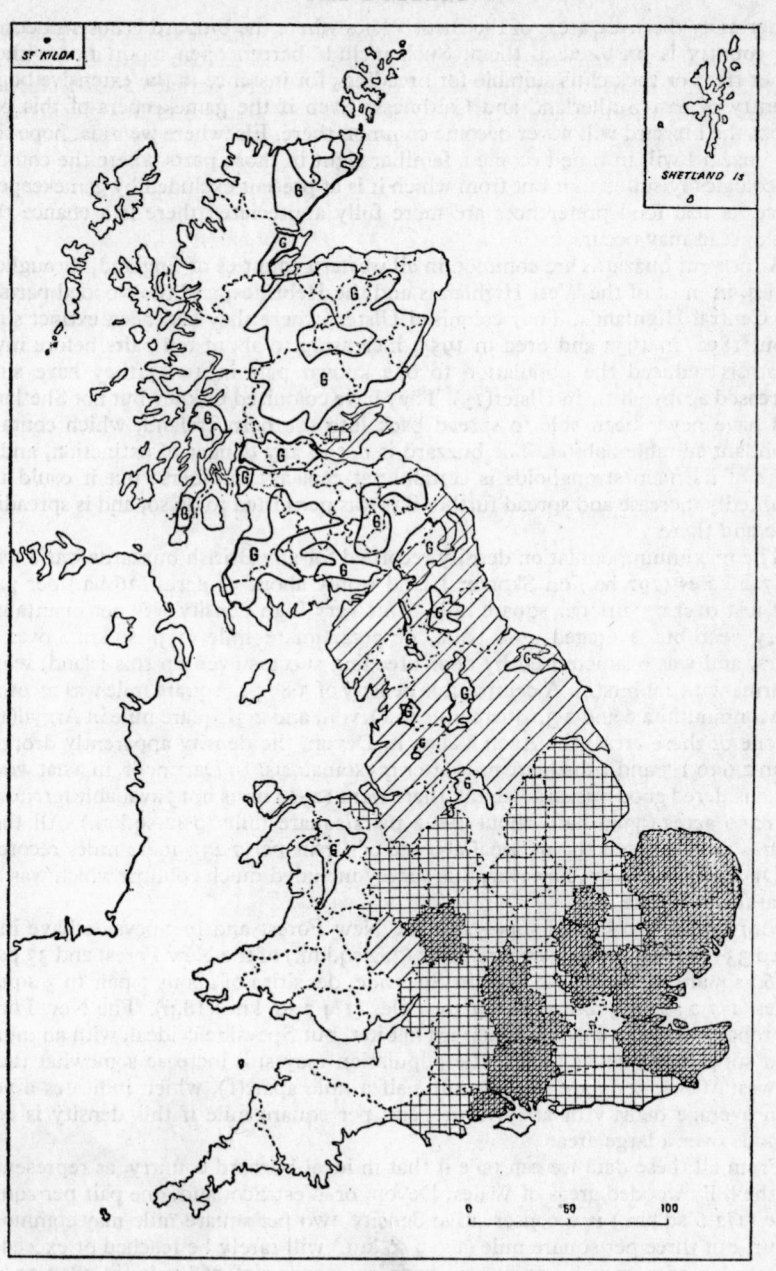

MAP 29. Distribution of game preserving areas (cf. maps 25-28) in relation to past and present distribution of breeding buzzards.

Certainly there are areas of the British Isles where the buzzard is absent because the country is unsuited to them. Such include barren open moorlands without either trees or rock cliffs suitable for breeding; for instance in the extensive boggy country of east Sutherland and Caithness. Even if the gamekeepers of this part relent the buzzard will never become common there. Elsewhere we must hope that the buzzard will in time become a familiar sight in those parts where the country is ecologically suited to it but from which it is at present excluded by gamekeepers. Once its real food preferences are more fully appreciated there is a chance that this spread may occur.

At present buzzards are common in all western counties of England, throughout Wales, in most of the West Highlands and the Hebrides, and the wooded parts of the Central Highlands. They colonised Ulster, where they had been extinct since about 1890, in 1954 and bred in 1955, increasing to about ten pairs before myxomatosis reduced the population to one known pair in 1961; they have since increased again a little in Ulster(15). They have colonised Orkney but not Shetland, and have never been able to spread back into southern Ireland, which contains abundant suitable habitat. The buzzard is not in any danger of extinction, and in some of its main strongholds is certainly at capacity numbers; but it could undoubtedly increase and spread further if it was permitted to do so, and is spreading here and there.

The maximum population density recorded for any British buzzards was 8 pairs on 722 acres (292 ha.) on Skomer Island – only about 90 acres (36 ha.) per pair, and just over 7 pairs per square mile. This very high density was not maintained every year but averaged 4·64 pairs, or 3·54/square mile (1·38/sq.km.) over 10 years, and was characterised by poor breeding success even on this island, which swarms with rabbits(4). A comparable density of 3·87 prs/square mile was recorded in Monmouth, 2·6 and 2·3/square mile in Devon, and 2·5/square mile in Argyll(11). In one of these areas, the Avon Valley in Devon, the density apparently dropped from 2·6 to 1·7 and 1·6/square mile after myxomatosis. In Dartmoor, in what would be considered good buzzard habitat, there were 12–14 nests in 15 available territories on 8250 acres (3340 ha.), about 1–1·2 pairs/square mile (0·42/sq.km.). All these figures are far above the national average of 1 pair per 7·23 square miles recorded in Dr Moore's survey; however, this survey included much country which was not ideal for buzzards.

More recent ecological surveys in the New Forest and in Speyside have indicated 33–37 pairs in 112·5 square miles (282 sq.km.) of the New Forest and 33 pairs on 60 square miles (155 sq.km.) in Speyside, densities of about 1 pair to 3 square miles (1/7·7 sq.km.) and 1/1·8 square miles (1/4·7 sq. km.)(18,p). The New Forest is probably rather a marginal buzzard habitat, but Speyside is ideal, with abundant food supply and nesting sites; the population may still increase somewhat there. In west Wales nests are spaced only half a mile apart(f), which indicates a very high average density of about four pairs per square mile if this density is continuous over a large area.

From all these data we can take it that in ideal buzzard country, as represented by the hilly wooded areas of Wales, Devon, or West Scotland, one pair per square mile (1/2·6 sq.km.) is a conservative density, two per square mile may commonly occur, but three per square mile (1/0·9 sq.km.) will rarely be reached or exceeded. These densities may be compared with an average of 768 pairs in 1832 sq.km. (707·2 sq.miles) of seven European study areas, equivalent to just over one pair per square mile, with a variation from 2·2 pairs/square mile in Lorraine to one pair in three square miles in parts of Germany(10,17). British buzzards are on average at least as common in good habitat as in Europe, perhaps actually commoner. If a more careful estimate were made of the total extent of ideal or good buzzard habitat in Britain, with more frequent sample densities of population, it would not surprise me to find that the total present estimated population in Britain, of around 15–20,000 buzzards was an underestimate, and that my own guess of 25,000 was nearer the mark.

Table 7   Breeding Densities: Buzzard: Britain and Europe

Country/ locality	Total area surveyed sq.km.(sq.mi.)	Total pairs observed	Average Home Range Ha.	Acres	Source
Switzerland			550	1236	Mebs, 13(10)
Germany (1)	72(27·8)	48	150	371	,, ,,
(2)	31(12)	16	190	470	,, ,,
(3)	113(43·8)	33	340	840	,, ,,
(4)	82(31·7)	10	**820**	**2026**	,, ,,
All Germany	298(115·3)	107	276	682	
Belgium	50(19·3)	24	210	519	,, ,,
Denmark	1336(515·7)	522	250	618	Holstein (iii)
France (Lorraine)	148(57·1)	115	**129**	**319**	Thiollay, 13(17)
All Europe except Switzerland	1832(707·4)	768	237	584	
Britain					
Dartmoor	33·4(12·9)	15	225	590	Dare, 13(3)
Skokholm (10 year average)	2·93(1·13)	4·64	**63**	**156**	Davis, 13(4)
Speyside (1970)	155·4(60)	33	472	1164	Weir, pers. comm.
New Forest 1962–66	291·3(112·5)	35	**830**	**2052**	Tubbs, 13(18) (ii)
All British areas	483·03(186·5)	87·64	542	1360	

NOTES   (i) Figures in **bold** type indicate largest and smallest ranges.
(ii) British figures are somewhat distorted by large sample from thinly populated New Forest.
(iii) Holstein, V. 1956. Musvaagen *Buteo buteo buteo* (L). Copenhagen.

Very detailed ecological work has been done on the buzzard in two areas of Britain, on Dartmoor just after myxomatosis from 1956–58 by Peter Dare(3) and in Speyside by Douglas Weir and Nick Picozzi from 1968–72(21). Unfortunately, neither of these studies has yet been published in easily accessible form, the former because it has never been written up except in a voluminous PhD thesis secreted in the library of Exeter University, and the latter because it is as yet incomplete. Peter Dare's thesis is essential reading for anyone who wants to understand the population dynamics of buzzards or, for that matter, any bird of prey. So detailed a piece of field work can really be appreciated only by fellow workers who know the labour involved. Even if it applies to only one small area, and to a particular set of years just after the outbreak of myxomatosis, it is so much more thorough than any other published British work that it must be consulted. Douglas Weir and Nick Picozzi were girding their loins for the task when last I saw them; but it will evidently be a year at least before their detailed results are published. However, they have been kind enough to let me use some of their preliminary results for this book. If and when both these detailed studies are properly published more will be known of the ecology of the buzzard than of almost any other species, for it has also been extensively studied in the New Forest by Colin Tubbs(18) and on the Continent of Europe by several ornithologists(10,22).

Peter Dare's study area of 8250 acres near Postbridge on Dartmoor varied from 925–1737 ft A.S.L., contained two villages and several scattered farmsteads, but only 1400 acres of enclosed farmland, with 3900 acres of moors and commons and 1100 acres of young forestry plantations. The rest was bogs, small woods, and high heather moors. This area, typical of upper Dartmoor, has a more rigorous climate than what one would think of as ideal buzzard country, say in the lower wooded Dart or Teign valleys. The main food animals available were rabbits (in the initial stages of recovery after myxomatosis), brown rats, wood mice (mainly nocturnal so not often caught by buzzards), water voles, short-tailed and bank voles, and common shrews, also many frogs and toads. Various other items of prey were taken, but rabbits, voles, moles and frogs were the most important.

Fifteen available territories in this area were occupied by 12, 14 and 14 pairs in 1956, 57, and 58. The average total range available per pair was 688 acres (253 ha.) in 1956 and 590 acres (225 ha.) in 1957–8. The buzzards occupying the territories did not defend or hunt in the whole of these available areas, but defended smaller territories varying from 130–580 acres and averaging 350 acres (134 ha.), a little more than half the total area available. The territories were separated by considerable areas of unoccupied undefended ground.

Ordinarily, 'territory' is a word I dislike using in relation to any bird of prey, particularly the larger species, since they do not usually defend from others the total area available to them, and frequently do not perform any obviously aggressive actions towards intruders. The buzzard, however, seems to perform more typical territorial boundary demarcation demonstrations than do most other British raptors, and this seems to be true for the genus *Buteo* as a whole. The augur buzzard *B. rufofuscus* in Kenya is strongly aggressive to intruders in its territory; and the Craigheads in the United States recorded strong territorial behaviour in red-tailed hawks *B. jamaicensis* and Swainson's hawks *B. swainsoni*(2). When dealing with buzzards, therefore, the term 'territory' as opposed to 'home range' seems appropriate.

This behaviour observed on Dartmoor appears quite typical of buzzards, and has also been observed in Speyside and in the New Forest. The owners of territories demonstrate their right to possession by perching on conspicuous perches at the edge of the territory; by soaring in fine weather; or by diving displays, mainly by the male in fine spring weather, and again in autumn. Soaring birds frequently visit the edges of their territory where they may encounter neighbours, circle quietly and part without actual fighting. Two neighbouring males occasionally perform diving displays on the boundaries. Little obvious fighting takes place in territorial defence. An intruding stranger buzzard often appears alert and uneasy, and retreats hastily when the lawful occupants appear. When actual trespass occurs the male usually follows a stranger quietly if at a height, or dives at it when perched or flying low. Females also repel trespassers; one on Dartmoor even left her nest to do so. Dare thought that this territorial behaviour might be more intense than normal, stimulated by the prevailing post-myxomatosis food shortage. However, all *Buteo* species appear to be vigorous defenders of territory, even when food is abundant; in this respect buzzards are more vigorous than are most birds of prey, which content themselves with advertisement and seldom actually attack one another.

In Speyside many territories abut, and boundaries are defended. There is not more than 5% overlap between summer breeding territories, which remain remarkably constant from year to year(21). By the use of a decoy buzzard the boundaries of winter territories have also been established in Speyside. The decoy attracts any buzzards there may be in the area, which fly at it and even attack it. While doing so they can be critically examined for recognisable plumage characters, rings, colour markings, or any other aid to individual identification. In this way it was shown that winter ranges had broadly the same characters as summer breeding territories(21). They did not usually overlap, boundary disputes and advertisement flights took place, and intruder buzzards were attacked. The winter range of a pair is normally in the same area as the following summer's breeding territory, and any slight adjustments occur at the end of the breeding season. The winter range is usually the lower altitude part of the summer range, and is contained within it(21).

On Dartmoor Dare found that the young of the year and unsuccessful breeding adults moved out of the area. Half the young had left by early October and all by the following February. The total population of adults on the 8250 acres varied from 17 in late 1955 to 30 at the end of 1956 and in early 1958. As 80–90 separate individuals were recognised, of which only 17 were young reared in the area there was clearly a rapid turnover in the adult population. Unsuccessful breeding birds which had lost eggs or young emigrated usually before July and the territory would then remain empty till October, sometimes to midwinter, before being occupied by new adults from some other area. Once new adults had arrived they generally stayed and bred at least once and successful breeders continued to occupy their territories. In thirteen cases of re-occupation of vacant territories new pairs arrived, already mated, in eight; in five cases one member arrived first, to be joined later by a mate. Two mate-replacements occurred in late February six weeks after the previous mate had died. During the breeding season March–June and through to the end of October, when broods of young were still present in the territories, little or no immigration took place(3).

The Dartmoor results were obtained in a poor food supply situation, but generally similar behaviour has been observed in Speyside in a good food supply situation, with larger territories available per pair than on Dartmoor. Territorial behaviour does appear to limit the numbers of buzzards that can live in any area. On Dartmoor some of the territories were much larger than others; of the 14 pairs, seven lived in 4·5 square miles (11·6 sq.km.) averaging 380 acres (152 ha.) per pair, while the other seven lived on 8·5 square miles (22 sq.km.) averaging 780 acres (315 ha.) per pair. Since not even the whole of the smaller ranges was actively defended by the territory owners there should theoretically be considerable room for compression of territory size to still smaller areas in more abundant food supply conditions such as in Speyside. However, this does not seem to occur, and in both Speyside and Dartmoor the number of territories remains remarkably constant despite variations in food supply. The undefended areas of 'no man's land' comprising almost half the whole area, may well be vital to the survival of young buzzards.

According to Dare the Dartmoor buzzards hunted assiduously during the daylight hours. They use a wide variety of hunting techniques, but three main methods; perching and scanning their immediate surroundings intently; walking or standing on the ground; and hovering low over open country. These methods are common to all *Buteo* species that have been carefully observed. Hunting effort is concentrated in those areas where prey is likely to be abundant. The buzzards respond quickly to changes in weather or variation in abundance of prey, and the roles of the sexes in hunting depends largely on the stage of the eggs or brood of young in the nest. In times of food shortages especially an intimate knowledge of the territory is an advantage, an experienced adult having a better chance to catch prey than a newcomer. The quantity and type of prey taken varies according to the time of day and the weather. In the New Forest buzzards have intensive hunting spells in early morning and at evening, and soar most often towards midday when thermal activity is greatest(o).

In autumn and winter, from September to February, Dartmoor buzzards hunt most often from perches. From March to June buzzards on Dartmoor hover more often than they perch, and perches are used for hunting only when some such factor as bad weather prevents hovering. In the New Forest buzzards hunt most from perches and seldom hover, behaviour probably associated with woodland habitat and avian prey. Carrion is eaten on Dartmoor when it can be found, and many buzzards may feed on the same carcase. Buzzards will also attend moor fires, as hawks attend grass fires in tropical Africa. No doubt these details of hunting behaviour vary from place to place; but if a buzzard is soaring high up it is safe to conclude that it is not hunting.

Within their territories buzzards have favourite hunting perches which may be dead trees, fence posts, rocks or telephone posts; such favourite perches are defended against other buzzards. It is perhaps necessary for a buzzard to remain for a certain minimum time on any perch for prey (which may have been alarmed by the bird's flight from one perch to another) to appear. Voles, which squeal, can probably be located by ear as well as by eye. When a buzzard sights prey from a perch it moves its head to and fro, probably to assist in pinpointing the exact position, descends in a gentle glide, and finally pounces. Large kills are taken to other perches to dismember, small are swallowed whole; these habits appear common to most *Buteo* species.

When hovering buzzards may hover at up to 300 feet (100 m.) above the ground, head to wind, with gently fanning wings. When prey is sighted the buzzard drops gently at first, by partly closing its wings but as it approaches the ground may either give up, or suddenly raise the wings above the back and plunge on the prey. Success is difficult to judge, because the object of attack may be a small beetle or a field vole; but if a kill is made the buzzard does not usually rise immediately from the ground, but picks at its feet, which hold the prey. As many as ten unsuccessful attacks are made for every successful pounce.

Other methods of hunting are used less often. Walking or standing about on the ground is likely to yield mainly invertebrates such as beetles, caterpillars, or earthworms. R. W. Hayman records an extraordinary case where five to seven buzzards frequented the same sown grass field from September to November 1968, spending much time on the ground, and seizing small invertebrate prey with a clumsy walk or, if need be, a waddling run(5). Low pursuit flights are seldom used, but nevertheless, in some areas especially the New Forest, buzzards do capture many birds and some must be caught in flight(18). One buzzard in Wales easily took a starling from a flock flying across an estuary, without apparently stooping at it or greatly accelerating the pace of pursuit(m), and another Welsh buzzard has been seen to take a woodpigeon with a stoop like that of a peregrine(c). On Speyside buzzards have been seen to kill woodpigeons and grouse in the manner of an eagle. Normally, however, spectacular methods of killing are not to be expected of the buzzard.

A buzzard's daily food requirement was estimated by Dare, with captive young birds, as about 140 grams (5 oz), which is more than 10% of bodyweight and consequently rather higher in proportion than in American *Buteos* studied by the Craigheads, which ate about 10% of bodyweight(2). Others, with less detailed data, consider this estimate too high, and that 80–100 grams per day would be nearer the mark, on the basis of food brought to the nest by adults, or with captive buzzards(1). Accepting the estimate of 140 grams, and that an average young rabbit weighs 250 grams (9 oz) (a full grown one weighs more than 1000 grams (2½ lb) and buzzards can kill rabbits larger than 250 grams) it is clear that a buzzard which catches a young rabbit has enough for more than one day. However, if rabbits are very scarce and hard to catch, a buzzard may have to catch seven or eight voles (which weigh 15–60 grams and average about 20 grams) to provide its daily ration. In hard weather in winter an adult buzzard can starve for two weeks and stay alive, but a growing brood in the nest must be fed daily. These figures indicate why the buzzard was so successful in the presence of abundant rabbits, and why the myxomatosis epizootic so affected the total population. In the absence of rabbits more moles and vipers are taken; but such prey is scarcer and harder to catch. Voles are most often taken in the winter, rabbits in spring and summer. Frogs are an important article of diet in March and April when they are spawning, and most of the birds caught by buzzards are young recently out of the nest in July and August. In Speyside such young birds include everything from robins to young capercaillie.

The amount of time spent hunting obviously must depend on the availability and weight of different types of prey. Dare's Dartmoor buzzards, in a low rabbit population, had to spend most of each winter day hunting and in high summer the males were active from dawn to dark, up to 16½ hours out of 24(3). One male, whose mate was on the nest the whole day, hunted for 8½/11 hours and made five small kills in that time; in another pair the male hunted for 11½/13½ possible hours, and the female for 6½/8 hours observed. The male brought 11 kills to the nest, the female two, but she hunted mainly near the nest while the male ranged widely. Evidently, if either of these birds had easily caught a rabbit they would not have needed to continue hunting. In the New Forest buzzards spend more time perching or hunting through the woodland in the manner of a goshawk or sparrowhawk, mainly in early morning and evening(0).

It is easy to understand why in Northern Europe, with still shorter winter days and heavy snow on the ground, buzzards are forced to migrate further south while those that live permanently in mild climates further south can remain where they are. Equally, one can understand why buzzards in Speyside, with a relatively abundant rabbit population up to midsummer, can rear large broods while those on Dartmoor immediately after myxomatosis could not.

The requirement of a pair of adult buzzards (inhabiting their territory all the year round) is about 101 kg. of food (223 lb). That of the brood from hatching to independence varies according to the number of chicks reared, but for each chick is estimated at 6890 grams (15 lb), made up of 250 grams in days 1–5, 765 grams in days 6–14, 910 grams in days 15–21, and 3465 grams in days 22–42, when the chick is reaching full size and rapidly growing its feathers; its appetite is then greater than that of an adult. 1500 grams (3·3 lb) are needed for the 10 days following first flight, before the young buzzard can kill any prey for itself. Young buzzards are regularly fed by their parents for up to two months after first flight and on occasion may still be fed seven months after first flight. However, once they can fly strongly they presumably catch some prey for themselves, and if they remain in the territory their appetite can be regarded as the same as that of an adult, needing 140 grams per day.

Taking the national average brood size of 1·37 young per occupied nest, and assuming that the young leave the adults' territory two months after first flight, an average territory must provide about 123 kg. (260 lb) of prey during the year. This is made up of nearly 500 average young rabbits (492) but of over 6000 average voles. From this Dare concluded that if buzzards had neither abundant voles nor fairly common rabbits in their territories they could not rear broods, for enough food must be continuously available for the first three weeks of the chicks' lives, during which time the female is dependent also on the killing ability of the male. In times of acute food shortage Dare noted that the parents went without and fed all that they caught to the young. Such facts indicate that the behaviour of buzzards is not entirely controlled by their own appetites.

The actual composition of the buzzard's diet has been exhaustively studied by many observers; but is too often expressed generally as 'mainly rabbits and voles' without giving full details. To summarise, mammals are preferred when available, and various species of voles are by far the commonest items. All continental studies indicated 40–60% of voles by number in the prey; for instance 1906 mice, voles and water voles among 2209 mammals and 2556 identified food items in a study of stomach contents of 1237 shot buzzards by G. Rorig in 1909; and 2486 small mammals out of 2532 mammals in 3588 vertebrate items in a recent study in Lorraine(17,20) The Lorraine buzzards appear to have eaten more birds and invertebrates than do most continental buzzards (814 and 2104). So important are voles in the diet of continental buzzards that clutch size, brood size, and brood survival are all affected by their abundance or otherwise, smaller clutches and broods being produced in bad vole years(10).

There is less detail available in the food of British buzzards and it is unfortunate that so few of those who took part in the buzzard survey provided accurate food data. The few who did observed that in all parts of Britain rabbits and other small mammals were the commonest prey, and that oddments such as eels and trout might even be taken, perhaps picked up dead. On Dartmoor Dare found 774 mammals (including 193 rabbits and 364 voles), 103 birds, 55 reptiles, and 131 amphibia in pellets; the birds included three young buzzards eaten by their nest mates, thrushes, finches, and corvids, but no young gamebirds or poultry. In addition there were countless insect remains. 508 items of prey brought to nests included 345 mammals (120 rabbits and 134 voles), 73 birds, 15 reptiles (13 vipers) and some amphibia. By weight, rabbits and voles would be the most important items.

In the New Forest buzzards feed much more on birds, especially young corvids and pigeons. In visits to 81 nests during the fledging period Tubbs found young jackdaws on 71 nests, jays on 50, stock doves on 42, song thrushes on 29, and woodpigeons on 21, often in large quantities, three or more per nest visited. Rabbits were scarce up to 1964, after which they have appeared on almost every nest; the only other regular mammalian prey was woodmice, present on 31 nests. Birds found on less than 10 nests, in other words species taken only irregularly included green woodpecker, pheasant (6 on 5 nests), woodcock, magpie, chaffinch, greater spotted woodpecker, tawny owl and carrion crow. Mammals taken irregularly included grey squirrel, mole, short-tailed vole and young hares. There were also a few reptiles and casual items found only once included red-legged partridge and five other bird species, adder and lizard(18). The Speyside results have not yet been summarised; but here again small mammals, especially young rabbits, predominate in the diet.

All these results show that a buzzard is a versatile hunter but that, even when birds are important in the diet, very few gamebirds are taken. In the 1909 German study 29 gamebirds occurred among 2556 items; in Lorraine 4 out of 814 birds and 3040 vertebrate items; in the New Forest, where gamebirds are relatively quite plentiful compared to some buzzard habitats, only 6 pheasant chicks among at least 800 other items; 6 pheasant chicks among 33 pairs in 11 years is less than one-fiftieth of a pheasant per year per pair. In Speyside buzzards are known to take rather more gamebirds, but it is estimated that the total take is only about three gamebird chicks per nesting pair per annum, a negligible proportion of the total population(p). Buzzards in Speyside take several gamebird species from grouse to young capercaillie; but some of the gamebirds brought to nests are undoubtedly picked up on roads or scavenged from other predators. One young capercaillie known to have been first killed by a fox was later brought to a nest(p).

No sensible ornithologist will deny that buzzards do take a certain number of gamebirds. In 1970 I myself saw a buzzard eating a red grouse beside a road, where it might have been injured by a car; and I saw another grouse in a buzzard's nest in 1972. However, I have located only two other published records of red grouse taken by a buzzard since the publication of the *Handbook of British Birds* in 1943, which did not record that grouse were ever taken(8). The damage done by buzzards to pheasants, grouse, partridge, or any other gamebird is negligible in relation to the other adverse factors affecting populations of these birds, and there is no excuse whatever for the continued persecution of the otherwise very useful buzzard by the gamekeeping fraternity. This is a typical example of the sort of result that is arrived at whenever the food habits of a raptor accused of taking large numbers of gamebirds, pigeons, or lambs, is investigated carefully by objective naturalists; and it is quite time such evidence was given the legal weight that is its due.

Although the ecological habits and hunting behaviour of the British buzzard have been well investigated I cannot find similarly detailed work on the breeding biology. I have searched the main British journals from the time of the publication of the *Handbook of Brisish Birds* in 1943, and for some time beyond that without locating a single good breeding behaviour paper on the buzzard. Dare did provide some good information from Dartmoor; but his visits to nests were incidental rather than intended to provide detailed breeding data, and most other papers recently published on the buzzard refer to status, breeding success, and kindred matters that at present preoccupy the minds of those who fear for our dwindling stocks of birds of prey. Full understanding of the breeding biology is, in my opinion, just as important as any other aspect of buzzard behaviour.

The breeding cycle, among established pairs that have wintered in their territories or in near-by winter ranges, begins on the first fine days of early spring. Display can be seen as early as February, earlier in a mild winter(3,j). Fine weather, enabling the birds to soar, is essential for the mainly aerial nuptial display; on cold wet foggy days they cannot display. Either a single bird, or a pair, mounts to a considerable height, as much as a thousand feet or more above the ground, and very often calls. A circling calling pair may attract other neighbouring buzzards, and then five or six, or even ten, may be seen circling together(k). The male, who weighs on average 130 grams less than the female, and consequently has lower wing loading, can mount faster than she can and, as a result, can readily gain a position some hundreds of feet above her. From here he dives at her, shoots past, and swings up again, often screaming as he does so; alternatively he may perform these diving or undulating displays by himself, the successive upward swoops being shorter than the downward dives, so that his course is gradually downward. After repeating the performance ten or twelve times he will seek to regain height before another bout of diving and upward swooping.

Sometimes buzzards call when perched; and a male will often dive at a perched female, swing up again, and repeat the performance; or the female may take wing and soar with him. The diving and upward swooping of the male is performed, not only before the female but also in the presence of a neighbouring male on the border of the territory. If a male is diving and swooping alone he may only be advertising himself rather than courting his mate.

Occasionally, but apparently rather rarely, a mutual circling display in which the male dives at his mate causes her to turn over on her back and present her claws to his(k). This is not often reported in British buzzards, but is very common in some other *Buteo* species. Still less often the pair may lock claws at this point and come cartwheeling down, their wings 'resembling the rotating sails of a windmill' as one observer put it; they separate after falling several hundred feet(j). This cartwheeling display is commonly seen in sea and fish eagles and kites, but more rarely in other birds of prey. Arguments may arise as to whether it is the male and female courting, or whether it is a fight between two rival males, but if such be-haviour follows a circling flight in which the two have flown together, calling, it is probably courtship. Some reported instances, however, such as the occasion when two struggling buzzards fell on to the back of a horse ridden by an exceedingly surprised Monmouthshire farmer, are more likely fights between rival males than mutual nuptial display(h).

In the New Forest buzzards are seen displaying over the woodland, in the manner of an *Accipiter* species, in nearly level flight with slow, deliberate wing-beats(o). It is possible that this type of display may be significant for raptors that breed in dense woodlands, and is a further indication that the New Forest buzzards are a long isolated population and something of a law unto themselves.

Displays continue, at least on the part of the male, till after the eggs are laid. They may be resumed to some extent, but less vigorously, in fine autumn weather after the brood of young have become independent. The fledged young birds themselves may go through the motions of display. An adult mated pair of buzzards then intending to remain in their territory for the rest of the winter advertise their continued presence in this way though, of course, they cannot breed at that time of the year.

Buzzards regularly reoccupy the same nesting sites and each pair has several nests or groups of nests in different woods. Nests may be up to half a mile apart, but are usually within 200 yards of each other(3,21,18). The nests of adjacent pairs may be 500 yards to 1¼ miles (490–3000 m.) apart. Where trees are available buzzards prefer to use them; but in relatively treeless country may build in a cliff, an earth bank above a stream, occasionally even almost on the ground on a slope. Analysis of 874 nest record cards at the B.T.O. shows that in southern England all nests are in trees except for one in a quarry and two on sea-cliffs, while about a quarter of Welsh buzzards build on cliffs(19). Most tree nests are in woods, but isolated or hedgerow trees are sometimes used. In northern England and the Scottish Highlands about as many nests are in cliffs as in trees, no doubt because there are fewer suitable nesting woods. There are, however, places such as the Island of Mull and Argyll where buzzards will nest in cliffs even though suitable tree sites are sometimes available to them.

When in a tree the nest site requires a secure fork, shelter and concealment, a wide field of view, and easy access(3). If two-thirds of these needs are available accessibility is of less importance; but buzzards prefer to breed in high trees. On Dartmoor heights of 29 nests varied from 15 feet (3m.) above ground in a hawthorn to 60 feet (20m.); in the New Forest they were from 40–75 feet above ground, usually in oak or Scots pine and in Speyside are 6–75 feet (2–25 m.) above ground. On Dartmoor 21/29 nests were in conifers, and this was apparently due to actual preference because there were plenty of other trees available; perhaps the rather rigorous climate made the shelter of a dense conifer attractive.

The average number of nests per pair in Speyside is three, but pairs have 1–11 nests(p). In the New Forest one pair had 14 nests, but two or three is usual(18). The same nest is not normally occupied for two years in succession but a number of such instances are recorded. In 97 pair/years in the New Forest only four pairs used the same nest for more than one consecutive year, and two for three years; but one used the same nest for 14 years and in Speyside one nest has been used for eight out of nine years. Thus, although there is considerable variation most buzzards prefer to change their nest often. They usually build up and line more than one nest, finally selecting one of these.

A newly built nest is a substantial structure of sticks, heather, or whatever may be readily available; it becomes more substantial with repeated use in the same territory, and is used by a succession of different adults, not only by the bird that built it. It is apparently the site, located in a suitable available territory, that draws the birds to occupy it. On Dartmoor most of the nests were near the centre of the territory and only occasionally towards the periphery, but this seems to be less true of Speyside and the New Forest. Recent work near Sedbergh suggests that nests on the periphery of home ranges are more likely to be used in good vole years, though why is rather obscure(6).

Building of the nest may begin or even be completed in February, two months before the eggs are laid, if the weather is fine and the birds active in display. During March and early April more material is added, sometimes a considerable amount, and the addition of green branches towards the end of the building period indicates, as a rule, which nest is to be used. It has been suggested that these green branches are a form of camouflage to help make the nest less visible in spring(16), when the trees are leafing out; but as the habit is common to most large birds of prey and is used in situations where it actually makes the nest more rather than less conspicuous we may rule this out. The ultimate function of these green branches is to provide a soft bed of leaves on which the eggs are laid; but quite why the birds bring green branches and not small dry sticks is still uncertain. Buzzards certainly select the material they bring for this purpose, preferring pine or spruce tips if these are available.

When the female is ready to mate she solicits the male by perching, fluttering her wings, and raising and lowering her tail. The male usually then flies straight on to her back and mates or may perch beside her and later mount her(k). Mating takes about 15 seconds. Most matings take place on the nest, but mating is recorded up to 150 yards (150 m.) from the nest, and on occasion no doubt occurs further away. Mating is recorded as early as mid January. From the time of coition the female is tied more and more to the nest site, and the male takes over all or most of the hunting duties formerly shared by the pair. He may sometimes have fed his mate during courtship, but from now on must catch most of the food required for the pair.

The laying date varies less than might be expected, in relation to temperature and leafage, from south to north. In Cornwall and Devon most clutches are laid early April to early May, with the majority of Cornish clutches laid between 9–20 April(3,16). In Lakeland most clutches are laid about a week later, 15–25 April, and in Speyside the peak laying dates are 10–20 April, with a spread from 29 March to 5 May(d,e). This indicates a remarkable consistency in the main laying period, from about 10–25 April, all over Britain. In any one area there may be a spread of more than a month. On Dartmoor Dare recorded no clutches before 5 April; four from 6–10 April; one from 11–15 April; seven from 16–20 April; five from 21–25 April; two from 26–30 April; one between 1 and 5 May; and two more from 6–10 May, a total spread of about 34 days.

Not every pair of buzzards breeds every year. As was brought out on a countrywide scale in Dr Moore's survey, which indicated that fewer buzzards bred after the onset of myxomatosis, non-breeding is probably connected with inadequate winter and spring food supply(11). In Europe buzzards breed less often and lay smaller clutches in years of poor winter food supply(10). Absolute proof of non-breeding in any raptor is hard to obtain, and the buzzard, breeding in woods, is a difficult species in this respect. However, if a nest is not located during incubation it often is once young have hatched.

On Dartmoor, in 40 pair/years eggs were laid in 29 cases; that is, 27% did not breed, in a poor food supply situation(3). On Skomer, in an exceptionally dense population of buzzards 11/51 pairs noted did not breed (19%)(4). In the New Forest, which appears to be somewhat marginal buzzard habitat, non-breeding was observed in 15/97 nests, and probably the proportion was actually higher since in the last three years of the survey 13/62 (21%) did not breed; in some years, as many as 25% did not breed(18). In Speyside in 1970, despite a good food supply, only 29/34 pairs laid, or 15% non-breeders(p). Some pairs do not breed for several years in succession; one in the New Forest did not lay or hatch in any of three years. Others lay every year. Non-breeding is not necessarily associated with, for instance, building a new nest, for in the New Forest in seven cases nests were built and not used but in eight others only old nests were associated with non-breeding. Nor is it connected with the actual size of a range or territory though it may be due, for instance, to the death of an adult in late spring or to immaturity(3).

British buzzards usually lay 2–3 eggs, sometimes 4, occasionally 1 or 5. Six have been recorded, and the *Handbook of British Birds* suggests that clutches of 1 may be laid by very old birds; the evidence for this is not given but may be based on egg collectors' series(23). The average for all Britain 1948–69, as recorded on 641 B.T.O. nest record cards is 2·56, but it has varied from 1·9 in 1962 to 3·0 in 1948 (with a small sample)(19). The mean of 91 Devon and Somerset clutches in 1948 was 2·8 and in Cumberland and Westmorland that of 67 clutches was 2·7(i). Individual females average higher clutches during their lifetime. One bird in the centre of Exmoor laid 27 eggs in seven years of an eight-year period; she was robbed one year but averaged 3·9 in the rest(i). Regionally, clutch size seems to increase from south to north, being 1·9 in the New Forest, 2·2 in S.W. England, 2·3–2·5 in N.W. England, and 2·7 overall in Scotland; the last figure, however is affected by the predominance of Speyside results with large clutches (averaging 2·9 from 1964–71) in favourable food supply. The analysis does not suggest that clutch size was seriously reduced after myxomatosis; it averaged 2·4 for three years after 1954 as compared to 2·7 for three previous years. This is further supported by Dare's Dartmoor results, where 14 clutches averaged 2·43 in 1956–8, very little less than the national average.

These figures may be compared with a mean of 1·96 in poor years and 2·85 in good vole years in Europe, while 298 European clutches average 2·45(10). British buzzards evidently lay clutches as large as those of their European relatives, and there is no real evidence of a reduction in clutch size in recent times, associated with myxomatosis, pesticides, or any other factor. New Forest buzzards consistently lay smaller than average clutches.

I have not located detailed data on the share of the sexes in incubation in British buzzards, but in this species both sexes take part, which is typical of *Buteo* species in general. The female does much more incubation by day and sits all night. She either does not kill or rarely kills for herself during incubation. Dare's observations suggest that she is tied to the nest during the whole incubation and the first half of the fledging period, but this does not seem to be invariable; other observers have reported kills by the female when off the nest(p). Recorded incubation periods in Britain vary from 36–38 days for each egg, with one old record of 28 days from Speyside. Continental records indicate that the period is 33–35 days for each egg, an egg taking 48 hours from chipping to hatch; according to the number of eggs the clutch hatches over 3–7 days. Most British clutches hatch in the second half of May.

Failure to rear young once eggs have been laid is too often due to egg loss. Analysis of the B.T.O. nest record cards shows that human predation is the most serious cause of egg loss, amounting to at least a third of all cases; farmers and gamekeepers rather than egg collectors are most often the cause of this. In the New Forest, loss of clutches varied from 6·3–25%, mainly due to predation by crows. On Dartmoor crows destroyed only one clutch directly but were indirectly aided to destroy three other clutches by inadvertent human interference. It is important not to disturb buzzards in the incubation period, for such disturbance can enable other predators to destroy the eggs. Overall egg loss on Dartmoor was nearly 40%, and 102 of 641 clutches on B.T.O. cards were lost. In Speyside, of every 1000 eggs laid, 733 hatch, a loss of just over 25%(3,18,p).

At hatching the young weigh 40–45 grams, and grow very fast. At 18 days they weigh 400 grams (0·86 lb), nearly half the weight of an adult, and at 28–32 days 800 grams (1·75 lb), almost the weight of an adult. Thereafter their weight gains decrease, and food is mainly used for feather production. When they make their first flight they may actually weigh less than adults, with a maximum of about 1000 grams (2·2 lb) compared to 1250 grams (2·85 lb) for a large adult female(1). They fly at 50–55 days as a rule, sometimes longer. On Dartmoor the fledging period averaged 53 days, and 40 records from the New Forest vary from 48–62 days(3,0). Here it seems that the length of the fledging period may be controlled by the situation of the nest and the ease of making the first flights. After leaving the nest the young cannot fly strongly for at least another ten days and are normally dependent on their parents for food for six to eight weeks.

Brood survival has been very extensively studied, both in Britain and in Europe in recent years. It appears to be directly affected by food supply. In Britain as a whole the average brood size is 1·37 young per pair from average clutches of 2·56 from 1948–69, varying from 0·9 in 1955 and 1960 to 1·6 in 1952 and 1969(19). There is no indication that brood survival has fallen off, and it does not seem to be directly connected with clutch size, myxomatosis, or with the prevalence of pesticides. Brood sizes in the south of England are generally less than those for the north of England and Scotland, and there are great regional variations. On Dartmoor 1956–58 the average was 0·45 young per pair overall, but in Speyside in 1970 the average was 1·8 per pair(p). One pair of Speyside buzzards has reared 26 young in eight years averaging 3·2/year; and one New Forest pair either did not lay or failed to rear any young in any of three years. The broods in the New Forest are again below all other areas, averaging 1·2, while all those from the Scottish Highlands average 1·9. On Skomer, in the densest known population of buzzards, brood size has varied from 0·66–1·03/pair overall, 0·73–1·34 per occupied nest, and 1·55–2·00 per successful nest(4). In Britain as a whole the number of young reared per successful nest varies from 1·4 in the New Forest to 1·7–1·9 in the rest of England and Wales and 2·2 in the Highlands of Scotland. In Speyside, of 733 young hatched from 1000 eggs 700 are expected to fly. These figures for Britain compare favourably with continental figures where, in about 400 cases over a period of years, an average of 1·2–1·4 young were reared(1,10). In Germany, brood survival is better (2·14/nest) in good vole years than in bad years, when it might be as low as 1·35/nest(10). Again, the breeding performance of British buzzards is at least as good as in Europe.

In rearing the young the second week of the fledging period appears to be critical. For the first 15 days of the fledging period, while the young are small and downy, the female remains on or near the nest and takes little or no part in hunting for herself or the brood. At this time the male must be able to catch enough for himself and his mate (280 grams) and for a growing brood in the nest which, in this area, at this stage would normally number two and needs another 150–200 gr./day, making a total of about 430–480 grams (0·9–1·1 lb) needed daily. This stage of the breeding cycle occurs about 25 May to 5 June in most cases, which coincides with the emergence of numbers of young rabbits. If the male can catch these, weighing 250 grams each, he still needs about two per day; if he must depend wholly on voles, weighing 20 grams each, he must catch 22–24 per day, or about 1·5 per hunting hour, dawn to dark, wet or fine, which is a higher rate of success than has been noted by direct observation. This again emphasises how important the rabbit is to buzzards in Britain, and helps to explain why large broods are reared in Speyside and smaller in parts of the country where rabbits are scarce. New Forest buzzards, which live largely on corvids and pigeons, have evidently arrived at a different balance between brood survival and food supply(18).

After day 21 of the fledging period not only can the young survive longer without food, but the female can also take part in hunting and so double the hunting effort. Losses among young buzzards are usually lower after this stage(3,10). Deaths among young New Forest buzzards however generally occur in the third or fourth week of the fledging period, after the female can hunt, and suggest quite a different period of maximum food availability(18). A certain amount of loss in the earlier stages is due to inter-sibling fighting (or the Cain and Abel battle as it is usually called), but more is due to the fact that the elder young are very much heavier and more active than the younger and so are more likely to get whatever food is available. Dead chicks are either eaten by the parents or fed to their nest-mates(3). In Speyside chicks are usually found below the nest, suggesting a lesser need in areas of abundant food to eat the dead young(p).

Towards the end of the fledging period the young buzzards are left almost entirely alone in their nests, with prey brought to them by either parent as and when caught. From 30 days onwards they do not have to be fed but can tear prey up for themselves. At this stage of the fledging period the total requirement for parents and brood, assuming that in most cases one or more of the young will have died from starvation, is about 420–480 grams (c. 1 lb) but both parents can now spend all day hunting. Even if they can find no rabbits they each must average only about one vole per 1½ hours to satisfy the brood, and the young themselves can remain on the nest eating what is available as they feel hungry, without having to be fed. At this time – early July or end of June – myxomatosis usually has struck again, so that there may be plenty of moribund young rabbits wandering in the open and easy to catch. Accordingly, it is not surprising that losses in the late fledging period, among young that have so far survived, are slight.

The young buzzards make preliminary short flights before finally leaving the nest, which they do of their own accord, without prompting or coaxing by the parents. When first they leave their quill feathers are not fully developed – in the blood as falconers put it – and it is at least another two weeks before they are strong on the wing and the quills fully developed. Dispersal begins from four to eight weeks after first flight. The young on Dartmoor all remained in the areas where they were reared until mid August, four weeks after leaving the nest, but by September they had been reduced by deaths or emigration and by mid October a general exodus had begun and only about a third of the young were still present(3). In Speyside dispersal begins in August about a month after fledging, but in the New Forest may be delayed for another month, until September(21). Dispersal normally begins in the first month out of the nest, and is usually nearly complete by the end of the third month. Few young remain in breeding areas after the end of December but young have been seen soliciting parents for food up to February, seven months after leaving the nest. The behaviour varies somewhat regionally or according to the severity or otherwise of the winter. Since a good many pairs fail during breeding, and at that time apparently leave their breeding territories, there is sometimes a considerable area of no man's land into which young buzzards can disperse; this does not seem to be true of Speyside. Adults begin re-demonstrating their presence in their territory in October, but by this time most young are independent.

Further light on the behaviour of immature buzzards after dispersal from the nesting area comes from Speyside(21). Of 41 young colour-ringed in the study area in 1969 only two were seen again and two others were recovered dead outside it. One of the colour-ringed birds, which had been ringed 10 miles (16 km.) N.E. as a nestling, set up a winter territory from mid October. Four other immatures did likewise but since they had no colour rings they were clearly immigrant immatures from elsewhere. All these young remained within the same small areas of about 100 acres (39 ha.) or less, and defended them more or less vigorously against other adult or immature buzzards. Two of these winter ranges actually overlapped, and all were in no man's land outside adult winter or summer territories.

Such behaviour again varies from place to place and from season to season. In Speyside in 1971–72, in an unusually mild winter, the young did not set up defended winter territories but were more nomadic, moving from place to place(p). On Dartmoor in 1956–58 all the young left the study area and did not attempt to establish winter ranges within it. Two adults attempted to establish a territory in 'no man's land' between known territories but failed to breed, and another pair may have failed because of persistent intrusions on their territory. Most buzzards passing through the Dartmoor study area in winter were dispersing juveniles, resented and repelled by the resident adults so that none stayed more than four or five days. In Speyside certain ringed young, which had disappeared as immatures from the study area, have returned to it at sexual maturity.

Thousands of buzzards have been ringed in the nest or as first-year young in Britain, but the majority of recoveries indicate that they do not move very far(b). Of a total of 106 such young birds recovered up to 1971 three were found at their nests having died there since ringing, six where ringed; 38 had travelled less than 20 miles (32 km.); 21, 11–20 miles; 13, 21–30 miles; 11, 31–40 miles; 1, 41–50 miles and 13 more than 50 miles (80 km.). These latter included two of six recoveries from young ringed in the New Forest, among them both the long-distance records. One of these was recovered at Rowlston, Yorkshire, 215 miles (324 km.) N.N.E. and the other, which also had the distinction of being the only British buzzard recovered abroad, was at Malmaison, Aisne, France, where it was pole-trapped, 270 miles (432 km.) E.S.E. Of the remaining New Forest recoveries none were less than 20 miles from home and the average distance travelled by young New Forest buzzards (89 miles or 142 km.) is about four times the average for all British buzzards (22 miles or 35 km.) and more than five times the average for all other British buzzards (17 miles or 27 km.). However the sample is small from the New Forest and apart from the two long-distance travellers the journeys of the other five were not remarkable, 20–35 miles. The available evidence indicates therefore that British buzzards are not likely to move far from where they are reared though evidently autumn dispersal is widespread. But again New Forest buzzards seem to be greater wanderers, and are so far the only British buzzards to cross to Europe, in a single case. No foreign-ringed buzzards have been recovered in Britain though continental birds are on the whole more mobile(9).

The British ringing records show that the huge majority of the recoveries are of birds shot, trapped or found dead in their first winter. 82/106 were so recovered, 14 aged one to two years, 5 aged two to three and only 5 over three years, of which the two oldest were birds of 11 and 12. This indicates a loss of 90% before sexual maturity in Britain; but this must be higher than is natural because so many of the ringing recoveries are of birds that are admittedly shot or have died from some other unnatural cause. Recent Speyside data indicate that of 700 young fledged (from 1000 eggs and 733 hatched) 233 on average are alive at the end of the first year, mortality of about 67% in the first year(p). Much more extensive ringing studies in Europe have shown that 63% of young die in their first winter and 79% before their third year, when they can normally breed(7, 13). Such figures appear typical of all *Buteo* species for which there are adequate data(i). Four out of five young buzzards die before they can breed, and in Britain the death rate may be even higher because of a continuing fairly high level of persecution in some areas, but not in others. Despite this high rate of mortality the buzzard has proved that it is able to survive and recover from both continual persecution, in the past more severe than at present, and such factors as catastrophic epizootics among its favourite prey, in the shape of rabbit myxomatosis. Probably, therefore, mortality of young would be very high even in a capacity population of totally undisturbed buzzards, such as might still be found in parts of Wales.

The life of a young buzzard, once independent of its parents in its first winter, is in any case likely to be precarious. The remaining full adults, somewhat reduced from the total summer population by deaths maintain and hold winter territories, and the young must do the best they can with what land remains available or live unobtrusively in adults' territories. To some extent they are tolerated by adults, and they can sometimes defend their own winter ranges, though this ceases in spring; as already mentioned, this behaviour varies from season to season and place to place.

The total number of young in the population at the end of the breeding season, say in October, is usually less than that of the adults, but may vary from almost the same number in an area such as Speyside, where the average brood is almost two per pair, to less than a quarter of the adult population in such an area as Dartmoor 1956–8 where the average brood is less than one young per two pairs. It seems possible that small numbers of young reared per pair might have a better chance of survival through their first winter than in areas where broods are large; mortality of the young might be density-dependent. However, there is as yet no evidence to support this suggestion.

The British population is augmented in winter by only a few continental buzzards. No European-ringed buzzard has ever been recovered here. In certain years, such as 1951, buzzards are included in autumn migration peaks on the continent, but few of these birds reach Britain(q). A buzzard seen in Britain in winter is normally one which has been bred here.

Once it is sexually mature the buzzard has a good chance of survival for several more years of breeding life. The life span has been calculated from European records of 5·38 years for all buzzards more than one year old(13). Taking the average British brood size, 1·37 young per nest, and 80% mortality before sexual maturity in the third year, a British buzzard must live just under eight years as an adult to replace itself with another sexually mature individual. In an area such as Speyside, with a mean brood of nearly two young, buzzards can replace themselves within five years but on Dartmoor (if the breeding success is still as low as 0·45 young per pair overall) they must average 22 years, which is unlikely. Four to six years as an adult is probably about the normal breeding life of a buzzard, or six to eight years altogether if two years as immatures is added. Odd buzzards live very much longer and, until recently a buzzard of just under 24 held the age record for wild ringed birds. Since 1961, however, that record has been beaten by both ospreys and red kites among birds of prey, by a herring gull, a curlew, and, of all things, an oystercatcher.

Far too many buzzards still die of unnatural causes that is, they are shot, poisoned, or trapped by gamekeepers. In 1912, at a very early stage of ringing, two young ringed in the nest at Scourie were captured at Invershin and shot at Durness respectively(b). Two young from the same nest at Eigg, in 1934, were shot three months later on the same day. A good many are trapped, some of them deliberately, for ringing, and released again, sometimes after a period of nursing. Most of the ringing records now state 'found dead' which may mean that they have died from unnatural or natural causes. Buzzards have been killed by cars and electrocuted on the high tension wires where they often perch, and one had the ill luck to be killed by a shell on a practice firing range. However, the most curious case of all is of one which drowned in the sea. It flew out to sea from the island of Eigg, was somewhat pestered by seabirds, and settled on the water. After resting, apparently calmly, for about five seconds, it tried to take off, could not, and finally perished after 20 minutes in the water. The body was recovered and there was no evidence of injury, nor had the bird been savagely attacked by seabirds and driven down(g).

If unnatural mortality, mainly caused by gamekeepers, can be further reduced, perhaps by endeavouring to ensure that there is a better understanding of the true

BRITISH BIRDS OF PREY

role of this useful bird as a predator in nature, then we may expect buzzards to increase and spread still further in Britain, and many more people will be able to enjoy the magnificent spectacle of their soaring displays in spring without having to seek them out in their present strongholds in the west and north. Unlike some other British birds of prey, they seem to do as well here as the same species on the Continent of Europe, and there seems to be no question of trying to save a beleaguered remnant population which may well be doomed anyhow.

174

CHAPTER 14

THE GOLDEN EAGLE

THE golden eagle has a special place in this book, not only because it is the largest and most magnificent raptorial bird still breeding in the British Isles, but also because it is the one I personally know most about. The golden eagle was the first raptor I ever studied, and it led me on to make detailed studies of African eagles, so that I can now relate my Scottish experience to eagles in other countries(3,5). In turn this led to a wider study of birds of prey as a whole, which is one of the reasons why I, who live elsewhere, am writing this book about British birds of prey at all(8).

Whenever I am in Scotland I spend most of my time in the Highlands and I am not happy until I have added some new snippet of knowledge to what I already know about the eagle. When I am in the hills, from long practice, I see the eagle as soon as it breaks the skyline, though nowadays I do not instantly cast myself into a wet sphagnum bog to glass the bird. When I am abroad a group of old friends – Adam Watson, Morton Boyd, Douglas Weir, and others – keep me abreast of eagle affairs. I am also in touch with a growing band of golden eagle enthusiasts in the United States, in Montana, Utah, Colorado and Texas, all areas where the eagle is being intensively studied, particularly from the viewpoint of what it eats. Correspondents in Europe write to me about eagles, usually to tell me I am wrong in something I have said. So I keep pretty well in touch even when I am not observing golden eagles myself – I am always observing some species of eagle.

I saw my first eagle in 1935, and I did not know what it was because I could not credit that the great bird would breed on a little cliff half a mile from and in full view of a motor road. I thought they must be buzzards; but they were eagles. They must have had young in a nest I did not discover till 1951, by which time this cliff had been deserted as a regular breeding haunt. The nest has now mouldered into the ground and only an eagle man could read the signs to know where it once had been. I saw my first definite eagle in 1936, and found my first eyrie the same day. Thereafter, however, I was much abroad, and I did not see an eagle's egg or chick until 1946, when I carried out the first of a series of detailed surveys of blocks of country to try to estimate the density of breeding pairs.

Fortunately, or sometimes, as we shall see, unfortunately, eagles are conservative creatures. In 1937, on one of my early ploys, I found an eyrie on a small cliff in the Cairngorms. At that time this pair bred regularly in an old pine overhanging the gully of a burn, into which I used to imagine falling as I climbed to it; but they still built up the cliff eyrie each year. Thirty years later, in 1967, I went to look for these nests and found the skeleton of the pine in the burn; but the cliff eyrie was in use and contained an eaglet, the first my companion of that day had seen. Not long ago, in Kenya, I spent an evening with Lord Strachan, and we spoke together of eagles' eyries he had known and photographed before the 1914–18 war, during which I was born and he lost the use of both legs, so that he could no longer go to the hill. I was able to assure him that two of the three eyries he had known were still 'on the go', and tell him of a place where he might still watch an eagle with a good glass from a road. That bird was breeding in 1972, and I hope he saw her.

People who study large birds of prey are very often solitary individuals; they must be that way inclined to endure the long tramps in bad weather over rough ground, the freezing vigils at eyries, or the thorns and the sweat and the heat of tropical situations. But there is a long-continued web of friendship and the best of company tying me to Scotland on the one hand and to many other people and other eagles in different parts of the world. We don't often meet; but when we do our tongues clack from morn to night, or whenever we can draw breath to thrash out a knotty point as we climb the inevitable steep hill.

In my early studies I became over-confident and made inaccurate dogmatic statements. I fell into error largely because I could not believe that the eagle would breed in certain lowland pine woods and because – alone and ropeless – I had funked climbing to an eyrie where I had a very narrow escape from death in 1936. I was gently put right by the late Bernard Tucker, who took a great interest in birds of prey though he did not publish much on the subject. By our mistakes we learn, and since then I have been more careful. The later results have been more accurate and have given a better idea of the truth of the matter than did my early efforts.

Although we think of the golden eagle as a very rare bird, and try to imagine that it is golden when we see it on a rare sunny day, in fact it is neither. Of the fourteen species of diurnal birds of prey in Britain only three at present exceed 500 pairs. The golden eagle may be the second or third commonest in the next group, of 100–500 pairs, beaten by the peregrine and perhaps the hen harrier, but probably commoner than the merlin; it may be the fifth or sixth commonest raptor in the British Isles.

I do not see any point in trying to gloss over this fact, which can be deduced by anyone who reads with intelligence the carefully guarded statements in status surveys or scientific papers published in recent years. In 1946, after my first endeavours to ascertain the facts of eagle population density in Scotland, I suggested that a census of known breeding sites be carried out. This was later discussed at a Scottish Ornithologists' Club meeting, which I could not attend, and at which both Seton Gordon and Dr Fraser Darling spoke against the proposal(j); their point was that the prevailing widespread ignorance on the subject was beneficial to the conservation of the eagle. Seton Gordon later reiterated this view in his book on the golden eagle; he hoped that such a survey would never be published because the results would give the arch enemies of eagles – gamekeepers and shepherds – the weapon they wanted to say that golden eagles were too numerous and ought to be destroyed(17). Gamekeepers and shepherds have been doing this anyhow for many years, and it can be shown that the 1954 Bird Preservation Act has had not the slightest effect in checking such abuses; so from this viewpoint the publication of reasonably accurate facts can make matters no worse than they are.

In 1946 there may have been something to be said for obfuscating the facts though, if such a survey had then been done and followed up, we should now be very much further advanced in our knowledge of the eagle. However the climate of public opinion at least has changed since then, and the illegal destruction of golden eagles by gamekeepers, who are the principal offenders, meets with general disapproval. Despite the view of the S.O.C. three of us, Adam Watson, Charles Palmar, and I, who had all been working on the same lines, determined to make our own estimate; and this estimate, variously garbled, has been the basis of every subsequent status survey published(14). The last time our figures were jointly brought up to date was in 1955; we then knew of 173 breeding places or territories (though 'territory' is a word I dislike using in connection with eagles) and estimated a total population of 270–280 pairs. The late James Fisher, working very much more in the dark than we were, made a very similar estimate in 1941(15).

Since then, some of the known sites have faded out, some because of deliberate persecution, others through increased casual interference by climbers and walkers, and a few probably for natural reasons we are unable to understand. This decrease has more than counterbalanced any small recent increases in certain areas, and the welcome tendency to spread to new breeding areas in South West Scotland, the English Lake District, Ireland, and Orkney, all of which have been colonised since the Second World War. I would still estimate that there may be between 250 and 300 pairs of golden eagles in Scotland and the Hebrides, and the species clearly has the resilience to increase quickly and spread to new areas if left alone.

We arrive at such figures by dividing the map of the Highlands into definable blocks of country, limited by clearly recognisable boundaries. On this we plot the known groups of nest sites, and estimate where there ought to be others. Traditionally, we are kneeling on the floor with the map spread out between us and whisky handy. Coins are taken from sporrans and placed on the map; we never seem to have enough tiddlywinks. Womenfolk go quietly away, occasionally plying us with fodder. Later, there may be an argument as to who placed a particular 50p piece on the map; but we do not fight about it.

I dislike using the word 'territory' in connection with the breeding area of any birds of prey, eagles included, for in the modern view it implies 'a defended area'. Eagles at least do not obviously defend their 'territory', though some other raptors, such as buzzards, do. For want of a better term I prefer to use 'home range' to define the area occupied year round by a pair of eagles. In Scotland this varies from about 8000 acres (3220 ha.) in one small local area (a population density not later sustained) to about 18,000 acres (7300 ha.), and averages 11,000–13,000 acres (4450–5250 ha.), apparently largely irrespective of the natural food supply available within the range(9). Some observers have thought that the density was exceptionally high in certain Hebridean sheep farming areas, but this is not so; it is just as high in some deer forests where there are no sheep(21). In some areas too the population is clearly limited by the lack of suitable trees or cliff nesting sites; but in most this is not a limiting factor, and in areas with a superabundance of good nesting cliffs, such as in Torridon, the coins make a nice even pattern on the map. Nowadays, when we set out to do an actual survey, we have a very good idea of how many pairs there ought to be and where. If there is apparently no pair where we expect one, or if we see a pair of eagles and cannot find a nest at once, persistent search will often reveal a nest in some silly little gully, on a ledge almost invisible behind trees and bushes, or in a crack where the eagle cannot make a large nest because she lacks headroom. I know of nests that are both inaccessible and invisible from any angle, but they are few; in most cases the nest is easy to see.

Sometimes we locate what we think is a possible or doubtful breeding site, either because it is too low or close to human habitations, or because in a remote and little disturbed situation, it seems too close to other known pairs which surround it. Such places must be checked, and in 1967 I visited one such, previously rejected, to find there an old established breeding site of many years' standing. Occasionally our theoretical estimates may be a little out in this way, but we have broadly concluded that the golden eagle is about as numerous as its own territorial habits will allow it to be in most of its major strongholds, which are the deer forests of West and Central Scotland, and that some lowland eyries which are regularly persecuted are in any case marginally viable. That is not a good reason for their being persecuted, which is clearly against the law. However, we no longer fear that the golden eagle is in imminent danger of extinction, as I did in 1946 when I began working on these lines.

If we say that the population of eagles is 270 active pairs, that is 540 breeding adults. In addition, there must be some unattached adults and subadults, perhaps only 50 or 60 altogether; and there are immatures. Where they are undisturbed the breeding pairs rear an average of about 0·8 young per pair per annum, including non-breeding pairs, so that the total recruitment in July of flying young should be perhaps 220. This optimum figure is, however, reduced by one form of persecution or another to about 140–150, for 80–90 pairs fail to breed successfully each year, mainly through human interference.

Perhaps three-quarters of the surviving young die before they are old enough to breed. They wander to low ground where they may still be shot or trapped, law or not. However some young from successful undisturbed areas, for instance in Argyll, probably enter areas where adults have been destroyed and may survive there better than they would if they had to compete with a capacity population of adults; but we cannot assess this accurately at present(25). Taking everything into account I estimate that an autumn population of about 720–740 eagles of all age classes is thus reduced to about 630–640 adults and immatures by the following spring.

In areas of poor breeding success the population is apparently often maintained by 'import', often of young birds, from more successful areas. It is not uncommon to find an adult mated with a subadult or an immature; or an immature occupying a home range, often a marginal one, by itself. In areas of high breeding success there must still be a small surplus of unmated adults and subadults, which manage to survive, keeping out of the way of breeding adults in 'no man's land', or perhaps even being tolerated by them in occupied home ranges. One sees such birds, but it is very difficult to make a good estimate of the numbers as they often cannot, in poor light or bad weather, certainly be differentiated from adults or, still more difficult, aged between birds of the year and older subadults.

Immatures do take up home ranges and hold them, even form pairs; Seton Gordon recorded a pair in Skye that were immature and did not breed for several years though they remained mated and later bred successfully(17). In Sutherland in 1967 two out of twenty territories I examined were occupied by immatures(6). Other less fortunate immatures move to lower ground, or into grouse moors, where they meet with a charge of shot or are trapped or poisoned. While, as experience with other eagles elsewhere shows, it is quite normal to find a *small* proportion of immatures mated with adults or occupying ranges by themselves, if this proportion is large it indicates an unstable population and too high a death rate among adults. These are the areas where one should look for pole traps and other such evil devices.

Philip Brown, in his book *Birds of Prey* estimates that at one time there may have been 3000 breeding pairs in Britain(10). He bases this largely on the possibility that, in purely natural conditions, there might have been three times the number now existing in the main strongholds of Inverness, Ross and Sutherland. I cannot believe that there ever were that number, and base this conclusion on the stability of eagle populations, not only in Scotland but elsewhere. Whatever the species concerned, the size of the home range locally varies little. My opinion is that for some time, perhaps for the last half century, the golden eagle has been at

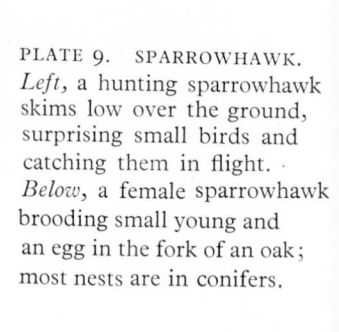

PLATE 9. SPARROWHAWK.
Left, a hunting sparrowhawk skims low over the ground, surprising small birds and catching them in flight. · *Below*, a female sparrowhawk brooding small young and an egg in the fork of an oak; most nests are in conifers.

PLATE 10. COMMON BUZZARD. *Above*, a buzzard at nest with two young, one several days the elder; if food is short the younger sibling may starve. *Below*, buzzards habitually feed on rabbits when they can, and prefer mammals to birds as prey.

capacity numbers – as many as a particular block of country will hold – in most of the deer forest country that is its main stronghold. It may even have benefited from such nineteenth-century atrocities as the highland clearances, which forcibly removed people from the upper glens towards the seashore and left these glens more secluded for sheep and deer. Quantities of mutton carrion then became available, a new food source.

Severe inroads were undoubtedly made on the golden eagle population in the era of the great collectors, in the mid- and late-nineteenth century. The works of Harvie Brown indicate that at the end of the nineteenth century it may have been less numerous than it is now; but he never carried out a population survey in the modern manner(18). Once collection was reduced, and landowners gave some protection to the eagle, I see no reason why vacant home ranges should not have been re-occupied and remain occupied from the early years of this century to the present day. In 1955 Seton Gordon, who is the grand old man of eagle studies, observed that there had been relatively little change in areas he knew as a young man, and such has been my own experience too, with some recent exceptions(17). In the last thirty years there have been minor fluctuations in areas we know well, but as a rule they have been slight. As a result, I cannot believe that there ever were much more than 500 pairs of eagles in Scotland, maybe another 50 in England and Wales, and perhaps 100–150 in Ireland; so that in the case of the golden eagle we may still have something like half the optimum population Britain could support if *Homo sapiens* was wiped out.

This view is, of course, belied by the 'vermin' lists of the game preservation era, in the early and middle nineteenth century especially; they include hundreds of eagles(2). However, having myself employed Africans to kill such 'vermin' as hyenas and porcupines, I know just how easily such lists can be inflated by people who know a soft spot when they see one. Vermin lists do not convince me that the population of golden eagles was ever as great as 3000 pairs.

Outside Scotland the golden eagle formerly bred widely in Ireland, the English mountains as far south as the Pennines, and in Wales. It disappeared from all these areas before the end of the nineteenth century. A pair re-colonised Ireland in 1954, bred for several years, then disappeared. They may have come from Kintyre, to which area they were said to fly to obtain mountain hares of the Scottish race; but hares are common in Antrim and there was therefore little reason for the eagles to fly to Kintyre(e). After many prospecting visits by immatures and adults a pair has recently established itself and bred in the Lake District. They probably came from Ayr, Dumfries, or Galloway where, despite heavy human persecution, a small population has managed to hang on and even increase since the Second World War. For the last several years a pair has bred in Orkney, the first time certainly since about 1844(a). In Western and Southern Scotland and the Hebrides the eagle may be slightly increasing, but any increase here is more than counterbalanced by a sharp increase in deliberate persecution and casual human interference in the last decade in Eastern Scotland and in some of the more popular climbing areas, such as west of Loch Lomond or in Glencoe. Taking the population as a whole the eagle is in slow decline; but this decline could rapidly be checked if human interference, deliberate or casual, could be reduced.

At present the golden eagle, and some other birds of prey too, are threatened by gamekeepers on grouse moors; ordinary walkers and rock climbers; and egg collectors, perhaps in that order of importance. Bird photographers and bird-watchers also play their part, causing desertion of some eyries, though we must suppose that this is not deliberate. Egg collectors are still prepared to take risks to obtain 'British taken' clutches, and they like to do so themselves, as did the elderly gentleman who was caught and fined £100 for taking golden eagles' eggs in Sutherland in 1968. Personally, I have never thought there was much point in trying to keep the whereabouts of nests secret from egg collectors; if there is one thing they can do it is find nests, and a golden eagle's nest is easy to find. The only question is whether one can escape unobserved with the eggs.

Ordinary walkers and climbers, bird-watchers, and bird photographers are probably a greater threat than egg collectors. Inadvertently, in many cases – the only exception being the bird photographer who just cannot resist a picture of the eggs or young – they disturb the eagles in the breeding season, sometimes repeatedly, so that they fail. One eyrie close to the Cairngorm chair lift, formerly regular, has not reared young since 1966; another Cairngorm site, in an area favoured by ice and snow climbers also often fails. Some sites are in areas that are just too popular, and do not have a hope. In some other cases it might be worth *trying* to interest mountain clubs or others in avoiding the eyrie areas at crucial times, or even making a public viewing point at an eyrie which has little chance at present, such as the one near the Cairngorm chair lift.

Shepherds are often quoted as a menace to the golden eagle, which is accused of taking lambs wherever it occurs alongside sheep. This question is discussed more fully in the chapter on 'Burning Issues'. I have heard a good deal of talk in hotel bars of an evening about 'rogue' eagles killing hundreds of lambs, but have also spoken with many shepherds in the hill, and only met one who said he had actually *seen* an eagle kill a lamb; he bore the bird no ill will and had rather admired its skill. From a lifetime's experience he was convinced that his flock had little to fear, and he was right. Shepherds may need convincing on this subject, but they are less of an immediate threat to adult eagles than are gamekeepers. They seldom actually kill or trap eagles, but may have a prolonged lunch under an eyrie with deliberate intent to keep the bird off, or burn a nest 'by accident', while heather burning in spring.

Stalkers and keepers in Western deer forests, who are interested in deer and salmon in that order of importance, either ignore the eagle or may give it some positive protection. The proprietors of these estates also like to see an eagle, and are sympathetic and sometimes actively protective towards them. The worst threat to the adult birds, in fact the only severe cause of adult mortality, comes from grouse moor gamekeepers, who actively and illegally hunt eagles with guns, traps, and poison, sometimes with the connivance of the proprietors or factors of the estates concerned, but sometimes in direct defiance of instructions given to them.

These matters are discussed at greater length later. For the present I would estimate that 80–90 pairs of golden eagles are destroyed or fail to breed every year throughout Scotland and this figure might be too low. In the survey of breeding success carried out by the Royal Society for the Protection of Birds overall breeding success was reduced, mainly by human interference, from a potential of 0·83 young/pair to 0·56 young/pair(13). This is a very serious proportion, more than a third of the estimated total juvenile population. It can be apportioned, probably, at about forty pairs deliberately destroyed or disturbed by gamekeepers and shepherds; about thirty due to casual or unintentional human interference; and the rest to egg collectors and natural losses. If egg collectors find any cause for glee in that they are no longer considered by me to be the worst offenders, then I hope any such rejoicing will be short lived.

Losses are worse in some parts of Scotland than in others. In the Monadhliaths, upper Speyside, and Deeside generally, out of 43 nesting sites known to us 24 either have disappeared altogether or now breed irregularly. Of these 16 can be ascribed to the depredations of grouse moor gamekeepers and eight to walkers and climbers. Other black spots are Islay, Easter Ross and Caithness, and even odd places such as the neighbourhood of Inchnadamph; anywhere where there are grouse in sufficient numbers to be worth preserving. The total loss can be assessed with fair accuracy. It is more difficult to do anything effective about it; and as I said earlier it is plain that the provisions of the 1954 Act have had practically no effect.

More recently, a sudden and totally unexpected threat developed in the West Highlands, potentially far more dangerous than any of those so far mentioned. The use of Dieldrin in sheep dips reduced the breeding success of eagles in Wester Ross from about 70% to about 30% per annum(22). In Argyll, likewise, it dropped from about 60% or higher in undisturbed mountain areas to about 30%(25). At 70% per annum, with an estimated mortality of about 75% before sexual maturity, golden eagles must live 11–12 years as breeding adults to replace themselves. At 30% per annum, with similar mortality, the eagles would need to breed for at least 28 years to replace themselves. While we know that golden eagles in captivity can live to be forty or more years old there is no evidence that they ever do in the wild state.

Projections of this nature are extremely tricky, for when breeding success is lower the few young that are reared may have a better chance of survival to maturity. However, the natural breeding rate of the golden eagle appears rather nicely adjusted to keeping the population stable, and it thus seemed inevitable that if the breeding success fell off to less than half the normal the eagle would become extinct within a couple of decades, just as the peregrine falcon became extinct over much of North America and Europe(19). Fortunately, a voluntary ban on the use of dieldrin in sheep dips has been largely effective. After 1967 the breeding success of eagles in West Scotland has returned to nearly normal, while at the same time the amount of dieldrin in the eggs has been reduced(23). These effects are further discussed under the chapter on pesticides and birds of prey.

However, these and other causes of reduction of adults or poor breeding success indicate that, although the golden eagle is not a rare bird, indeed is one of the commoner British birds of prey, its position is still insecure and needs constant watching. The point to emphasise is that even 740 eagles – the maximum – is a *small* population. It could be quickly wiped out by really systematic persecution, or by the effects of some new and unpredictable factor such as the use of certain chemicals for sheep dips. The latest threat is a narcotic, alpha-chloralose, ostensibly used for poisoning crows and gulls, but effective also against eagles and other birds of prey(28).

A fair proportion of all the eyries in Scotland are now checked annually by Nature Conservancy or R.S.P.B. personnel, or by people who enjoy doing it at weekends. However, there is still a great deal that is unknown about the biology of the golden eagle. Numbers and breeding status have been fairly well studied; but the full story of the breeding cycle, for instance, has to be pieced together bit by bit from various accounts, many of them old, and not all from Britain. None, I think could give a good account of how a golden eagle spends its day, or the proportion of time spent hunting. The difficulties here are obvious, for one sees an eagle about once a day, and if lucky for one minute, when on the hill. Attempts are being made in America to study this aspect of eagle behaviour by radio telemetry, much used on larger animals such as cougars and bears; but the technical difficulties of making a small enough transmitter sufficiently powerful are immense.

The strength of a golden eagle is often exaggerated. The largest animal normally killed as an adult in Scotland is the brown hare, which can weigh up to 4 kg. (9 lb). In Europe the largest normal prey is the alpine marmot, and in America the largest favoured prey is the rather smaller jack rabbit. There are occasional authentic cases of golden eagles taking or attacking prey much larger than this. In America a golden eagle is said to have attacked an adult pronghorn antelope, which was in difficulties in deep snow(1). In 1942 a Swedish game warden reported a case of a golden eagle killing an adult roebuck weighing perhaps 30 kg. (66 lb), also in snow(b). In this case the attack was not observed, but the marks of the eagle's wings in the snow were kept undisturbed and the roe was examined by a veterinarian who could find nothing wrong with it except the talon marks of the eagle on the neck.

Until recently I should have scouted these tales as fables, or physically impossible. However, the African crowned eagle, a somewhat smaller but proportionately more powerful bird than the golden eagle, certainly does kill bushbuck weighing 20 kg. (44 lb) or more; so I am less inclined to assert that a golden eagle could not possibly kill an adult roebuck(7). Seton Gordon recounts attacks on red deer or even cows; but in many such cases mere swooping at the animals is interpreted as an attack, though the eagle has no intention of striking or killing.

Normally a golden eagle would not attempt to kill an animal the size of a roebuck; it could not possibly carry it away. As a rule a golden eagle cannot carry a whole hare or a new-born lamb, and must dismember such larger prey before carrying away portions. Experiments with a captive golden eagle, released with weights attached to its legs from a tower, indicated that it could not easily fly with more than 1100 grams (2½ lb)(1). This is not the same thing as lifting heavy prey from the ground against a wind, and in these situations a golden eagle can lift and carry for a short distance about 7 kg. (15 lb)(m). I have known winds in Scotland against which I could run downhill knowing that I could not fall, and in which I am sure it would only have been possible to land a light aircraft under full power. In such a wind a golden eagle could rise from the ground without apparent effort, carrying a heavy animal entire.

The food requirements of a golden eagle and its diet are pretty well known; this is understandable since this is the major area where the activities of golden eagles impinge upon the interests of game preservers and sheep farmers. More work on the subject has been demanded and done. From the work of the Craighead brothers in the United States we know that a golden eagle requires 6–7 grams of food per 100 grams of bodyweight to survive, winter and summer, or about 230–280 grams, (8–10 oz) per adult eagle per day(12). This estimate has been confirmed for Britain by the London Zoo keeper Derek Wood (who has been described as one of the world's most unobtrusive experts)(l). When gorging a golden eagle eats more than this, even up to 1500 grams (3¼ lb) in a day(27). The heaviest stomach contents recorded for a wild golden eagle (in U.S.A.) was 560 grams (1¼ lb)(1). After a huge gorge an eagle need not eat again for some time, if in good condition. Falconers' eagles can survive for three weeks without food and can then consume seven days' supply at once. These results, obtained from captive birds, have been broadly borne out by observations of the prey brought to the nest by wild birds; but we need more accurate data on this.

An eagle wastes, or does not eat, a proportion of what it kills. When the prey is small

THE GOLDEN EAGLE

it may be swallowed entire at a gulp; if it is large, such as a hare, it must be dismembered and carried in pieces to the eyrie, or part left lying. In the dissection
process the eagle takes a large meal, and may return later for the abandoned
portions if another scavenger has not been there first. This 'waste factor' is calculated at about 20–30% of all live kills, so that a golden eagle must *kill* about 107 kg.
(235 lb) of food per year, of which it actually *eats* about 80 kg (175 lb). Some of the
food is carrion, especially in winter, when dead animals may make up 40% of the
diet. This means that an eagle does not have to kill that total amount of living
prey(9).

In 1964, Adam Watson and I, after working together on this subject for several
years, concluded that the average home range or territory would have to produce
for the pair of adults, their brood (at 0·8 young/annum) and for any immatures and
unattached adults in the area (at 20% of the total population) a grand total of
271 kg. (620 lb) of prey per year of which 249 kg. (550 lb) would actually be eaten.
Of this we estimated that 50 kg. would be carrion, 127 kg. mammals, and 72 kg.
birds (110 lb, 280 lb and 160 lb)(9). These proportions no doubt would vary from
place to place, according to the abundance of different types of prey. Since no one
else has produced a better estimate or seriously contested these figures we can
assume they still apply. The amounts of living prey given represent 70 mammals
the size of a mountain hare and 126 grouse-sized birds per year.

To enumerate here all the species of animals and birds known to be killed by the
golden eagle would take up too much space. Suffice it to say that, when they can
catch them, golden eagles prefer to feed on medium-sized mammals, such as
rabbits, hares, prairie dogs, or marmots. If these are abundant they will kill little
else. If large gamebirds are abundant in the home range many of these will be
eaten too, and some pairs living near the seashore feed largely on seabirds. One
Scottish pair must feed almost entirely on puffins, and others eat many Manx
shearwaters or fulmars. However, a golden eagle will eat anything from the carcase
of a dead deer to a grasshopper, and will catch such unlikely items as a meadow
pipit, a weasel, or a fox cub in Scotland. Golden eagles are even recorded as
catching fish – salmon and pike(17); this becomes less incredible when one re-
members that a peregrine falcon has been known to *catch* a fish – by just wading
into an Alaskan stream and grabbing one(11).

It has always struck me as very odd that golden eagles eat so few gulls. Gulls of
several species are among the commonest large birds in many parts of Scotland,
and often breed in colonies on lochs within eagle territories. One would think that
well-grown young gulls would be easy prey, but apparently they are not often
taken. If these same gulls lived alongside African fish eagles we should soon see a
decrease in the gull population, as most of the young would be eaten; and perhaps
the same might apply if we still had sea eagles in Britain. Some pairs of golden eagles
take a great many fulmars, which one would suppose more distasteful than gulls;
but the St Kildans ate fulmars and not gulls, and gulls are apparently unpalatable
to Eskimos, who are not choosy(k). I am not prepared to believe that eagles cannot
catch gulls, for I have seen one miss a gull by inches after a magnificent stoop; but
gulls usually ignore a soaring eagle and apparently apprehend little danger from
it. Even in Sutherland, where there are any number of gulls, the eagles fed their
young largely on much scarcer grouse and ptarmigan.

Extraordinarily few people have ever seen an eagle kill. I suppose I have walked
5–6000 miles through the hills on my eagle surveys and at other times, constantly
on the alert for eagles, and I have seen it happen twice. Adam Watson, who lives in

eagle country and has travelled it, summer and winter, far more than I, can recall eight kills – a hare, two grouse and five ptarmigan. Seton Gordon, with much longer field experience than either of us, records in his book few observations of his own, but a selection of accounts from gamekeepers, stalkers, and others, some of them incredible to me(17). I think the consensus of opinion would be that the eagle normally kills animals well within its strength to lift, and that it takes the majority of its prey on or close to the ground. There are authentic records of eagles catching grouse and even wild geese on the wing; and from America an unusual record of an eagle taking a red-shouldered hawk that was pestering it, by a sudden turn and twist in flight(c); but most prey is undoubtedly taken on the ground.

When an eagle is soaring high up it is not hunting, though it may still stoop at something that takes its fancy. For the most part it hunts by flying low over the slopes, sometimes working along a hillside where it can soar without effort even in a light breeze. When it sees prey it makes a quick attack, which may only last a few seconds. On available evidence an eagle's eyesight has four to eight times the resolving power of the human eye, so that the bird undoubtedly has the ability to perceive any possible movement in a whole glen 1000–1500 feet below it. It is then a matter of making an attack which may take the prey by surprise. Here knowledge of the ground, probably possessed by an experienced bird resident in the same area for some years, must be an advantage.

Although it normally kills on the ground eyewitness accounts show that a golden eagle can take grouse on the wing easily if it wishes; and perhaps this occurs more often than we think. In several recorded cases the eagle stooped at and pursued the grouse faster than they could fly, even going fast downwind, dived below them, turned up, and caught one from below in the foot. One instance recounted by Seton Gordon suggests that the eagle struck the grouse with its wing or breast; but in nearly all cases the taloned foot is the killing instrument(17).

From experience with other eagles I know that one seldom casually sees them kill, but that if one sets out to watch for this one sees it happen more often. It usually happens very quickly, so it is not surprising that one sees it so seldom by chance. We may take it, I think, that an eagle is equipped to kill swiftly and efficiently when its chance comes; but there are no really good data on the proportion of time spent hunting, on hunting success, and so on; this needs more observation.

One would think that the density of eagle populations would depend directly on the abundance of natural prey or carrion available, as seems to be the case with several other British raptors. However, this is not so. In our 1960–64 survey Adam Watson and I chose four areas, either well or very well known to us, and which varied greatly in their food potential(9). Area I was in dry heather country of eastern Scotland, abounding in hares, rabbits, several species of gamebirds, deer, and some sheep. Area II was in typical West Highland grass hill country with hardly any heather or grouse, but a large population of sheep and some rabbits; all our work was done after myxomatosis affected the rabbits. Area III was on the Torridonian sandstone formation, characterised by a fair amount of heather, moderate grouse and ptarmigan populations, abundant deer, but few sheep. We included Area IV, in north west Sutherland, because we knew there were many eagles there with, apparently, an extremely poor food supply of grouse, hares, or ptarmigan, though there were plenty of deer and, on low ground, many sheep.

We found that in all these areas the size of the home range varied from 11,400 acres (4600 ha.) in Area I, with the best food supply, to 17,884 acres (7250 ha.) in

Area II, which had potentially the worst natural live food supply. Area IV, however, with an extremely poor natural food supply had an average home range of 13,015 acres, very little less than the richest area. I re-surveyed this area IV in 1967 more thoroughly, and found in it two additional pairs, so that the average home range in this area actually was 11,500 acres, about the same as in the food-rich Area I. Since 1964 Area I has lost two of its pairs from apparently natural causes, so that actually the richest natural food supply supports fewer eagles than one of the poorest. To give an idea of the poverty of the food supply in Area IV, I walked an estimated 360 miles in this area and saw *one* hare, and found another in an eagle's eyrie, while at one stage I walked 86 miles between successive flushings of grouse. In Area I it would be easy to flush in a day as many grouse as one would flush in a month in Areas IV or II.

The amount of natural food available thus does not directly determine the size of an eagle's territory. Some observers have felt that the amount of 'unnatural' food, in the shape of abundant sheep carrion on overgrazed crofting land in the Western Isles, results in an extraordinarily small home range per pair of eagles(21). This is not actually the case, for these Hebridean home ranges are about the same as those in Sutherland or in upper Deeside. It is evident that any shortage of natural live prey, hares, grouse, or rabbits, can be made up, at least for the adults, by feeding on abundant carrion, at least in winter and spring. In 1967 I calculated that in an average home range in Sutherland 500–700 dead lambs would be available in May and June and that the eagles, if they wished, could feed their young entirely on dead lamb. They were, however, living almost entirely on the scarce grouse and ptarmigan, and I saw no lambs in any eyrie, though I did find castings of sheep's wool where adults roosted.

I must conclude from the evidence that the size of an eagle's home range does not depend directly on the amount of live natural food available, and I doubt if it depends on carrion either; in Sutherland eagles are as abundant in high deer forest country devoid of sheep as they are on low ground with heavy sheep mortality. What does control the population of eagles we do not know for there is little obvious boundary fighting between pairs, and apparently hardly any of the active territorial defence seen in any species of *Buteo*, including the British buzzard. I have had to walk many thousands of miles to see two or three possible boundary disputes between eagles, the most recent being the display seen from the top of Ben More of Mull described in Chapter I; this is as near as I have ever come to seeing a real boundary dispute. That such disputes may occasionally occur when eagles try to breed too close to one another is exemplified by the discovery, by Bob McKechnie, of two dead Torridon males locked in each other's talons(g). In that year there were two nests on opposite sides of a valley only a mile and a half apart, and conflict would seem almost inevitable in such circumstances. For the most part we conclude that eagles manage to avoid this sort of direct contact, perhaps by showing themselves by high soaring on fine days, without any loud calling, but sometimes reinforced by undulating advertisement displays.

Since food supply does not appear directly to affect the population of adult eagles I would like to test thoroughly and accurately, the effect of food supply on breeding success. Broadly speaking, eagles in the west where natural live food supply is poor or bad rear fractionally fewer young that those in the east where food supply is abundant(25). In 1957 Adam Watson calculated that the eagles in Area I reared on average 0·8 young per pair per annum, but that without human interference this would have been 1·1 young per pair per annum. More recent figures from here give a high average of 1·4 young reared per successful nest(26). At the same time, eagles in the West reared on average 0·7–0·8 young per pair per annum; but again recent figures from S. Argyll indicate that the number of young per successful nest (1·2–1·4) is little if at all inferior to that in areas of good food supply(25). The difference is certainly not proportionate, for the natural food supply in the east is five to eight times as good as in the west; on our 1964 figures the natural food supply in Area I, our best, was eight times as good as that in Area II, our worst; yet from this same Area II recent figures for breeding success indicate that, in undisturbed localities, it is just as good as in Area I(25).

From 1964–1968 inclusive the Royal Society for Protection of Birds carried out a five-year survey of the breeding success of golden eagles in Scotland as a whole. The results of this have recently been summarised by Mike Everett, and I have used his figures to prepare Text Table 8(13). In a grand total of 489 occupied territories and 395 breeding pairs the results were unknown in 80 cases; I have excluded these from the calculations. Overall, an average of 0·56 young per occupied territory, 0·73 young per pair which bred, and 1·18 young per pair which succeeded were produced. These figures are as low as they are because 118 out of 315 pairs with known results failed – 37·5%; most of this failure was due to human interference, higher in some areas than others.

The areas may be subdivided into four (Monadhliath, Perthshire, Speyside, and Deeside) with good food supply, and three (Wester Ross, South Argyll, and Galloway) with poor food supply. In the areas with good food supply 132 pairs (75%) bred in 175 known territories. 70/111 known nests were successful (63%), rearing 0·55 young/territory, 0·77/pair which bred, and 1·21/successful nest. In the three areas of poor food supply, 110 pairs (78%) bred in 141 territories; and on the 97 known results, 56 (57%) succeeded, producing 0·44 young/territory, 0·59/ pair which bred, and 1·02/successful nest. If the small sample from Galloway, where breeding success is very poor, largely because of human interference, is excluded, the figures become, 94 pairs bred in 129 territories, with 12 unknown results, giving 82 positive results in 117 territories. In these 53/82 (64%) succeeded, producing 0·46 young/territory, 0·65 young/pair which bred, and 1·05 young/ successful nest.

From these figures it appears that about the same proportion of pairs did not breed in both types of area (25 and 22% respectively); and that the proportion which succeeded was only slightly higher (63%) in areas of good food supply than in areas of poor food supply (57%). If the Galloway figures are excluded the proportion of nests succeeding becomes almost the same (64% cf. 63%). However, the number of young reared per territory, per pair which bred, and per successful nest in areas of good food supply are all somewhat higher than in areas of poor food supply. The difference, however, is only of the order of 15–20%, and is not, accordingly, proportionate to the relative abundance of natural wild food, which may be five to eight times as abundant in areas of good food supply as in areas of poor food supply.

When it comes to the survival of the adults through the winter carrion, in the form of usually plentiful dead deer or sheep, should suffice to maintain life. Hence, it is not surprising to find about the same proportion of non-breeding pairs, about a fifth to a quarter, in areas of good and bad food supply. When it comes to rearing young, however, natural food must be found; the only carrion used is dead lamb, and that is not used much. Hence, in areas of poor natural live food supply the breeding success, in terms of young reared per pair, per pair which bred, and per

Table 8 Breeding Success: Golden Eagle: Scotland 1964-8

Data from Everett, M. 1971, 14(13). Original figures modified to eliminate unknown results from columns 7–9. Figures in brackets are minima.

AREA STUDIED	(1) Occupied territories	(2) Pairs which bred	(3) Pairs which failed	(4) Pairs which succeeded	(5) Results unknown	(6) Total young reared	(7) Young per occupied territory	(8) Young per pair which bred	(9) Young per successful nest
Areas of good food supply									
Monadhliath	20	13	7	6	0	7	0·35	0·54	1·17
Perthshire	40	35	6	16	13	(19)	0·70	0·86	1·18
Speyside	54	38	17	19	2	(21)	0·41	0·58	1·10
Deeside	61	46	11	29	6	38	0·69	0·95	1·31
Total	175	132	41	70	21	85			
Mean							0·55	0·77	1·21
Areas of poor food supply									
Wester Ross	(59)	48	13	34	1	35	0·61	0·75	1·12
South Argyll	64	46	16	19	11	19	0·37	0·54	1·00
Galloway	18	16	12	3	1	3	0·19	0·20	1·00
Total/Mean	141	110	41	56	13	57	0·44	0·59	1·02
Miscellaneous	173	153	36	71	46	(89)	0·70	0·83	1·25
Total/Scotland	489	395	118	197	80	(231)	0·56	0·73	1·18

% non-breeding, good food supply   25%
% non-breeding, poor food supply   22%
% non-breeding, overall Scotland   19%
Potential breeding success eliminating all failures = 0·83 young per pair overall.

successful nest ought all to be lower – and they are, according to the R.S.P.B. survey figures.

One feels like saying, Q.E.D! However, unfortunately human interference, either deliberate or inadvertent, is now such a severe limiting factor that it distorts the figures. In Galloway human interference is such that very few young (3/19) flew from the known breeding sites. In Speyside, Deeside, and other areas with good food supply there is still much interference from gamekeepers, and nowadays from tourists and climbers; about half the pairs that were regular in the early fifties now fail from one or other of these causes. In Argyll re-examination in 1972 of the pairs existing in our Area II in 1962 shows that some have disappeared altogether in the more popular climbing areas while others in more remote places do as well as ever they did; in this case the human interference is mainly from climbers, bird photographers and walkers, with even egg collectors largely absolved(25). Even in Sutherland, which one would think sufficiently remote, there was a strong positive correlation between human interference and poor breeding success. In 1967 I found that in areas close to roads only really inaccessible sites had a chance of rearing young; but in the more inaccessible deer forests, where even the stalkers sometimes did not know where the nests were, eyries accessible by an easy scramble produced young(6). Unfortunately, in this respect, the eagle is conservative; it will keep on trying in the same general area, though it may build a new nest, despite human interference that effectively prevents later breeding.

Ideally, to get a true picture of the effects of food supply on breeding success one should study two areas, of about equal size or containing the same number of pairs, for several years, obtaining a continuous series of breeding records and correlating these with estimates of prey abundance, plant cover, amount of snow lying, and other factors that might affect the eagle in different times of the year. Unfortunately, it would now be impossible in Eastern Scotland to locate an area of the requisite size which is sufficiently undisturbed to give a true picture; too high a proportion of the pairs would fail either through gamekeepers or through walkers and climbers. It would be easier to find such an area in the West, but here again interference would have some local effect.

A better way to get at the same information would be to select, say, twenty pairs, known to breed regularly in undisturbed areas with a good or fair food supply and compare their performance with twenty pairs in areas of poor food supply. One would expect to find that a low natural food supply would depress overall breeding success, probably first by reducing the proportion of pairs that bred at all, and later by somewhat higher brood losses and fractionally smaller numbers of young reared per successful nest. However, I would not expect – and neither would anyone else who knows about eagles – that this effect would be in direct proportion to the available food supply, natural or carrion; that is, it would not be five times as good in areas of good food supply as in areas of bad. At present, in fact, the maintenance of the population in areas of good food supply probably depends in large measure on 'import' of surplus birds produced in the western areas of poor food supply.

Although we know a good deal in this way of the biology of the golden eagle and its population dynamics we are still lamentably ignorant of the full details of the breeding cycle. I do not know of a single case in Scotland where an observer or a group of observers has systematically watched a nest from before egg laying to the first flight of the young. This data is now being obtained by the team of R.S.P.B. watchers at the only English golden eagle's eyrie in Cumberland; and whether this isolated pair can be regarded as strictly typical is open to doubt. The grand old man of eagle studies, Seton Gordon, undoubtedly has spent many thousands of hours watching at eagles' nests, and the best accounts of the breeding cycle at present available are from his eight-year study of one nest in Skye(17). However, with due respect to him, his observations were not systematically summarised. If he had only been able to summarise the main details of his work, which is no doubt recorded in field notebooks, in a few tables those of us who like to study the comparative biology of eagles would have been very much in his debt. As it is, one is frustrated by the feeling that, in this species and others, much more is known than has been published.

Putting together the breeding biology of the eagle from fragmentary information from several countries it appears that, like other eagles, the pair remains mated for the life of any one individual. If one dies, the other does not pine, as is reported in some fables, but at once gets a new mate, which may be an immature. Thus a site known to have been occupied continuously for a century or so has not, for all that time, been occupied by the same birds, but by a succession of different individuals. Sometimes a home range is occupied for a year or two by a single bird, which later acquires a mate; and sometimes immatures occupy a territory or mate with an adult. Such immatures may even lay eggs while still retaining immature plumage; there are two records at least of this. However, if I found in any area that the proportion of immatures occupying ranges or mated with adults was high I should suspect that the golden eagle was in trouble there, since this implies a shortage of adults.

An adult pair normally remain in their home range year round and do not wander far from it. Even those that live in high mountains such as the Cairngorms, which are deeply snowclad in winter, remain there and do not migrate to lower ground, though they may perhaps spend more time in the lower parts of their ranges. In most eagle ranges there is a tract of lower ground which remains snow-free for most of the winter while the high tops are snow clad from November to April. These snow-free areas may be vital winter range, for in them may be found the dead deer and sheep which provide 40% of the winter food supply as carrion while on the snowy tops only ptarmigan remain; but even these hardy birds may move lower down in winter.

On fine days, at any time of the year when the weather permits soaring, display may be seen; it is especially common on fine sunny days in winter(k). As one would expect of an eagle that lives in mountain country the golden eagle is a magnificent flier. I have not sufficient space to expatiate on the beauty and majesty of an eagle's flight, and must content myself with saying that some of the evolutions performed, especially in nuptial display, are both breathtaking and electrifying in their speed and precision.

Seton Gordon doubts if an eagle could fly against a hundred mile an hour gale. However I recall one day on Sgurr na Ciche of Wester Ross when the wind was such that slabs of turf the size of a good-sized carpet were being torn from the rock faces and flung hundreds of yards. My brother and I – then both big strong heavy men – going down a steep grass slope against the wind had to bend double and *run* to make progress; it seemed as if we could have taken wing ourselves, given a couple of little sails. In the pass above the grass slope an eagle was soaring, motionless, wings flexed, as if nailed to the sky. When he saw us he turned downwind, not in the least affected by the tremendous turbulence that was throwing slabs of turf about, and swept magnificently down into Glen Dessary, where his mate was no doubt at her nest.

With such power and command available one would expect the aerial displays of the golden eagle to be magnificent, and they are. The commonest is the undulating advertisement display in which a single bird, soaring high, performs a series of steep downward dives followed by an upward swoop, ten or twelve times. This is often performed over the skyline of a ridge or mountain top, and I suspect that in such situations it is the male eagle who is displaying himself to a neighbour, as do male buzzards. Pairs of eagles have nest-sites 2–3 miles (3·2–4·8 km.) apart, so that when two neighbouring males or pairs are on the wing together on a fine day they can easily see one another and avoid contact or trespass. Females, however, also perform this undulating display alone, perhaps less often than males, and sometimes close to the ground(17). In some cases they may be stimulated to perform by the presence of the male partner. This undulating display is extremely common among birds of prey; almost all big eagles do it, some more often and more vigorously than others. In the golden eagle it is especially common in late winter and early spring but also occurs in high summer when the young are in the nest or just fledged; such year-round display is also true of other eagles that remain in their home range. Golden eagles actually perform less often than most such permanently resident eagles, perhaps because they live in very open mountain country where they can see each other without spectacular advertisement.

Still more magnificent mutual displays are sometimes seen in which the pair soar very high on a fine day and break off in a series of tremendous dives, swooping up again to mount on air currents to a new pitch before repeating the process. Rather rarely the male, soaring above the female, dives at her and, as he rushes at her she whirls over and presents her claws to his. This 'symbolic food pass' again is a very common form of display among large birds of prey, but is seldom recorded in the golden eagle; I have seen it twice myself and it has been seen by Seton Gordon and only a few other observers(h). Usually, after the first pass, the male swings up again and may repeat the performance. However I have not yet seen, or found any record of the culmination of this beautiful evolution, in which the pair lock claws and come whirling down for several hundreds of feet. This whirling display is actually recorded in only two *Aquila* species that I know of(3).

Mating occurs on the ground near the nest and doubtless on the nest itself. Very few people have seen it; but from Seton Gordon's observations it may occur from six weeks before to at least a month after incubation has started, in the former case once in deep snow. The male alights near the female and walks over to her to jump on her back, maintaining his position by slowly waving his wings while the act is completed(17).

In their range golden eagles have from one to eleven nests. Usually they have two to four, of which one will be used most often though they may build up others. The average in all sites I know of personally is 2·6. There is good evidence that an old wives' tale to the effect that eagles move their nests when disturbed is a fact(25). Repeated breeding failure through human disturbance, whether from gamekeepers or walkers, does cause the eagle to build more nests. They are often not used in the first year, perhaps because they may often be built in late sprin and early summer after the failure of the occupied site, but when they are used they have a better chance of success than old, well-known sites. I know of one recent case where an eagle, regularly 'hammered' by grouse moor gamekeepers, succeeded in rearing young in a small gully where the keeper did not go; when the nest was discovered he was given a bounty, though he had persistently prevented these wretched birds from breeding for many years! In Argyll it is clear that the eagles which suffer badly from human interference frequently move their nest. By so doing an eagle may shift from a well-known and much frequented site to a little known one, where the pair succeeds for a year or two before the new nest becomes sufficiently bulky and obvious to attract attention.

Nests may be built at altitudes of 50–3000 feet (16–900 m.) above sea level. The lowest are on sea-cliffs and the highest are all in the Cairngorms, where there are a number between 2700–3000 feet (830–900 m.) A.S.L. Those in the West Highlands are invariably considerably lower than those in the Eastern Highlands, and in Argyll the mean altitude is about half that of the highest mountain in the eagle's home range. This figure, however, would not apply to either the Cairngorms or to Sutherland. In the Hebrides, and in low-lying western coastal areas, there are nests on considerable inland cliffs at less than 500 feet above sea level.

In the Highlands most nests are in cliffs; tree nests are seldom found outside the old pine forests of the eastern highlands, but there are odd ones in Jura, Mull, Rannoch, Corrour, and Easter Ross(d). Actually only about a dozen pairs, perhaps 5% of the total, have regular tree nests; and some of these also have rock sites which they sometimes use. Most tree nests are in old Scots pines, but larch, birch, willow, rowan, and oak are also known; only one nest, in a larch, has ever been known in an artificial plantation(17).

Sometimes a cliff nest is partly supported by or overshadowed by a tree or group of small saplings. The tree nests include the biggest known, one which was 17 feet deep when I last saw it, and several others at least eight feet deep. Cliff nests are usually smaller, but some become turret-shaped, up to six feet high. They tend to spread laterally on a broad ledge, the nest cup being made one year in one place and years later in another. The size of the nest is also controlled by the timber available; where there are plenty of pine trees the nest is always large, even when recently made, but in the treeless far north and west it is relatively small, and can be almost invisible.

All cliff nests start with a scrape, surrounded by branches, heather or whatever material may be available. If the eagle has headroom they gradually increase in size but seldom exceed two or three feet in depth and five or six feet in width. Oddments besides sticks worked into the nest structure may include stags' antlers or a coil of wire. About a third of the cliff nests may be reached (by an agile man) with a scramble; about another third by anyone prepared to do a short rappel; and the remainder only by mountaineering techniques needing an assistant(6). These are the ones which, in well-known localities, often succeed in rearing young where others fail. The proportion in each category varies surprisingly little, but of course in areas where there are abundant steep high cliffs the nests are likely to be generally more inaccessible than among rounded heather hills, where the eagle may be forced to breed in a small gully or even on the steep bank of a burn.

Two common statements, that eagles' eyries usually face north, and that eagles regularly rotate the use of their alternative nest sites are, I think, inaccurate. Analysis of known eyrie sites does not indicate that they necessarily face north; they must be placed wherever possible on the most suitable nesting cliff. It is largely an accident of glaciation that more suitable cliffs face north than south. If, however, the nests face west or south, the directions from which the hottest sunshine is likely, they are often shaded by an overhanging or angle of cliff or by bushes and trees. Little critical examination of this oft-repeated statement has been made.

Rotation of eyries is, likewise, certainly not regular. Pairs have favourite nest sites which they use year after year though they may build up several; and I do not think that there is any evidence that (excluding human disturbance) pairs that have only one nest are any less successful than pairs with several sites used in alternate years. In high sites the choice in any year may be dictated by the amount of snow lying, the bird being forced in some years to use a nest it might not otherwise have selected. My own feeling is that individual females may have nests which they prefer, and that the many alternative nests on cliffs close by may be old structures used by earlier inhabitants of the site. Such old nests take seven to ten years to moulder into the ground, depending on the climate, altitude, etc.; and they may be kept sufficiently well renovated though not used to be laid in again after many years if the preferred nest fails; witness the one I found in use in 1967 thirty years after I first saw it.

Golden eagles build at almost any time of year; in fact I think the only time of year they do not build is when their nests are entirely covered in snow or when they have a brood in the nest or just out of it, when they must spend most of their time hunting. If a pair fails to hatch or loses its young early much building may be done in May, June and July, often at the nest where the disaster occurred, sometimes at alternates(6). I have seen an eagle building in August; and Seton Gordon records building in November and December. Serious building is, however, concentrated in late February or early March(17).

Some eagles add great quantities of material early in the year, others very little. Larger branches are picked up and carried in the feet, and I have watched an eagle building by grabbing living heather in its feet and flying off backwards with it. Towards the end of the building period green sprigs and branches are added, usually of pine if that tree is locally available, if not of almost any green material that is handy. Small green sprays are torn off neighbouring trees and brought in the bill; sometimes they are brought for some distance, for instance a sprig of larch recorded by Seton Gordon, which he estimated must have been carried 1200 feet (390 m.) uphill(17). Both sexes build, but probably the female more than the male. One can usually tell which of several alternates is going to be used in March by the amount of green material in it. Very often the cup is filled with woodrush *Luzula sylvatica*, a soft material that grows in profusion on ledges near many eyries. Bringing a green branch often is associated with nest relief and green material continues to be added to the nest through the incubation period and during the first half of the fledging period. If the eggs are deserted the eagle may cover them with quantities of green material.

From 10–25% and sometimes, I suspect, more of all eagle pairs do not lay in any particular year. There is slight evidence that non-breeding may occur more often in areas of poor food supply. If there is green material in the nest and no eggs the egg collector may not have been there. The onset of incubation is indicated by flattening the cup, and by flecks of down adhering to the nest-edge or the heather round about. These are a sure indication that the eagle has settled to sit, and if they are seen and the eggs are gone, then look for the egg-collector's bootprints or the place where the shepherd had his lunch and kept the eagle off 'by mistake'.

Usually two, sometimes one, occasionally three, and very rarely four eggs (two records) are laid at intervals of 90–120 hours, or three to four days. The average clutch size of 37 nests on B.T.O. nest record cards is 1·84 and in Speyside is 1·7 in all nests examined(27). Sometimes one egg is infertile, and the same female may lay one fertile and one infertile egg for several successive seasons. Normally only the female incubates, but in a pair watched by Seton Gordon for eight years the male took an almost equal share even, once, perhaps sitting all night; the male at the Lake District pair also incubates so that incubation by males may be more frequent than is thought(f). The incubation period on available records is 43–45 days; but really good accurate records are lacking.

The female is not normally fed on the nest by the male. In the pair watched by Seton Gordon for eight years he never saw the male feed the female. In this particular case the female was certainly off the nest long enough to catch prey for herself but even in most cases where the male does not incubate the female seems to leave the nest to feed. No doubt her appetite is reduced during incubation, as in other eagles(9), and carrion is usually abundant at that time of the year, so that if no other prey offers she can satisfy her hunger by flying to a carcase perhaps only a few minutes away from the eyrie. In areas of poor food supply, unless the female regularly feeds on carrion, she would have to hunt for long hours to obtain wild prey, so risking loss of the egg through cold. Alternatively, she would have to be fed by the male, if not at the nest, then somewhere in the vicinity. In other species of eagles where the female alone incubates it is normal for the male to feed her, and incubating females normally kill only when males take a large share of incubation(3). Female golden eagles have been seen to leave their nests to kill grouse or rabbits close at hand, but this cannot be usual. The incubation habits of the golden eagle thus appear somewhat aberrant and require further study.

Incubation begins with the laying of the first egg which may, exceptionally, be laid as early as 1 March, is quite often before 10 March, especially in nests at lower altitudes, and almost always before 25 March. Very late laid clutches up to mid April have been recorded, but these result in very late fledging of the young. If the eggs are addled the female will sit on long after the normal hatching date, in one case known to me until 8 July, by which time she must have been sitting for about 115 days(6).

The differences in laying dates results in a difference of about three to four days in age of the chicks when they hatch. This difference is usually fatal to the younger chick. The hatching weight is about 90–100 grams, but when the second chick hatches the older already weighs about 250 grams and is active, whereas the newly-hatched youngster is so feeble it can hardly raise its head. Shortly after the hatch the older begins to attack the younger, and may often kill it within the first week; if the younger survives to three weeks it has a good chance of being reared, though it may still be attacked. The overall average for Scotland is 1·18 young reared per successful nest, but in some areas the result is better, up to 1·4 per successful nest. In other words, in Scotland as a whole, the younger chick is killed by the elder in about four cases in five, and the majority of chick mortality is due to this cause.

As we have seen in earlier discussion, broods of 1·3–1·4 per successful nest may occur alike in areas of good and bad food supply. The elimination of the younger chick by the 'Cain and Abel battle'(16) (as the inter-sibling strife was aptly named by Seton Gordon in the twenties) occurs in the presence of abundant food, and is not in any way prevented by the parents. The golden eagle is actually rather unusual among *Aquila* species in the relatively high proportion of second chicks reared; in several other species, including the closely allied Verreaux's eagle, the younger is almost invariably eliminated(8). The usual explanations for this extraordinary process, to the effect that it is in some way related to abundance or shortage of food, simply will not do. It is not, and what the purpose of it may be remains obscure.

Many believe that the larger eaglet is normally a female, and that therefore a greater proportion of females survives. This postulates non-random distribution of the sexes in the egg and, while this may occur, for instance in hen harriers or kestrels, it is unlikely in golden eagles. Perhaps a slightly greater proportion of females than males would be reared, since females are generally more aggressive, must gain weight quicker, and may therefore have a slightly better chance, when they are the younger chicks, of surviving the tussle. Against that, there is no evidence in other eagles where this battle occurs that anything but an equal sex ratio results. Young golden eagles can actually be sexed with fair accuracy before they leave the nest, and falconers who obtain single young could also help in this respect. I would expect the sex ratio of young reared to be equal, though there is no good evidence one way or another.

The chicks gain weight rapidly. One weighed by Niall Rankin weighed 450 grams (1 lb) at 8–9 days old, doubled its weight in the next week, and more than quadrupled it when 22–23 days old(17). At 37–38 days old, on 9 June, it weighed 3200 grams, thirty-two times its birth weight. Thereafter its gains were smaller and, as recorded in other eagles, this is probably because of the rapid production of feathers at that stage(8). It reached its maximum weight, about 3750 grams (8¼ lb), at 48 days, but thereafter lost weight, weighing 3350 grams(7¼ lb) at 66 days; a week later it flew. Its weight was then well below that of the average adult which varies from 3350–4400 grams in males, averaging 3924 (8½ lb), and 4050–5720 in females, averaging 4692 (10¼ lb). This eaglet was, presumably, a male.

During the early fledging period the female remains near the nest, either brooding the chicks or feeding them as necessary. One female, watched through the night by Mrs Seton Gordon stood over but did not brood the chick despite the cold, and eaglets are often left alone for some hours when only two weeks old(16). The male begins to bring more prey as soon as the chicks hatch, which is signified by a change in the female's posture; she 'sits high' with her wings partly opened. Even when he has not incubated the male apparently takes a large share in brooding chicks; but again we lack good quantitative data. While he is brooding the female leaves the nest area, and presumably hunts for herself; but I can find no record of the female returning to the nest with prey and of the male feeding on it, as occurs in some other eagles I have watched where both sexes brood the young.

After the chicks are 21 days old (by which time usually only one survives), the female spends long periods off the nest by day but usually remains in the area, perched somewhere along the top of the nesting crag. She may return to brood the young in rain, hail, snow or strong sunshine, all of which may occur in Scotland in early June. At this time, apparently, the male brings all prey and does not brood the chicks. He may feed the chicks if alone with them, but normally the female returns when he arrives with prey and feeds them. After 40 days, by which time the young are partly covered with feathers and require less assistance with food, the female spends long periods away. At the end of the fledging period visits by either parent are confined to a few moments when either sex may bring food.

Late in the fledging period the eaglets wander about the nest or along the nest ledge when they can, often seeking shade; they hurry back when prey is brought. They make their first flight 70–80 days after hatching, without parental coaxing, and often when the adults are not there. If too closely approached at this stage a young eagle will fly prematurely, but does not seem to be harmed by this; its parents find it and feed it, or it flies back to the nest. When the first flight is made the quill feathers are not fully developed, and the young remain not far away, perching on trees or ledges for 15–20 days after first flight. By this time their quills are strong and they can fly expertly, thereafter accompanying their parents, though often returning to the vicinity of the eyrie.

Some young separate from their parents about October and popular belief is that they are driven away. There is little real evidence for this statement, however, and there is good evidence that young will visit the eyrie site again and again during their first winter and perhaps into the following spring. Such a young bird may not be much in evidence but may be tolerated by the adults and may even, perhaps more often than we suppose, be loosely attached to them well into the following spring(25). It is, of course, extremely difficult to keep track of young eagles after they have flown and even more so after they have become independent of the adults, and there is practically no evidence as to what happens to them until they are old enough to breed.

There are now nine ringing recoveries available, however, all of which indicate that, like young buzzards, young golden eagles disperse but do not travel very far from where they were bred. None had travelled more than 62 miles (100 km.) in a straight line but all had moved more than 15 miles, showing that young normally leave their parents' territories. Of the nine recoveries, two were of rings only, from a pair of eaglets ringed in Glen Affric; the rings were found near Kingussie and near Carrbridge respectively, both famous grouse moor areas. One,

PLATE 11. COMMON BUZZARD. Mainly distributed in western Britain, a confiding juvenile such as this stands no chance in eastern game-preserving districts.

PLATE 12. GOLDEN EAGLE. *Above*, a male brings a grouse to the eyrie; at this stage the male brings all prey, feeding himself, his mate, and the eaglet. *Below*, the golden eaglet at about 60 days lacks nobility but still looks fierce; at this stage it is left alone in the eyrie most of the time.

ringed in Galloway, was caught in a crow trap near Peebles and released. Most informative of all, one young bird ringed in the Cairngorms in June 1966 was caught on one of several gin traps set in the open near an eyrie on the Cawdor estates in the upper Findhorn Valley in its second spring; it lived, but its leg was severed and it was thereafter kept in captivity. The gin traps (themselves then illegal when set in the open) had undoubtedly been set near the eyrie by a gamekeeper in order to catch the adults, and the fact that this young female was caught 'by mistake' not only exposed this practice but also indicates that such young birds may occupy a vacant range where one or more of the adults are regularly destroyed. It also shows that young birds, which are often seen near eyries in spring, may not necessarily have been reared in them.

Most of the young birds reared in Scottish eyries probably wander to lower ground, often grouse moors in the east, where they are too often quietly shot or trapped. They may not move far from their home nesting area and, in areas where the adults are not molested and are at capacity numbers, the young must be tolerated by them. However, in some cases I have found immatures living in stretches of country not suitable for adult breeding pairs, and no doubt they keep out of the way of adults if they can. Since the Scottish eagle population is only slowly declining, and since the decline would soon stop if the present level of persecution could be reduced, it seems that about 0·8 young reared per occupied territory is sufficient to maintain the population at full strength in the absence of deliberate or accidental human interference. Young birds may have a better chance of survival if they do not have to compete too actively with adults in their first winter.

There appear to be no good studies of the moult in British golden eagles, but this has been quite thoroughly studied in the American race(20). The amount of white visible in the tail and at the carpal joint of the wing is reduced in successive moults as new feathers grow in, becoming darker with age. Jollie described three main stages, juvenile, immature, and adult, and considered that adult plumage is attained in three and a half years, though a further moult may be needed to rid the plumage finally of immature looking feathers. Golden eagles can perhaps breed in their fourth year and almost certainly in their fifth. In the pair watched by Seton Gordon the pair took up residence at the eyrie site in spring 1943, when they were probably 1¾ years old, and bred for the first time in 1946, when they were probably in their fifth year(17).

From available data we can attempt to calculate how long golden eagles live in the wild state. We know that captive golden eagles can live for 40 to 45 years (though many do not), but such ages are unlikely in the wild; I discount Seton Gordon's record, which he accepts, of a 93-year-old bird called 'Lightning'. We lack really good records from long-continued observations of particular recognisable individuals, though Seton Gordon's Skye pair lived at least eight years as adults and probably at least 13 altogether. There is another, more dubious record, from a Californian egg collector, of a bird that lived for 21 years(i); but since she was never allowed the privilege of motherhood we cannot say whether she would have lived as long under this additional strain.

From the available data on population dynamics we conclude that in the absence of human interference the number of young reared per pair per year is 0·83. If three-quarters of these die before they are sexually mature, that is, in their fifth year, this is equivalent to 0·21 sexually mature replacements per adult pair per year. On this basis golden eagles must live on average nearly ten years as adults, and 14 or 15 altogether, to maintain a stable population. Since the population appears able to maintain itself nearly stable at a considerably lower figure, 0·57 young per occupied territory per year in nearly 500 Scottish cases, we can assume either that an eagle must be able to live longer than this or that mortality of young is actually lower. At the same rate of juvenile mortality (which may not always apply, as in areas where adults are trapped juveniles may survive better) the mean life span as adults would be something like 14 years, or 18 altogether. However, these are the sort of conundrums that must be left to further research to unravel.

CHAPTER 15

THE KESTREL

PROBABLY the commonest of all British birds of prey, the kestrel is certainly the most familiar to ordinary folk. It is even familiar, these days, to people who travel up and down motorways at speed, for kestrels hunt voles in the long grass on the embankments and sides of cuttings, or at clover-leaf intersections, and are often seen hovering there with the traffic roaring past a few yards away. Kestrels breed in many cities and are often seen hovering over the open parts of London parks; Richmond Park, for instance, has one of the highest population densities of kestrels recorded in Britain(j). Out in the country kestrels are seen most days hovering over open fields; and even in the treeless wastes of eastern England, where the old hedgerows have been grubbed out to make way for the combine harvester and intensive farming leaves very little good hunting ground for kestrels there are still a few of these decorative little falcons to be seen. On any moorland they are more or less common, and they are probably the only British diurnal raptor that the average person could expect to see almost every day, summer or winter, when walking or driving through the countryside.

The kestrel may not be much more common locally than the sparrowhawk, but is seen more because it is conspicuous, hunting in the open by its characteristic hovering which at once attracts attention, not very shy, and relatively brightly coloured. In former times the kestrel must have been much less common than the sparrowhawk, but as the forests of Britain were felled and burned to make way for sheep grazing and later for agriculture the kestrel must have multiplied while the sparrowhawk disappeared. Kestrels will breed in patches of woodland but cannot live in closed forest; they must have open country, heath, pasture or cultivated fields near by. They are ideally suited in open moorland with plenty of small cliffs wherein they can nest, but there are a good many parts of Britain where they cannot breed as commonly as they should for lack of enough suitable nesting sites. The Orkney kestrels have got over this difficulty by taking to nesting on the ground; but then, Orkney birds are different(2). Even woodpigeons nest on the ground in Orkney.

The kestrel may have suffered less than most from the persecution shown to all birds of prey in the game preserving era, but it certainly suffered severely. I am old enough to remember a time when kestrels were relentlessly pursued and shot by gamekeepers, and one of the minor tragedies that befell me when I was a student at St Andrews was being watched by a gamekeeper when visiting a kestrel's nest in a quarry and later being told with glee by him that he had shot the bird – which he thereafter did every year. Even in 1961, in Berkshire, I found ingrained prejudice against the kestrel still very strong; they would eat all the young pheasants I was told, when I ventured, ignorant as I am, to suggest that they might actually be harmless. One wonders what if any effect all the informative factual propaganda that has gone out over the radio, through the press, books, and other media may have had on minds so bigoted and blocked against observed fact.

However, the sporadic persecution meted out to the kestrel in many parts of Britain apparently did not succeed in reducing the overall numbers very much, and in some parts of Britain not at all. Kestrels rear good-sized broods and breed in their first year, so recovery is potentially swift. Parslow's 1967 survey considered that up to 1959 there had been little change in its status during the twentieth century; and J. S. Ash, in a survey of a Hampshire game preserve in 1952–59 noted no marked change in the kestrel, which was always the commonest species seen, outnumbering all other birds of prey put together(1,15). It seems, therefore, that in this one species the population may have been more or less stable from 1900–1960, and perhaps for quite a long time before that too.

From 1960–63 there was some decline in the numbers, especially in southern and eastern England, where kestrels were probably affected by pesticides. In a survey by Prestt in 1965 59 localities noted no change in the status of kestrels, four noted an increase, and 71 (53%) a decrease; the survey covered less than half of Wales and Scotland, however, and if these had been included there would have been a greater number of areas showing no change(17). The increases were in built-up areas, where kestrels have increased as breeding birds in cities and suburbs, and the decreases were from the eastern and southern agricultural and cereal-growing areas. In these areas the kestrel's decline resembled that observed in sparrowhawks, peregrines, and other raptors. The most severe decline was observed south of a line from Nottingham and Leicester to Hampshire, Sussex, and Kent, and was less severe locally in wooded areas such as the Norfolk and Suffolk brecklands. A less marked decline, perhaps only temporary, occurred in central England, south-east Scotland, and Ireland. The worst decline was, in fact, observed in those areas where agricultural pesticides were most used. Since 1963 there has again been some increase in the number of kestrels seen in some eastern counties, such as Kent, Surrey, and Lincoln.

Such surveys should be carried out annually over a period of years to get a true result. The kestrel is a partly nomadic species which, in some parts of its very wide range in the Old World, concentrates in large numbers to breed in areas where the small mammals on which it feeds are at peak numbers preceding a crash in population. A vole plague of this nature occurred in southern Scotland in 1890–92, and both kestrels and short-eared owls then became numerous, laying large clutches and rearing large broods(16). Kestrels occurred at a density of at least one pair per 400 acres (160 ha.), which is not actually a very high density compared to some recorded in modern times but is higher than the density in that area today. The numbers of kestrels breeding or seen in the same area in different years fluctuates greatly. Thus J. S. Ash in Hampshire saw, year round, five times as many kestrels in 1957 as he did in 1959, but there was comparatively little difference in the numbers seen in the breeding season in these two years, though 1959 was still a poor year, with only about a fifth of the kestrels breeding as in 1954(1). In Oost Flevoland, in Holland, where there was no possibility of the population being limited by lack of nesting sites, because experimental blocks in the newly reclaimed polder were more than amply supplied with kestrel nesting boxes, the population first fell from 32 pairs in 1961 to 16 in 1962, then rose gradually to 62 pairs in 1965 (with fewer nest boxes)(4). Such surveys can therefore mislead if carried out for only one year and not continued over a series of years.

Nothing in the data available at the British Trust for Ornithology on the number of young kestrels ringed per year, or on clutch size, brood size, and breeding success supports the idea of a general decline throughout Britain. There has been no obvious decline in the number of young ringed per year, which fluctuates up and down according to the enthusiasm of ringers and the ease of locating occupied nests(20). The mean clutch size in 1969–71 (4·81) is practically the same as that in 1951–53 (4·80). The average size of brood reared in 1960–62, 3·42, was low despite high clutch size, 4·93 in the same period, but again there is little long-term variation and broods in 1971 are actually larger than in 1951. The drop in brood size in 1960–62 suggests that in those years breeding success may have been low despite the laying of large clutches, and that pesticides might have been the cause of this. The peregrine falcon and other species seriously affected by pesticides reached a low population point about that time. However, since 1962 when certain pesticides were restricted breeding success has swung back up to normal, and some local increases have been reported from parts of eastern England where the kestrel had become scarce.

Although these figures do not support the idea that the kestrel has generally declined the fact remains that in cereal-growing areas in eastern England the kestrel is now rather a rare bird. Clearly there has been a marked decline here, whatever may have caused it. Factors contributing to it may include, besides the use of agricultural pesticides, the destruction of possible nesting places and the intensive methods of farming in use, which may reduce the supply of small mammals on which the kestrel feeds. In southern England kestrels often nest in hedgerow elms because there is nowhere else for them to nest; accordingly if these are grubbed out to make fields larger or because of Dutch elm disease nesting places of kestrels go too, and the kestrel must disappear. As in the case of the merlin, there is no obvious single simple explanation for the observed decline of the kestrel in parts of Britain, though there are several likely causes which, acting together, could have brought it about.

No country-wide survey of the kestrel has been carried out to estimate what the total population of Britain might be. Being neither large nor rare the kestrel attracts less attention than the buzzard or the peregrine, though it is just as interesting in its way. In 1967 the population of Leicestershire was estimated at 150–180 pairs, or one pair per 3500 acres (1420 ha.)(10). The population of Sussex was estimated at about 600 pairs in 1968, and there was thought to have been only a slight decline since 1938(18). The population density in Sussex varied greatly according to habitat from one pair per 2250 acres to nearly four times that density, one pair per 600 acres.

If the average density in Sussex and Leicester, about one pair per 2000 acres, or roughly 3 square miles (7·8 sq. km.), is typical of the whole of southern and central England, then there could be 15–20,000 pairs of kestrels in these areas alone. I suspect that the number would actually be higher, for in parts of southern England very much higher population density is reported. I have been told of a density of four pairs on 100 acres in 1972; and in 1967 19 nests were found in Richmond Park, of which seven were robbed by boys and two were repeats after being robbed by the same pairs(i). This is equivalent to about one pair per forty acres (16 ha.), that is about ten times as numerous as the kestrels in the border vole plagues of 1890–92. Such a very high density would not be typical of a larger area; but it suggests that the figures for Sussex and Leicester might be pessimistic for S.E. England as a whole.

There are few figures available for any typical moorland area to enable me to make a guess as to the number of kestrels there could be in Scotland or Wales. At Eskdalemuir there were seven pairs on 4157 acres (1680 ha.), about 600 acres (240 ha.) per pair, during a good vole year in 1970(16). I would think that kestrels would certainly be more numerous in moorland and upland agricultural areas of most of western and northern Britain than in the agricultural south east. There could well be another 50,000 pairs, maybe more, in these areas not subject to pesticides and not intensively farmed, where with a more abundant supply of small grass-loving rodents the kestrel could survive on a smaller area per pair. As a crude guess, I would think that there could be about 65–80,000 pairs of kestrels in Britain and an unknown but large number in Ireland.

The kestrel is certainly the only British diurnal raptor likely to top the 100,000 pair mark in all parts of Britain, but it would not surprise me to find this an over-estimate. There are very large tracts of moorland and mountains in Scotland and elsewhere where the kestrel is relatively rare, partly because of a lack of suitable nesting sites. When doing surveys of country inhabited by golden eagles I see very few kestrels. In the absence of any good figures from anywhere of this type it is impossible to guess how much this might affect the total population estimate, but certainly the relatively high density of Eskdalemuir is not typical of the West Highlands or Sutherland, and probably not of other parts of the Cheviots.

No one man could do a thorough country-wide survey of the kestrel to ascertain the population. It would need a co-operative inquiry such as that done for the buzzard and it would need to be continued for several years to cover fluctuations. The kestrel is not a threatened species in Britain, so there are probably many other priorities which will prevent any such inquiry being started. Nevertheless, I believe it would be worth while to establish the population of what is probably the com-monest diurnal bird of prey in Britain, and it is the sort of work like the current Common Birds Census that could be carried out satisfactorily by amateur ornithol-ogists in their spare time. My own feeling is that the kestrel would outnumber the sparrowhawk and buzzard very considerably; but that in terms of total live-weight the buzzard might equal or even slightly exceed the kestrel in Britain, not in Ireland, for a buzzard is equal to about four kestrels. However, these are merely conjectures, and I expect it will be many years, if ever, before a better answer is achieved.

Kestrels are able to build up to very high local populations if food is abundant partly because they are not strongly territorial. They only defend from other kestrels an area of about 35 yards radius – about an acre or 0·4 ha. – round their nest site, and several kestrels can be seen hunting in the same favourable places without interfering with one another(4). This behaviour probably derives from the nomadic nature of the kestrel in other parts of its range, where it is more strongly migratory and gregarious than in Britain. Evidently, for a nomadic species, it would be desirable for a large number to be able to congregate and breed in areas of abundant food supply for a year or more, moving to other areas following the cyclic fluctuations of the prey. Species that live in open country often tend to be more nomadic than those which live in woodlands, which tend to be strongly territorial. However, this rule is not universal, as demonstrated in Britain by the extraordinary allegiance to particular sites shown by the merlin, which is even more an inhabitant of open country than the kestrel. In Britain and southern Europe generally the kestrel is not really nomadic; nevertheless the kestrel does congregate and breed in areas where there are abundant voles, sharing this habit with the short-eared owl, which is decidedly nomadic even in Britain.

Kestrels therefore do not have a permanent home range with the nest site some-where near the centre of it, hunted over by a particular pair and not by others, as occurs for instance in the buzzard, golden eagle, peregrine and probably the merlin. They more closely resemble sparrowhawks which breed in certain woods at high density but hunt some distance away from the nest site, several often hunting in certain favoured areas. Nevertheless, many kestrel breeding sites are occupied every year for many years, some for centuries, by a succession of different individuals. One may wonder whether this accommodating nature is not part of the secret of the kestrel's success, for the merlin, about the same size as the sparrow-hawk and kestrel, but more inclined to stick tenaciously to a certain area of moorland, is very much less common than either kestrel or sparrowhawk.

Even so, there seems to be an upper limit to the number of kestrels any given area can maintain, though this fluctuates considerably year by year. To ascertain this upper limit in a bird such as the kestrel, which does not build its own nest but is dependent on cliffs, old birds' nests, buildings, or nest boxes, one must ensure that lack of nesting sites does not limit the number of kestrels able to breed. Both the European and the American kestrels *Falco sparverius* readily use nest boxes, and the provision of enough nest boxes often means that the population multiplies several times over. In the polder of Oost Flevoland in Holland kestrel nest boxes were erected all over 9 sq. km. (3·475 sq. mi.) experimental blocks, in rows of nine boxes at intervals of 330 metres (350 yards). There were thus 81 boxes per block. One of the blocks was later split into two parts and the number of boxes in one part doubled. This, however, had no effect on the total population of breeding kestrels, showing that the number of boxes first erected was adequate(4).

In the first part of the block, over six years, 227 boxes accommodated 101 pairs of kestrels. In the second part 358 available boxes accommodated 97 pairs of kestrels. In both halves of the block the population of kestrels fluctuated sharply. In 1962, each half had eight pairs, while in 1965 there were 32 and 30 pairs, almost four times as many. Unfortunately, A. J. Cavé who did this work did not say whether the kestrels were always more or less evenly distributed over the blocks, the pairs in years of low population being about the same distance from each other but further apart than in years of high population. If that were so, then although kestrels are not strongly territorial, they would be showing the same sort of even spatial distribution pattern between pairs that seems to be regular in almost all other birds of prey breeding in Britain or Europe, excepting some colonial harriers such as Montagu's.

Evidently the same sort of experiment could be carried out, for instance, on otherwise barren but recently afforested land in the Cheviots, with a high vole population but nowhere for kestrels to nest. It would not cost very much and it would produce results of great interest. The nest boxes need only be six feet off the ground, and the sitting kestrels can apparently be caught on the nest with a net for ringing and other studies, without causing them to desert.

In some of their range kestrels are colonial, as the lesser kestrel almost always is. In Japan kestrels breed in small colonies in cliffs as do lesser kestrels in south Europe(3); and in the Steppes of south Russia and west Siberia, where trees are rare, they breed in small colonies in other birds' nests, as do red-footed falcons in Hungary. James Ferguson-Lees has recently recorded that he saw similar colonial nesting, along with both lesser kestrels and red-footed falcons in a grove of trees at Askania Nova reserve in the Russian Steppes, and also in Jordan(9). True colonial nesting of this nature has not been seen in Britain, but there are two recent cases of two pairs of kestrels nesting very close together, one on the buildings of a disused lead mine in Cardiganshire and the other on an electricity pylon in Derbyshire. In the first case the kestrels' nests faced in opposite directions, and they could not easily see one another; on the pylon, however, they obviously could. In this case, and in the colonial nesting cases mentioned, the nests were only 8–15 yards (2½–5 m.) apart, well within a 35-yard radius, so that evidently even that normally defended territorial limit can be relaxed on occasion. It would be interesting to festoon an electricity pylon with nest boxes and see if this resulted in a colony of kestrels; it would at least make that particular pylon more bearable.

The kestrel's mode of hunting is well known. Normally it hovers with beating wings over open country or, if the wind is strong, poises without beating its wings. Such hovering and poising amounts to aerial perching, and permits the kestrel to examine minutely the ground immediately below it. In hovering the kestrel swings up to a pitch from level flight, stops with the body held at rather a steep angle, spreads the tail, and winnows the air with its wings. The head remains steady while any variation in the air currents is absorbed by movements of the body and wings. Evidently the large, fan-like spread tail considerably increases the lift obtained. If it fails to spot anything the kestrel moves on a little way and tries again; it may only move a few feet between hovers, or travel a hundred yards or more. If it sees possible prey it glides steeply downwards, controlling the rate of descent by varying the angle of its wings, as a parachutist slips air from his parachute, and, when a few feet above the quarry, raises the wings vertically above the back and plunges feet foremost into the grass to grasp the prey. The whole action is beautifully controlled and a joy to watch.

Alternatively, a kestrel may hunt from a perch, usually on the bare branch of a tree. From here it can descend to take mammals or any other prey. One male hunted in this way for many days between 15 August and 5 September, feeding almost entirely on large black slugs in that period(h). This kestrel skinned the slugs carefully, then swallowed them whole and, being left-footed, got its left foot slimy and dirty in the process. Perching is less often seen than hovering, partly because it limits the kestrel's range of vision whereas, in hovering a whole field can be examined in a short time. In very open country a kestrel must hunt hovering as there are no perches. Hovering must use much more energy than perching, so that the kestrel that perched for weeks in one place subsisting on an apparently unattractive diet of doubtless nutritious slugs was actually being sensible and taking it easy.

Because hovering and perching are the normal methods of hunting no one should imagine that kestrels cannot turn to other methods at need. When voles run short they eat many birds and though most of these are fledging starlings or young waders such as lapwings in open country, they do occasionally attack larger birds and can catch some birds in flight(4). They attend starling roosts and sometimes succeed in catching them in flight, and have been known to kill turnstones, Kentish plovers, adult moorhens and godwits(n). One kestrel selected a starling blind in one eye from a flock and would have killed it if it had not been disturbed(j). Occasionally kestrels rob other birds of prey such as little owls or even a peregrine falcon. This peregrine chased a chaffinch which took cover in a bush, where it was caught by the kestrel which then flew off with it; the peregrine did not pursue. Perhaps this piracy sometimes leads to taking on more formidable prey than can be handled, for a kestrel has been seen to attack a weasel and be killed by it, perhaps attracted in the first case by a vole the weasel was carrying(k). Another kestrel actually attacked a weasel running across a road but dropped it. A weasel weighs about as much as a male kestrel.

Kestrels are not infrequently drowned, probably when pursuing waders or other birds near water. One plunged into sewage sludge, but emerged and flew away(c).

They are decidedly crepuscular, often hunting very late in the evening, and occasionally even long after nightfall, but in moonlight(f). At these times they probably catch long-tailed field mice, which are common prey but are largely nocturnal, so are not often caught by diurnal birds of prey. There are several records of kestrels following the plough, and dropping on the turned furrows to take mice or other prey so exposed; on the evidence of earth in their castings they are thought to eat earthworms, the rest of the worm being completely digested(o). They occasionally feed on carrion, always, in the few records, dead birds(b). They may eat scraps left by picnic parties, snatch small fish from the surface of water like a tern, or catch crabs(a,g). When prey is scarce or the weather is hard they sometimes cache surplus kills, returning to them later, and have also been seen robbing a little owl that was trying to store food in a hole for its own use(l). Occasionally they catch bats.

Kestrels are, in fact, very enterprising and versatile hunters which can, if their normal prey is lacking, turn to a variety of other prey. At Oost Flevoland in poor vole years more birds than usual were taken(4). However, they cannot kill anything very large, and have difficulty with animals of their own weight, averaging about 200 grams (7 oz). They prefer to kill slow-moving creatures on the ground rather than birds in flight, which they can only just manage, and they probably kill 90% or more of their food on the ground. They are especially likely to kill small mammals, voles, rats, mice and shrews.

All the food studies that have been done in Britain and elsewhere indicate that voles, if available, are the preferred prey. Examples have been collected in Appendix Table I and from this it will be evident that voles and other small mammals form 60–80% of the prey, and on this account they are regarded as farmers' friends and protected(6,7,8). On migration in Africa kestrels eat many insects, especially large grasshoppers caught at bush fires or in the grass, and flying termites (everything eats flying termites). However in Britain and Europe insects are not important constituents of the prey taken, at least by weight. In Ireland, where voles are absent, kestrels feed mainly on other small mammals and may occasionally kill a baby rabbit(8).

The food requirement of a kestrel is probably about a fifth of bodyweight, about forty grams per day(5). Two average-sized voles suffice for one kestrel, or one young starling, with some to spare. In areas where both kestrels and buzzards occur and both feed largely on voles a kestrel can satisfy its needs in a third of the time needed by a buzzard. The small food requirement means that the kestrel cannot do very much harm to game-preserving interests, even in the rare instances where some game-bird chicks are taken. Kestrels do take a few young game-birds, but very few. Game-birds are not identified at all in the British food studies, but kestrels have occasionally been recorded as taking them in Britain, though never to the extent alleged by gamekeepers. In Oost Flevoland, in six years, a total of only 36 young pheasants was recorded among 198 pairs of kestrels, a minute fraction of a pheasant chick per kestrel per year. Once again, persecution of the kestrel by game-preserving interests, which still continues to some extent, is entirely unjustified.

The main prey of British kestrels, the short-tailed vole *Microtus agrestis* fluctuates cyclically in numbers, with population peaks about every four years followed by sharp reductions or 'crashes'. However, such fluctuations do not occur simultaneously all over Britain, and population peaks in the Highlands of Scotland are out of phase with the rest of Britain(20). The Orkney vole *Microtus arvalis* apparently does not fluctuate to the same extent, possibly because it is heavily preyed upon by harriers, kestrels and short-eared owls; such predation could help to prevent the voles from reaching a population peak leading to a crash. The number of kestrels breeding in any one year apparently is directly related to the abundance of voles. In Cavé's study at Oost Flevoland he found that in bad vole years fewer kestrels bred and that many female kestrels laid but deserted their eggs, so that fewer broods were reared. He considered that this was due to the inability of the males to provide their mates with enough food, and that scarcity of voles was aggravated by wet weather preventing the kestrels from hunting effectively(4).

In Britain we have no good quantitative evidence of this sort, but the number of young kestrels ringed per year is probably greater in years of good food supply than in other years, because more complete broods are reared, found, and ringed. Allowing for the varying efforts of individual ringers and such events as the Second World War (which reduced the numbers ringed) David Snow found that there was quite good correlation between peaks of kestrels ringed and probable peak vole years(20). For instance, there were vole peaks in 1926, 1929–30, 1932–33, 1935, 1937–8, 1952–3, 1957, 1961, 1962–3, and 1964; and corresponding ringing peaks in 1926, 1933, 1938, 1944, 1948–9, 1952, 1957, 1961, and 1964. Most of these ringing peaks agree quite well with peak vole years. The figures have been larger and more reliable in recent years because of the generally increased interest in birds of prey.

Once again, there is no good British breeding study of kestrels, and the details of breeding behaviour must be put together from scattered sources. In what follows I have made frequent reference to a detailed study carried out in Oost Flevoland, Holland, which is a fine example of how to get good results from an experimental situation(4). Adult British kestrels remain close to their breeding places year round, and adults do not migrate far; but they do not hold a home range or territory through the winter either. In spring they return to the breeding place and perform vigorous courtship displays. The male repeatedly dives at the female, either in flight or when she is perched on the ground, passing so close that he almost strikes her, screaming shrilly(3). In flight she turns over and presents her claws to his, as do most other birds of prey. At this stage, as in other falcons, the female is dependent on the male for food, and does little hunting for herself. Mating normally takes place on a ledge or cliff or branch of a tree, sometimes some distance from the nest site and is often accompanied by presentation of prey by the male.

The male is said by some observers to select the nest site, but others say that the female does so, and this seems more likely. One male returned to the nest box in which he was reared, but in Oost Flevoland, although the breeding kestrels are drawn from those which have wintered in the neighbourhood they do not regularly return to the nest box in which they were reared(4). Such behaviour is comparable to that of some other small birds of prey such as the merlin or sparrowhawk but is unlike that of the larger, more strictly territorial species.

The nest may be in a hole in a tree, a natural cliff ledge, a building or man-made structure, the old nest of another bird in a tree or on a ledge, or in a nest box. An analysis of the sites described on the B.T.O. nest record cards in recent years (Text Table 11) shows that in southern England the commonest site is a hole in a tree, 177 out of 291 nests being so placed. The next most common site is an old nest of a crow, heron, or other large bird in a tree (57/291), followed by outbuildings or structures (27/291), and cliff ledges (24/291). Old nests on cliffs and nest boxes are very seldom used, the latter mainly because there are not enough nest boxes. In northern England and Scotland a ledge on an inland or sea cliff is the most favoured site (143/354), followed by old nests in trees (76/354). Buildings or structures are used in the north about as often as natural forks or holes in trees, and old nests on cliffs are used more often than in southern England. Again, nest box records are scarce for lack of nest boxes. There is some suggestion that in higher parts of southern England, such as Dartmoor, old nests in trees are preferred to natural holes; which might be due to the ability of a few people to find such sites, lack of good natural holes, or natural preference for a more sheltered site by the kestrel.

Kestrels breed on a variety of man-made structures and buildings, the records including old mine chimneys, barns, churches, buildings in cities, viaducts, bridges, cranes, and electricity pylons(d). When on a building or a viaduct the kestrels can use a hollow where a block has fallen out, which resembles a cliff ledge. However, on some other structures such as pylons they may have to wait till another bird has built a nest on it and then use that; the two kestrels nesting on a Derbyshire pylon used old carrion crows' nests(9). Falcons make no nests themselves and require some sort of soft foundation on which to lay their eggs: bare concrete or metal will not do. One nest in a ruined cottage in Denbigh was only four feet from the ground level, but most nests are much higher, up to 70 feet (22 m.) in tall trees. In buildings kestrels not infrequently nest very close to barn owls; the B.T.O. cards include records of barn owls breeding four or five feet from kestrels in Northants, the Isle of Man and Kirkcudbright, while one kestrel's nest in Northumberland was ten feet from that of a long-eared owl. Apart from the two cases of very close nesting on buildings and pylons already mentioned, the nearest recorded distance between kestrels' nests in Britain is 200–250 yards, in Richmond Park and Kempton Park(i). Almost all kestrel nests are at less than 1500 feet (480 m.) above sea level; they are not likely to breed on crags on high mountains.

Kestrels will use whatever usable site is available to them, but if there are no trees, buildings, or cliff ledges they may not breed in otherwise suitable habitat. In Orkney, apparently since 1945, kestrels have taken to nesting on the ground, usually in luxuriant tall heather, but sometimes under a bank or in a rabbit burrow(2). Kestrels prefer longer heather than merlins in the same area and seldom nest in medium-length heather. Such nest sites may be re-used up to three times if not destroyed by spring fires. The incubating kestrel sits very tight and may allow herself to be handled; or if in a hole may crawl away up it on being disturbed. Ground nesting has the advantage that the young cannot fall out of the nest, but few young do that anyhow and ground nesting exposes them to attack by predators such as foxes, which are absent in Orkney. Perhaps the habit is more widespread in Scotland than is supposed, for I have sometimes seen kestrels in spring where there was no obvious breeding place.

Eggs are laid at two-day intervals, sometimes longer, so that a clutch of five eggs takes at least nine days to deposit. Larger clutches are known of seven, eight, or even ten, the latter perhaps laid by two different females in the same nest. Analysis of the clutch size on B.T.O. nest record cards shows clutches of from one to seven eggs, the single egg clutches being apparently complete but perhaps the remnants of a larger earlier clutch reduced by boys or predators. Four or five eggs is commonest. The average of 534 clutches is 4·72, slightly greater (4·75) in N. England and Scotland and slightly less (4·68) in S. England(14). If this small difference is consistent it supports the theory that clutches of the same species become larger from the tropics north towards the poles. There is some annual variation, for instance from 4·38 in 1966 to 4·95 in 1968; or, over three-year periods 4·60 in 1966–68 to 5·00 in 1957–59. There is no evidence that kestrels have been laying any smaller clutches in recent years, and these clutches are also up to average when compared to continental clutches.

Normally the female alone incubates, and is fed by the male, but males rarely take a small share of incubation. When bringing prey the male may take it to the nest site or box, or may perch near by and call, when the female will leave the nest and receive the prey from him. In Oost Flevoland it was found that although clutch size was not dependent on vole abundance female kestrels would often desert their eggs in years of poor food supply, or when hunting conditions were difficult because of continuous rain. The proportion deserted from year to year varied from nil to 60% and averaged almost exactly 20% in 375 clutches. This was by far the greatest cause of egg loss in Oost Flevoland, infertile eggs being only 6·8% of the total laid, and predation from all causes, including human interference, 12·7%. Such figures will vary from place to place and the somewhat artificial situation at Oost Flevoland, with the kestrels nesting entirely in nest boxes built for them, may have been unusually favourable(4).

Table 9   Kestrel: Clutch and Brood Size

Data from British Trust for Ornithology Nest record cards.

Area	No. of clutches or broods	1	2	3	4	5	6	7	Mean
Clutch size									
S. England	234	–	5	14	70	108	35	2	4·68
N. England Scotland	300	3	4	22	72	138	57	4	4·75
Total, Great Britain	534	3	9	36	142	246	92	6	4·72
Brood size									
S. England	264	13	29	65	96	54	6	1	3·65
N. England Scotland	405	12	43	96	132	100	22	–	3·82
Total, Great Britain	669	25	72	161	228	154	28	1	3·75

In view of the fact, clearly established at Oost Flevoland but not so far even indicated in Britain, that nearly twice as many female kestrels as males are reared, it seems curious that the adult sex ratio is not unbalanced and that bigamy is not often reported in kestrels. It was not even reported at Oost Flevoland where the sex ratio among young kestrels is almost two to one in favour of females. In the hen harrier, where the sex ratio in the young is somewhat in favour of females, and in the sparrowhawk where it is said to be even, bigamy or polygamy appears to be common. This is obviously something that future kestrel watchers should look out for.

In Britain the earliest eggs may be laid before the end of March, usually in late April and into May with a few late clutches even in June. Exact laying dates are hard to establish from the existing data, but in southern England most clutches are laid by 30 April and further north by 10 May. The laying date may be affected by winter and spring food supply. In Oost Flevoland kestrels laid early in good vole years with favourable weather and laying was delayed by rain. Later clutches were smaller than earlier clutches, averaging 5–6 up to 10 May, then 4–5, and less than 4 only after 31 May; the same feature has been generally observed in Britain. The

Table 10   Kestrel: Three Year Averages, Clutch and Brood Size

Period	Clutches	Eggs	Mean	Broods	Young	Mean
1951–53	30	144	4·80	23	88	3·83
1954–56	24	111	4·63	25	87	3·48
1957–59	25	125	5·00	23	91	3·96
1960–62	28	138	4·93	33	113	3·42
1963–65	78	365	4·68	101	374	3·70
1966–68	202	930	4·60	268	990	3·69
1969–71	132	635	4·81	174	673	3·87
Total	519	2,448	4·72	647	2,416	3·73

Data from British Trust for Ornithology Nest Record Cards and Morgan, R., in prep., 15(14).
No marked differences in clutch or brood size since 1950, but slight possibility of pesticide effects, 1962, with large clutches and relatively small broods.

oocytes from which the eggs develop begin development in autumn, and the number of eggs laid can thus be reduced by hard conditions in winter though not apparently by the abundance of voles in spring. Also, cold conditions in spring mean that there is less energy available for egg production. Such effects vary a good deal from year to year, or from one bird to another in the same area, but the general indications are that a warm, open spring will result in larger earlier clutches(4,20).

Incubation does not normally begin till several eggs of the clutch have been laid, but may start with the first egg and always starts before the clutch is complete. Each egg hatches in 27–29 days, and the whole brood hatches over a shorter period than the laying period, 3–5 days as opposed to 7–9 in clutches of 4–5. This results in a brood of more even age than would have been the case if the female began incubating with the first egg. The young are not aggressive to one another and, provided that food is plentiful, there is a good chance that all will be reared. Most nestling losses occur in the first week of the fledging period after which losses are slight. Once the young have hatched it seems that the male is able to supply the increased amount of food required, and the brood losses are not high even in years when a large proportion of females have deserted their eggs apparently because the males could not satisfy their mates(4). Since the male, after the young have hatched, must suddenly increase his rate of killing, it is hard to understand why he should be unable to feed the female earlier.

Table 11   Kestrel: Nesting Site Preferences

	S.W. and S.E. England	N. England and Scotland
Hole or fork in tree	177	62
Old nest in tree	57	76
Building/bridge	27	60
Ledge on cliff	24	143
Old nest on cliff	2	10
Nest box	4	3
Total	291	354

Data from B.T.O. nest record cards.

When first hatched the young weigh 14–18 grams, then increase rapidly to a maximum weight in males of 250 grams (9 oz) at 20–22 days and 280 grams (10 oz) at 26 days in females. Feathers show through the copious down coats at 12 days and they are fully feathered on the body by 20 days. At that age they can feed themselves on prey brought by either parent. Once they are fully feathered they lose weight slightly before leaving the nest at 27–34 days, usually 28–30 days. Males are both lighter and more active than females, and leave the nest two or three days earlier. The young can thus be sexed with certainty by accurate weighing at the end of the fledging period, females averaging 240–245 grams and males 220. In Oost Flevoland this revealed that 63–64% of nestlings were females, almost two females for every male. This is a higher proportion of females than in any other known raptor, and must surely indicate a non-random distribution of the sexes in the egg stage(4).

During the early fledging period the female remains in the nest with the brood and is fed there by the male, who must sharply increase his rate of killing as soon as the brood hatches, and continues to increase it until the female can leave the feathered brood and take part herself. Up to a late stage and sometimes for the whole fledging period the female and brood are still mainly or entirely dependent on the male. The appetite of a growing young kestrel is estimated at about 35% of its bodyweight, and the male must supply at least one vole per nestling per day to maintain their weight and 1·5–2 voles to enable them to make normal rapid growth. A male, with a brood of four, must thus catch his own requirement and that of his mate (about four voles per day) and another six to ten to satisfy the brood. This means catching about one vole per hour from seven in the morning to eight at night. In a good vole year and fine weather this will not be difficult; in Oost Flevoland as many as 28 voles have been brought in in a day, and in fine weather kestrels brought 22–44 grams of food per hour against only 12 grams per hour in rainy weather. In a year when voles are scarce kestrels turn more to birds, especially young starlings, which are generally abundant when the kestrels have large young in late May or June. At this time they may also kill larger birds. In Ireland, where there are no voles and the only small mammals available are mice and shrews kestrels apparently feed more upon birds than they do in Great Britain(8).

In Britain, analysis of the B.T.O. nest record cards shows that brood size is normally about one less than the clutch size. The average of 609 broods is 3·75, again slightly higher in north England and Scotland, (3·82), than in southern England (3·65). Three-year periods averaged from 1951–71 vary from 3·42 in 1960–62 to 3·96 in 1957–59, and again show no reduction in the size of brood reared in recent years. Apart from one period, 1960–62, the variation in brood size closely follows the clutch size averages, but in 1960–62 clutches were large, averaging 4·93, and broods relatively small. This suggests that at this period, when the peregrine and sparrowhawk reached their lowest population and breeding success, the kestrel may also have been adversely affected by pesticides. However, since 1962 the situation has reverted to normal, and it is impossible now to say whether the poor breeding success in 1960–62 may not have been due to some other cause. 1962, however, was a good vole year so broods should have been up to normal.

Figures from nest record cards do not necessarily reflect the true annual productivity of the kestrel, for they apply only to successful nests as a rule. Cases in which the same brood was followed through to the end have been analysed by Shrubb(18). In 79 nests with clutches of 4·4–4·9 in different areas 64% of eggs hatched, losses being due to predation, robbing of nests by humans, and infertility.

85% of the young hatched flew successfully, the losses again being entirely due to robbing by humans. All these losses resulted in average broods of 2·1 from average clutches of 4·5; but if human interference could have been eliminated the average brood size would have been 2·5 overall. In Oost Flevoland, where a controlled situation permitted more satisfactory analysis, about 30% of eggs failed to hatch, the main cause being desertion, followed by infertility and predation, 6·8% and 3·3%(4). If this figure were applied to average British clutches they would be reduced from 4·72 eggs to 3·30 young. In Flevoland, 16·6% of young died from all causes, and a similar scale of loss in Britain would reduce broods of 3·30 to 2·75. The true annual productivity of a pair of breeding kestrels is therefore probably 2·5–2·75, in the absence of human interference. Clutches and broods in Britain are somewhat smaller than they were in the artificial, and perhaps specially favourable situation in Oost Flevoland, so that a figure of 2·5 young per pair which breeds, as calculated by Shrubb, is probably quite accurate.

After the young kestrels leave the nest they remain in the area for some time and continue to be fed by the parents until they are strong on the wing, when they follow the parents to hunting areas. What happens in the post-fledging period does not seem to have been fully observed by anyone. However, it is likely that the young kestrels are largely dependent on their parents for about a month after they leave the nest and are therefore not able to fend for themselves until late July or August.

Although Cavé considered that in Oost Flevoland the laying date, and through this factor clutch size, were dependent on food supply, and that females were likely to desert because they were not supplied with food in poor vole years, he also concluded that the most young were likely to be reared from the largest clutches, of seven eggs. Young from large clutches also weigh no less than those in smaller clutches, suggesting that they did not suffer from any lack of food. This does not support Lack's view that in large broods each fledgling gets less to eat and accordingly is smaller and weaker than in small broods(11). It also indicates that even with a very large brood male kestrels catch enough food to maintain growth among the young at the same rate as in smaller broods. This makes it very difficult to understand why a few weeks earlier a male cannot feed a single incubating female sufficiently well, and suggests that frequent desertion of eggs might be due to some other cause than simply food supply. The kestrel data do not support the theory that the optimum brood size is not usually the largest that the parents ever rear, for in Oost Flevoland brood size increases with clutch size, and the largest numbers of fledglings were reared from unusually large clutches of seven eggs(4). However, again, the somewhat unnatural conditions concerned may have had an effect, and these observations need confirmation in a truly wild situation.

In Britain the movements and mortality of kestrels after they leave the nest have been studied by Sir Landsborough Thomson and more recently by David Snow(12, 20). Still more recent ringing returns do not suggest any variation in the pattern established up to 1965. Young kestrels just fledged move in any direction at random, with some tendency to move east and south-east. In their first autumn and winter they tend to move predominantly south and south-east, some crossing the Channel to Europe, mainly over the Hampshire and Sussex coasts. In March and April, if they survive, they return to near the areas where they were bred; 16/18 recoveries at this time were within 30 miles of where the bird concerned was ringed. The young can breed in their first summer when less than a year old, and most probably do. In their second and subsequent winters ringing returns show that they tend to remain closer to their nesting areas, though they evidently move some distance from

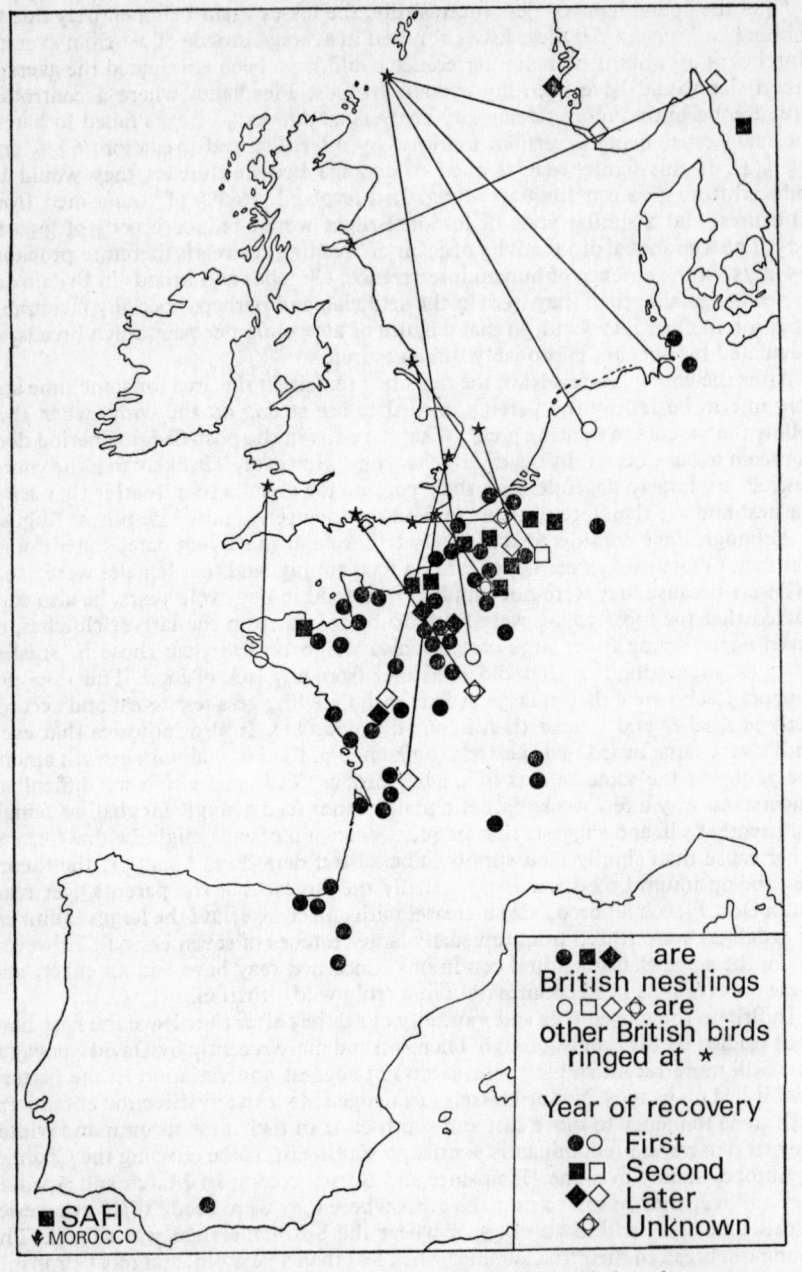

MAP 30. Kestrels ringed in Britain and recovered abroad.

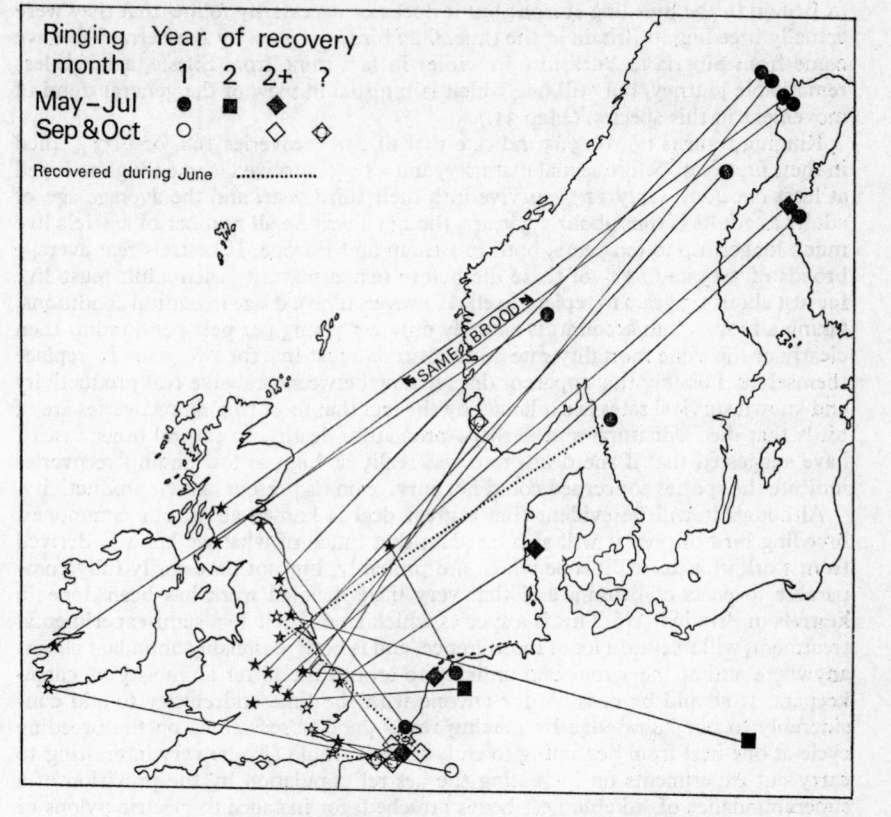

Ringing Year of recovery
month   1   2   2+   ?
May–Jul   ●   ■   ◆
Sep&Oct   ○   ◇   ◇

Recovered during June ....

SAME BROOD

MAP 31. Kestrels ringed abroad and recovered in Britain.

the actual nest site and do not attempt to hold a territory or range through the winter.

Some kestrels migrate to the continent. Most of these birds pass through Western France as far as the Pyrenees, but probably go no further; some reach Spain but so far no British kestrels are known to travel to Africa with the hordes of migrant European kestrels in winter. A return movement of British kestrels from S. France probably begins in January or February and takes a more easterly course than the southern movement. British ringed birds have also been recovered in Schleswig-Holstein and Sweden, but these records are abnormal. Ireland is a subsidiary wintering area for kestrels ringed in north England and Scotland. Two nest-mates ringed on the Isle of Man were recovered within two days of each other, one in Ireland and one in northern Spain(20). (Map 30.)

Continental kestrels visit Britain in winter, mainly in the eastern counties. Most of them apparently come from Scandinavia and travel roughly south-west; these include two from the same brood ringed in N. Sweden and recovered in west Scotland and south-west Ireland respectively. Others come from Holland or N. France, moving generally west(13). A few foreign-ringed birds have been recovered in Britain in the breeding season; but it does not necessarily follow that they were actually breeding in Britain at the time. One bird, reported by Bannerman to have come from Siberia to Yorkshire in winter in fact came from Silesia, a much less remarkable journey, but still one which is unusual in view of the general trend of movement in this species. (Map 31.)

Ringing returns up to 1965 indicate that of 258 recoveries 168, or 61·3% died in their first year, before sexual maturity, and 38·7% survived long enough to breed at least once(20). Only 11% survive into their third year, and the average age of adults as adults is thus about 1·3 years, though a very small number of kestrels live much longer, up to ten years, both in Britain and Europe. If kestrels rear average broods of 3·75 and 61% of these die before sexual maturity each adult must live for just about 1·3 years to replace itself. However, if brood size in natural conditions, taking all losses into account, is actually only 2·5 young per pair per annum, then clearly at the same mortality rate adult kestrels must live for two years to replace themselves. Possibly this apparent discrepancy between probable real productivity and known survival rates is explained by the fact that most ringing recoveries are of birds that died unnatural and perhaps premature deaths. In several other cases I have suggested that if the death rate was really as high as the ringing recoveries indicate the species concerned could not survive on its present known productivity.

Although it will be evident that a great deal is known about our commonest breeding bird of prey it will also be plain that much of what we know is derived from work in areas of Europe which are probably, but not necessarily fully comparable to parts of Britain, and that very little detailed work has been done in kestrels in Britain itself. This is a species which lends itself to a semi-experimental treatment, will tolerate a lot of interference, and is both reasonably abundant almost anywhere and at the same time unlikely to arouse the bitter animosity of game-keepers. It should be possible for anyone with the time and energy to add considerably to our knowledge by making really good observations on the breeding cycle at one nest from beginning to end, while it would also be very interesting to carry out experiments on increasing the kestrel population by the provision of a superabundance of suitable nest boxes attached, for instance to electric pylons or poles in areas where they cannot be attached to existing trees. There are some situations, such as young forestry plantations, where controlled experiments with different numbers of nest boxes per square mile could be carried out to see just how many kestrels could live in particular areas.

This would probably result in an increase in the number of kestrels in Britain, just as the provision of abundant nest boxes increases the population of great tits or pied flycatchers. However, since the objections of game preservers cannot even be taken seriously in this species, no one should complain at that, any more than they object to an increase in great tits. The only sufferers could be rats and mice; and even they would not be exterminated by kestrels. If such things were done, we could confidently look forward to a time when there were certainly 100,000 pairs of kestrels in Britain, and this pretty species could become more numerous than at any time in British history.

CHAPTER 16

THE MERLIN

THE merlin is one of the smallest of British falcons and diurnal birds of prey, and one of the least known, although it is relatively common and not particularly shy. No doubt this is because it is small, for among students of birds of prey there is a decided tendency to concentrate on large and rare species, to the exclusion of commoner small species which may be just as rewarding or beautiful, especially when it comes to amassing quantities of scientific facts. This is much more difficult with a big eagle, for instance, when the most energetic field worker may well find that the magical *sine qua non* of statistical significance eludes him.

Although the merlin has often been photographed at the nest and its beautiful red eggs have been in demand by egg collectors for many years little of significance has been written about it in recent years. It does not even get a mention in about a third of the volumes of British birds, going back to 1943, the date of the *Handbook of British Birds,* and very little detail has been published about its habits. To find a good account of its breeding behaviour one must go back to Professor Rowan's work in 1921(8). He studied merlins in an area of Yorkshire and did some fine pioneer work, including in his watches several all-night sessions, during one of which he noted that the male sat all night – a very rare thing in birds of prey. Yet his observations were not complete and he was hampered by the relentless destruction of even the young birds he was watching as soon as they left the nest by the gamekeepers who assisted him. As he points out, it is relatively easy to find merlins' nests and observe the birds once you know how; but no one from that day to this has made or at least recorded a special study of the merlin in Britain. For a fairly good modern account one must go to America, where merlins were studied for a season on an island in Lake Michigan(1,5). A really good modern study of the merlin is badly needed, and the field is wide open for someone with the energy and opportunity to do this work.

No detailed data are available on the number of merlins in Britain. I have included it in the group of species with 100–500 pairs, for I should be exceedingly surprised if a thorough survey revealed that there were more than 500 pairs. I should be equally surprised if there were less than 100 pairs and, at a guess, I would say the total is likely to be nearer the higher than the lower figure. However, there is no doubt that it is not a very common bird, and that it has decreased rather sharply in recent times.

In his 1967 general survey of all British raptors Parslow observes that a decline in the population of merlins had been noted before 1900(7). One would have expected such a decline to have been reversed in more recent times, when there was a glimmer of a more enlightened attitude among grouse moor gamekeepers, who are and have been the merlin's only serious enemy. However, it apparently has not been reversed, and a general decline affecting Ireland, England and Wales, and the Scottish mainland at least was evident right up to 1950 when other raptors were showing an increase. Here and there there were local increases, for instance in Devon, while in Ireland its status has perhaps changed less than elsewhere. But the merlin did not show the expected increase in numbers as observed in several other British raptors in and just after the Second World War, and apparently continued to decline.

Since 1950 there has been a more marked decline affecting the species throughout its British range. It has decreased since the mid fifties in 31 counties of England, Wales and Scotland, including six out of seven counties in Wales where it was formerly common, all in N.E. England and S. Scotland, in Sutherland, Caithness, and Shetland. By 1964 it had disappeared altogether from several well-known areas in Yorkshire and from Durham, and there was only one successful breeding pair on one island in Shetland where there were formerly 10–12 breeding pairs in the fifties. Although it is impossible to quantify the decline for lack of good population figures in former years it is evident that it is widespread, recent, and severe. In only a few areas has the merlin not declined; for instance it colonised Cornwall for the first time in 1954(7).

In the early years of the decline it was suggested that it was largely due to loss of habitat through increased forestry plantings on lowland moors, which were formerly favoured breeding habitat for merlins. There is without doubt some substance in this view. Very large tracts of suitable and formerly merlin haunted moorlands have been planted up with conifers, and the process, which has accelerated since the end of the Second World War, and which has entirely changed the face of much of upland Britain since I was a boy, is continuing. However, the total amount of forest planted does not amount to more than quite a small fraction of the total area of moorland, and cannot account wholly for the decline. It could not, for instance, account for the decline noted in Sutherland, Caithness, or Shetland, where no large areas of suitable moorland have yet been planted with trees. The cause of the recent accelerated decline must be sought elsewhere.

Merlins frequent upland moors during the breeding season, but in the winter move to lower ground, especially sea coasts, dunes, and salt marshes. On the upland moors their prey should be relatively free of contamination by organochlorine pesticides, but once they move to low ground and hunt close to coastal marshes they are almost certain to feed to a large extent upon contaminated birds. The recent decline in merlins, while less exactly documented, resembles that for peregrines which breed in Arctic or sub Arctic areas, or for the few pairs of peregrines which breed in the high Cairngorms but which migrate to warmer coastal areas or temperate farmlands in winter. In its breeding areas the merlin may be almost free of this pesticide threat; but in winter it is likely to acquire the poisons, and its breeding success might be adversely affected thereby.

However, one must admit that good evidence for any substantial falling off of breeding success from this cause is non-existent. In the early sixties many eggs were said to have failed to hatch in Northumberland; but at that time everyone studying birds of prey was looking out for such effects, which may have been over-stressed(a). Analysis of the available nest record cards at the B.T.O. gives a mean clutch size of 3·94 for 53 clutches before 1962 and 3·97 for 64 clutches after 1962. Brood sizes have apparently actually risen rather than otherwise in the same time. Before 1962 30 broods old enough to ring averaged 2·97 and 54 after 1962 averaged 3·37. These figures would not bear out the suggestion that the decline in the merlin is due to poor breeding success caused by increased pesticide use, though the apparently increased brood size since 1962 could have been aided by the restrictions on some of these compounds which have been in force since then.

What, then, is the real cause of the decline of the merlin, and how serious is it? The available evidence suggests that clutch and brood size is still up to standard, and there is still plenty of suitable moorland habitat, though this has been reduced to some extent by forestry plantings. Sporadic persecution by grouse moor game-keepers has never ceased, at least in Scotland, but it is doubtful if this can be the cause of the decline because, if it were, the population of merlins, like that of other British raptors, would have shown a sharp increase in the late forties and early fifties; it did not, rather, the steady slow decline continued. Disturbance of merlin-haunted moorlands has undoubtedly increased with the greater mobility of people, but to some extent this should have been set off by a decrease in egg collecting, particularly in north England where many merlin nests were formerly robbed. Moreover it cannot explain observed losses in Shetland, or Caithness, where there is literally no one on that vast barren desolate expanse of windswept moor north of a line from Berriedale to Forsinard. It is a real puzzle, and needs careful and early investigation.

Probably the decline is due to a combination of various factors, persecution, increased disturbance of some haunts, pesticides, and other causes, such as the hard winters of 1947 and 1963. Another possibility is the impetuous nature of the merlin itself. This is one of the most dashing of all birds of prey, pursuing its quarry at speed with a single-minded tenacity and ferocity that cannot be bettered by many a larger and more spectacular raptor. An unusually high proportion of merlins seem to kill themselves by dashing into houses, wire fences, and other obstacles when in pursuit of prey. Further details are given later; but of 122 ringing recoveries no less than 32, or about a quarter, were killed by dashing into houses, striking wire, being knocked down by a car, drowning, or were found with broken wings or other injuries suggesting that they might have so hurt themselves(b). This is a far higher proportion than in either the kestrel or sparrowhawk, in which the causes of death have recently been discussed by David Glue(2). Although I hesitate to suggest that this could be the main cause of the decline there is no doubt that Britain has become, to an increasing degree, festooned with wire in the last thirty years, and a species as prone to strike wire as the merlin must have suffered. Again, however, it is difficult to believe that this could be the cause of decline in the merlins in north east Scotland and Shetland, where there is comparatively little wire, especially as the Orkney merlins have not declined to the same extent, despite a superfluity of ex-naval barbed wire which results in an impenetrable tangle of spiky fencing all over Orkney.

Merlins are very easily overlooked in their breeding and winter haunts, so that when the species is properly investigated it may be found more common than I fear it may be. I hope so, for this is a splendid little bird, quite inoffensive to man, yet possessing all the fire and dash of the peregrine. A merlin in full pursuit of agile quarry follows every twist and turn of the prey's evolutions with equally swift manoeuvres. In 1972 I saw one pursuing a wader on Stoer Head, in Sutherland. The two came hurtling over my head from the east, and before I could bring binoculars to bear on them had disappeared behind a ridge into a dip in the ground two hundred yards away; in that distance, in about 20 seconds, the merlin had risen and stooped at its quarry three times. I did not see the end of the chase, but assume that since the merlin did not reappear from within the shallow valley it may have finally killed its desperate prey. Dr Ludwig Koch claims to have timed a merlin with a stopwatch at 240 m.p.h. (385 k.p.h.), and suggests that it is the fastest of all British falcons(4). I could not agree that this is so, for according to aerodynamic laws the fastest falcon in full stoop is likely to be the heaviest, the gyrfalcon; and I have certainly never seen a merlin travelling at any speed approaching 200 miles per hour. However, the person who eventually does the much-needed detailed study of the merlin will find it a quicksilver little bird very rewarding for its size.

Merlins feed largely on birds, which they catch almost entirely in full aerial chase. In doing so they are less inclined to make the spectacular steep diving stoops with which peregrines normally kill, but are more inclined to hunt near the ground almost in the manner of a sparrowhawk, skimming low over the moorland until some bird is caught unawares and, when it takes to flight, relentlessly pursuing it with twists and turns of almost miraculous rapidity until it finally kills or abandons the chase. Alternatively, a merlin may use cover, such as a bank or hedge, to come close to birds located from some distance away and snatch one by surprise with a lightning twist in flight. Since it so often hunts close to the ground it is less often seen killing than the peregrine which normally kills from a height; but the merlin will continue its pursuit of quarry close to human beings without being deterred, and will chase prey into buildings and sometimes kill itself in attempting to catch prey amongst obstacles. One which came aboard the weather ship *India* when 300 miles S. of Iceland and 500 miles W. of Cape Wrath pursued small migrants all over the ship, but managed to catch only one wheatear in a week, between 23.9 and 1.10, when it left(e).

Some prey is taken on the ground, perhaps more than is supposed. A small proportion of the food is small mammals, which must be caught on the ground, while the few gamebird chicks that are taken and some of the other birds are probably also taken by surprise on the ground. A merlin probably could not catch a gamebird chick except on the ground, for the chicks would not readily fly far until they were too big for a merlin to catch. Good quantitative data on the composition of the merlin's food are lacking in Britain; but every account agrees that most of it is small moorland birds such as larks, pipits, finches, wheatears and stonechats, with some moorland waders such as dunlins, redshanks, lapwings or snipe. Bergmann lists 713 items in Norway, of which 90% were small birds, 4·5% gamebird chicks, and 5% small rodents, the rest being insects. A brood of young merlins on an island in Lake Michigan learned to hunt by pursuing large insects. On occasion merlins attack and kill quite large birds, such as green woodpeckers or adult lapwings; but there is no doubt at all that the majority of their prey is small birds weighing less than 100 and mainly less than 50 grams.

The persecution still suffered by merlins from gamekeepers on grouse moors is wholly unjustified. The merlin cannot normally kill any bird much larger than 100 grams in weight, which is soon exceeded by growing grouse chicks; adult grouse and ptarmigan weigh 500–700 grams. A merlin has been known to kill a Manx shearwater in Shetland, but even the larger passerines are normally beyond its powers(c). It sometimes roosts in the company of starlings without attacking them(f), and in Norway fieldfares have been known to breed close to a breeding merlin and derive protection from the falcon, which chased away other predators(3). Merlins have been seen stooping playfully at magpies without intent to kill them and although they will stoop at and irritate much larger birds such as crows and buzzards they could not possibly kill these. The salient fact is that on a grouse moor the grouse chicks can only be vulnerable to a merlin in the early stages of their existence, and that they will not often be taken even then because they do not fly. In Speyside it is estimated that young red grouse form less than 3% of the diet. Merlins do kill a few young grouse when they have their own young to feed; but some of these chicks would die anyhow, and the effect of merlins on the stock of grouse on 12 August is entirely negligible. The excuse offered to Professor Rowan in 1921 for shooting merlins, that they would cause disturbance on driving days is merely ludicrous for, as he observed from his hide, merlins and adult grouse pay no attention to each other at all(8).

Merlins are not wasteful, killing only what they need at the time. They may cache food which cannot immediately be eaten. J. W. Greaves records a merlin burying the body of a meadow pipit nine inches down in heather, and there is an Irish record of a female recovering the body of a previously hidden skylark(d). Other observers have seen merlins caching part-eaten prey until it can be used up. These records are of special interest in view of the paucity of records of birds of prey hiding or caching food generally.

With its powers of flight and spirit the merlin has been in demand by falconers for centuries. Because of its small size it was used as a lady's hawk, but it was and still is used by many falconers to catch larks. A merlin is too small to be used for game-hawking, for though it can be trained to attack adult gamebirds it cannot normally kill them. Lark hawking, however, gives the merlin every chance to show its powers of flight, and the lark often escapes in the end. In this form of the sport the merlin is released to fly at the lark, which mounts skywards, while the merlin or merlins also soar up in circles. The pursuit may go so high that the lark disappears in the field of binoculars, but in the end it is seen hurtling earthwards with the merlin stooping repeatedly at it. Wild merlins are generally very much quicker and more agile in pursuit of larks than are trained birds, which generally catch their prey near or on the ground, pursuing it if necessary into dense cover(6). Nowadays, many falconers who take young merlins fly them for a season and then allow them to go back to the wild rather than keep them for a full year. This humane process may actually lead to a higher survival rate in young merlins than would be the case in the truly wild state while the young merlin, when released, is already an experienced hunter with a good chance of survival later, if it is not shot.

Merlins do not frequent their breeding haunts the whole year round as a rule, unless these are on relatively low-lying moorlands without a severe climate. In winter on upland moors gamebirds such as grouse remain all the year round for they can feed under the snow, but practically no small birds remain for the merlin to catch. Accordingly it leaves, and usually moves close to the coast where it often lives along the tideline, finding prey there even in the most severe weather. Alternatively, it may catch sparrows on the outskirts of coastal towns. In Speyside merlins occur on the floor of wide valleys in autumn and winter from September to March (but uncommonly from November to February) and from April to August are found on the uplands bordering Strathspey, where they breed on the open moorlands. In March they are seen gradually moving uphill to their breeding grounds(9).

Further south merlins may return to their breeding grounds earlier, in March or even in February on Dartmoor, but a normal date of return in north England is early April. They resort to the same favoured areas each year and, once a merlin haunt is located, it is relatively easy to find the new nest site each year. One site in Speyside known to egg collectors in 1940 is still in use, and in Yorkshire Rowan found only four sites regularly used in 20 square miles, despite an apparent abundance of suitable alternatives(8). These sites continued in use no matter how often the wretched merlins were shot by keepers; in one case the site was used for 19 consecutive years although the pair was destroyed each year and no young were ever reared, proving that the site is continually attractive to a succession of different individuals.

A check on breeding areas in spring is therefore the best population index of

British merlins. If the birds are not in their accustomed haunts then something has happened to them. The site is naturally not occupied by the same birds each spring for many years, but by a succession of different individuals. Being small, the merlin is relatively short-lived; but any survivor of a pair will obtain a new mate if it can and the site will evidently be colonised by other merlins if both the resident birds die. No other method of checking the population, such as the number of nest record cards or ringing returns sent in to the B.T.O. (which have not varied much in the last 20 years) is likely to be as reliable as this.

Merlins do not perform spectacular aerial display flights. The male is said to arrive first on the nesting ground and to advertise his presence by short calling flights from one perch to another; this behaviour resembles that of a male peregrine flying from ledge to ledge(11). When the female arrives some aerial chasing may be done, but this is unusual. Exceptionally, a male and female may mount to several hundred feet above the ground, then dive at speed earthwards, rising again to repeat the performance. In one observed case this followed a prolonged period of chasing one another along and among the branches of an oak tree, the aerial display lasting an hour occurring after the birds had mated.

Before egg laying the male feeds the female at or near the hollow in the heather where the nest will be. From now on until the young are well grown the female is dependent on the male and does not normally hunt herself. The actual site of the nest may be only a few yards from the site of the previous year. Merlins mate on the ground near or at the nest, or on a boulder or treetop, and mating is often preceded or accompanied by the presentation of food by the male(8).

Most nests are in deep heather, sometimes in other vegetation such as bracken, but seldom in short open growth. The site is often near the head of a valley with a steep slope below it and a wide outlook. In flatter country the nest may be on a steep slope or a bank over a stream so that the sitting female has an outlook; but nests can also be in deep growth on flat ground where she cannot see a yard. The sitting bird collects a certain amount of material into the nest by nipping off the tops of grasses or heather stems growing around it, and may perhaps walk a few feet to collect pieces of bracken. However, nest-building proper is unknown, as in all other falcons.

The vast majority of nests are on the ground, 118 out of 159 nests on B.T.O. cards being so placed. The next most common site is the old nest of another bird, usually a crow, in a tree, which is very often a hawthorn growing high up in a valley; 29/159 nests were of this type, but the sample may be biased by certain

Table 12   Merlin: Clutch and Brood Size

(Data from B.T.O. nest record cards)

	1	2	3	4	5	6	Total	Mean
Clutch size								
Before 1962	3	1	9	23	17	0	53	3·94
After 1962	0	6	13	23	21	1	64	3·97
All clutches	3	1	22	45	38	1	109	3·96
Brood size								
Before 1962	5	6	8	7	4	0	30	2·97
After 1962	3	7	16	23	5	0	54	3·37
All broods	8	13	24	30	9	0	84	3·21

Table 13   Merlin: Site Preferences

(Data from B.T.O. nest record cards)

	Wales and S.W. England	N. England	Scotland	Total
On ground	18	80	20	118
Old nest in tree	19	7	3	29
Other sites	2	4	6	12
Total	39	91	29	159

observers who recently became aware of this habit and who search each year for such nests. It seems more common for Welsh and west of England merlins to nest in trees than in northern England or Scotland, and this no doubt reflects the availability of suitable trees high enough up the mountain slope for merlins to nest. Occasionally, other sites are used, such as a cliff ledge, an old hooded crow's nest on a cliff, even a small heathery island in a lake(a). A nest is also recorded on top of a small isolated sand-dune grown with marram grass in an area of nearly barren coastal sandhills. Nests may be found at any altitude from near sea level to 2000 feet (0–600 m.), but most (61/145) are between 1000 and 1500 feet (300–450 m.), a level very commonly planted with conifers in recent years.

One to seven eggs are laid, at two-day intervals. There are three apparently full clutches of one egg only on B.T.O. nest record cards, but these may have been reduced from a larger clutch. Four eggs are commonest (46/117) but five nearly as common (38/117) averaging 3·96 overall. Only one nest in ten contains less than three or more than five eggs. Both sexes incubate, but the female does most, incubating for about three-quarters of the daylight hours. In the only night watch ever done the male incubated all night; but we must assume that this is unusual and that the female normally sits at night. She sits very tight and will flush only when closely approached. The male feeds her, arriving with prey, calling, and passing it to her usually on the ground but sometimes in an aerial pass, when she leaves to feed. He then very often goes to the nest and incubates until she has finished feeding and wishes to return. Incubation does not usually begin until the entire clutch is laid, but sometimes begins earlier; this usually results later in fledglings of an even age or with one younger than the rest. Eggs are laid from early May to early June, usually 10–20 May in the south and 20–30 May in northern England and Scotland. Northern Scottish egg dates are less than two weeks later than southern English as a rule, indicating once more that the egg laying date is not necessarily correlated with temperature.

The young hatch after 28–32 days' incubation and the female remains on the nest with them. The male increases his rate of killing as soon as the young hatch and brings 3–6 kills per day during the fledging period. Normally, the male brings all prey and the female feeds the young, receiving the prey from the male away from the nest. Exceptionally, however, the male may visit the nest and feed young, probably when the female is not there. If the female is shot the male is then said to take over the rearing of the young himself. In the later stages of the fledging period the female leaves the young alone in the nest and prey is brought by both sexes.

The young are clad in voluminous down coats, start to grow feathers at about 14 days old, and make their first flight at 25–30 days. From about 20 days they are independent of parental assistance with food, and are then left alone in the nest. Even when still downy the female does not brood them at night after ten days; they huddle together to keep warm(8). The brood may be reduced by losses from cold, starvation, rain or other such causes, but usually a rather high proportion, often all of the young hatched fly, the average of 84 broods on B.T.O. nest record cards being 3·23 as compared to an average clutch of 3·96; this is equivalent to 82% fledged of eggs laid, which is a very high proportion. However, recorded broods may have been to some extent further reduced by deaths later in the fledging period and they represent only what happens in successful nests. Probably the real figure, allowing for failures, non-breeding pairs, and other such factors is only 2–2·5 young per pair per annum. Even so, this is a high rate of breeding success and there is nothing in the data recently available to suggest poor breeding success which could account for the decline in merlins.

The requirement of a pair of merlins with a brood of three young is estimated at 450 small birds during the breeding season. This seems rather a high figure but is quite realistic since the requirement of the adults is likely to be about 20% of their bodyweight, about 35–50 grams per day, equivalent to one or two small birds each per day, allowing for waste. The total is made up of 80 during courtship, 80 during incubation, 140–180 during the fledging period, and 100 in the post fledging period.

The effect of a pair of merlins and their brood on the available prey can thus be broadly assessed. In one area of Yorkshire there were regularly only four pairs of merlins in about 20 square miles, so that each pair had a range of about 3000 acres (1200 ha.)(8). Since there should be at least two to three small birds per acre even in moorland of this type, it is unlikely that the merlins could exert severe hunting pressure on their prey. In Orkney ranges are considerably smaller, perhaps 1500 acres (600 ha.), but here the young of moorland birds such as lapwings and curlews are so abundant in early summer that the predatory effect of the merlins is probably even less. It would seem that shortage of food supply in the breeding season cannot be the cause of the observed decline either; and in any case this would not be borne out by the high fledging success recorded in relation to the number of eggs laid.

After the young make their first flights they remain close to the nest for a few days and then gradually move away from it. They are fed by the parents near the nest and soon learn to fly to the adult bringing food, receving it by an aerial food pass or on the ground. Most young in Britain leave the nest in early July and by early August have become independent of parental aid in hunting. At that stage both adults and young begin to move out of breeding areas on to lower ground.

Large numbers of young merlins have been ringed in the nest and there is a good series of 101 recoveries which show quite clearly what happens to them (Map 32). Of those ringed as young in the nest most are recovered in their first winter close to the nest. Three were dead in the nest after ringing, and one of these had been eaten by its nest mates. 48 had travelled less than 20 miles (32 km.), 35 20–50 miles, 13 50–100 miles, seven 100–200 miles (160–320 km.), and only four more than 200 miles within Britain. These four include a bird ringed at Orphir, Orkney, recovered injured at Aberlady Bay when eight months old; one ringed in Mid Yell, Shetland, which killed itself on wires near Kirkcaldy when nine months old; one ringed at Scalloway, Shetland, recovered at Lurgan, Armagh when seven months old; and one ringed at Wolsingham, Durham, recovered three months later at Blandford, Dorset, where it was shot. Those which had travelled 100–200 miles all came from Orkney, Shetland, north Scotland or north England, suggesting that

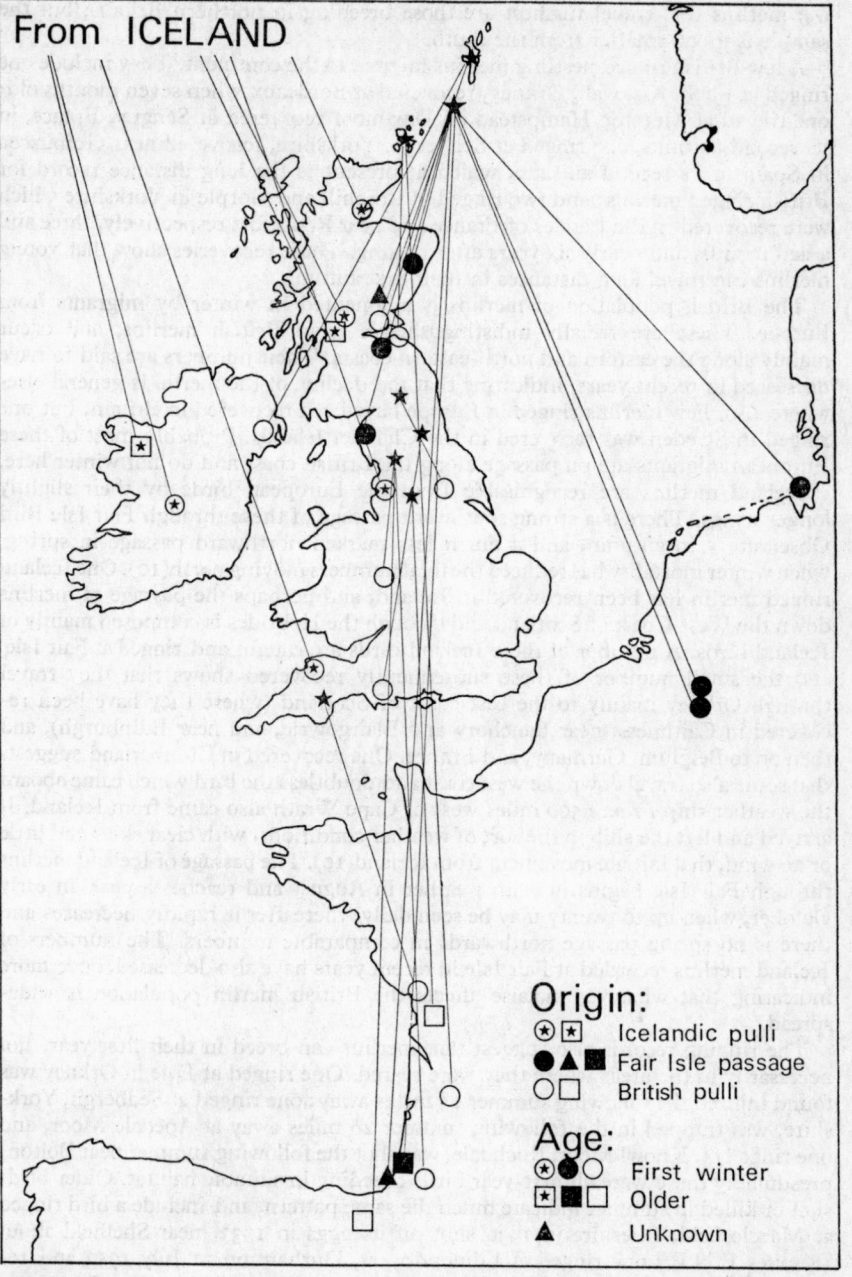

From ICELAND

Origin:
⊛ ⊠ Icelandic pulli
● ▲ ■ Fair Isle passage
○ □ British pulli

Age:
⊛ ● ● First winter
⊠ ■ □ Older
▲ Unknown

MAP 32. Recoveries abroad of British-ringed merlins, and of merlins ringed on passage at Fair Isle.

the merlins that travel furthest are those breeding in northern Britain; but the sample is much smaller from the south.

A few British ringed nestling merlins migrate to the continent. They include one ringed at Firth, Kirkwall, Orkney, recovered at Bordeaux when seven months old; one ringed at Moreton Hampstead on Dartmoor recovered at Senguy, France, in its second autumn; one ringed at Sedbergh, Yorkshire, recovered near Guipuzcoa in Spain in its second autumn, which at present is the long distance record for British ringed merlins; and two ringed at Rosehill and Gorple in Yorkshire which were recovered in the Landes of France and near Rochefort respectively, three and a half months and nearly six years after ringing. These recoveries show that young merlins can travel long distances in their first autumn.

The British population of merlins is augmented in winter by migrants from Europe. These are racially indistingushiable from British merlins, and occur mainly along the eastern and north-eastern coasts. Their numbers are said to have decreased in recent years, indicating that the decline of the merlin is general elsewhere also. Few merlins ringed in Europe have been recovered in Britain, but one ringed in Sweden was recovered in the Channel Islands. Probably most of these European migrants are on passage along the British coast and do not winter here.

Iceland merlins are recognisable from the European birds by their slightly longer wings. There is a strong southward passage of these through Fair Isle Bird Observatory in autumn, and a much less marked northward passage in spring, when winter mortality has reduced the total numbers moving north(10). One Iceland ringed merlin has been recovered in Ireland, and perhaps the passage of merlins down the West Coast of Scotland and through the Hebrides is composed mainly of Iceland birds. A number of these Iceland birds are caught and ringed at Fair Isle, and the small number of these subsequently recovered shows that they travel through Orkney mainly to the east coast of Scotland (where they have been recovered in Caithness, near Banchory and Blairgowrie, and near Edinburgh), and then on to Belgium, Germany, and France. One recovered in Cumberland suggests that some also travel down the west coast and doubtless the bird which came aboard the weather ship *France* 500 miles west of Cape Wrath also came from Iceland. It arrived and left the ship in the sort of weather conditions, with clear skies and little or no wind, that initiate movement from Iceland(10). The passage of Iceland merlins through Fair Isle begins in calm weather in August and reaches a peak in early October, when up to twenty may be seen daily; thereafter it rapidly decreases and there is no spring passage northwards in comparable numbers. The numbers of Iceland merlins recorded at Fair Isle in recent years have also decreased, once more indicating that whatever malaise affects the British merlin population is widespread.

The ringing records also suggest that merlins can breed in their first year, not necessarily in the areas where they were reared. One ringed at Evie in Orkney was found injured the following summer 15 miles away; one ringed at Sedbergh, Yorkshire, was trapped in the following summer 26 miles away at Apedale Moor, and one ringed on Knowl Moor, Rochdale, was shot the following summer near Bolton; presumably these were all first-year birds breeding in suitable habitat. Older birds shot or killed in summer indicate much the same pattern, and include a bird ringed at Macclesfield, Cheshire in 1930 shot off its eggs in 1933, near Sheffield about 18 miles E.N.E.; one ringed at Edmondbyers, Durham on 21 July 1953 and recovered in May 1956 at Coldfell, Cumberland, 25 miles west; one ringed at Garsdale, Yorkshire in 1928 and trapped at Dalry, Kirkcudbright in June 1932; and others. The oldest British merlins on record are a bird ringed at Goathland, Yorkshire in June 1938 and found dead on the road, presumably killed by a car in September 1944, when over six years old; one ringed at Gorple, Yorkshire, recovered five years and nine months later near Rochefort, France, presumably on its way north again; and one ringed on Skiddaw in Cumberland in 1926 which was found injured at Lydiate, Lancashire, in March 1934, perhaps about to breed in this locality, 80 miles south of the place where it was ringed, as an adult almost eight years old.

The recovery circumstances of merlins are also of unusual interest. Of the total of 122 records, including passage birds ringed at Fair Isle, 32 struck wires, dashed into buildings or trees, got entangled in sacks or were drowned, died or were found injured in circumstances suggesting violent accident. Several were eaten by domestic cats and must have been injured before they could be caught – or perhaps they were preoccupied with prey they had themselves killed. This is a far higher proportion of violent accidental deaths than is known in any other British diurnal raptor, and must be largely due to the impetuous hunting habits of the merlin; the most common single cause of accidental death is by collision against wires. Most merlins recovered before 1955 were admittedly shot (31/63), those found dead being the next most common cause. After 1955 some were still admittedly shot (7/47 cases) but the proportion 'found dead' rises sharply (13/47). It may be that this is partly due to greater forbearance on the part of gamekeepers but is more likely due to merlins being shot and thrown away, not reported, but found later by someone else, often decayed so that the cause of death could not be established.

One merlin ringed near Goathland, Yorkshire, in 1912 had the honour to be recovered in October 1914 by officers of Scotland Yard near Middlesborough; its nest mate was – unkindest cut of all for the ringer – 'shot by a friend' at North Cave, Yorkshire, in September 1913. One young bird which was caught near Stocksfield on 10 August 1929, when it stunned itself against a window, was kept for a month in a cage till it was well enough to be released, ringed on 10 September, only to have the ill luck to be shot in May 1931 at Wolsingham, where it was presumably breeding. A young bird was caught in a trap used to lure adults near Newcastle in August 1931, was released again, but persisted in its folly and drowned itself in a water tank on 27 October. One first winter young bird ringed at Fair Isle on 3 September 1957 came aboard a boat at Bremerhaven, Germany on 11 October 1957, and died there; and an adult female ringed on Skokholm on 19 April 1965 was found dead and beheaded, presumably by some larger predator which did not care to eat it, on Skokholm on 26 April, a week later.

From all these ringing recoveries we can build up a good picture of the life of merlins away from their moorland breeding grounds. They are migrants, some of which leave Britain, but most of which travel longer or shorter distances within Britain and return to breed, if they survive, in an area not very far from where they were ringed but probably seldom the same locality. This pattern of movement is rather unlike that of any other British raptor, most of which are either frankly sedentary, never moving very far, or definitely migratory, leaving Britain altogether in winter. It seems clear that the merlin is more likely to hurt itself by its impetuous methods of hunting than even the sparrowhawk, which seems equally impetuous but may be more skilled in dodging obstacles at speed at close range. Merlins are also still likely to be shot by grouse moor gamekeepers in Britain or by gunners in France.

Analysis of the age at which merlins have died or been killed over the years from

1912 to date (which included a long period up to 1955 when they could expect to be shot by grouse moor gamekeepers more promptly than they are today) does not indicate an unusually high rate of mortality. Of the young ringed in the nest, 60% did not live to their second summer to breed. However, 22 young survived to their first breeding year, and 11 to their second, while 12 lived more than three years. The average age of all the birds that could breed is over two years. Brood size in recent years has averaged 3·23 per successful nest. On this figure, with 60% mortality before breeding, 1·3 sexually mature replacements per pair are produced so that a pair needs only to live on average for a little over a year and a half as adults to be able to replace themselves. The ringing records indicate that merlins live as adults for over two years.

However, if the real productivity of merlins, taking into account all failures, non-breeding pairs, and so on, is actually lower than the observed productivity per successful nest, say 2·5 young per pair, then only one sexually mature bird survives to breed, and the species can just maintain itself. If overall productivity is, less than 2·5 per pair the merlin must decline slowly. These theoretical calculations which are admittedly based on biased data resulting from the high proportion of unnatural deaths in ringing recoveries, suggest the need to carry out a detailed survey of overall breeding success in several areas for a number of pairs. On available evidence, however, merlins produce enough young per successful nest to maintain the population so that it seems unlikely that poor breeding success is the real cause of the observed decline.

In fact, none of the possible reasons discussed fully explains the recent observed decline of the merlin. It is not easily attributable to pesticides, to increased persecution, or human disturbance of habitat, and not fully accounted for by loss of habitat under dense coniferous woodlands, hard winters, or a proliferation of wire. The merlin, the smallest and most dashing of British falcons, is declining for reasons unknown, and accordingly deserves a full ecological study as soon as possible.

CHAPTER 17

THE HOBBY

THE hobby could contest with the merlin the title of being Britain's least-known bird of prey. It would probably win if Britain only were considered, for although its exact status here is obscure it is certainly rarer and less widespread than the merlin, and is rather difficult to study in its known haunts. Practically nothing of any real value has been written about the hobby in Britain in the last thirty years and like the merlin the hobby gets an occasional brief mention in major British journals since 1940. Going back even further than that less of value has been written about it than about the merlin(8,9). On the other hand, it has been more fully studied in Europe than has the merlin, through the work of Schuyl and Tinbergen, and others(11,14). Even these observations, however, are incomplete in several respects, and no one seems to have watched a pair of hobbies right through the breeding season.

I am not familiar with the hobby in its British haunts, but I see far more hobbies in Kenya each year than most people in Britain see in their lifetime. The hobby is strongly migratory and large numbers pass south through East Africa in November and again northwards in March. I have seen as many as two hundred hobbies in a large scattered flock, hunting flying termites, and have driven for miles through country where rainstorms had recently brought out these insects, seeing a hobby every few minutes. Especially I remember one evening in November 1948, when I was lounging at dusk, enjoying a sundowner outside my tent in a remote part of the thornbush of Embu district. A flock of hobbies streamed overhead for ten or fifteen minutes, going to roost on a steep hillside behind me. I did not count them, but suppose that two or three hundred must have passed over in that time. They had been hunting flying termites in the evening, following a rainstorm, and were all going to bed with full crops.

In Britain the hobby is not especially rare in certain areas, but is always uncommon and hard to locate. No exact estimate of its status is possible, but there are probably not more than a hundred pairs, perhaps considerably less. In Parslow's 1967 survey he lists a total of about 74 regular breeding pairs in Hampshire, Surrey, Sussex, Wiltshire, Dorset and Berkshire, and another eight in counties a little further north or west where it is a less regular breeder(10). On the other hand he suggests that there may only be one irregular pair in Somerset where, as I understand it, hobbies have been seen more commonly in recent years, so that there really may be rather more. In Oxfordshire, by all accounts, it has decreased in recent years and disappeared from one or two places where it formerly bred(e). Parslow observes that numbers fluctuate from year to year, as one would expect with such a strongly migratory species, and that there has probably been little change in its status for twenty-five years, if not for a century. Others say that the hobby has markedly decreased in recent years and yet others tell me that there are certainly far more than is generally supposed. Since I have not managed to see a hobby in Britain myself, largely because I spend very little time in hobby country, I am not in a position to judge, and accept as sound Parslow's view that there are probably rather less than 100 pairs in Britain.

There can be little doubt that the reasons for the hobby's rarity are ecological rather than due to persecution. It was, and no doubt still is, persecuted to some extent by gamekeepers and, since so many breeding haunts are in popular southern counties the nests were frequently robbed by egg collectors, but it seems clear that hobbies would be far more common than they are if conditions really suited them in Britain. They are distributed over most of the counties in which they regularly breed at a density of 50–100 or even more square miles (130–260 sq.km.) per pair, and it is impossible to believe that they really need any such area to live in. They are somewhat more concentrated in Hampshire where Tubbs gives an average of 7 square miles (18 sq. km.) per pair over three years, in 116·25 square miles of the New Forest where the hobby is about as common as the kestrel(15). In Britain two pairs have been recorded nesting within five hundred yards of each other, but if this spacing were regular there would be a pair of hobbies per 50 acres (20 ha.) and some 15,000 pairs in Sussex, where there are actually about ten(10). If the hobby were really suited in Britain it would surely increase, but it seems to have varied little in recent years, even when persecution by keepers and egg collectors was reduced during and just after the Second World War, leading to an upsurge in the numbers of several other British birds of prey.

Abroad, in France especially, the hobby is much more numerous. In Lorraine there is a pair per 3000 acres (1200 ha). in wooded country, about the same density as that of the kestrel in Sussex(13). I have been shown where a hobby nested in a small clump of pines on sand-dunes in the south of France, admittedly well supplied with migrant birds and the only place where it could have nested in a large flat treeless expanse. One can think of plenty of such places in Britain, but without hobbies. They are just not common in Britain, and probably never will be. However, it would be nice to know rather more accurately how many there are, and to study them fully to see whether there is any good reason for their scarcity.

Hobbies appear to like mixed heathlands and woodlands, but will live in a big wood if no smaller woods are available(8). They hunt almost exclusively in flight, and must evidently have fairly open country in which to hunt, though they can catch insects or birds close to the ground and between trees. Their flight is sur-passingly beautiful and leisurely, resembling that of a gigantic swift yet without the fuss and hurry of a swift; the hobby always appears perfectly in control of its movements at speed. They are also capable of soaring very easily to great heights, and I suspect that they migrate normally at great heights. In Kenya I once saw hobbies soaring up until they disappeared into the base of a thundercloud; they were then out of sight of the naked eye, more than 2000 feet (600 m.) above me, but I watched them with × 12 binoculars. They seemed to have no hesitation in disappearing into the cloud, never reappeared, and might have been lifted another 10,000 feet within it. They were on the move, in company with red-footed falcons.

In their winter quarters, where I know them best, hobbies are mainly insectivor-ous. They specialise in flying termites which emerge in millions after tropical rainstorms. In Kenya, when the short rains begin in earnest in November, hobbies appear in the neighbourhood of a thunderstorm as if by magic. They fly in graceful arcs through the moist air in the wake of rain, catching the termites on the wing, sometimes several hundred feet above the ground. It appears to be no effort for them at all, but even a hobby must catch quite a few termites to make a reasonable meal, and they accordingly weave to and fro above a nest from which the insects are emerging for a long time. They will continue until the daylight is so dim that their colours cannot be clearly seen, and they do not mind getting wet. It often happens that a heavy drizzle falls for some time after the first intense rain of the thunderstorm has passed, but this does not discommode the hobbies. They shake themselves dry every few minutes, with a shiver and a fluffing of feathers, like an osprey emerging from the water, and continue hunting in conditions far too wet for most birds of prey in the tropics. This makes it all the stranger that they should be deterred by the British climate, if that really is the main reason why they are rare in Britain.

Hobbies pass on to the south of Kenya and spend the period December to February in the great belt of woodland covering most of the southern third of Africa(4). It is then wet in these parts, and there is abundant insect life, including flying termites, for the hobbies to feed on. Then, in early spring, they start moving north again, and pass through Kenya in March. Again, this is a time when the 'grass rains' as we call them, the first few heavy storms of the year, wash the dust and smoke out of the atmosphere and bring out further hordes of termites. The hobbies then seem to be travelling in a more purposeful manner, in tighter flocks, and feeding less leisurely en route. They pass through Somalia, but presumably the hobbies that follow this route are not those that come from Britain but, like many of the other migrants to East Africa, come from Russia and Siberia(1). Where in Africa British hobbies may winter is obscure, for there are very few records from West Africa, and little information from scanty ringing returns(2). The peak of this northerly migration is reached late in April and early May in Somalia, and the last of the hobbies have left Africa by the end of May.

Hobbies arrive on their breeding grounds in Britain occasionally before the end of April, but more often during May, and they do not normally lay eggs till June(8). There are old records of very much earlier arrivals, in February and March, all in the nineteenth century; but in most areas hobbies are not expected to appear before 7–15 May. The favoured habitat seems to be heathlands with clumps or lines of pine trees scattered over it, but hobbies are also to be found where big woods alternate with heath or in cultivated country or pasture land interspersed with patches of woodlands. They are practically confined to low altitudes, and presumably the availability of suitable open heathlands at low altitudes is one ecological feature limiting the numbers of the hobby in Britain. In this respect they are sometimes similar to Montagu's harrier.

Hobbies either arrive paired or are paired very soon after arrival(8). They perform protracted spectacular aerial displays in the neighbourhood of the breeding site, often in the evening. The pair soar up to a great height, and the male then dives repeatedly at the female. Sometimes she turns over and presents her claws to his, or they may dive at breathtaking speed to near the ground, throwing up again to mount once more to a height. One display is described in which the male dived earthwards, corkscrewing in flight and, when he turned upwards close to the ground produced a sound akin to the drumming of snipe(i). They are noisy in display, uttering a call like 'kirik' or 'quirik', also apparently used when hunting.

Even at this early stage of the breeding cycle the female is largely dependent on the male for food. This is in line with what is observed in other falcons, and many other birds of prey such as harriers. The male hunts small birds and presents them to the female, sometimes in an aerial pass at great speed, sometimes in a complicated ceremony on a branch. In the latter the male arrives with the prey, calls, and transfers the food from his foot to his bill. The female then joins him and both birds, the male, with the bird in his bill, sidle along the branch, standing high on their legs and exposing the chestnut belly and thighs, calling a subdued 'wer-wer-wer'. The female snatches the prey, and flies to another branch to eat it. The male may leave her feeding or fly round her(16). This sort of behaviour is somewhat similar to but more elaborate than the ritualised bowing ceremonies of male peregrines feeding their mates(6).

On migration in the tropics hobbies can probably catch enough insects in a day to satisfy their individual needs fairly easily. However, when a male feeds a female and later a brood as well at the nest it is difficult to catch enough insects, so that it is not surprising that in the breeding season hobbies feed largely on birds. The male, at least partly, feeds himself on insects; but the female catches little and depends on what he brings for the young. This is not necessarily associated with an acute shortage of insects because African hobbies *Falco cuvieri*, which may normally be largely insectivorous, also feed mainly on birds in the breeding season(5).

A hobby weighs on average 180–225 grams (6½–8 oz), the female being heavier, and probably requires about a fifth of its bodyweight per day as food, 36–45 grams. This is provided by one lark or starling-sized bird, but only by a very large number of even quite large insects. Hobbies do eat many insects during the breeding season, notably such conspicuous species as pine hawkmoths, cockchafers, and some of the larger beetles; but a male trying to feed a female in courtship would be obliged to bring her many such, while one decent-sized bird will suffice her need. The birds are caught in flight, singing skylarks being a vulnerable target; but hobbies do very occasionally catch mice on the ground and have also been known to rob kestrels of mice they have caught, snatching them from the kestrel's foot at speed(14).

Many hobbies are noisy and aggressive to humans near their nest sites, which are then fairly easy to locate generally; others are silent, and may hunt some distance from the eventual nesting wood. Just before egg laying they may become more noisy, performing mutual display flights with much screaming. The nesting site will have been chosen by the beginning of June, and a clump or line of trees is sometimes preferred to a large wood. However, these are used in about a quarter of all recorded cases, while rarely a single tree or a hedgerow tree is chosen. Since it is more difficult to find nests in big woods the records may not accurately reflect the hobbies' real preferences(8,b).

No nests are made, the eggs being laid in the nest of another bird, usually that of a carrion crow, but also sometimes those of other corvids or herons, and occasionally in squirrels' dreys. There seems no doubt that in most areas pine trees are preferred to deciduous woodland, 30 out of 38 recent cases in B.T.O. nest record cards being in pines with eight in deciduous trees, three of these in hedgerows. Either an old or a new nest of another bird may be used, and if it has a wool lining placed there by the crow this is sometimes removed; old nests are used more often than new. The exact nest site is difficult to locate if in a large wood, but may be easy to find in a line of trees or a small copse. It may not be so easy to examine for most nests used are 30 to 50 feet up, and occasionally over 80 feet up (10–15 m.; occ. 25 m.). One nest is recorded 12½ feet from the ground in a lone pine on a heath(a). The maximum height above sea level is about 500 feet (150 m.), but most nests are much lower.

One to four eggs are laid, normally two or three, on alternate days or sometimes at three-day intervals. The average of 35 clutches on B.T.O. nest record cards is 2·8, which appears to be up to standard for the hobby in Europe also. According to egg collectors' accounts the same female lays in successive years on approximately the same date, within a day or two, and the main laying date in southern England is 14–20 June(8).

Only the female incubates, and she is fed at the nest by the male. He usually arrives with prey, takes it to a branch of a tree some distance from the nest, calls, and the female leaves the nest to receive it from him, either on the perch or in a spectacular aerial pass at speed. The male may either drop the prey which is caught by the female or she may turn over on her back and seize it from his claws. The incubating female will require one or two birds per day, and the male at this stage has time to spend many hours perched near the nest not hunting.

Incubation begins normally with the second egg, and the incubation period is 28 days. Some incubating hobbies are shy, others sit tight and continue to sit even when humans are close to the nest. When disturbed they are usually noisy and aggressive, but not so much as when they have young a little later. If robbed by egg collectors it is claimed that about half lay another clutch 11–21 days later, but probably this would only happen if the eggs were nearly fresh when taken. Unfortunately many of those who studied hobbies in Britain seem to have been egg collectors, who learned very little about the later stages of the breeding cycle because they never allowed it to proceed. Nethersole-Thompson, attacking E. M. Nicholson (who had observed that a certain collector regularly took all the hobbies' eggs from certain parts of England), writes: 'Now, though I know that no serious field naturalist ever gives a thought to Mr Nicholson's childishness a deliberate lie like this must be countered. I should like to say, with knowledge of the facts, that this "unscrupulous collector" is a creature of Mr Nicholson's imagination. When malicious lies replace facts the growth of knowledge is much impeded.' Quite so! This passage comes at the end of a paper describing 'visits' to fourteen hobbies' nests in one season, in which apparently not even one pair continued to be observed by this 'serious field naturalist'(9).

Recent data from B.T.O. record cards mercifully indicates that these mental aberrations are no longer quite so prevalent. Out of 100 eggs in 35 clutches 72 hatched from 91 in which the outcome was known, or almost 80%. Losses were mainly due to infertility, including a single clutch of one egg, and one egg was taken by crows. Hobbies defend their nests vigorously against corvids and other large birds, but one has also been seen in difficulty with a pair of magpies, which approached from either side of the nest along branches apparently hoping to be able to reach the eggs, or perhaps merely baiting the hobby(g).

I cannot find any accounts of the later stages of the fledging period in British journals, but this has been acutely observed, especially in the behavioural aspects in the Netherlands by Schuyl and Tinbergen(11). It is reasonable to assume that British hobbies behave in much the same way as Dutch, and the habitat described in Tinbergen's papers is evidently rather like a southern English heath. The young hatch nearly simultaneously, or with an interval between the second and third, and are not aggressive to one another, so that any losses among the brood are not due to this cause. For the first ten days of their lives they are closely brooded by the female, even in fine weather. Thereafter they are not brooded except at night, but the female remains near the nest, perching on trees near by, until the young are covered in feathers. She may then, but does not always, take some part in hunting, and even at this late stage the male brings most of the prey. The young start growing feathers at about 12 days old, are covered with feathers by 21 days old, and make their first flights at 28–32 days. Probably young males are more active and fly earlier than do the heavier females, though often the broods fly together on the same day.

The male brings most of the prey throughout the fledging period, and it is mainly birds, not insects. In the first few days he brings a kill every three or four hours, averaging about four or five per day. Later this must be increased to a kill every $1\frac{1}{2}$ hours, perhaps eight to ten birds per day. In the early stages he brings the prey fully plucked, but later apparently has not time for this and brings them unplucked for the female to prepare(14). Observation shows that the male does not start hunting at first light, but in mid July begins about 4.40, and in one observed case brought his first kill a quarter of an hour later, at 4.55. The last kill of the day may be brought as late as 20.00, and hunting continues during fifteen or sixteen hours of daylight. The number of kills brought per day must depend on the size of the prey chosen, and in some areas fewer kills are brought than in Holland. Thiollay, for instance, found in Lorraine that only two to three kills were needed early in the fledging period rising to four to five per day towards the end(13). The male's hunting time appears tied to the activities of diurnal birds and if he hunts in the dusk for insects he is hunting for himself, not the brood or the female. Insects probably form a relatively insignificant part of the diet by weight, though they appear commonly in castings, and their wings are found beneath feeding trees.

The birds most commonly taken are not, apparently, fledglings but adults of species that fly in the open, particularly skylarks which in Holland are the prey most often taken. Over half the birds taken are larks and pipits but they include also finches, sparrows, swallows, warblers and such oddments as a juvenile cuckoo and a crossbill. Hobbies apparently dislike green woodpeckers and there are several records of violent attacks upon these birds, which are driven to the ground but not killed(d). No gamebirds are taken, no doubt because the hobby nearly always kills in flight; but the prey includes a few small mammals such as voles and shrews taken on the ground or, as mentioned earlier, pirated from kestrels.

Male hobbies in Britain must be able to catch enough prey to feed the broods, for the losses in the fledging period are relatively slight from starvation, though apparently heavy from other causes. Of 35 young on B.T.O. nest record cards whose fate was followed to fledging 16 were lost, seven from unknown causes, two eaten by a tawny owl, one from anaemia and six from human interference; three of these were because the adult female was shot and three others from a heath fire. If these two cases are eliminated the ten losses among the 29 others equal a little more than a third. This is probably quite normal. On the available small set of British figures, out of 100 eggs laid about 80 would hatch, and of these about 28 would die of natural causes, leaving 52 reared. On an average clutch size of 2·8 this is approximately 1·4 young per pair per annum, and there is no reason at present to suppose that this would be markedly lower than in Europe.

Ringing data in the hobby are not adequate to establish mortality rates with any certainty, but supposing that these are the same as in other small falcons, about 60% before sexual maturity in the second year, adult hobbies must live as adults for about two and a quarter years to replace themselves. There is no reason to suppose that they do not have a life span of about this order.

The post-fledging period, after the young have flown, has been fully observed in the hobby, far more thoroughly than in most birds of prey(11). Immediately after making their first flight the young hobbies are weak and uncertain on the wing, and have difficulty in controlling themselves when landing on branches. A few days later, however, they are flying quite strongly and expertly, and seven days after their first flight they can fly to meet the food-bringing parent to receive the prey. Normally, the female remains perched at the nest site during this stage, but may sometimes assist in hunting. The young birds fly to meet the parent and receive the prey from it on a branch, but if the female is present she will fly to the calling male, take the prey from him, and fly to another branch with the hungry young in pursuit. They do not have to be fed at this stage but can break up prey for themselves. They drop the wings and shoulder girdles below the perch where they feed, so that the type of prey taken is easily identified.

From seven to eight days after first flying the young make longer and longer practice flights round the nest area, and only ten days after their first flight they start chasing large insects, sometimes with success; young have been seen to catch chafers on the tenth day after flying. Young males develop these abilities quicker than the heavier young females(11,14). Although they begin to chase birds such as swallows soon after this they do not at first succeed in catching them, but continue to catch insects, and to play at chasing birds and each other. They spend hours perched on trees not far from the nest and beg for food from any flying adult. Towards the end of the post-fledging period they start following the adults away from the nest area on hunting flights but remain largely dependent on them for 33–34 days possibly longer. At that stage the whole family moves out of the nesting area, and thereafter are seldom observed.

The young probably become independent of parental assistance sometime in mid to late September, and hobbies normally migrate out of Britain and Europe at the end of September and in early October. Occasionally hobbies may remain later, and have been recorded much later; one female apparently adult, was reported to spend the winter near Abberton reservoir in Essex, and was seen several times between November and January(j). This must be a quite exceptional case, however, for most hobbies are in southern Africa by November. During the autumn hobbies habitually attend starling roosts in the evening, and no doubt catch their daily needs there with great ease(f). They apparently single out individual starlings from the great flocks and pursue these.

There are only six recoveries to date of hobbies ringed in Britain, four of which were recovered in Britain(7,c). Four were young ringed in the nest and two were adults, or at least one year old. Of the young two were recovered within twenty miles of the place where they were ringed; one, ringed near Salisbury, was recovered 100 miles away near Ludlow, Shropshire, the following summer when it was doubtless breeding; and one ringed on Salisbury Plain in early August 1936 had reached the Landes of France by 16 October, where it was shot. Another reached Portugal in September. Of the six, three were shot, two in Britain and one in France; one was sick when ringed and died later; and of the other two one was found dead and the other killed by a car. One of the birds shot in Britain was shot in 1968 at Bovey Tracey, after the passage of the 1954 Protection Act.

There is some passage of continental hobbies through Britain in autumn and also in spring. One young bird ringed in Finland in July 1953 was shot at Hickling, Norfolk in September 1953, and there is evidence of a small autumn passage on the east coast. Hobbies have been recorded in Shetland, Fair Isle, and in the Orkneys, at Loch Fyne and in Ardgour(3). Since the hobby has only once bred in Scotland, in well-wooded Perthshire in 1887, any hobbies that appear in Scotland are probably continental passage birds. The hobby has been recorded 13 times in Ireland, mostly in the south-east, and these too were probably passage birds(12). The same might apply to two hobbies seen by H. E. Pounds on Ramsey Island off

Pembrokeshire on 30 May 1939; they were flying north one after the other, but may, of course have been about to breed in the Welsh border country(h).

The hobby is a relatively rare bird in Britain but is apparently not endangered at present and is holding its own, unless it has been severely hit by the recent resurgence of egg collecting, always one of its main enemies accounting for perhaps a third of all clutches laid in Britain in former times, but apparently reduced between 1940 and 1970. It deserves closer study here, not only to establish its status more exactly, but because there are certain aspects of the breeding behaviour still rather inadequately observed and recorded. Anyone who has the good fortune to be able to study hobbies could with advantage observe the ecological conditions under which they nest in Britain so as to try to ascertain whether there are any obvious or not so obvious ecological reasons why the species does not increase. Although it is, through the continental work, a comparatively well-known species, no one need suppose that the last word has been said. The study is not likely to produce large sets of figures for the statistically minded; but the aesthetic rewards of watching these incomparably graceful little falcons in their natural habitat would be great.

CHAPTER 18

THE PEREGRINE FALCON

UNTIL the last decade or so, the peregrine falcon would have been a hot contender for the title of the world's most successful bird. Probably its only rivals would have been a few other very wide-ranging species, such as the osprey or barn owl, and maybe one or two seabirds such as the roseate or caspian tern; but these are not so uniformly successful and adaptable. Peregrines occur on all continents as residents, and on many oceanic islands. Where the climate forces them to migrate, that is, in the Arctic or in high mountain ranges that are snowed up in winter, they do. Hence perhaps the German *Wanderfalke* and 'to peregrinate', a facetious verb meaning 'travel' or 'journey'; which came first, the falcon or the verb I would not know. In warmer climates peregrines are resident year-round, and here inhabit all types of country from tropical forests to semi-desert; all they ask is a place to breed and a food supply they can catch. They are found from 15,000 feet to sea level and have, in fact, adapted to a greater variety of habitats than either the barn owl or the osprey. So – a hot contender indeed for the title; and surely no one would regret it if the peregrine won.

Not only is the peregrine cosmopolitan and able to fit into almost any habitat, but it is a matchless flier and a spectacular predator, killing almost all its prey in flight with a stoop of dazzling velocity and accuracy, either striking the luckless bird dead in mid air or gripping it – 'binding to it' – and bringing it to the ground further on. No other species, except one or two other large falcons such as the lanner or the gyr, and maybe some eagles, can match the peregrine's combination of power, speed and precision. Swifts and albatrosses may be able to fly further without effort, and some other birds of prey, storks, and even pelicans can soar better, but none can provide quite the same thrill of pleasure derived from just watching a peregrine playing about in the updraught of a clifftop, its every aerial move accomplished with magnificent grace and certainty.

It is no wonder that this splendid bird causes its admirers – be they falconers, ornithologists, or poets – to wax lyrical(1). There is no other bird quite like the peregrine. Even the other large falcons, magnificent fliers though they are, kill much more prey on the ground than does the peregrine, and seem also, to me, to lack the neatness, the 'finish' of a peregrine. To me the peregrine has a presence the others lack, heightened by the deep, raucous, hacking voice, unmistakably angry rather than just anxious, that quite clearly warns you to keep away from the nest site, and which may be reinforced by actual attack if you persist.

I have seen a good deal of British peregrines, mainly on big sea-cliffs where they appear tiny as they perch on some halfway ledge among flowering rose roots and campion, surrounded by nesting seabirds. We also have peregrines in tropical Africa – smaller and darker than British peregrines but otherwise much alike – and here I know them better and have photographed them at the nest. I used some-times to see a pair that bred in the middle of Nairobi, and I have watched African peregrines perform evolutions that left me quite breathless with excitement or admiration. I have studied eagles more than I have watched peregrines; but the two are often found together, and I would be hard put to say which gives most pleasure.

Of all the great falcons used in falconry the peregrine is the favourite. No other is so keen or so biddable(13). Lanners, sakers, and gyrs especially are all superb birds, but lanners and gyrs at least are more difficult to train than peregrines, and will not, as a rule, 'wait on', bells jingling, 100–200 feet above the falconer while he slips the spaniel to flush the grouse his setter has pointed. If a peregrine was as powerful as a saker or a gyr it is doubtful if anyone would want to own these others at all; but then perhaps it might not be able to fly in quite the same matchless style. Peregrines have been in great demand by falconers for centuries, were once protected by Royal decrees, and reserved for the use of nobles and kings. Alas, any protection they now have is largely ineffective.

More recently, since the last war in fact, peregrines have been used to clear airfields of birds on the runways. If not actually fatal to the pilot and others aboard, the damage done to high-speed jets by 'bird strikes' can be extremely costly. The R.A.F. maintains a wing of falcons purely to prevent such damage on airfields where, for instance, gulls think that the runways were built for them. In this way at one R.A.F. base alone peregrines have saved the British taxpayer around £375,000 per year in preventing such damage, not preventable in any other known way(f). For this reason alone, even if they were hideous and dangerous to other interests, they would deserve careful husbandry and protection. Yet not a penny is spent by the Government directly protecting them, gamekeepers still kill them with impunity, pigeon-fanciers and others ravage some eyries if they can.

With all these virtues and points to admire it is sad to have to relate that the peregrine has fallen on evil times. In all developed countries of western Europe, Britain included, and North America it has become scarce or even – in eastern North America – extinct(11). Even the northern migratory populations, which hardly see men in their northern haunts, are either somewhat or drastically reduced. They, and those that live in high mountains in summer, must migrate or move to lower ground to avoid the winter snows. Their movements may take them to tropical Africa or America, and in so doing they pass through industrialised and intensively farmed areas where, since peregrines must eat, they feed upon contaminated prey and concentrate the poisons in their own bodies.

The primary cause of this decline seems absolutely clear. It is not due to persecution by gamekeepers, egg collectors, or pigeon fanciers, which the peregrines survived in a mild way until the fifties of this century. It is primarily due to pesticides used in agriculture, but is now aggravated in some areas by increasing malicious interference by pigeon fanciers or demand on a reduced population by falconers. A peregrine is worth a large sum today to a falconer, and there are those who will break the law readily enough to get one. If a falconer takes such risks, or pays large sums of money for his bird he may keep it alive, fit, and working for his entertainment but, unless it escapes, it will never breed to replenish the dwindling stocks of wild birds. The peregrine which, in my boyhood, could be seen on any good Scottish sea-cliff has become a rarity in many areas of Britain where it used to be quite common.

Such a spectacular creature as the peregrine has many devotees, and consequently a great deal is known throughout the civilised world about its past history and present or recent status. There are still parts of the world where its status is obscure – for instance it has only just been discovered breeding on the island of Fiji – but in most of Europe and North America breeding sites have been known for a long time. I do not think it would be untrue to say that it is this band of devoted peregrine lovers who brought to light the threat of slow poisoning of the whole environment with organochlorine chemicals used in agriculture. In 1965 scientists from all over the world assembled in the U.S.A. for a conference on the peregrine and other birds of prey, and the results have been brought together by Professor Hickey in *Peregrine Falcon Populations; their Biology and Decline*. I doubt if any other species of bird has ever attracted so much skilled attention, or had a conference of this nature all to itself(11).

Basically, from 1950–65 a population crash occurred among breeding peregrines in most of Europe including Britain and North America. It was, as Professor Hickey observed, one of the most extraordinary recent events in environmental biology. Why, one could ask, should the population of the world's most successful bird drop suddenly in this way, especially as the species had already proved itself resilient and able to recover from severe persecution during the Second World War ?(23,19). The assembled scientists set themselves to ascertain the reasons for this extraordinary phenomenon and although the results were in some ways confusing and conflicting they clearly pointed at pesticides as being the main cause of the decline.

So far as British peregrines were concerned, the changes in status are extremely well documented, especially by Derek Ratcliffe of the Nature Conservancy who has studied peregrines continuously, at least since 1945(18–21). In 1939, at least 570 and probably 630 eyries were occupied in Great Britain, and probably another 200 in Eire and N. Ireland; the total population may have been about 820 pairs(8, 9). The population had probably been stable from about 1900 onwards, with the single exception of certain West Highland districts where a slow creeping decline had been continuing for many years. This slow decline in the West Highlands was probably associated with ecological changes in the vegetation, leading to the virtual disappearance of red grouse, probably because of excessive burning and over-grazing by sheep(14). In the rest of Britain the peregrine appeared to be flourishing. It was persecuted to some extent by gamekeepers, and eggs or the young were taken from some eyries each year by egg collectors and falconers, but this sporadic persecution had little overall effect. There were plenty of eyries on remote inland cliffs or undisturbed sea-cliffs where the peregrines reared young unmolested year after year. Recruitment into the population was sufficient to ensure that, if an adult was shot, another appeared in the same territory a short time later, sometimes even within the same breeding season. It seemed clear that not only were most available territories occupied, but that there was a considerable surplus population of adults which could not find a vacant territory in which to breed, and were therefore ready to step into any available vacancy caused by persecution. Quite often Ratcliffe found three adults at a nest site, one of them perhaps a surplus, unmated bird. Steady persecution of the pre-1939 type did, however, prevent spread of peregrines into marginal territories, or the re-occupation of long-deserted territories. If they are not persecuted peregrines will colonise very small cliffs, and may even breed on the ground on a steep slope, as they do in the Arctic. In 1939, but for persecution, mainly by gamekeepers, peregrines probably would have colonised a good many such possible haunts, and the numbers would have been higher.

During the Second World War the peregrine was relentlessly shot out in parts of Britain because of the fear that the falcons might intercept and eat military carrier pigeons bearing important messages. Destruction was practically complete in S. England, parts of Wales, and Northern Ireland, but in North England and south Scotland it was less complete and in north Scotland and Eire negligible or not done at all. At the same time the reduction of keepering allowed the colonisation of some marginal sites by pairs of peregrines. I recall my astonishment in 1946, when visiting a small cliff by a waterfall not far from my home town, to find a peregrine sitting on eggs; pre-war the gamekeepers in that area would never have tolerated those peregrines, and they have since 'disappeared' again, and not through pesticides either. They have succeeded in breeding again lately, only to be wiped out afresh(h). The destruction of the peregrine in this way shows that while sporadic slight persecution does not have much overall effect on the population, systematic persecution can wipe out such a bird of prey quite quickly. Probably about a quarter of all the breeding pairs were wiped out in four years, and if the same level of persecution had been uniformly applied the peregrine could have been virtually exterminated in that time.

At the end of the war legal protection was restored to the peregrine, and the species quickly recolonised old haunts. Recovery was nearly complete by 1951 and apart from certain south coast areas practically complete by 1955(18); by that time, however, a few of the previously persecuted pairs had again dropped out, including my pair by the waterfall. There were then probably 550–560 pairs of peregrines in Great Britain and another 185 pairs in Eire and N. Ireland. Within the decade following the end of the war the population had increased by 30% in the south and about 10% overall.

From 1955 onward, the peregrine began to decline again. In Cornwall, where the peregrine was practically wiped out between 1939 and 1945, at least 17 of 20 known eyries had been reoccupied by 1955; but by 1959 only seven were occupied and of these only two produced young(23). In 1960 no peregrines bred successfully in Cornwall. Similar effects were observed elsewhere, and obviously something quite alien to the normal behaviour of this resilient and successful bird was happening. The symptoms of the affliction included egg-breaking by the parent birds, first observed about 1948–49, and frequently noted in the fifties. Falcons were observed actually eating their own eggs, and broken eggs were found in many eyries. This undoubtedly reduced overall breeding success. At first, the reason for this extremely odd behaviour was not understood, and was ascribed to, for instance, nervous reaction of the sitting falcons to increased disturbance by birdwatchers, rock climbers, and other intruders, which certainly did increase once people could get about again after 1945.

In 1960 the pigeon racers, complaining about excessive loss of their homing pigeons, which they attributed to an excessive population of peregrine falcons, initiated a B.T.O. inquiry into the status of the peregrine. In itself, this was a magnificent example of the habitual bigoted ignorance displayed by people who would persecute birds of prey without adducing any real evidence for so doing. The results of the inquiry not only refuted the pigeon racers' claims that the peregrine population had increased out of all bearing, but proved that 40% of all previously known territories were now unoccupied, while only 20% actually reared young(19). By 1962 half the known territories were deserted, and only 13% bred successfully. In effect, what this meant was that in a group of 100 pairs of peregrines which, prior to these effects, would have reared broods of two to three or about 250 young birds per year, production by 1962 would be only 30–35 young per year. While 250 young per hundred pairs per year was probably in excess of the needs of a stable population and resulted in a considerable 'surplus' population, clearly 30–35, only about one-eighth of normal production, would be inadequate

Table 14   Fluctuations in the Peregrine Population of Britain and Ireland
1930-71

(Figures compiled from Ratcliffe, D. A., 18(18–21); Ferguson-Lees, I. J., 18(8); and other sources.)

	Total known territories	Occupied territories					
		1930–9	1945	1955	1961	1963	1971–2
S. England	110	93	15	60	29	5	5
Wales	149	125			39		
N. England	68	60	185	200	31	26	45
S. Scotland	59	52			29		
E. and S.E. highlands	142	129	130	125	130	130	130
N. and N.W. highlands	190	173	170	170	146	134	120
Total, G.B.	718	632	500	555	404	305	350
% of 1930–9		100	75	87	64	48	55
N. Ireland		25	12	22	15	?10	8
Eire	200+	163	163	163	110	?60	55
Total, Ireland	200+	188	175	185	125	?70	63
% of 1930–9		100	93	99	67	37	33
Grand total	918	820	675	740	530	375	413
% of 1930–9		100	82	90	64	45	50

NOTES   (1) Figures for 1961–71 calculated from % occupation of eyries; since eyries occupied by only one bird quite frequent, actual population is lower than 2 per eyrie.
(2) Figures for 1961–71 based on results of 1968–9 survey, which indicated continuing decline post 1967.
(3) Most recovery since 1963 low has occurred in N. England and S. Scotland rather than Wales.

to maintain the adult breeding stock and the peregrine would swiftly become extinct.

The decline began and was worst in southern England and Wales, areas where a relatively dense population of peregrines preyed upon abundant birds of arable land as opposed to few moorland birds. It also affected the peregrines breeding on sea-cliffs, but was less severe in upland inland areas, especially in Central Scotland. The reasons for the decline are discussed more fully in Chapter 26 along with other instances of poisoning by organochlorine pesticides or polychlorinated biphenyls in the sea. It appeared quite clear that these substances were the major cause of the decline, though it was aggravated by increasing public demand for recreation in peregrine breeding areas, increased persecution by pigeon fanciers and gamekeepers despite legal protection, and increased pressure on the surviving broods of young by falconers. Peregrines could and did successfully withstand all these other pressures in the past.

Not only did the survey initiated by the pigeon racers demonstrate that, far from being over-abundant, the peregrine was in rapid decline, but it also proved that the amount of damage done by peregrines to homing pigeons was very slight.

The peregrine feeds almost entirely on living birds, the great majority of which are caught in full flight. They are either struck dead in the air by a blow from the hind claw, delivered with great force at the end of a swift, near-vertical stoop, or the peregrine seizes the bird and carries it to a perch. Peregrines will occasionally eat other things such as occasional mammals and even fish – one has been seen to wade into an Alaskan river and grab a fish in passing(5). A very small proportion of the prey, perhaps less than one kill per thousand, is taken on the ground. Any insects found in the peregrine's diet may have been eaten by the bird taken as prey, which ate them first.

The British peregrine survey recorded 1240 items of prey, varying from small passerines to large gulls, mallard, and black grouse. The commonest items of prey were red grouse, domestic pigeons, Turdines (fieldfare and blackbird) and wheatears. Of these, 230 domestic pigeons were much the most numerous, and rock doves and wood pigeons added to this brought the total of pigeons up to 294. In the survey peregrines were found to kill tawny and little owls but no diurnal birds of prey; but elsewhere they have been known to kill buzzards, kestrels, sparrowhawks, and even other peregrines. At least 117 species of birds are known to be taken in Britain, and at least 145 in Europe, varying from a greylag goose (which the falcon certainly could not carry) to such oddments as water rails and nightjars(19,24). In coastal areas seabirds such as auks or petrels are important in the diet and the prey taken is that most readily available. The normally entirely maritime Manx shearwater has been found at one peregrine eyrie 50 miles from the sea and 70 miles from the nearest colony and a puffin has also been found in a highland eyrie(c,h). Such cases prove that, odd as it may seem, these seabirds do sometimes travel overland.

Out of the 1240 items recorded in the survey there were 123 gamebirds, mainly red grouse; 168 waders, 294 pigeons, and 366 medium-sized passerines, cuckoos and woodpeckers. This indicates a strong preference for prey weighing from 100–500 grams, one-eighth to one-half the peregrine's weight. These data agree with all earlier reports and indicate that there had been no change in peregrine food habits in recent years – as was apparently claimed by the pigeon owners.

A peregrine does not kill when it is not hungry, and wastes little of its prey. It plucks off the feathers from the body and sometimes the wings, but eats the head, intestines, and feet of most prey. Often one finds the breastbone, with the feathered wings still attached, but with all the meat neatly removed. Smaller bones, skin, etc. are swallowed, partly digested, and the indigestible portions cast up in a pellet, as in other birds of prey. Probably not more than 10–15% of any kill is thus wasted.

The food requirement of a peregrine is about 83 grams per day in summer rising to 104 grams in winter, about 11·5–15% of the falcon's own weight(6). The daily requirement, year round, for a pair of British peregrines is taken at 235 grams killed or, for the 1930–39 population of 650 pairs at maximum in Great Britain, 55,383 kg. (122,000 lb) per year(19). The requirement for feeding young and immatures is estimated at 35,501 kg (78,000 lb), the total for all 650 pairs of peregrines in England, Wales and Scotland in 1930–39, 90,884 kg. (202,000 lb). Adding 10% to this for waste, the amount killed required to feed British peregrines is 99,972 kg, or roughly 100,000 kg. – 100 metric tons (98·42 long tons) of birds. At the present time this would actually be less, about 60%, or about 60 metric tons (59 long tons).

The speed at which a peregrine falcon can stoop is a subject of much conjecture and estimates have varied from over 100 to 275 m.p.h. (160–410 k.p.h.). The latter is said to have been measured at a Naval Research Laboratory during the Second World War, by photographing a peregrine in full stoop. The bird was also said to have been breathing all the time, although at that speed incoming air would normally burst the lungs. However, the peregrine's nostrils are equipped with a series of baffles which could slow down the wind velocity and help it to avoid this danger(17). Whether one accepts this extreme high estimate or not is a matter of choice; but few who have watched wild peregrines stooping at their prey, or even playing about a cliff face, will credit recent observations which suggest that peregrines cannot fly faster than 85 miles per hour (128 k.p.h.)(d). In this case the measurements were made by attaching a small air-operated speedometer to trained falcons, the speedometer itself being calibrated against that of a car driven fast along a road. Most people will be ready to accept that a peregrine can travel at somewhere between 100 and 200 miles an hour in full stoop, and many will agree that over 150 seems perfectly feasible.

In the absence of air resistance or friction a falling object accelerates at the rate of 32 feet/sec./sec.; that is, when it has fallen 480 feet, it is travelling at 160 feet/second or 109 miles/hour (185 k.p.h.). A stooping peregrine presents a drop-shaped silhouette, with a heavy solid fore-end tapering to a pointed tail. Such a shape would help to minimise air resistance and friction, and it therefore seems perfectly feasible that a peregrine which has stooped almost vertically for 1000 feet, such as the one I watched shooting past an Ayres' eagle in Kenya, could be travelling at 150–200 miles an hour. In level flight peregrines have been timed at 50–55 m.p.h. and it is very difficult to believe that in full stoop they are travelling at less than twice that speed. A skilled mathematician with a knowledge of aerodynamics can calculate the terminal velocity which a peregrine could not exceed, no matter how far it fell, because of the air resistance and friction encountered. This is about 180 m.p.h. (288 k.p.h.) assuming that the wings are closed and the dive vertical(e).

It will be obvious that it is its speed which limits a peregrine to the aerial method of attack. If it habitually took birds on the ground it would run severe risk of injury through impact. Peregrines do take some prey on the ground, but it is usually small and light, such as waders in estuaries or young, unfledged lapwing chicks(19). It is actually pointless for a peregrine to stoop at full potential speed when killing – 65–85 m.p.h. will do nicely.

The efficiency of the peregrine in making its kill is the subject of much argument. G. Rudebeck, who made a special study of killing success among migrating raptors in Sweden, recorded only 16 kills in a total of 260 attacks(22). Sometimes a peregrine may be seen to make repeated unsuccessful stoops at, for instance, pigeons or, in estuaries, waders, which are very agile in flight, and are apparently able to detect the falcon coming up from behind and dodge it at the crucial moment. However, Derek Ratcliffe believes, and I agree with him, that a great many of the so-called attacks recorded are not real attacks at all, and that when a peregrine means business it has little difficulty in catching its prey. Treleaven, a Cornish falconer who knows peregrines well, distinguishes between high and low-intensity chasing: in the latter the peregrine cannot resist 'having a go' but does not really try. When it does try the quarry has very much less chance of escape(g). More data is needed on the killing efficiency of all birds of prey, in Britain and elsewhere. However one feels that if a trained peregrine averaged only one in sixteen successful kills out of attempts made it would not be worth the large sum which is willingly paid for one at present.

In falconry, the peregrine is mainly used for killing game-birds that are put up for it, and rooks, the method in each case being different. Game-birds such as grouse, ptarmigan, or partridges – all of which peregrines can kill with ease – will not voluntarily leave the ground when a peregrine is in flight overhead; they are aware that it is extremely dangerous to do so. Accordingly, the game-birds are first located by a pointer or setter. The falcon is then released, flies round for some distance and gains height, to return and 'wait on' about 100–200 feet above the falconer. From that height it can very possibly see the quarry, crouching invisible to observers on the ground. A spaniel is then released to flush the game-birds concerned, they fly, the peregrine stoops at them and either kills or misses. I have once had the pleasure of watching a trained falcon take a grouse – an old cock that tried to escape by flying low down into a steep valley. She stooped from her pitch, overhauled him with ease, and plucked him out of the air with the nonchalance of a swallow collecting a floating feather for its nest.

A good falcon will succeed in killing two out of three times, and may sometimes persist in the chase for a long distance. On the other hand, the falcon may not kill the grouse or partridge because it does not really try; it puts in a stoop, which misses by a few inches, and it is almost unbelievable that it could not have killed if it really tried to do so. Admittedly, in this form of falconry, the falcon is being given every chance to kill efficiently; one might compare the performance to easy clay-pigeon shooting as against duck flighting on a windy night in winter. Again, however, the skill with which some trained falcons will kill their prey under apparently difficult circumstances argues in favour of the view that the falcon can kill when it has a fair chance.

In rook hawking the technique is completely different(13). In this case the falcon is released from the hand after making an upwind approach as near as possible to the quarry. The peregrine then attempts to force the rooks upwind, at the same time circling to get above them, so that it can put in a killing stoop. It makes a series of short stoops, rather in the same manner as wild peregrines will make when pursuing an agile wader near the sea coast, but must immediately regain height after each. The pursuit and series of stoops takes place downwind, and finally the rook glides down towards cover. If the peregrine does not then kill, it will fail, and the rook will escape. While the falcon can kill perfectly healthy rooks recent German evidence indicates that it takes a higher proportion (40%) of diseased or subnormal rooks than exist in the population as a whole (23%)(7,19). This supports evidence obtained from other predators, mainly mammalian such as lions or wolves, that unhealthy animals are killed for preference, which seems perfectly natural and what is to be expected.

Probably the available food supply, summer and winter, controls the breeding density and local habits of British peregrines. Prior to the pesticide decline the densest populations of breeding pairs occurred on the south coast of England and in Wales. In such areas, populous as they are, the peregrine had access to abundant birds in open fields, and to large numbers of domestic pigeons. There was abundant food all the year round, so that it was not necessary for such peregrines to leave their territory in winter. On seabird cliffs in north Scotland the food supply alternates between a superabundance in summer, with thousands of auks, petrels and gulls breeding on the cliffs, to virtual starvation in winter when the seabirds have deserted the cliffs and all the peregrine can find is a few small birds and perhaps a small population of feral pigeons and wild rock doves living in caves all winter. On low-lying grouse moors peregrines likewise can find food all the year round and need not move in winter. However, in high mountains, such as the

Cairngorms, which may only be a few miles from such low-lying grouse moors with resident pairs, some high-nesting peregrines are forced to move out of their breeding territory once it becomes snowed up in autumn and can only return in the following spring. In the interim they may move to lower ground in the same area or possibly travel further, to the seashore, where many peregrines winter. In this way, it appears, peregrines which breed in remote highland areas which they are forced to leave in winter, may acquire pesticide residues from their prey while pairs permanently resident on lower ground only a few miles away do not.

In Britain, the distance between peregrine nest sites varies from 1·6–6·5 miles (2·6–10·4 km.), the least distance being on the southern English cliffs, and the greatest in highland areas of West Scotland; these differences appear to be correlated with year-round food supply(19). In most of the country on sea-cliffs peregrine eyries are from 2–4 miles apart, averaging about 3 miles (5·4 km.) apart both on coastal and inland areas of England, S. Scotland, and Wales. In the West Highlands even sea-cliff eyries may be over 5 miles apart, and in general the Highlands of Scotland support far fewer peregrines than might be expected. Average available home range sizes are 20 square miles in Wales, 37 square miles in east central Scotland, and 85 square miles in the West Highlands (54, 76 and 223 sq.km.). These figures apply to areas where there is no lack of suitable nesting sites, and indicate that peregrines require larger home ranges in Britain than do golden eagles. In odd extraordinary cases peregrine sites may only be 500 yards apart, an even higher density than that of Peale's falcon in the Queen Charlotte Islands of British Columbia, which is otherwise the highest recorded density of breeding peregrines(2). Peale's falcons breed less than a mile apart on cliffs supporting enormous summer colonies of sea-birds.

The distribution of breeding peregrines in Britain is controlled by the availability of suitable cliff sites. In southern England this means that they are confined to the coast, but in mountainous Wales, northern England, and Scotland, they also breed inland. In Britain they have never bred in old nests of other birds in trees (as they do in parts of Germany and Sweden); nor are any nests in big hollow trees recorded in Britain. If peregrines in Britain could evolve the habit of breeding on old nests of, for instance carrion crows, they would undoubtedly be able to extend their range to inland areas where they are now absent.

Peregrines prefer a large cliff when they can find one; but if a large cliff is lacking in an otherwise favourable territory they will make do with one 50 or even 25 feet high. A good many eyries can be walked into, but those on large sea-cliffs are only accessible by ropework. In 170 eyries examined by Ratcliffe 125 were on cliffs of more than 100 feet and only four on cliffs of less than 25 feet. A relatively small face in the midst of a large range of tiered cliffs may often be used, the total height of the entire cliff-face being more important than the actual height of the face chosen for the nest ledge. Altitude above the sea is affected by the high proportion on sea-cliffs; most inland nests are 1000–2000 feet above sea level, with only a few above 2000 feet (600 m.)(18).

Occasionally, peregrines will breed on buildings, the most celebrated case being Salisbury Cathedral, where peregrines have certainly reared young on at least one occasion but not in this century. Other known sites in Britain include an old mine chimney, and there are a few records of man-made cliffs in quarries. Considering the number of domestic pigeons in some towns it is somewhat remarkable that peregrines do not breed more often on buildings. From the viewpoint of food supply Trafalgar Square is an ideal breeding site, with an inaccessible nesting ledge at the top of Nelson's Column. In other countries peregrines have bred on sky-scrapers or tall buildings in New York or Montreal, in Nairobi, and in ruins in Spain and Germany(11).

Part of the reason seems to be the lack of a suitable nesting ledge. Peregrines prefer to have a ledge on which there is soft earth or vegetation in which to make a scrape for the eggs, or the old nest of another bird. Thus, in Nairobi they nested at least once successfully behind the coat of arms on the Law Courts, only 60 feet above the ground. However, when these were defaced on Kenya's independence in 1963 the falcons were deprived of the old nests and accumulated rubbish in which they had bred. For a year a pair frequented a futuristic concrete sculpture on the side of the President's Office, but this had no earth or accumulated rubbish in it and if they laid the eggs rolled out; they have not been seen since. The peregrines which bred successfully for sixteen years on the Sun Life Building in Montreal did so largely because they were provided with a box containing earth in which to make a scrape. Individual preference no doubt also plays a part; it was the same female which bred all the time on the Sun Life building, appearing as a yearling, and recognisable thereafter year after year until she died(11).

It has always seemed to me that a possible explanation for the failure of pere-grines to breed in towns more often is their way of killing. Kestrels, which kill their prey mainly on the ground, frequently build in towns or ruins as well as in natural rock sites. The peregrine, killing in the air, must invariably, in a town, bind to and carry its prey without dropping it, or it will lose it in the traffic-filled streets below. This is certainly rather an unnatural behavioural restriction on a wild peregrine, and it is my theory to explain why peregrines do not more often take advantage of the abundant and relatively easily caught food supply of domestic pigeons living in many towns. In the improbable event that I ever erect a skyscraper I shall endeavour to ensure that a suitable earth-filled niche is provided about half-way up for any peregrine that may pass.

In natural British cliff sites aspect has no effect on the choice of the nesting ledge. In districts where suitable crags face in all directions peregrines are in-different to aspect. However, it so happens that in much of Britain the most suitable crags face north and east, probably the result of glacial activity in the Ice Age. Thus, in practice, more eyries tend to face north and east than west and south. Peregrines avoid narrow ravines for nesting, and prefer a cliff with an open outlook. Of 170 nest sites examined by Ratcliffe only 16 were in such ravines, and of these only nine were regularly used(18).

In the nesting territory individual pairs may regularly use one ledge year after year or may have a number of alternate ledges, sometimes as much as four miles apart on different cliffs. The favourite type of ledge is one about 18 inches wide or more, with a sheer fall of rock above and below. It may be overhung but not necessarily; caves or holes are not essential. Some believe that it is essential for the ledge to be soft and earthy, or at least gravelly, so that the peregrines can go through the ritual of making a scrape in which to lay the eggs. However, this is contested by Ratcliffe, who considers that the behaviour of individuals varies in this connection. British peregrines frequently make use of the old nest of a raven, or sometimes that of a buzzard or eagle instead of making a scrape; this habit is shared by both Arctic and tropical peregrines, which may breed in the old nests of eagles or buzzards. In such cases the peregrines do not have to make a scrape for the eggs at all, and sometimes will lay their own eggs on the undisturbed wool lining of the raven's nest.

In the days when the peregrine population was mildly persecuted but had not yet been reduced by the effects of pesticides, a suitable nesting cliff was held with great tenacity. Even if successive females were shot by gamekeepers new ones appeared either in the following year or, occasionally, even in the same season(18). The immediate neighbourhood of the nesting ledge is defended against other peregrines, and other large birds are usually attacked if they pass near it. Ravens and peregrines, which frequently nest close together on the same range of cliffs, are constantly at war with one another, but the strife does not lead to many fatalities and normally does not prevent both species from breeding successfully. In some areas where the choice of nest site is extremely limited on small cliffs the raven, nesting early, may get there first and succeed in appropriating the nest site before the peregrine. Possibly, in a few cases, peregrines evict ravens from suitable nest sites. In Scotland, there is competition between peregrines and golden eagles for some nesting cliffs, and although the peregrine is obviously aggressive to the eagle and the eagle not obviously aggressive to the peregrine, there is reason to suppose that the number of breeding peregrines in such terrain is limited by the presence of golden eagles.

Nesting ledges and cliffs in Britain vary from 2700 feet (820 m.) A.S.L. in the Cairngorms to near sea level on sea-cliffs. Of 170 peregrine eyries on inland cliffs 95 were 1000–1500 feet A.S.L. and only 10 above 2000 feet. The highest eyries, as in the case of the golden eagle, are all in the massive hills of eastern Scotland where, in summer, there is an abundant food supply of ptarmigan and grouse but where in winter the peregrines are forced to leave their territories because of snow. In western Scotland peregrine eyries inland are lower, and the peregrine is generally rather rare, much less common than the golden eagle.

Resident pairs frequently roost near their nesting ledge for much of the winter, and in early spring spend the night near the place where they are about to lay. Females often roost on the nesting cliff, the males on another cliff some distance away. If both the pair survive the winter they perform spectacular aerial displays, soaring together, diving and swooping up again, either singly or together, or whizzing one after the other from a great height to near the sea along some sea-cliff, to regain height on the updraught and repeat the performance. Males feed the females copiously during courtship, and may pass the food to the female in the air or on a ledge, when they frequently bow slowly up and down, uttering a chittering call(5). This ceremony is thought to overcome the female's natural aggression towards the male – being much larger, she otherwise might kill him when the two are at close quarters. This has not, so far as I know, been observed among British peregrines, but has been carefully observed in Alaska. Unmated males frequent the nesting cliff and fly out in invitation towards any passing female they may see, calling, and returning to re-alight on a ledge until a female is attracted(16). Mating takes place on the cliff top or on ledges, and is frequent until the eggs are laid, after which it apparently ceases.

Despite the number of devotees this falcon attracts, a really good account of the breeding cycle in British peregrines is lacking. The best British accounts available are those by the egg collector Nethersole-Thompson in 1931, and by Francis Heatherly in 1910(10). Usually, in British species, when a good account of the breeding cycle is lacking, it is possible to find one in the continental literature applicable to similar ecological situations; however, in the case of the peregrine, even this is lacking, and the details of the breeding cycle must be put together from scattered accounts and various sources.

Peregrine eggs have long been in demand by egg collectors because of their rich colouring. They are rounded ovals with a buff or biscuit-coloured ground colour with ashy grey shell marks almost obscured by superficial freckles, spots or heavy blotches of deep brick red. They vary a great deal, but it is said that eggs from the south coast of England would be recognised by any skilled collector. Others deny this; but Irish eggs are larger on average. The normal clutch is three to four, averaging 3·4 in 98 clutches examined by Ratcliffe, which is probably typical, though the mean of 21 recent Scottish clutches is 2·96 and the mean of 102 clutches on B.T.O. nest record cards is 2·85. These may have been affected by pesticides(a,25).

Full clutches of two are sometimes laid, and one, five, or even six have been recorded. The eggs are laid at intervals of two to three days, so that a clutch of four takes a week or so to lay; incubation normally begins when the second-last egg has been laid, but may not begin till the last egg is laid(16). This behaviour means that the eggs hatch more nearly simultaneously than is the case in many raptors.

In southern England the earliest full clutches may be laid before the end of March, but more usually by 10 April. In northern Highland Scotland most clutches are complete by 21 April and there is less variation in laying dates from south to north than prevailing temperature and snow conditions would lead one to expect. Both sexes incubate, but there are no good quantitative data from Britain as to the share taken by each. The female or falcon is said to take the major share by day and no doubt sits all night. She is fed on the nest by the male or tiercel, who comes with prey to the ledge or calls her off to receive it. This type of behaviour is very common in other birds of prey; but it is also true to say that when both sexes incubate the female has the opportunity, while off the nest, to kill for herself, and may then even feed the male(3). It is not known whether this occurs in British, or any other peregrines.

Incubation takes 30–32 days for each egg and, since incubation proper does not start till the penultimate egg is laid, the young from a clutch that took five to seven days to deposit hatch over two to three days. In the peregrine intersibling aggression, or the Cain and Abel battle between young does not seem to occur. At first the female remains in the nest brooding the young, and the male brings all the food. On arrival, he calls, and the female often leaves to receive it from him, either on a ledge some distance away or occasionally by an aerial pass, the prey being dropped and caught by the female or taken foot to foot from the male. The male must increase his killing rate immediately after the hatch to provide for the growing brood, but I am unable to locate any data on how much prey he then kills. In fact, data of this sort are badly needed for the peregrine.

The young peregrines are clad in white down at first, and they grow a second coat of down after about ten days. They then look, when standing, as if they were clad in voluminous white fur coats, and the thick down must go far towards keeping them warm. The falcon is then released from her brooding duties to some extent, and spends more time off the nest than on it. At this time she can be exceedingly aggressive to a human intruder; I have actually been struck by a falcon – in Africa – with young at this stage, and falconers attempting to take young on the Sussex cliffs used regularly to be attacked(12). A female peregrine at this stage is perfectly capable of terrifying a large dog and can presumably do the same to a fox. This could be of biological advantage in nest sites which are easily accessible, at least by day.

The young start to show feathers through the down at about 18 days old, the characteristic moustachial streak showing as a brown patch. By 21 days old they start wing-flapping practice, and thereafter, as they become feathered, they are left alone in the nest, and no longer need brooding, though the female remains at the nest site for much of this time and usually roosts in the nest with them. The demands of the brood at this stage for food are large, and it would be of advantage for the female to be released to take her share in the killing. However, it appears from most of the available data that throughout the fledging period the male brings all or most of the prey, while the female remains at the nest site or near it. Some recent Scottish observations by Douglas Weir indicate that the female does hunt after 20 days and that in her absence the male may shelter the young in a storm(h). In the eyrie on the Scilly Isles observed by Francis Heatherly in 1910 the female disappeared part-way through the fledging period – whether shot or alarmed by the photographers so that she would not go back to the nest is uncertain. The male in this case took over the rearing of the brood entirely, and they flew successfully in due course(10). Fuller observations are needed.

The young leave the nest after 35–42 days in it; there is no information on whether the larger females are slower to fly than the smaller males, or on the ratio of the sexes reared. This may be 1:1 but the occurrence of bigamy in adults indicates a surplus of females later. Falconers who take broods late in the fledging period could presumably supply such information. The young are not immediately able to fend for themselves, but remain near the nest site for up to two months, leaving the nest in mid-June in S. England to mid-July in north Scotland. They have plenty of time to grow strong on the wing before they have to leave the area, and they often accompany their parents about the territory while still dependent on them for food.

I do not think there is any data at all on the post-fledging behaviour of young wild peregrines, with particular reference to the time when they make their first kill. Young peregrines taken by falconers are kept 'at hack', in an open house from which they can fly in any direction, but at which they are fed as necessary. When their return to the hack house becomes irregular the falconer assumes that they are able to kill for themselves, and catches them for final training at this stage(12,13). The behaviour of the young in the hands of falconers proves that they do not have to be taught to kill by their parents but can do so independently. However, it would be pleasant to have confirmation of this from observation on wild birds.

Four hundred records from all parts of the peregrine's temperate range indicate that the average brood size reared is 2·6 per successful nest, varying from 1·87 in parts of Britain to 3·05 in the eastern United States(11). The number of young reared per pair per annum would be lower than this. The average brood in Britain, 1·87 as recorded by Ratcliffe, is well below the average for peregrines in their temperate range, but his figures may already have been affected by the pesticide decline. 89 broods on B.T.O. record cards average 2·08, but some were still young enough to sustain further losses. Broods from 24 Cornish eyries pre 1948 averaged 2·4, which is about the same as the European average or only slightly lower(23).

As we have seen, before the incidence of pesticides the average production of British eyries was adequate not only to maintain the population but to allow a considerable surplus, and it is possible that the low average brood size may have been partly because the peregrine was at 'capacity' numbers in most of its British range. In central Highland Scotland, the only area not now seriously affected by pesticides, in 168 territory years 125 were known to be occupied, 94 laid, and 68–72 young fledged, almost exactly 1·0 per territory per year, 1·33 per occupied territory, 1·76 per pair which bred, and 2·38 per successful nest(h). This may be a truer picture of overall productivity in the peregrine. In other words, when left alone and if it breeds, the peregrine normally rears two to three young from three to four eggs, sometimes one only, and very occasionally four.

The young separate from their parents in the autumn but there is, so far as I know, no evidence to support the common statement that they are driven away. Up to 1970 218 peregrines had been ringed in Britain, all but five of which were young in the nest. Of the latter there were 26 recoveries up to 1965, of which four had travelled less than 10 miles (16 km.), nine 10–50 miles (16–80 km.), seven 50–100 miles (80–160 km.), four 100–200 miles (160–320 km.), and only one more than 200 miles. This bird, which was ringed in Sutherland and recovered in Wexford, showed roughly the same pattern of migratory movement as is shown by continental peregrines recovered in Britain. The next longest traveller, however, a Lundy peregrine which was recovered five years later as an adult, apparently drowned, in Lough, Ireland, had travelled 190 miles (305 km.) N.N.W. Among the 26 records there are three cases where two young from the same nest were recovered. One of these was the Sutherland bird recovered in Wexford; its nest-mate was recovered in Banffshire 110 miles (176 km.) S.S.E. of where it had been ringed. Of the other pairs, two ringed in Inverness were recovered in Ross and Inverness 48 and 80 miles (72 and 128 km.) N.; and two Cumberland young were recovered in Ayrshire and the Isle of Man 85 miles (136 km.) N.W. and 72 miles (125 km.) W.S.W.(b). (Map 33.)

The data indicate a more or less random dispersal of young from the breeding site, probably to greater distances than in either the buzzard or the golden eagle. The five-year-old Lundy peregrine, recovered in March in Ireland, was presumably a breeding adult in that area, and the Sutherland bird which moved 445 miles south to Wexford and was recovered there in its first winter indicates that there is probably free interchange of individuals between different areas in Britain.

Continental peregrines recovered in Britain all come from Sweden, Norway, or the Lofoten Islands. The eight records all indicate that these North European peregrines migrated in a south-south-westerly direction for several hundred miles. One of these continental birds was shot, and of the British young birds 26 were shot and 12 'found dead'; two of these had been drowned, and had presumably died a natural death. One of the shot birds had been shot after the passage of the 1954 Bird Protection Act, and peregrines known to have been ringed and shot by game-keepers are not reported. There have, in fact, been few recoveries since 1950.

Ringing records elsewhere have indicated that very few peregrines live more than ten years (4/108 records) the oldest known being a 14-year-old European bird(4). Evidently, with an average brood size of 2·6 per successful nest and probably 2 per nest, in normal conditions, adults would not need to live very long to replace themselves. Assuming 70% mortality before sexual maturity in the second year of life (as indicated by available ringing data) 30 out of every 100 young peregrines become adult and can breed. Adults would thus have to live only a ittle more than three years as adults to replace themselves. Scottish observations indicate that females are replaced normally at about four years, but that some live five or six years(h). In the wild state the oldest known life span is of the celebrated Sun Life female in Montreal; she lived for 12 years, first appearing as a yearling and breeding for 11 years before she disappeared, and had three different males in her lifetime(11). The longest continued occupation of an eyrie in Britain by the

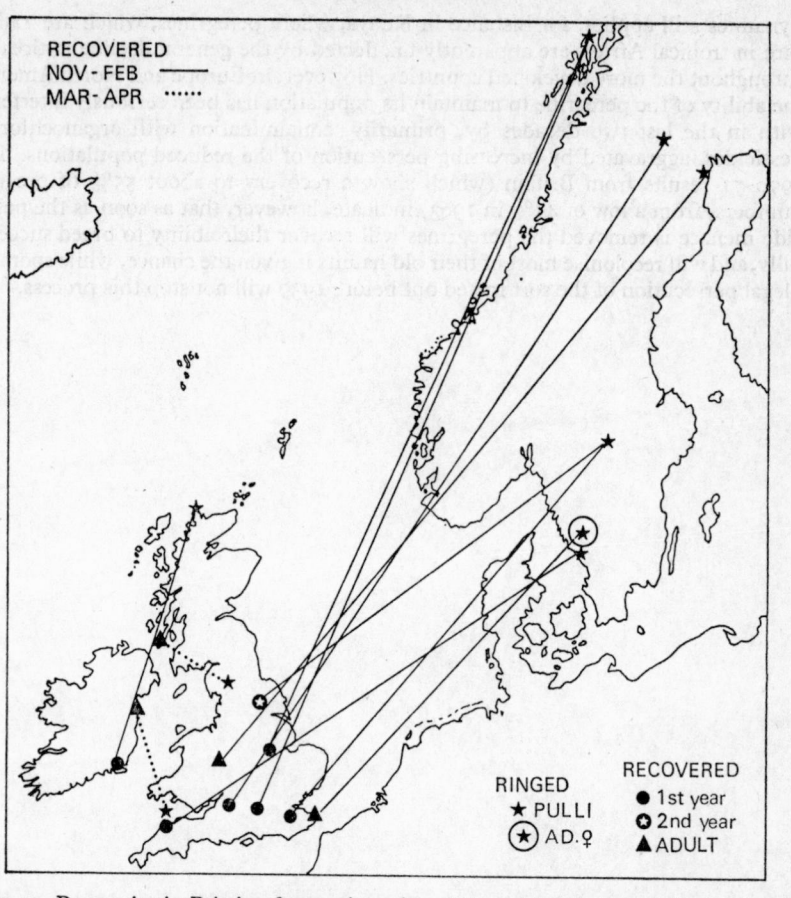

RECOVERED
NOV-FEB ——
MAR-APR ······

RINGED
★ PULLI
⊛ AD.♀

RECOVERED
● 1st year
✪ 2nd year
▲ ADULT

MAP 33. Recoveries in Britain of peregrines ringed abroad showing Scandinavian origin and of the three most distant British-ringed birds, showing more random dispersal.

same female observed by Ratcliffe was seven years, and it is common for the female to be replaced every year in areas where some persecution occurs(18).

All the data indicate, in fact, that the breeding biology of the peregrine, prior to pesticide incidence, enabled natural populations to build up a surplus of immatures and adults. This accounts for the frequent occurrence of third adults at breeding sites, and of intruder females which may mate with bigamous males or interfere with the successful breeding of the rightful pair. In the case of the Sun Life peregrines in Montreal, an intruding pair on one occasion attempted to take over the site, with a fight which resulted in the death of the rightful male. The indications from available data are that a wild adult peregrine probably lives four to five years on average. The average age of 30 European and American ringed birds recovered as adults was 5·5; in other words these birds lived for an average of 3·5 years after becoming sexually mature at two years old.

There are still parts of the world where this favourable type of population dynamics still applies, for instance in Kenya, where peregrines, which are rather rare in tropical Africa, are apparently unaffected by the general decline noticeable throughout the more developed countries. However, in Europe and North America the ability of the peregrine to maintain its population has been seriously interfered with in the last two decades by, primarily, contamination with organochlorine pesticides, aggravated by increasing persecution of the reduced populations. The 1970–71 results from Britain (which show a recovery to about 55% of pre-war numbers, from a low of 45% in 1963) indicate, however, that as soon as the pesticide menace is removed the peregrines will recover their ability to breed successfully, and will recolonise most of their old haunts if given the chance, while sporadic illegal persecution of the sort meted out before 1939 will not stop this process.

CHAPTER 19

BOREAL MIGRANTS

THE gyrfalcon and rough-legged buzzard are of special interest among migrant birds of prey in Britain because they visit us more or less regularly in winter, and because they both come from the Arctic where the life of many predatory mammals and birds is controlled by cycles of abundance in their prey. There is also the vague hope that one or both might someday breed in Shetland. Recently this vague possibility has been strengthened since the snowy owl, another characteristic Arctic species, has bred successfully in Shetland for several years past. If the snowy owl can do it, why not the gyrfalcon?

Gyrfalcons breed all round the North Pole in the tundra, and sometimes the northern taiga or coniferous woodland zones, where the woodland is sufficiently open to permit them to hunt. Those that visit Britain in winter come from Greenland, Iceland, or northern Scandinavia. The birds from these three localities were formerly separated as distinct races, *Falco rusticolus candicans, islandus,* and *rusticolus* respectively. All races of the gyrfalcon have, however, been submerged by Vaurie in his *Birds of the Palearctic Fauna*; he considered that there was a cline of paler and darker birds from north to south while no races could clearly be separated on measurements(15).

Whether one accepts this or not, the fact is that as a rule the milder the climate inhabited by gyrfalcons the less likely they are to migrate south in winter. Thus it happens that those from Iceland, milder in winter climate, visit us less often than do the magnificent white, black-flecked Greenland falcons, of the type *candicans*, which visit Britain almost annually. Nowadays if one is heard of in the south, an army of 'twitchers' can be expected to converge on it, breaking down farm fences, parking their cars in crops, and no doubt hounding the wretched bird from one perch to another to get a view of it in flight. Sometimes these magnificent birds are still greeted by a charge of shot; this happened to one in Anglesey in 1972(b).

I have never had the fortune to see a wild gyrfalcon either in the Arctic or in Britain; but I have watched a trained bird fly in Shropshire, and the impression left is unforgettable. One expects a gyr to resemble a bigger peregrine; but it is much more solid, heavy-bodied, and flies with a majestic, almost deliberate wingbeat. When it comes down in a magnificent stoop from on high it looks like some monstrous living missile. And, when travelling at 100 m.p.h. (160 k.p.h.) in such a stoop, it is developing energy of 56,000–80,000 foot pounds, or ten to fifteen times the muzzle energy of an elephant rifle!

Gyrfalcons have long been in demand by falconers because of their magnificent stature and power and their peerless form and plumage. Keen falconers make special expeditions to the Arctic to capture eyasses in the nest, and as a result special protective measures, not always successful, are applied in Iceland, Sweden (where the penalty may be six months in jail) and some other relatively accessible breeding areas to prevent an excessive toll of young falcons. Although gyrfalcons seem to have had a legendary reputation in the past, the fact is that in modern times they seem to have been less successful as trained hawks. They are apparently disinclined to 'wait on' over the party when game hawking, and are consequently of relatively little use in this sport. The late Ernest Vesey went specially to Iceland to obtain young Iceland falcons, which were then expertly trained in Islay; but none of them seem to have been very successful, and, although magnificent fliers, were very independent and difficult to control, while at least one would not stoop at quarry close to the ground(9,10). When one looks at the theoretical energy figures I have calculated above this reluctance to come too close to the ground at great speed seems to me quite natural.

I have long felt that the main reason for the failure of trained gyrs as compared to peregrines is the difference in their hunting methods in the wild. Gyrs kill much more prey on the ground than do peregrines, which habitually kill in the air. The hunting methods of gyrfalcons have recently been clearly described by Sven-Axel Bengtson in Iceland(2). From this account it seems that gyrs habitually hunt by swift flight skimming along close to the ground, or from low perches, on rocks or telegraph poles. They soar high in the air too, but at such times they may not be hunting in earnest.

Their commonest prey in Iceland is ptarmigan, but they also take many wild duck, waders and gulls. Elsewhere they take some mammals (especially lemmings when abundant) and occasionally larger birds such as blackcock, though these are not often found out in the open where the gyrfalcon can hunt. All these are usually taken on or near the ground, the falcon hurtling a few feet above the barren moors to surprise them if it can. In just the same way I have watched lanner falcons which are in the same species-group as gyrs hunting small rats on the high moorlands of Semien and Bale in Ethiopia. Such falcons may appear to be travelling extremely fast, but probably are not.

The lanner is not much bigger than a peregrine, and is nearly as fine a flyer when performing at some height above the ground, but its mode of hunting is rather different. It too, apparently, makes a less successful trained falcon than does a peregrine(c).

It is unlikely that a falconer, however skilled, can inculcate into his trained birds methods of hunting that are unnatural to them; and if wild gyrfalcons are not inclined to wait on and kill in the air then no trained gyr is likely to either. The peregrine, as the falconers' favourite bird, cannot be replaced by the gyr. Moreover, the gyr, coming as it does from much colder regions, simply will not fly at all on a warm August afternoon after grouse. It feels the heat, poor thing; and the Arab sheikhs who, unable to obtain peregrines, now want to have gyrs, are wasting their money and endangering this splendid falcon for nothing.

The biology of the gyrfalcon wherever it occurs is apparently closely tied to that of grouse and ptarmigan in the Arctic. In Iceland, in summer, ducks form a greater total proportion of the food taken, 48·5% by number and 62·0% by weight; but even here ptarmigan, at 41·4% by number and 34·5% by weight, are the commonest single species of prey taken(2). In Alaska, in summer, ptarmigan may form up to 90% of the prey taken by weight; they are preferred even in years when they are comparatively scarce(4). In years when lemmings or other small rodents are abundant a large number of these are taken, especially arctic ground squirrels; but since lemmings are very small they are relatively insignificant items of prey by weight. Ground squirrels, which individually weigh almost as much as a ptarmigan, may form up to 75% of the gyrfalcon's prey in some Alaskan localities. The gyrfalcon takes comparatively few small birds, which are inadequate for its food needs. A gyrfalcon probably needs about 120–180 grams (4½–6½ oz) of food a day, according to sex, perhaps more in the very cold arctic climate, especially in winter. It is therefore easy to see that lemmings and small passerines, weighing only about 50 grams or less, would not be more than a snack for a gyrfalcon, hardly worth the trouble of catching.

Small passerines and ducks migrate south out of the Arctic in winter, and the ground squirrels and lemmings either hibernate or are then buried under snow. The ptarmigan, however, remain feeding on exposed willow shoots and other plants. They may move from one part of the country to another, and concentrate where food is accessible, but they do not migrate far from the Arctic latitudes, and they are therefore the main winter standby of the resident gyrfalcons(4). In Iceland, and apparently elsewhere, ptarmigans fluctuate in numbers according to a ten-year cycle, and are killed more often in years when they are more abundant.

In Iceland, near Lake Myvatn the ptarmigan population steadily increased from 1960–66, and then crashed to a quarter or less of its 1966 level. In three years, from 1964–66 inclusive, the gyrs in five known eyries bred in 12/14 possible cases and, in eyries where the young fledged reared broods averaging 3·25. In three later years, 1968–70, with low ptarmigan populations, these same pairs bred only five times in 14 possible cases, and reared smaller broods averaging 2·5. One pair bred in all three good years 1964–66, rearing three and five young in two years and hatching five in the third year, but did not breed at all in the bad years 1968–70. These figures are too small, but are indicative of the close relationship between the ptarmigan cycle and the breeding of the gyrfalcon, even in an area where the abundant population of ducks in summer could have been expected to mask this effect(2).

In the Alaskan tundra and in northern Norway too ptarmigan are vital to gyrfalcons. The gyrfalcon breeds early, laying in April, when snow still carpets much of the ground, and the young falcons fledge in early to mid-July, about the time that ptarmigan chicks hatch out(4). It is the population of adult ptarmigan which has survived the winter which is important for successful breeding. If large numbers of these concentrate in a particular area in spring the gyrfalcon in that area may be able to lay large clutches and breed satisfactorily; if the ptarmigan population is low they cannot breed at all, or few pairs will breed. In Norway gyrfalcons also breed more successfully in peak lemming years; but these, at least sometimes, agree with peak ptarmigan years, and ptarmigan are still more important as prey than lemmings, however abundant(6). Young gyrfalcons, becoming independent of their parents in late summer, mid-August to September, then find weak-flying young ptarmigan and duck relatively abundant and consequently have a better chance of survival. However, the overriding factor controlling the breeding of gyrfalcons is the spring and early summer population of adult ptarmigan; the young falcons just happen to come in for a feast that is available in late summer.

Gyrfalcons normally breed on ledges of cliffs, which need not be high or steep, or in the nest of some other bird, especially of the rough-legged buzzard or ravens. They lay two to seven eggs and rear broods of one to five in the years when they breed. The average clutch in Alaska is 3·8 and the average brood is 2·34(4). In Alaska brood size also depends on the abundance of ptarmigan. In a good year it may be 3·0, in a bad year less than half that, 1·3. Since every pair of gyrfalcons does not breed every year (non-breeding varying from 10–60% according to the spring abundance of ptarmigan) the overall annual productivity is considerably lower than mean brood size. In Iceland, near Lake Myvatn, over ten years of varying ptarmigan population, 28 pairs bred in 41 possible cases(3). Some eyries were robbed by falconers; but 10 broods, including one of five, averaged 2·7, varying from 3·25 in the good years to 2·5 in the bad. The real productivity of the gyrfalcons in this area was thus about 1·9 per pair per year over ten years, but varied from 2·8 per year in good to 0·54 per year in bad years. In a more extreme climate, such as Alaska or Greenland, such variations may be still greater.

Against this background of dependence on ptarmigan we may assess the possibility of gyrfalcons ever breeding in northern Britain. It seems to me highly unlikely. There are no ptarmigan in Shetland, which is the most likely place. The snowy owl could breed in Shetland because it feeds predominantly on mammals; but even then the owls had to modify their natural tastes a good deal and feed far more on birds than they would have done on, say, Baffin Land(a). Given that gyrfalcons are unlikely to be able to breed without a good population of ptarmigan in their haunts it seems most improbable that they would even try in any part of Britain north of the Monadhliaths. This area might be too warm for them in summer; and in that hot bed of gamekeeperdom they would certainly be illegally persecuted if they appeared.

The gyrfalcon population in the Arctic thus fluctuates according to the abundance of the favoured prey; and when a ptarmigan crash comes quite large numbers of the falcons may be forced to move south in winter, especially from Greenland. The numbers seen in Britain in winter are always too small, averaging two per year since 1958, to be able to connect the records with fluctuations in the ptarmigan population of Greenland or Iceland(14). The British records have not been fully collated, except during the last 13 years when rare Palearctic migrants have been more carefully noted. One year in which there were apparently more than usual was 1910–11; but it is not possible to say whether this year was a year in which the Greenland ptarmigan population crashed(1). Since most of those that come here are the white Greenland form, Greenland is the most interesting country from this viewpoint. The Iceland gyr occurs less often and the Scandinavian gyrfalcon has only occurred twice, in 1845 and 1867(14,1), a period when winters were apparently more severe than they are now.

Most of the gyrfalcons that visit Britain are seen in the Outer Hebrides, northern Scotland, or Shetland; but some occur in the south of England. Most of them appear between October and March, as one would expect; but there are also records in May, June, and September(14). It seems rather doubtful if many of these wandering individuals would be able to survive to return and breed in Greenland or Iceland, especially if they are immatures. However, that is no excuse for shooting them as they appear, which still sometimes happens. On the rare occasions when one appears, it should be given every chance to live. They are so few that they could do no one any real harm, and nowadays they often give pleasure and excitement to hundreds of bird-watchers.

There is better evidence that the irregular irruption of rough-legged buzzards in Britain are connected with the cyclic abundance of prey in the Arctic. Like most of their genus rough-legged buzzards feed mainly on small rodents which, both in the tundra and wooded taiga zones normally go through cycles of three or four years' duration. The most famous of these animals are the lemmings, which every few years, reach spectacular levels of abundance. Large numbers of especially immature animals irrupt, even sometimes swimming out to sea and drowning in thousands. Voles, however, go through the same sort of cycles, if less spectacular, in the taiga woodland. These cycles are, indeed, characteristic of small rodents in harsh climates(16).

The predatory Arctic birds affected by such cycles include the snowy and other owls, the rough-legged buzzard, and several skuas(11). For rough-legged buzzards, breeding both in taiga woodland and tundra, voles may be more important than lemmings. The rodent cycles have two interacting effects on the buzzards. Firstly, if rodents are abundant in spring, the buzzards may all breed and lay large clutches of eggs. Secondly if, as often happens, the abundant rodent population continues to multiply through the summer, the buzzards rear large broods. Thus, they have a far greater potential for rapid increase in a good year than does the gyrfalcon, in which breeding success is controlled by the steadily dwindling population of adult ptarmigan, whereas the rough-legged buzzard can take advantage of the increasing summer hordes of fast-breeding rodents. In the gyrfalcon the population may rather more than double in a good year; but in the rough-legged buzzard it can treble, or even more.

This is an over-simplification of a complicated situation; but in years of poor food supply in spring rough-legged buzzards may not breed, or may lay small clutches while in good years almost all breed and lay large clutches. Taking non-breeding pairs into account the average clutch could vary from less than one egg per pair to more than four. In good years the average brood may exceed three, with six and even seven young recorded. An eight-year average in one area was 2·7 young per nest.

Thus, in a good rodent year, the spring population of adult rough-legged buzzards is more than doubled by late summer and autumn(7). Sometimes, however, the abundant rodent population crashes while the young buzzards and other predators are still in the nest, in which case the young die and breeding is virtually a failure. If, however, the voles and lemmings are still abundant when the young buzzards leave the nest they have little difficulty in catching them, and must have a better chance of survival than do young gyrfalcons, which must learn to catch larger, less abundant, and more active avian prey. Assuming that a rough-legged buzzard's daily need is about 10% of bodyweight(5) (about 80–120 grams per day) this would be provided by four to six average-sized voles or lemmings, which would be easily caught in a few hours.

Voles, lemmings, and other rodents are subject to more violent fluctuations of population than are ptarmigan because they produce litter after litter through the summer while ptarmigan rear only one relatively small brood of chicks. In years of vole or lemming abundance they become extremely numerous in late summer, eat down the vegetation until there is little left, and are then obliged to move out in hordes or die where they are. Even after their own summer increase the total available population of predators is unable effectively to control the supply of rodents, since even in good years their rate of increase is far lower than that of voles or lemmings. The latter may multiply a hundredfold whereas the rough-legged buzzard, for instance, would at most treble. To some extent a local super-abundance of food attracts nomadic avian predators from other areas(d); but this cannot happen until late in summer, when young and avian predators can leave their breeding territories. This is a factor common to other nomadic birds of prey, such as kestrels, which live in hot arid areas.

The end result is that the starved rodents, having eaten themselves out of house and home, die in huge numbers, leaving a very small population of survivors. The rough-legged buzzards, having fared well up to now, suddenly find themselves deprived of food and, if they can fly strongly, must irrupt or migrate out of the area. Thus, major southward irruptions of rough-legged buzzards and other avian predators, in North America, Europe, or North Asia, tend to occur immediately after years of rodent abundance.

Irruptions of rough-legged buzzards into Britain seem to have occurred more regularly in the past than in recent years. Possibly this is related to the irregularity of rodent cycles in more recent years. Apparently, for a long time between the mid-thirties and mid-sixties the normal four or five-year rodent cycles seem completely out of gear in Scandinavia as a whole(8,d). Thus there were no regular years of abundance, though in some years rodents were locally abundant. Bannerman lists irruptions of rough-legged buzzards into Britain in 1839–40, 1858–59, 1875–76, 1880–81, 1891–92, 1903–04 and 1915–16(1). These occurred at irregular intervals of four to 19 years, but with multiples of four or five predominating, suggesting that they were connected with four or five-year cycles of abundance of rodents in northern Europe.

Since 1915 there has been only one major irruption, in the winter of 1966–67, when at least 67 rough-legged buzzards visited Britain between October and April(12). Careful note has been taken of the occurrence of rough-legged buzzards in Britain since 1958, and these records have been analysed by Sharrock(13). Probably, about 270 individuals visited Britain in the ten years 1958–67 inclusive; but 40% of all the records were in 1966–67. The same individual, as it moves about from place to place, is nowadays reported by a number of different people, so that the number reported is always more than those that actually occurred. There was a minor peak, of about 50 records, in 1960–61; but it was of less than half the magnitude of the 1966–67 irruption.

It is tempting to suggest that the prevalence of relatively regular irruptions in the mid-late-nineteenth century, and their absence from 1915–67 may have been connected with the apparently irregular rodent cycles in Scandinavia, at least in the latter half of this period. These, in turn, may have been connected with long-term climatic fluctuations, for in Victorian times winters were apparently more severe than during most of this century. Such severe winters may now again be becoming more frequent, after the exceptionally hard winter of 1963. This is a pure guess; but perhaps we shall see more regular irruptions of rough-legged buzzards between now and AD 2000.

The 1966–67 irruption was quite closely observed. The buzzards began to arrive on 1 October, and peak immigration was noted about 19 October, the main influx to south-east England occurring from 27–29 October. Rough-legged buzzards had been reported from 20 counties by the end of October. The birds moved gradually south but did not reach west England or Wales. They occurred also in Inverness, Kincardine, and Shetland. They were commonest in east England, with 14 and 11 in Suffolk and Norfolk, and 12 and 4 in Kent and Sussex; 6 were noted in Shetland. Many of these birds spent the whole winter in Britain; they had begun to disappear by February, and had left East Anglia by late April (Map 34).

This well-documented irruption apparently coincided with a year of low rough-legged buzzard breeding populations in N. Finland, Norway and N. Lapland, but quite a large population in south Lapland, with good breeding success. Apparently, therefore, it was not correlated with a very large, late summer population of European rough-legged buzzards in much of their range. However, it appears to have been clearly correlated with a rodent crash in these areas. 1966 was a peak year for voles over almost all Scandinavia(8,d). This was, as usual, followed by a population crash in which the numbers fell by at least 80% before the spring of 1967, and probably by a greater proportion since figures for vole populations given

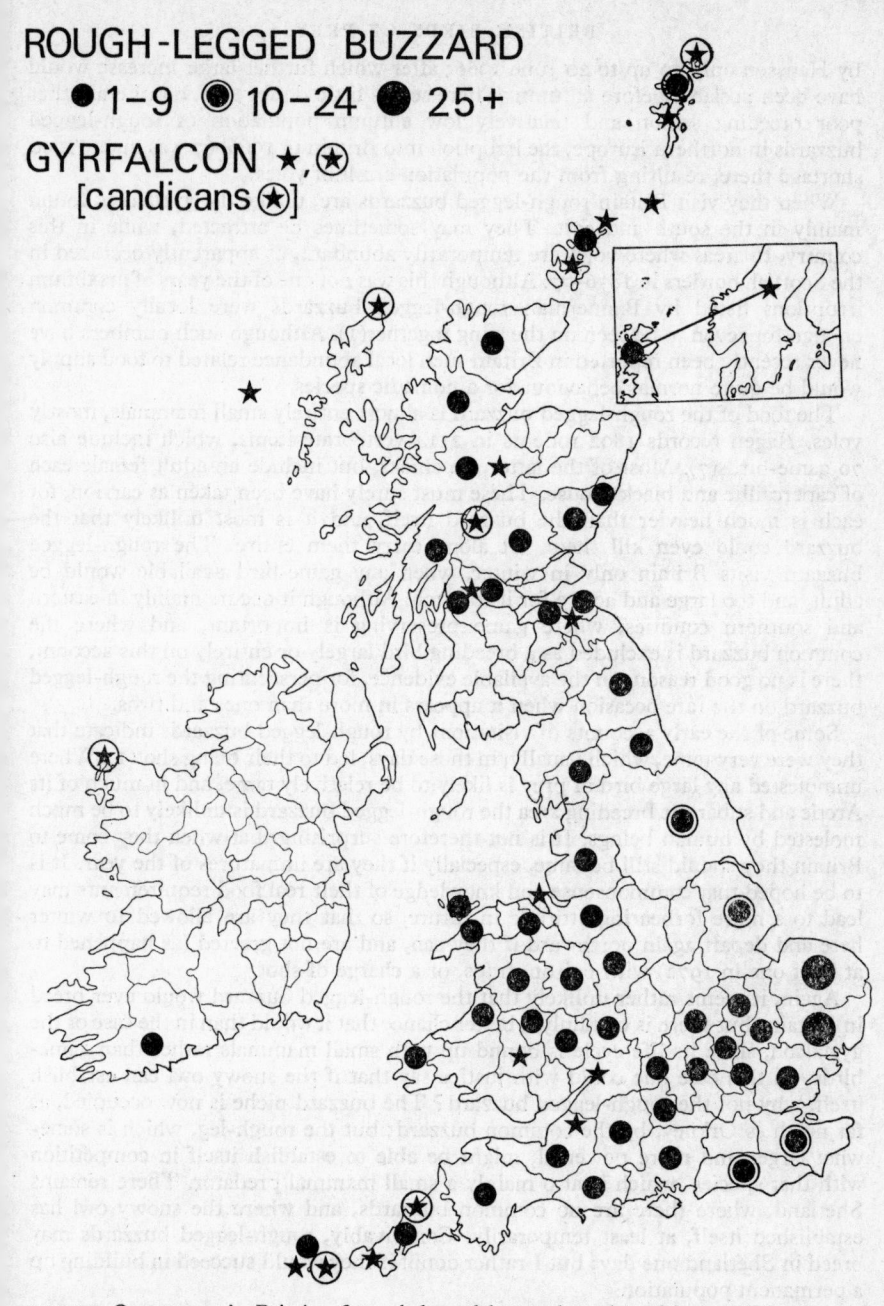

ROUGH-LEGGED BUZZARD
● 1–9 ◉ 10–24 ● 25+
GYRFALCON ★,✪
[candicans ✪]

MAP 34. Occurrence in Britain of rough-legged buzzards and gyrfalcons (all but one of six Greenland gyrfalcons in spring). The inset shows the only recovery of a rough-legged buzzard ringed abroad.

255

by Hansson only go up to 20 June 1966; after which further large increase would have been possible before autumn. There seems little doubt that, despite a rather poor breeding season and relatively low autumn population of rough-legged buzzards in northern Europe, the irruption into Britain in 1966–67 was due to food shortage there, resulting from the population crash of voles.

When they visit Britain rough-legged buzzards are, unlike the gyrfalcon, found mainly in the south and east. They may sometimes be attracted, while in this country, to areas where voles are temporarily abundant, as apparently occurred in the Scottish borders in 1876–77. Although this was not one of the years of maximum irruptions listed by Bannerman rough-legged buzzards were locally common enough for seven to be seen on the wing together(1). Although such numbers have never recently been reported in Britain such local abundance related to food supply would be quite normal behaviour for a nomadic species.

The food of the rough-legged buzzard is almost entirely small mammals, mostly voles. Hagen records 1802 rodents in 2114 vertebrate items, which include also 70 game-birds(7). Most of the latter are chicks, but include an adult female each of capercaillie and black grouse. These must surely have been taken as carrion, for each is much heavier than the buzzard itself, and it is most unlikely that the buzzard could even kill them, let alone carry them entire. The rough-legged buzzard visits Britain only in winter, when any game-bird available would be adult, and too large and active for it to catch. Although it occurs mainly in eastern and southern counties, where game preserving is important, and where the common buzzard is excluded as a breeding bird largely or entirely on this account, there is no good reason, on the available evidence, for persecuting the rough-legged buzzard on the rare occasion when it appears in more than ones and twos.

Some of the early accounts of visitations by rough-legged buzzards indicate that they were very tame, which usually, in those days, led to their being shot(1). Where unmolested any large bird of prey is likely to be relatively tame, and in much of its Arctic and subarctic breeding area the rough-legged buzzard is unlikely to be much molested by human beings. It is not therefore surprising that when they come to Britain they should still be tame, especially if they are immatures of the year. It is to be hoped that commonsense and knowledge of their real food requirements may lead to a more forbearing attitude in future, so that they are allowed to winter here and depart again northward if they can, and are not greeted (as happened to at least one in 1972) with poison, traps, or a charge of shot.

Again, it seems rather unlikely that the rough-legged buzzard would ever breed in Britain; but there is certainly a better chance that it would than in the case of the gyrfalcon, since its life cycle is bound up with small mammals rather than game-birds. In this case one could with justice say that if the snowy owl can establish itself, why not the rough-legged buzzard? The buzzard niche is now occupied, as far north as Orkney, by the common buzzard; but the rough-leg, which is somewhat larger and more powerful, might be able to establish itself in competition with that species, which is also mainly a small mammal predator. There remains Shetland, where there are no common buzzards, and where the snowy owl has established itself, at least temporarily. Conceivably, rough-legged buzzards may breed in Shetland one day; but I rather doubt if they would succeed in building up a permanent population.

CHAPTER 20

VAGRANTS

ONE third of all the diurnal species of birds of prey occurring in Britain are only more or less occasional vagrants. They do not breed here even occasionally; and (with one exception, the sea eagle) there is no evidence that they ever did in the historical past; or that (with two other possible exceptions) they may in the future. Nowadays they are better recorded than they used to be, for an army of bird-watchers, all on the lookout for rarities, scours the countryside at most weekends. Anything unusual is widely reported and dozens of people converge on it. Many of these observers now have experience in Europe or further abroad, and are not likely to mistake, for instance, a male red-footed falcon if they have a good view of it. In this way we probably now obtain a fuller and more accurate record of rare vagrants than would have been the case fifty years ago, when people could not get about with the same ease, binoculars were expensive, and a much smaller proportion of British people had either the money or the opportunity to gain experience outside Britain.

The eight vagrant species include the black kite, the Egyptian and griffon vultures, the pallid harrier, the spotted eagle, the lesser kestrel, and the red-footed falcon. To these must nowadays be added the sea eagle, which has been discussed in another chapter because it was formerly a breeding species but now occurs only as an occasional vagrant; I shall not discuss it again here. The other seven are the true vagrants, that either never have bred here, or did so in a past so distant that no believable record of it remains.

The first, the **black kite**, can fairly claim to be the world's most successful bird of prey, largely because it has adapted to life with man, particularly in towns. In Asia especially, black kites occur in almost incredible numbers, thousands together, in any large town; and the highest known breeding densities of any bird of prey, other than of truly colonial species, is recorded of the black kite in New Delhi(2). Black kites are also very abundant in tropical Africa and in parts of Australia. In fact they occur throughout the warmer parts of the Old World, breeding as far north as the southern temperate zone, and throughout the tropics.

Quite how black kites behaved before man became numerous we cannot now say; but the several races were probably all birds of open woodlands rather than dense forest or open country, and all were either nomadic or migratory, as they are today. The nearly omnivorous black kite is both a predator and a scavenger. It is not a powerful predator, and cannot kill anything very large; but a combination of boldness and agility enables it to take prey such as young chickens or rats from human backyards. One has very little chance of rearing a brood of chicks on open range in Africa or India, particularly if they are white. Taking young chicks is, however, almost the only harm that kites do. Otherwise, they are extremely useful birds, cleaning up all sorts of edible scraps, feeding on locusts or flying termites where these may be available, or even on fatty fruits such as oil palm fruit, and regularly patrolling roads early in the morning, searching for the night's kills.

In Nairobi, black kites roost in numbers in the railway stores yard in the centre of the town; and each morning a group of them flies along the main Mombasa road soon after dawn, going about as far as the Kenya Meat Commission's factory at Athi River, 16 miles away. Here they remain much of the day, and no doubt, if they have not already eaten part of a road kill, they may get some scraps before winging gently back to Nairobi in the evening. So far as I can see, this sort of behaviour is typical of black kites in any tropical African city, including such large modern places as Johannesburg; while in a town such as Addis Ababa, almost entirely devoid of sanitation, the kites scavenge the smaller items from the streets by day and the hyenas the larger corpses by night.

In Europe, doubtless because of the high standards of sanitation in towns, black kites are relatively much less numerous than they are in Asia or Africa. This may not always have been so; probably in mediaeval times black kites were abundant scavengers in European cities, just as red kites scavenged in the streets of London. Where the two species occur together the black kite seems to be able to dominate the red kite for possession of the profitable if unattractive scavenger niche. It is smaller than the red kite, but bolder, more aggressive, and more piratical. A black kite will attack a much larger raptor which may be in possession of a scrap which it wants; and very often gets it. The red kite, by comparison, appears to be a rather shy bird of woodland, and is perhaps more dependent on natural prey and carrion which it can find in the open. However, in Europe, both species may be found breeding in the same wood, sometimes in quite large numbers(7).

In Europe the black kite is a summer migrant, which seems to be increasing and extending its range. It is tempting to ascribe this spread to the mounting death toll of birds and animals on roads, but I do not know of any really good evidence for this. Certainly black kites are on the wing very early in the morning, when few people are about; and they could probably find road kills and feed on them, or carry them away, before the motor traffic became really heavy – at or around office-opening time, just after breakfast.

Black kites are not only masters of soaring flight, almost as graceful as red kites; but are also extremely agile and manoeuvrable close to the ground, among trees, or even among festoons of telephone wire, which defeat many other large birds. They constantly pick up kills from roads; yet are so alert that very few are themselves killed by speeding cars, even in areas of high traffic density. They have adapted not only to dirty old mediaeval European or tropical man, but to modern technological man; and they are among the few birds of prey in the world that will certainly increase and spread along with the human population explosion. They are often despised and anathematised with unpleasant epithets; but their adaptability and success, when almost all other birds of prey that come in contact with man are in retreat or danger, is to be admired and extolled. They do not even seem to suffer from the effects of pesticides.

In Britain black kites have been seen more frequently in recent years. There are only 12 records within the last century or so, but of these seven have been seen since 1960. The most ever seen in one year was four in 1966, but at least one of these may have been seen more than once. Within the last ten years black kites have been recorded from such extremes in the British Isles as Shetland, Norfolk, and the Scilly Isles. Individuals were seen in all three of these localities in 1966, and it seems to me extremely unlikely that they were all the same bird. The greater frequency of observation in recent years is probably a compound result of the increased number of bird-watchers and the spread and increase of the black kite in Europe. Most of the British records are in spring, when the birds are on the move north to breeding grounds; and all the records identified by race refer to the nominate European race *Milvus migrans migrans*, as one would expect.

The increased occurrence of the black kite in Britain suggests that the day may come when it tries to breed here. It is to be hoped that any pair that tries to settle are not either shot or poisoned, but are allowed to go about their business unmolested. They could scarcely do any harm to any human interest, for nowadays poultry in Britain are not normally reared on free range, and young pheasants kept in wire pens would also be safe if they are confined until they are too big for the kite to kill. In any case, kites would find dead birds on roads so abundant that they would hardly need anything else, and could collect these between four and six on a summer morning, when few people are about and the road traffic is light.

It is in no way likely that either the Egyptian or the griffon vulture will ever breed in Britain. The **Egyptian vulture** is a rather scarce breeder in the Mediterranean basin, and is more abundant in the tropics, especially India, where it is a town scavenger and breeds on buildings as well as in rock clefts. There are only two records of the Egyptian vulture in Britain, and it has not been seen here within the last century, the last known record being in Essex in 1868. It barely deserves the title of a British bird at all.

The Egyptian vulture's main claim to fame in recent times is the discovery that it was a tool-user, picking up stones in its bill and throwing these rather incompetently to break ostrich eggs. It thus joins the very select company of man, two or three higher apes, the sea otter (which uses stones to break open molluscs held against its chest), a finch in the Galapagos islands, and perhaps a bower bird, which uses a 'paint brush' to decorate its bower. It is perhaps salutary to reflect that the despised Pharaoh's chicken, which scavenges *inter alia* human excrement, and is the only bird that regularly does, is of this exclusive tool-using club.

The Egyptian vulture is a solitary breeder, and subsists, where it does not scavenge on man's dejecta, on the scraps left by the larger scavenging vultures at kills, or by picking off pieces of meat from places where their larger bills cannot effectively work. The **griffon vulture** is one of these large scavenging vultures, strongly gregarious and colonial in its nesting habits. It is one of a group of five species of the genus *Gyps*, all of which breed mainly in rocky cliffs in tropical or sub-tropical lands, closely allied to two other species (formerly in the genus *Pseudogyps* but now included with *Gyps*), which are colonial breeders in trees. All these huge birds, with wingspans of seven to nine feet have long bare necks and feed on the soft flesh and entrails of large dead animals. They collect together at a carcase, thrust their long necks into any orifice or opening, and quickly clean it up, leaving only the bones which, in some areas, are then eaten by hyenas or other such mammalian scavengers.

The European griffon is still quite common in Spain, Greece, and north Africa. It has occurred twice in Britain, in 1843 and 1927, when two birds appeared in Derbyshire. Again, it barely merits recognition as a truly British bird, and there can be no likelihood that it ever bred here or will breed here. To breed, griffons depend on carrion over a long period of time but will travel a hundred miles per day to get it(4). Their incubation and fledging periods are very long and while, in the Highlands of Scotland anyway, they could certainly find enough carrion for most of the summer and also cliff nesting sites, they would probably be unable to breed because of their very lengthy breeding cycle.

All species of griffons thrive best in lands where primitive herdsmen maintain large herds of domestic stock in overgrazed or poor conditions, and where veterinary services are inadequate. Such conditions, typified by the highlands of Ethiopia or India (where most domestic stock, cattle especially, are left to die naturally and are not killed as they approach old age) provide a much more regular and reliable year-round food supply than is found in any tropical game park, where the griffons have to compete with powerful mammalian predators and scavengers, and a sickly or weak animal is usually killed and eaten by these and does not just lie there for the griffons. Primitive herding or shepherding conditions are still, to some extent, found in the mountains of Spain or Greece; but with progress in sanitation and disposal of carcases the griffon has retreated from France as a breeding bird, except in the Pyrenees. As mentioned, I do not believe it is only available food supply which limits the range of the griffon; but also probably the very long breeding cycle, and the climatic conditions. Griffons are normally inhabitants of warm or hot dry areas; and large vultures are always uncommon in tropical forests or woodlands in the Old World.

The **pallid harrier** is a very common migrant to Africa and India in winter, from its central European and Asian breeding range. It is evidently very closely allied to Montagu's harrier in all its habits, so much so that where they breed together female Montagu's have been known to solicit male pallid harriers for food(5, 6). The main breeding range of the pallid harrier lies to the east of Montagu's; it is probably more a bird of grass steppe than of heathlands. Rarely, it has bred in Germany, Czechoslovakia, and southern Sweden(6). The breeding in southern Sweden and Mecklenburg occurred in 1952 and one of the three records accepted by the B.O.U. List Committee was at Driffield, Yorkshire, in the autumn of that year(8). The other two were adult males in spring, at Fair Isle and in Dorset.

All the British records have been since 1931, and it may be that this harrier is making sporadic attempts to increase its range northwards and westwards, into that normally occupied by Montagu's harrier. However, it seems unlikely that this trend will continue, for the evidence from tropical Africa, which is the main wintering ground of the species, indicates that this harrier is on the decrease. Probably this is not due to anything that happens in Africa itself, but to a combination of increased cultivation of central European steppes for grain, and perhaps increased use of pesticides. It is possible that some of the pesticides might be picked up in parts of Africa, but in winter this harrier normally inhabits open plains where pesticides are not likely to be used much, if at all. Again, it seems extremely unlikely that it will ever become a British breeding bird, or that it ever was.

It is conceivable, on the other hand, that the **greater spotted eagle** may once have been a breeding bird in Britain, though there is no positive evidence of this. At present, this species is an inhabitant of large central European and West Asian forests, and breeds no nearer Britain than eastern Germany. It is a migrant, arriving in its breeding quarters in spring, and leaving in late summer for Africa, where it spends the winter mainly in Sudan and Eritrea – though recent records are conflicting on this point. The forests in which it breeds in Europe are mainly swampy or near rivers, where the eagle tends to hunt in open marshy country, often walking about on the ground. No such terrain now occurs in Britain; but it is possible that in the dim and distant past there may have been extensive swampy valleys, for instance those of the Thames and Test, in woodlands of southern England, where this eagle might have bred.

There are twelve records of the greater spotted eagle in Britain, involving 14 birds; but it has only twice been recorded this century and not for more than 50 years, the last occasion being in Hereford in November 1915. The numbers of both this species and its slightly smaller relative the lesser spotted eagle *Aquila pomarina* have been decreasing in Europe since the end of the Second World War. So much so, in fact, that recently some very interesting experiments have been carried out to see whether the breeding success of the lesser spotted eagle can be increased by inducing other raptors to rear the second-hatched chick, which would otherwise be killed in the nest by its elder sibling. In view of the general decrease in both species of spotted eagles in Central Europe it seems unlikely that its British status, that of a very occasional vagrant in this century, will change in any way. The spotted eagle too can hardly now be regarded as a British bird.

The **lesser kestrel** and the **red-footed falcon**, the two remaining vagrants, are most decidedly birds of a feather, which often migrate together in flocks and feed, in their African winter quarters, on much the same insect food. Their breeding range overlaps, but that of the lesser kestrel is more southerly, which probably explains why there are fewer recent British records of this species than of the red-footed falcon. The B.O.U. List Committee accepts about twelve records of lesser kestrels, mainly adult males; but only one since 1926. Most of the records are from the nineteenth century, and mainly from southern and eastern counties. They include, however, records from as far north as Aberdeen and from the Scilly Isles; and there is one Irish record, near Dublin in 1891.

Lesser kestrels are hard to distinguish from common kestrels in the field, so it is possible that they may have occurred more often than is indicated above and been overlooked or mistaken for ordinary kestrels. The best field distinction, in my experience, is the almost plain unbarred underwing of the male, which shows up very pale when the kestrel hovers. Females are harder to distinguish, but are also smaller and paler.

In its breeding habits the lesser kestrel is normally quite distinct from the common kestrel, for it is strongly colonial, breeding in old buildings and in natural rock cliffs; it is not known to breed in the old nests of other birds in trees, but a colony in a pollarded tree full of holes has been recorded. Although it is a common breeder in big buildings in cities, it has never been very thoroughly studied. Anyone with the opportunity to take a prolonged holiday in sunny Mediterranean climates in spring could substantially add to our knowledge of this engaging and beautiful little bird. I found a colony once, in Morocco, which would have been ideal for observation, for the nests were on overhung ledges on either side of a gorge, and could have been overlooked by anyone lying on top of the cliff.

The habit of lesser kestrels, of nesting and roosting in towns, sometimes leads to entertaining moments. Guy Mountfort recounts one such, at Cordoba, concerning my friend Roger Peterson. The rest of the party were spellbound in admiration of the frontage of the thousand-year-old cathedral, and Roger gazed upwards with them, apparently equally moved. However, he was actually watching the lesser kestrels breeding in the tower. I know what he felt, for I once was stuck in Rome, working for F.A.O. for a period. I could only get a walk in the evening after work in the streets round the Colosseum and Circo Massimo; and though I contemplated making a study of the territorial behaviour of the multitudinous forum cats I hoped not to have to stay there long enough to make this worth doing. One evening, after dark, I was walking past the Victor Emmanuel monument, a large ornate building with two stone horses on top. The Italian passers by, watching me gaze raptly upwards at the floodlit front, assumed that I was admiring the superb structure, and politely hushed their otherwise extremely loud voices as they passed in order not to break my intellectual reverie. Had they but known, I was watching the southward migrating lesser kestrels roosting on the right-hand horse, and wondering why they picked only the right-hand animal, when the left-hand one appeared equally suitable to me.

Red-footed falcons occur very much more commonly in Britain. The B.O.U. List Committee accepts more than 160 records, of which about 60 occurred from 1958–68. These pretty little falcons are now identified annually, often several in a few days. In their case there is little difficulty in distinguishing males at least from any other British falcon, for they are dark slate grey, with red thighs and legs; adult females and young are more difficult, but adult females have grey backs and tails barred blackish, and are almost unstreaked below, unlike the rufous females of either common or lesser kestrels.

Most of the records are in spring, and from southern and eastern England. No doubt this is because the northward spring migration of the western nominate race *F.v. vespertinus* of this falcon takes a more westerly swing than does the southward autumn migration when this species is, of course, actually more numerous, following the breeding season. Autumn migrants pass mainly east of Greece and Crete; but in spring this falcon is common at Malta, and apparently crosses the Mediterranean on a broad front(1,9). More are then seen in Spain and southern France, and some of these birds swing still further west and reach Britain. However, there are a few British autumn records too, and although the majority of the records are from southern and eastern England there are also records from Scotland and Wales, and even a few from Ireland; one of these was a bird seen in Galway in September 1966.

Time will tell whether the red-footed falcon is becoming a more frequent visitor to Britain, or whether the more numerous records in recent years are just due to the greatly increased number of critical field observers. If it is actually becoming more numerous, it is another species which might eventually colonise Britain as a breeding bird. Unlike the lesser kestrel, which breeds almost exclusively in rocks, the red-footed falcon uses the abandoned or empty nests of corvids, mainly rooks, but sometimes other species. Rookeries in Hungary are occupied in late April or May, when the rooks are rearing young, and the falcons apparently do not eject rooks from occupied nests but use empty ones, mainly in the top of the trees. They therefore could be nothing but welcome guests if they chose to stay and breed in Britain for they would not even harm the rooks.

Probably however, our cool wet climate would discourage them, for most of the European breeding range is in countries with a hot summer. In Hungary, frogs are an important food item at breeding colonies, in one study making up 75% by weight of all prey taken(3). In the parts of England where breeding by these falcons would be most likely – Hampshire and East Anglia – frogs have either largely disappeared or become very scarce, probably through the effects of agricultural pesticides, which frogs absorb directly through the skin as well as from their food(a). However, the red-footed falcon also feeds much on insects and on small mammals, so might be able to survive in Britain, at least in small colonies. Insects, too, are likely to be scarcer in Britain in summer than in the main haunts of breeding red-footed falcons.

It would be nice to think that of the eight present vagrant species the formerly resident sea eagle might be effectively reintroduced as a breeding bird; and that the black kite and the red-footed falcon might actually extend their breeding range to include Britain, for the first time known. We would then have 17 breeding species in Britain; and although some of these would inevitably be rare, even if given careful protection, our bird of prey fauna would be richer than it ever has been, so far as we know, within the last two thousand years. These are, however, only rather remote possibilities; and for the most part the vagrant third of our bird of prey fauna is likely to remain what it is now, an interesting and exciting but effectively unimportant segment of the whole complex of predators in Britain.

CHAPTER 21

CHANGES IN HABITAT AND STATUS

To quote my favourite author once again 'When two wise men cannot agree over the price of an onion who shall say what happened in the time of Yu'. Indeed, when systematists cannot agree whether the steppe buzzard is a good species or not it may seem a little pointless to conjecture what that bird's status may have been five or ten thousand years ago. Nevertheless, I find it intriguing, and I do not think it is wholly without relevance to some present-day problems, to speculate on what may have been the composition of the British bird of prey fauna before man became sufficiently numerous in Britain to make serious inroads on the habitat.

To do this it is not necessary to go so far back in time that 'it would be impious to doubt whatever happened then' but merely to about three thousand years ago when the climate of Britain was much the same as it is now (vile), but when the country was inhabited by a sparse population of primitive agriculturists and pastoralists, lacking effective tools, so that they could make little impression on the sea of deciduous forest in which they subsisted(8). Apart from the cold and wet, which would make burning the vegetation difficult, conditions then in Britain were perhaps not very dissimilar to those of, for instance, some of the central Amazonian jungles where forest and savanna at present mix with extensive swampy areas, and where a varied fauna of birds of prey exists unmolested alongside a small population of no doubt happy, culturally rich, and politically enlightened, but materially backward and decidedly homicidal Amerindian tribesmen. In those days Britain must have supported a natural unmolested population of birds of prey, probably composed of the same species existing today, but in very different numbers and proportions. How this healthy population has shrivelled to the persecuted remnant surviving today is surely of some interest.

The ice sheets of the last glacial period retreated from Britain 12,000–14,000 years ago. They extended as far south as the Severn estuary and before they retreated there were no doubt gyrfalcons and rough-legged buzzards hunting over Arctic tundra on what is now Dartmoor. In the succeeding 9–11,000 years boggy tundra gradually gave way to birch and pine forests and then to more luxurious deciduous timber species such as oak and beech. At one time forests extended to over 3000 feet (920 m.) A.S.L.(3), which would have meant that the whole of England and Wales, apart from the tops of a few hills in Snowdonia and the Lake District, and even all but very small areas of the Highlands of Scotland would have been covered with woodland, no doubt stunted by cold and wind, but still woodland in which, for instance goshawks but not golden eagles could exist.

This situation may be compared with the upper limit of tree growth today, which is about 1000–1500 feet (320–470 m.) in England and Wales and higher, 1700–1800 feet (510–550 m.) in Central Scotland(11), so that if man and his works were suddenly obliterated, leaving the vegetation to revert to normal, there would still be some large areas of open country above the limit of trees. In recent times the peregrine falcon has been confined to sea-cliffs in lowland districts and to crags in mountain areas; three thousand years ago its distribution may well have been similar, though it may have been scarcer than it has been in recent times in some

264

mountain districts that were then predominantly covered with forest among or over which the swift peregrine would find it difficult to catch prey. Perhaps this is one reason why the peregrine never has taken to breeding in trees in the open agricultural country of southern England, where its prey abounds and where it could perfectly well appropriate old crows' nests. British peregrines just did not evolve in that way.

The sheet of forest covering most of Britain would have been modified by two main natural influences, cold at high altitudes and waterlogging in lowlands and valleys. Here and there, also, poor soil may have made it almost impossible for forest to flourish, resulting in open patches of grassland or heath. These open patches would doubtless have been the areas most attractive to primitive pastoral people, and they would settle therein. As they took to agriculture, so they would hack into the forests, starting on the edges of the open patches where they lived. A very similar process can be seen taking place in parts of southern Ethiopia today. This thin population of pastoralists and small-scale agriculturists, however, would have made little overall impact on the vast extent of the forests, in which there were plenty of bears, lynx, wolves, and deer.

In those conditions it seems likely that the goshawk and the sparrowhawk were the commonest raptors in Britain; they alone would have been able to thrive in the heart of the deep forests. Since it seems probable that about 60% of the total area of Britain and Ireland, about 75,000 square miles (194,000 sq.km.), was covered with forest or woodland(3), it is likely that there were over 50,000 pairs of sparrowhawks and something like 7000–8000 pairs of goshawks in Britain. On the other hand, birds such as the kestrel and common buzzard, which prefer to hunt in open country, were almost certainly much less numerous than they are today. The kestrel, now our commonest raptor, numbering perhaps 65–80,000 pairs, may then only have numbered a few hundred pairs, for it would have been virtually excluded by forest from all but the far north of Scotland, in a cold wet climate where it is not common today and probably never has been. In vast swampy valleys such as those of the Thames and the Test in S. England, the fens of East Anglia, the Humber and the Somerset levels, marsh harriers would have abounded, feeding on waterfowl and frogs. Hobbies and honey buzzards, liking open patches among forest and warm climate, would have been a good deal more numerous than they are today, but probably not very much more widespread for climatic reasons. Merlins must have been decidedly rare and peregrines confined to cliffs near open country in which to hunt. Kites, so much associated with man, would not have been so numerous as they became later.

The Roman conquest of Britain was accompanied, like most colonial periods, by increased prosperity and more efficient agriculture. However, a map of Britain in Roman times shows that there were still vast tracts of forest over most of southern and central England while we suppose that the Romans had little effect on Scotland or Ireland. The main tracts of forest remained largely untouched, and were used for hunting and some charcoal burning. No doubt the kestrel, the buzzard, and the kite became more numerous, associating with improving but still very primitive agriculture, and feeding on the rodents that would undoubtedly abound under these conditions. However, there can have been no serious attempts to drain swamplands affecting the marsh harrier, which must then have been numbered by the thousand pairs.

In the fifth century AD the Saxons, who more or less exterminated or drove out the Celts into more inhospitable Welsh or Scottish fastnesses, cleared many valleys and extended agriculture(9). They ceased to cultivate the poor chalk soils which then reverted to downland pasture, but cultivated the lighter forested soils and left the heavy clays alone; the clays remained mainly forested for about another 1000 years. Similar ravages on natural forest country have recently been perpetrated by Anglo-Saxon people in North America, New Zealand and Australia; and, in a less efficient and industrious way, other people are doing the same thing. The end result of this process is a patchwork of small fields and weed fallows eating haphazardly into what was formerly forest. Any species of bird or mammal that requires the seclusion of *large* areas of *deep* forest is likely to disappear, but as a whole the resulting mosaic of different habitats makes for a much richer and more varied fauna. Such species as sparrowhawks and goshawks would still have found secluded woodland areas large enough to breed in and would have hunted also in open country, while buzzards, kites, and kestrels would have quickly colonised the farmlands and become abundant. Again, species such as the peregrine, golden eagle, sea eagle, honey buzzard, hobby, and marsh harrier would probably have been relatively little affected by these changes.

The Normans seem to have temporarily checked the trend towards a more open grassland agriculture. They adopted a scorched earth policy, systematically devastating certain areas to overawe the Saxons, but at the same time reserved certain large tracts of land, not necessarily all true forest, for hunting purposes. These included the New Forest which today owes its very existence and the unique population of birds of prey it supports to the selfish despotism of the Norman kings(9,10). Other such areas were Dartmoor, probably then mainly forested, and the Peak forest; perhaps a third of England was then still covered with such forest, and no doubt very large areas in Scotland and Ireland, which were then very thinly populated. The stoppage of forest clearing was only temporary, however, and by the twelfth century it had again accelerated. Increased tillage and shepherding led to more and more open ground and in the forests themselves cattle and swine were pastured. This certainly would lead to the elimination of forest regeneration, just as in the New Forest today the vegetation is very largely affected by the presence of large numbers of ponies, which browse on almost anything below a certain level(10).

Grassland and arable continued generally to increase, fluctuating in extent according to the price of corn or cloth. At one time, in the mid-fourteenth century there were four sheep per head of human beings, and about two acres of cultivation were needed to keep one Briton alive year round(8). Areas not actually cultivated reverted to fallow grazed by stock, and did not return to forest, so that the area opened up was several times that actually needed for subsistence. The primitive methods of agriculture, drawing upon stored fertility in the forest soils after new fellings, would continually deplete the remaining forest areas merely to keep the same number of people alive. To one who lives in Africa all this has a familiar ring; similar, equally wasteful, destructive processes are seen in progress in many tropical forest areas today, with a good deal less excuse, since our knowledge has improved since the dark ages.

The steady depletion accelerated through the demands of industry. Wood was the only fuel available for glassmaking or iron smelting, and though attempts were made to preserve coppice woodlands for these purposes they were inadequate. Large oak trees were left as standards above the coppice woodland, and the end effect was to create a more open tall woodland with a denser shrub layer beneath(3).

By 1685 oak had to be imported for shipbuilding and by 1700 only 16% of Britain was covered with forest.

In Scotland extensive forests persisted in the highland glens up to 1600, but thereafter they were very rapidly destroyed for iron smelting. The destruction lasted about three centuries and was almost total, accelerated by the introduction of large-scale sheep farming in the nineteenth century; sheep effectively prevent regeneration. By the early 1800s forest had reached its lowest ebb in Britain, covering only about 5% of the country(3). 90% of the forests had been destroyed in 4000 years of agricultural development accompanied by a steady increase of population. The human population of Britain increased from about two million in the fourteenth century to six million in 1700 and nine million in 1800, increasing thereafter to 27 million at the end of the nineteenth century and 50 million in the middle of the twentieth; it is still increasing, and Britain today is more densely populated overall than India(8). In 1700 Britain had a predominantly rural population exceeding 60 to the square mile, which would be counted as a fairly dense population in for instance, much of tropical Africa today, and which is certainly sufficient to have drastically affected all wild life, including birds of prey, through alteration of the habitat alone. However, in such conditions elsewhere in the world, dense populations of certain raptors can thrive, and no doubt this was also true of Britain(2).

The effect of all these changes would have been to favour those birds of prey such as buzzards, eagles, harriers, merlins, and kestrels that prefer open country; and further reduce those such as goshawks and sparrowhawks that need forest or woodland. As we know, sparrowhawks can manage quite well in small woods in mixed arable country; but if the total area of forest was reduced, by 1800, to 5% of the country, and most of that in small patches of coppice, it seems to be evident that the goshawk, probably still quite common and widespread two centuries or so before, would already have become scarce long before the real era of game preserving even started. The drainage of fenlands, valleys, and swamps must undoubtedly have been the main factor in the reduction of the marsh harrier, and the increase in human population would have led to increased abundance in the kite. Today, in tropical Africa, the black kite is an uncommon bird, mainly a passage migrant, in the uninhabited woodlands, but occurs in thousands associated with human beings; even a little village means that one suddenly sees a few pairs of kites(2). I see no reason why this should have been any different in Britain, where the red kite was certainly largely commensal with man.

Up to about 1800 the main effect of human change and development in Britain on birds of prey was thus connected with habitat changes. There was already some persecution during the latter part of the eighteenth century, but it probably was relatively mild. Although it is impossible even to guess what the population of most of the breeding species may have been it is certain that none had been reduced to their present-day precarious figures, except perhaps the goshawk, while such species as the kite, though perhaps reduced by improved sanitation and loss of woodland habitat, were probably still several hundred times as common as they are today. Reduction by persecution of certain of the species, such as golden eagles in England and Wales, had begun.

Since 1800 there has been a small increase in forest habitat. This was first brought about by private plantings, but these hardly kept pace with continuing depletion while after 1800 they were often associated with game preserving and were no sort of haven of refuge for birds of prey. The shortage of home grown timber in the

First World War led to the establishment of the Forestry Commission which, since I was young, has planted very large areas of quick growing conifers over much of upland Britain(3). Some of these forests are now very large, but are criticised on the ground that they are composed entirely of gloomy conifers, mostly Sitka spruce and Scots pine. To my mind the Forestry Commission has been rather unfairly criticised, for although it is true that the plantings are mainly of conifers they have undoubtedly enriched the habitat as a whole, and they certainly provide good refuge for the birds of prey and other predators. Hen and Montagu's harriers especially have benefited from forestry.

The planting policy of the Forestry Commission is largely dictated by economics, and those who anathematise them for planting nothing but Sitka spruce might well complain equally bitterly if they were required to pay a much higher price for forests designed eventually to be more beautiful but less profitable – for that's the choice. Foresters, who are not soulless men, would no doubt be glad of the opportunity to grow some really fine mature trees in open forest after thinning, rather than clear fell the whole crop at a certain age for pulpwood – which is what happens now. The public cost in subsidy is enormous anyhow, so perhaps there should be a review of policy, with more amenity and mature woodlands in mind. This too would benefit birds of prey; the present dark, closed forests are not ideal, though they are better than nothing, and give us a fair chance to re-establish certain species such as the goshawk in relative freedom from excessive persecution.

The destruction of forest and marshland habitat and its replacement by open cultivated country, which was the main environmental feature affecting British resident birds of prey up to 1800 would have depressed the woodland and marshland species, encouraged the open country species associated with agriculture and man, and left some others practically unaffected. If one cast up a balance sheet in 1800, it is likely that the mainly aquatic osprey and the sea eagle were largely unaffected by the changes, though ospreys would have lost some habitat on inland meres in fenlands, and sea eagles had already been to some extent deliberately reduced by human persecution. The red kite had probably reached its peak numbers about two centuries before, and had declined, but was still abundant. The honey buzzard must have suffered through loss of woodland habitat, though to what extent it is hard to guess since England must anyhow have been mainly marginal for this species. The hobby may, on the other hand, have been favoured by the increase in open country in formerly forested southern areas. Hen and Montagu's harriers, common buzzard, golden eagle, kestrel, merlin, and peregrine must have increased, some of them at least a hundredfold, since man started to exploit the forests, though the peregrine would probably have been less affected generally because of its overall dependence on cliff nesting sites. The only species seriously reduced by forest and fen destruction would have been the sparrowhawk, goshawk and marsh harrier; and of these the sparrowhawk could still find enough small woodlands to breed quite abundantly while it was not persecuted seriously, and even the marsh harrier may still have been present at least by the hundred pairs.

From now on, however, and at an accelerating pace as the nineteenth century progressed, persecution became the dominant decimating factor. It may be said that this is all 'old hat', and need not be repeated again here, since the climate of opinion in the nineteen-seventies is quite different. To some extent this is true; it is now apparently the general public wish that birds of prey should not be persecuted. Nevertheless, persecution remains the worst threat to many British birds of prey, and the attitude of mind prevalent in the nineteenth century is still very far from dead, while some nineteenth-century abominations such as commercial egg collecting and pole trapping have sharply worsened in the decade 1960–70. The new environmental factor of persistent agricultural pesticides, which has had a disastrous effect on certain species, has tended to obscure the continuing importance of deliberate human persecution of birds of prey.

Game preserving, and with it the destruction of birds of prey, was already well established in England by 1800 but did not become really important in the wilder parts of Scotland until much later. It was stimulated in Scotland by the return of their estates to highland owners who had been outlawed after 1745, since when many of them had been maintained in France by their tenants, who paid one rent to the Crown and one to the laird abroad. Queen Victoria in many cases pardoned these people, and in others, such as the Frasers, their lands were won back by feats of arms in the service of the Crown. The end result, so far as habitat management in Scotland was concerned, was the clearance of pastoral people from the highland glens by the proprietors so that they could become sheep walks, grouse moors, or deer forests. Those who wish to acquaint themselves with the details of this infamy, infinitely more disreputable than anything ever done to people in any African colony in the last half-century can read about it elsewhere(4).

So far as birds of prey were concerned, the clearances would probably have been beneficial to moorland species if they had not been accompanied by the active persecution of, first, eagles, buzzards, and kites because they were seen eating dead sheep, and later of any species of bird of prey because they might or did eat grouse, or other game-birds. This persecution was already rampant in England early in the nineteenth century, and the golden and sea eagles had already been almost or quite exterminated there. It was accelerated in Scotland in the second half of the nineteenth century by the development of railways and by the invention of the breech-loading shotgun.

A sportsman travelling north of Perth in 1850 still had to go by carriage, or by boat to his destination. Railways reached Perth in 1849, Inverness in 1861, and Thurso in 1874(6). Thus virtually the whole of the Scottish grouse moor country and deer forests were developed after the turn of the nineteenth century. The breech-loading shotgun was invented in 1853 and it quickly had a disastrous effect, as might be expected, on birds of prey, while it also made shooting more popular. In the days when one had to walk everywhere in all sorts of weather and use a heavy muzzle loader one had to be very keen, fit, and skilled to bring back two brace of birds in the evening. With a breech loader and improved transport systems many more people took up the sport of shooting, and the demand for sporting properties increased. Attempts were made even in ecologically unsuitable areas, such as Orkney, to develop grouse moors; but they did not always persist(b).

In Scotland as a whole the heavy stocking with sheep and deer led to a slow creeping decline in ecological potential which has had some effect on, for instance the peregrine falcon and perhaps also the merlin(5). Any such creeping ecological decline, however, had a negligible effect compared to the direct persecution of birds of prey with guns, poison, and traps, notably pole traps. Any species that became extinct was rendered extinct by persecution, not by ecological factors or habitat changes after 1850, by which time large new tracts of woodland were being planted by many proprietors on formerly denuded ground(3).

Egg and skin collectors are frequently blamed for the extinction or dramatic reduction of certain birds of prey and, in the late-nineteenth century, when collecting was the done thing, they certainly had a severe and sometimes crucial effect.

However, their effect was not fatal except when species had already been brought to the verge of extinction by habitat changes, gamekeepers, or both combined. Thus the osprey in Scotland, which otherwise might have made a slow come-back from a remnant, was given the *coup de grâce* by persistent egg and skin collectors. The last clutch of sea eagle eggs in Shetland were taken by a collector in 1910 and although by then the sea eagle may have been too far reduced to make a come-back it is certain that this collector deprived it of what slender chance it may have had(1).

Four species, the sea eagle, osprey, marsh harrier, and goshawk actually became extinct in part or the whole of Britain through persecution, not all at the same time. In the case of the goshawk and marsh harrier undoubtedly the primary factor in reduction of numbers was the destruction of habitat, which in the case of the goshawk reduced the potential population from perhaps 7000 pairs to a hundred or less, and in the marsh harrier from at least a thousand (probably several thousand) to under a hundred. Who can doubt, however, that, but for the *coup de grâce* given by the gamekeepers and skin and egg collectors, the goshawk and the marsh harrier would have survived in limited remnant habitats and that the goshawk would actually have increased in the later part of the nineteenth century as big woods matured and were kept relatively secluded in the interests of game preservation(7). The sea eagle and the osprey did not die out because of habitat destruction but were persecuted to a remnant by gamekeepers (for they, not shepherds or farmers, were the people with the arms and the poison to do it) and then given the final knockout by collectors.

By about 1910 the breeding species in most of Britain had thus been effectively reduced from fifteen to eleven, though the marsh harrier still lingered in Ireland to 1917 and a single, doomed pair of sea eagles bred in Skye to 1916. One other, the red kite, was in imminent danger of extinction, being reduced to less than ten pairs. The same no doubt applied to the honey buzzard, but in the case of the kite the population reduction between 1800 and 1900 must have been from perhaps ten thousand pairs to under ten, while that of the honey buzzard would not have been of that order, since this species was probably never abundant, for climatic reasons, even when woodland covered much of southern England.

Of the remaining nine species the hen and Montagu's harriers had undoubtedly been drastically reduced, the hen harrier from thousands of pairs breeding all over the open country of Scotland, north England, Wales and Ireland to a remnant breeding in Orkney, the outer Hebrides, and Ireland; but the Montagu's harrier proportionately much less, because its original range and numbers were probably much lower in the first instance. It might have been reduced by habitat destruction and other means from perhaps two hundred to twenty pairs, while the hen harrier had been reduced by ten times that extent.

At the same time the sparrowhawk was much reduced, but managed to survive country-wide by cunning. The buzzard had been pushed back into unkeepered areas of west England, Wales, and the West Highlands, and exterminated in Ireland. The golden eagle had finally been exterminated in England, Wales and Ireland but probably survived in sufficient numbers in highland deer forests to maintain a strong viable population which could rapidly increase given the chance. The kestrel and the merlin, widespread in suitable habitat, likewise remained fairly numerous, the merlin probably more abundant then than now. The peregrine falcon, persecuted in inland districts, would have survived on the sea-cliffs which were one of its favourite breeding habitats, probably in smaller numbers than in say 1930, but relatively little affected by either habitat changes or persecution. The hobby was probably persecuted severely, for its habitat corresponded largely with intensive game preserving areas; but again it was probably reduced from several hundred rather than several thousand to under a hundred pairs since its ecological requirements apparently do not really fit it for life in much of Britain.

Since 1910 the situation has improved, in some cases greatly. Three of the species which became extinct, the osprey, goshawk, and marsh harrier have re-established themselves, in all cases in dangerously small numbers; of these the marsh harrier, once up to twenty pairs, seems likely to become extinct again in the near future. The goshawk may only have been re-established through the agency of man, in the person of falconers, whose hawks escaped and bred; but it may also have come back naturally. The species that have returned are all wholly or partly migratory, the goshawk being, in our latitudes, the most sedentary of the three. The sea eagle has not returned, partly at least because it is sedentary in temperate latitudes. It will be the most difficult of any extinct species to re-establish because of its large home range, slow potential rate of reproduction, and the persecution it will meet with in areas suited to it.

The red kite has increased perhaps fivefold since 1900, and has doubled since 1950; it will make a come-back given the chance. The hen harrier is aggressively increasing, aided by forestry plantations and some reduction in persecution, though this is still the main threat to its further increase. Montagu's harrier and the hobby, for ecological reasons, have not fluctuated so much in this century. The sparrow-hawk, buzzard, golden eagle, kestrel, and peregrine have probably all increased since 1910, the buzzard to a spectacular extent; it is only held back by persecution from further increase. The status of the merlin is and has been obscure, but it is certainly reduced as compared to the twenties and thirties of this century, for reasons unknown. On balance, therefore, the situation has improved, often greatly in particular species; but the threats to survival continue to exist, and certain new ones have appeared in recent times.

The most important new threat is the prevalence in the environment of persistent organochlorine insecticides, DDT, dieldrin, and others. The importance of this threat is that it strikes at certain species even if, in other respects, they receive effective protection. The species most affected are bird-eating hawks and falcons, the peregrine and probably the merlin, the sparrowhawk and goshawk, and probably the marsh harrier. The golden eagle, the red kite and the buzzard were also adversely affected, for a few years, when dieldrin was used for dipping sheep. The kestrel has been reduced in cereal growing districts, though the effect of pesticides may well be aggravated in this species by food shortage caused by intensive methods of agriculture, and shortage of nesting sites. Certain other species, such as the buzzard and the hen harrier, which feed mainly on mammals, or in areas little affected by pesticides, have been relatively unaffected.

Pesticides and their effects are discussed more fully in a later chapter. Here all that I need say is that no species has as yet been rendered extinct by pesticides, and that the acute threat posed to certain species by their use has shown some sign of receding since voluntary methods of control have been brought into operation. If any species is actually threatened with extinction in Britain through pesticides it may well be the very scarce marsh harrier rather than the sparrowhawk or peregrine, which have received most of the publicity in this connection. That does not alter the fact that pesticides have reduced the otherwise flourishing populations of these two species by 40–60% at various times in the last two decades.

Persecution of one sort and another continues, often virtually unabated. Persecution by gamekeepers on sporting estates has received a new fillip in the last decade because of the high demand for shooting and the high rents paid. It has never, in fact, been effectively reduced by any other than economic reasons, or by wars. Forbearance hardly comes into it, and it can be shown that the 1954 Protection of Birds Act has had practically no effect. Other forms of persecution are still, in my opinion, secondary to that meted out by gamekeepers.

Peregrines are not only persecuted by gamekeepers but by pigeon fanciers too, and their eggs and young are taken sometimes by egg collectors and falconers. Egg collectors still threaten the really rare species such as the osprey, honey buzzard and kite; and male marsh harriers may recently have been shot for their skins(a). On other species, such as buzzards or golden eagles collectors have a much less severe deleterious effect than do gamekeepers, who are the main enemy of golden eagles, law or not. In the last decade a new threat, sheer numbers of bird-watchers, twitchers, bird photographers, and simple walkers and other people out to enjoy the open air, have without doubt adversely affected the status of certain species. They may be the main reason why the marsh harrier does not recolonise certain suitable habitats in Norfolk and Suffolk, and they probably cause the annual loss of about a sixth of all the golden eagle eyries in Scotland.

All these factors make it harder for the remnant of a once flourishing population of British birds of prey to recover to a healthy state of numbers. For two very rare species, the marsh harrier and the honey buzzard, lack of suitable breeding habitat is crucial, even if protection is completely efficient, and even if any pesticide threat is removed. Neither will ever again be common in Britain as long as the human population and its agriculture remains at the present level. Likewise, Montagu's harrier and the hobby, breeding in reduced southern habitats, are unlikely ever again to be numerous, even if they achieve fifty or a hundred pairs. Of the other presently rare or extinct species, the red kite and the osprey can recover to healthy population levels if left alone; and if it is possible to re-establish the sea eagle it too could thrive in moderate numbers. There is now much more suitable habitat for the goshawk than in 1800, though undoubtedly this habitat, in the new forestry plantations, is not ideal under present methods of management aimed at pulpwood rather than mature timber with a good population of large woodland birds. All the other species, with more than 100 pairs are not so acutely threatened, though among them the merlin, apparently declining for reasons unknown, perhaps merits the most urgent attention.

Whether the position of British birds of prey will again improve or worsen depends on public opinion backed by adequate legal provisions realistically enforced. At present public opinion seems in general in favour of protection for birds of prey; but the sheer numbers and mobility of the public, including the actively interested ornithological public are one of the main threats to certain species. Forbearance will have to be shown if this threat is not to increase in future; the alternative is the unpopular one of further restricting access to breeding areas, which is anyway not very easy to do. The legal provisions, as discussed later, exist in theory, but are flouted regularly and with impunity by the worst offenders, gamekeepers and their employers; and when cases are successfully brought the penalties inflicted are often derisory(c). Vested interests would, without doubt, increase the levels of pollution in the environment by the sale of potent poisons to a gullible public if not actively dissuaded from doing so.

The outlook for British birds of prey, if fractionally better than it was when I was a boy, is still rather bleak, and is certainly worse in 1972 than in 1952 or 1962;

it has, indeed, sharply worsened in the last decade. What seems to be needed is a determined attempt to improve the status of some very rare species such as osprey, goshawk, and kite, whose status can be improved without actually having to recreate habitats now gone, such as extensive reedbeds for marsh harriers. This needs to be coupled with a determination to prevent abuses of the existing legal provisions in the case of the commoner species, if necessary coupled with stronger legal provisions and a real will on the part of magistrates to penalise the main offenders. If these steps were taken several species would come back out into the open from the dark remnant wood, where they have skulked in fear for a century, and more, and would once again flourish to give general pleasure.

CHAPTER 22

FOOD HABITS AND THE EFFECTS OF
PREDATION ON PREY

CONSIDERING that what they eat and how much of it is the main bone of contention affecting the existence of most birds of prey in Britain it is both surprising and regrettable that their food requirements and preferences have not been as well documented as they might be. In only a few species do we have anything like the detail available for the same species in Europe. The few species well studied from this viewpoint have generally, like the peregrine and the red kite, been the subject of special surveys(10,18). However, even in some species which have been thus surveyed, such as the buzzard, little of value has been published on their food preferences. The results from the country-wide buzzard survey were too scrappy to be worth publishing. For several species that might be of economic importance, or are the subject of frequent complaint, a good deal is known on a qualitative basis, but little that can be quantified. The hen harrier, an unpopular species, can be said to eat voles and moorland birds; but for a good quantitative assessment of how many of each we must go to Norway(14). In short, for several British species, we have a good idea what they eat, but could not say precisely how much of each type of food, certainly not on a country-wide basis.

Undoubtedly, far more is actually known than has been recorded. Large numbers of food records must be available in field notebooks all over Britain. Bird-watchers often do not trouble to publish such facts, because they think them trivial, unless they see something unusual, such as a buzzard killing a woodpigeon in flight or a kestrel eating slugs. If one were to assess the food habits of any species on the basis of these unusual records it would be misleading, and for that reason I have not attempted to extract them from the literature except for incidental interest. By laborious search through journals one can locate a good many scattered food records; but again, they are often only qualitative, not quantitative. One often reads, for instance 'the main food brought to the nest was voles and young rabbits' giving no exact idea of how many of each. To summarise such vague records might also be misleading, and it is also a task which would have taken much more time than I could spare.

Again, there are for instance thousands of records of osprey kills in R.S.P.B. field record books at Loch Garten, but never adequately summarised and published, though I hope this may shortly be done. What is now needed is for the British Trust for Ornithology, R.S.P.B., Nature Conservancy, or other bodies who are interested in setting out the detailed facts on this subject, first to extract what is available in the literature or other sources, and then to organise a country-wide co-operative inquiry among interested ornithologists to fill the gaps. The ten or a dozen people who are really interested in the golden eagle could, for instance, dig out hundreds of actual prey items from their notes; and if a hundred different people sent in only half a dozen records of kestrel prey per year for two years, that would provide a sample of 1200 prey items, adequate for quantitative analysis. One cannot have too many records; 100 is inadequate: 3–500 will do; 1000 is adequate; 10,000 unarguable.

One might ask why it is necessary to go to these lengths if, for instance, it is generally accepted that a buzzard eats voles and rabbits. I would again stress that what these birds eat is the main cause of opposition to their existence. Opposition to birds of prey is entrenched, powerful, well-organised, and rich, by comparison with conservation bodies: it is often also bigoted to a degree. There may be little hope anyhow of convincing such people that a bird of prey is relatively harmless to their interest; the peregrine survey has not convinced all pigeon racers. But 10,000 prey records from all over the country, set out in detail, is a far better argument than any amount of general statement. It is at least a body of evidence carefully gathered, which is much more likely to convince a man of law than is a general opinion.

There are, fortunately, many thousands of prey records gathered in various parts of Europe for the same species that occur in Britain. I have summarised a great many of these in Appendix Table 1. When these continental records come from areas ecologically similar to Britain they can be taken as a very good indication of what any of the species will eat in Britain too; and in a few cases it is possible to document this fact with comparable British data. Where this can be done the correlation is good; our raptors do generally eat the same food in Britain as they do in Norway or Holland. However, even with the bulk of European evidence available there will be some in Britain who will say that without comparable British data the case is not proven. In Germany a species may eat voles; but in Britain it lives exclusively on young pheasants!

We first need, therefore, to establish in detail what any British bird of prey eats, and this can be done in three ways. The first but least-used method is the direct observation of kills, or of feeding on carrion. As explained in the texts of several species, this is difficult because one rather seldom sees a bird of prey kill, and if one does it is often impossible to determine what it has killed. Also one could say with certainty that a golden eagle killed a hare or a white-feathered ptarmigan at long range, but a kestrel dropping into a meadow of long grass and gulping something small is a different matter. However, I feel certain that if all the records of this sort could be extracted from bird watchers all over the country they would amount to a considerable total, which would be especially valuable because of its relative exactitude, and the fact that such observations would cover both winter and summer.

The most common method of estimating food preferences in detail is to record what is found in or near nests, either from the bodies of animals lying there or brought by the parent, or by making collections of bones, castings, and other remains such as feathers at plucking posts for later analysis. This again has the advantage of being a direct method of estimating, and is the best at present available. However, it suffers from several disadvantages. The first is that it covers only or mainly the breeding season, which is only two to four months of the year; what the bird concerned eats outside the breeding season is not revealed. We simply assume that it eats the same, but this may not be the case at all. A golden eagle, for instance, may catch rabbits for its young, but itself subsist largely on meat from a deer or sheep carcases; and a male sparrowhawk, feeding his mate and young, may take quite a different range of prey to a female in winter.

A second disadvantage is that when a collection of bones from nests is examined the bones of the larger animals which cannot be swallowed or broken up tend to appear in greater proportion than is justified by the actual numbers of such species killed. Small animals and their bones are broken up and swallowed altogether; large bones are left lying in the nest. A golden eagle may only have picked up a couple of lambs dead on the hillside; but the bones of those lambs remain prominently visible on the nest, bleached white and staring accusingly when the small bones of many young rabbits may entirely disappear. Records of prey found at the nests, or seen to be brought by the parents are therefore more directly valuable than records of analysis of remains after the breeding season is over; these must be interpreted with some insight, making due allowance for what may have disappeared(9).

The analysis of castings is a well-known method of learning what a bird of prey eats. These are, of course, the indigestible remains of bones, fur, feathers, scales, etc. that are cast up in pellets not only by hawks and owls but also, for instance, by gulls and herons. The analysis of castings is particularly valuable in that it gives a good idea of what birds of prey eat outside the breeding season and away from the nest(11,13,20). They can be collected beneath or on nests, under roost perches in winter, or where an adult bird rests or roosts while the young are in the nest. Castings may indicate that the diet of adults is different to that of the young. For instance in 1967 I found that young Sutherland eagles were being fed mainly on large birds, but the few castings I found of adults indicated that they were subsisting largely on deer and sheep carrion(4).

The main difficulty in analysis of castings is that of different degrees of digestion in different kinds of prey. The bones of fish and frogs are much more easily and completely digested than those of birds or mammals. The skulls and incisor teeth of rodents usually appear whole in buzzard castings; but it has been reckoned that to get a true idea of the number of frogs eaten by a buzzard any definite frog remains in castings should be multiplied by at least four(9). A misleading idea of the prey of sea eagles would be derived from castings. The obvious remains in these would be the beaks and feathers of puffins, eiders, etc., mixed with slime and a few fish scales, which might have come from several otherwise completely digested fish, but which cannot be quantitatively analysed(2). Likewise in a kestrel or buzzard casting there are often many insect remains, too small and broken up to determine how many insects are represented. A kestrel may have eaten many earthworms and one rat; but only the remains of the rat will appear in the casting, with some earth which we assume comes from the worms(10).

Taking all these disadvantages into account, a careful analysis of the prey of any species usually reveals that it feeds on a large variety of animals, mammals, birds, reptiles, amphibians, fish, or invertebrates, sometimes all of these, but usually with a marked preference for one class or another. In such an analysis the prey most often taken is not necessarily the most important for survival. In the sparrowhawk, for instance, the house sparrow is by far the commonest prey taken in Holland and Germany, while in Dumfriesshire the chaffinch is the most common prey item. However, 205 chaffinches weigh far less than do 73 woodpigeons, so that by weight the woodpigeon is actually the more important item of prey in Dumfriesshire. Kestrels eat many insects; but hundreds of insects are needed to provide as much sustenance as one vole.

Thus, to get a true picture of the food habits the prey must not only be analysed by number but also by weight. This is not always easy because the weights of many species of birds or animals may not be recorded. They are, for instance, very seldom quoted in standard bird reference books. The weights of animals eaten also varies with their age, and this is far from easy to estimate from the remains found, or even from prey brought to the nest by the parents. In the case of the osprey records at Loch Garten a fairly accurate idea of the species of fish brought, and a less accurate estimate of their length, and from that their weight, can be obtained by careful observation. Obviously, at the best there is a large margin of error (Text Table 2, p. 60). In other species, where the prey brought may be much more varied, this error becomes greater. However, with care it is possible to arrive at reasonably accurate estimates of the weight of each type of prey, and consequently its relative importance in the diet of the raptor concerned. Estimates, carefully made and supported by data on methods, are always better than mere guesses.

Adequate British data, either by number or by weight (which can always be calculated if the number is recorded) on the diet of the British breeding birds of prey is available in published form for only two species, the peregrine and the golden eagle. For the osprey, kite, and sparrowhawk British data is available but is not yet published; I have been able, through the kindness of the researchers concerned, to include here the kite and sparrowhawk data, and some of the osprey results. Fair British data is available for the kestrel and the buzzard, though in view of the abundance, wide distribution, and versatility as hunters of these species it is hardly adequate to base an analysis of their British diet on even a large sample from one area. For the honey buzzard, kite, sea eagle, hen harrier, goshawk, sparrowhawk and buzzard good or fair data is available from continental sources, in areas ecologically similar to British conditions. For the marsh and Montagu's harrier, merlin and hobby, inadequate published quantitative data is available, although in all cases the composition of the diet is well known in qualitative terms. About some of these, such as the hobby, there is little argument; but on the other hand the merlin is still accused of doing damage on grouse moors and continues to be illegally persecuted on that account. This general assessment underlines how much more work needs to be done on this subject in Britain; we have really good food data for less than a third of the British breeding species.

A general summing up of the food preferences of the British breeding or formerly resident species, based on qualitative methods but sometimes supported by quantitative material either from Britain or Europe or both reveals the following. Seven species, the kite, marsh harrier, hen harrier, Montagu's harrier, buzzard, golden eagle, and kestrel are primarily dependent on live or dead mammals, the latter as carrion. Of these the kite, marsh, hen, and Montagu's harriers, buzzard and golden eagle also eat many birds, and in some areas may take more birds than mammals. Birds are the primary diet of the goshawk, sparrowhawk, merlin, and peregrine falcon. The marsh harrier is probably the only British species to which amphibia may be really important, though frogs are also regularly eaten by buzzards.

No British species feeds exclusively on reptiles, though in the tropics there are groups of eagles and hawks that feed on hardly anything else(5). However, the harriers, buzzard, kestrel, and golden eagle all eat some reptiles; and in the deserts of north Africa the golden eagle makes a staple of thorny-tailed *Uromastix* lizards(5). This indicates that it is scarcity of reptiles in a cold wet climate and not low palatability which results in so few reptiles appearing in British prey lists.

Fish are the staple of the osprey and the sea eagle; but in the breeding season especially the latter also takes many birds, and some mammals. One species, the honey buzzard, is almost exclusively insectivorous; and the hobby is also mainly insectivorous outside the breeding season but takes many birds to feed its young. Several other species, notably buzzards and kestrels, feed heavily on insects or other invertebrates, such as slugs or earthworms when these are very abundant and easily caught; and when on migration in the tropics such species may be more insectivorous than they are in Britain.

Table 15 Food Preferences of British Breeding Species

Species	Preferred food	Frequently taken food	Occasional food
Osprey	Fish (99%)		Mammals, birds
Honey buzzard	Insects (wasp larvae)		Reptiles, birds
Red kite	Mammals to 250 gr.; carrion	Birds, esp. young corvids	Reptiles, insects, amphibia, fish
Sea eagle	Fish	Birds (water or sea); mammals to 5 kg.; carrion	Small mammals, reptiles, amphibia
Marsh harrier	Mammals to 200 gr.	Birds, mainly young; amphibia	Insects, birds' eggs etc.
Hen harrier	Mammals to 200 gr.	Birds, esp. moorland spp.	Insects, amphibia, reptiles
Montagu's harrier	Mammals to 100 gr.	Birds, esp. small spp.; reptiles	Insects, amphibia, birds' eggs
Goshawk	Birds to 1200 gr. (85–90%)	Mammals to 1500 gr. (10–15%)	Reptiles
Sparrowhawk	Birds to 500 gr. (98%)	Mammals to 100 gr. (2%)	Reptiles, amphibia
Buzzard	Mammals to 500 gr.	Birds to 600 gr; amphibia, reptiles, insects, carrion	Earthworms (sometimes in quantity)
Golden eagle	Mammals to 4 kg.	Birds to 1200 gr; carrion	Reptiles, amphibia
Kestrel	Mammals to 100 gr.	Birds, usually small or young; insects	Reptiles, amphibia, earthworms, slugs
Merlin	Birds to 100 gr.	Insects	
Hobby	Insects	Birds to 100 gr., esp. when breeding	Mammals, occasionally taken by piracy
Peregrine	Birds to 600 gr. (99%)		Small mammals to 100 gr.

For other data see Appendix Table I.

On this general basis alone we can class a good many of the British breeding species as harmless or neutral to man's interests, and a few as actively beneficial in that their favoured prey is certain mammals, which can be agricultural pests, or insects that can be a nuisance. The actively beneficial species are the honey buzzard feeding on wasps, and the buzzard and kestrel feeding mainly on pest mammals. The neutral species, which can also lay claim to being in some degree beneficial, include the kite, all three harriers (though in some areas the hen harrier is open to attack because it eats game-birds), merlin, and hobby. The remaining species, the osprey, sea eagle, goshawk, sparrowhawk, golden eagle, and peregrine either do some damage to man's interests or could do so. Two, the osprey and goshawk, are at present so rare in Britain that any damage they do should be ignored, though it may anger individuals locally; and a third, the sea eagle, is still only a nebulous hope for the future. The case of the sparrowhawk, golden eagle, and peregrine needs, and has received, more critical attention; and while every sensible observer will admit they do some damage to certain interests it may safely be said that the claims of damage done are in all three cases exaggerated. One could say that these birds are neutral except in certain areas where they may need watching. In this category one could also put the hen harrier, which is now sufficiently common and widespread to rise out of the extremely rare class.

A more critical and accurate assessment of the effect of any species of bird of prey on the prey animals in its environment is necessary if we are to arrive at a better idea of the good or harm that can be done by any species. To do this, a number of factors must be taken into account, such as: (i) The size and weight of the bird of prey concerned; this controls its appetite. (ii) The population of the species in any given area; basically this means that the average size of home range or territory of a number of pairs or individuals must be established. (iii) The period of the year in which the raptor is present – year round or, in migrant species, summer or winter only. (iv) The population of preferred prey animals in the range of the raptor concerned. (v) The habits of the prey animals concerned at different levels of population; these can affect their vulnerability to attack by a predator(8, 21).

To obtain a full picture of the effect of any bird of prey on its food animals is thus a complicated and protracted process, requiring detailed research, preferably by scientists of more than one discipline, over a period of consecutive years. All serious students of birds of prey will admit that it has seldom been successfully attempted. and that all published studies are open to criticism. However, they would also claim that the few detailed studies available from Britain or elsewhere give a far truer picture of the state of affairs than any general opinion or accusation, from whatever source.

Despite occasional statements to the contrary, birds of prey, like other predators, do not normally kill unless they are hungry(18). Trained falcons or eagles flown by falconers have to be carefully worked up if they are to give their best performance; a trained golden eagle must be starved till it is really hungry before it will, for instance, attack foxes. If trained falcons kill out of sight and cannot be recovered before they have been fed they will often not respond to the falconer's call, and may be lost. They've eaten, and that's that, until they are hungry again. In very unusual circumstances, such as, for instance, when a raptor or other predator is in a confined space with a superabundance of its prey it may kill more than it can immediately use. For instance, a leopard inside a chicken coop or goat pen may kill a hundred chickens or ten goats and not eat any; and American kestrels have been known to kill bat after bat when thousands are rushing together out of roost caves(5). Such situations are, however, most unusual in nature, and even the killing of a surplus of food sufficient for a few days is rather unusual.

Sometimes one finds that a large apparent surplus of food is provided at the nest, particularly in the early fledging period. When the chicks hatch any male bird of prey increases his killing rate if he can; and one may then find half a dozen grouse on a golden eagle's eyrie, or a superabundance of small birds on a sparrow-hawk's nest. These kills are, however, not wasted; they are fed to the young or are eaten by the parents in due course. Among raptors in the tropics such surplus supplies are unusual, perhaps because they rapidly putrefy, or because prey is normally easier to catch daily, in stable weather conditions. In temperate or cold climates kills do not rot quickly; we like to hang a grouse for a week or so ourselves. The parents eventually eat any surplus themselves, sometimes carrying the kills away. Their own appetites are thus satisfied, so that they do not have to kill more prey. Storage of surplus of this sort may, in fact, be a biological necessity in cold wet climates such as that of Britain, where the young still require a continuous food supply, though hunting on a few fine days may be easy but very difficult on days of storm. Not enough is known about this; but it is reasonable to suppose that prey is more easily caught in clear weather than in rain and wind, which makes the prey lie low and impairs the raptors' flying efficiency.

With these small reservations, the food taken by any raptor depends on its appetite. The bigger the raptor the lower the proportion of its weight that it must eat daily; this is a general rule applying to all animals, since body weight increases as the cube and body area as the square of any measurement. Thus, a small, highly active sparrowhawk probably consumes 25% of its bodyweight per day, while a buzzard requires 8–12%, and a golden eagle only about 6–7%(8). There is now sufficient data available from careful controlled studies of captive birds to enable us to set this out graphically. I have done this in Fig. 6, while Text Tables 16 and

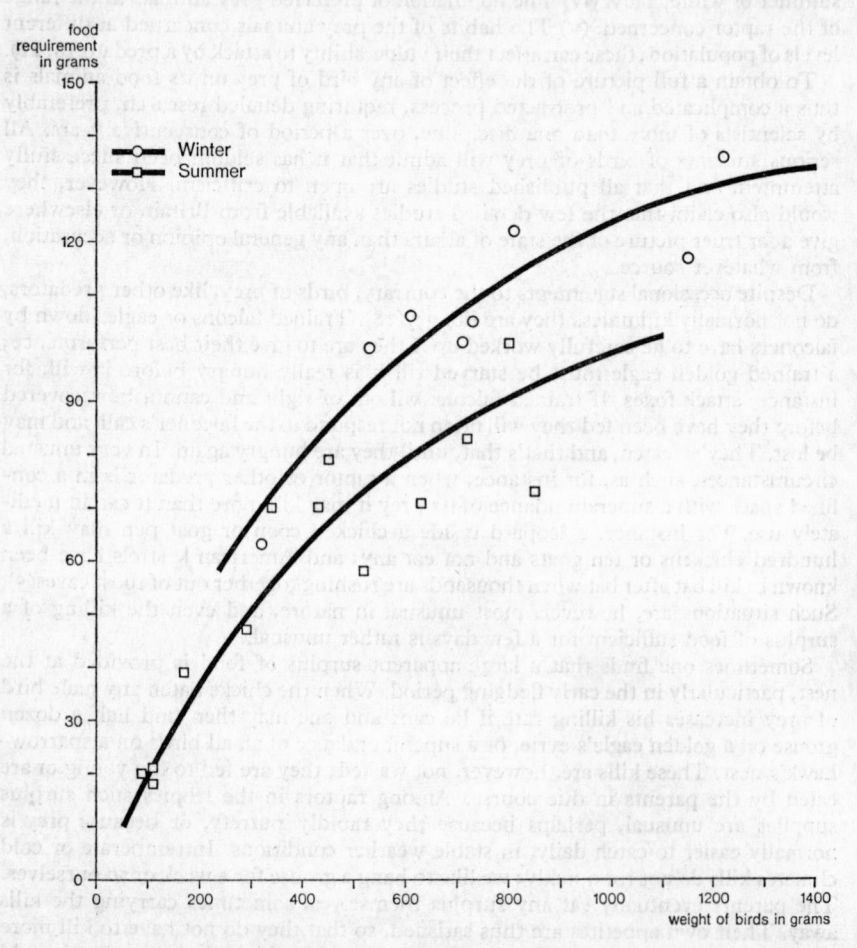

FIG. 6. The relationship between food requirement and body weight in birds of prey. (Data from both British and American species, winter and summer.)

280

Table 16 Actual Measured Food Consumption (grams)

SPECIES		WINTER			SUMMER		
		Body weight	Food eaten	% Body weight	Body weight	Food eaten	% Body weight
*Aquila chrysaetos	♂	3705	253	6·8	3705	231	6·2
(2)	♂	3740⎱	206·5	4·5	3740⎱	206·5	4·5
	♀	5220⎰			5220⎰		
Buteo jamaicensis	♀	1218	136	11·2	♂ 855	73	8·6
	♂	1147	117	10·2			
Buteo lineatus					♀ 636	71	11·2
					♂ 519	58	11·2
*Falco peregrinus	♂	727	105	14·4	♂ 721	83	11·5
	♂	716	101	14·1			
	♂	607	106	16·9			
Falco mexicanus	♀	811	122	15·0	♀ 801	103	12·9
Falco sparverius					♀ 112	21	18·4
					♀ 107	18	16·9
					♂ 91	20	22·3
*Circus cyaneus (3)	♀	526	100	19·0	♂ 343	70	12·1
Accipiter cooperi	♂	319	63	19·7	♂ 288	47	16·2
					♀ 453	79	17·3
					♀ 437	70	16·0
Accipiter striatus					♀ 167	39	23·3

	Mean % body weight eaten	
Buteo spp.	10·6	10·33
Large falcons	15·1	12·2
Small falcons		19·9
Accipiters	19·7	18·2
Hen harrier	19·0	12·1

NOTES (1) * denotes British species.
(2) Data from Fevold, H. R. and Craighead, J. J., 1958. Auk 75 312–317, and D. Wood, London Zoo, in litt.
(3) Variation between winter and summer in single examples of different sexes is probably inaccurate.

17 give the bodyweight and estimated or actual food requirements of all the British breeding raptor species.

The largest present resident raptor, the golden eagle, in which males are more than 26 times the weight of the smallest, the male sparrowhawk, eats only about ten times the daily ration of a sparrowhawk. In other words, an equivalent weight of sparrowhawks needs two and a half times as much food as of golden eagles. Moreover, a golden eagle may kill a large animal, gorge itself, and then not feed again for days, or take a snack off the remains of the kill. A sparrowhawk must feed more often. Golden eagles can starve for weeks if need be; and even small active sparrowhawks or merlins must be able to survive for some days without food in hard times. If they could not they would soon die of starvation in winter, when many inexperienced young do die.

Appetite is increased on average 10–15% by cold and exercise; decreased by warm weather and idleness(8). A wild raptor may be expected to eat rather more than a captive bird kept continuously in a cage, but there is little reason to suppose that it eats much more than a trained falcon which is regularly and vigorously exercised. A man in hospital eats only a little less than he does when active outdoors. The measured food demand of such trained birds has been used to estimate the wild raptors' requirements; and all evidence indicates that this is the best available method. A wild bird might eat 10% more than a trained bird; but not twice as much.

The basic requirement of the food eaten is also increased to a varying degree by the amount wasted, that is, what is not actually digested or which cannot be swallowed, such as some of the larger bones, feathers, fur, scales or stomach and gut contents. The amount of this waste factor varies according to the type of prey taken. In a simple case, such as that of a buzzard subsisting entirely on voles, these would be swallowed whole, and all that would be cast up and wasted would be what the buzzard cannot digest, the fur, the incisor teeth, and often the hard skull and some other bones, perhaps 10% by weight. If the same buzzard cannot catch voles, but can find abundant earthworms or frogs, the proportion digested is greater and the amount wasted less, perhaps 5% by weight. If, on the other hand, this buzzard is catching half-grown young rabbits in June, then it will waste more of each kill. For a start it will degut and probably dismember the body, which may be too heavy to carry entire; the stomach, a tight-packed bag of vegetable matter, is normally rejected as uneatable. The buzzard might carry away the hindquarters after making a good meal itself as it tears the prey apart, and might only return for the forequarters later, if another scavenger does not eat them first. When it actually finishes the rabbit, it will leave the larger limb bones and the skull, and though it will eat the skin the fur will later be cast up as a pellet, with some of the smaller bones which have been swallowed but not digested. In such a case the waste might amount to 25%.

Similarly, a golden eagle feeding on carrion in winter wastes a little fur or nothing; feeding on grouse and hares in summer it would waste 10-20%. An osprey, habitually feeding on smallish fish, casts up only the scales, and consumes and digests all but the larger bones of its biggest catches; in this case the waste would certainly be less than 10%. Sea eagles feeding on fish digest all but the scales; but if, as is usual in the breeding season, they feed more on water birds and mammals, they cast up beaks, bones and feathers. In most cases it is safe to add 10-20% of the amount eaten to estimate the amount of food a bird of prey must kill or find dead daily to remain in good health. In the sparrowhawk, for instance, the average daily requirement is about 53 grams; but it has been reckoned that sparrowhawks must kill about 82 grams of prey daily to obtain this need, a waste of over 50%. This figure may be actually too high, but is indicative.

In this way we can estimate quite accurately the total weight of prey required by a raptor daily, monthly or yearly. From this we can also calculate how much a pair and their brood will need. This again varies from place to place and season to season, according to breeding success. Reverting to the buzzard, which is the best-known British case, an average pair need 101 kg (223 lb) of food per year(9). Each chick they rear to independence needs another 19 kg (42 lb) before it leaves the parental territory in autumn. To these figures must be added say 15% for waste, so that a territory rearing one chick to independence must produce about 140 kg (311 lb) of food per year. On Dartmoor just after myxomatosis, when the buzzard pairs were rearing less than half a chick per annum, the requirement would fall to about 120 kg (267 lb); and on Speyside at present, where they rear about two young per year, it rises to 180 kg (400 lb). One can adjust such figures according to the

Table 17   Estimated Daily Food Requirements

Based mainly on data in Craighead, J. and F. 1956. Ch. 8(6)

SPECIES		Body weight (gr.)	% body weight (minimum)	Eaten (minimum)	+ for cold/exercise (total)	Waste %	Total (maximum)	Approx. mean maximum killed
Osprey	♂	1400	10	140	15 (155)	10	170 }	180
	♀	1570	10	157	16 (173)	10	190 }	
Honey buzzard	♂, ♀	1170	10	117	12 (129)	5	136	135
Red kite	♂, ♀	950	10	95	20 (115)	15	132	130
Sea eagle	♂	4020	6	242	25 (267)	15	308 }	355
	♀	5120	6	308	30 (338)	15	403 }	
Marsh harrier	♂	520	12	62	15 (77)	15	88 }	110
	♀	760	12	93	18 (111)	15	128 }	
Hen harrier	♂	360	12	43	10 (53)	15	62 }	75
	♀	480	12	57	15 (72)	15	83 }	
Montagu's harrier	♂	270	15	41	8 (49)	15	57 }	65
	♀	340	15	51	10 (61)	15	70 }	
Goshawk	♂	1020	15	153	25 (178)	20	214 }	250
	♀	1350	15	203	33 (236)	20	283 }	
Sparrowhawk (2)	♂	140	25	35	7 (42)	25	56 }	75
	♀	940	25	65	13 (78)	25	98 }	
Buzzard (3)	♂	810	10	81	9 (90)	15	104 }	110
	♀	940	10	94	10 (104)	15	120 }	
Golden eagle (4)	♂	3920	6	235	23 (258)	25	322 }	355
	♀	4690	6	282	28 (310)	25	389 }	
Kestrel	♂	180	20	36	8 (44)	20	53 }	60
	♀	220	20	44	10 (54)	20	65 }	
Merlin	♂	190	20	38	8 (46)	25	55 }	65
	♀	230	20	46	10 (56)	25	70 }	
Hobby	♂	180	20	36	8 (44)	20	53 }	60
	♀	230	20	46	10 (56)	20	67 }	
Peregrine	♂	620	11	68	14 (82)	20	98 }	130
	♀	1010	11	111	22 (133)	20	160 }	

NOTES   (1) These figures, which are based on the recorded requirements of captive birds, winter and summer, exercised and not exercised, are a good approximation of requirements but not necessarily completely accurate.

(2) The theoretical figure for the daily food requirement of the sparrowhawk (mean 55 gr.) agrees closely with estimates by Uttendorfer and Tinbergen (Ch. 12(17, 18)); but they give a higher total mean (82 gr.) than the theoretically calculated mean here.

(3) Dare (Ch. 13(3)) estimates the daily food requirement of a buzzard at 140 gr., cf. the calculated requirement of 90–104 gr. Picozzi, however, conconsidered 90 gr. per day nearer the mark; this agrees closely with the theoretical figure.

(4) The theoretical calculated figure for the golden eagle is rather higher than that given by Brown and Watson (Ch. 14(9)), which is based upon other data besides that of Craighead and Craighead.

(5) Based on the Craighead data, the food of the peregrine increases from about 11% in summer to 15% in winter. Ratcliffe (Ch. 18(19)) gives 235 gr. per pair per day (118 per peregrine per day), including wastage, considerably below the requirement calculated here, which may be too high.

facts as long as the principle is understood. The total requirement is the amount eaten by the parents, and their brood of any known size, plus the waste factor, which can vary according to whether the food is mainly voles, frogs, or rabbits.

If the composition of the diet is well known it is also simple to calculate how many of each species of prey are required to provide the annual ration. In the sparrowhawk for instance, which is abundantly documented both in Britain and Europe, most of the prey is small birds of less than 50 grams' weight(21,a). In this case, the total need for parents and an average brood of two young (under present-day conditions where pesticides reduce breeding success) would be about 44 kg. (97 lb). In Dumfriesshire, from which area adequate food data are available, the food is 98% birds and 2% mammals, by numbers; since the mammals taken are nearly all very small, voles or shrews, weighing 20 grams or less, they are even more unimportant (1·1%) by weight. The 98% birds include, among 1255 items, 12 corvids, 17 game-birds (1·3%), 135 other non-passerines, and 1091 passerines varying from a mistle thrush to a willow warbler. The 135 non-passerines are only 11% by number; but since they include 73 full-grown woodpigeons and 30 lapwings they are far more important by weight, about 37%. The small songbirds, by far the most common prey, 88% by numbers, are only about 58% by weight. Thus in this area, in approximate terms, of the total requirement of an average pair of sparrowhawks and their brood, about 25·5 kg. (45½ lb) is songbirds; 15·4 kg. (34 lb) woodpigeons, lapwings and other non-passerines; and only 1·3 kg. (2¾ lb) game-birds, mostly young pheasants. One could claim that this small toll of pheasants was amply compensated for by the 12 jays, two crows, and two adult male sparrowhawks recorded among the items taken(a).

Such figures may be easily calculated for any species in which the composition of the prey is well known. They vary from area to area according to the abundance of the prey available or the preference of the raptor concerned. Thus, in the peregrine falcon, Ratcliffe found that of the total daily requirement of a pair of peregrines of 235 grams (including wastage) 46% by weight was made up of domestic pigeons in England, Wales, and Southern Scotland, but only 20% in the central Scottish highlands and only 5% in coastal northern eyries where there are practically no pigeons and peregrines subsist largely on sea-birds(18).

Such data indicate that, on a national scale, a large sample of food items should be recorded. What is taken in one area may be typical for that area, but differ in many particulars from the prey taken by the same species in another area. For instance, in Dumfries the chaffinch is the most numerous single item of sparrowhawk prey; in Holland and Germany the house sparrow is most often taken. To get a true picture of the prey of the golden eagle in Scotland it would be better to record thirty items of prey from ten different eyries in different parts of the west and east than three hundred kills from Inverness-shire or Perthshire alone. Such work still needs to be done for many British birds of prey. When it is done it is perfectly possible that it might indicate that a species is beneficial or harmless on balance in one area and harmful in another. The hen harrier, for instance, which feeds on voles and moorland birds in Orkney without adversely affecting the abundance of either, may be regarded as neutral there(3); but in Aberdeenshire research may show that the toll of young grouse in the breeding season is such that an over-abundance of hen harriers might have to be controlled.

The overall effect of a bird of prey on the prey animals in its home range varies according to the population of the latter. Working from a simple theoretical case, let us say that golden eagles eat, year round, 30% of grouse by numbers and 20%

by weight. Since the home range of golden eagles is about 11–12,000 acres (4400–4800 ha.) per pair all over Scotland, and since they rear on average, if undisturbed, about two young per pair in three years it is easy to calculate the number of grouse required by the eagles. The total food requirement of the pair and their young is about 207 kg. (456 lb). If 20% of this is grouse by weight, that is 41·4 kg.; and, since a grouse weighs about 600 grams, that is 70 grouse. Add 20% for waste, and the total requirement is 87 grouse, or about a grouse per 125 acres (50 ha.)

If a constant level of predation on grouse were maintained by pairs of golden eagles irrespective of the abundance of grouse, then evidently the effect of such predation on a sparse grouse population would be very much more severe than on an abundant one. Grouse can be as abundant as a pair per three acres, but seldom exceed 1 per 5 acres (2 ha.) in the breeding season, and can exceed a bird per acre in autumn; that is, 4400–11,000 grouse, occasionally even 25,000 in an average eagle's range. Evidently, a total toll of 89, many of them perhaps sick, or surplus non-territorial birds that would die anyhow in winter would not be important at the high population level. However, where the stock of grouse is small, say one pair per 50 acres, as could be the case in many West Highland areas, a total requirement of 87 grouse per pair of eagles would mean that 12–20% of all grouse were killed, which might have a marked limiting effect on the stock. Yet it is paradoxical that golden eagles are not generally persecuted in areas where grouse stocks are very low, because the grouse are hardly worth bothering about anyhow, but are severely persecuted in the areas where grouse are most abundant and the eagles can do least harm.

In practice, the same level of predation irrespective of the population of the prey would never be exerted by any bird of prey anywhere. The evidence indicates that birds of prey exert a selective influence on their prey, taking what is most abundant and easily caught(6,21). Factors increasing the vulnerability of prey to attack include numbers, size, conspicuousness, and habits. Abundant birds which tend to move in flocks, such as sparrows and several finches, are more likely to be taken than any others by sparrowhawks(21). Birds which are conspicuous either because of their colour or their behaviour are more likely to be taken. Cock partridges, running about crazed with sexual excitement in spring, are more likely to be taken by goshawks than are the females they are pursuing; and in dense American woodlands the drumming male grouse are more likely to be killed than the quiet, cryptically coloured hens(6,12). Ospreys or sea eagles are more likely to take relatively sluggish fish inclined to bask on the surface in still lakes than quick-moving species which swim deep in fast-flowing streams. Thus pike may be more often taken than trout in relation to their numbers, though this is conjectural since it is hard to estimate the actual population of either. Sheer size may save a bird from predation if it is big enough. There is nothing much more conspicuous in Britain than a crowing cock pheasant on a stubble field; yet the bird is safe because it is too big for any available local predator. Something like Bonelli's or the martial eagle of Africa is required to deal justly with cock pheasants. If we had these species the pheasants would crow only from thick cover which the eagle could not penetrate.

The habits of birds or animals, and their agility or flying powers likewise affect the rate of predation. Male skylarks and tree pipits in full song in the air are vulnerable to hobbies, but would be quite safe if they stayed on the ground(19). Sparrowhawks generally kill species found out in the open, attacking them from within dense cover, but kill comparatively few of quite abundant birds that live continually in thick shrubbery where the hawk cannot easily fly(21). Likewise, in the open, sparrowhawks can catch larks and pipits, but hardly ever catch the more abundant and obvious swallows or martins because of their superior flying powers. Voles are never very obvious animals when their population level is low, for they then live in dense vegetation and are difficult to find If their numbers increase to plague proportions, however, as sometimes happens they not only are easier to see because they are so numerous, but eat down the cover in their own habitat and so make themselves even more obvious to any predator(8).

The effect of a predator also varies according to its own habits. Certain species, such as some harriers, and kestrels do not have strong territorial requirements, and can accordingly concentrate, at least to hunt in areas where voles are very abundant without actively competing with one another(22). Buzzards, on the other hand, in the same sort of open moorland terrain, would have strong territorial requirements and residents would repel strangers(15). The population of buzzards would not be any higher in vole-plague years than in normal years. The individual buzzards, provided with an abundance of easily caught voles, might well eat proportionately more voles than they would in a normal year. Even so, the abundance of voles in the territory would be such that the resident buzzards would not be able to have much real effect in reducing the numbers of voles. If none of the more nomadic predators entered the area the voles would build up in numbers till they ate themselves out of house and home, the population would crash and the resident buzzards would then suffer from a vole famine after a feast. This situation might affect breeding success in that the buzzards might rear larger broods in a vole plague year(15). Even that would make only a slight overall difference to the population of buzzards, probably only an average of one more chick per year.

All these examples indicate how difficult it is to assess with even reasonable certainty whether a bird of prey is harmful, beneficial, or neutral. It is true to say that if a bird of prey cannot do very much harm it probably cannot do very much practical good either. All that one can say is that those species which feed for preference on animals generally regarded as harmful to human interests, such as rabbits or woodpigeons or rats, are clearly beneficial, while those which feed for preference on animals beneficial to human interests such as insectivorous birds, are on balance harmful. If goshawks confined their attention to woodpigeons and rabbits, or even if more than half their diet was of these species (as in Britain it well might be) they would be regarded as beneficial on balance. But equally, one can say that a goshawk with a home range per pair of 7000–10,000 acres (2800–4000 ha.) could not possibly make much practical difference to the rabbit and woodpigeon population and so would be effectively neutral. If careful research, however, showed that the goshawks took a large proportion of nesting woodpigeons at the peak breeding times in summer, the situation might then be different again. They might then be exercising effective control of nesting woodpigeons and so be beneficial.

To take a more concrete example, in the West Highlands golden eagles in summer eat 30% lambs by weight; 60% large birds, mainly grouse and ptarmigan, but also crows, fulmars, curlews etc.; and 5% each of deer calves and other mammals(16). This estimate includes no carrion, which is certainly eaten by some adult eagles in summer as well as winter. The 30% of lambs looks harmful until one understands that at least half of them were picked up dead; that the total take of live lambs so represented is under 1% of those available; and that these might anyway have been weak, separated from their dams, and likely to die. The 60% of large birds, mainly grouse and ptarmigan, would be regarded as harmful rather than otherwise if game preserving, other than deer, was taken seriously in these areas. As things stand most shooting tenants on West Highland estates do not bother about more than an occasional day's rough grouse shooting, and take what they can get in this way, while ptarmigan are normally left strictly alone; it would not improve the stalking to shoot them on the tops. So here the effect of the eagle on the grouse and ptarmigan population is not important, and is compensated to some extent by taking crows, which are regarded, with or without reason, as being harmful species on grouse moors. 5% of the diet each composed of deer calves and other mammals, such as scarce mountain hares, is not going to make much real difference to the population of either, while it is clearly inadequate to control colonies of rabbits there may be on the low ground. Thus we would end up with the eagle being more or less neutral, with a small but negligible amount of undoubted damage to sheep.

The wider the range of prey the more complicated this sort of assessment becomes. A buzzard eating rabbits or voles, or young crows, is regarded as beneficial. If it eats earthworms it is being harmful, if it has any effect at all on their population. A sparrowhawk that concentrates on sparrows which can be pests, is being actively beneficial; but if it must feed largely on insectivorous songbirds in the absence of sparrows it is being essentially harmful. Sentiment also comes into it; one may happen to like jays or chaffinches, or be trying to carry out research upon them, and so regard the sparrowhawk that kills them as a nuisance. However, any true researcher would only accept predation as a necessary and unavoidable feature of the species' biology, an interesting fact to be recorded, and nothing else.

Any assessment of whether a bird of prey is harmful or otherwise to human interests is a separate matter to whether it effectively controls the numbers of its prey. It is generally accepted nowadays that birds of prey do not effectively control or, in the long run, reduce the numbers of their prey. If they have any marked effect, it is to smooth slightly the large fluctuations in population that would otherwise occur. All animals and birds, of whatever species, if they are to survive in the long run, must breed sufficiently fast to combat the effects of three main enemies, predation, disease, and starvation(1). Of these three, predation takes the least toll, with small local exceptions; even human wars do not kill like plagues or famines have and will again.

It is also certain that, in the absence of predation, the population of any prey species would rise faster, till it overcrowded the environment, became more subject to disease, or died of starvation if disease did not strike. If 30–50% of red grouse on a well managed moor are not shot in autumn they will die in winter anyhow, as they are more than the environment can support year round(23). A few of these need not be grudged to hungry foxes or hen harriers in winter, nor need anyone feel guilty about enjoying roast grouse on the menu. Predation, by mammals or birds of prey is a fact of life for which every species which is eaten has evolved compensatory patterns of behaviour and population control. If they did not, they would cease to exist.

Birds of prey are only one class of predators available. In Britain, many of the others have already been eliminated, and those predatory mammals that remain are usually either persecuted or scarce. No species of mammal, bird, or insect is likely to become extinct, or even to be seriously reduced by the presence of even a capacity population of birds of prey. As I shall explain in Chapter 24, the birds of prey themselves have evolved population control mechanisms which prevent them from ever becoming too numerous for their environment to support them. Persecution of birds of prey on the basis of whether they are harmful or beneficial to human interests can have no evolutionary significance in the long run. We would do better to leave them alone, observe them till we understand their habits better than we do, and then, if we must, make a judgement based upon the known facts and not upon conjecture or prejudice.

CHAPTER 23

SOME BURNING ISSUES

FOR centuries birds of prey have aroused interest, enthusiasm, or dislike from human kind. In most parts of the undeveloped world, for instance in Africa where I live, any dislike they generate is only sporadic and mild, and they are usually more or less ignored(2). In Britain, in some European countries, in North America and Australia, in fact in most of the 'developed' world dominated by civilised white men, the general dislike for birds of prey often develops into sustained systematic campaigns of eradication or extermination, often quite indiscriminately, against particular birds of prey. In France, which would certainly consider itself one of the world's most civilised countries, the once abundant population of birds of prey has been grievously reduced in the last ten to twenty years, not only by the use of pesticides, but by direct persecution and shooting. Legal protection has only just been given to French birds of prey. Dozens of totally harmless honey buzzards are shot each year in Malta or Spain(1); and Australians have been wantonly destroying wedge-tailed eagles on an enormous scale for many years(5).

However nowhere in these other countries do narrow sectional interests arrogate to themselves the right to *break the law* in destroying birds of prey to a greater extent than in Britain; and it can be shown that existing legal provisions are quite inadequate to prevent the present continuing level of destruction. Persecution has lessened somewhat since I was a boy and certain species have been able to re-establish themselves in areas from which they were formerly banished. However in 1972 I heard of egg collectors taking rare birds' eggs, including four pairs of kites; of shepherds and gamekeepers destroying golden eagles and breeding peregrines; of gamekeepers destroying every sparrowhawk's nest they can find in a certain area and rendering research results on buzzards and hen harriers less useful than they might be by unwarranted illegal interference.

I have discussed conservation of birds of prey with several sympathetic land-owners and estate agents, who admit that birds of prey are illegally destroyed by their keepers and shepherds, whom they say they cannot control. Peregrine eyries in south-west Scotland have been robbed by falconers and destroyed by pigeon fanciers. Public opinion and the law desires that all these birds should be protected; but both are flouted by these sectional interests, who consider that they have every right to ignore the law and other people if it does not happen to suit them.

In the midst of this general antagonism there appear to me to be certain burning issues which deserve fuller factual discussion. Each is concerned with the adverse effect of one or more species of diurnal birds of prey on the legitimate interests of a section of the public or an industry. They are:

(i) The golden eagle (or the sea eagle, rendered extinct in Britain for this reason) and sheep; is the amount of damage done to sheep farmers by eagles sufficient to entitle them to kill eagles illegally if they think fit?

(ii) The golden eagle, peregrine falcon, hen harrier and other species as affecting game preserves. Do these raptors really endanger the success of game rearing enterprises or seriously affect the economic value of shooting estates?

(iii) The peregrine falcon and the racing pigeon owner; do peregrines really so much endanger racing pigeons that this section of the community can claim the right to exterminate the endangered peregrine illegally whenever possible, in the face of a plain desire on the part of a very large number of bird watchers and others that peregrines should be allowed to remain alive ?

In a detailed analysis of these issues I believe we shall get at the factual root, if any, of complaints against birds of prey in general. I omit lengthy discussion on the quite serious question of the rights and wrongs of egg collectors and egg collecting, which has apparently increased rather sharply in recent years after being more or less moribund for two decades(a). Few people nowadays have much sympathy for egg collectors who deliberately rob the nests of rare raptors; even proprietors who would like to see their gamekeepers permitted licence to destroy protected species or if caught, let off lightly, would show no sympathy to the less destructive egg collector. There are more than enough eggs now in collections for any foreseeable scientific purposes (where they have sometimes been useful) and egg collectors are generally regarded as aberrant individuals who should be heavily penalised if caught, though in actual fact they do less harm to some species such as golden eagles than do the gamekeepers who kill breeding adults. But the gamekeeper pressed by his employer to rear the maximum number of pheasants or grouse; the shepherd anxious about his flock and his livelihood; the shoot proprietor who pays vast sums of money to county councils in rates and who provides valuable enter-tainment for foreign business men; the pigeon racer who carefully rears his birds only to see them disappear. These surely have some right on their side, and their attitude towards birds of prey deserves some sympathy. Or do they, and should they get as much sympathy as they do, when so many other people like to see birds of prey alive ?

No useful purpose can be served by heated emotional discussion of these matters. Facts are what is needed, and will speak far more cogently than generalised emotional accusations. Accordingly, I aim to deal with these issues as fairly and factually as I can, although I admit at the start to bias in favour of birds of prey, not only because I like them and I have studied them all my life, but also because I know they are largely blameless. There are certainly cases when the opposite view deserves to be heard; but we must look at these issues in the cold light of established facts, not of opinion or emotion.

Most of the complaints voiced against birds of prey share three main charac-teristics.

(i) They are scarcely ever based upon a solid body of factual evidence. They are usually broad generalisations about wholesale damage, and a request for precise factual evidence, as to exactly where, when, and how many usually results in no specific data and can too easily degenerate into a bellicose 'Are ye tellin' me ah'm a leear ?'; which merely indicates that there is no substance in the complaint, and that the complainant is incapable of rational discussion.

(ii) When the complaints are carefully and painstakingly investigated by teams of competent naturalists, who are only too anxious to have the company of the complainants in the arduous field work necessary, but who often cannot obtain this co-operation, they are invariably found to be either wholly without substance or at worst grossly exaggerated. I know of absolutely no exception to this rule, anywhere in the world.

(iii) When the carefully documented factual information is available and the report published its findings, if they happen to disagree with the previously ex-pressed sweeping complaints, are seldom accepted, and are often very rudely

PLATE 13. KESTRELS at the nest. *Above*, kestrels nesting in a window box 17 floors up in a London block of flats; the male brings a mouse to the brooding female. *Below*, a more typical nest-site in an old crow's nest; female with four downy young, whose similar size shows that incubation began when the clutch was nearly complete.

PLATE 14. KESTRELS. *Above left*, female kestrel at a nesting hole in a stump, a common natural situation in England; *right*, a young kestrel about to fly from a nest in a hollow tree. *Below*, the hunting kestrel has caught a mouse and flies with it to a perch to feed.

rejected. Thus the well-documented factual report has little effect on the people it was meant to help. Often too it has little effect on the political lawmakers, who should be expected to take a more responsible view of the situation. Emotions and votes are still too often preferred to hard established fact.

In Britain the legal situation with regard to all three burning issues I have mentioned is perfectly clear. All species of birds of prey are protected all the year round, and anyone who deliberately kills them or interferes with them at their nests is committing an offence. All the rarer species, such as the golden eagle, peregrine, harriers, hobby, merlin, honey buzzard and goshawk are given special protection in addition, with liability to heavier fines and imprisonment if the offender is caught. I do not believe that today, nearly 20 years after the passage of the 1954 Bird Protection Act, anyone has any grounds for pleading ignorance of the law on the subject, any more than they have for supposing that they can drive a car without a licence. The law gives all birds of prey protection, some stronger than others; only two common species, the buzzard and kestrel, still have 'ordinary protection' all the year round. No one may shoot, trap, poison, or otherwise kill a bird of prey, or take its eggs or young, or, in the case of those specially protected, photograph it at its nest without committing an offence unless, in the last two cases, he is a falconer with a permit to take young, or a photographer, or an observer permitted by the proper authorities to study and watch the birds at the nest without causing any interference with their normal activities.

The law is deliberately and continuously flouted. Between March 1971 and June 1972 the deaths of 194 birds of prey were drawn to the attention of the R.S.P.B. These are only the cases that have come to light; the R.S.P.B. does not go around snooping, or it would undoubtedly hear of a great many more. The birds included one red kite, poisoned in Somerset, perhaps by a keeper who could not be caught. It was one of a pair which had been frequenting a certain area for months, and everyone hoped it would be the first definite case of breeding outside Wales. One osprey and two rough-legged buzzards were shot in Lincolnshire and 18 golden eagles were shot, poisoned or trapped in Scotland. 30 buzzards were shot in Shropshire, and 15 buzzards poisoned on one estate in Wales. In addition I have been told that 9 out of 11 peregrine eyries with young in Galloway in 1972 were robbed by unauthorised falconers in one weekend, and that four out of five active peregrine eyries in the Cheviots were destroyed by pigeon owners. Even if these details are incorrect, some such offences have certainly been committed. I have already mentioned the four pairs of kites robbed by egg collectors. There can be no doubt that there is a steady trickle of offences against the law the whole time, and that these are deliberate.

The easiest of these burning issues to dispose of is that of the peregrine and the pigeon racer which, as noted above, still is an issue which causes those who think they are aggrieved to break the law. This one is easy to deal with because it already has been the subject of a very exhaustive inquiry by the British Trust for Ornithology, the results of which were published in a paper by Derek Ratcliffe(11). When the peregrine falcon began to recover from the persecution it had received during the war years the racing pigeon owners of Great Britain complained to the Home Office that the falcons were becoming far too numerous and that the losses they suffered were intolerable. They did not produce any concrete evidence of such losses, and to do them justice it would have been difficult to do so. However, the matter was very carefully examined by competent naturalists, and the results have been published in full for anyone to read.

Briefly, this survey, carried out in 1960–61, found that the first of the complaints, that the peregrine was becoming too numerous, was nonsense. In fact, the reverse was the case, and peregrines were in the throes of a catastrophic decline, at that time not understood, and from which they still have not recovered. Of 718 possible territories, of which at least 630 were believed to be occupied pre-war, 431 (66%) were examined; the sample was thus adequate for a sound result. In 173 territories, or 40%, there were no peregrines; and in another 118 (28%) there were peregrines but not proven to breed. Only in 140 territories (32%) did the peregrines lay, and only in 82 (19%) did they rear young. Far from increasing, the peregrine was proven to have decreased to less than two-thirds of the pre-war population and it decreased still further in later years to a low point about 1963, when the total population was estimated at 45% of the pre-war numbers. Later surveys in 1971 show that it has since recovered to about 55% of pre-war numbers(12). This was one of the fullest and most careful surveys of a bird of prey carried out anywhere in the world, and there can be no question that the results are accurate and completely refute the allegations of large increases in the peregrine population made to the Home Office by the pigeon racers.

The naturalists who did the survey also collected all prey remains they could find, so as to estimate the numbers of pigeons killed by British peregrines in relation to the total number known to exist. As expected, it was found in England, Wales, and southern Scotland that the commonest prey of the peregrine falcon was the domestic pigeon, though many of these were not registered racers. In some other parts peregrines ate mainly game-birds or sea-birds. 1240 prey records involving 73 species of birds included 294 pigeons, 230 of which were domestic pigeons. Domestic pigeons made up 18·5% of the total by number, and 29% by weight of the prey overall, and in England, Wales and Southern Scotland 46% by weight. These were, however, the very areas in which the decline of the peregrines was most severe, so that even if the peregrine was taking a number of domestic pigeons the total kill over a vast area was not likely to be large.

The total possible kill of domestic pigeons was in fact carefully calculated at 67,768 per annum, on the basis of the pre-war figure of 650 pairs of peregrines; the 316 pairs in England, Wales and S. Scotland were estimated to kill 52,649 pigeons per year pre-war. However, the peregrine population in these areas had fallen by 1961 to a much smaller figure. In these areas, of 450 known territories, 254 were visited, and of these peregrines were only present in 74, or 29%. In the territories where they were present they only bred successfully in eight. Their total take of domestic pigeons could thus be reduced from a hypothetical 52,649 pre-war to 7897 altogether.

However, in order to avoid the possible accusation that they were favouring the peregrine the biologists who did the survey suggested a much higher possible figure country wide of 24,200 pigeons for 1961 and 16,500 for 1962. Of these most would have been killed in England, Wales, and S. Scotland. The figure of 16,500 amounted to 0·3% of the total homing pigeon population of about five million birds. If a more realistic figure had been used, of about 7887 birds killed by a much reduced peregrine population in the main homing pigeon areas in England, Wales and S. Scotland, the percentage kill would have been just over 0·1%. In other words, peregrines are liable to kill about one pigeon in 800, not all of them registered homers(11).

These are the facts of this particular burning issue. Anyone capable of elementary arithmetic can take the figures given in Ratcliffe's paper, sit down with a calculator,

Table 18 Food of the Peregrine Falcon in Britain

Sources: Ratcliffe, D. A., 1962, 1963 (18 (18, 19)); Weir, D., 14(27); and Brown, R. H., Brit. Birds 23: 10: 269–72.

Area studied	Game birds	Pigeons (domestic)	Sea-birds, gulls	Waders, ducks	Cuckoo, swift, passerines, (corvids)	Other	Total
ENGLAND, WALES, S. SCOTLAND							
Ratcliffe 1962	24	159 (145)	4	54	340 (7)	—	581
Ratcliffe 1963	50	190 (175)	14	85	186 (15)	—	525
R. H. Brown	22	96 (74)	—	4	65	3(mamm.)	190
Total	96	445 (394)	18	143	591 (22)	3	1296
Mean weight (gr.)	550	400	300	150	100	50	
% by weight	16·3	56·1	1·6	6·6	19·6	neg.	
INLAND SCOTTISH HIGHLANDS							
Ratcliffe 1962	14	12 (10)	5	14	20 (3)		65
Ratcliffe 1963	96	92 (75)	20	90	152 (25)		450
Weir (unpub.)	72	61 (53)	25	56	53 (6)		267
Total	182	165 (138)	50	160	225 (34)		782
Mean weight (gr.)	550	400	300	200	120		
% by weight	35·5	38·0	5·6	11·4	9·5		
COASTAL SCOTLAND							
Ratcliffe 1963	3	43 (10)	111	36	16 (6)		209
Mean weight (gr.)	550	400	300	200	150		
% by weight	3·1	17·0	62·0	13·4	4·5		
GRAND TOTAL: BRITAIN	281	653 (542)	179	339	832 (62)		
% by number	12·3	27·7	7·9	14·8	36·3	neg.	
% by weight	24·8	41·8	8·6	9·9	14·8	neg.	

NOTES (1) Variation in mean weights of passerines and waders allows for greater or lesser proportion of heavy species in total.

(2) % domestic pigeons by weight: England, Wales, S. Scotland 49·9%; inland highland Scotland 26·5%; coastal Scotland 7·4%.

and get the same result. The pigeon racer's complaint was proved to have practically no substance on both the main counts. The peregrine falcon had not increased; and it killed only a very small fraction of the total population of racing pigeons. Even at that the figures quoted assume that every pigeon the peregrine kills is a racer and not a lost bird or a feral bird from a farm dovecot. In Scotland we say that 'facts are chiels that winna ding'. But in this case they do ding, and Scottish pigeon racers still illegally destroy peregrine eyries. They need no sympathy for doing so.

A very similar result was arrived at in Sweden when this same issue was objectively assessed there(9). As a result the peregrine was given complete protection, and the pigeon owners were refused leave to destroy peregrine eyries. In Sweden they were able, by picking the route to be followed in pigeon races, to avoid obvious hazards at certain peregrine eyries. This might not be so easy to do in

Table 19 Lambs as Eagle Prey

EAGLE SPECIES	Lambs, kids (1)	Rabbits, hares	Other mammals (2)	Game birds (3)	Other birds	Reptiles, fish, carrion	Total
GOLDEN EAGLE							
E. Scotland (Watson)	2	80	31	98	4	—	215
E. Scotland (Weir)	1	19	4	72	1	—	97
Argyll (Merrie)	7	13	2	22	6	—	50
W. Ross, winter (Lockie)	5	7	11	21	—	126	170
W. Ross, summer (Lockie, Balharry)	93	97	236	345	133	—	904
Lewis (Lockie)	11	80	12	11	10	14	138
Scotland (Stephen)	0	186	9	148	14	—	357
Scotland (Brown)	4	19	4	34	3	1	65
Total, Scotland	123	501	309	751	171	141	1996
% by number	6·1	25·1	15·6	37·6	8·5	7·2	
% by estimated weight	18·4	37·6	23·1	14·1	1·4	5·4	
Montana (Reynolds)	3	1149	454	173	203	6	1988
Alaska (Murie)	—	6	646	23	22	—	697
Texas (Packard, Bolen)	93 (5)	785	303	20	20	2	1223
Utah (Arnell)	—	477	20	6	144	1	648
California (Carnie)	—	145	244	4	64	46	503
Other U.S.A.	4	182	48	21	2	12	269
Total, U.S.A.	100	2744	1715	247	455	67	5328
Switzerland (Stemmler)	8	28	195	45	13	1	300
Europe (others) (6)	5	(101)161	(60)	98	11	—	275
Total, Europe	13	139	255	143	24	1	575
Grand total	236	3384	2279	1141	650	209	7899
% by number	3·0	42·7	28·8	14·4	8·3	2·8	
% by estimated weight	7·2	52·0	34·9	4·3	0·1	1·5	
WHITE-TAILED EAGLE (4)							
Norway (Willgohs)	80	29	58	—	663	576	1406
Europe (others)	—	—	19	—	156	65	240
Total	80	29	77	—	819	641	1646
WEDGE-TAILED EAGLE							
Australia (Leopold)	25	113	110	—	56	65	369

NOTES (1) In all species the majority of lambs found in eyries were considered to have been picked up dead.

(2) 'Other mammals' include everything from large prey such as red deer or antelope calves to moles and rats, and young of carnivores such as foxes which could be dangerous to sheep.

(3) In Britain the proportion of game-birds is higher than in America, but in N. Europe (e.g. Estonia) may be higher still.

Britain, but the idea is worth considering in case British pigeon racers may feel able at some time to take a more constructive attitude.

Eagles and sheep. This is a somewhat more difficult issue, for shepherding is not a sport like pigeon racing, but the traditional occupation of a respected body of countrymen. Moreover, what they produce, succulent mutton which I myself enjoy eating, and wool which keeps me warm, is valuable food and clothing. One can, of course, say that the uplands of Britain are unsuited to sheep; that the whole industry is dying and only kept on its feet by massive subsidies; that we can eat beef or pig or chicken and wear nylon. Also, and with truth, that it would be better to reafforest the whole area to prevent the steady creeping ecological deterioration through leaching and erosion which results from destruction of original forest cover, and excessive heather burning to obtain sheep grazing(10). However, here and now, there are millions of sheep in the Highlands of Scotland and the Lake District, and the shepherds are perfectly entitled to express anxiety if golden eagles or sea eagles or any other eagle are killing enough sheep seriously to affect the welfare of their flocks or their livelihood.

Wherever the golden eagle occurs alongside sheep it is accused of doing damage in the lambing season. Complaints of this nature are comparatively moderate in Scotland when compared to some other countries. In America extermination campaigns from aircraft have been waged against golden eagles, and have unfortunately been fairly successful, wiping out the breeding eagles in large tracts of country and making heavy inroads among migrants from further north in winter(13). Attempts have been made to control this pointless butchery; but through adroit political wriggling they have been rendered largely ineffective. In Norway and other countries of Europe the shepherds likewise object to eagles and accuse them of killing sheep; in this case they accuse both the golden eagle and the sea eagle, which is larger and more likely to pick up dead sheep as carrion(15). In Australia the wedge-tailed eagle, a slightly larger bird than the golden eagle, has been persecuted relentlessly for decades because it is said to kill lambs, in a country where sheep ranching really is an important part of the economy(5). In southern Africa the Verreaux's eagles and martial eagles of the Karroo are likewise accused(b).

These complaints have been carefully investigated in Scotland by Lockie and Stephen; in America by the University of Montana, the Audubon Society, Texas A and M University, and others; in Australia by Dr Starker Leopold and the C.S I.R.O.; and in South Africa by biologists of the Percy Fitzpatrick Institute at Cape Town. In Text Table 19 I have summarised most of the results of these

(4) In the white-tailed eagle the majority of items under reptiles etc. are fish; the majority of birds taken are seabirds and diving ducks.

(5) This figure may represent too high a proportion because of the method of sampling, regarding all large bones as probably lamb.

(6) Sources of information. *Golden eagle.* Scotland: Lockie, Watson, Balharry, and Merrie in litt.; Weir, 14(27). America: Arnold, 14(1); Murie, A. 1944. U.S. Nat. Parks series, 5; Carnie, S. K. 1954. Condor, 56, 3–12: and unpub. theses and reports by Reynolds, H. V. 1966 (Montana), Arnell, W. B. 1971 (Utah), and Packard, R. L. and Bolen E. C. 1969 (Texas). Europe: Stemmler, K. 1955. Der Steinadler in der Schweizer Alpen; Schaffhausen. Uttendorfer et al. 10(14). *Sea eagle:* Fischer, W. 7(5) and Willgohs, 7(10). *Wedge-tailed eagle;* Leopold, A. S. and Wolfe, T. O., 1969; C.S.I.R.O. wildlife research. Figures for rabbits and hares and other mammals estimated from total of 161.

findings, which in some cases have been financed by the wool growers themselves and in others by conservation bodies. With no exception, the eagles are exonerated of doing serious damage, though in every case it has been found that a few lambs are taken, and a smaller number actually killed, a fact that will be readily admitted by anyone who has studied eagles.

A feature of most of the complaints against eagles is that they are seldom based on direct observations of a kill. The eagle is seen to feed upon or carry away a lamb, or wool is found at the eagle's eyrie. When I have questioned shepherds on the subject I have very seldom met one of any race who could tell me clearly how often he had seen an eagle kill a sheep, with details of where and when. If they can, it normally amounts to under five in a lifetime. Seton Gordon, in his book on golden eagles(4), recounts two instances in his own long lifetime in eagle country, and only about a dozen other cases that have come to his notice in correspondence.

Of course, one can argue that one seldom sees an eagle kill anyhow; we know they kill grouse and hares, but we seldom see it happen. However, the long list of several thousand items of prey which is available from the various studies that have been done indicates beyond doubt that the golden eagle prefers to eat moderate sized mammals, from one to six pounds in weight, when it can get them. When it cannot it eats many game-birds, corvids, and various other prey, including quite a selection of carnivores such as foxes. It may indeed be argued that the golden eagle is almost as effective in controlling foxes (unfortunate animals which are hated even more than the eagle) as are men. Lambs are taken because they are moderate sized mammals; and adult sheep are only eaten as carrion after they are dead.

In fact, most of the lambs that are found in eyries are also carrion. In about half of all cases it is possible to determine whether a lamb has been killed by an eagle or has been picked up dead. If an eagle kills a live lamb it must exert great crushing force with its talons, which penetrate the flesh and cause bruising and bleeding, clearly visible when the carcase is skinned. If the lamb is picked up dead the eagle does not have to exert such force and, since the lamb is dead, the blood does not flow, so that no bleeding takes place. The difference in appearance is quite characteristic, and has been fully described by Lockie in Britain, and by other scientists in the United States(7).

It is not always possible to determine whether a lamb carcase in an eagle's eyrie has been killed by an eagle or not. When killing a mammal any eagle tends to grip the head and thorax, but it may not later bring these parts to the eyrie. A lamb is normally too heavy to carry whole, so the eagle usually dismembers it, and may bring the unmarked hindquarters only, perhaps returning for the forequarters later if other scavengers have not eaten them. Lockie points out that if the eyes of the lamb are missing crows or ravens have been at it before the eagle; and this is confirmed by American evidence. Using these criteria he calculated that, of 22 lambs examined in one eyrie over five years, ten could be definitely identified as picked up dead or killed; of these, three had been killed by the eagle, and seven picked up dead. On this basis this eagle had killed a total of seven lambs in five years and picked up 15 others, only about 1/1000 of the 20–25,000 lambs, live or dead, available in that eagle's home range in the same period. He observed that in Wester Ross eagles ate more lambs in poor lambing years when there were more dead lambs lying about.

One cannot even be certain that the few live lambs taken would have lived. In 1972, at about 2700 feet on one of the Five Sisters of Kintail I came on a lamb, live and apparently healthy, standing beside its dead mother, already pecked by ravens. I felt that in June there was just a chance that it might survive; but it seemed a good deal more likely that a fox or an eagle would find it weak and starving and make an end of it.

In Lewis, where there were complaints from one area (originated by a game-keeper) of a large increase in the numbers of eagles and serious inroads on lambs, the situation was examined by Lockie and Stephen(8). They found that despite reports of increase in eagles there were only two occupied eyries in the area concerned, and only one lamb, known to have been killed by an immature eagle was noted; none were found in eyries. They found that the eagles were eating rabbits, grouse, golden plover, hares, and rats. They also found that the sheep population had increased by 40% in five years; that the whole area was heavily overgrazed; that the ewes suffered from deficiency disease; and that lamb mortality was heavy because the ewes had not enough milk. All these symptoms are typical of what happens on overgrazed range, in Britain, Texas, Western Australia, or Masailand. Mortality among the young of domestic stock is heavy and, except in Masailand, (where the blame is laid upon the Deity) eagles and other predators get the blame for man's inefficient management of his own resources.

The American investigators were actually able to prove that ranchers unjustly accused eagles of killing lambs. They found one lamb that had died just after birth, and watched it for some days. In due course an eagle found and fed on the carcase, and while it was doing so the rancher happened to drive up and at once accused the eagle of killing the lamb. Whether he was later convinced by the investigators or not, his first reaction was one of prejudice, leaping to conclusions on inadequate evidence. In Britain, shepherds who find lambs' wool and feet near or in eyries assume that the eagle has killed a large number of lambs. The fact is that a lamb is very woolly and its wool is white, while the uneatable hocks of the same lamb may be found in a different place later, carried out of the eyrie and dropped. What looks like a lot of wool may only have come from two or three lambs, all or most of them picked up dead.

Eagles do kill lambs occasionally, as has already been said. One very large female in West Inverness several years ago was reported to kill quite a number in her home range. This female was said to be exceptionally large and powerful and was observed to lift from the hillside a lamb estimated to weigh seven kilograms, against a wind. She perhaps corresponded to that common bogey-bird, the rogue eagle that kills hundreds of lambs in a season, the subject of talk in hotel bars of an evening from Kintyre to Durness. Perhaps her exceptional size had something to do with it(d).

For most of the fledging period at almost all eagle eyries, the female takes little part in hunting until the young are well feathered, which in Britain is in the latter part of June. By that time the lambs, which weigh about eight pounds at birth, are very much larger and heavier and could not normally be lifted by any eagle, certainly not by the smaller male, who up to then has been providing all the prey. I mentioned earlier that golden eagles have difficulty in flying with more than two and a half pounds attached to their legs, though this must vary with the size and power of the bird, the type of terrain, and the air conditions. A large female in a strong wind could lift a lamb from the hillside when a male could not; but she could not lift the same lamb in conditions of calm.

So there it is. Eagles do kill a few lambs, but they pick up dead far more than they kill, and the number they kill or pick up in any area is only a very small fraction of what is available, while it cannot be proved that these lambs would have survived if the eagle did not kill them. The evidence for wholesale killing is non-existent and, as stated in the chapter on the golden eagle, the numbers of eagles are slowly declining through human persecution and are in any case strictly limited by the territorial behaviour of the birds themselves. Any report of serious damage should be investigated by competent people and sympathetically dealt with; but the result is likely to be that the complaint grossly exaggerates the reality on very slender evidence.

I have been told that it is one thing to produce this sort of evidence and another to convince the shepherds themselves that it is so. I would retort that if people cannot be convinced by a massive bulk of factual evidence gathered by naturalists, who have spent very much more time investigating the matter than any of the complainants, and have evaluated the evidence in an objective manner backed by data they are unreasonable anyhow and should not be listened to. I would not like to think that Scottish shepherds are, as a whole, so unreasonable that they cannot be convinced by factual evidence; and I have met a number who admit that golden eagles do little or no harm to their flocks. In Scotland we are not in such a bad case as in Texas where, despite the publication of a mass of factual evidence, the sheep ranchers continue to vituperate against predators and demand their extermination. In Australia I believe, after centuries of large-scale but rather ineffectual persecution of the wedge-tailed eagle, the Government has recently withdrawn bounties on eagles, as a result of Dr Starker Leopold's report and a fuller report, as yet unpublished, by the C.S.I.R.O. to the effect that the wedge-tailed eagle does very little damage and quite a lot of indirect good to sheep(5).

This disposes of two of the three main burning issues. The third, the relation between birds of prey and game preserving, is the one which causes the most widespread and severe damage to birds of prey, and which generates more heat than any other. Again, game preserving is a sport, and not a livelihood for most of its devotees, except for the gamekeepers themselves. However it is also a large source of income for many county councils through rates levied on the value of shootings. For instance, about four million acres in England and Scotland is grouse moor. Common capital values are £1.20 per brace of grouse shot; and rents can run to £8 per brace or, on good moors, £800/gun/week(c). To me it is perverse that anyone wants to pay that sort of money to shoot a hundred or more grouse; but there is no doubt that big money is involved. At an average of one grouse per two acres in autumn, and 30% of grouse shot, that is 300,000 brace, equivalent to £360,000 to county councils and nearly £2½ million in rents. It is not surprising that shooting is a recognised industry, which in practice has practically monopolised land use over vast areas of mountain and moorland for the past century or so. Oddly enough, one of the first real game preserves, the New Forest, is now an unkeepered refuge for rare birds of prey.

In this case it must freely be admitted, and is admitted by anyone who studies birds of prey, that they do kill some game-birds and that in some cases these almost amount to the staple food of the bird of prey concerned. What must be evaluated is whether the number of game-birds killed by any bird of prey is sufficient to make such serious inroads into the game-bird population that it reduces the bags shot, and accordingly the value of the sporting property and the rates paid to the county council. There are two aspects of this question: the actual number killed; and the disturbance produced by certain large birds of prey during, for instance grouse driving. These are different aspects of a related matter, and I propose to deal with the numbers taken by birds of prey first.

Of the 24 species of birds of prey in the British list we can surely exonerate all the rare vagrants, the scarce winter migrants, and all the species with less than a hundred breeding pairs. None of the vagrants is ever sufficiently common to do any serious harm. Several of them do not take game-birds anyway. In this way we can eliminate at once any right to persecute the black kite; the white-tailed sea eagle (which would take some game-birds and possibly lambs if it were, as is hoped, once again a resident in Britain); the Egyptian and griffon vultures, which would not eat game-birds anyhow; the pallid harrier, which might eat a few young game-birds; the greater spotted eagle, which is mainly a frog eater; the red-footed falcon, which is insectivorous; and the two scarce but regular winter migrants the gyrfalcon and the rough-legged buzzard, one of which prefers game-birds while the other lives almost entirely on small mammals. Reference to the details of offences committed since March 1971 shows that both gyrfalcons and rough-legged buzzards are included therein – both shot.

We can also exonerate, on grounds of extreme rarity, the four species with less than ten breeding pairs, the osprey, honey buzzard, marsh harrier and goshawk. The last two do eat game-birds, and the goshawk, if numerous, would probably have to be kept under control for this reason. The osprey does eat fish, including trout. The honey buzzard is totally blameless on any count. Again, an osprey figures in the list of species illegally shot, in Lincolnshire, in the 15 months prior to writing this book. The fact that it was not a breeding osprey surely matters little.

I would assume that we can surely also exonerate all those species that are not extremely rare but are represented by less than a hundred pairs. Of these, the commonest, the hobby, is anyway entirely harmless to game preserving interests. Montagu's harriers take a small proportion of wild-bred game-birds in their food, but are so rare that they can safely be neglected. Red kites eat very few game-birds. Again, I draw attention to the fact that a red kite is among the species illegally poisoned between March 1971 and June 1972, probably by a gamekeeper; it contained about 500 parts per million of strychnine(a).

Elimination of all these, which surely no sportsman worth the name – and there are many – would contest, leaves us with seven species represented by more than 100 breeding pairs in Britain, which might be sufficiently numerous or effective as predators to have some real influence on game-bird stocks over large tracts of country. These are the golden eagle, peregrine falcon, hen harrier, and merlin with 100–500 breeding pairs; and the buzzard, sparrowhawk, and kestrel with more than 500 breeding pairs. Two of them, the golden eagle and the peregrine are already implicated in one of the other two burning issues discussed in this chapter.

Again, we can eliminate several of these species right away. The merlin is too small to do any serious damage on a grouse moor, and would scarcely ever see a young partridge or a pheasant in its life. The buzzard and the kestrel, on the basis of factual evidence, kill very few game-birds and are worthy of being considered as positively beneficial to the farming community by reason of the number of rabbits and rodents they kill. This leaves us with the peregrine falcon, the golden eagle, the hen harrier and the sparrowhawk, only four out of the 24 British species that really need to be seriously considered as dangerous enemies of British game stocks.

Of these, the only one that is liable to occur in country inhabited by pheasants or partridges today (for the peregrine has virtually disappeared from agricultural country) is the sparrowhawk. The male sparrowhawk is the smallest of British birds of prey, and the species' feeding habits have been more thoroughly studied than those of any other raptor in the world. In Appendix Table 1 I have listed a massive total of over 90,000 items recorded by various authorities in Britain, Germany, and Holland. From this it is abundantly plain that the sparrowhawk lives almost entirely on small woodland birds and that, while it does take a few game-birds, the number is relatively small.

As pointed out in the chapter on the species a sparrowhawk, weighing on average 137 grams in males and 257 in females, normally does not kill birds weighing more than 100 grams. In the breeding season, moreover, the female does not take much part in hunting until well on in the fledging period, about mid-June, by which time most young wild pheasant poults will weigh more than 200 grams and will not be taken. The danger to gamebird stocks from sparrowhawks which otherwise, by reason of their numbers and cunning could be considerable, is exaggerated; and the collected facts from many areas of Europe and Britain show that the accusations of severe damage to game-bird stocks by the sparrowhawk are largely baseless. In any case, the sparrowhawk has disappeared from many of the best game-rearing areas for another reason, agricultural pesticides.

The other three, the golden eagle, peregrine falcon, and hen harrier are all mainly inhabitants of uplands and grouse moors today. They seldom see a pheasant and rarely a partridge except in winter so those who rear or preserve these species need not worry about them. The case of the grouse moor proprietor must be considered more carefully. We know that grouse moor gamekeepers do kill all these species, and that in Eastern Scotland the golden eagle is declining more from this cause than any other. In such a case one is bound to ask (i) does it matter to the species, (ii) is it justified and (iii) if not justified, is it preventable, either by persuasion or legal compulsion.

In all three cases it does matter to the species concerned. At least a third of the whole golden eagle population in Scotland lives in the eastern highlands, east of a line drawn from Caithness south through East Sutherland and Easter Ross to near Inverness, the eastern Monadhliaths, Loch Ericht, and Central Perthshire. In this area the golden eagle has rapidly declined in recent years, mainly through persecution by grouse moor gamekeepers, including those employed by some very eminent persons indeed. In other parts of Scotland the eagle is threatened by shepherds, and by hill walkers, ornithologists, photographers, and climbers; but none of these kill the adults as does the grouse moor gamekeeper.

In the peregrine, the largest surviving healthy populations of this splendid bird are in the Central Highlands of Scotland. These are probably providing the recruits for the difficult climb back to normal population in a species that only a few years ago seemed headed for early extinction. In the hen harrier, if this species is not allowed to recolonise the Scottish mainland by gamekeepers, we shall be reduced once more to small isolated colonies in the outer Hebrides and Orkney, where some untoward circumstance could quickly wipe out the whole stock. In all three cases, therefore, the persecution *does* matter to the species concerned.

One may say that it is against the law of the land, and against the wishes of a majority of ordinary people. This, however, will not convince some of those who own these estates, or who are told to produce a good stock of grouse. In some cases these people are still living mentally in the nineteenth century. I believe too that gamekeepers sometimes destroy these birds of prey in direct defiance of orders given to them by their employers or by the factors of the estates. In others the employer either commends the destruction or tacitly turns a blind eye to it. In the latter case it is the employer who should be penalised, not only his gamekeeper.

As everyone will admit, peregrine falcons and golden eagles do take grouse. In the peregrine survey the red grouse was, after domestic pigeons, the most common item of prey, and in certain areas it is almost a staple. However, this must be evaluated against the size of a peregrine's home range and the appetite of a peregrine. An average peregrine must kill about 130 grams (4½ oz) of food daily to keep alive. A grouse weighs 500–700 grams (1¼–1½ lb), so that even allowing for waste one grouse suffices for two peregrines for two days. The peregrine survey, and other food surveys of the peregrine indicate that in areas where red grouse are common, they form about a fifth of the total prey by number, but are more important by weight. Even if red grouse form half of the peregrine's prey by weight, a pair of peregrines and their brood would not kill more than 100 grouse in a year. Anyone can do these sums for himself, and get the same answer.

The home range of a pair of peregrines in the Central Highlands is larger than that of a pair of golden eagles, about 24,000 acres (9500 ha.). In well-stocked grouse moor country such as that in Nairn, East Inverness, Moray, Banff, Aberdeen, Kincardine, and Angus, there might be anything from 5000 to 25,000 grouse in such an area. The killing by peregrines of 100 grouse is obviously not going to make any great difference to the total stock, particularly as it is likely that some of these grouse will be sick or injured birds better eliminated anyhow, or killed in high moorlands where the modern car-borne sportsman hardly ever goes.

The peregrine shares its territory with the golden eagle, which is larger but commoner, with an average home range in grouse moor country of 10–12,000 acres (4000–4800 ha.). The food of the golden eagle has been shown to be about one-third large birds, by number; and in 1964 Adam Watson and I calculated that golden eagles would take about 126 grouse-sized birds – not all of them red grouse – per pair per annum. Possibly a few pairs might take rather more, but in areas where hares were abundant I should expect eagles to take fewer grouse.

Again, one may compare the number of grouse taken with the number available in the territory. A golden eagle with a range mainly composed of grouse moors, with a population of 5000–15,000 grouse in its home range, would obviously not have any very great effect on the stocks. In a single case in eastern Perthshire where this was actually investigated it was found that the eagles would take from 0·6 to 2% of the grouse available in spring in their home range(6). Obviously, however, the effect of the eagle on grouse stocks must vary according to the density of the grouse population. In such a place as north-west Sutherland, where one year I walked 86 miles between flushings of grouse, it was possible to calculate that eagles would eat most of the grouse available in the territory if they fed on them to the same extent as in the eastern highlands. But then, in these areas grouse are anyway so scarce that they are not worth preserving. I fancy that the worst animosity to golden eagles on grouse moors is shown in those areas where the stocks are moderate, large enough to be worth preserving, but small enough for the eagle to make considerable inroads into them.

However, the point must also be made that it has been shown that the population of grouse in any area is mainly dependent on good moor management, the heather being burned in small patches so that the grouse can have growth of several ages in their territories. The population can be doubled or halved by good or bad management. It has also been shown that the population of grouse existing in spring is determined the previous autumn, and that the grouse killed by predators during the winter are the surplus non-territorial birds that would die anyhow(14). It is even said that the abundance of these surplus grouse is what attracts a large population of predators into any area; more grouse should be shot each autumn to avoid this situation. Thus one can argue that a good proportion of the grouse killed by golden eagles or peregrines can scarcely affect the spring breeding stock, for they would die anyhow. It is only spring predation that is important to stocks in the shooting season; and it was in connection with spring predation that it was estimated that eagles only took 2% or less of the available stock.

The hen harrier is in a somewhat different case to the peregrine and golden eagle. It kills surplus adult grouse in winter but is unable to kill healthy adult breeding grouse and is most important as a killer of chicks in the breeding season. Here again, the available evidence from elsewhere is that the hen harrier only kills a few game-birds and that its main prey is small mammals, especially voles, and other moorland birds. However, good Scottish figures on the prey, or even full data from Orkney where the harrier is not persecuted, have not yet been published, though there is reason to believe that hen harriers on eastern grouse moors do kill quite a number of young grouse.

Whether these depredations make any real difference to the bags at the end of the season has yet to be evaluated. Indeed, this is one of the most important aspects of the evidence that needs to be gathered. There are estates which formerly persecuted golden eagles and other raptors but which do not now do so. Do these estates now obtain poorer bags in consequence? Col. Meinertzhagen records instances in eastern Ross where the conservation of predators not only did not decrease bags, but actually increased them several times over. However, we need more recent objective evidence on these points.

I think that I have now laboured these points sufficiently to make clear that the three species most concerned on grouse moors, the golden eagle, peregrine falcon, and hen harrier, do not or cannot do sufficient damage on well-managed grouse moors to justify any alteration in the law to permit their destruction at present. They only kill a small number of grouse, and of these a good many would die of other causes anyhow. Forced into a corner in this way, the opposition of landowners and gamekeepers tends to argue that it is not the numbers of grouse killed but the disturbance caused on grouse moors that is damaging. The golden eagle, in particular, is said to clear a moor of grouse if it appears in the sky, and a good day's driving is spoiled. This could be, as I can see, particularly annoying in these days when many people can only manage a day or two's grouse driving each year, staying in a hotel and going out for a day rather than taking a lodge for the season at an astronomical price of around £6 per brace of grouse shot.

It may be said that the golden eagle is just as likely to drive grouse on to a moor from somewhere else as off it(14). It could certainly be claimed that when this happens the eagle will not be given the credit while, if it clears a moor, it will certainly be blamed. To be fair, I would think it is likely that golden eagles prefer to hunt in certain parts of their range, and that accordingly they would be more likely to drive grouse out of certain areas than others. However, an astute grouse moor owner should be able to observe such facts, if they occur regularly, and act accordingly – and not by killing the eagle.

Of the three species concerned, it is chiefly the golden eagle that is accused of disturbance. The peregrine falcon has the reverse effect, causing the grouse to squat tight, for they know well enough that the falcon can only kill in the air. Although hen harriers are reported to disturb grouse as badly as an eagle and can catch grouse on the ground, I have watched hen harriers hunting low over abundantly stocked grouse moors in eastern Scotland without raising any grouse. I have often seen grouse and ptarmigan fleeing in panic from an eagle, so I am familiar with the phenomenon. The actual validity of this complaint about disturbance requires careful objective investigation; but I think it likely that when such an investigation is done it will show that the complaints are exaggerated. In 1921 Professor Rowan, studying the merlin, was unable to persuade the gamekeepers in the area not to shoot the young merlins. They would, he was told, cause disturbance at grouse drives. Even in 1921 he despaired of such reasoning; but in such respects the reasoning powers of some grouse moor gamekeepers have not advanced one whit since 1921.

Thus, when we come to examine the burning issues objectively they are found to be very flimsy bogies. No serious damage can be proven in the case of any bird of prey, and only a few species could do even slight damage to pigeon racers, shepherds, or game preserving interests. The birds of prey are shown to take a small proportion of the available prey of pigeons, lambs, or game-birds in any area, and to take many surplus animals that for other reasons would not survive anyhow.

Nothing in this examination would convince any dispassionate judge that there was any need to alter the law at present to permit destruction of rare or common birds of prey. In the event that certain species, for instance the goshawk and the hen harrier, became much more numerous in the future it might be necessary to keep their numbers under control. If so, it should be done on the basis of biological investigation and not, as at present, illegally, and on the basis of outworn nine-teenth-century ignorance and prejudice.

CHAPTER 24

TERRITORY, SPACING AND NATURAL
POPULATION CONTROL

In any resident breeding population of birds of prey (or of any other species) in Britain or elsewhere, it is usually claimed that food supply is the primary factor controlling the population. If there is no prey to eat, naturally there can be no raptors of any sort. Such conditions are, of course, found only in extreme desert environments or the Arctic, and in any temperate or tropical environment there is usually a superabundance of possible prey. This is because the populations of the prey, in their turn, must in the long term be able to survive the ravages not only of predators, but of climate, disease and starvation as well. All these are usually capable of making more drastic inroads into prey populations than any number of predators, which often only skim off the periodical surplus. Accordingly, it is usual to find that in the home range or territory of any raptor there is more prey than that raptor can possibly eat, even if it could catch it all in prevailing conditions of cover or weather conditions.

Of course the effects vary greatly from place to place and species to species; and the study of this subject is almost infinitely complicated. However, the obvious primary factor of food requirement is not the only one which comes into play in the natural regulation of raptor numbers. The population of several species of birds of prey is also self-limiting through its own behaviour and spatial requirements. However carefully protected, some species of birds of prey would never attain any greater population than is permitted by their own territorial or dispersion behaviour, even in the presence of superabundant prey animals.

Among British breeding species it is only possible to study this aspect of behaviour in a few cases, since most species are or have been so badly persecuted, or their habitat so much interfered with that we cannot suppose they behave in the same way as would, for instance, members of the same genus in the protected environment of an African National Park or the vast boreal forests of Siberia. Even in the so-called National Parks of Britain our birds of prey are far from immune from human interference: for instance they often harbour gamekeepers and always are visited by many people. In Snowdonia or the Cairngorms you are not told to stay in your car; and there are no lions or elephants or puff adders to induce the timid to do so. In a few species, however, the natural methods of population control do appear to override the all-too prevalent effects of human interference, either with the raptors themselves or with their habitat; and even where the habitat is largely artificial, as it is all over Britain, the patterns of natural population regulation do tend to appear.

To study the interactions of food supply and needs, and territorial requirements which may or may not be based on these, it is necessary to find a population of raptors which is at or near capacity numbers, that is the maximum that that particular environment can maintain. A characteristic of most such raptor populations is that they are relatively stable, changing little from one year to the next. A breeding site temporarily unoccupied one year will be reoccupied in a future year. We know enough now about the behaviour of certain unmolested capacity populations of raptors, notably in tropical Africa, to be able to observe similar behaviour patterns, even in Britain.

Any species suited to such study must also be common and widespread. It is no use even contemplating the study of natural methods of population control in Britain in any of the vagrant, rare migrant, or extremely rare breeding species such as the goshawk, osprey, marsh harrier, or kite. Some of these have been well studied abroad, notably the goshawk. It is possible that in certain parts of southern England the existing population of hobbies or even of honey buzzards may actually be at local capacity numbers. It appears, for instance, that in the New Forest, where it is protected, the hobby is nearly as numerous as the kestrel; is relatively far more numerous than anywhere else in southern England; and that the rather small numbers are fairly stable from year to year(23). However, even at that, I doubt if anyone wishing to make a study of natural regulation in a hobby population would pick the New Forest as first choice for a study area. The few pairs of Montagu's harriers breeding on southern heathlands may behave, individually, quite typically for their species; but no one could say that Montagu's harrier is at capacity numbers on, for instance, Exmoor, or that its population is not unnaturally depressed by a variety of human interference factors, probably including the insidious effects of persistent agricultural pesticides.

Eliminating these rare or vagrant species, we are left with the seven species with more than 100 breeding pairs in Britain, all of which are probably at capacity numbers in some sufficiently large part of their British breeding range to be worth studying from this aspect. Fortunately, these species include quite a good variety of types, which can be compared with other species elsewhere in the world. They include, for instance, three falcons, nearly half the total; but of these one, the kestrel, is a semi-nomadic and migratory mammal-eating species which can be expected to behave rather unlike either the bird-eating, ground-nesting merlin, or the bird-eating, cliff-nesting peregrine. We know that the population of the latter has, in recent years, been adversely affected not only by persecution and human interference but by pesticides; but fortunately it is such a spectacular and well-loved bird that a great deal is known of its past history and mode of natural population regulation(18).

Our species also include one harrier, the hen harrier, whose Orkney population has been stable, and therefore probably at or near capacity numbers since the fifties. Moreover it has been devotedly studied in several respects for many years, so that here we probably have a better source of material for the study of regulation of harrier numbers than in any other harrier species anywhere else in the world. We have one typical woodland hawk, the sparrowhawk which, although grievously decreased by persecution and the more insidious effects of pesticides, is still at capacity numbers in some parts of its British range, and displays typical population regulation patterns even in some other parts where it is persecuted(17). In the common buzzard we have a good example of a generalised, medium-sized bird of prey, depending mainly on mammals, but highly versatile in its hunting methods. And finally, we have one big eagle, the golden eagle, which is certainly at capacity numbers in several parts of its range, and has been quite extensively studied from the viewpoint not only of its food supply and requirements but also of its spatial needs. Britain does not at first sight appear as promising a study area as, for instance, the Serengeti or the Amazon jungles; but the mine of available information here is richer than one would at first think, while there are still many good nuggets in it for the quarrying.

Table 20 Types of Territorial Behaviour in Common British Birds of Prey

Type 1 Regularly spaced breeding pairs maintaining ranges by strong territorial behaviour.
    2 Regularly spaced breeding pairs without obvious territorial defence.
    3 Breeding pairs regularly dispersed, with areas of undefended common hunting ground.
    4 Nesting pairs spaced well apart, but only small area round nest defended.
    5 Almost non-territorial; hunts in communal areas, defends only small area near nest.

Type	Species	Preferred food/ habitat	Type of territorial behaviour
1	Common buzzard	Mammals, birds/ woodland, open country	Strongly territorial winter and summer. Defends nesting and large feeding area by display, conspicuous perching, attack on trespass.
2	Golden eagle	Mammals, birds/ open mountainous country	Regular espacement summer and winter in apparently undefended home ranges of remarkably uniform size irrespective of food supply: population very stable. Espacement may be assured by methods unseen by human observers.
	Merlin	Birds/open moorlands	Regular wide espacement of breeding pairs in summer stable, as far as known, without overt defence of range; in winter non-territorial.
3	Sparrowhawk	Birds/woodland	Breeding pairs regularly spaced at variable distance throughout available habitat. Little overt territorial behaviour other than some display. Hunts outside nesting territory, when non-territorial.
	Peregrine	Birds/cliffs on seashore or in mountains	Nest site strongly defended; a larger area less often. On sea cliffs 'linear' range occupied year round; in mountains large ranges more akin to Type 2. Extensive 'no man's land' between defended areas, summer or winter. Linear distance between pairs varies in different parts of Britain.
4	Hen harrier	Mammals, birds/ open moorland	Not strongly territorial in summer, non-territorial in winter. Individual female nesting areas grouped in larger male territories, varying according to number of associated females from year to year. Polygamous in summer, gregarious in winter.
5	Kestrel	Mammals, birds/ open country, some woodland	Almost non-territorial, nomadic. In summer defends only small area round nest, may become colonial; gregarious and migratory in winter.

PLATE 15. MERLINS. *Above,* merlins perch on stumps, rocks, or hummocks, and hunt their prey skimming low over moors. *Below,* merlin at nest in heather; one egg has been accidentally kicked out of the nest, but was later retrieved.

PLATE 16. HOBBY and PEREGRINE. *Above left,* adult hobby at nest with two young in a Scots pine; this is one of our least-known species; *right,* a hobby just out of the nest; such young learn to catch insects before hunting birds. *Below left,* an adult peregrine; this swiftest and most magnificent of British breeding falcons is menaced by agricultural pesticides; *right,* a young peregrine displays typically powerful feet.

The seven most numerous British species display widely different types of territorial behaviour, which I have set out schematically in Text Table 20. The differences are in the degree in which the whole area potentially available to a pair of birds of prey is treated as a territory, in the generally agreed sense that a territory is a defended area. The British species vary from the strongly territorial buzzard to the relatively non-territorial kestrel, which only defends from other kestrels a small area round the nest. Between these extremes, about five discernible types of territorial, spacing, or dispersion behaviour are shown, and the majority of the species do not obviously defend even a large part of the area available to them. This reinforces my view that 'territory' is a bad word to use in describing the areas occupied by birds of prey.

No two species behave exactly alike though two pairs of species, not closely allied systematically, appear to have evolved rather similar dispersion patterns. These rather uneasy pairs are golden eagle–merlin, and sparrowhawk–peregrine. The least territorial species in the nesting season, the hen harrier and the kestrel, are both likely to be gregarious in winter, though this tendency is displayed more strongly in the kestrel in other parts of its range than in Britain. The most strongly territorial species, the common buzzard, is also the most inclined to defend a winter feeding territory.

The type of terrain does not clearly affect the mode of territorial behaviour, and experience elsewhere suggests that this is linked more to systematic relationships than to anything else. All *Buteo* species that have been studied seem to be strongly territorial, and since they are among the easiest to study, being large and common, may even have led some observers into the belief that all raptors must necessarily behave the same way. Likewise nearly all big eagles that have been studied display a regular highly stable espacement of pairs over the breeding range from year to year without obvious fighting or territorial behaviour. It is possible that woodland species may be more obviously and actively aggressive than those which live in open country, though this does not apply to the commonest and most widespread woodland genus, *Accipiter*. When we know more about it we may find that open country species may be able to defend their sometimes large ranges by more subtle means than, for instance, the obviously aggressive buzzard, which behaves in a similar way whether it lives in open Sutherland moorlands or Devon or Welsh woods, but whose behaviour may have evolved in woodland.

The type of prey preference, mammals, or birds, or both in some degree, does not appear to affect the type of territorial behaviour shown. And this, as Lewis Carroll would have said, is really odd because, if food supply actually controls the numbers and dispersion of birds of prey, one would expect it to be tightly bound up with the type of territorial behaviour which achieves the dispersion pattern.

One of the best-known species in Britain is the hen harrier. It is at least semi-social, and polygamous, exhibiting behaviour that will probably be found typical of most of the world's harriers, if and when they are properly studied elsewhere. Mapping of hen harrier nesting sites shows that the same females, or a succession of different females, use the same general area from year to year; if a site is unoccupied in one year it is normally re-occupied again sometime(1). Although on the map these nests appear in groups, the nest-sites of individual females within the group are rather regularly spaced 300–500 yards apart. (Fig. 7). These loose groups themselves perhaps represent the territories of individual males who may, as they grow older and more capable, take on additional female partners, even including in their harems females that may in other years have been mated to other males.

The groups, and hence perhaps the males' territories or ranges, change from time to time, but this aspect of the hen harrier's behaviour has not yet been very critically analysed, nor have the results been published. Clearly, much more work is needed before we can understand just how it works. However, it seems that the Orkney habitat is only capable of supporting a certain number of females and their broods, and that these are mated to or dependent upon a smaller number of males, always averaging about two females per male, but varying from one with a young male, rising to a normal maximum of three or four in his prime, and decreasing again with his old age(4).

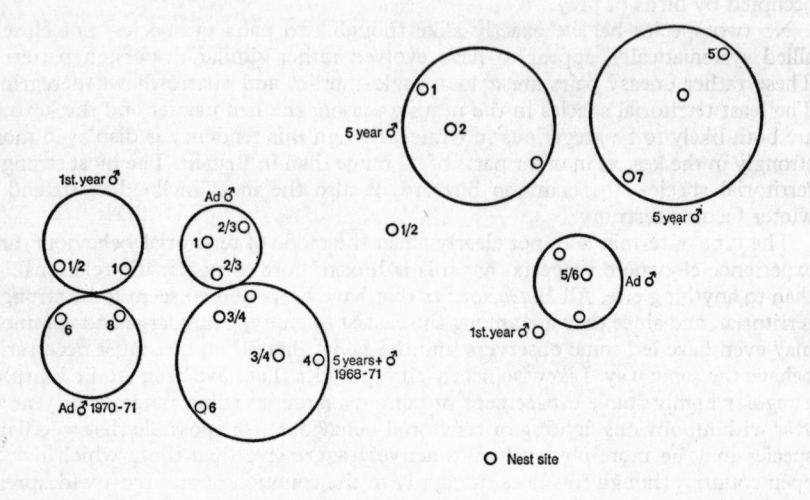

FIG. 7. Hen harrier territories, diagrammatic (to conceal real locality), showing nest sites and polygyny; Orkney 1971. (J. Cadbury and E. Balfour.)

In the hen harrier little obvious defence of nesting territory is seen by adjacent males, and nesting females may defend only a small area close to their nest. Yet a spacing mechanism of some sort clearly operates to ensure regular dispersal over large areas of comparatively featureless open moorland. Almost the same nesting sites are used year after year, much further apart than the area actually defended by a female. Otherwise, even Eddie Balfour could not have walked over an apparently undistinguished bog, observed in his inimitable way 'She should pe chust apout here', clapped his hands, and up she got. If no harrier appeared, probably the nest was roughly where he expected it, and had either been abandoned or had come to grief from some usually unknown cause.

From what little we know of the other British harriers, the marsh and Montagu's harrier, a somewhat similar nesting pattern occurs, though in both cases the females may nest even closer to one another (only 30–50 yards apart in Montagu's harrier) than do individual female hen harriers(19). Unfortunately the only other harriers that have been fully observed elsewhere are the same species, the marsh, Montagu's and hen harriers in Europe, and the American race of the hen harrier(7,12). In essentials they do not seem to behave differently in Holland, Hungary, or Wisconsin. It also appears that the pied harrier, breeding in Siberia, behaves rather like a hen harrier(16); and I cannot myself perceive much difference in the behaviour of the African and European marsh harriers, which may be conspecific.

The mode of natural population control through regular espacement shown by the hen harrier in Orkney is thus likely to be fairly typical of harriers on their breeding grounds world-wide, at least in temperate climates. In view of the amount of data already available on the species in Orkney, the lack of persecution there, and the apparent absence of any severe pesticide effects (not, apparently, the case in Wisconsin), Orkney is an ideal area for the study of the mechanism of self-regulation in harrier populations, which is not at present fully understood.

In winter all harriers appear to be non-territorial and to roost communally(7,13). This has been well observed in the American race of the hen harrier, and though some of the Orkney hen harriers occupy and hunt over the same ground year-round they too roost in numbers in certain places. The marsh harrier is too rare in Britain to show this tendency, but it roosts communally, in small groups, in Africa in winter(2). Montagu's and the pallid harrier likewise roost in regular places, in larger groups in their African winter quarters; individuals of these two species may mix at the roost. From the American studies of roosting hen harriers in winter it seems that the 30–40 individuals in any one roost fly direct from the roost to hunting areas, which vary from time to time. Thus the hen harriers seen hunting over Orkney moorlands in winter may not be the same birds that nested there in summer. Presumably, the individuals in these communal harrier roosts also vary from time to time; but too little is known about this aspect of harrier behaviour generally. All one can say is that any loose territorial behaviour shown by hen harriers in summer is lost in winter.

The merlin occupies the same habitat as the hen harrier, open moorland, but feeds in a completely different way, on birds which it catches in flight, and not on mammals caught on the ground. Its mode of population regulation is not clearly understood and has apparently never yet been fully studied. However, Rowan's pioneer studies established that merlins occupy large home ranges in which nesting sites are fairly stable from year to year, but are colonised or recolonised by fresh birds as the existing owners die or are shot(20). Given this pattern it appears extremely unlikely that merlins would ever become over-numerous, even if they were strictly protected and allowed to rear their broods unmolested every year. Their territorial behaviour is more reminiscent of that of the golden eagle than of other falcons and is certainly very different to that of the hen harrier inhabiting the same study area. However, the merlin has been too little studied anywhere for a sound understanding of any aspect of its biology.

The kestrel too lives in the moorland habitat of the hen harrier, but further south inhabits mixed agricultural country with woodlands. It displays yet another mode of territory and population regulation. It is, for all practical purposes, non-territorial, as breeding pairs defend only an area of about 35 yards all round the nest site, about an acre, probably less than 1% of the available area per pair(6). In Britain the population of kestrels is relatively stable, does not migrate far, and is certainly not truly nomadic. However, in some other parts of its range the kestrel is truly nomadic; that is, the entire population wanders and concentrates to breed where food supply, usually rodents living in open country, is temporarily abundant. Such rodents are typically subject to very violent local fluctuations in population numbers, so that, given enough nesting sites in one area, it would be advantageous for the kestrels not to be strongly territorial. Large numbers could then concentrate to feed on any available rodent plague without having to spend much of their time repelling each other from large territories.

In Britain the conditions on the Central European and Asian steppe, which may be considered ideal nomadic kestrel habitat, do not apply. However, in neighbouring Holland, in an area somewhat similar to East Anglian fenlands, the kestrel population has been shown to fluctuate very greatly over a period of a few years, the maximum being almost four times the minimum, despite a superabundance of available nesting sites in the form of nest boxes specially erected for the kestrels(6). In much of rural Britain it may be the lack of suitable nesting sites more than any other factor which limits the total numbers of kestrels. This can only be determined by experiment, by saturating any area with nest boxes till most of them are always unoccupied.

In theory, if kestrels behave like, for instance merlins, which presumably repel other merlins somehow from their large home ranges, it should be possible to achieve a kestrel population of one pair per acre (which is all they will defend), if there are enough catchable rodents for them to eat. That is quite evidently unlikely; but the kestrel population, given enough nesting sites, would probably stabilise around some figure, perhaps an average of a pair to 200 acres (80 ha.) on, say, Cheviot moorlands, fluctuating from as many as one pair to a 100 acres (40 ha.) to as few as a pair to 400 acres (160 ha.) over several years. In all cases these 'home ranges' would be far larger than the acre or so of nesting territory which the individual pairs would actually defend from other kestrels, so that here we would have a case of nomadic species controlled only by food supply, and not by territorial spacing behaviour at all. It would be illuminating to carry out controlled experiments with kestrels along these lines, in different parts of Britain. They could provide a far clearer answer than even detailed studies of the natural population. Even London parks, such as Richmond Park, would make quite good study areas.

In the sparrowhawk there is evidence that the population is at present severely restricted by the use of pesticides, and in this species the information from the past is not sufficiently accurate or comprehensive to show what changes may have occurred since 1950(17). The sparrowhawk is also persecuted, and to some extent at least its population is limited by the availability of suitable woods in which to nest. However, in parts of its range in Britain, natural patterns of dispersion do appear among nesting sparrowhawks, especially in large areas of forestry plantations which are at the right stage of growth.

From such areas we learn that, given similar woodland cover, the sparrowhawk pairs space themselves regularly apart. If one puts pins or coins on a map to show the breeding places they make a very nice regular pattern. They average 0·4 miles apart in Dumfries; 0·7 miles apart in southern Kincardine; 1·0 miles in Central Wales; and 1·5 miles in the Spey basin of Inverness (0·6, 1·1, 1·6 and 2·4 km.)(17). In other words, sparrowhawks are almost four times as common in Dumfries, in terms of linear distance as they are in Speyside; and the area of country potentially available to each Speyside pair is fourteen times as great as in Dumfries. However, it is not known whether pairs hunt over the whole of the area potentially available to them; and some at least visit hunting grounds not occupied by breeding sparrowhawks.

Table 21   Home Ranges/Territories of Sparrowhawk, Buzzard, Golden Eagle and Peregrine

Sources	Area of study	D=Average distance in miles between adjacent pairs (Range min-max)	Theoretical defended circular territory (sq.ml.)($\pi \times \frac{1}{2}D^2$)	Actual calculated area available per pair (sq.ml.)
Sparrowhawk				
(1)	Dumfries	0·4	0·126	0·16 } × 6·2
	Central Wales	1·0	0·78 } × 14	1·0 } × 14·1
	S. Kincardine	0·7	0·39	0·49 } × 4·6
	Inverness (Spey basin)	1·5	1·77	2·25
(2)	Holland			2·7
	Germany (Sachsen)			4·25
Buzzard				
(3)	Skomer			0·21
(4)	Dartmoor	0·88(0·28–1·75)	0·78	0·9 } × 2 } × 15·7
(5)	Inverness			1·8
(6)	New Forest			3·3
(7)	Germany			0·96 } mean 770
(8)	Denmark			1·02 } prs. = 0·93
(9)	France (Lorraine)			0·49
Golden eagle (in order of natural food abundance)				
(10)	Aberdeenshire	3·02(1·5–4·6)	28·2	17·8
	Wester Ross	4·4(3·3–6·0)	61	These theoretical 23·5 circular ranges overlap
	N.W. Sutherland	3·2(2·1–4·9)	33	17·9
	Argyll	3·8(2·2–5·6)	36	27·8
(11)	Lewis	—		15·6
Peregrine falcon				
(12)	S. English sea-cliffs	1·6	2	Linear cliff plus undetermined inland area
	Welsh sea-cliffs	2·9	6·6 } × 4·9	
	N. Scotland sea-cliffs	3·5–4·0	9·7	
	Inland central Wales	3·1	7·6	20
	Inland N. England, S. Scotland	3·0	7·1	18·8
	Inland Perth, Inverness	4·5	15·8 } × 4·3	37
	Inland W. Highlands	6·4	32·3	85

Sources (1) Newton, 1971. (2) Tinbergen, 1946. (3) Davis and Saunders, 1965. (4) Dare, 1961. (5) Weir, unpub. (6) Tubbs, 1967. (7) Mebs, 1964. (8) Holstein, 1956. (9) Thiollay, 1967. (10) Brown and Watson, 1964. (11) Lockie and Stephen, 1959. (12) Ratcliffe, 1962.

NOTE   The figures in the last column assume that the birds concerned can hunt over the whole of the area available to them; they may not in fact utilise the whole area.

N.B.   If it is desired that these figures should also be expressed in metric units 1 sq.mi. = 2·59 sq.km. and 1 mile = 1·61 km.

Considering these four areas in more detail the Dumfries area may appear ecologically more akin to Central Wales than to either Inverness-shire or southern Kincardine; both are relatively wet areas with planted or natural woodlands and large tracts of open sheep walk. However, Dumfries has much more arable land than central Wales. S. Kincardine in and near the lower basin of the Dee, is really rather similar to the Spey basin of Inverness. It is, however, less wooded than Speyside, has more arable land, and a drier warmer climate, all factors which should encourage a larger population of small birds. In winter, especially, the Spey basin is relatively devoid of small birds.

The area of ground available per pair in Inverness is over four and a half times as great as in south-Kincardine. Nest sites in central Wales are two and a half times as far apart as in Dumfries; and here the area of ground potentially available to a pair of sparrowhawks is more than six times as large (6·2). Between the two extremes, the Spey basin and Dumfries, which are nearer to one another geographically but ecologically less similar than Dumfries and central Wales, the nest sites are nearly four times as far apart in the Spey basin, while the area potentially available in Speyside per pair of sparrowhawks is over fourteen times as great as in Dumfries. Without good quantitative evidence I am unable to accept that differences of this magnitude are to be wholly explained by facile assumptions that they are due to differences in the available food supply.

In the case of the sparrowhawk it appears that whatever method of natural population regulation applies in different parts of the country it results in regular espacement of breeding pairs over a given area of suitable habitat. In sparrowhawks, however, it also seems quite clear that the birds hunt outside their nesting ranges, if ground not occupied by breeding pairs is available to them. Whether this would be the case if, as must once have been so, the whole country were covered with suitable woodland habitat is doubtful. Lacking such neutral ground over which to hunt sparrowhawks might then have been obliged to space themselves more widely apart in the breeding season, as apparently they do in large Dutch woodlands(21). In Tinbergen's study of the sparrowhawk the population from year to year was stable, and the nest sites were all occupied in most years, usually by different birds. In other words, this population of sparrowhawks was apparently at capacity level. Yet the size of individual home ranges, in apparently more suitable sparrowhawk habitat, was very much larger than in Dumfries.

I have paired the peregrine, rather uneasily, with the sparrowhawk. Both eat birds, both are at present severely affected by agricultural pesticides and to some extent by illegal persecution. However, for the peregrine we have available far better data on the breeding sites before the Second World War, and a fine population study by Derek Ratcliffe on which to base conclusions(18). Even when it is at capacity numbers, however, the peregrine's distribution is limited by availability of cliff nesting sites; and almost all the nesting sites are natural cliffs. Artificial cliffs, such as buildings or quarries, are not much liked even if available. No cliffs, no breeding peregrines! However, in most of the larger mountainous tracts of Britain, in Wales, Cumberland, or the highlands of Scotland adequate cliffs are usually available, sufficiently widespread to give the peregrine a choice of possible breeding ledges within a home range.

Thus, in these areas pre-war the peregrine was at capacity numbers and its distribution could be mapped quite exactly (Fig. 8). This is not the case today, when pesticides have affected the population; but in the highlands of Scotland at least, certainly in central Inverness-shire, peregrines are still at or near capacity

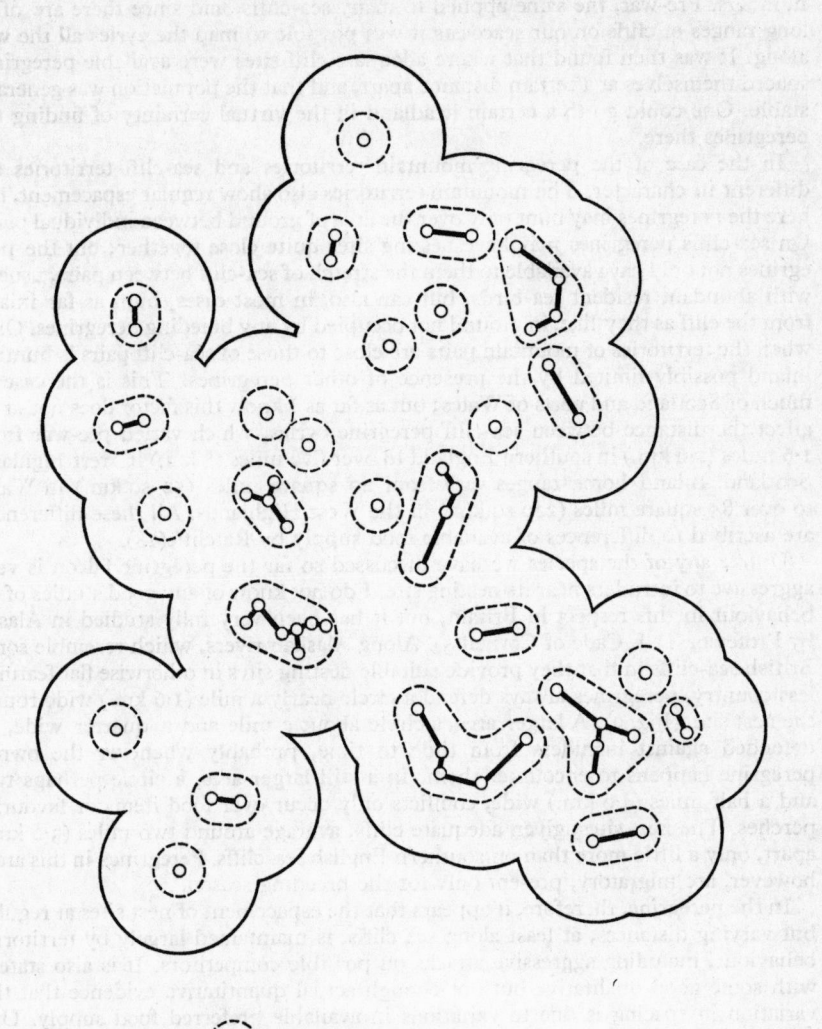

FIG. 8. Peregrine falcon: breeding sites in an inland study area. Average distance between sites 2.9 miles. (Adapted from D. A. Ratcliffe, 1962.)

Single nest site

Alternative nest sites, one pair

numbers. Pre-war, the same applied to many sea-cliffs, and since there are often long ranges of cliffs on our seacoasts it was possible to map the eyries all the way along. It was then found that where adequate cliff sites were available peregrines spaced themselves at a certain distance apart, and that the population was generally stable. One could go to a certain headland in the virtual certainty of finding the peregrines there.

In the case of the peregrine mountain territories and sea-cliff territories are different in character. The mountain territories also show regular espacement, but here the peregrines may hunt only over the area of ground between individual pairs. On sea-cliffs peregrines may have nesting sites quite close together; but the peregrines not only have available to them the stretch of sea-cliff between pairs, usually with abundant resident sea-birds, but can also, in most cases, hunt as far inland from the cliff as they like, in ground not occupied by any breeding peregrines. Only when the territories of mountain pairs are close to those of sea-cliff pairs is hunting inland possibly limited by the presence of other peregrines. This is the case in much of Scotland and parts of Wales; but as far as I know this factor does not at all affect the distance between sea-cliff peregrine eyries, which varied pre-war from 1·6 miles (2·6 km.) in southern England to over five miles (8 km.) in west highland Scotland. Inland home ranges vary from 20 square miles (52 sq.km.) in Wales to over 85 square miles (220 sq.km.) in the West Highlands. All these differences are ascribed to differences of available food supply by Ratcliffe(18).

Unlike any of the species we have discussed so far the peregrine falcon is very aggressive to intruders near its nesting site. I do not know of any good studies of its behaviour in this respect in Britain, but it has been very fully studied in Alaska by Professor T. J. Cade of Cornell(5). Along Alaskan rivers, which resemble some British sea-cliffs in that they provide suitable nesting sites in otherwise flat feature-less country, peregrines always defend a circle nearly a mile (1·6 km.) wide round the nest site. (Fig. 9). A larger area, a circle about a mile and a quarter wide, is defended against intruders from time to time, probably whenever the owner peregrine happens to encounter them. In a still larger area, a circle perhaps two and a half miles (4·0 km.) wide, conflicts only occur over food items or favourite perches. The nest sites, given adequate cliffs, average around two miles (3·2 km.) apart, only a little more than on southern English sea-cliffs. Peregrines in this area, however, are migratory, present only for the breeding season.

In the peregrine, therefore, it appears that the espacement of nest sites at regular but varying distances, at least along sea cliffs, is maintained largely by territorial behaviour, including aggressive attacks on possible competitors. It is also stated, with some good qualitative but not enough actual quantitative evidence that the variation in spacing is due to variations in available preferred food supply. Un-fortunately, in the peregrine today, the possibility of studying these aspects of behaviour is limited by the abandonment of so many breeding sites since the fifties, due to the effects of agricultural pesticides. These even appear to affect peregrines nesting on remote sea-cliffs, where otherwise food availability at different seasons could be quite readily estimated, and where human persecution is likely to be minimal. Our understanding of these aspects of the peregrine's behaviour must largely rest upon past research, except in central Scotland where the population is still healthy.

The common buzzard is, apparently, an even more aggressive bird than the peregrine to others of its own kind, though it is not at all aggressive to human beings and perhaps less to other birds such as corvids, which a peregrine will often harry

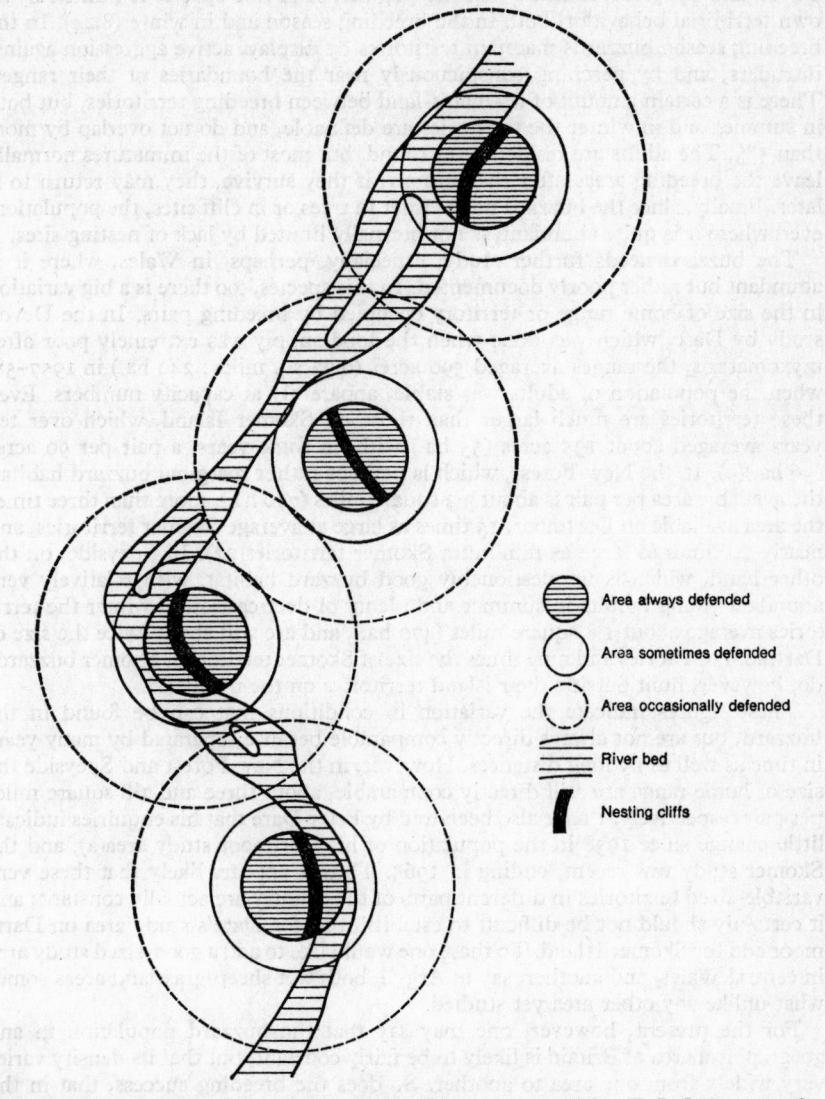

FIG. 9. Peregrine: defended territories, Yukon River, Alaska. (After T. J. Cade, 1960. See also Brown and Amadon, 1969.)

unmercifully. Both the detailed studies that have been done on the buzzard, in Devon and Speyside, indicate that the population of this species is limited by its own territorial behaviour, both in the breeding season and in winter(8,24). In the breeding season buzzards maintain territories by display, active aggression against intruders, and by perching conspicuously near the boundaries of their ranges. There is a certain amount of no-man's-land between breeding territories, but both in summer and in winter the territories are definable, and do not overlap by more than 5%. The adults are resident year round, but most of the immatures normally leave the breeding areas after the autumn; if they survive, they may return to it later. Finally, since the buzzard nests either in trees or in cliff sites, the population, even where it is quite abundant, is not normally limited by lack of nesting sites.

The buzzard needs further study, especially, perhaps, in Wales, where it is abundant but rather poorly documented. In this species, too there is a big variation in the size of home range or territory occupied by breeding pairs. In the Devon study by Dare, which was done when the food supply was extremely poor after myxomatosis, the ranges averaged 590 acres (0·92 sq. miles: 240 ha.) in 1957–58, when the population of adults was stable, apparently at capacity numbers. Even these territories are much larger than those on Skomer Island, which over ten years averaged about 135 acres (55 ha.) with, in some years, a pair per 90 acres (36 ha.)(9). In the New Forest, which is perhaps rather marginal buzzard habitat, the available area per pair is about 3·3 square miles (770 ha.), more than three times the area available on Dartmoor, 15 times as large as average Skomer territories, and nearly 20 times as large as minimum Skomer territories(22). In Speyside, on the other hand, which is unquestionably good buzzard habitat, with relatively very abundant young rabbits in summer and plenty of deer carrion in winter the territories average about 1·8 square miles (470 ha.), and are still about twice the size of Dartmoor territories and nine times the size of Skomer territories. Skomer buzzards do, however, hunt outside their island territories on the mainland.

These figures indicate the variation in conditions that can be found in the buzzard, but are not always directly comparable because separated by many years in time as well as by long distances. However, in the New Forest and Speyside the size of home range are still directly comparable, about three and 1·8 square miles per pair respectively. I have also been told by Peter Dare that his enquiries indicate little change since 1958 in the population of his Dartmoor study area(a), and the Skomer study was recent, ending in 1965. Thus it appears likely that these very variable-sized territories in different parts of the country are actually constant; and it certainly should not be difficult to establish this for Dare's study area on Dartmoor and for Skomer Island. To these one would like to add a good-sized study area in central Wales, and another, say in Argyll, both wet sheep/grassland areas somewhat unlike any other area yet studied.

For the present, however, one may say that the buzzard population in any geographical area of Britain is likely to be fairly constant, but that its density varies very widely from one area to another. So does the breeding success, that in the Speyside study area in recent times being four times as great as that on Dartmoor 15 years ago, but only about two and a half times than that on Skomer Island where the territories are smallest.

Thus far, most of the species discussed show wide variation in the size of home range or territory they require, and in their way of ensuring espacement of breeding pairs, which often have not been fully observed or understood. However, whatever part of the country may be concerned, and whatever species may be living therein at capacity numbers, a regular pattern of espacement of breeding pairs emerges, though there are usually wide differences in the distance apart in the same species in different parts of Britain. The golden eagle appears to be something of an exception to this general rule, and to maintain home ranges of remarkably similar size in different parts of Scotland, irrespective of the ecological conditions, and of the available food supply.

In five study areas of Scotland, in widely varying ecological conditions, golden eagle breeding sites always average three to four and a half miles apart, and the total areas available per pair varies from 10,000 acres (Lewis) to 18,000 acres (Argyll), usually 11,500 acres to 14,000 acres (4050, 7300, 4650, 5700 ha.)(3). In fact, I doubt if the variation in size of actual home range used by a pair is even as great as this, for when one puts the coins on the map in the traditional manner one sees that there are quite large tracts for some reason not occupied by breeding eagles and that the breeding pairs are spaced at remarkably regular intervals. The maximum and minimum differences between pairs are somewhat misleading.

In the golden eagle the numbers are not normally limited by the lack of nesting sites, though in relatively cragless and treeless areas such as the Monadhliath mountains and parts of Sutherland and Caithness there are fewer breeding eagles per hundred square miles than elsewhere, and the birds may then breed on any little cliff that is just usable. Usually, however, there are adequate good cliffs and/or trees available; and having established the situation of one pair's nesting site it is easy to predict where the next may be.

This method may be applied to any bird of prey provided one knows the normal spacing of the species in any area of country; an experienced observer can establish this to his own satisfaction in a few days' work. In the golden eagle the espacement of pairs is apparently very much more regular than in any other British species, except, perhaps, the merlin, with which I have, again uneasily, paired it in respect of dispersion behaviour but which is inadequately studied. The golden eagle, unlike the merlin, is resident in its home range the year round; in this respect it is more like the buzzard or the peregrine, both of which have home ranges or territories of widely varying size.

The regular espacement of the golden eagle in the highlands may be due to the fact that the whole of the habitat is mountainous, and therefore rather similar, showing less variation perhaps than the habitats of buzzard, peregrine, or kestrel. However, there are very wide differences in the landforms found in different parts of the eagle's habitat, in rainfall and climatic conditions, in vegetation and in food supply. The extremes are, perhaps, the steep grassy and craggy mountains of Argyll and Wester Ross, practically devoid of grouse, hares or ptarmigan; and the rolling heathery hills of, say Atholl, with only a few small cliffs, but by comparison swarming with hares, grouse and ptarmigan. The dispersion pattern of golden eagles in these two contrasting areas is very nearly the same; and nothing that I have found in any part of Scotland, Morvern, Knoydart, West Perthshire, Lochinver, or the Ben Alder massif leads me to believe that these areas are markedly different in this respect. Given freedom from persecution and an adequate place to nest the eagle pairs are always regularly spaced apart. (Fig. 10).

The particular pattern of dispersion and territorial behaviour of a species may be due more to specific or generic affinities than anything else. For instance, all harriers appear to be semi-social and bigamous or polygamous; all buzzards (Buteo spp.) are strongly territorial and very aggressive to each other; and all big eagles seem to have a very regular pattern of dispersion over any tract of country,

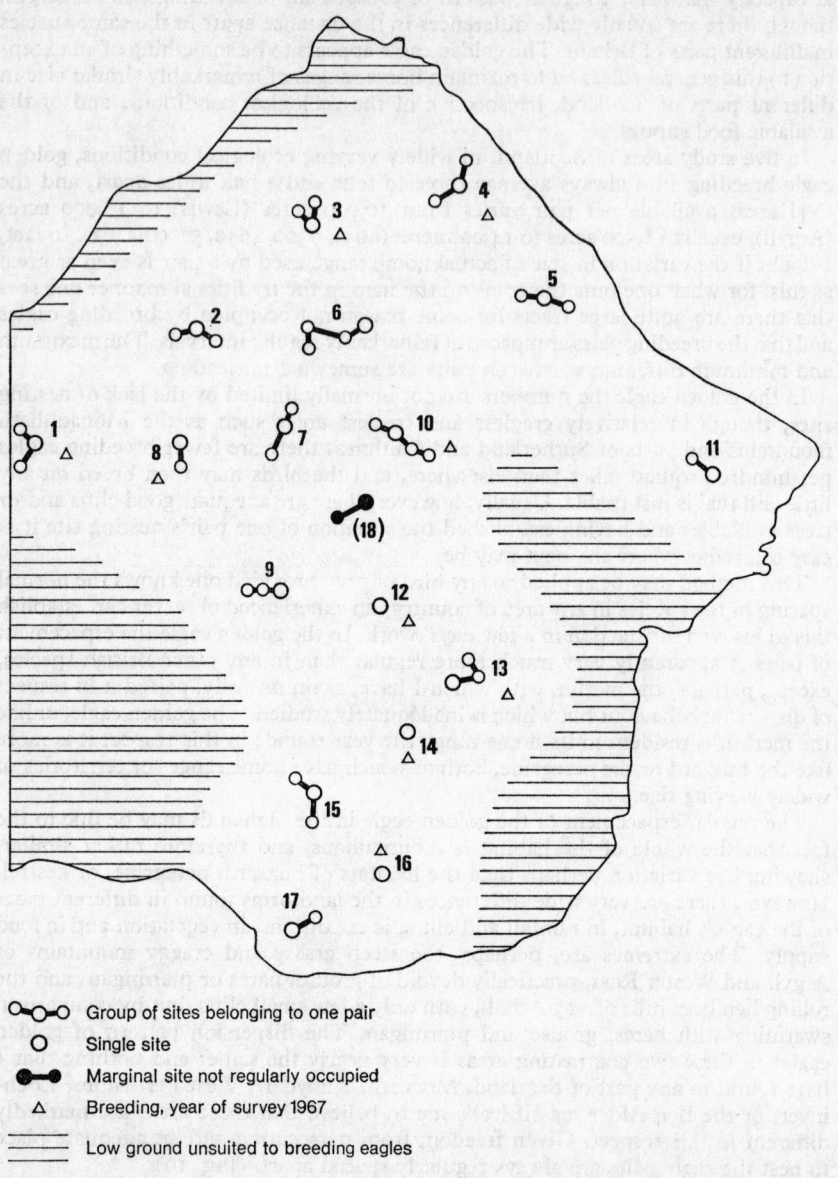

FIG. 10. Even dispersion of breeding sites in a capacity population of golden eagles, Scotland.

The map legend reads:

- Group of sites belonging to one pair
- Single site
- Marginal site not regularly occupied
- Breeding, year of survey 1967
- Low ground unsuited to breeding eagles

though in some, for instance Verreaux's eagle, the size of the range varies a good deal from one part of the total area inhabited to another. Presumably these patterns have evolved in order to enable the species to survive over a very long time, and it is therefore perhaps unlikely, except in nomadic species, that they would quickly change in the light of rapid changes of habitat or of food supply brought about by human activity in the last century or two. For instance, in the buzzard, whose territory varies greatly in size, there is little real evidence that the catastrophic reduction in food supply following myxomatosis greatly affected the total population of territorial adults, though it did perhaps adversely affect their breeding success(15).

Most such variations in dispersion pattern are ascribed to variations in food supply, but I do not consider that this case is always adequately proved. To do so requires a careful quantitative assessment of the food supply of preferred prey animals, as well as the numbers of the bird of prey concerned and its population dynamics, including breeding success, over a period of years. It is usually impossible for one man to do both successfully; and ideally this problem should be tackled by a team, composed of a plant ecologist, mammalogist and ornithologist with access to advice from geologists and topographical geographers. I do not think any such attempt has ever been made in Britain, and until it is we are unlikely to have the quantitative data needed to prove the case that dispersion patterns are always or usually based mainly or entirely on available food supply.

The detailed surveys of the peregrine falcon provide some general information supporting the theory that food supply controls nesting density for this species(18). Pre-war, the peregrine was most numerous on southern English sea-cliffs, nesting at an average of a pair per 1·6 miles (2·6 km.), with access to rich farmlands inland where suitable prey, including domestic pigeons, was probably abundant. On Welsh sea-cliffs peregrines were less numerous; and on northern Scottish sea-cliffs the nests were 3·5–4 miles (4·8–8·7 km.) apart; on these northern cliffs sea-birds may be quite abundant in summer but in winter, when the peregrines are still there, the areas are an ornithological desert. Inland, the density varied from an average of 3·0 miles (4·8 km.) between pairs in N. England and S. Scotland, to 4·5 miles (7·3 km.) in Central Scotland and 6·4 miles (10·3 km.) in the West Highlands. Anyone acquainted with the general food potential of these areas might be somewhat surprised that the density of peregrines is greater in southern than in central Scotland, where game-birds are relatively very abundant; however, this is explained by the fact that these southern peregrines could also easily fly to lowland farmlands where, inter alia, there were plenty of pigeons. In the West Highlands, catchable food supply, flying birds in open country, is obviously scarce.

On sea-cliffs it is difficult to judge the total area used by any peregrine pair, because they hunt an unknown distance inland as well as along the cliff. Only where mountainous country abuts on sea-cliffs could the breeding peregrines meet with direct competition from inland-nesting birds, and there is no real evidence that this affects the spacing pattern observed. Ratcliffe observes that there is scarcely any evidence that peregrines maintain a territory in Britain by territorial behaviour or defence. Yet he concludes, on general evidence, that this must be so, and that the size of the territory of home range is connected with the availability of food.

In the case of the nomadic, non-territorial kestrel, the work of Cavé in Oost Flevoland seems to prove that the numbers of kestrels breeding in any year is controlled largely by the abundance of voles, and that behaviour and breeding success is also much affected by the weather and hunting conditions; bad weather in winter can affect breeding success in advance(6). This conclusion is also generally indicated by British brood records and ringing data. Although there are some aspects of these studies, such as the ability of the male to supply large broods with food even in bad vole years, which are difficult to reconcile with the view that food supply controls both numbers and breeding success, this view must at present be accepted in this species. The same may well apply to such other more or less non-territorial and semi-colonial species as the osprey and Montagu's harrier.

However, in the buzzard, which is much more strongly territorial in its behaviour than even the peregrine, and which is also resident in Britain year round in or near its nesting range, I find it hard to believe that the food supply on Skomer Island is nearly ten times as abundant as on Speyside; rabbits are relatively abundant in both places and the scientists who did the Skomer study did not think food supply was an important limiting factor(9). I likewise find it hard to believe without better quantitative data that the food supply for sparrowhawks is almost 14 times as abundant in Dumfries as in Speyside. In studies on both these species food supply has been advanced as the main reason for the wide differences in size of home range or territory found; and I certainly do not think this case is adequately proven.

In the golden eagle I am personally convinced and, with Adam Watson, have provided a good deal of quantitative evidence in favour of this theory, that the existing dispersal pattern has little to do with available food supply, which generally appears superabundant if carrion is included(3). If one considers only the available preferred wild food supply hares, rabbits, grouse, and ptarmigan, one finds enormous variations in the amount of wild prey available between areas with almost exactly similar linear distance between pairs. One area may have five to more than a hundred times as much live wild food as another; yet in both the eagles manage to survive and breed at a density of one pair per 11,000–12,000 acres (4500–4900 ha.). When one considers carrion, in the form of dead sheep and deer, one finds that it is generally superabundant, especially in winter and spring. However, although carrion may be important to adults and to young during the winter after they leave the nest, the adults in the breeding season may prefer to depend on natural live prey. This is certainly necessary for rearing the young, and varies enormously in abundance irrespective of the nesting density. Again, poor food supply may affect breeding success, but among unmolested pairs, on available data, even this effect is only marginal(10).

In the golden eagle, and for that matter among other large African eagles, I do not consider that the evidence supports the view that breeding density is controlled by food supply. Accordingly, the remarkably regular dispersal of the breeding pairs over wide areas of similar habitat, which appears typical of big eagles, is presumably controlled by the birds themselves. Quite how is not yet understood, for eagles are not actively territorial as are buzzards, which in any given area have a somewhat similar regular dispersal pattern. In both the golden eagle and Verreaux's eagle, which is its African equivalent, even when several pairs are soaring together, and can obviously see one another, any sort of territorial demonstration or fighting is rare(11).

Food supply has not been quantitatively and accurately assessed in relation to territory size in any British species; the data for the golden eagle is as good as any available. Even in Dare's detailed buzzard study, although food supply was generally thought to be the main controlling factor, good quantitative evidence was lacking(8). In several cases general assertions are made, sometimes with some qualitative evidence to back them, as in the peregrine, but without full quantitative detail.

I therefore consider that the available facts only enable us to say that in any part of Britain, or any other country, the population of any resident bird of prey will reach a certain level and then remain relatively stable at capacity numbers, which will in some species vary from area to area on a constant dispersal pattern. The numbers may in some cases be controlled by such other factors as availability of nesting sites. However, where the population is not held at less than the potential natural level by this means, it is not only controlled by the available food supply, but also by other factors such as the behaviour of the birds themselves. This often has not been fully observed or understood; and there is evidently a rich mine for further research along these lines, both in Britain and elsewhere.

CHAPTER 25

BREEDING BEHAVIOUR

THE breeding behaviour of birds of prey has been more thoroughly studied than any other aspect of their lives. This is easily understandable since the nest, which may be a large permanent structure used for many years, is one certain means of locating an individual otherwise hard to find in a large home range or territory, which in large species may be twenty square miles or more. A breeding bird must return to the nest if it contains eggs or young, and an observer concealed in a hide can then, with proper care, watch exactly what it does.

There is also a special fascination in watching the behaviour of birds of prey with their young. There is no contrast in nature more entrancing than that between the rending wrenching strength of an eagle tearing the flesh and skin from the bone, and the extraordinary gentleness with which the morsel of food is patiently presented to a weak and feeble chick. Of course, as the chick grows, so it gains strength, and gobbles the food presented to it; but the observer close to the nest, perhaps only thirty feet away, still is thrilled by the intimate spectacle.

Somehow, it seems, that piercing glare, visually several times as acute as human eyesight, must detect him in hiding. However, birds of prey are not usually particularly shy or difficult to observe and photograph at the nest. They are much easier, for instance, than a duck or a greenshank; but no duck or greenshank ever looked like an eagle or even a merlin at close quarters.

In the chapters on the various species breeding in Britain I have described their individual breeding behaviour, and accordingly I shall avoid repetition of much detail here. Although breeding behaviour is better understood than other aspects of the lives of British birds of prey, there are still some lamentable gaps in our knowledge. Some species, such as the hen harrier, are very well known; others, such as the merlin or hobby, are much less well known. In yet others, such as the honey buzzard, there is much detailed knowledge of the behaviour available from Europe, but very little published in Britain. The behaviour of the kestrel, for instance, is very well known now as a result of Dutch studies; but I have yet to find a good account of the breeding of the kestrel in Britain, although it is by far the commonest British breeding species.

On a world-wide basis it is often true that the more spectacular and rare a species is, the more it has been studied. Thus, some of the big eagles, which are relatively uncommon, may have been exhaustively studied by enthusiasts for decades, while much commoner, smaller, but potentially just as interesting species nesting in the same area have been more or less ignored(7). I classify the knowledge of breeding behaviour of birds of prey in five categories, as follows: (i) Unknown; the nest has never been found; this applies to many tropical species but not, of course, to any British or European species. (ii) Little known; one or two nests may have been found, and odd observations made, but little detail is available. (iii) Well-known; a good general idea of the nesting habits, nest sites, clutch size, etc., is available; and some sustained observations have been made in at least one case. (iv) Very well-known; the general nesting behaviour is understood, and detailed accurate observations are available throughout most of the breeding cycle for at least one nest, leaving only a few details to add. (v) Intimately known; observations in detail made over many years and at many different sites, including such advanced details as records of the changes of mates and longevity of individuals.

If these criteria are applied to the 15 British breeding species (of which one, the sea eagle, no longer breeds here, but once did and may again) none are unknown or little known. On British published data alone, the honey buzzard, red kite, sea eagle and goshawk could only be called little known; but of these, the red kite will advance into the very well known category when the studies of the Welsh Nature Conservancy are published; and the honey buzzard, sea eagle, and goshawk are either very well or intimately known (goshawk) on the basis of published European studies.

In the 'well known' category I would place the marsh and Montagu's harriers, merlin, hobby, and peregrine. Of these, the peregrine might just be elevated into the very well-known category on British data alone, and certainly would reach that status on the basis of additional American and European data. The hobby, and the two harriers would also be considered very well known on European data, but the merlin is apparently not better than well known anywhere. Of all the British breeding species it is the one most in need of detailed study. A year or two's systematic work would greatly advance our knowledge of this species.

The sparrowhawk, buzzard, golden eagle, and kestrel are very well known in Britain, the kestrel being the most doubtful member of this group. Of these, additional continental data on the sparrowhawk, buzzard and kestrel might advance them to the intimately known category, especially the sparrowhawk. The golden eagle is not better than very well known anywhere in its vast range. It is doubtless intimately known to Seton Gordon, from his studies in Skye, not published in full detail; and it is approaching that status in some regions of America, while the British studies of the pair in the Lake District should likewise make the breeding behaviour intimately known. However, from the published literature it is certainly not as well known even as some quite rare African eagles.

The osprey and the hen harrier are perhaps intimately known in Britain, though the details of some aspects of the hen harrier's breeding, notably in the fledging period, are not yet fully described. The studies of the osprey have not yet been analysed, and published in full; this is now being done by the R.S.P.B., but too late to include in this book. The breeding behaviour of the hen harrier has been thoroughly understood for many years through the work of Eddie Balfour in Orkney, a magnificent long-term study which has not attracted the world-wide attention it deserves. A few more years' work on the hen harrier, directed to a few additional objectives, such as the details of parental behaviour during the fledging period, or observing how individual males manage their polygamous affairs, will make the Orkney hen harriers perhaps the best known species of birds of prey anywhere in the world. Certainly they are already in the 'top ten'.

This general survey of our knowledge of breeding behaviour indicates that there are still some considerable gaps. Co-ordinated and directed research, either by a group of people who may be interested in doing it on their own initiative, or through some such organisation as the B.T.O. or Nature Conservancy, could soon fill in some of these gaps. However, detailed knowledge of such matters as the share of the sexes in the incubation and fledging periods, or the amount of food eaten by the parents and young is only to be gained by protracted spells of concentrated observation. In Britain this means sitting in a hide, usually cold and often damp, and sometimes bored stiff, for many hours at a time, and recording exactly what is seen. As I have mentioned, in my opinion this is best done by teams of observers, with a clear idea of what they are trying to observe, and with the results recorded or extracted on to pro-forma sheets, which can be bound in loose-leaf form and readily analysed at the end of each day, week, month, stage of the breeding cycle, or the season.

When such work is done, it is usually found that although there are differences between the behaviour of different species of birds of prey, a common thread runs through the breeding cycle of most species. It would be very surprising indeed to find that the behaviour of one buzzard species differed greatly from that of another member of the genus *Buteo* in any other part of the world. Some surprises do occur with detailed study; the best example I have recently come across is the remarkable disproportion between male and female kestrel chicks reared in nest boxes in Holland(10). Also, and perhaps fortunately, not all birds of the same species behave the same; because one female golden eagle shares the duties of incubation with the male it does not follow that all will. Observations in enormous detail at one nest will not give so good a picture of a species' breeding cycle as observations in good detail at one nest, supplemented by adequate confirmatory observations at six others. However, by studying the available literature, a good deal of which has been summarised in this book and other standard works, one can obtain a good idea in advance as to what is likely to happen at any nest. That should not, of course, make one assume that the predicted is inevitable; surprises can occur and will be noted by any careful observer.

All birds of prey nest within a territory or home range. As already mentioned, I dislike the use of the word territory in general when dealing with birds of prey, for in a good many species the whole area occupied and hunted over by a breeding pair is not defended from others of the same species. Some species, for instance the harriers and the kestrel, are not strongly territorial. Even some species such as the sparrowhawk and peregrine, which nest quite well separated may not display strong territorial behaviour, or may sometimes hunt on common ground used by several pairs. Of the British species, only the common buzzard really seems to be strongly territorial; but some other species, such as the golden eagle, may ensure their regular espacement pattern by subtle territorial behaviour understood by other eagles but not, at present, by humans.

The territory or home range may be occupied seasonally in the case of summer migrants or, for instance in the merlin which nests on high moors and moves to lower ground in winter. Alternatively it may be occupied year-round, as in the golden eagle, peregrine, or buzzard; in the buzzard the winter territory defended is not necessarily quite the same as the summer nesting territory(25). What one can say is that once a territory has been defined in one year, and a nest site located within it, that is the most likely place to look for the birds in later years. Even in the sparrowhawk, which nests in apparently featureless conifer woods, or in the merlin which nests on rolling moorlands, with apparently an unlimited selection of suitable nest sites, the same small general area is resorted to year after year, and the nest will usually be found within a few yards of that of earlier years(19). Of course, there is some movement to alternate sites; but it is best to look carefully first at the known past nesting site in an old established territory.

The same nest site is not always occupied by the same birds, but appears to attract, year after year, a succession of different birds. In the case of birds such as the osprey or the golden eagle, which make huge nests which remain visible for many years even after they are deserted it is fairly easy to understand how this comes about. It is unlikely that both members of a pair of these large, relatively long-lived species, which pair for the life of any individual, and may be paired for five years or more will die at the same time. A bereaved survivor attracts another mate and naturally returns with him or her to the old nesting site. A new mate may not like the old mate's nest, and may insist on building another; but usually the old nest is simply accepted and refurbished by a succession of different birds. It may be occupied for half a century by ten or 15 different individuals.

This faithfulness is less easy to understand in smaller species, such as the sparrow-hawk or merlin, which apparently return to the same nesting sites (but not necessarily the same nests) with great fidelity, but in which both the individuals attracted to this spot may be new adults that have never nested there before. In part this may be explained by an apparent tendency, as yet not fully documented, on the part of young birds to return to the same general area in which they have been reared after an absence of one or more years. The new birds that re-occupy an old site may be the offspring, or at least the fairly close relatives of birds that nested there before. However, this sort of theory can only be proved by extensive colour ringing; and as yet there is no good evidence to show that this is how the same nest sites come to be preferred year after year even when the individuals occupying them are different. One must just be grateful for the fact that this is so, for it makes the study of birds of prey much easier.

The presence of the owner in the nesting territory or home range is demonstrated by display, usually aerial, and sometimes also vocal. Most of the British and well-known European species do not perform such spectacular or noisy displays as do some of the tropical species, for instance the African fish eagle and the crowned eagle. However, in essentials, the display behaviour is very similar, and the exact form it takes is usually dictated by specific and generic affinities. In virtually all members of the genus *Accipiter*, including the sparrowhawk, goshawk, and over 40 other species distributed world wide, nuptial display consists of soaring with spread tail and calling in the early morning, with the same basic feature of rather slow stylised wing flapping, shallow undulations in flight, and diving back down to the forest, sometimes towards the nest-tree(19). All the big falcons perform spectacular swooping and diving displays, often together, sometimes accompanied by screeching or raucous calling; all male harriers that have been well observed perform spectacular tumbling dives towards the ground; and almost every big eagle I know at some stage performs spectacular undulating and swooping flights high in the air, sometimes attracting attention to the performance by calling.

The common forms of nuptial display are: (i) Perching and calling; the male sits on a commanding perch and emits a loud, far-carrying display call. Sometimes females also perform such displays. (ii) Soaring and calling; the bird soars high up, often in circles or figures of eight, elaborating the display by vigorous diving and swooping in undulating flights, and sometimes attracting attention by calling. As a very general rule, species which breed in heavy woodland or forest are more vocal than those which live in open country; the buzzard, for instance, is much more inclined to call than the golden eagle. (iii) Mutual displays, in which the male soars above the female, then dives towards her; she turns over and presents her claws briefly to his, or he may swing up again without any such response. Many of the British species perform such displays more or less often; and they are sometimes extremely spectacular performances.

The most spectacular mutual displays of all are the 'mock fighting' displays of fish and sea eagles including the European sea eagle(11). In these the female, turning over on her back to meet the diving male, then locks her feet with his and either spins or whirls downward for several hundred feet, separating just above the ground or water. This beautiful variant has been described in poetry by Walt Whitman, referring to the American bald eagle(27), and occurs in most members of the genus *Haliaeetus*, some kites, and a few other species; it has been described in the buzzard, but is apparently rare in any British species. To the participants it must resemble the vigorous birling of an excited young couple in an eightsome reel. Displays of this type can be distinguished from real fighting by observing the relative size of the participants; the female is always bigger, and would at the start be flying below the male.

These displays are normally seen before rather than during the breeding season. In the golden eagle, for instance, soaring displays are most often performed on fine days in winter and early spring(d). Certain displays, such as the whirling descent flights of male harriers, probably represent a peak of sexual excitement reached only rather late in the nuptial display period; and often male birds of prey continue displaying above or near the nest site after eggs are laid or young have hatched. However, if the breeding proceeds normally display is usually inhibited by other activities, for the male then has work to do feeding female and brood. If the nest fails, or eggs are not laid, birds such as golden eagles or peregrines which remain in their home ranges year round may continue to indulge in out-of-season displays. Such displays doubtless help to maintain the pair bond in species which remain mated to one another for the life of any individual; probably all the larger species are in this category, though harriers are certainly fickle(2).

When the female is ready to mate she usually remains near the nest site, where she is very often fed by the male. Actual mating usually occurs on or near the nest, and may be preceded by solicitation on the part of the female, who may crouch, flutter her wings, display certain markings such as the white nape feathers and eye stripe of the female sparrowhawk, and sometimes utter begging calls. Males may present food to the female at mating, or bring a twig or spray of leaves. Mating may occur many times a day over a short period, or less often over a much longer period. In the osprey, for instance, it may occur more than a hundred times within three weeks(b); and in golden eagles males have been known to feel moved to mate six weeks before egg laying, without any apparent female invitation(13). Not enough is known about mating behaviour in most species.

A pair may go as far as to display in their territory, mate, build up the nest, but not lay eggs. Positive evidence for such non-breeding is rather hard to obtain, as it is necessary to search far more thoroughly than when an obviously occupied nest is found. However, non-breeding is now well documented in the golden eagle and buzzard, and probably occurs even in smaller species such as the sparrowhawk or harriers, though proof is then even harder to secure(23,24). However, when one finds a nest repaired but empty, one need not always suppose that a predator, or more likely a human egg collector has been there and taken the eggs. They may never have been laid. Usually, when this occurs, the birds concerned then leave the vicinity of the nest site and move to other parts of their range, behaving again as they do during the winter. However, it is always as well, when non-breeding is suspected, to check again when there should be young in the nest. Sometimes old nests are repaired and not used while the pair breeds in a new nest which is not discovered during display or incubation but becomes more obvious once the young are growing in it.

It is likely that when non-breeding occurs it may be connected with food supply though nowadays the effect of pesticides must also be feared. In the buzzard, many pairs did not breed immediately after the catastrophic reduction of rabbits by myxomatosis. In the golden eagle there is some evidence that, in areas of poor food supply, fewer pairs may try to breed than in areas of very good food supply. In this case, however, a more careful look at the situation raises some further queries. Even in areas where the natural food supply of live animals is short, golden eagles should always be able to find enough carrion in early spring. It therefore seems unlikely that a female would be unable to muster enough energy to lay an egg from sheer shortage of food; she might only have to fly a mile or less to find a dead deer or sheep.

In this case, I have wondered whether food supply as such is the whole explanation, or whether it is necessary for the female to be presented with food in a certain courtship ritual by the male(6). I have no evidence for this theory in the golden eagle, in which males have not been seen to feed females. However, in several other eagles the female is fed by the male before and during the incubation period; and perhaps if she is not so fed she may go off to hunt for herself, and lose interest in breeding(5). Non-breeding, as a result of the male's failure to catch enough food to enable the female to breed would be a neat natural form of population control related to food supply. However, there is no positive evidence that this is what occurs in the golden eagle and the suggestion requires observational proof.

Most birds of prey build their own nests, but no falcon does. If any falcon is found breeding in a stick nest, it is that of a crow, heron, buzzard or eagle, temporarily appropriated by the falcon, which seldom actually ejects the rightful owner from a new nest, but usually uses an old or abandoned one; hobbies sometimes use newly built crow's nests. In some smaller species, notably the sparrowhawk and harriers, a new nest is built each year, easily recognisable from old nests of the same pair in the same area(19). In others, such as the kite or the honey buzzard, sometimes a new nest is built, or an old nest of the same or another species may be added to. In yet others, including all the largest species, new nests are seldom built and the same old nest or group of nests is repaired annually.

Such annually repaired nests often become enormous structures. The largest I have personally seen was a golden eagle's nest occupying the whole of the top half of a Scots pine, about 17 feet deep and known, at that time, to have been used intermittently for at least 40 years and probably half a century. Ospreys and sea eagles also make enormous nests; but those of common buzzards or kites, the next stage down in size, never become so large, nor are they used for so long. Goshawks, much larger than sparrowhawks, build much bigger nests, and are more likely to use the same nest in a second year, though they too normally build afresh each year. Harriers annually make small or large nests on the ground, the size being probably most affected by the type and degree of wetness of the terrain – bigger in wet places(4).

Most of the large species that return to the same nest or site yearly have several alternative sites, and it is often supposed that these are used in regular succession, as a kind of sanitary measure. The idea is that in a long breeding season a nest becomes so fouled with droppings, bits of prey, and parasites, that it will be avoided next year if possible. Any parasite that can survive the Scottish winter in the frozen grasp of a golden eagle's nest deserves to thrive; but in fact the evidence for anything of this sort is very slim. Eagles have from one to 11 nests, usually two or three, one of which may for some reason be preferred to the others and be more regularly used. I know of no evidence to suggest that those which have only one, or regularly use only one nest of several alternates, breed any less successfully than those which have many and use a different nest each year. In fact, I would suspect that the reverse is the case, and that the frequent re-use of the same or a favourite nest is often a response to freedom from human disturbance, which certainly causes eagles to build and use more nests than they do in completely undisturbed localities(17). A new nest may sometimes mean a new mate; but just as often, I believe, a new mate will calmly accept and use the dwelling of his or her predecessor.

In most species both sexes take some part in building the nest, but the female does more than the male, and in some does it all. In the goshawk, according to Holstein, the nest is built largely by the male; however, this needs confirmation as it would be virtually unique in the whole order of Falconiformes. In the osprey, on which very detailed information is available in Britain, the male begins to repair the nest as soon as he arrives at the site (9,b). When the female joins him she also brings sticks, but the male continues to bring more than the female until after the young hatch. The female then brings in more than the male, possibly because he is busy catching fish for the whole family while she remains near the nest with little to do. In such cases, bringing nest material may be a biologically valuable displacement activity, helping to keep the female near the nest, where she is needed. In the hen harrier the female does most of the nest building, and the male only occasionally brings any material. In the honey buzzard, again according to Holstein, the male brings most of the material and the female works it into the structure(14). Perhaps this achieves some economy in time, in a species whose breeding cycle is abnormally compressed at the beginning as it is a summer migrant. The entire process varies from species to species and in many has not been exactly observed.

In species such as the golden eagle, which remain in their territory year round, and seldom build a new nest but repair old ones, nest building may be seen at any time of the year, even in winter(13). If a pair fails to breed successfully or loses its eggs they often build up nests in May and June. Ospreys, likewise, build 'frustration eyries' as they have come to be called. In most species, however, the building of a new nest or the repair of an old one is concentrated in the early spring, just before the eggs are laid. In some cases a nest may be begun in one year, and completed and used in the next.

When egg laying approaches all birds of prey line their nests with green sprays of trees, some selecting Scots fir if it is available, rushes, moss, or other softer material than the thick sticks which may form the main structure. Deliberate or not, this makes a softer bed on which the eggs are laid. In all species the eggs are laid at intervals of more than one day; and if the clutch is large, as in harriers, kestrels, or sparrowhawks, it may take a week or ten days to deposit. However, the female usually begins to sit before the clutch is complete, and in large species, such as the golden eagle or osprey, always begins to incubate with the first egg. Falcons, harriers, sparrowhawks, or goshawks normally begin incubating after several eggs have been laid. As smaller species usually lay larger clutches of eggs (four to seven as opposed to one to three in large species) the late onset of incubation means that there is less difference in size between individual members of the subsequent brood, and in very large species such as eagles, the gap of three or more days between the laying of the first and last eggs later has a critical effect on the survival of the young.

The eggs of birds of prey are usually rather rounded ovals, with a whitish or bluish ground colour sometimes, but not always, spotted with red-brown to a varying degree. Those of harriers are unmarked pale blue, and in the falcons the eggs have a buffish or pinkish white ground so heavily obscured by red-brown and brick-red markings that from a distance they appear wholly dark red. Among the most beautiful are those of the sparrowhawk, clear pale blue, with rich red-brown blotches; and those of the honey buzzard, highly variable, white or pale buff, spotted, clouded, and blotched with red or red-brown, the marking sometimes obscuring the ground altogether.

Having been an egg collector in my youth I can appreciate the fascination of possessing a cabinet full of beautiful eggs, and the sense of achievement derived from a stiff climb to secure what is in fact, a trophy. However, I have never been able to understand the desire to take clutch after clutch of even common species, which has been and still is so harmful, while it would be absurd now to pretend that Oology, as a science, can add much of value to our knowledge of a species, when hundreds of clutches already lie in cabinets in museums and private collections, seldom or never examined with care by anyone.

In most birds of prey the female incubates alone, and may be fed on the nest or may leave it to feed herself. If the female must leave the nest to feed she must expose the eggs to cold, wet, or predators such as crows which can be serious enemies of birds of prey. It is therefore biologically advantageous either for the male to feed the female or to share the duties of incubation with her, so that she can leave the nest long enough to catch prey for herself. In the first of these alternatives, the male is naturally forced to catch more prey than he himself needs; but when females are incubating their appetites are probably reduced, so that they can manage with a kill brought once every few days(5).

Too little is known in detail about incubation behaviour in British birds of prey; but in many of our species the female incubates alone, though she is not always fed by the male. No male harrier has ever been proved to incubate, though this was once suspected in a hen harrier, after the eggs were addled(c). In the golden eagle, males have not been seen to feed females, which leave the nest to feed. Normally, if a male incubates, it is only by day, and for comparatively brief periods, often when the female is off the nest feeding on prey he has brought. This is true, for instance, of the osprey, in which the male takes a large share(9). In the merlin we have one of the few known instances of a male incubating all night, a duty which normally falls to the female(21). However, when more observers have watched through the night we may find that this is more common than is supposed! As a general rule females do from 80–100% of all incubation in all species.

Incubation periods are long to very long; the shortest are those of small falcons, about 28 days, and the longest those of large eagles, about 45 days. Within the same genus the incubation periods tend to be rather similar, irrespective of the size of the bird. Thus the peregrine hatches its eggs in 30–32 days, almost the same time as the merlin or kestrel, only about a fifth or a quarter of its weight; and the marsh harrier, twice as heavy as Montagu's, takes only a little longer to hatch; the incubation period of Montagu's harrier is not satisfactorily established. The goshawk, according to one authority, takes 45 days to hatch, but a more normal estimate is 36–38 days, while the sparrowhawk, a fifth of the goshawk's weight, hatches on average in 35 days. There is less proportionate difference between the incubation periods in the large and small members of these groups (averaging less than 10%) than between, for instance, the buzzard, which hatches in 34–37 days, or the osprey hatching in 36 days and the golden eagle hatching in 43–45 days. The golden eagle, less than four times the weight of these species, has an incubation period almost 25% longer. With these exceptions, there is a general correlation between increase in size and length of incubation period, a principle recognised long ago by Aristotle(20).

The end of the incubation period can usually be detected, without disturbing the birds on the nest, by the behaviour of the incubating parent. For some 24–48 hours before it breaks free the hatching chick can be heard cheeping in the egg; it breaks out just as in any other bird by making a hole with the egg tooth on the bill-tip and finally splitting the shell. While the chick is actively trying to break free the parent 'sits high', slightly raising the body and part opening the wings; and often peers beneath its body in a seemingly surprised yet expectant manner. Those species which lay large clutches, such as harriers, often have vigorous chicks a week old in the nest at the same time as the later laid eggs are still hatching. However, in all these species, the onset of true incubation is deferred until several eggs have been laid, so that the hatching period is always shorter than the laying period. In the peregrine falcon, incubation does not begin till the second last egg is laid, so that the young all hatch almost together.

The difference in hatching dates means that there is a large difference in size, and particularly weight, between the earliest and latest hatched chicks. In harrier broods the eldest may be part-feathered while the youngest is weak and downy. Normally, some of these latest-hatched chicks die, because they are unable to obtain enough food, so that the brood is reduced by degrees. In some cases the young are actively aggressive towards one another and then the natural disadvantage of smaller size is aggravated by fratricidal strife. In those species which lay larger clutches and rear large broods, such as the harriers, the sparrowhawk, and smaller falcons, the young are not usually aggressive towards one another and any deaths occur through starvation or weakness. In species which lay small clutches, however, especially in the golden eagle, but also, for instance in the common buzzard, goshawk, and, most surprising, the insectivorous honey buzzard(14), fratricidal strife in some degree may cause the death of the weaker chick.

The battle between siblings in eagles' nests was first immortalised as the 'Cain and Abel' battle by Seton Gordon; it has since been solemnly discussed by German observers as 'the problem of Cainism'(26). In the golden eagle, and in other large eagles of about the same size, such as Verreaux's or the wedge-tailed eagle, the second hatched chick in a normal clutch of two eggs, weighs only about 100 grams while the elder weighs about 250 grams(1). The contest which shortly begins is as unequal as that between a fit and active heavyweight boxer and a lightweight just out of a hospital bed. It has been suggested by both Lack and Wynne Edwards that this contest is a response to inadequacy in the food supply(15,29). However, observations on several species have shown that this is not the case, and that it regularly occurs in the presence of far more abundant food than the chicks could possibly eat. Its purpose remains obscure; but in many eagles it accounts for 75–100% of the mortality among second hatched chicks, and in some the second chick is invariably eliminated. In the golden eagle in Britain this happens in about four cases in five where two young hatch; there is some slight evidence that the second chick is less often killed in areas of abundant food, but the difference is marginal.

The Cain and Abel battle has recently been more critically observed, in the lesser spotted eagle and other species, by Bernd Ulrich Meyburg(18). His observations show that the first hatched chick is not always or immediately aggressive to the second hatched, which may live with it in the nest for two or three days, being fed by the parent, grow and become more vigorous, before it is suddenly attacked. Once it is attacked, it has little chance, for the elder pursues it remorselessly round the nest, apparently in a frenzy of fury, hacking at its back and head, squatting on it, and finally driving it to the cold and exposed nest edge. Sometimes the younger bird actually seals its own fate by first attacking the elder. Once it has been attacked, it becomes submissive and makes no attempt to defend itself, grows weak and is unable to beg for or obtain food from the adult, and soon dies or falls out of the nest. Once it is dead it may be fed to the older young bird or even eaten by its parent.

If an attempt is made to save the younger chick by removing it, or the elder, from the nest, hand rearing it up to a point, and replacing it later, the other will still go at the one replaced hammer and tongs, and kill it if it is not again saved. The hand-reared youngster, even if younger, may actually be bigger and heavier; but once the aggressive instinct of the other has been fully aroused a chick replaced stands little chance until the late stages of the feathering period. When the small young one in the nest is well feathered the second can be replaced and will be accepted and reared by the adult eagles to independence.

In this way the breeding potential of some scarce birds of prey can be nearly doubled. In the period when it is out of its own nest the eaglet can either be reared by human hands or be placed in the nest of another bird of prey, such as a black kite or a buzzard, which may have to be assisted to rear this large cuckoo in its nest by a supply of extra food placed there by humans. In recent attempts to rear young goshawks in sparrowhawks' nests it was clear that the sparrowhawks could not catch enough food for the young goshawks, which had to be removed and reared by hand(a). Such methods are somewhat desperate but could be useful, for instance, in re-establishing sea eagles in Britain.

Newly hatched birds of prey are very feeble and weak, have heavy heads and partly closed eyes, and are covered with a thin first coat of down, later replaced by a second, thicker, and more serviceable coat. They cannot feed themselves, and must be very gently induced to feed by the parent, usually the female. The adult tears off a shred of flesh from whatever prey may be available, and very gently holds it out on the hooked tip of the beak to the young bird, which must reach up to get it. The young bird reacts to anything red held out to it, by reflex action. I think everyone who has watched the gentleness of a big bird of prey feeding its tiny weak chick is entranced by it; but in a few days the chick is vigorous enough to reach up and snatch greedily at the proffered morsels, so that many pieces of prey are swallowed one after another in a few minutes.

During the fledging period the roles of the parents are normally clear cut. Usually, the female broods and feeds the chicks alone; the male may take some part in the brooding, but even when he does he very seldom feeds the young, even if the female is not present. Young may solicit males, which often seem ill at ease and do not remain long at the nest. Probably, they are actually afraid of their larger and usually fiercer female partners. Male golden eagles and sea eagles have been known to feed young in the nest with the female present; but this is extremely unusual behaviour in a bird of prey(28).

This relatively clear cut division into the roles of food-bringer and brooder/ feeder means that the male must normally kill far more than he himself needs to satisfy his mate and brood. Instead of only a female with a reduced appetite he must also provide for several rapidly growing and voracious chicks. Usually he doubles or trebles his rate of killing as soon as the chicks hatch and his hunting instinct is no longer solely controlled by his own appetite. A surplus of prey often accumulates in the nest. At first the chicks eat little, and the female subsists on part of the kills brought by the male, swallowing what the chicks do not take, and feeding herself after they are satisfied. However, by the time the chicks are half-grown they may eat as much as an adult; and if shortage of food is to show up at any stage of the breeding cycle it should be now, when the strain on the male is greatest. However, in at least some species, such as the kestrel or the golden eagle (for quite different reasons), most brood losses occur in the early fledging period and are not necessarily due to the inability of the male to provide food(10). He is normally able to provide for his young brood, which is another argument against a simple division of available land area purely on the basis of food availability.

In many species, once the young are partly feathered and more active, normally from one-half to two-thirds way through the whole fledging period, the female can leave them alone in the nest and thereafter assist the male in killing prey. The male's effort is then theoretically halved, and certainly much eased. Often, long before this, the female has taken to perching in the neighbourhood by day rather than remaining on the nest brooding the young. She can then, if needed, return to cover the young in a storm of rain, in the unlikely event (in Britain) of really hot sunshine, or to protect them from predators. She still feeds the young, who are normally unable to tear up prey themselves until two-thirds to three-quarters grown and well-feathered, though they will try to feed themselves from an earlier age if alone in the nest.

The stage at which the female leaves the young in the nest and starts to hunt depends on various factors. In the harriers, for instance, the frequent occurrence of bigamy or polygamy forces the females to hunt earlier than they would in monogamous matings(2). In the osprey and the peregrine, and in at least some kestrels and merlins, the male continues to bring prey right up to the end of the fledging period; he may then be killing five or six times his own requirements. However, it is usual, once the young are feathered, for both parents to bring prey to the nest. In the last stages of the fledging period the young do not have to be fed but tear up carcases brought in by either parent, and any surplus of prey brought in favourable hunting weather is eaten at leisure when hunting is not possible. In practice, the female probably does not kill all the prey she brings to the nest but is suspected of receiving some of it from the male and later taking it to the young.

Female nestlings, which when adult may be up to twice as heavy as males, grow faster in the nest, but are less active. Wherever this aspect has been carefully studied male and female fledglings can be sexed either by eye colour, as in harriers, by the thickness of their legs, or simply by weighing them(4,19). Some early observers believed that in the golden eagle, where the elder chick normally kills the younger, this led to a preponderance of females reared(12). However, in this case it is likely that the ratio of males and females reared is about equal, though a female might have a somewhat better chance if hatched from the second egg than a male. In the hen harrier and kestrel more females are reared than males; but while in the hen harrier this disbalance later increases until there are two adult females for every male, in the kestrel on present evidence it seems to disappear(10).

The young normally fly when they are ready to, and of their own accord. They usually lose a little weight before finally taking the plunge. Coaxing behaviour by the parents to induce the young to leave the nest, by tempting them with food, has been recorded by a number of observers; but some of these accounts are uncritical, and certainly coaxing behaviour is unusual. From tree nests the young climb out on to branches, practise wing flapping, and so on before actually flying. Young harriers walk away from the nest into the surrounding vegetation as soon as they can, and when ready to fly may climb tall reeds and make short exploratory flights before moving any distance. On rock ledges eaglets walk out of the nest into any shady place they can find. When the young leave, they usually make a determined effort, and travel some distance. If disturbed by humans at this stage they may fly prematurely; but they usually come to no harm from this. Whether they fly naturally or prematurely, they are quickly found by the parents, either by eye or by ear, and fed away from the nest; or they may themselves return to the nest when the parent brings food. Sometimes a young bird does not return to the nest to receive food for a few days after its first flight, but does so when it can fly more strongly.

Once the young have flown it again becomes extremely difficult, at least after the early stages of the post-fledging period, to locate them and observe what happens. The post-fledging period has not been adequately observed in most species, but it is clear that in all the young continue to be dependent on their parents for some time. Young hobbies and sparrowhawks remain near the nest for several weeks and are fed there by either parent(19,22). They often fly to meet the adult and receive the prey a little distance away. Young harriers soon learn the aerial food-pass technique practised with such skill by their parents. Depending on the size of the preferred prey and the difficulty of killing it they may learn to kill for themselves early or late in the post fledging period. Young hobbies soon learn to kill insects, but chase birds ineffectively for some weeks before they can actually catch them(22). Young peregrines are probably dependent on the adults for at least a month to six weeks before they themselves can kill their own prey. Young eagles, which normally leave the nest in early to mid July, are dependent on their parents until October, and perhaps sometimes long after that. In the osprey one case is described where the young learned to kill their own fish within a week of leaving the nest; but this seems so unusual that it requires confirmation(16).

The number of young leaving the nest is always less than the number of eggs laid, and varies within the same species from pair to pair, and place to place, perhaps according to the level of food supply, though the true effect of the last has not been quantitatively estimated. There must usually be some further mortality in the post-fledging period before the young become independent; but its extent is virtually unknown. The overall breeding success of any bird of prey is usually expressed in terms of the number of young that fly per pair. Much too often, all that is recorded is the number of young flown per successful nest; but this gives a misleading picture of total productivity. This can only be assessed by careful study of a number of pairs over a number of years, recording all the non-breeding pairs and those that fail in the incubation or fledging period as well as those that sucessfully rear young. The number of young reared per pair per annum overall is often only about half the average brood size in successful nests.

It is often supposed that at the end of the post-fledging period the young are driven away by the adults, but the actual evidence for this is in most species slight or non-existent. In non-territorial species, such as the kestrel or harriers, there is no conceivable reason why the parents should act thus, when they do not repel other strange adults. In the buzzard, which is a strongly territorial species, most young appear to leave the breeding area when they become independent, but are rarely driven away. Some remain, at least in some areas, living quietly on what they can find, in 'no man's land' between the defended winter territories of adult pairs. There is some recent evidence which suggests that in mild winters adult buzzards may be less likely to repel such young than in harder winters(25). In all probability, in most species, the young simply become independent and leave the area of their own accord. There are cases where the young of golden eagles have been suspected of staying with their parents till the following spring, and still being tolerated in the nesting territory(17). However, in such cases it is obviously exceedingly difficult to be certain that the same young bird and not a stranger is always concerned.

Once the young become independent one usually loses track of them altogether. Ringing records reveal quite a good picture of their wanderings, but probably give rather a misleading picture of the rate of mortality, since so many recoveries are of birds that have been shot, killed by cars, electrocuted, or met with some other violent end. These records always indicate a high rate of mortality between leaving the nest and sexual maturity, which may occur from one to five years later. In the kestrel, which can breed in its second summer, at least 50% are lost; but in buzzards, which become sexually mature in their third year, about three out of four young die before they can breed. At present there is no better way of working out the possible survival rate and age structure of the population than from ringing records; but if a species is sufficiently common, and can be aged reasonably accurately in the field (as for instance buzzards can be) counts of adults and immatures may give a better idea of mortality than do ringing records. This method, recently tried with African fish eagles and bateleurs, has not yet been fully tried with any European species(8).

The basic statistics needed to calculate the possible age to which any bird of prey on average lives are the number of young reared per pair overall, the mortality before sexual maturity, and the age at sexual maturity. To take a simple theoretical case, if each pair rears on average one young per pair, and three-quarters of these young die before sexual maturity in their third year, each adult produces 0·5 young in the nest and 0·125 young sexually mature birds able to replace dead adults. In other words, each adult must live for an average of eight years as an adult and eleven years altogether to replace itself. In theory, if the same rate of post fledging mortality applies in each case, buzzards on Dartmoor must live about four times as long as buzzards in Speyside to maintain a stable adult population. Such variation seems highly unlikely, and it seems more probable that some other natural compensating factor, such as reduced mortality among the young, would occur to balance the situation. However, here we are entering the realm of conjecture, which applies to so much of the habits of birds of prey away from the nest and outside the breeding season, where they are much more difficult to observe.

Table 22 Reproductive Potential: British Species

Including only those for which adequate data is available and excluding human interference except pesticide effects. (Figures in brackets estimated.)

SPECIES	Clutch size	per successful nest	Young per pair which bred	per pair overall	Age at maturity	% lost before maturity	Adults reaching maturity per pair of breeding birds	as adults	Age overall
Osprey	2·64	2·33	1·34	1·04	3	75	0·26	8	11
Red kite	2·04	1·32	0·67	0·52	3	75	0·13	15	18
Marsh harrier	4·0	3·0	2·3	(2·0)	2	70	0·6	3·3	5
Hen harrier	4·6	2·4	1·58	(1·5)	1	60	0·6	3·3	4
Sparrowhawk									
normal	5·0	3·8	3·8	(3·5)	1	60	1·4	1·4	2·4
pesticide areas	5·0	2·9	1·9	1·8	1	60	0·72	2·8	3·8
Buzzard									
overall	2·56	1·37	1·15	0·94	3	70	0·28	7·2	10·2
Dartmoor	2·43	1·33	0·62	0·45	3	70	0·135	15	18
Speyside	2·9	2·2	2·1	1·6	3	70	0·48	4	7
Golden eagle	1·8	1·2	0·9	0·83	5	75	0·21	9·5	14·5
Kestrel	4·72	3·73	2·7	(2·5)	1	60	1·0	2·0	3·0
Merlin	3·96	3·21	(2·7)	(2·5)	1	60	1·0	2·0	3·0
Hobby	2·8	2·25	1·4	1·4	1	60	0·56	3·5	4·5
Peregrine									
normal	3·4	1·87	1·76	1·33	2	70	0·40	5·0	7·0
pesticide areas	2·9	2·08		0·53	2	70	0·16	12·5	14·5

NOTES (1) In general, these figures suggest that wild mortality rates must actually be lower than those indicated, generally based on ringing records.

(2) Human interference reduces the estimated breeding potential by up to 40% (golden eagle) and as a result average wild life spans must be higher to maintain stable population, perhaps achieved by lower juvenile mortality.

CHAPTER 26

PESTICIDES AND BIRDS OF PREY

IN many raptors in Britain, continental Europe, or North America at present, statistics on breeding success derived even from long periods of careful observation are suspect because of the adverse effect of pesticides on the breeding biology of these species. In the sparrowhawk, for instance, there is a complete range from normal breeding to total failure(a); but overall breeding success is at present apparently about half the normal rate, as estimated from pre-war British records; in cereal growing areas it is usually even lower(18). In studying the biology of any species in Britain at present it is necessary to try to assess objectively the possible adverse effect of pesticides on the breeding success. Pesticides are, of course, not the only adverse factor involved; human disturbance, deliberate or accidental is an even more serious factor at present for some species, such as the golden eagle. However, while human disturbance should be controllable if properly tackled, the effect of pesticides is prolonged, insidious and can all too easily result in extermination. It causes public concern that the entire environment on which we ourselves depend is becoming poisoned. The birds of prey which fail to breed from this cause are perhaps valuable as more sensitive indicators of this insidious overall poisoning than we are ourselves(4,11).

In the extreme view, all birds of prey and many other species, are adversely affected by all pesticides (including herbicides), which ought therefore to be banned. Extreme views are unlikely to be either objective or sound, and the banning of all pesticides would be totally impracticable at present. Fortunately a more balanced approach has been possible in Britain than in some other countries where pesticides have been used on a larger scale. The facts are that some birds of prey do not appear to be adversely affected by pesticides at all; some others are affected to some degree; and yet others severely or perhaps even critically endangered by these substances. Even among these last, the species concerned are not adversely affected by all the pesticides in use.

There seems little point in trying to assess in this book the effect of pesticides on any other but the British breeding species. The rare vagrants and the boreal migrants should be studied in their countries of origin rather than in Britain. Even in some of the British and European breeding species the effect is not clear-cut. The depressed population, for instance of the peregrine, is not only due to the key factor of pesticides, but is severely aggravated by increased human disturbance and illegal persecution(23). In some species which are very rare in Britain, such as the goshawk or honey buzzard, it is impossible to say, on British evidence alone, what the effect of pesticides may be; at best one can suspect. In the case of some such as the goshawk, however, there may be good evidence from Europe of the adverse effect of pesticides; and it may reasonably be expected that the same effects would appear in Britain if we had enough goshawks to study.

Counting the sea eagle, of the 15 British breeding birds of prey, the effect on some cannot accurately be assessed because they have not been adequately studied. In this category I would at present include only the honey buzzard and the merlin. Of these two, it is reasonable to suppose that some of the apparent decline of the bird-eating merlin is due to the effect of pesticides. Merlins and their eggs contain quite high pesticide residues, probably not acquired in moorland breeding quarters but in winter on low ground. However the available data on their breeding success does not indicate serious pesticide effects (Ch. 16). There is no real evidence that the insectivorous honey buzzard has been seriously affected in Britain; and it is still apparently quite abundant along its main migration routes in Europe. Anyway, when honey buzzards are shot in numbers along their migration routes, who can say that their decrease is mainly due to pesticides?

Species which are apparently little if at all affected by pesticides include the mammal-eating hen harrier and buzzard, and the insectivorous or bird-eating hobby. Although the hobby seems to have disappeared as a breeding bird in some parts of England there is little evidence that this is due to pesticides, and the population is considered to be nearly stable, perhaps slightly increasing, in so far as its status is known(20,a). Both the hen harrier and the buzzard would increase and spread to other parts of Britain if they were permitted to do so by gamekeepers; in their case human interference and illegal persecution is a far more important limiting factor than pesticides, even though they may contain quite high residue levels in their bodies.

The osprey, red kite, sea eagle, marsh and Montagu's harrier, golden eagle, and kestrel all are or have been at some time more or less severely affected by pesticides. Several of the ospreys breeding in Speyside are sterile or unsuccessful breeders while, in Connecticut and New York State, a very large population breeding in colonies on the seashore has practically disappeared in the last 20 years(1). They were still relatively flourishing in 1950, but seriously endangered by 1960 and practically gone by 1970.

Although the evidence is not conclusive, there is a strong likelihood that the breeding success of red kites in Britain was depressed by the use of dieldrin in sheep dips in 1963–66; this depressing effect, at that time, was unlikely to have been aggravated by human disturbance(6). In some parts of its continental range, notably in East Germany, the small remaining population of sea eagles is so critically affected that the birds are artificially fed on prey which may be less contaminated than what they could obtain naturally (10,19). In other parts, such as in Norway, they may be less affected; but both in Norway and in Britain, sea eagles would feed to a considerable extent on sea-birds and diving ducks, some of which, such as puffins, appear themselves to be endangered through chemical contamination of the ocean itself(8). The sea eagle could be expected to suffer, and one might question the wisdom of trying to re-introduce sea eagles only to find them unable to breed because of pesticides.

In the marsh and Montagu's harrier it is not possible to say, on British evidence, that their decline is wholly due to pesticides. However, marsh harriers have disappeared from one former regular haunt where they were quite effectively protected, and the few harriers examined have contained high pesticide residue levels. In Britain Montagu's harrier may be more adversely affected ecologically than for other reasons; but both it and the marsh harrier have apparently declined to some extent at least in other parts of their range, while the wintering African population of the closely related pallid harrier has almost certainly decreased since 1950(3). In the case of these harriers the evidence is circumstantial, but implicates pesticides.

In the golden eagle it is proven that the use of dieldrin in sheep dips between 1960 and 1966 reduced breeding success from about 70% to about 30%(13). Since the voluntary ban on dieldrin as sheep dip came into effect the breeding success of undisturbed pairs of West Highland golden eagles has reverted to normal(14). In the kestrel, too, the population in the eastern cereal-growing counties, where most of the pesticides are used, is either greatly reduced or absent. Part of this decrease may be due to the grubbing up of old hedgerow trees which provided nesting sites, or to more efficient methods of farming which mean less vole-infested grassland and more weed-free cultivated grain. Gamekeepers cannot be blamed in this case, because kestrels used to be relatively common in these counties when gamekeepers were apparently larger, more numerous, and more aggressive than they are now. They may have played their part, but the observed decline of the kestrel in eastern cereal-growing counties is more likely to be due to pesticides(22).

Three species, the goshawk, sparrowhawk, and peregrine falcon appear to be critically affected or endangered by pesticides. Of these the goshawk cannot be studied in Britain, but has declined very sharply in some European countries where it flourished before 1950. This decline is almost certainly not mainly or entirely due to increased human interference with breeding sites, which are always hard to find. In the peregrine falcon and the sparrowhawk the evidence from Britain and Europe that the decline is due mainly to the effects of pesticides is clear, and is reinforced for the peregrine by the evidence from North America, where this falcon has become extinct over large tracts where it was formerly quite common. Even the migratory races of the peregrine, breeding in the far north but migrating to temperate climates in winter appear to be more or less threatened(11).

This assessment shows that, of fifteen species concerned, only three are at present known to be severely or critically affected in Britain, but another seven are to some extent affected either here or in some other part of their range. Three species are little if at all affected; and two are so little known that one cannot say what the effect if any may be. In one of these pesticides are suspected as a cause of the decline. Thus, when one looks at it clearly the effect, though sufficiently serious, is not as bad as has often been implied. Even the species most critically affected, the goshawk, sparrowhawk and peregrine falcon, are not at present headed for early extinction. When 3000 goshawks per year can be shot on licence in Finland any such statement would be an absurdity; and in both the sparrowhawk and peregrine in Britain there is some recent encouraging evidence of increase from a low point reached about 1963. In the peregrine the British population has apparently recovered to about 55% of the pre-war level from a low of about 45%; and in this species continuing illegal interference and persecution certainly aggravate pesticide effects.

The evidence implicating certain pesticides as the main cause of any decline that has occurred is partly circumstantial, but strongly supported in recent years by actual experimental or investigational proof. I visit Britain only at intervals, so that the stages in the decline have perhaps been clearer to me than to those who live alongside it. In 1955 I heard only mutterings, which had become louder and clearer by 1958, still louder in 1961, and by 1964 had become a positive bellow of apprehension. In 1967 they were still loud, but by then a few more hopeful signs – such as at least no further worsening of the position – had become evident. In 1970 and 1972, when I did the work for this book it was said that the decline had ceased, and that there was even some improvement in some of the affected species – excepting the marsh harrier, which continued to decline to its present tiny remnant, and is the only species apparently heading for re-extinction in Britain.

The main circumstantial evidence is that nearly all the decline has taken place since 1950, when certain agricultural chemicals came into widespread general use. The main decline apparently started in the mid-fifties, when aldrin and dieldrin seed dressings caused acute poisoning in the sparrowhawk and peregrine(a). Further circumstantial evidence is derived from the regions worst affected by the decline, which are the cereal-growing areas in eastern and southern Britain, where these agricultural pesticides are most often used. Finally, positive circumstantial evidence that the decline in breeding success of certain species was due primarily to chemical residues in the environment was provided by the improvement noted after the withdrawal or restriction of use of certain compounds, especially dieldrin in sheep dips. The breeding success of both golden eagles and red kites improved again after dieldrin was banned as sheep dip, and some effects were observed even in the buzzard(6,14).

Of less than 300 chemical compounds at present marketed in Britain as fungicides to kill fungi, insecticides to kill insects, or herbicides to kill weeds, only a few can be directly or indirectly implicated as the main cause of the decline of any species of bird of prey. Excepting deliberate poisoning with phosdrin and alpha chloralose, aldrin and dieldrin have been the most significant(a). In every case, as I have stressed at intervals, any decline caused by pesticides is more or less severely aggravated by other factors, such as destruction of habitat, or illegal or unwitting human interference. In some cases, for instance, in the golden eagle and buzzard, human interference is at present a far more serious threat to the species than are pesticides but if dieldrin sheep dip had not been banned the reverse would be true for the eagle. In others pesticides may be the primary offender; but in both the most seriously affected British species, the sparrowhawk and peregrine, illegal human persecution aggravates the pesticide effect.

The only fungicidal compounds likely to affect birds of prey are mercurial seed dressings, which have been used for a very long time in British agriculture. Most cereal seed is automatically treated with organo-mercurial dressings, which are highly toxic to fungi. In large doses they are also deadly to fish, birds, and mammals, but cases of direct poisoning have seldom been reported in Britain. It is not thought that mercurial fungicides are a serious danger to wild life, including birds of prey, in Britain; but the situation is apparently different in Sweden and parts of America or Japan(15). In Sweden a different type of mercurial seed dressing is normally used, and the dressings applied may be heavier. Mercury is also more widely used in industrial processes. At least one lake became totally poisoned through such industrial waste, and had to be restored at heavy cost to the local taxpayers. In certain parts of America, too, mercurial compounds have accumulated in fish and birds to such an extent that even salmon and pheasants are at least dangerous to eat – a truly dreadful thought! Thus, although the situation in Britain in this respect at present appears not to be dangerous, it must always be watched. Mercury is one of the heaviest metals and can accumulate insidiously in the environment; once there, it is very hard to get rid of.

No other common fungicide, mainly compounds of copper, is of real present importance as a threat to birds of prey, or apparently to other wild life. Herbicides, which are designed to kill weeds or unwanted shrubs, likewise have no direct effect. Any effect they have is indirect, and is unlikely to be as serious as that of other factors. The control of weeds in cultivated land, which results in large increases of yield in cereal crops, is likely to affect mainly seed-eating birds which would otherwise feed on these weed seeds. Their population might decline as a result; and any birds of prey dependent on them could proportionately decline. There is at present no evidence that any bird of prey in Britain has declined from this cause. Herbicides are also sometimes used to destroy bushes or tall weeds growing alongside roads; but any effect of this process on birds of prey must be slight, and indirect. Herbicides in Britain are much less likely to affect birds of prey than in Vietnam, where the defoliation of large tracts of jungle has no doubt adversely affected many woodland birds of prey, and such more potent predators as tigers, by depriving them of nesting and other cover.

We can therefore neglect herbicides, weed killers, and most fungicides in this connection. The main other class of compounds used is insecticides, and these are the only compounds seriously affecting the recent decline of birds of prey. Even then, not all insecticides are implicated, but only certain highly persistent compounds known as chlorinated hydrocarbons, including DDT, lindane, dieldrin, aldrin, heptachlor and others. Another very common and highly poisonous, but less persistent group of insecticides, known as organo-phosphorus insecticides, including parathion, malathion, disulfoton, and others, are not seriously implicated. Some of these, notably one now disused called tepp (of which an ounce could fatally poison nearly 500 men) and parathion are potentially deadly to human beings as well as insects and accordingly dangerous to use. Parathion is used on quite a large scale in Africa to kill pest finches of the genus *Quelea* on roosts; but even when millions of dead finches are carpeting the ground inches deep after a successful aerial spray it has not been noted that any considerable death of birds of prey or other predatory animals results. Probably this is because the finches roost in very localised areas only a few acres in extent, and can be sprayed only once or twice a year even there, while the organo-phosphorus compounds are rarely transmitted to predators because of their rapid breakdown.

Of the chlorinated hydrocarbon insecticides DDT is the most widely used and known, and nowadays the most infamous. I am old enough to remember how the advent of DDT, relatively non-toxic, or so it appeared, to birds, fish, and mammals was greeted with immense relief by those agriculturists and others who regularly had to use very much more toxic substances, such as arsenic, to kill dangerous pest insects such as locusts. Directly, DDT is about as poisonous as aspirin; but unlike aspirin it tends to be stored in the body and not excreted, and it and its derivatives, chiefly DDE, are extremely stable. It is this stability which makes it valuable as a persistent insecticide. Used in malaria control, for instance, it can be sprayed on the interior of hut walls and any mosquito which alights to rest there will die. The stability also means, however, that if any areas are sprayed or dusted with DDT it remains as an environmental contaminant for a very long time.

The DDT in the environment is taken up first by earthworms or insects, then by the birds, or mammals that eat these insects or worms; and finally by the birds of prey that eat these. It thus becomes concentrated through the ascending stages of a food chain, and while not serious perhaps to the insectivorous birds themselves, may occur in such concentrations in their predators that it becomes serious, if not actually lethal. Occasionally, DDT has been used in such amounts that it was actually lethal to insectivorous or fruit-eating birds, as when spraying elm trees against Dutch Elm disease in America(4). However, the effects are more often sub-lethal, even in the birds of prey; that is, they do not kill, but adversely affect the species in some other way(5,15). In birds of prey the most common effect has been reduced breeding success, which can rapidly lead to a great reduction in the population if not to early extinction.

Dieldrin, aldrin, endrin and heptachlor are all related substances which have done more harm to wildlife in Britain than any others(15). When they were invented their adverse effects were not foreseen, for although all were more toxic than DDT, they appeared no more poisonous to mammals or man than DDT, and their persistence in the environment, not then fully realised, would have been regarded as an advantage rather than otherwise. They were not put on the market without extensive tests for toxicity, mainly on rats. It is normally unjust to accuse suppliers and manufacturers of chemicals of irresponsibility in this connection, as is often done nowadays. They are only trying to provide a needed remedy for a pest or disease, and to make a good living while giving this service, and are not deliberately and irresponsibly plastering the environment with deadly poison.

Dieldrin and aldrin have been used to control wireworms, carrot fly, and especially wheat bulb fly. Dieldrin was also used in sheep dip to a considerable extent. The effect of these compounds was most serious when used as seed dressings. Between 1956 and 1961 large numbers of birds died in spring, a spectacular example being a total of 5668 woodpigeons, 118 stock doves, 59 rooks and 89 pheasants dead in 1480 acres of woodland(14). Hawks and other predators were also found dead, but the direct effect was worst on seed-eating birds. The death of the woodpigeons which actually dug up the treated grain was not itself serious; but their dead bodies contained the poisonous compounds and, if eaten by other predators, including birds of prey, these also were poisoned. At this time the rapid disappearance of the sparrowhawk from many areas was not only due to sub-lethal effects such as reduced breeding success but to acute direct poisoning of the adults.

The sub-lethal effects of these pesticides on birds of prey were not at first appreciated or understood. It was easy to understand that a raptor eating a pigeon which had taken a dose of dieldrin would itself ingest the poison and die. However, this did not wholly explain the rapid disappearance of certain species from certain tracts of country. Good quantitative evidence of the extent of the decline in certain species was not obtained till the peregrine survey conducted by Ratcliffe in 1961–62(23) This showed that the peregrine had greatly declined in certain areas, especially those where the habitat included agricultural land. It was reinforced by status surveys of other species by Prestt, all of which showed a marked decline in one or more species investigated(22). The situation was complicated in some cases by drastic reduction of potential food supply after 1955, due to myxomatosis in the rabbit; by the unusually hard winter of 1963, which killed many kestrels; by increased persecution in the interests of game preserving; and by increased access to the countryside by many people, with consequently increased disturbance of birds of prey. However, the observed effects seemed to implicate pesticides quite clearly, if only on the basis of circumstantial evidence.

The distribution of the peregrine was well known and well documented pre-war, and it was expected that this resilient and successful bird would soon recover from wartime persecution to re-occupy old haunts. An early warning that it was not doing so was sounded by Treleaven in 1959 in Cornwall when he found that of 17 eyries re-occupied by 1955 only seven were occupied and only two produced young(27). This was confirmed, countrywide, by Ratcliffe's survey, which showed that of 461 eyrie sites visited only 251 were occupied and only 76 succeeded. The overall brood size was very low, 0·325 young per territory, 0·59 per occupied territory, and 1·97 per successful territory. In England, Wales, and southern Scotland only 30 young were reared from 16 successful out of 255 territories, averaging 0·12 per territory. In the highlands of Scotland, however, 60 successful out of 206 territories produced 120 young, or 0·58 per territory, almost five times the rate in England and Wales. The fact that in both areas the number of young reared per successful eyrie was still about two indicates how useless it is, in population studies of breeding biology, to record this particular statistic alone.

The indications were thus clear that the decline was serious and that it was worst in areas where peregrines hunted over agricultural land. Some unprecedented factor, suspected to be the new pesticides in use, was implicated. This was naturally unwelcome, both to the farmers who had hailed these compounds as heaven-sent remedies for intractable pests, and the entomologists and chemical firms who thought they were supplying or recommending a valuable product. Other possible explanations, such as dwindling food supply, persecution, or climatic change could not have produced the type of localised decline observed, and there was no evidence for any new disease affecting peregrines. Ratcliffe accordingly concluded that the decline was most likely to be due to the use of certain chlorinated hydrocarbon pesticides; and suggested that the peregrines might even be obtaining these directly through feeding on pigeons that had been dusted with such compounds to keep them free of pests(23).

Past and present population data were far less reliable for some other species affected, such as the sparrowhawk, which had shown a drastic decline, while some other species such as the golden eagle and buzzard appeared largely unaffected. At the same time ornithologists alerted by the peregrine's plight began to look more carefully at the situation in various other species, and observe their breeding success more critically. A good many cases of such curious habits as egg-eating or breaking were then reported, mainly because they were noted when they had previously been missed.

Country-wide surveys by Prestt in 1965 recorded a decline in the sparrowhawk in 86% of the areas studied, while in 41/49 counties reporting a decrease this was said to be recent(22). Even the increasing numbers of gamekeepers could not find sparrowhawks. On one 4000 acre estate in Hampshire J. S. Ash reported an average of 53 killed per year between 1949 and 1953, but only 13 per year from 1954–59, indicating at least a fourfold decrease(2). The decrease of the sparrowhawk between 1953 and 1963 was, in fact, catastrophic, at least as severe as and possibly worse than in the peregrine at the same time. The sparrowhawk actually became extinct in some eastern counties such as Lincolnshire by 1960. Again, the decline was mainly in the eastern cereal-growing counties where chlorinated hydrocarbon compounds were most used in agriculture, particularly as seed dressings which could be eaten by the seed-eating finches, sparrows, and pigeons that are the sparrowhawk's most important prey.

Bird-eating species among the birds of prey were most affected, and mammal-eating species less or not at all affected. There was no anxiety on this score for the golden eagle until the late fifties, after which there was a sharp decline in breeding success. Observations in the West Highlands showed that, unlike the peregrine and sparrowhawk, the population of adults had not yet declined, 39 eyries being occupied in 1961–63 out of 40 used from 1937–60; but that the proportion of pairs not laying eggs, or with broken eggs had sharply increased. The non-breeding pairs increased from 1/40 to 16/39; and while I personally doubt that in any population of golden eagles anywhere in Scotland non-breeding was ever as low as 1 pair in 40, there must have been a marked increase in this factor from about 20% to about 40%. Eyries with broken eggs increased from 5/40 to 8/39, and from 1/9 (11%) in 1937–50 to 5/9 (56%) in 1963. Breeding success dropped from 26/40 eyries rearing young 70(%) to 10/39, or 29%. It seemed clear that after 1961 some hitherto unknown factor was reducing the breeding success of West Highland eagles through increased non-breeding and breakage of eggs, to less than half the normal figure; and it was easy to calculate that if this continued a decline in the adult population similar to that seen in peregrines and sparrowhawks would soon follow(13).

The new factor suspected in this case was the introduction of dieldrin in sheep dips. DDT had been used in sheep dips from the late forties, followed by BHC and dieldrin in the early and late fifties. Eagles fed substantially on dead sheep, especially in winter, and could directly absorb these substances with their food. In Australia, at that time, chlorinated hydrocarbon pesticides had been banned as sheep dip because of export problems. The very hard winter of 1963 may have aggravated the effect of the insecticides on golden eagles, as these substances are normally stored in fat, which would be metabolised in a hard winter.

Although the circumstantial evidence implicating chlorinated hydrocarbons as the main cause of the observed decline in birds of prey was already strong in the early sixties, real experimental or factual proof was demanded, and was naturally hard to supply. The direct toxic effects of these pesticides on birds were not at first known, and when dead bodies were examined for pesticide residues the amounts present sometimes seemed insufficient to cause death. However, by 1965 it had been shown that the whole of the British Isles were contaminated to some degree by chlorinated hydrocarbon pesticides; that birds of prey and fish-eating species such as herons and many sea-birds contained higher amounts of residues than fruit- or seed-eating birds; that among these, those that fed on vertebrates had higher residue levels than feeders on invertebrates; and that most wild birds' eggs contained residues of organochlorine pesticides(5,17).

The amounts of pesticide residues in the eggs, liver, and breast muscle of the birds examined were generally of the same order of magnitude. Residues in fat were much higher than in other tissues, indicating that these substances were stored in fat. In effect, this means that in a hard winter, when fat reserves are used up, considerable amounts of the toxic substances are released into the bird's system in a short time. This might have worse effects than would be observed in a mild winter, when fat reserves remain partly or largely unused.

Among the birds of prey, those which fed on birds, the merlin, sparrowhawk, and peregrine, had the highest residue levels. Birds excrete pesticides more slowly than do mammals, so raptors feeding on birds automatically feed on prey with higher levels of residues in their bodies(17). Those which fed on both mammals and birds, the hen and Montagu's harrier, kite, buzzard, golden eagle and kestrel had the next highest, the residues in some kestrels, possibly habitual bird-hunters, being very high. Only one specimen of the insectivorous hobby was examined, and it contained very low residues. It also became clear that different species of birds might react differently to the pesticides concerned, some being more sensitive than others. For instance, the fish-eating heron contained generally higher residue levels than any bird of prey but did not show the same pattern of decline. Among birds of prey the buzzard had in some cases relatively high residues, but showed no evidence of decline.

Experiments were carried out both in Britain and other countries to determine the effects of these insecticides on birds of prey and other species. In America the species most affected were the bird-eating peregrine and the fish-eating osprey and bald eagle. Captive bald eagles were successfully killed by feeding them diets containing measured amounts of DDT(7). Before they died they showed symptoms of nervous disorders, such as tremors, or lack of balance. Lanner and peregrine falcons that had died, either in the wild or captivity, had similar levels of pesticide residues in their livers as those in dogs that had been killed experimentally, 5·3–9·3 parts per million of dieldrin and heptachlor epoxide in the birds of prey and 3·3–7·4 parts per million in the dogs(11). Lanners and peregrines with 0·8–2·0 parts per million of these substances had died of other causes.

The sub-lethal effects causing population decline were more difficult to determine, and, even in 1970, the third report of the research committee on toxic chemicals was inclined to be rather non-committal in its findings on this subject(26). The most common and remarkable feature associated with the population declines of peregrines and sparrowhawks had been the increased incidence of egg-eating and egg-breaking by the parents. This apparently unnatural behaviour was also observed in golden eagles, especially between 1961 and 1966, when dieldrin was in use as sheep dip(13,16). While it was clear that such increased egg-eating and egg-breaking, coupled with fewer pairs breeding, greater disturbance of nesting pairs, and increased persecution by gamekeepers would lead to lower breeding success and eventual extinction of the species concerned, it was not clear just how the process worked. Human interference and interference at the eyries by other peregrine falcons could, however, be rejected as the cause of egg-eating or egg-breaking, as this unnatural behaviour also occurred in undisturbed pairs.

The final answer came from yet another elegant piece of research by Derek Ratcliffe(24). He examined hundreds of peregrine, golden eagle, and sparrowhawk eggs in museums and collectors' cabinets, and devised an 'eggshell index' of relative weight, the weight of the shell divided by the product of length and breadth. Without the help of egg collectors and their carefully dated clutches it would have been impossible, or at least very much more difficult, to do this research. Egg collectors can thus claim to have been, for once, and inadvertently, useful to the conservation of birds of prey. The results showed that in all three species, but especially in the sparrowhawk and peregrine the eggshell index, almost constant from 1900 to the mid-forties, decreased sharply after 1945 and reached a much lower level in the fifties; this lower level was maintained almost unchanged up to 1970. (Fig. 11 and Text Table 23).

In other words, after 1945 the eggshells of peregrine and sparrowhawk had become weaker and more liable to breakage. This was due both to reduction in eggshell thickness and in density, each of which would make the shells more fragile. In the peregrine the eggshell index fell by 19·1% all over Britain after 1946, but fell more, by 19–22% in England, Wales, and S. Scotland than in the central and eastern Highlands, where it fell by only 4·4%. In the sparrowhawk the index for Britain as a whole fell by 17·2%, but fell more (20·9%) in south and east England than in other areas of Britain (13·9%). The effect could even be tied to individual female peregrines whose eggs had been taken year after year by collectors. One, in Lancashire, had a shell index of 1·92–2·03 in 1943–5 and 1·29–1·36 from 1947–49. In the golden eagle, the decrease in eggshell index was noted in the West Highlands, where eagles fed substantially on sheep carrion impregnated with dieldrin, but not or less in the eastern Highlands where the food, hares, grouse, and deer carrion, was mainly natural(24).

Further positive proof that this effect is produced by chlorinated hydrocarbon insecticides comes from experiments with captive birds fed on diets with and without these substances. Chlorinated hydrocarbon insecticides in the diet have been proved to reduce the eggshell thickness in quail and mallard(9). Birds of prey are normally difficult to breed in captivity, but this has been successfully

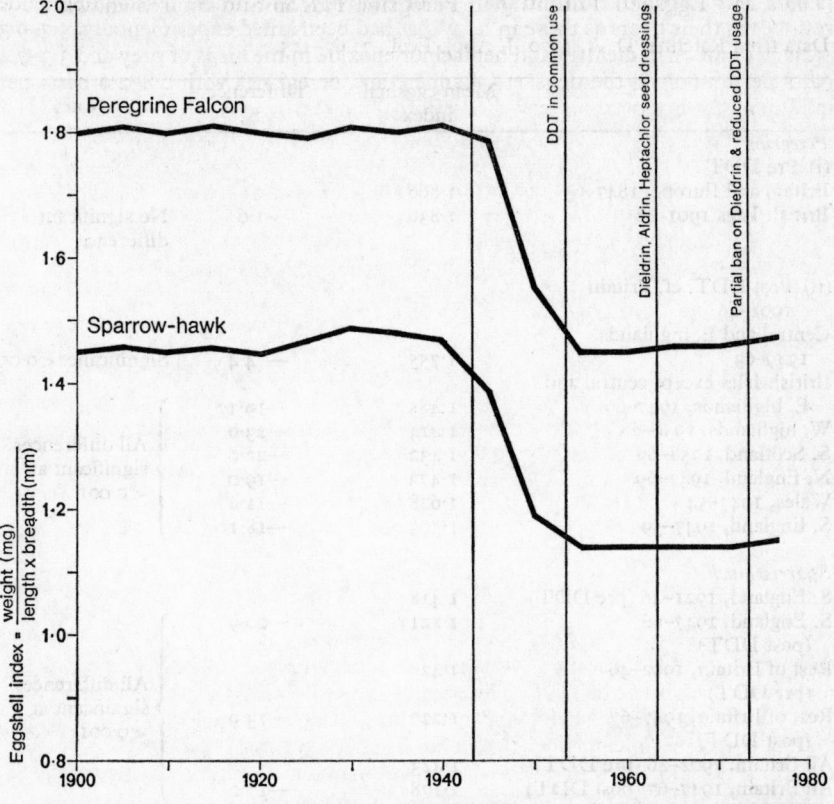

FIG. 11. Relationship between eggshell thinning and usage of organochlorine insecticides' showing: (i) minor fluctuations up to mid 1940s; (ii) serious drop continuing to 1960s; (iii) some slight recovery since 1963, as yet not significant. (Data adapted from D. A. Ratcliffe, 1970.)

achieved in the American kestrel, which can be induced to use nest boxes in a cage. In this species too it has been shown that feeding the kestrels a diet containing DDT resulted in lowered eggshell strength and poorer breeding success, exactly the effects observed in wild British peregrines and sparrowhawks(21).

Any reasonable person must therefore accept as proved that the presence of residues of chlorinated hydrocarbon insecticides in the environment leads to reduction in breeding success, and eventually in the adult population, of certain birds of prey, especially the bird and fish-eating species. It has little effect on others, notably the mammal-eaters such as the buzzard perhaps because mammals excrete pesticides more rapidly than do birds(a). In some other cases, such as the marsh harrier, the effect may be reasonably suspected but not proved. It may have even worse effects on some other species, such as the American brown pelican, which has become extinct in most of its N. American range, through eggshell thinning(12).

Table 23   Eggshell Thinning in Peregrine Falcon and Sparrowhawk

Data from Ratcliffe, D. A. 1970. J. Appl. Ecol., 7: 67–115.

	Mean eggshell index	Difference %	Notes
Peregrine			
(i) Pre DDT			
Britain and Europe, 1847–65	1·866		
British Isles 1901–46	1·836	—1·6	No significant difference
(ii) Post DDT. cf. Britain 1901–46			
Central and E. highlands, 1949–69	1·755	— 4·4	Significance <0·05
British Isles except central and E. highlands, 1947–69	1·485	—19·1	
W. highlands, 1956–68	1·414	—23·0	
S. Scotland, 1958–69	1·432	—22·0	All differences significant at <0·001
N. England, 1947–69	1·473	—19·0	
Wales, 1947–54	1·628	—11·4	
S. England, 1947–59	1·503	—18·1	
Sparrowhawk			
S. England, 1921–46 (pre DDT)	1·418		
S. England, 1947–66 (post DDT)	1·121	—20·9	
Rest of Britain, 1902–46 (pre DDT)	1·425		All differences significant at <0·001
Rest of Britain, 1947–67 (post DDT)	1·227	—13·9	
All Britain, 1902–46 (pre DDT)	1·423		
All Britain, 1947–67 (post DDT)	1·178	—17·2	

COMMENTS (i) In peregrine, slight reduction of eggshell thickness in central highlands does not prevent successful breeding; few eggs available from S. England and Wales after mid 1950s.

(ii) In sparrowhawk, there was no significant difference in eggshell thickness between S. England and other regions pre 1946 (1·418 cf. 1·425). Since 1946 eggshell thickness has decreased markedly in all regions, but in areas not so much affected as S.E. England by pesticides does not appear to reduce breeding success (Newton, I. 1974, op. cit. 12(8)).

The final effect is compounded of decreased eggshell strength and parental behaviour, those birds affected being otherwise quite healthy but more inclined to break and eat their own eggs. The end result of greatly decreased breeding success (which, in natural conditions, has presumably evolved to the level which can successfully maintain a capacity population) is a more or less rapid decline in the adult population. The rapid population decline in the peregrine and sparrowhawk observed since 1955 may have been partly due to direct poisoning, but was aggravated by decreased breeding success, which also now prevents the population from recovering to its former level in the affected areas.

Still more recent circumstantial evidence strengthens the case against these insecticides. As a result of public disquiet voluntary restrictions were placed on the use of dieldrin, aldrin and heptachlor as spring seed dressings for wheat, and on dieldrin as sheep dip, while the use of DDT has also been reduced. Once dieldrin ceased to be used as sheep dip in the West Highlands the breeding success of eagles reverted to normal, increasing from 0·31 young per pair per annum in 1963–65 to 0·69 young per pair in 1966–68. At the same time the level of dieldrin in eggs dropped from 0·86 parts per million in 1963–65 to 0·34 parts per million in 1966–68; and the eggshell index in affected pairs likewise returned to normal(14,24).

The hard-pressed peregrine falcon has also shown some recovery in numbers from a low point reached about 1963, from about 45% of pre-war numbers to about 55%. The recovery has occurred in the very areas where it might have been expected, namely in southern Scotland and northern England, where the peregrine's food is partly natural and partly derived from domestic pigeons and other birds feeding in contaminated agricultural areas. On northern sea-cliffs, where the peregrines feed on sea-birds, which themselves may be threatened not only by organochlorine insecticides but also by polychlorinated biphenyls and heavy metal residues there has been no appreciable recovery in peregrine breeding success. In other words, where peregrines are dependent on the products of the final sump, the ocean, they are still adversely affected, while those in inland localities feeding on natural uncontaminated prey are either less affected or, in central Scotland, hardly affected at all(25).

In the sparrowhawk there is much less reliable past population data available for comparison, but recent work in Dumfries suggests that even though the sparrowhawk probably still breeds much less successfully there than it did pre-war, the population may have doubled in the last few years(18). In this species too the eggshell index and breeding success are not reduced, or are less severely reduced, in areas where agricultural pesticides are not used much, mainly the grassland areas of the western parts of England, Wales, and Scotland.

I have been a practising agriculturist most of my life, so that I can fully appreciate the arguments of the entomologists who seek to control the insect pests afflicting crops and of the chemical firms who supply the products, to the effect that Britain and the world cannot now do without these substances. To attempt to do so in Britain, Europe, or North America would both raise the cost of living in the developed countries and reduce the available surplus of food needed to prevent famine in under-developed countries. It is an undeniable fact that it is impossible at present for any agriculturalist to foresee how to feed the expected, indeed the inevitable and appalling increase of human population, likely to reach 5500 million before the end of this century, without very much more intensive methods of agriculture resulting in higher yields per acre. These higher yields cannot be achieved on the necessary scale without the use of pure improved crop varieties, which will not give the full potential return unless they are kept free of weeds by weedkillers and free of insect pests by insecticides.

There are many who claim that what is called, rather sneeringly, 'the environmentalist lobby' overstates its case, and that the dangers of environmental poisoning implied by the observed decline in breeding success of the peregrine, sparrowhawk, osprey and bald eagle are overdrawn. Undoubtedly there are environmentalists who do overstate the case and overstress the dangers. However, one may retort that this is not a good excuse for obfuscating the facts by chemical firms whose profit motive is bound to be suspect; or for fighting, at this stage, pettifogging rearguard actions, for instance by suggesting that no one has properly established that pre-war there were really 25 peregrine eyries in parts of Cornwall(27). There were, and there are not now, and it is no use burking this issue.

Britain is fortunate in having both a relatively educated, informed and concerned public, and a body of scientists working both on the conservation side and in commerce and agriculture who have generally been able to agree among themselves on necessary measures. At present, a screening process whereby any new chemical is studied, not only by those who make it and sell it, but also by the Nature Conservancy's laboratories, is in effective operation. I think it unlikely that many British people really understand what is happening in the environment around them, for probably not more than one in five could accurately name ten species each of trees, grasses, mammals, birds, or fish. However, the prospect of trying to explain the dangers of environmental contamination to, for instance, Ethiopian peasants, who certainly could pass such a test (at least in Amharic) makes the imagination boggle.

It is unlikely that the relatively quiet and unspectacular efforts of these scientists to agree among themselves as to what is needed, and put into effect, will attract as much public attention as the louder outcries of the lunatic environmentalist fringe; but they are more likely to do actual good. Their efforts may not bring back the peregrine to the cliffs of Dover or the sparrowhawk to East Anglia, (though even these apparent miracles are not impossible) but they are likely to be able to watch and prevent the situation from actually worsening. Continuation of this commonsense collaboration is the best hope of mitigating the adverse effects of pesticides on British birds of prey.

CHAPTER 27

CONSERVATION

In the future the conservation of British birds of prey may be better achieved by closer attention to a few quite simple basic principles. These are, not necessarily in order of importance:

(i) The conservation of adequate areas of undisturbed breeding habitat.
(ii) Adequate legal provisions effectively enforced.
(iii) Better enlightenment of the public on the true function of birds of prey.
(iv) Freedom from unnecessary disturbance in the breeding season.
(v) Effective control of environmental contamination.

The degree to which any of these principles affect a particular species varies. For instance, the first is at present crucial for the marsh harrier, which depends absolutely on undisturbed reedbeds in which to nest. It may not be possible to ensure that adequate areas of such habitat exist or are developed; but without them it is certain that the marsh harrier cannot survive as a breeding species. In this case it is also obviously important that marsh harriers should not be shot by game-keepers or skin collectors near the breeding habitat, and that ornithologists who wish to enter the marsh harrier on their British lists should defer visiting the areas concerned till the end of the breeding season, say in late July, when both the young and the adults will be on the wing. Evidently, too, the level of pesticide residues in marsh harrier food in the British environment should be monitored regularly, as otherwise this factor could defeat the best efforts to protect breeding pairs. How-ever, all these other factors are more or less secondary to the need to provide adequate areas of undisturbed reedbeds in which the marsh harrier can breed.

In most species the worst dangers at present arise from the second principle. The legal provisions, especially the penalties, are not adequate, and are not effectively enforced. In the past, whenever I have reported the presence of pole traps on any ground in Scotland to the police, I have been met with a polite dis-inclination to do anything about it, and in some cases a tendency to ask aggressive questions as to how I came by this knowledge. I believe that this attitude may now have changed; but I shall believe things are better when a police constable in such a case at once takes out his notebook and suggests I go with him to the spot.

In theory the law is quite adequate on the subject; it protects all birds of prey, and gives stronger protection to the rarer species. Anyone who kills a bird of prey, takes its eggs, takes a falcon eyass without a permit, or even photographs certain rare species at the nest without a permit commits an offence. It is in the enforce-ment that the law is unsatisfactory, for the penalties are both inadequate in modern money terms and ineffectively applied by magistrates. Cases are from time to time reported in the press or the R.S.P.B. magazine, *Birds*, and as a rule the fines reported, even when convictions have been secured, are often pettifogging.

The highest fine I have heard of in Britain in recent years was that inflicted upon an elderly gentleman who took two clutches of golden eagles' eggs in Sutherland. Had he not had the stupidity to ask if he could have his eggs back he and his assistant might not have been fined the £100 each of which they were mulcted, by a sheriff perhaps unusually sympathetic to the conservation cause. In contrast, the two men who were responsible for robbing the osprey's nest in Speyside in 1971 were fined only £50 each, although their action deprived thousands of people of pleasure and the R.S.P.B. of hundreds of pounds in donations expected over the course of the summer(c).

The fines inflicted on gamekeepers who set pole traps, or who are caught shooting or poisoning birds of prey are even more ineffective. They rarely exceed £10-15, and no doubt are usually paid by the employer. They seldom appear to deter the gamekeeper concerned for long, but only make him more careful, and resentful of the conservation personnel who caught him. If gamekeepers, or better still their employers, were given a jail sentence without the option for setting pole traps or poisoning a carcase in the open the situation would be quite different. Such doubtless draconian measures may be impossible or difficult in law; but at least adequate fines, permissible even under the present law, should be inflicted; and the employer who is ultimately responsible, should also be brought to court.

One may compare this situation directly with the fines inflicted upon poachers of pheasants, grouse, or salmon. No one need have any sympathy with poachers who blast or poison salmon rivers or who (as they used to do in the past at least) drive away with a still living and suffering wounded stag in the boot of their car. They deserve all they get. However, the prevalence of such offences in the recent past, particularly just after the war when the black market in meat flourished, has led to strengthening of the law and to the ability of magistrates to inflict disproportionately heavy penalties. If I, tempted beyond endurance, get out of my car and shoot a brazen cock pheasant on the roadside, I not only lay myself open to a heavy fine but to confiscation of my gun, refusal on the part of the police to issue me a shotgun licence again, and even confiscation of my car on the grounds that I used it to approach the bird.

Shooting a pheasant in eastern England might almost be regarded, in many cases, as a more serious offence than peddling drugs! Recently a man in East Anglia, who shot one pheasant with an air gun at night, was fined the equivalent of £120, including the value of his gun which was taken away from him(d). For all I know he may have been a hardened and cunning poacher whom the police had been trying to catch for some time. However, it seems to me as likely that he was just out after one of the thousands of pheasants hand-reared in the area. When I see a gamekeeper in East Anglia, fined £100 and deprived of his gun licence for shooting a migrant osprey or rough-legged buzzard, I will have a stronger belief in the impartiality of the officials who enforce the law.

The main enemies of birds of prey are men; and obviously the worst enemies are those who actually kill adults and young of the birds concerned rather than those who only take eggs, destroy the young in the nest, or take the young for training, while leaving the adults alone. Gamekeepers and their employers are the only important class of persons in Britain, other than a very few skin collectors, who deliberately kill adult birds of prey. They are, accordingly, potentially the worst offenders, and should be dealt with most severely when caught.

Naturally, many gamekeepers do not come into this category. I have met many who do their utmost to conserve rare birds of prey that may be nesting on their ground, even when it goes against the grain. However, I have also met gamekeepers who, law or not, kill every bird of prey they think they can get away with, set pole traps on their land, use poison indiscriminately, and boast about it, saying, for instance: 'We make the laws here!'

CONSERVATION

A great deal of heat has recently been generated by the practice of pole trapping, which has long been and is regular on many estates. It is as well to make clear that pole trapping is objectionable not only because birds of prey are caught, for corvids, blackbirds, gulls and others sometimes also suffer. It was made illegal in 1904, when opinion on conservation was a good deal less liberal than it is said to be nowadays, because of the vile cruelty of the practice. The pole trap is set in the open, on top of a pole, post, or cairn of stones, in such a position that a bird of prey or other species will naturally be inclined to perch on it. If caught, the wretched bird first flutters off, and then hangs by the chain of the trap, its legs probably smashed, upside down and struggling exhausted, if not in agony, for hours, perhaps days, until the gamekeeper who set the trap chooses to come that way again. It is idle to pretend that anyone but a gamekeeper normally sets a pole trap. The setting of a pole trap on any land should automatically carry a heavy sentence, preferably jail; and no employer should be able to evade responsibility by saying his keeper did it without his knowledge. He ought to know what his keeper does, and keep him under effective control, as the best employers do.

It has been suggested to me by many people, including the R.S.P.B. and employers of gamekeepers and shepherds, that the real trouble is not the inadequacy of the law but the fact that the public in general, and specifically these possible offenders, are not yet enlightened as to the true function of birds of prey in the ecosystem, and that greater and more continual efforts should be made to enlighten them before applying the existing or future legal provisions with greater severity. I do not personally agree with this view. Great efforts have already been made, in the press, on the radio, on television, and by the publication of numerous books and articles, popular and scientific, to enlighten the public, and in particular gamekeepers and their employers. I believe there are even training courses for gamekeepers at which these matters are discussed though, not having attended such a course, I cannot say how well or accurately this may be done. All I can say is that the massive propaganda effort which has been mounted to date seems to me not only to have failed, but to have failed signally and almost completely, except when preaching to the half-converted, the rather rare minority that takes a general interest in nature as a whole.

I do not say that the effort should not be intensified and continued; but I do say that anyone who can read and write and who looks at television has already had the facts put before him many times, to take note of if he cared to. As I mentioned earlier, there is also no excuse for ignorance of the law, which has, in the main, been in force for nearly twenty years. I do say that any intensified propaganda effort should be coupled with more severe penalties for those who cannot or will not learn the lesson, and especially for those who deliberately ignore facts of which they are perfectly well aware. I am convinced, myself, that the 'soft sell' has failed, and that what is needed is a good hard bang on the ear. I do not, to my regret, have the power to deliver it myself; but there are those who do and who evade their responsibility in a manner deserving only contempt.

Egg collectors, pigeon fanciers, falconers, bird photographers, ordinary bird watchers, and even walkers who have no interest at all in birds of prey all do some damage, deliberate or inadvertent, by taking eggs or young, or causing desertion of the nests, without actually killing the adults. Of these, the egg collector inspires least sympathy, and is usually dealt with most severely if caught. In their case the law as it stands is inadequate as a deterrent, for it is necessary to prove that the eggs were taken; even if they are obviously recent there is no offence in possession

351

once they have been blown and placed in a cabinet drawer. The number of egg collectors who do real damage is small, and do not include those small boys who take a few common birds' eggs, or even, with a tremendous effort, a clutch of buzzards' or kestrels' eggs. Serious egg collectors, however do a disproportionate amount of damage in relation to their number; for instance one collector in 1972 was responsible for failure in four out of 26 active kite's nests, nearly a sixth of the whole. They are most interested in rare birds, and are sometimes driven by peculiar criminal motives. This last must apply to the two attempts, both of which effectively prevented breeding in that year, to rob the Loch Garten osprey eyrie and no other. Egg collecting of this nature can only be deterred by more severe penalties; but it should be looked at more objectively, and it must be admitted that, as a whole, a small number of warped egg collectors is a very much less potent threat to most birds of prey than a host of well-armed gamekeepers with the sympathy of the law on their side.

Pigeon fanciers are only a threat to the peregrine, and their case has been adequately discussed in Chapter 23. They deserve no sympathy for killing young peregrines in the nest or destroying the eggs, and should be dealt with accordingly if they are caught. Falconers, also interested in the peregrine, are a somewhat different matter. They are not interested in destroying the eggs or young of peregrines, goshawks, or any other species that can be trained. Indeed they will not act against the adults of any species, and will normally visit nests only to obtain young for training. Any damage they do is only severe if they adversely affect the bionomics of a scarce or threatened species. It is for instance unpardonable on their part to aggravate the environmental factors now militating against survival of the peregrine, their favourite and most admired falcon, by taking, or even buying the young. It should, in fact, be illegal to sell, offer or possess for sale any British bird of prey. However, pre-war, the small number of young taken by falconers yearly in British eyries had no real adverse effect on the peregrine population, and the same would be true of, for instance, the buzzard today. The kestrel has, in recent years suffered from would-be falconers, the film *Kes* having stimulated attempts by boys to keep kestrels.

One must distinguish between true falconers, and people who just want to keep a bird of prey in their backyard, either for prestige or for other reasons. This practice is particularly prevalent in the United States, where in 1969 there were reputed to be more peregrines in captivity than alive in the wild, and where those who kept these and other birds of prey included several scientists who should have known better. I suppose there may be some peculiar psychological twist that makes some people want to dominate and control a wild and regal bird of prey or make money out of displaying such birds. However these are not to be confused with true falconers.

Falconry is an ancient and an elegant sport, and true falconers devote thousands of hours of time and the greatest care to their charges, worrying, for instance, about exactly right diets and diseases that may afflict their hawks. They have included some of the greatest past experts on birds of prey, superseded in modern times by the new generation of active field observers, but who in their day did more to interest the public in conservation of raptors than any others. Men such as the late G. E. Lodge and Captain C. W. R. Knight, or Philip Wayre and Jack Mavrogordato, to name a few, would no more think of taking action likely to endanger birds of prey, especially threatened species such as the peregrine, than they would wish to batter an old lady to death in Hyde Park for the contents of her bag.

I could wish that falconers kept better records of such details as moult to adult plumage, the age to which their hawks survive, disease problems, amount of food consumed, and survival rates of captive as opposed to wild hawks, for in these ways they could add considerably to our knowledge of birds of prey, and would find themselves less often regarded as cranks who only want to keep wild hawks in captivity. The life of a properly trained hawk, regularly exercised, and given veterinary care when necessary, is obviously better than that of a hawk in a zoo cage; and there is some evidence that survival rates of such trained young hawks may actually be higher than the 50–75% mortality they can expect between first flight and sexual maturity in the wild(2). In 401 recorded cases, 113 (28%) died (some after several years), 154 (38%) were lost (of these some would survive as wild birds), and 134 (34%) were returned to the wild alive.

To avoid the slight public odium in which they are held, and which has been brought upon them by the actions of the more disreputable members of their fraternity, falconers need stricter rules among themselves, which should preferably acquire legal force. It should be illegal for anyone to keep a hawk of any sort unless he is a licensed member of a falconer's club with strict rules. Within such clubs young new members should not be allowed to keep the more advanced and difficult species unless they have proved, by an apprenticeship with common species, that they can man a hawk properly. This is no more than any true falconer would demand of himself; and if such measures were effectively enforced by falconers themselves British birds of prey would have little to fear from them.

Bird photographers and bird watchers are again in a somewhat different category. They too are only interested in the wild bird alive, and are not interested in taking its eggs or young, but in obtaining a trophy picture, or recording the species on their lists. Bird photographers vary in their degree of responsibility, but as a rule are most anxious not to disturb their subjects unnecessarily, for they will not secure good photographs if they do. The only damage they can do is near the nest, when putting up a hide too precipitately will sometimes cause the adults to desert. This threat is fairly well under control in Britain, since to photograph any rare species one must have a permit, and this is not given unless the person concerned is a responsible individual, and not at all in the case of such very rare or shy species as the marsh harrier and the red kite.

It is, of course, possible to try to photograph some species without a permit; but the construction of a hide in a tree or on a mountainside will normally be observed by someone, unless it is in thick woodland; and the long-continued activity associated with taking a good series of photographs at various stages in the nesting cycle will usually mean detection. Away from nesting areas bird photographers, unlike gamekeepers or dubious falconers can do no harm at all; and the worst harm is done by those rather casual photographers who, finding a raptor's nest, feel that they must have a picture of the young or eggs. Bird photographers cannot now claim, as they once did, and with justice, that they above all are the people who interest the public in conservation of rare species. However, they still have a very important part to play especially in television films, book illustrations, and recording aspects of behaviour not easily described in writing. British birds of prey are not affected adversely by responsible bird photographers, only by the irresponsible, and only in the breeding season.

The same, basically, applies to the ordinary bird-watchers and listers, who want to see and record a bird of prey, but have little long-term interest in it. Outside the breeding season they can do no harm at all; if five hundred people go to twitch a gyrfalcon on the coast of Norfolk in December they only benefit the Government by the taxes they pay on petrol and the local landlords by the amount of beer they consume. They may irritate the local farmers; but far worse would happen if a Beatle were heard vocalising in the area. On the other hand, the listers and twitchers, lacking any real long-term interest in the species concerned, sometimes act irresponsibly. The worst present threat to the security of the marsh harriers at Minsmere is not the gamekeepers in the surrounding country, or egg collectors, but the relatively large number of people who, although they cannot get a permit to go to Minsmere because the small reserve will daily accommodate only a certain number, still try to get in by the back door to twitch marsh marriers, bitterns, and bearded tits(a). Such people need to learn forbearance, and to remember that they have at least a 50% better chance of seeing a British marsh harrier in July or August than in April or May, while they would also then be able to visit parts of the reserve denied to them in spring.

Finally, there is the threat posed by people who do not even know or care that birds of prey may be living in a certain area, but are interested in rock climbing, mountain walking, fishing, or some other outdoor pursuit which takes them into the breeding habitat. These people mean no harm whatever, and would often be horrified if told that they did harm to any species concerned. Yet they undoubtedly do cause some harm, especially perhaps to species which breed in spectacular mountain country and national parks. The golden eagle and peregrine seem among the worst affected in this way, but so is the beleaguered red kite. Even pre-war there were golden eagle eyries in the southern Cairngorms that sometimes failed because too many people picnicked in the neighbourhood of the nest. These particular pairs have now given up altogether, and several others which used to succeed regularly have faded out in the last decade, when more and more people take the chairlift to the summit of Cairngorm, or walk up on to the Ben MacDhui plateau from Deeside. One can draw a map of the eyrie sites that have been disturbed in this way, and it is obvious that they lie close to the main routes into the mountains. Certain favourite rock climbs also adversely affect breeding eagles.

It is more difficult to know what to do about this situation because the damage done is not normally intentional, and because the erection of notices saying 'please keep away, eagles breeding' might finally seal the fate of certain pairs that still stand a slender chance of success. The easily gulled British public might be better deterred by a notice saying: 'Warning: eagles at large.' In some cases I feel that it would be worth trying to interest, for instance, rock climbers in keeping clear of certain cliffs at certain times of year. Perhaps also enabling people to see and watch a kite's nest from a hide would mean that fewer people would wander about half-looking for kites when on a walk in the Welsh mountains.

However, some damage from this source can hardly be avoided without undue interference with the liberties of individuals. Perhaps, as long as a species is not actually threatened by such activities, and as long as other more serious threats (such as grouse-moor gamekeepers in the case of golden eagles) can be contained, the disadvantages of publicising the whereabouts of breeding sites to induce people to keep clear of them outweigh any other possible advantage. However, as people become more and more mobile this problem is bound to worsen, and measures to combat it should at least be considered.

The first three of the four principles have now been adequately covered, while the problems of environmental contamination by pesticides were separately discussed in the last chapter. Evidently, it will be necessary to keep a continuing check on the contamination of the environment by pesticides and to monitor, country-wide, the breeding success of birds of prey that might be affected by such contamination. This is being quite adequately done at present by the Nature Conservancy, though they have not adequate staff or funds to cover all eventualities and could benefit from the help of experienced amateurs. There are also certain species such as the merlin which may be affected but are too little studied for any certainty on their status.

There remain one or two other threats to birds of prey which need mention. One recent threat is the increasing use of the narcotic alpha-chloralose in place of strychnine as a poison for avian predators. Phosdrin and cyanide have also been found in recent cases. Alpha-chloralose, which has sometimes been used with great effect by conservationists to protect, for instance, flamingo colonies in the Camargue from an excessive population of marauding herring gulls, has recently been introduced in order to control avian predators, principally crows, in Scotland and elsewhere. As in the case of the introduction of certain pesticides the motives leading to its use were good. It was felt that alpha-chloralose, being a narcotic, would result in a less painful death than strychnine, which kills by agonising convulsions; and that by putting it for instance into eggs, the crows it was meant for would be killed and not birds of prey. Unfortunately, recent evidence suggests that in the hands of the unscrupulous this particular narcotic is even more dangerous than strychnine, killing many birds of prey as well as crows[3]. A parallel case in Africa is the use of the concentrate of toxaphene cattle dip to kill jackals, hyenas, lions and other predators. It was never intended for such purposes, but is extensively used, and is very lethal, while the carnivores concerned seem actually to relish the taste of toxaphene, so sealing their fate.

This example also shows how necessary it is to keep a constant watch on the situation, so as to detect and attempt to combat any new threat to birds of prey before it becomes so serious that species are endangered. Within the last 20 years British birds of prey, which were thought to have recovered to a fresh high peak of numbers in the late forties and early fifties through the partial retreat of several previously severe threats, such as egg collecting and game preserving, have had to withstand several new threats, the most severe being the introduction of myxomatosis in the rabbit and the pollution of the environment by agricultural chemicals. Some species have not recovered from the last, nor are they likely to in the foreseeable future. Others were and are less or little affected, while the rabbit has recovered sufficiently well to provide a useful source of food for birds of prey without again becoming the appalling agricultural pest it once was. We may now be feeling a little complacent that the worst of environmental pollution by pesticides is over. However, more recently again the insidious adverse effects of polychlorinated biphenyls, which are industrial breakdown products, have become increasingly evident in certain species, notably in puffins feeding in the north Atlantic[1]. Only constant vigilance can detect such possible threats in time and combat them, perhaps not even then.

Some of the present day threats to birds of prey are old, such as gamekeepers, public ignorance, destruction of habitat, and egg collectors. Others, such as the increasing demand for falcons by true falconers and others less scrupulous including dealers and showmen interested in making a profit are old dangers with a new virulence, derived from the present precarious position of some of the bird-eating hawks. Yet others, notably environmental pollution, are largely or completely new. The best way in which to combat all these threats is to co-ordinate efforts to study birds of prey through effective continuing research on populations, and to back up any conservation measures proposed with real legal teeth, effectively closed with a snap on the offender. If such steps are more effectively taken than they are at present no more of our birds of prey should become extinct, while others now rare may increasingly flourish, and yet others may be reintroduced to breed with us again before the century is out.

APPENDIX TABLES

Notes on Appendix Table I

(1) The figures given herein are those collected from papers readily accessible to me during my study of British species and are not completely exhaustive. They are, however, considered to be representative, and in some species for which large numbers of prey items are available (e.g. goshawk, sparrowhawk, buzzard and golden eagle) not seriously arguable.

(2) Prey items have been divided into broad categories indicating main preferences and to some degree possible harmfulness or usefulness. E.g. among mammals carnivores have been separated from herbivores and among birds the supposedly harmful corvids from other species. Among birds, however, other non-passerines include predatory species such as owls or other raptors; for instance the golden eagle is known to kill several *Buteo* species, large and medium sized owls (great horned and barn owl e.g.) and several falcons and *Accipiter* spp. occasionally.

(3) No attempt has been made to disguise the fact that raptors do sometimes take prey which is useful to or preserved by man; for instance, eagles do take some lambs, mainly dead as carrion, and many gamebirds; goshawks feed on gamebirds to about 20% by weight, but also take large numbers of pigeons and include many sparrowhawks and owls among other non-passerine kills, while they are a considerable controlling influence on corvids.

(4) There is an obvious need for better and more complete data in Britain on certain species, for instance hen harrier (studies being done not yet published) and our commonest species, the kestrel and sparrowhawk, the latter in other areas besides the present main study area in Dumfries.

APPENDIX TABLE I — *Food of selected British raptors*

Column groups: **MAMMALS** = Lagomorphs … Total Mammals; **BIRDS** = Gamebirds … Total birds; **OTHER VERTEBRATES** = Reptiles … Total other vertebrates.

SPECIES	Lagomorphs (rabbits, hares)	Small mammals (voles, rats, shrews)	Carnivores (foxes, stoats, etc.)	Large mammals (mainly carrion)	Misc. & unidentified mammals	Total Mammals	Gamebirds	Other non-passerines	Corvids	Small passerines	Misc. & unidentified birds	Total birds	Reptiles	Amphibia	Fish	Total other vertebrates	TOTAL ALL VERTEBRATES	INVERTEBRATES	TOTAL ALL ITEMS
RED KITE																			
Lorraine, France	30	426	7	6	—	469	3	67	19	131	—	220	11	49	207	267	956	259	1,215
Other, Europe	48	51	—	—	60	159	24	237	163	—	158	582	few	few	few	10+	751+	many	751+
Total Europe	78	477	7	6	60	628	27	304	182	131	158	802	11	49	207	277	1,707	259	1,966+
% by number	3·9	24·4				32·0	1·4		9·4			40·6				14·1			
Wales: Nest kills	32	44	7	2	—	85	1	62	40	15	—	118	—	—	—	—	203	—	203
Pellets etc.	—	—	—	391	464	855	—	5	—	—	310	315	2	2	7	11	1,181	180	1,361
Total Wales	32	44	7	393	464	940	1	67	40	15	310	433	2	2	7	11	1,384	180	1,564
% by number	2·2			25·2		60·0	0·06		2·6			27·5				0·7			
Total: RED KITE	110	521	14	399	524	1,568	28	371	222	146	468	1,235	13	51	214	288	3,091	439	3,530
% by number	3·1	14·8		11·3		44·2	0·80		6·3			34·5				8·2	87·6	12·4	
HEN HARRIER																			
Norway	6	326			1	333	40	43		128	27	238	2			2	573	7	580
Europe	7	346				353	17			77	1	95	3			3	451	31	482
North America	3	32				35				16		16					51		51

SPECIES	Lagomorphs (rabbits, hares)	Small mammals (voles, rats, shrews)	Carnivores (foxes, stoats. etc.)	Large mammals (mainly carrion)	Misc. & unidentified mammals	Total mammals	Gamebirds	Other non-passerines	Corvids	Small passerines	Misc. & unidentified birds	Total birds	Reptiles	Amphibia	Fish	Total other vertebrates	TOTAL ALL VERTEBRATES	INVERTEBRATES	TOTAL ALL ITEMS
HEN HARRIER (cont.)																			
Total outside Britain	16	704			1	721	57	43		221	28	349	5			5	1,075	38	1,113
% by number		63·3				64·8	5·1			19·6		31·4							
Total	16	704			1	721	57	43		221	28	349	5			5	1,075	38	1,113
% by number		63·3				64·8	5·1			19·6		31·4							
Orkney: (1) at nest	5	18				23		4		9	6	19					42		42
(2) pellets	3	29			23	55					30	30					85	12	97
Total	8	47			23	78		4		9	36	49					127	12	139
% by number		33·3				56·1						35·1							
Total: HEN HARRIER	24	751			24	799	57	47		230	64	398	5			5	1,202	50	1,252
% by number	2·0	60·2				64·0	4·5	3·8		18·4		31·8							
MARSH HARRIER																			
Europe	23	196				219	28	54		65		147	1	12	11	24	390	9	399
Lorraine, France	8	734	1			743	0	44		57		101	1	27	5	33	877	60	937
Total	31	930	1			962	28	98		122		248	2	39	16	57	1,267	69	1,336
% by number	2·3	69·5				72·2	2·1					18·6		2·9					

MONTAGU'S HARRIER

Europe	32	317	349	32	257	289	88	108	211	957
Vendée, France	1	804	805		81, 30 eggs	111	2	2	745	1,663
Total	33	1,121	1,154	32	338	400	90	110	956	2,620
% by number	1·2	43·0	44·2	1·2	12·9	15·2	3·4	4·2		36·2
% of vertebrates	2·0	67·2	68·7	1·9	20·3	23·8	5·3	6·6		

GOSHAWK (EUROPE)

											Total wt.	Total
(a) Germany (Uttendorfer)	373	77	4	259	713	1,113	3,249	1,675	2,272	8,309		9,022
(b) Germany (Kramer)	47	28	2	16	93	149	1,076	588	430	2,243		2,336
(c) Lorraine, France	6	6	1		13	2	149	78	266	495		508
(d) Germany (Brull)	563	9			572	404	1,591	277	1,031	3,303		3,875
Total	989	120	7	275	1,391	1,668	6,065	2,618	3,999	14,350		15,741
% by number	6·9				9·8	11·6	18·2	18·2	15·6	90·2		
Mean weight gr.	500	50	200	100	100	600	400	300	80			
% by weight	9·8				10·2	19·8	18·2	28·0	6·3	89·8		neg.

SPARROWHAWK (EUROPE)

												Total	Total all
(a) Germany (Uttendorfer)	62	1,318	5		1,386	110	748	719	400	56,510	58,087		59,473
(b) Germany (Kramer)	2	983	11		997	136	271	345	35	26,840	27,592		28,589
(c) Tinbergen		96			96	0	110	48	3,932	3,032	3,115		3,211
(d) All other		11			11	2	30	19	2,009	2,009	2,060		2,071 · 4
Total Europe	64	2,408	16		2,490	248	1,084	1,131	88,391	90,854			93,344 · 93,348
% by number					2·8	0·3	1·2	1·2	95	97			
Mean weight gr.	100	20	200		40	400	400	50					
% by weight	0·1	0·8			1·1	0·5	8·4	4·4	85·6	98·9			98·9

(BRITAIN)

Dumfries	27	27	17	128	12	1,059	39	1,255	1,282		1,282
Mean weight gr.	25	25	100	30–500	200	15–90	40				
% by weight	0·6	0·6	1·5	2·1	4·4	54·4	1·4	99·4			

	Total				Total ALL	
Total ALL	2,517	89,450	92,109	94,626	94,630	
% by weight	1·05	85·1	92·95	98·95	98·95	

APPENDIX I continued

SPECIES	Lagomorphs (rabbits, hares)	Small mammals (voles, rats, shrews)	Carnivores (foxes, stoats, etc.)	Large mammals (mainly carrion)	Misc. & unidentified mammals	Total mammals	Gamebirds	Other non-passerines	Corvids	Small passerines	Misc. & unidentified birds	Total birds	Reptiles	Amphibia	Fish	Total other vertebrates	TOTAL ALL VERTEBRATES	INVERTEBRATES	TOTAL ALL ITEMS
COMMON BUZZARD																			
Britain																			
Dartmoor (Dare)	193	505	1	9	66	774	—	5	5	49	44	103	55	131	1	187	1,064	many	1,064 +
New Forest (Tubbs) (estimated from figures given)	58	108	—	—	—	166	7	171	356	96	—	630	4	—	—	4	800	many	800 +
Britain (scattered sources; minimal data)	68	82	6	9	—	165	7	25	33	23	—	88	22	3	2	27	280	3,000 +	3,000 +
ALL Britain	319	695	7	18	66	1,105	14	201	394	168	44	821	81	134	3	218	2,144	3,000 +	5,144 +
Europe																			
Germany (Uttendörfer)	41	968	3	—	3	1,015	5	←202→				207	123	67	1	191	1,413	many	1,413 +
Germany (Rörig)	45	1,896	10	—	297	2,248	29	10	←44→			83	72	186	6	264	2,595	many	2,595 +
Fenno-Scandia (Bergmann)	2	193	—	—	40	235		←73→				73	30	20	—	50	358	—	358
France (Thiollay)	11	2,486	19	14	—	2,530	4	78	37	662	—	814	34	164	46	244	3,588	2,104	5,692
Total Europe	99	5,548	32	14	340	6,028	38	121	37	662	319	1,177	259	437	53	749	7,954	2,104 +	10,058 +
Total Buzzard	418	6,243	39	32	406	7,135	52	322	431	830	363	1,998	340	571	56	967	10,098	5,104 +	15,202 +
% by number of vertebrates		61·6				70	0·5		4·2	8·1		19·6		5·6		9·4			

																Total
ROUGH-LEGGED BUZZARD																
Germany (Rörig)	6	1,367	6	22	1,403	9	8			19	2					1,424
Germany (Uttendorfer)	16	843			859	8				7					35	899
Norway (Hagen)	18	1,830			1,871	132	25	23	46	21	232				86+	2,114
Total	40	4,040	29	22	4,133	149	33	30	3	54+	21+	284	19	2	123+	4,437
% by number of vertebrates	91	93				3·3						6·4				4,560+
																2,200+
GOLDEN EAGLE																
ALL Scottish data	501	133	40	373	12	1,059	751	62	48	135	197	1,788	54	13	5	13
European data	139	14	28	226	—	407	143	4	16	—	2	167	—	18	—	18
American data	2,754	1,622	43	140	—	4,559	247	69	133	14,339	702	49	67	5,328		
Total	3,384	1,769	111	739	12	6,025	1141	135	197	44,269	1,788	54	13	85	7,899	7,899
% by number	42·7	1·4				77·2	14·4	2·5		22·7	0·11					
% by weight	52·0	1·6				95·5	4·3	0·3		4·4	0·13					
KESTREL																
Britain (minimal)	272	1,737	274	2,738	36	36	4	47	656	739	46	142	4	3	146	323
Europe (main sources)		2,737														3,633
Total	1,3009	3,011	36	51	39	17·3	695	785	19·8	142	5	2	149	3,946		3,946
% by number of vertebrates	78	78	0·9	0·3												5,840+
PEREGRINE																
ALL British sources (Text Table 18)	3	7	1		8	84		16		2·5	197	2,284	18	85		1,996
Europe (Uttendorfer)										0·3		167		0·11		575
Total	10 neg.	1	11 neg.		3	8		62	735	312	2,342			20	11	2,287
% by number						50·5	4·8		39·2							5,504

Notes on Appendix Table II

(1) The data contained herein are sometimes indicative only because they have had to be calculated from incomplete figures. The main headings indicate the essential data to obtain a true picture of breeding rates in any species. In many older studies only the pairs which actually bred, or those which bred and succeeded, have been fully recorded so that in some of these the results given under certain headings are merely comparative. Fuller results have usually been available since 1960, when the effect of pesticides appeared to become increasingly apparent and serious as a depressing factor on raptor populations. Thus, early and apparently higher figures for marsh harrier breeding success do not necessarily indicate that British breeding success is at present depressed.

(2) Most of the buzzard data is both post myxomatosis and post pesticide influence, indicating that there had been no serious falling off in breeding success in this species, and that breeding success in Britain overall is little inferior to that in Europe.

(3) In the golden eagle, the main factor depressing breeding success both in Britain and America is human interference, which appears to be actually lower in the breeding season in America than in Britain. The figures suggest that American golden eagles rear a greater number of young per successful nest than do British eagles.

(4) The figures for capacity unmolested populations of large African eagles suggest that in the tropics a lower breeding rate can maintain a stable or even increasing (fish eagle) population. Without human interference it is likely that in the golden eagle about 0·8–0·9 young/pair/annum overall would maintain a capacity population, while in tropical species about 0·4–0·5 young/pair/annum overall is adequate.

(5) The figures for the peregrine indicate (a) the falling off in overall breeding rates post pesticides, except in one population (Weir, 1964–1971) which is essentially the same as Ratcliffe's Central and Eastern Highlands 1961–1962. This is probably a good approximation of the true natural breeding rate of peregrines; (b) the uselessness of recording only the results from successful nests, which are often several times as great in pesticide affected areas as those for the pairs which actually bred, and may be ten times as great or more as those for the known territories.

(6) Future observers are urged to (1) concentrate on the same area or group of pairs for several successive years, not less than three to obtain best results; (2) record results from unoccupied sites as well as occupied sites; the pair may still be in the territory in such cases, but not so readily visible or observable as when the breeding site is occupied. The *maximum* number of pairs observed in any defined area is more likely to be the true population than the *minimum* number. This, however, may vary as to whether the territorial behaviour of the species concerned is nomadic (kestrel) or highly conservative (golden eagle). In the former, a variation between 8 and 30 pairs in the same area probably represents actual variation, while 12–24 pairs in the golden eagle does not.

APPENDIX TABLE II *Summarised breeding data for some British species*

SPECIES/COUNTRY/AUTHOR	Pairs studied	Pairs which bred	Pairs successful	Young reared	Young per pair overall	Young per pair breeding	Young per successful nest
OSPREY							
Britain (Weir)	45	35	21	47	1·05	1·34	2·23
RED KITE							
Britain (Davis & Davies)	362	321	161	215	0·52	0·67	1·32
France (Thiollay)	27	23	20	25	0·93	1·08	1·24
MARSH HARRIER							
Britain (Axell)	42	49	42	111	2·65	2·25	2·62
France (Thiollay)	20	11	7	26	1·3	2·35	3·71
Holland (Haverschmidt)	?	?	14	45	?	?	3·2
Sweden (Bengtson)	?	26	18	57	?	2·2	3·2
Germany (Creutz)	?	68?	55	193	?	2·8	3·5
Finland (Hildén, Kalinainen)	?	79	50	117	?	1·49	2·35
HEN HARRIER							
Britain (Balfour)	562+	562	331	794	1·4	1·58	2·4
GOSHAWK							
France (Thiollay)	8	5	4	9	1·1	1·8	2·25
SPARROWHAWK							
Holland (Tinbergen)	24	13	7	24	1·0	1·82	3·4
Scotland (Newton) (affected by pesticides)	330?	244	152	473	1·44	1·94	3·1

APPENDIX II continued

SPECIES/COUNTRY/AUTHOR	Pairs studied	Pairs which bred	Pairs successful	Young reared	Young per pair overall	Young per pair breeding	Young per successful nest
BUZZARD							
Britain (Dare)	40	29	14	18	0·45	0·62	1·28
Britain (Tubbs)	185	166	73	102	0·55	0·61	1·39
Britain (Davis)	62	40	26	44	0·7	1·1	1·68
Britain (Weir 1970)	34	29	21	47	1·38	1·6	2·2
TOTAL/MEAN/BRITAIN	321	264	134	211	0·65	0·8	1·57
France (Thiollay)	107	90?	?	106	0·99	1·18	1·19
Germany (Wendland)	69	39	32	54	0·78	1·38	1·68
Germany (Mebs)	?	95	95?	158	?	1·66	1·66
GOLDEN EAGLE							
Britain (Brown)	20	11?	7	8	0·35	0·72	1·14
Britain (Watson)	65	55	37	44	0·68	0·8	1·2
Britain (Weir)	167	105	63	72	0·43	0·68	1·14
Britain (Everett)	489	395	197	231	0·56	0·73	1·18
Britain (Merrie)	114	84	51	54	0·47	0·64	1·06
TOTAL/MEAN/SCOTLAND	909	650	355	409	0·45	0·63	1·14
U.S.A. Montana (McGahan)	36?	32	32	41	1·12	1·28	1·28
U.S.A. Montana (Reynolds)	92	56+	50	73	0·79	1·3	1·46
U.S.A. Utah (Murphy)	31	23	18	26	0·84	1·11	1·44
For comparison:							
UNMOLESTED AFRICAN SPP.							
Fish eagle (Brown)	138	82	50	70	0·51	0·85	1·4
Verreaux's eagle (Gargett)	223	150	114	114	0·51	0·76	1·00
Crowned eagle (Brown)	39	21	15	15	0·38	0·71	1·00

KESTREL							
Britain (Shrubb)	79	79	44	145	1·82	1·9	3·3
Holland (Cave)	198	198	152	570	2·86	2·0	3·7
PEREGRINE							
Britain (Ratcliffe, 1962)	796	616	475?	900?	1·1	1·45	2·2
Britain (Ratcliffe 1965, all)	461	251	76	151	0·32	0·6	2·0
Britain (Ratcliffe, Central and Eastern Highlands)							
Britain (Weir 1964–1971)	87	71	21	46	0·65	1·68	2·38
Switzerland (Herren pre 1960)	125	94	70	168	0·52	1·68	1·94
Switzerland (Herren post 1960)	65	38	33	64	1·34	1·0	1·8
W. Germany (Mebs pre 1960)	63	27	18	33	1·0	0·54	1·18
W. Germany (Mebs post 1960)	?	116	36	79	?	0·68	1·04
E. Germany (Kleinstauber pre 1960)	?	73	38	76	?	0·6	2·2
E. Germany (Kleinstauber post 1960)	?	128	?	77	?	0·28	2·0
(all quoted in Hickey, 1968)		50	?	14			?

BIBLIOGRAPHICAL REFERENCES

CHAPTER 1

Main references

1. Cade, T. J. 1967. Ecological and behavioural aspects of predation by the Northern Shrike. The Living Bird; 6:43–85.
2. Cone, C. D. 1962. The soaring flight of birds. Scientific American; 206:130–142.
3. Pumphrey, R. J. 1948. The sense organs of birds. Ibis; 90:171–199.
4. Walls, G. L. 1942. The Vertebrate Eye. London.
5. Welty, J. C. 1964. The life of birds (flight). Constable, London.

CHAPTER 2

Main references

1. Ash, J. S. 1960. Birds of Prey on a Hampshire game preserve, 1952–59. British Birds; 53:7:285–300.
2. Axell, H. E. 1964. The Marsh Harrier in East Anglia. Bird Notes; 31:3:95–98 (and pers. comm.).
3. Brown, P. and Waterston, G. 1962. The return of the Osprey. Collins, London.
4. Davies, P. W. and Davis, P. E. 1973. The ecology and conservation of the Red Kite in Wales. British Birds; 66:183–224, 241–270 (and mss. and pers. comm.)
5. Gordon, S. 1955. The Golden Eagle, King of Birds. Collins, London.
6. Nethersole-Thompson, D. 1931. The field habits and nesting of the Hobby. British Birds, 35:142–148.
7. Parslow, J. L. F. 1967. Changes in status among breeding birds in Britain and Ireland. British Birds; 60:1:2–47.
8. Prestt, I. 1965. An enquiry into the recent breeding status of some of the smaller birds of prey and crows in Britain. Bird Study; 12:3:196–221.
9. Ratcliffe, D. A. 1968. Population trends of the Peregrine Falcon in Great Britain. Peregrine populations, Ch. 21. Ed. Hickey; University of Wisconsin Press, Milwaukee.

Short references

(a) Pounds, H. E. Brit. Birds; 41:153. (b) Weir, D., pers. comm.

CHAPTER 3

Main references

1. Bannerman, D. A. 1956. The Birds of the British Isles, Vol. V. Oliver and Boyd, Edinburgh.

2. Benson, C. W. and White, C. M. N. 1957. Check List of the Birds of Northern Rhodesia. Government Printer, Lusaka.
3. Brown, L. H. 1971. African Birds of Prey. Collins, London.
4. Brown, L. H. and Amadon, D. 1969. Eagles, Hawks and Falcons of the World. Country Life/Hamlyn, Feltham.
5. Christensen, S. *et al.* 1971–72. Flight identification of European raptors. British Birds; 64:247–266, and 435–465. 65:52–78 and cont.
6. Hickey, J. (Ed.) 1968. Peregrine Falcon Populations. University of Wisconsin Press, Milwaukee.
7. Landsborough-Thomson, A. (Ed.) *et al.* 1964. A New Dictionary of Birds. Nelson, London.
8. Laszlo, S. 1941. The habits and plumages of Montagu's harrier. Aquila; 46–51:247–268.
9. Nice, M. M. 1953. Incubation periods of birds of prey. Vogelwarte; 16:4:154–157.
10. Peters, J. L. *et al* 1931–68. Check-list of Birds of the World. Mus. Comp. Zoology; Cambridge, Mass.
11. Sibley, C. G. 1960. The electrophoretic patterns of avian egg-white proteins as taxonomic characters. Ibis:102:215–284.
12. Snow, D. W. (Ed.) 1971. The Status of birds in Britain and Ireland. Blackwell, Oxford.
13. Stresemann, V. and Stresemann, E. 1960. Die Handschwingenmäuser der Tagraubvögel. J. für Orn.; 101:4:373–403.
14. Vaurie, C. 1961. (a) Systematic notes on Palearctic birds, No. 44: Falconidae, the genus *Falco*: Part 1, *Falco peregrinus* and *Falco pelegrinoides*. Am. Mus. Novitates; 2035:1–19.
15. Vaurie, C. 1961. (b) Systematic notes on Palearctic Birds, No. 47: Accipitridae, the genus *Buteo*. Am. Mus. Novitates; 2042; 14.

Short references

(a) Note on *Circus cyaneus hudsonius* in E. Anglia; Brit. Birds; Dec. 1971.

CHAPTER 4

Main references

1. Abbott, C. G. 1911. The Home Life of the Osprey. New York.
2. Ames, P. L. 1961. A preliminary report on a colony of Ospreys. Atlantic Naturalist; 16:26–33 (and Peterson, R. T., pers. comm. 1960–70).
3. Bannerman, D. A., 1956. op. cit. 3(1).
4. Brown, P. and Waterston, G. 1962. op. cit. 2(3).
5. Meinertzhagen, R. 1954. The Education of young Ospreys. Ibis, 96:153–155.
6. Osterlof, S. 1951. Fiskgjusens flyttning. Var Fagelwarld, 10:1–15.
7. R.S.P.B. record books; Speyside Ospreys, esp. 1969–71.
8. St John, C. 1849. A tour in Sutherland.

Short references

(a) Bentham, H. H. Brit. Birds; 38:135. (b) Clancey, P. A. Brit. Birds; 39:218.
(c) Humphreys, G. R. Brit. Birds; 38:195. (d) Long, D. A. C. Brit. Birds; 61:178.

BIBLIOGRAPHICAL REFERENCES

(e) Niestle, A. Brit. Birds; 61:465. (f) Palmer, M. G. Brit. Birds; 43:124. (g) Sandeman, P. W. Brit. Birds; 50:147–149. (h) Swaine, C. M. Brit. Birds; 40: 252. (i) Weir, D. pers. comm.

CHAPTER 5

Main references

1. Bannerman, D. A., 1930. Birds of Tropical West Africa Vol. 1. Crown Agents/ Oliver and Boyd, Edinburgh.
2. Buxton, A. 1932. Sporting interludes at Geneva. Country Life, London.
3. Gibb, J. 1951. The birds of the Maltese Islands. Ibis; 93:109–127.
4. Hagen, Y. and Babbé, A. 1958. The food of some Honey Buzzards *Pernis apivorus* (L.) in Norway. Pap. Norwegian State Game Research. Ser. 2.2:3–28.
5. Holstein, V. 1944. Hvespavaagen *Pernis a. apivorus* (L.). H. Hirschprung Forlag. Copenhagen.
6. Munch, H. 1955. Der Wespenbussard. Neue Brehm Bücherei, 151. Wittenberg-Lutherstadt.
7. Parslow, J. L. F. 1967. op. cit. 2(7).
8. Snow, D. W. (Ed.) 1971. op. cit. 3(12).
9. Thiollay, J. M. 1967. Ecologie d'une population de rapaces diurnes en Lorraine. Terre et Vie; 2.(1969) 116–183.
10. Trap-Lund, Ib. 1962. Observations on a Honey Buzzard digging out a wasp's nest. British Birds; 55:36.
11. Ulfstrand, S. 1958. De ärliga fluctuationerna i bivräkens (*Pernis apivorus*) sträck over Falsterbo. Medd. fran Falsterbo Fagelstation. 11 VF. 17:118–144.

CHAPTER 6

Main references

1. e.g. Baxter, E. V. and Rintoul, L. J. 1953. The Birds of Scotland. Oliver and Boyd, Edinburgh.
2. Davies, P. W. and Davis, P. E. 1973. op. cit. 2(4).
3. Morrey Salmon, H. 1970. The Red Kites of Wales. Welsh Wildlife in Trust; Ch. XI: 67–79. North Wales Naturalists Trust, Bangor.
4. Thiollay, J. M. 1967. op. cit. 5(9).

Short references

(a) B.T.O. ringing records. (b) Nisbet, I. C. T. British Birds; 52:239–40. (c) Weir, D. pers. comm.

CHAPTER 7

Main references

1. Arnold, E. L. and Maclaren, P. I. R. 1939. Notes on the habits and distribution of the White-tailed Eagle in Iceland. British Birds, 34: 4–10.

2. Baxter, E. V. and Rintoul, L. J. 1953. op. cit. 6(1).
3. Brown, L. H. and Amadon, D. 1969. op. cit. 3(4).
4. Dennis, R H. 1968–69. Fair Isle Bird Observatory reports.
5. Fischer, W. 1959. Die Seeadler. Neue Brehm Bücherei, 221. Wittenberg Lutherstadt.
6. Gordon, S. 1955. op. cit. 2(5).
7. Helander, B. 1970. Havsörnen in Sverige, 1964–69. Svenska Naturskydds-foreningen: Uddevalla.
8. Oehme, G. 1961. Die Bestandsentwicklung des Seeadlers *Haliaeetus albicilla* (L) in Deutschland, mit Untersuchungen zur Wahl der Brutbiotope. Beitr. zur Kenntnis Deutscher Vögel. Fischer, Jena; pp. 1–61.
9. Waterston, G. 1964. The White-tailed Eagle; British Birds: 57:11:458–466.
10. Willgohs, J. F. 1961. The White-tailed Eagle *Haliaeetus albicilla* (Linne) in Norway. Norwegian Universities Press, Bergen.

Short references
(a) Ratcliffe, D. A. pers. comm.

CHAPTER 8

Main references

1. Andersson, G. K. A. and Larsson, A. 1970. Bruna kärrhöken *Circus aeruginosus* i Sverige ar 1969. Far Vägelwarld; 30:99–105.
2. Axell, H. E. 1964. op. cit. 2(2) and in litt.
3. Bengtson, S-A. 1967. Observations on the reproductive success in 26 nests of the Marsh Harrier (*Circus aeruginosus*) in Skäne province, Sweden. Ool. Rec.; 2:23–28.
4. Brown, L. H. and Amadon, D. 1969. op. cit. 3(4).
5. Colling, A. W. and Brown, E. B. 1946. The breeding of the Marsh and Montagu's Harriers in N. Wales in 1945. Brit. Birds; 34:233–243.
6. Craighead, J. and Craighead, F. 1956. Hawks, Owls, and Wildlife. Stackpole Co., Harrisburg, Pennsylvania.
7. Creutz, G. 1968. Gelegestärke und Jungendzahl bei der Rohrweihe (*Circus aeruginosus* (L)). Bonn. Zool. Beitr.; 19:3/4:340–345.
8. Haverschmidt, F. 1953. Observations on the Marsh Harrier with particular reference to clutch size and breeding success. Brit. Birds; 36:258.
9. Hilden, O. and Kalinainen, P. 1966. Über Vorkommen und Biologie der Rohrweihe *Circus aeruginosus* (L) in Finnland. Ornis Fennica: 43:3/4:85–124.
10. Hosking, E. 1943. Some observations on the Marsh Harrier. Brit. Birds; 37:2–9.
11. Mead, C. J. 1973. Movements of British Raptors. Bird Study; 20:4:259–286.
12. Moore, N. W. 1967. Pesticides and Birds; a review of the situation in Great Britain to 1965. Bird Study; 12:3:222–252.
13. Parslow, J. L. F. 1967. op. cit. 2(7).
14. Thiollay, J. M. 1967. op. cit. 5(9).
15. Thiollay, J. M. 1970. Observations sur l'ecologie d'une population de Busards des Roseaux *Circus aeruginosus* en Camargue. Nos Oiseaux 30; 8/9:214–229.
16. Weis, H. 1923. The life of the Harrier in Denmark. London.

BIBLIOGRAPHICAL REFERENCES

Short references

(a) Buxton, J. in litt. (b) Macmillan, A. T. 1967. Scot. Birds; 5:1, 25–26. (c) Pinowski J. and Ryszkowski, L. 1961. Ecologia Polska B. Tom.; 7:(1)55–60. (d) Schipper, W. and Walmsley, J. G., in litt. (e) Soper, M. F. 1958. Notornis; 6:p. 6.

CHAPTER 9

Main references

1. Balfour, E. 1957. Observations on the breeding biology of the Hen Harrier in Orkney. Bird Notes; 27:177–183 and 216–223.
2. Balfour, E. 1962. The nest and eggs of the Hen Harrier in Orkney. Bird Notes; 30:69–73.
3. Balfour, E. 1970. Iris colour in the Hen Harrier. Bird Study; 17:1:47.
4. Balfour, E. and MacDonald, M. A. 1970. Food and feeding behaviour of the Hen Harrier in Orkney. Scot. Birds; 6:157–166.
5. Cadbury, J. and Balfour, E. mss. Observations on the biology of the Hen Harrier in Orkney. R.S.P.B. Research Report (and in litt.).
6. Craighead, J. and Craighead, F. 1956. op. cit. 8(6).
7. Hamerstrom, F. 1968. A harrier population study. Ch. 31, pp. 367–383 in 'Peregrine Falcon populations' ed. Hickey: University of Wisconsin Press, Milwaukee.
8. Mead, C. J. 1973. op. cit. 8(11).
9. Parslow, J. L. F. 1967. op. cit. 2(7).
10. Ruttledge, R. F. 1966. Ireland's Birds. Witherby, London.
11. Watson, A. and Dickson, R. C. 1972. Communal roosting of the Hen Harrier in south-west Scotland. Scot. Birds; 7(1):24–48.

Short references

(a) Arnold, E. C. Brit. Birds; 33:276. (b) Balfour, E. pers. comm. (c) Griffith, P. R. *et al.* Brit. Birds; 47:1:125. (d) Picozzi, N. pers. comm. (e) Tucker, B. W. Brit. Birds; 38:275. (f) Turner-Ettlinger, D. M. Brit. Birds; 44:205. (g) Weir, D. pers. comm.

CHAPTER 10

Main references

1. Bannerman, D. A. 1956. op. cit. 3(1).
2. Bannerman, D. A. and Priestley, J. 1952. An Ornithological journey in Morocco in 1951. Ibis; 94:678–682.
3. Brown, L. H. 1971. op. cit. 3(3).
4. Brown, L. H. and Amadon, D. 1969. op. cit. 3(4).
5. Buxton, A. 1946. Fisherman Naturalist. Collins, London.
6. Colling, A. W. and Brown, E. B. 1946. op. cit. 8(5).
7. Elgood, J. H., Sharland, R. E. and Ward, P. 1966. Palearctic migrants in Nigeria. Ibis; 108:84–116.

372

8. Laszlo, S. 1941. op. cit. 3(8).
9. Mackworth Praed, C. W. and Grant, C. H. B. 1953. The Birds of Eastern and North Eastern Africa, Vol. 1. Longman's, London.
10. Mead, C. J. 1973. op. cit. 8(11).
11. Parslow, J. L. F. 1967. op. cit. 2(7).
12. Robinson, W. 1950. Montagu's Harriers. Bird Notes; 24:3:103–114.
13. Thiollay, J. M. 1968. La pression de predation estivale du Busard cendré *Circus pygargus* (L) sur les populations de *Microtus arvalis* en Vendee. Terre et Vie; 3:321–326.
14. Uttendorfer, O. *et al.* 1939 and 1952. Die Ernährung der Deutschen Raubvögel und Eulen. Neumann-Neudamm. Neue Ergebnisse über die Ernahrung der Greifvögel und Eulen. Stuttgart; Eugen-Ulmer.

Short references

(a) Allin, E. K. Brit. Birds; 43:158. (b) B.T.O. nest record cards. (c) Dent, G. Brit. Birds; 33:51. (d) Hosking, E. Brit. Birds; 37:3. (f) King, B. and Roche, K. B. Brit. Birds; 50:352. (g) Robertson, D. W. P. 'Bird Pageant' Batchworth, London. 1954. (h) Vincent, J. quot. in Bannerman (1) above.

CHAPTER II

Main references

1. Baxter, E. V. and Rintoul, L. J. 1953. op. cit. 6(1).
2. Brown, P. 1964. Birds of Prey. Andre Deutsch, London.
3. Brull, H. 1964. A study of the importance of the Goshawk *Accipiter gentilis* and Sparrowhawk *A. nisus* in their Ecosystem. Report, I.C.B.P. Conference on Birds of Prey, Caen; I.C.B.P.
4. Craighead, J. and Craighead, F. 1956. op. cit. 8(6).
5. Edlin, H. L. 1956. Trees, woods and man. Collins New Nat., London.
6. Eng, R. L. and Gullion, G. W. 1962. Predation of Goshawks upon Ruffed Grouse in the Cloquet Forest Research Center, Minnesota. Wilson Bull.; 74:227–243.
7. Ferguson Lees, I. J. *et al.* 1964. Report on I.C.B.P. conference on birds of Prey, Caen. I.C.B.P.
8. Holstein, V. 1942. Duehögen. Copenhagen.
9. Kramer, R. 1967. Die Populationsdynamik bei Habicht und Sperber ... in der Südlausitz. Der Falke; 14:2:40–41.
10. Kramer, V. 1955. Habicht und Sperber. Neue Brehm Bücherei, Wittenberg-Lutherstadt.
11. Meinertzhagen, R. 1950. The Goshawk in Britain. Bull. B.O.C.; 70:7:49–59.
12. Newton, I. 1972. Birds of Prey in Scotland: some conservation problems, Scot. Birds; 7:5–23.
13. Ruttledge, R. F. 1966. op. cit. 9(10).
14. Snow, D. W. (Ed.) 1971. op. cit. 3(12).
15. Tansley, A. G. 1968. Britain's Green Mantle. Allen & Unwin. London.
16. Sulkava, S. 1964. Zur Nahrungsbiologie des Habichts *Accipiter g. gentilis* (L). Aquilo. Tom 3, 1–103, Oulu, Finland.
17. Thiollay, J. M. 1967. op. cit. 5(9).

Short references

(a) Newton, I. pers. comm.

CHAPTER 12

Main references

1. Bannerman, D. A. 1956. op. cit. 3(1).
2. Brown, L. H. and Amadon, D. 1969. op. cit. 3(4).
3. Cadbury, J. and Balfour, E. mss. op. cit. 9(5).
4. Landsborough Thomson, A. 1958. The migrations of British Hawks (Accipitridae) as shown by ringing results. Brit. Birds; 51:85–93.
5. Mohr, H. 1960. On the development of behaviour patterns in young Sparrowhawks and Hobbies. Inst. Zool., Giessen.
6. Newton, I. 1973. (a) Success of Sparrowhawks in an area of pesticide usage. Bird Study; 20:1–8. mss.
7. Newton, I. 1972. (b) op. cit. 11(12).
8. Newton, I. 1974. (c) Changes attributed to pesticides in the nesting success of the Sparrowhawk in Britain. J. appl. Ecol; 11:95–101.
9. Newton, I. 1973. (d) Studies of Sparrowhawks. Brit. Birds; 66:271–278. mss.
10. Owen, J. H. 1916–22. Some breeding habits of the Sparrowhawk. Brit. Birds; 10:2–10, 26–37, 50–59, 74–86, 106–15. 12:61–65, 74–82. 13:114–124. 15:74–77.
11. Owen, J. H. 1926–27. The eggs of the Sparrowhawk. Brit. Birds; 20:114-120.
12. Owen, J. H. 1932. The hunting of the Sparrowhawk. Brit. Birds; 25:238–243.
13. Owen, J. H. 1936–37. Further notes on the Sparrowhawk. Brit. Birds; 30:22–26.
14. Parslow, J. L. F. 1967. op. cit. 2(7).
15. Pounds, H. E. 1936. Notes on the flight of the Sparrowhawk. Brit. Birds; 30:183–189.
16. Snow, D. W. (Ed.) 1971. op. cit. 3(12).
17. Tinbergen, L. 1946. Die Sperwer als roofvijand van zangvogels. Ardea; 34:1–213.
18. Uttendorfer, O. *et al.* 1939 and 1952. op. cit. 10(14).
19. Witherby, H. F. *et al.* 1943. The Handbook of British Birds, Vol. III, Witherby, London.
20. Young, J. 1972. The Pheasant and the Sparrowhawk. Birds; 4:4:94–99.

Short references

(a) Baggaley, W. Brit. Birds; 41:60. (b) Blank, T. H., Game Conservancy, Fordingbridge, in litt. (c) B.T.O. ringing results. (d) Flynn, J. E. Brit. Birds; 35:19. (e) Newton, I. pers. comm. and in litt.

CHAPTER 13

Main references

1. Brown, L. H. and Amadon, D. 1969. op. cit. 3(4).
2. Craighead, J. and Craighead, F. 1956. op. cit. 8(6).
3. Dare, P. J. 1961. Ecological observations on a breeding population of the Common Buzzard *Buteo buteo*, with particular reference to the diet and feeding habits. Ph.D. Thesis; Exeter University.
4. Davis, T. A. W. and Saunders, D. R. 1965. Buzzards on Skomer Island. 1954–64. Nature in Wales; 9:3:116–124.
5. Hayman, R. W. 1969. Buzzards, pedestrian and hovering. Devon Birds; 22:4:66–69.
6. Holdsworth, M. 1971. Breeding biology of Buzzards at Sedbergh during 1937–67. Brit. Birds; 64:9:412–420.
7. Mayaud, N. 1955. Coup d'oeil sur les reprises en France de Buse Variable *Buteo buteo*. Alauda; 23:225–248.
8 McNally, L. 1964. Food at a Buzzard's nest. Scot. Birds; 3:1:26–27.
9. Mead, C. J. 1973. op. cit. 8(11).
10. Mebs, T. 1964. Zur biologie und Populationsdynamik des Mausebussards (*Buteo b. buteo* L.). J. für Orn; 105:3:247–306.
11. Moore, N. W. 1957. The Buzzard in Britain. Brit. Birds; 50:5:173–197.
12. Moysey, G. F. 1970. Census of Buzzards in Devon and Cornwall during 1966. Devon Birds; 32:1:11–19.
13. Olson, V. 1958. Dispersal, migration, longevity and death causes of *Strix aluco*, *Buteo buteo*, *Ardea cinerea* and *Larus argentatus*. Acta Vertebratica (Stockholm); Vol. 1, No. 2.
14. Prestt, I. 1965. op. cit. 2(8).
15. Ruttledge, R. F. 1966. op. cit. 9(10).
16. Ryves, B. H. 1946. Bird Life in Cornwall. Country Life, London.
17. Thiollay, J. M. 1967. op. cit. 5(9).
18. Tubbs, C. R. 1967. A population study of Buzzards in the New Forest during 1962–66. Brit. Birds; 60:10:381–395.
19. Tubbs, C. R. 1972. Analysis of nest record cards for the Buzzard. Bird Study. 19:97–104. mss.
20. Uttendorfer, O. *et al.* 1939 and 1952. op. cit. 10(14).
21. Weir, D. N. and Picozzi, N. in prep. Territory and population studies in the Buzzard in Speyside (partly reported in 'Work on Buzzards'; Research on Vertebrate Predators in Scotland; Progress report by Nature Conservancy; cyclostyled).
22. Wendland, V. 1952. Populationsstudien an Raubvögeln: 1. Zur Vermehrung des Mausebussards (*Buteo buteo* L.) J. für Orn. 93, 144–153.
23. Witherby, H. F. *et al.* 1943. op. cit. 12(19).

Short references

(a) Brown, R. H. Brit. Birds; 41:53. (b) B.T.O. ringing records. (c) Buzzard survey, original questionnaires. (d) Campbell, B. Brit. Birds; 40:182. (e) Coombes, R. A. H. Brit. Birds; 41:53. (f) Davis, P. pers. comm. (g) Day, M.

Brit. Birds; 42:187. (h) Gilbert, H. A. Brit. Birds; 44:411. (i) Mayo, A. L. W. Brit. Birds; 41:349 (and other records in Brit. Birds on clutch size). (j) Moule, G. W. H. Brit. Birds; 44:101. (k) Nelder, J. A. Brit. Birds; 42:226. (l) Picozzi, N. pers. comm. (m) Robinson, J. S. C. Brit. Birds; 44:412. (n) Ryves, B. H. 1946; Bird life in Cornwall. (o) Tubbs, C. R. pers. comm. (p) Weir, D. N. pers. comm. (q) Autumn rush of Buzzards, 1951 rep. in British Birds; 46:129.

CHAPTER 14

Main references

1. Arnold, L. W. 1954. The Golden Eagle and its Economic status. U.S. Fish and Wildlife Serv. Circ. 27:35 pp.
2. Baxter, E. V. and Rintoul, L. J. 1953. op. cit. 6(1).
3. Brown, L. H. 1955. Eagles. Michael Joseph, London.
4. Brown, L. H. 1966. Observations on some Kenya Eagles. Ibis; 108:531–572.
5. Brown, L. H. 1970. Eagles. Arthur Barker, London.
6. Brown, L. H. 1969. Status and Breeding Success of Golden Eagles in north-west Sutherland in 1967. Brit. Birds; 62:9:345–363.
7. Brown, L. H. 1971. The relations of the Crowned Eagle *Stephanoaetus coronatus* and some of its prey animals. Ibis; 113:240–243.
8. Brown, L. H. and Amadon, D. 1969. op. cit. 3(4).
9. Brown, L. H. and Watson, A. 1964. The Golden Eagle in relation to its food supply. Ibis; 106:1:78–100.
10. Brown, P. 1964. op. cit. 11(2).
11. Cade, T. J. 1960. Ecology of the Peregrine and Gyrfalcon populations in Alaska. Univ. Calif. Pub. Zool.; 63:151–290.
12. Craighead, J. and Craighead, F. 1956. op. cit. 8(6).
13. Everett, M. 1971. The Golden Eagle survey in Scotland, 1964–68. Brit. Birds; 64:49–56.
14. Ferguson-Lees, I. J. *et al.* 1963. Changes in the status of birds of prey in Europe. Brit. Birds. 56:4:140–148.
15. Fisher, J. 1941. Watching Birds. Penguin, Harmondsworth.
16. Gordon, S. 1927. Days with the Golden Eagle. Williams & Norgate, London.
17. Gordon, S. 1955. op. cit. 2(5).
18. Harvie-Brown, J. A. and Macpherson, H. A. 1904. A fauna of the North-West Highlands and Skye. Edinburgh.
19. Hickey, J. (Ed.) 1968. op. cit. 3(6).
20. Jollie, M. 1947. Plumage changes in the Golden Eagle. Auk; 64:549–576.
21. Lockie, J. D. and Stephen, D. 1959. Eagles, lambs, and land management on Lewis. J. Anim. Ecol.; 28:1:43–50.
22. Lockie, J. D. and Ratcliffe, D. 1964. Insecticides and Scottish Golden Eagles. Brit. Birds; 57:89–101.
23. Lockie, J. D., Ratcliffe, D. A. and Balharry, R. 1969. Breeding success and organochlorine residues in Golden Eagles in West Scotland. J. Appl. Ecol.; 6:381–389.
24. Mead, C. J. 1973. op. cit. 8(11).
25. Merrie, D. mss. Golden Eagles (*Aquila chrysaetos*) in south Argyll.

26. Watson, A. 1957. The breeding Success of the Golden Eagles in the N.E. Highlands. Scot. Nat.; 69:3:153–169.
27. Weir, D. N. mss. Status of the Peregrine, Raven and Golden Eagle in part of the Central Scottish Highlands.
28. Weir, D. N. 1971. Mortality of hawks and owls in Speyside. Bird Study; 18:3:147–153.

Short references

(a) Balfour, E. pers. comm. (b) Bjorn von Rosen, Count, in litt. (c) Broun, M. Auk; 64:317–318. (d) B.T.O. nest record cards; and Mead, C. J. pers. comm. (e) Deane, C. D. 1962. Brit. Birds; 55:272–274. (f) Everett, M. pers comm. (g) Palmar, C. pers. comm. (h) Ross, W. M. Brit. Birds; 35:82. (i) Spofford, W. R. pers. comm. (j) Waterston, G. in litt. (k) Watson, A. in litt. (l) Wood, D. in litt. (m) Weir, D. pers. comm.

CHAPTER 15

Main references

1. Ash, J. S. 1960. op. cit. 2(1).
2. Balfour, E. 1955. Kestrels nesting on the ground in Orkney. Bird notes; 26:245–253.
3. Brown, L. H. and Amadon, D. 1969. op. cit. 3(4).
4. Cavé, A. J. 1968. The breeding of the Kestrel *Falco tinnunculus* L. in the reclaimed area Oostelijk Flevoland. Netherlands journ. zool. 18(3) 313–407.
5. Craighead, J. and Craighead, F. 1956. op. cit. 8(6).
6. Davis, T. A. W. 1960. Kestrel pellets at a winter roost. Brit. Birds; 53:7:281–284.
7. Ellis, J. S. C. 1946. Notes on the food of the kestrel. Brit. Birds; 39:113–115.
8. Fairley, J. S. and Maclean, A. 1965. Notes on the summer food of the Kestrel in Northern Ireland. Brit. Birds; 58:4:145–148.
9 Ferguson-Lees, I. J., Frost, R. A. and Young, J. 1972. Kestrels nesting close together. Brit. Birds; 65:256–258.
10. Griffiths, M. E. 1967. The population density of the Kestrel in Leicestershire. Bird Study; 14:3:184–189.
11. Lack, D. 1954. The natural regulation of animal numbers. Oxford.
12. Landsborough Thomson, A. 1958. The migrations of British falcons (Falconidae) as shown by ringing results. Brit. Birds; 51:179–188.
13. Mead, C. J. 1973. op. cit. 8(11).
14. Morgan, R. in prep. Analysis of B.T.O. nest records for the Kestrel.
15. Parslow, J. L. F. 1967. op. cit. 2(7).
16. Picozzi, N. and Hewson, R. 1970. Kestrels, Short-eared Owls, and Field Voles on Eskdalemuir in 1970. Scot. Birds; 6:4:185–191.
17. Prestt, I. 1965. op. cit. 2(8).
18. Shrubb, M. 1970. The present status of the Kestrel in Sussex. Bird Study; 17:1:1–15.
19. Simms, C. 1961. Indications of the food of the Kestrel in upland districts of Yorkshire. Bird Study; 8:43:148–151.

20. Snow, D. W. 1968. Movement and mortality among British Kestrels (*Falco tinnunculus*). Bird Study; 15:2:65–83.

Short references

(a) Batten, L. A. Brit. Birds; 52:314. (b) Bell, A. A. and Ash, J. S. Brit. Birds; 58:469–70. (c) Beven, G. Brit. Birds; 59:45. (d) B.T.O. nest record cards. (e) B.T.O. ringing records. (f) Clegg, T. M. Brit. Birds; 59:193–194. (g) Cooke, D. A. P. Brit. Birds; 55:590. (h) Goodfellow, P. F. 1969. Devon Birds; 22:71–73. (i) Harris, M. P. Brit. Birds; 58:342. (j) Hayman, R. W. Brit. Birds; 42:90. (k) Hurrell, H. G. Brit. Birds; 59:4:151. (l) Moreau, W. M. Brit. Birds; 40:217. (m) Selwyn, S. Brit. Birds; 59:39. (n) Simmons, K. E. L. Brit. Birds; 54:243. (o) Stevenson, P. P. L. (and other instances), Brit. Birds; 41:279 and 39:131.

CHAPTER 16

Main references

1. Craighead, J. and Craighead, F. 1940. Nesting Pigeon Hawks. Wilson Bull; 52:241–248.
2. Glue, D. E. 1971. Ringing recovery circumstances of small birds of prey. Bird Study; 18:3:137–146.
3. Hagen, Y. 1947. Does the Merlin sometimes play a role as a protector of Fieldfare colonies? Var. Fagelwarld; 6:137–141.
4. Koch, L. (Ed.). An Encyclopaedia of Bird Life. London.
5. Lawrence, L. de K. 1949. Notes on nesting Pigeon Hawks at Pimisi Bay, Ontario. Wilson Bull; 61:15–25.
6. Lodge, G. E. 1946. Memoirs of an artist-naturalist. Gurney and Jackson, London.
7. Parslow, J. L. F. 1967. op. cit. 2(7).
8. Rowan, W. 1921. Observations on the breeding habits of the Merlin. Brit. Birds; 15:122–129, 194–202, 222–231, 246–253.
9. Weir, D. N. mss. Merlins on the Spey slope of the Cairngorms, 1964–71.
10. Williamson, K. 1951. The Migration of the Iceland Merlin. Brit. Birds; 48:434–441.
11. Witherby, H. F. *et al.* 1943. op. cit. 12(19).

Short references

(a) B.T.O. nest record cards. (b) B.T.O. ringing records. (c) Edwards, O. Brit. Birds; 38:218. (d) Greaves, J. W. Brit. Birds; 310–311. (e) McLean, I. and Williamson, K. Brit. Birds; 51:157–8. (f) Scott, R. E. Brit. Birds; 61:527. (g) Wells, T. P. Brit. Birds; 44:37.

CHAPTER 17

Main references

1. Archer, G. F. and Godman, E. M. 1937. Birds of British Somalialand and the Gulf of Aden: Vol. 1. Gurney and Jackson, London.

2. Bannerman, D. A. 1930. op. cit. 5(1).
3. Bannerman, D. A. 1956. op. cit. 3(1).
4. Brown, L. H. 1971. op. cit. 3(3).
5. Brown, L. H. and Amadon, D. 1969. op. cit. 3(4).
6. Cade, T. J. 1960. op. cit. 14(11).
7. Mead, C. J. 1973. op. cit. 8(11).
8. Nethersole-Thompson, D. 1931. op. cit. 2(6).
9. Nethersole-Thompson, D. 1931. My observations on the Hobby in 1931. Oologist's Record; 11:4:80–86.
10. Parslow, J. L. F. 1967. op. cit. 2(7).
11. Schuyl, G. and Tinbergen, N. 1936. Ethologische Beobachtungen am Baumfalken (*Falco s. subbuteo* L.) J. fur Orn; 84:387–434.
12. Snow, D. W. (Ed.). 1971. op. cit. 3(12).
13. Thiollay, J. M. 1967. op. cit. 5(9).
14. Tinbergen, N. 1932. Beobachtungen am Baumfalken (*Falco s. subbuteo* L.). J. für Orn; 80:40–50.
15. Tubbs, C. R. 1968. The New Forest; an Ecological History. David and Charles, Newton Abbot.
16. Witherby, H. F. *et al.* 1943. op. cit. 12(19).

Short references

(a) Attlee, H. G. Brit. Birds; 41:61; and Pounds, H. E. Brit. Birds; 41:251. (b) B.T.O. nest record cards. (c) B.T.O. ringing records. (d) e.g. Clifford, B. Brit. Birds; 40:251 and Goater, B. Brit. Birds; 41:22. (e) Elliott, H. F. I. pers. comm. (f) Glue, D. E. Brit. Birds; 61:526–7. (g) Mayo, A. L. W. Brit. Birds; 46:415. (h) Pounds, H. E. Brit. Birds; 33:111. (i) Pounds, H. E. Brit. Birds; 41:153. (j) Pyman, G. A. Brit. Birds; 47:308.

CHAPTER 18

Main references

1. Baker, J. A. 1967. The Peregrine. Collins, London.
2. Beebe, F. L. 1960. Marine Peregrines of the northwest Pacific coast. Condor; 62:145–189.
3. Brown, L. H. 1955. op. cit. 14(3).
4. Brown, L. H. and Amadon, D. 1969. op. cit. 3(4).
5. Cade, T. J. 1960. op. cit. 14(11).
6. Craighead, J. and Craighead, F. 1956. op. cit. 8(6).
7. Eutermoser, G. 1961. Erläuterungen zur Krähenstatistik. Deutscher Falkenorden; 6:49–50.
8. Ferguson-Lees, I. J. *et al.* 1963. op. cit. 14(14).
9. Ferguson-Lees, I. J. 1951. The Peregrine population of Great Britain. Bird Notes; 24:200–205, 309–314.
10. Heatherley, F. 1913. The Peregrine Falcon at the Eyrie. Country Life, London.
11. Hickey, J. J. *et al.* (Ed.). 1968. op. cit. 3(6).
12. Illingworth, F. (undated) Falcons and Falconry. Blandford Press, London.
13. Lodge, G. E. 1946. op. cit. 16(6).

14. McVean, D. N. and Lockie, J. D. 1969. Ecology and Land Use in upland Scotland. University Press, Edinburgh.
15. Mead, C. J. 1968. Ringed Peregrines in Great Britain. Ch. 32 in 'Peregrine Falcon populations', ed. Hickey. (11 op. cit.).
16. Nethersole-Thompson, D. 1931. Observations on the Peregrine Falcon *Falco peregrinus peregrinus*. Ool. Rec.; 11:4:73-80.
17. Peterson, R. T. 1950. Birds over America, p. 136. Dodd Mead, New York.
18. Ratcliffe, D. A. 1962. Breeding densities in the Peregrine *Falco peregrinus* and Raven *Corvus corax*. Ibis; 104:13-39.
19. Ratcliffe, D. A. 1963. The status of the Peregrine in Great Britain. Bird Study; 10:2:56-90.
20. Ratcliffe, D. A. 1965. The Peregrine situation in Great Britain, 1963-64. Bird Study; 12:2:66-82.
21. Ratcliffe, D. A. 1967. The Peregrine situation in Great Britain, 1965-66. Bird Study; 14:4:238-246.
22. Rudebeck, G. 1950-51. The choice of prey and modes of hunting of predatory birds with special reference to their selective effect. Oikos; 2:1:65-88 and 3:2:200-231.
23. Treleaven, R. B. 1961. Notes on the Peregrine in Cornwall. Brit. Birds; 54:4:136-142.
24. Uttendorfer, O. *et al.* 1939 and 1952 op. cit. 10(14).
25. Weir, D. N. mss. op. cit. 14(27).

Short references

(a) B.T.O. nest record cards. (b) B.T.O. ringing records. (c) Gaston, A. J. Brit. Birds; 57:466; King, B. Brit. Birds; 58:297; and Wormell, P. Brit. Birds; 58:149. (d) Glasier, P. in litt. (e) Ministry of Defence: in litt. (f) Pennycuick, C. in litt. (g) Ratcliffe, D. A. pers. comm. (h) Weir, C. pers. comm.

CHAPTER 19

Main references

1. Bannerman, D. A. 1956. op. cit. 3(1).
2. Bengtson, S-A. 1971. Hunting methods and choice of prey of Gyrfalcons *Falco rusticolus* at Myvatn in Northeast Iceland. Ibis; 113:468-475.
3. Bengtson, S-A. 1972. Observations on nesting gyrfalcons (*Falco rusticolus*) in the lake Myvatn area in 1969. Naturfraedingurinn; 42:67-74.
4. Cade, T. J. 1960. op. cit. 14(11).
5. Craighead, J. and Craighead, F. 1956. op. cit. 8(6).
6. Hagen, Y. 1952. The gyrfalcon (*Falco r. rusticolus* L) in Dovre, Norway. Norske Videnskaps-Akademi; Oslo.
7. Hagen, Y. 1952. Rovfuglene og Viltpleien. Gyldendal Norsk Forlag, Oslo.
8. Hansson, L. 1969. Spring populations of small mammals in central Swedish Lapland in 1964-68. Oikos; 20:431-450.
9. Lewis, E. 1938. In search of the Gyrfalcon. Country Life, London.
10. Lodge, G. E. 1946. op. cit. 16(6).
11. Pitelka, F. A. *et al.* 1955. Ecological relations of jaegers and owls as lemming predators near Barrow, Alaska. Ecol. Monogr. 25:85-117.

12. Scott, R. E. 1968. Rough-legged Buzzards in Britain in the winter of 1966–7. Brit. Birds; 61:449–453.
13. Sharrock, J. I. R. 1969–73. Scarce migrants in Britain and Ireland during 1958–67. Brit. Birds 62:169–189, 300–315; 63:6–23, 313–324; 64:93–113, 302–309; 65:187–202, 381–392; 66:46–64, 517–525.
14. Snow, D. W. et al. 1971. op. cit. 3(12).
15. Vaurie, C. 1961. Systematic notes on Palearctic Birds. No. 45; Falconidae: The genus *Falco* (part 2). Am. Mus. Novitates, 2038; pp. 3–8.
16. Wynne-Edwards, V. C. 1962. Animal dispersion in relation to Social Behaviour. Oliver and Boyd; Edinburgh and London.

Short references

(a) R.S.P.B. data on snowy owl. (b) R.S.P.B. offences reported. (c) Wayre, P. pers. comm. (d) Ulfstrand, S. in litt.

<h2 style="text-align:center">CHAPTER 20</h2>

Main references

1. Bannerman, D. A. 1956. op. cit. 3(1).
2. Galyushin, V. M. 1971. A huge urban population of birds of prey in Delhi, India. Ibis: 113:4:522.
3. Horvath, L. 1955. Red-footed falcons in Ohat woods near Hortobagy. Acta Zoologica. Vol. 1. 3–4:245–287. Budapest.
4. Houston, D. 1972. Vulture breeding biology. (Preliminary account given to B.O.U. conference, Reading, 1972): Ibis; 114:3:442.
5. Laszlo, S. 1941. op. cit. 3(8).
6. Lundevall, C. F. and Rosenberg, E. 1955. Some aspects of the behaviour and breeding biology of the Pallid Harrier (*Circus macrourus*). Proc. 11th I.O.C., pp. 599–603.
7. Meyburg, B. U. 1969. Die Besiedlung des Naturschutzgebietes Kuhkopf-Knoblochsaue mit Greifvögeln in Jahre 1967. Orn. Mitteil; 11:223–230.
8. Snow, D. W. (Ed.) 1971. op. cit. 3(12).
9. Stanford, J. K. 1952. The ornithology of northern Libya. Ibis; 93:3:455.

Short references

(a) Moore, N. W. pers. comm.

<h2 style="text-align:center">CHAPTER 21</h2>

Main references

1. Baxter, E. V. and Rintoul, L. J. 1953. op. cit. 6(1).
2. Brown, L. H. 1971. op. cit. 3(3).
3. Edlin, H. E. 1956. op. cit. 11(5).
4. e.g. Mackenzie, A. 1881. The Highland Clearances. Inverness, A. and W. Mackenzie.
5. McVean, D. N. and Lockie, J. D. 1969. op. cit. 18(14).

6. Moore, N. W. 1957. op. cit. 13(11).
   Newton, I. 1972. op. cit. 11(12).
   Stamp, L. D. 1969. Man and the land. Collins New Nat., London.
9. Tansley, A. G. 1968. op. cit. 11(15).
   .Tubbs, C. R. 1968. op. cit. 17(15).
11. Yapp, W. P. 1956. High level woodlands. Bird Study; 3:3:191–204.

Short references

(a) Axell, H. E. pers. comm. (b) Balfour, E. pers. comm. (c) R.S.P.B. prosecutions; coll. R. Porter.

CHAPTER 22

Main references

1. Allison, A. C. (Ed.) *et al.* 1970. Population control. Penguin, Harmondsworth.
2. Arnold, E. L. and Maclaren, P. I. R. 1939. op. cit. 7(1).
3. Balfour, E. and Macdonald, M. A. 1970. op. cit. 9(4).
4. Brown, L. H. 1969. op. cit. 14(6).
5. Brown, L. H. and Amadon, D. 1969. op. cit. 3(4).
6. Brull, H. 1964. op. cit. 11(3).
7. Cavé, A. J. 1968. op. cit. 15(4).
8. Craighead, J. and Craighead, F. 1956. op. cit. 8(6).
9. Dare, P. J. 1961. op. cit. 13(3).
10. Davis, T. A. W. 1960. op. cit. 15(6).
11. Davies, P. W. and Davis, P. E. 1973. op. cit. 2(4).
12. Eng, R. L. and Gullion, G. W. 1962. op. cit. 11(6).
13. Fairley, J. S. and Maclean, A. 1965. op. cit. 15(8).
14. Hagen, Y. 1952. Food of hen harrier; quoted in Bannerman, D. A. 1956. op. cit. 3(1).
15. Holdsworth, M. 1971. op. cit. 13(6).
16. Lockie, J. D. 1964. The breeding density of Golden Eagle and Fox in relation to food supply in Wester Ross, Scotland. Scot. Nat; 71:2:67–77.
17. Moore, N. W. 1957. op. cit. 13(11).
18. Ratcliffe, D. A. 1963. op. cit. 18(19).
19. Schuyl, G. and Tinbergen, N. 1936. op. cit., 17(11).
20. Simms, C. 1961. op. cit. 15(19).
21. Tinbergen, L. 1946. op. cit. 12(17).
22. Thiollay, J. M. 1968. op. cit. 10(13).
23. Watson, A. *et al.* Grouse management. Game conservancy, booklet 12. Fordingbridge.
24. Weir, D. and Picozzi, N. in prep. op. cit. 13(21).

Short references

(a) Newton, I. in litt. (b) Watson, A. in litt.

CHAPTER 23

Main references

1. Bannerman, D. A. 1956. op. cit. 3(1).
2. Brown, L. H. 1971. op. cit. 3(3).
3. Ferguson-Lees, I. J. *et al.* 1964. op. cit. 11(7).
4. Gordon, S. 1955. op. cit. 2(5).
5. Leopold, A. S. and Wolfe, T. O. 1970. Food habits of nesting Wedge-tailed Eagles in south-eastern Australia. CSIRO. Wildl. Res; 15:1:1–17.
6. Lockie, J. D. 1963. In report on Cambridge Conference on Birds of Prey. Bird Notes; 30:205–219.
7. Lockie, J. D. 1964. op. cit. 22(16).
8. Lockie, J. D. and Stephen, D. 1959. op. cit. 14(21).
9. Lundquist, T. 1963. Peregrines and homing Pigeons. Brit. Birds; 56:149–151.
10. McVean, D. N. and Lockie, J. D. 1969. op. cit. 18(14).
11. Ratcliffe, D. A. 1963. op. cit. 18(19).
12. Ratcliffe, D. A. 1972. The Peregrine (*Falco peregrinus*) Population of Great Britain 1971. Bird Study; 19:117–156 (Ms).
13. Spofford, W. R. 1964. The Golden Eagle in the Trans-Pecos and Edwards Plateau of Texas. Audubon Conservation Report, No. 1. New York.
14. Watson, A. *et al.* op. cit. 22(23).
15. Willgohs, J. F. 1961. op. cit. 7(10).

Short references

(a) Porter R. pers. comm. and in litt. (b) Siegfried, W. R., in litt. (c) Watson, A. in litt. (d) Weir, D. N. pers. comm.

CHAPTER 24

Main references

1. Balfour, E. 1957. op. cit. 9(1).
2. Brown, L. H. 1971. op. cit. 3(3).
3. Brown, L. H. and Watson, A. 1964. op. cit. 14(9).
4. Cadbury, J. and Balfour, E. mss. op. cit. 9(5).
5. Cade, T. J. 1960. op. cit. 14(11).
6. Cavé, A. J. 1968. op. cit. 15(4).
7. Craighead, J. and Craighead, F. 1956. op. cit. 8(6).
8. Dare, P. J. 1961. op. cit. 13(3).
9. Davis, T. A. W. and Saunders, D. R. 1965. op. cit. 13(4).
10. Everett, M. 1971. op. cit. 14(13).
11. Gargett, V. 1969. Black Eagle Survey; Rhodes Matopos National Park: a Population Study, 1964–68. Ostrich Supplement; 8:397–414.
12. Hamerstrom, F. 1968. op. cit. 9(7).
13. Meinertzhagen, R. 1956. Roost of wintering harriers. Ibis; 98:535.
14. Merrie, D. mss. op. cit. 14(25).
15. Moore, N. W. 1957. op. cit. 13(11).

16. Neufeldt, I. A. 1967. Notes on the nidification of the Pied Harrier *Circus melanoleucus* (Pennant) in Amurland, U.S.S.R. Journ. Bombay Nat. Hist. Soc.; 64:2:284–306.
17. Newton, I. 1973. op. cit. 12(6).
18. Ratcliffe, D. A. 1962. op. cit. 18(18).
19. Robinson, W. 1950. op. cit. 10(12).
20. Rowan, W. 1921. op. cit. 16(8).
21. Tinbergen, L. 1946. op. cit. 12(17).
22. Tubbs, C. R. 1967. op. cit. 13(18).
23. Tubbs, C. R. 1968. op. cit. 17(15).
24. Weir, D. N. and Picozzi, N. in prep. op. cit. 13(21).
25. Weis, H. 1923. op. cit. 8(16).

Short references

(a) Dare, P. J. pers. comm.

CHAPTER 25

Main references

1. Arnold, L. W. 1954. op. cit. 14(1).
2. Balfour, E. 1957. op. cit. 9(1).
3. Balfour, E. 1962. op. cit. 9(2).
4. Balfour, E. 1970. op. cit. 9(3).
5. Brown, L. H. 1966. op. cit. 14(4).
6. Brown, L. H. 1970. op. cit. 14(5).
7. Brown, L. H. 1971. op. cit. 3(3).
8. Brown, L. H. and Cade, T. J. 1972. Age classes and population dynamics of the Bateleur and African Fish Eagle. Ostrich; 43:1:1–16.
9. Brown, P. and Waterston, G. 1962. op. cit. 2(3).
10. Cavé, A. J. 1968. op. cit. 15(4).
11. Fischer, W. 1959. op. cit. 7(5).
12. Gordon, S. 1927. op. cit. 14(16).
13. Gordon, S. 1955. op. cit. 2(5).
14. Holstein, V. 1944. op. cit. 5(5).
15. Lack, D. 1954. op. cit. 15(11).
16. Meinertzhagen, R. 1954. op. cit. 4(5).
17. Merrie, D. mss. op. cit. 14(25).
18. Meyburg, B. U. 1969. Zur Biologie des Schreiadlers (*Aquila pomarina*). Deutscher Falkenorden; 39–66 (1970).
19. Newton, I. 1973. op. cit. 12(9).
20. Nice, M. M. 1953. op. cit. 3(9).
21. Rowan, W. 1921. op. cit. 16(8).
22. Schuyl, G. and Tinbergen, N. 1936. op. cit. 17(11).
23. Tubbs, C. R. 1967. op. cit. 13(18).
24. Watson, A. 1957. op. cit. 14(26).
25. Weir, D. N. and Picozzi, N. in prep. op. cit. 13(21).
26. Wendland, V. 1958. Zum Problem des vorzeitigen Sterbens von jungen Greifvogeln und Eulen. Vogelwarte; 19:186–191.

27. Whitman, Walt; quot. in Armstrong, E. A. Bird Display, 1942 edition. Cambridge University Press.
28. Willgohs, J. F. 1961. op. cit. 7(10).
29. Wynne-Edwards, V.C. 1962. op. cit. 19(16).

Short references

(a) Newton, I. in litt. (b) R.S.P.B. record books. (c) Turner-Ettlinger, D. M. op. cit. 9(f). (d) Watson, A. pers. comm.

CHAPTER 26

Main references

1. Ames, P. L. and Mercereau, G. S. 1964. Some factors in the decline of the Osprey in Connecticut. Auk; 81:2:173–185.
2. Ash, J. S. 1960. op. cit. 2(1).
3. Brown, L. H. 1971. op. cit. 3(3).
4. Carson, R. 1963. Silent Spring. Hamish Hamilton, London.
5. Cramp, S. and Conder, P. 1965. Fifth report of the B.T.O. and R.S.P.B. on Toxic Chemicals (and four earlier reports) R.S.P.B., Sandy.
6. Davies, P. W. and Davis, P. E. 1973. op. cit. 2(4).
7. De Witt, J. B. and Buckley, J. L. 1962. Studies on Pesticide-Eagle relationships. Audubon Field Notes,; 16:6:541.
8. Flegg, J. J. M. 1972. The Puffin on St Kilda 1969–71. Bird Study 19:7–17.
9. Heath, R. G. *et al.* 1969. Marked DDE impairment of Mallard reproduction in controlled studies. Nature, 224:5214:47–48.
10. Helander, B. 1970. op. cit. 7(7).
11. Hickey, J. J. *et al.* (Ed.) 1968. op. cit. 3(6).
12. Jehl, J. R. 1969. The Brown Pelican, a vanishing American. Environment Southwest, June 1969 (see also Blus *et al.* Nature, Feb. 1972, 376).
13. Lockie, J. D. and Ratcliffe, D. A. 1964. op. cit. 14(22).
14. Lockie, J. D., Ratcliffe, D. A. and Balharry, R. 1969. op. cit. 14(23).
15. Mellanby, K. 1967. Pesticides and Pollution. Collins New Nat., London.
16. Merrie, D. mss. op. cit. 14(25).
17. Moore, N. W. 1967. op. cit. 8(12).
18. Newton, I. 1974. op. cit. 12(8).
19. Oehme, G. 1961. op. cit. 7(8).
20. Parslow, J. L. F. 1967. op. cit. 2(7).
21. Porter, R. D. and Wiemeyer, S. N. 1969. Dieldrin and DDT effects on Sparrowhawk eggshells and reproduction. Science; 165:199–200.
22. Prestt, I. 1965. op. cit. 2(8).
23. Ratcliffe, D. A. 1963. op. cit. 18(19).
24. Ratcliffe, D. A. 1970. Changes attributable to pesticides in egg breaking and eggshell thickness in some British Birds. J. Appl. Ecol.; 7:67–115.
25. Ratcliffe, D. A. 1972. op. cit. 23(12).
26. Third Report of the Research Committee on Toxic chemicals. H.M.S.O. London. 1970.
27. Treleaven, R. B. 1961. op. cit. 18(23).

BIBLIOGRAPHICAL REFERENCES

Short references

(a) Moore, N. W. in litt. (b) Ratcliffe, D. A. pers. comm.

CHAPTER 27

Main references

1. Flegg, J. M. 1972. op. cit. 26(8).
2. Kenward, R. E. 1971. Mortalities of falconers' birds. The Falconer, Vol. V, 314–316.
3. Weir, D. N. 1971. op. cit. 14(28).

Short references

(a) Axell, H. E. pers. comm. (b) Gouldsbury, P. A. 1972. Birds; May–June, p. 62 (c) R.S.P.B. news; Birds, March–April, 1972, p. 34. (d) R.S.P.B. records and Porter, R. in litt.

INDEX

Numbers in **bold** type refer to main species descriptions. B=Bibliographical reference